D0848644

# REAL ESTATE LAW

By

**GEORGE J. SIEDEL III**

Associate Professor of Business Law
Graduate School of Business Administration
The University of Michigan

ST. PAUL, MINN.
WEST PUBLISHING CO.
1979

**Library of Congress Cataloging in Publication Data**

Siedel, George J.
 Real estate law.

 Includes index.
 1. Vendors and purchasers—United States. 2. Real property—United States.
3. Land use—Law and legislation—United States. 4. Landlord and tenant—
United States. I. Title.
KF665.S53    346′.73′043    79–13467

**ISBN** 0–8299–2048–X

Siedel Cs. Real Est. Law MCB

To George and Justine Siedel

*

III

# PREFACE

---

This book was prepared in response to a need for a real estate law textbook and reference that combines text, short case summaries, actual court decisions, and problems. This need has long been expressed by students enrolled in my undergraduate and graduate real estate courses at the Graduate School of Business Administration, University of Michigan, by real estate professionals in my Graduate, Realtors Institute Course, and by my teaching colleagues.

Four major areas of real estate law are covered in this book: (1) the general nature of the legal system and real property, (2) the transfer of real estate, (3) land use and regulation, and (4) landlord and tenant law. The transfer of real estate (Part Two) is an area of special concern to the real estate professional, the homeowner, and the investor in real estate; the chapters in this section have been arranged in chronological order, from the search for real estate through the closing, to illustrate the interrelationship of the various topics covered. The same approach has been used within certain chapters; for instance, the chapter on financing the real estate purchase begins with the mortgage application and follows the mortgage process through foreclosure.

Every chapter in the book opens with a text summary of the law that includes numerous illustrations and case examples. The text includes extensive footnotes to assist real estate professionals and students who wish to verify statements in the text or to conduct research in a particular area.

The text in each chapter, with the exception of Chapter 1, is followed by several edited cases. The use of cases is essential in the study of real estate law, for it is only by reading court opinions that students fully realize how the law is developed and refined in order to resolve disputes before the court. Furthermore, the court opinions contain specific situations that can be used in class discussions to explore a broad range of legal issues discussed in the text. In editing the cases, I have used asterisks to indicate places where sections of the original court opinion have been deleted, although no asterisks have been used to indicate the omission of case citations.

Each chapter, with the exception of Chapter 1, concludes with ten problems. These problems might be used as additional illustrations of legal principles discussed in the text. They might also be

v

assigned as research problems or used to test the reader's understanding of real estate law.

In using this book, students and real estate professionals should keep in mind two assumptions of fundamental importance in any law course taught to lay persons. The first assumption is that most persons handle their own legal problems without the assistance of an attorney. The average person frequently faces legal issues yet finds it simply too expensive and time-consuming to seek the advice of an attorney every time he encounters a legal question. The second assumption is that a person acting as his own lawyer must pay the financial—or even criminal—consequences if he makes a mistake. Ignorance of the law is rarely an excuse.

Given these assumptions, it becomes critically important for lay persons to be able to recognize those legal problems that are significant enough to justify professional counsel and to be able to communicate effectively with an attorney when advice is sought. It is hoped that the materials in this book will assist readers in developing the ability to recognize important legal issues and that this ability will remain long after specific real estate law rules have been forgotten. In dealing with future real estate problems, it should be remembered that this book was not written or intended to provide specific legal advice and should not be used as a substitute for the advice of professional counsel.

I am especially indebted to Dr. Alfred L. Edwards, Director of the Division of Research at the Graduate School of Business Administration, for providing research support that enabled me to complete this book. My special thanks are due to two persons hired by the Division of Research to work on this project. L. Fallasha Erwin, a tax attorney, verified case summaries, quotations, and citations in the text; he also read and commented on the text, and assisted in preparing the problems that follow each chapter. His advice and painstaking review were invaluable. Joan H. Kmenta served as the principal editor for the book. Mrs. Kmenta, who is not an attorney, offered many valuable suggestions that were incorporated into the text to clarify the law in terms understandable to lay students. I am also deeply indebted to Ms. Terri L. Lomax for her excellent work in typing the final manuscript. Finally, I would like to thank my wife, Helen. Without her occasional typing and editing and her continual encouragement and support, this book would never have been completed.

Although many other people advised and assisted me in preparing the manuscript, I would like to thank especially Professors Arthur F. Southwick, Donald H. Skadden, Donald L. MacDonald, and Richard D. Boley for reading selected parts of the manuscript. My thanks

# PREFACE

also go to Ms. Patricia L. Cornett for her editorial assistance on early drafts and to Ms. L. Pamela Brown and Ms. Joan E. Haley for typing preliminary drafts of the manuscript. I would like to thank Mr. Lewis J. Haeck for providing library and research facilities. I am also indebted to a number of students who were enrolled at the time of their assistance in the University of Michigan Law School; they include Stephen A. Cooper, Marcia K. Fujimoto, Stephen L. Gaines, Harold E. Hammersmith, Jay A. Kennedy, Brent D. Rector, Arlene Rosen, and Clifford J. Scharman.

Chapter 1 of this book has been adapted from Chapter 1 of *The Law of Hospital and Health Care Administration,* © 1978 by The University of Michigan, which I jointly authored with principal author Arthur F. Southwick. This chapter is used with the permission of The Health Administration Press. Chapter 14 is derived from my contribution to the *Environmental Law Handbook* (State Bar of Michigan, 1975).

Finally, I want to thank the students in my classes, who have used and tested many of the materials and cases in this book. Their comments and encouragement have made teaching real estate law and preparing this book both challenging and stimulating. In a landlord and tenant case, a judge once observed that the tenant had made a costly legal mistake, but "such is the tuition in the school of hard knocks where lessons are learned that will be of incalculable value in determining the course of future policies and operations." † If the numerous examples and cases in this book serve as vicarious experience for students so that some of the "tuition in the school of hard knocks" can be avoided, my debt to them will be partially repaid.

GEORGE J. SIEDEL III

Ann Arbor, Michigan
May, 1979

\*

---

† Gulbenkian v. Patcraft Mills, Inc., 104 Ga.App. 102, 121 S.E.2d 179 (1961).

# SUMMARY OF CONTENTS

# SUMMARY OF CONTENTS

# TABLE OF CONTENTS

# TABLE OF CONTENTS

# TABLE OF CONTENTS

# TABLE OF CONTENTS

# TABLE OF CONTENTS

# TABLE OF CONTENTS

# TABLE OF CONTENTS

# TABLE OF CONTENTS

## PART THREE.  LAND USE AND REGULATION

# TABLE OF CONTENTS

# TABLE OF CONTENTS

## PART FOUR. LANDLORD AND TENANT

# TABLE OF CONTENTS

## APPENDICES

# TABLE OF CONTENTS

# TABLE OF CASES

Principal cases are in italic type.   Nonprincipal cases are in roman type.
References are to Pages.

# TABLE OF CASES

# TABLE OF CASES

# TABLE OF CASES

# TABLE OF CASES

# TABLE OF CASES

# REAL ESTATE LAW

## Part One

## THE LEGAL SYSTEM AND THE NATURE OF REAL PROPERTY

### Chapter 1

### INTRODUCTION TO THE LEGAL SYSTEM

> "How do you like the law, Mr. Micawber?" "My dear Copperfield," he replied, "to a man possessed of the higher imaginative powers, the objection to legal studies is the amount of detail which they involve. Even in our professional correspondence," said Mr. Micawber, glancing at some letters he was writing, "the mind is not at liberty to soar to any exalted form of expression. Still, it is a great pursuit. A great pursuit!"
>
> Charles Dickens, *David Copperfield*

The study of law is essential to the person in a profession relating to real estate. With the many social and technological changes of recent years, law has assumed great, some would say exaggerated, importance in real estate transactions. Unfortunately, real estate professionals cannot have an attorney constantly at hand when they are confronted with the myriad statutes, administrative regulations, and court decisions that have become so important to real estate law. Consequently, they must have a fundamental understanding of the law so that they can at least perceive serious legal problems that do require professional legal counsel.

A knowledge of real estate law is also important for the person who deals with real estate law less frequently—the home buyer, the landlord, the tenant, and the investor. Although the purchase of a home is the most important contract most people ever sign, in most cases the transaction will be conducted without the assistance of an attorney. It is only after making a large financial commitment that an occasional home buyer painfully learns the adage: "Ignorance of the law is no excuse." In order to avoid financial embarrassment, the person who deals with real estate only occasionally, as well as the pro-

1

fessional, should at least know when professional legal counsel is necessary during the course of a real estate transaction.

In this chapter some general concepts essential to any study of law will be examined, with special emphasis on three areas: the sources of the law, the court system, and legal procedure. First, however, a working definition of law will be useful. Defined in its simplest and broadest sense, law is a system of principles and rules devised by organized society for the purpose of controlling human conduct. Society must have certain specified standards of behavior and the means to enforce the standards. In the final analysis the purpose of law is to avoid conflict between individuals and between government and citizens. Conflicts do inevitably occur, however, and then legal institutions and doctrines supply the means of resolving the disputes.

Since law is concerned with human behavior, it falls short of being an exact science. Much of law is uncertain. Rules of law often fail to guarantee particular results in individual controversies. Lawyers are many times unable to predict with authority the outcome of current conflict. As economic and social conditions change, laws must be changed, and these changes frequently produce legal uncertainties. Yet in one respect uncertainty about the law is a virtue and the law's greatest strength—its opposite, legal rigidity, produces decay by discouraging initiative with respect to the economic growth and the development of social institutions.

## I.   SOURCES OF LAW

Law can be classified as either public or private law, depending upon its subject matter. That body of law which concerns the government or its relations with individuals is classified as public law. In contrast, the term private law refers to the rules and principles that define and regulate individuals' rights and duties. Without doubt these two broad classifications of law have become intermixed in modern societies, and it is not always possible or advisable to assign arbitrarily a given rule of law to one classification or the other. Yet the classifications are useful in understanding Anglo-American legal doctrine.

The concept of private law embraces much of the law of contracts, property, and tort. In its broadest sense the law of property regulates the ownership, employment, and disposition of property, including the creation and operation of trusts. The law of contracts is concerned with such matters as the sale of goods, the furnishing of services, the employment of others, and the loan of money. Tort law defines and enforces those respective duties and rights that exist between the parties. Contract law and tort law are often intertwined with property law and will be covered in more depth in later chapters.

In contrast to private law, the purpose of public law is to define, regulate, and enforce rights where any part or agency of government is a party to the subject matter—areas such as labor relations, taxation, anti-trust, and municipal corporations. In general the primary sources of public law, substantive and procedural, are the written constitutions and statutory enactments of a legislative body, complemented by a third source, administrative law. In the following paragraphs we examine these sources of public law along with the primary source of private law, the judicial decision.

## A. CONSTITUTIONS

The United States Constitution is aptly called the "supreme law of the land," for the Constitution provides a standard against which all other laws are to be judged. In the most basic terms, the Constitution is a grant of power from the states to the federal government. All powers not granted to the federal government by the Constitution are reserved in the individual states. The grant of power to the federal government is both express and implied. The Constitution, for example, expressly authorizes Congress to levy and collect taxes, to borrow and coin money, to declare war, to raise and support armies, and to regulate interstate commerce. But Congress may also enact laws that are "necessary and proper" for exercising these powers.

The Constitution can be divided into two parts. The main body establishes and defines the power of the three branches of the federal government: (1) the legislative branch makes the laws; (2) the executive arm enforces the laws; and (3) the judicial branch interprets them. As we will see, this simple breakdown is often imprecise and incorrect, especially in regard to the sources of the law.

Following the main body of the Constitution are twenty-six amendments. The first ten, the Bill of Rights, were ratified shortly after the adoption of the Constitution. According to James Madison, the amendments served to calm the apprehensions of persons who felt that unless a specific declaration were made, the federal government might be considered to possess these rights. The provisions of the Bill of Rights include the well-known rights to free speech and free exercise of religion, to be secure from unreasonable searches and seizures, to bear arms, to demand a jury trial, to be protected against self-incrimination, and to be accorded due process. Despite the granting of these rights, however, the scope of the first ten amendments is limited; in and of themselves, they only apply to the federal government. Does this mean that without a provision in the state constitution a state government could take away any or all of the aforementioned rights?

The answer, at least before the ratification of the Fourteenth Amendment in 1870, was yes. However, the concluding phrases of the Fourteenth Amendment provide this safeguard: " . . . nor shall any State deprive any person of life, liberty, or property, without due process of law, nor deny to any person within its jurisdiction the equal protection of the laws." The Fourteenth Amendment is especially important for two reasons. First, the Supreme Court has generally defined due process as specifically including the rights set forth in the Bill of Rights. Consequently, neither the state nor the federal government may infringe upon these rights. Secondly, what constitutes the "State" or "state action" has been broadly defined by many courts. For instance, in Shelley v. Kraemer,[1] the United States Supreme Court held that a private agreement by property owners not to sell or lease to a Negro could not be enforced in equity. Such enforcement, the court held, would constitute state action in denying the Negroes equal protection of the law in violation of the Fourteenth Amendment.

In addition to the federal Constitution, each state has its own constitution, which is the supreme law of that state but is subordinate to the federal Constitution. The state and federal constitutions are often similar, although state constitutions are more detailed and cover such matters as the financing of public works and the organization of local governments.

## B.  STATUTES

The second source of law, statutory law, is the law enacted by a legislative body, normally the United States Congress, a state legislature, or a local governmental unit such as a city council. Often, the statutes passed by each of these bodies will affect a real estate transaction. For instance, a person selling real estate in most cases must comply with antidiscrimination legislation enacted by federal, state and local legislative bodies.

Although, as noted below, statutes have priority over conflicting judicial decisions as a source of law, judges are faced with the task of interpreting statutes; and this is especially difficult if the wording is vague or ambiguous. In interpreting statutes the courts have developed several rules of construction, and in some states these rules are themselves the subject of a separate statute. Whatever the source of the rules, they are designed to help clarify the intention of the legislature. The following section from the Pennsylvania "Statutory Construction Act" illustrates the type of guidelines a court uses to determine legislative intent.

> The object of all interpretation and construction of laws is to ascertain and effectuate the intention of the Legislature. Every law shall be construed, if possible, to give effect to all its provisions.

> When the words of a law are clear and free from all ambiguity, the letter of it is not to be disregarded under the pretext of pursuing its spirit.

1.  334 U.S. 1, 68 S.Ct. 836, 92 L.Ed. 1161 (1948).

When the words of a law are not explicit, the intention of the Legislature may be ascertained by considering, among other matters—(1) the occasion and necessity for the law; (2) the circumstances under which it was enacted; (3) mischief to be remedied; (4) the object to be attained; (5) the former law, if any, including other laws upon the same or similar subject; (6) the consequences of a particular interpretation; (7) the contemporaneous legislative history; and (8) legislative and administrative interpretations of such law.[2]

## C. ADMINISTRATIVE LAW

Administrative law, a third source of law, is that division of public law that relates to administrative government. According to Sir Ivor Jennings, a British scholar, "Administrative law is the law relating to the administration. It determines the organization, powers and duties of administrative authorities."[3] Whenever a question arises concerning the organization and the power of an administrative authority, fundamental principles of constitutional law become relevant. Further, a true understanding of administrative law requires more than a definition of the rules governing the powers and procedural methods of administrative bodies. Few people realize that the significance of administrative law goes far beyond procedural matters. In fact, this division of public law is the source of much law that directly affects the rights and duties of individuals and their relation to governmental authority.

The administrative or executive branch of government, in contrast to the legislative and the judicial branches, is often said to include all those departments of government that have the responsibility of putting the laws into effect. This definition oversimplifies, and hence misleads, because administrative government often does make law and even exercises a considerable amount of judicial or quasi-judicial power. In Anglo-American governments, the phrase "administrative government" embraces all departments of the executive branch and all governmental agencies created by legislation for specific public purposes.

Examples of administrative agencies or tribunals abound. In the United States they exist at all levels of government: local, state, and federal. Well-known federal agencies are the National Labor Relations Board, the Interstate Commerce Commission, the Federal Communications Commission, the Civil Aeronautics Board, the Federal Trade Commission, and the Food and Drug Administration. At the state level there are worker's compensation commissions, labor relations boards, boards of medical registration, and numerous other agencies.

---

2. 1 Pa.Const.Stat.Ann. § 1501 et seq. (1972).

3. See generally, I. Jennings, The Law and the Constitution (1959).

The lawmaking and judicial powers of administrative government result from delegated, or subordinate, legislation. The United States Congress delegates to various administrative bodies the right to initiate statutory law, typically called regulations or rules. Although it is an administrative agency, the federal Food and Drug Administration, for example, has the power to make rules controlling the manufacture, marketing, and advertising of foods, drugs, and cosmetics. The Internal Revenue Service regulates tax administration. Many other examples could be given.

The amount of delegated legislation has increased tremendously in this century, particularly since World War II. The reasons are clear: economic and social conditions inevitably change as societies become ever more complicated, and legislatures cannot directly provide the mass of rules necessary to govern the society. Not only does the legislature lack time; but also many of its elected representatives lack sufficient information and ability to formulate detailed laws that would implement the social policies expressed in primary legislation. Delegating legislative authority makes it possible to put this responsibility in the hands of experts.

All legislation, whether federal or state in origin and application, must be consistent with the federal Constitution, and the Supreme Court of the United States has the power to declare that an act of Congress or the act of a state legislature is unconstitutional.[4] The issue of constitutional law is also raised when Congress delegates legislative authority to administrative government. Congress may not abdicate its responsibility by delegating complete authority even in the case of specialized subject matter. Primary legislation must generally stipulate which regulations an administrative body is empowered to make. At the level of state government, the legislature's power to delegate authority is similarly limited. Furthermore the administrative body receives judicial or quasi-judicial power to enforce regulations; and this again raises a question of American constitutional law because the federal Constitution vests "judicial power" in the Supreme Court.

## D.  JUDICIAL DECISIONS

The last major source of law is the judicial decision. Judicial decisions are subordinate, of course, to the Constitution and also to statutes so long as the statute is consistent with the Constitution. Despite this subordinate role, however, judicial decisions are the primary source of private law, especially real estate law.

1.  **Common Law.** Historically, judicial decisions came either from common law courts or from equity courts. The common law— that is, the law that is common to England—originally developed there

---

4. Marbury v. Madison, 5 U.S. (1 Cranch) 137, 2 L.Ed. 60 (1803) estab- lished the court's power to declare federal legislation unconstitutional.

after the Norman invasion in 1066. Two factors especially influenced the subsequent development of the common law in England. First, the English court system was centralized with the appearance of the royal courts—the Court of Common Pleas, the Court of King's Bench, and the Exchequer. An important procedural device utilized by the courts and developed during the reign of Henry II (1154–1189) was the writ, an order purchased by the plaintiff which directed the defendant to appear before the King's Court. Each writ, or form of action, differed from the others and carried with it the development of a separate body of substantive law, prompting Maitland to note that, although the old forms of action are buried and no longer used, "they still rule as from their graves." [5]

Second, the common law courts developed the principle of *stare decisis*, of abiding by decided cases. Under this doctrine, courts would look to past disputes involving similar facts and determine the outcome of the current case on the basis of the earlier decision. The use of earlier cases as precedent has made for stability in the Anglo-American legal system, since a person embarking on a new enterprise may rely on the judicial decisions already rendered in similar circumstances. The use of earlier decisions to determine the substance of the law distinguishes the common law from the civil or Roman law system, which relies principally on a comprehensive code of laws to decide a case currently under consideration. Civil law is the basis for the law in Europe, Central and South America, Japan, Quebec, and Louisiana.

In the United States, *stare decisis* is a concept that is applied vertically, but not horizontally to equal or lower courts in the same system or to courts from other systems. An Ohio trial court, for example, would be bound by the decisions of the higher Ohio courts, that is, the state's appellate courts and supreme court, but would not be bound by decisions of other Ohio trial courts or by the decisions of out-of-state courts. Likewise, the federal trial court (the district court) would be bound by an appellate court decision for its own circuit, but not by the federal appellate decisions of other circuits or by decisions of other district courts. The one exception occurs when a federal court hears a diversity of citizenship action; it must then determine the law by following the decisions of the highest state court. Although they are not bound to do so, courts in one system often examine judicial solutions in other systems in order to decide cases for which there are no precedents.

While *stare decisis* provides stability to the Anglo-American judicial system, the doctrine could also lead to stagnation if courts were forced to adhere blindly to precedents. Consequently, courts are given some flexibility in modifying the legal rule when the facts vary from the precedent, or they may even completely overturn their own earlier decisions. As Justice Musmanno noted in Flagiello v. Pennsylvania

5. F. Maitland, The Forms of Action
at Common Law 2 (1965).

Hospital, "*Stare decisis* channels the law. It erects lighthouses and flys [*sic*] the signals of safety. The ships of jurisprudence must follow the well-defined channel which, over the years, has been proved to be secure and trustworthy. But it would not comport with wisdom to insist that, should shoals rise in a heretofore safe course and rocks emerge to encumber the passage, the ship should nonetheless pursue the original course, merely because it presented no hazard in the past. The principle of *stare decisis* does not demand that we follow precedents which shipwreck justice." [6]

The doctrine of *stare decisis* should not be confused with another important common law doctrine also referred to in its Latin form, *res judicata*. *Res judicata* literally means "a thing or matter settled by judgment." In practice, this means that once a legal dispute has been decided by a court and all appeals exhausted, the parties may not later bring suit regarding matters decided already by the court.

2. **Equity.** Equity developed as a source of law because of deficiencies in the common law. By the Middle Ages common law procedures had become rigid, and courts could provide no relief to many parties who had just claims. For instance, the common law generally acted only after the fact; damages could be awarded to an injured party after an injury, but a wrongdoer would not be ordered to cease his illegal behavior before the injury occurred.

As a result of such inadequacies, parties began to seek relief from the king when the common law could provide no satisfaction. The king, through his chancellor, often aided these parties and eventually established a separate court, the Court of Chancery, to hear the cases. These courts, which attempted to "do equity" and to act in good conscience where the common law courts could not provide relief, developed the law of equity, which differed from the common law in two major respects. First, the courts of equity developed their own remedies—for example, the injunction—whereby the court could provide relief before a wrong occurred. And, secondly, the procedure in the chancery court differed from that in the law courts. Most notably, the parties in the Court of Chancery had no right to a jury trial, and certain rules or maxims were applied, for example, "He who comes into equity must have clean hands." Gradually, with the development of these rules, equity became almost as inflexible as the common law, prompting Dickens to write in *Bleak House*: "Never can there come fog too thick, never can there come mud and mire too deep, to assort with the groping and floundering condition which (the) High Court of Chancery, most pestilent of hoary sinners, holds . . . in the sight of heaven and earth."

Although the dual system of law and equity was adopted in the United States, both here and in England law and equity eventually

6. 417 Pa. 486, 208 A.2d 193 (1965).

came to be administered by the same court. The relevant Michigan statute, for example, provides that the "circuit courts have the power and jurisdiction possessed by courts of record at the common law . . . and possessed by courts and judges in Chancery in England." [7] Despite the merger of law and equity into one court, however, procedural and remedial distinctions remain. For example, the parties in an equitable action are still not entitled to a jury trial, and the equitable maxims are still applied by the courts.

The law derived from judicial decisions is often referred to as the unwritten law because it is not a part of a formal statute or constitution. This term is misleading because court decisions are in fact written, and many are published in bound volumes.[8]

## II.  THE COURT SYSTEM

The primary method of resolving disputes in the United States is through the court system. This will involve one of fifty-two court systems in the United States, since each state and the District of Columbia has its own separate system, in addition to the federal court system. The large number of different courts makes study of the law in the United States extremely complex, especially when courts in different states use divergent approaches in deciding cases. Nevertheless, although students of the law must often study a "majority" approach and several "minority" approaches to the same legal issue, the complexity also adds a great deal of strength and vitality to the American legal system because a wide number of resolutions to a particular problem may be tested in individual states before a consensus is reached regarding the best solution. As Justice Brandeis noted in his dissenting opinion in New State Ice Co. v. Liebmann, the states should serve as "laboratories" to "try novel social and economic experiments without risk to the rest of the country." [9]

---

7. Mich.Comp.Laws Ann. § 600.601 (1961).

8. In this book citations are given when cases are mentioned, not only to show where the complete court opinion can be found but also to indicate when and where the case was decided. The citation "374 Mich. 524, 132 N.W.2d 634 (1965)," for example, shows that the case was a 1965 Michigan case and that the complete opinion may be found in volume 374, page 524, of the Michigan reports, and in volume 132, page 634, of a regional collection of cases, North Western Reporter, second series. "309 F.Supp. 548 (D.C.Utah 1970)" indicates that the case was de-

cided in 1970 by the United States District Court in Utah and may be found in the Federal Supplement. "504 F.2d 325 (5th Cir. 1974)" means the case was decided in 1974 by the U.S. Court of Appeals for the 5th Circuit and may be found in the Federal Reporter, second series; and "118 U.S. 356, 6 S.Ct. 1064, 30 L.Ed. 220 (1886)" means the case was decided by the U.S. Supreme Court in 1886 and may be found in three different sets of reports: the United States Supreme Court Reports, the Supreme Court Reporter, and Lawyers Edition.

9. 285 U.S. 262, 52 S.Ct. 371, 76 L.Ed. 747 (1932).

## A. STATE COURTS

The federal court system and many state court systems utilize a three-tier structure comprising the trial courts, the intermediate courts of appeal, and a supreme court. In the state court system, the lowest tier (the trial courts) is often divided into the court of limited jurisdiction and the court of general jurisdiction. Typically, the courts of limited jurisdiction hear criminal trials involving lesser crimes, that is, misdemeanors and civil cases where the amount in dispute is limited, normally to less than $10,000. These courts of limited jurisdiction often include a small claims court, in which lawyers are not allowed to practice and standard legal procedure is not followed.

The state courts of general jurisdiction hear the more serious criminal cases involving felonies, and the civil cases involving larger amounts of money. In some states only the courts of general jurisdiction may grant equitable relief, such as issuing an injunction. Because of the tremendous volume of cases, the courts of general jurisdiction are often divided into special courts: a family or domestic relations court, a juvenile court, and a probate court.

The second tier of many state court systems is the intermediate appellate court. This court has appellate jurisdiction, that is, the power to hear appeals from final judgments of the trial courts. The court also has limited original jurisdiction, with the result that certain cases (for example, a *mandamus* action to force a government official to perform his duty) may originate in the appellate court. In exercising their appellate jurisdiction, appellate courts generally are limited to the record from the trial court and to questions of law, not of fact.

The highest tier in the state court system is the supreme court. This court hears appeals from the intermediate appellate court and possesses original jurisdiction similar to that of the lower appellate court. The supreme court is often charged with other duties, for example, adopting rules of procedure and supervising the practice of law in the state.

## B. FEDERAL COURTS

The bottom tier in the federal court system is the district court, also called the federal trial court, which hears criminal cases involving both felonies and misdemeanors that arise under federal statutes. The district court hears civil cases involving actions arising either under federal statutes, such as federal civil rights actions, or under the Constitution. The district court may also hear suits in which a citizen of one state sues a citizen of another state (that is, where there is "diversity of citizenship") if the amount in dispute is over $10,000. In such a case, the court will apply the law of one of the states since in general there is no federal common law.

Appeals from the district courts go to the United States courts of appeals, the second level in the federal system. The United States has eleven circuits, each of which has a court of appeals functioning in the same manner as the state appellate courts. At the top of the federal court system is the United States Supreme Court. The Supreme Court hears appeals from the United States court of appeals and from the highest state courts in cases involving federal statutes, treaties, or the U.S. Constitution.

## C. ALTERNATIVE METHODS OF RESOLVING DISPUTES

1. **Administrative Law.** In addition to the court system, two alternative methods of resolving disputes are popular in the United States. First, adjudication of legal rights as defined by any particular area of administrative law is most often accomplished by an administrative agency or tribunal created by statute or constitution; hence, many private disputes controlled by administrative law are not resolved by courts at all. For instance, a compensation claim by an injured employee against a private employer for injury suffered in the course of employment is ordinarily adjudicated by a state workmen's compensation commission. Undoubtedly far more disputes are settled today by administrative adjudicative bodies than by the ordinary courts. Moreover an administrative agency often has the statutory responsibility and power to initiate enforcement of statutory pronouncements. It frequently happens that the same agency brings the initial proceeding, hears the case, and decides the dispute. In the United States, for instance, the Federal Trade Commission is empowered by Congress to initiate a proceeding to compel an alleged offender to cease and desist from using unfair methods of competition.

In general, the tasks or goals of procedural administrative law should be the same as those of common law in deciding matters of private law: to provide a "day in court," an independent "judge" or body to decide the dispute, and a rationally justified decision. Statutes, of course, will prescribe the powers of administrative authorities. The roles of ordinary courts will most often be limited to preventing administrative authorities from exceeding their powers and to granting remedies to individuals who have been injured by wrongful administrative action.

2. **Arbitration.** The second alternative method of resolving disputes is submitting the dispute to arbitration; that is, a neutral third party decides the dispute, often providing a quicker, less complicated and less costly solution than a court action. Probably all courts will enforce an agreement to arbitrate a dispute that already existed at the time of the agreement. And in a majority of states an agreement to arbitrate future, as well as existing, disputes will also be enforced.

## III.  LEGAL PROCEDURE

The law, either public or private, that creates and defines rights and duties is called substantive law, and most of this book is devoted to the substantive law as it relates to real estate.  Procedural law, on the other hand, provides the means of enforcing and protecting rights granted by the substantive law.  Procedural law, as it relates to the litigation of a case, may be divided into six stages, each of which will be discussed below.  It should be noted at the outset, however, that many real estate law disputes are resolved by negotiation or arbitration before the litigation process begins.

### A.  COMMENCEMENT OF LEGAL ACTION

When claims do go to court, the first stage is commencement of the legal action.  A claimant who begins a lawsuit or an "action" becomes the plaintiff and the other party to the action is the defendant.  The plaintiff commences his action by filing a complaint in court, which states the nature of his claim and the amount of damages he is seeking.  The complaint and all papers subsequently filed in court are the pleadings.  A copy of the complaint, along with a summons, is then served on the defendant.  The summons will advise the defendant that he must answer the complaint or take other action within a limited time—for example, 20 days—and that if the defendant fails to act, the plaintiff will be granted judgment by default.

### B.  THE DEFENDANT'S RESPONSE

In the second stage of the litigation process, the defendant can pursue several courses of action either successively or simultaneously.  At the outset, the defendant will file an answer to the complaint, either admitting, denying, or pleading ignorance to each allegation in the complaint.  The defendant may also file a complaint against the plaintiff (a countersuit) or against a third party (a third party action), thus bringing a "third party defendant" into the litigation.

The defendant in a lawsuit has one other option available at this stage in the proceeding:  to ask that the court dismiss the plaintiff's complaint.  The defendant may base the motion on a variety of grounds:  the court's lack of jurisdiction, a prior judgment on the same matter, or the failure of the opposing party to state a legal claim, assuming that the facts alleged by the plaintiff are true.  Although the terminology differs from state to state, the motion to dismiss is usually called a motion for summary judgment or a demurrer.  When the motion to dismiss is granted by the court, the judgment is final;  thus the losing party can appeal the decision immediately.  In many real estate cases, the trial court will grant a summary judgment dismissing the case, the losing party will appeal, and the appellate court will then decide whether to uphold the trial court decision or to remand the case, sending it back to another court for further action.

## C. DISCOVERY—THE DEPOSITION

In most cases, especially in urban areas, there is a four- or five-year delay between commencement of the action and the trial. During this time, each party engages in the third stage of the litigation process, discovery, which is an attempt to "discover" if the other party has a strong case and, if so, to settle the case as favorably as possible.

Five methods may be used by parties to discover the strength of the other party's case. All are limited to matters that are relevant to the subject matter and not privileged. The most common and effective discovery device is taking a deposition, whereby one party subpoenas a witness whose sworn testimony is taken down in writing by a court reporter. The opposing attorney will also be present during the deposition to make appropriate objections and, if he wishes, to cross-examine the witness. Besides being useful as a discovery device, the deposition serves at least two other major purposes. First, it may be read into evidence at the trial itself if the witness is unable to testify. Second, it can be used to impeach the testimony of a witness. For these reasons, especially the latter, persons making a deposition should answer the questions exactly as if they were testifying in court. The following excerpts from a malpractice trial illustrate the use of a deposition during trial as well as the importance of keeping accurate records. In this testimony, one of the defendant physicians had been called to testify by the plaintiff's attorney. Readers should keep in mind that no part of this examination deals with the physician's actual treatment of his patient: [10]

Q. BY MR. HARNEY: When did you graduate from college?

A. I graduated from Osteopathic College in—

Q. I didn't ask about Osteopathic College.

A. I finished at the University of Utah in 1934. After I finished at the University of Utah—

Q. No. I asked when did you graduate from college? Did you graduate from the University of Utah?

A. I completed all the requirements for my Bachelor's Degree in 1934.

Q. Did you graduate, Doctor, or perhaps you don't know what the word means.

A. I do know what the word "graduate" means.

Q. Did you graduate from the University of Utah?

A. I did not graduate from the University of Utah.

10. Senate Subcomm. on Executive Reorganization, Medical Malpractice: The Patient vs. The Physician, 91st Cong., 1st Sess. 57–60, 65–66, 69–71, 139–142 (1969).

Q. In your deposition you testified under oath that you received a degree; isn't that correct?

A. I have since received a degree from the University of Utah on the basis of my credits and work I did at the University of Utah and University of Southern California.

Q. Now, in your deposition you testified as follows:

"Q. Doctor, would you give us your educational background, please, beginning with undergraduate college? Tell us where you went to school, the approximate years, and what degrees you received, and so on, right on up the line.

"A. University of Utah; I got out of there I think it was 1932.

"Q. How many years were you there?

"A. Four.

"Q. Degree?

"A. Bachelor of Arts.

"Q. Major?

"A. Engineering."

A. That is true.

Q. You received the degree of Bachelor of Arts in 1932?

A. As I said, I have since received information from the University of Utah that I am eligible for my Bachelor of Arts degree and it would be given to me.

MR. HARNEY: I move to strike that answer. That is all kinds of hearsay, conclusionary, non-responsive matter.

THE COURT: That will be stricken.

Q. BY MR. HARNEY: Now, do you have a degree from the University of Utah or not?

A. I do not have a degree right now, no.

Q. When you testified in your deposition, which was taken on February 27, 1963, that you had a Bachelor of Arts degree from the University of Utah, that was not a true statement, was it?

A. It was true to the extent that I have been notified that I will get my Bachelor's Degree.

MR. HARNEY: I move to strike that.

THE COURT: It can remain.

MR. HARNEY: I asked if it was a true statement. Obviously it wasn't. He didn't ever get a degree.

THE COURT: We will let the jury decide that.

Q. BY MR. HARNEY: You still don't have a degree from the University of Utah, do you?

A. All I have is a letter notifying me that I have adequate—

Q. I say, you don't have a degree?

THE COURT: Answer yes or no, Doctor.

THE WITNESS: No.

Q. BY MR. HARNEY: And you know what a degree is, don't you?

A. I do.

Q. And you knew what a degree was when your deposition was taken?

A. I did.

Q. And you testified that you had a degree in engineering; is that right?

A. Yes, sir.

\* \* \*

Q. BY MR. HARNEY: Did you spend the entire four years in undergraduate school at the University of Southern California?

A. No, sir. I was working full time and trying to go to school too.

Q. All of the time you spent at the University of Southern California was strictly on the undergraduate level?

A. Yes.

Q. Not medical school?

A. Pre-medical undergraduate.

Q. Not medical school?

A. That's correct.

Q. In your deposition when you testified you were going to medical school there, you were mistaken; is that right?

A. Pre-medical school.

Q. No. In your deposition when you said "going to medical school; I did not graduate" you were mistaken about that, weren't you?

A. You might say I was mistaken.

Q. There is no question about it, is there?

A. I made the correction on my deposition.

Q. No. When you testified under oath as follows:

"Q. What were you doing at University of Southern California?

"A. Going to medical school. I did not graduate.

"Q. Why not?

"A. Uncle Sam called me."

When you said you were going to medical school there, it wasn't true, was it?

A. No. It was pre-medical school.

Q. But when you said you were going to medical school, that was not a true statement?

A. There are a lot of statements in this deposition—I changed them and corrected them to the best of my knowledge.

Q. Now, my only question, sir, is: When you gave that testimony at your deposition, it was not true, was it?

A. It was an error.

Q. Was that due to faulty recollection?

A. There were a lot of questions that were asked there that were due to faulty recollection.

* * *

Q. Did you take a residency at UCLA in anesthesia?

A. I did not take a residency where I was appointed as a—

Q. No. The question is, Doctor, did you take a residency at UCLA Medical school? You did or you didn't.

A. I did not take a full-time residency.

Q. Did you take a residency, as that word is used in medical terminology?

A. No.

Q. Now, in your deposition you testified as follows:

"Q. You said you interned a year?

"A. Yes.

"Q. From '49 to '50?

"A. Yes.

"Q. Where was that?

"A. In Chicago.

"Q. What—

"A. Rotating internship. We worked six hospitals. Then from '50 to '53 I was in general practice in Orlando, Florida. I came to California in May of 1953. Then I did a preceptorship in anesthesia for three years.

"Q. Where?

"A. Los Angeles.

"Q. Under whom?

"A. Doctor M. Howard Farber, F-a-r-b-e-r.

"Q. Where is he located?

"A. I think he is now on Santa Monica Boulevard. He was on Vermont. And then I—

"Q. That was two years?

"A. Yes. Then I went to UCLA and I had a residency in anesthesia."

That wasn't true either, was it?

A. I made a correction on my deposition at the time.

Q. But when you gave the testimony under oath, being questioned by Doctor Dunbar in this deposition, you knew that you didn't have a residency at UCLA; isn't that correct?

A. May I explain, your Honor?

THE COURT: You can answer yes or no.

Q. BY MR. HARNEY: What is there to explain? You knew it or didn't know it, Doctor.

A. I had not done a formal residency, no.

Q. You misused the word "residency" in that deposition, didn't you?

A. Misused the word "residency" where you would apply it as obtaining a certificate upon completion or being a salaried employee, yes.

* * *

Q. Well, I understand you got out of high school in 1933 and you said in the deposition you went in the Navy from '34 to '36 and USC from '36 to '41. Now, where did you get the four years in at the University of Utah?

A. To get the entire picture of this thing, you have to get all of my scholastic record together.

Q. Well, I am going to do that if I can.

A. I hope you do.

Q. I am sure going to try.

A. I was an orphan—

Q. Doctor, without going into that part of it, I want to know where you spent the four years at the University of Utah.

A. Because I had attended two other universities before I went to the University of Utah. I attended school, college and high school, where I could attend, where I could get a job and eat. I had to work and eat, as I lived by myself.

Q. I did too, Doctor, and I certainly admire you and myself, but the question is: Where did you get the four years in at the University of Utah?

A. The amount of credits and time that I had possessed from Northwestern University and University of Nebraska—

Q. When did you attend Northwestern University, now?

A. In 1929. I took courses at—

Q. When you were 13 years of age?

A. Yes, sir.

Q. At Northwestern University?

A. At University of Nebraska.

Q. When you were 13 years of age before you got out of high school, four years before you got out of high school, you went—

A. I finished high school, one high school, Central High School in Omaha, Nebraska, and when I transferred from Omaha, Nebraska, to Kansas City I had to go back into high school and take some more credits. I left Kansas City and went to Chicago. I had to take some more credits. I went from Chicago to Salt Lake City and my credits were not in order for the requirements there and I had to go back and take some more credits at West High School, and it seemed like wherever I went, each and every one of them always came up with something, "you are short one credit here," or "you are short of this" or "you are short on that." I was determined to go through school. I didn't care if they said I had to start over in kindergarten, I wanted to go to school.

Q. All right. Now, where did you spend the four years at the University of Utah? Was that in 1912, '14, '18, '32, '39, or what?

A. It would be around 1932, '33 or '[3]4.

Q. That would be two years, then?

A. '32, '33, '34.

Q. Two years, not four?

A. Three years.

Q. Three years?

A. Yes.

Q. I thought you didn't get out of high school until '33.

A. I just told you I was short on credits and they said you have to go take this. It seems all the time I was in school no matter where I went, this has to be made up, you have to do this, you have to do that. It is exceedingly difficult while you are working to try and go to school.

Q. I realize that, Doctor, because I worked my way through school. I understand.

Now, do you mean to say that the University of Utah let you in before you had your high school diploma?

A. I had a diploma—as I recall, I had a diploma from high school in Omaha.

## D.  OTHER METHODS OF DISCOVERY

A second method of discovery, written interrogatories, is similar to the taking of depositions except that the questions are in writing when they are presented to the witness. The procedure for using written interrogatories sometimes varies, depending on whether or not they are directed toward an adverse party or other witnesses.

A third method of discovery allows a party to inspect and copy documents and tangible things in the possession of the opposing party, and to inspect and copy things produced by a witness served with a subpoena *duces tecum*, that is, a subpoena requiring the witness to bring with him certain books and documents.

A physical or mental examination, the fourth discovery device, may be used when the physical or mental condition of a person is in dispute and good cause is shown for the examination. If the party being examined demands to see a report of the examination, that party waives any privilege he may have regarding the testimony of other persons who have conducted similar examinations, although in some states the privilege may be waived by bringing a lawsuit.[11]

In the final discovery method, the opposing party is requested to admit certain facts. By using these requests for admission, the parties may save the time and expense involved in unnecessary proof and may substantially limit the factual issues to be decided by the court.

In addition to the above methods of discovery, a pretrial conference will be held a few months before trial so that the judge and parties may determine what issues are in dispute, discuss settlement, and set a date for trial if settlement is not possible. The pretrial conference also aids discovery because the court will require that parties specify all damage claims in detail, produce all exhibits to be used in the trial and, in some jurisdictions, exchange lists of all witnesses to be called at trial. With all these discovery devices available, the calling of an unexpected witness or presentation of other evidence which truly surprises opposing counsel is extremely rare.

## E. THE TRIAL

Approximately eighty-five percent of all cases are settled before trial. For the remaining fifteen percent, if either party has requested a jury trial and if the case is one at law rather than equity, a jury is selected. When the jury is seated, each attorney makes an opening statement in which he explains what he intends to prove during the trial. The plaintiff then calls his witnesses and presents other evidence, and the defense attorney is given the opportunity to cross-examine each of the witnesses. After the plaintiff has rested his case, the defendant's attorney frequently asks the court to direct a verdict for his client. A directed verdict will be granted if the judge, after viewing the facts most favorably to plaintiff, feels that the jury could not reasonably return a verdict in the plaintiff's favor that would be in accord with the law. If the directed verdict is denied, the defendant proceeds with his evidence and witnesses, subject to cross-examination by the plaintiff.

When all evidence has been presented, either party may move for a directed verdict. If the judge denies the motions, he will instruct the jury as to the law, and the jury will deliberate until reaching a verdict. Many times, after the jury has reached its decision, the losing party asks the court for a "judgment notwithstanding the verdict."

11. Cal.Evid.Code § 996 (West 1965).

The motion will be granted if the judge decides that the jury's verdict is against the weight of the evidence.

The judge and the jury, of course, play key roles in the trial. The judge has the dominant role; he can decide whether evidence is admissible, charge the jury on the law before deliberation begins, and take the case away from the jury by means of a directed verdict or a judgment notwithstanding the verdict. This power narrows the role of the jury to deciding the facts in the case, ultimately determining whether or not the plaintiff has proved his case by weight of the evidence.

To illustrate the interplay between judge and jury, assume that Tom, an invitee, is suing Dick, the occupier of Blackacre, for injuries sustained on Blackacre. The judge must explain to the jury the legal standard of care, that is, that Dick must keep the premises in a reasonably safe condition and must safeguard Tom from dangers of which Dick knew or should have known. It is then the jury's responsibility to determine whether Tom met the burden of proving that Dick did not meet the standard of care. However, if the judge concludes that reasonable minds could not differ on the facts, he can take the case from the jury and enter a directed verdict.

## F.   CONCLUDING STAGES

The next stage in litigation is the appeal. In the appellate court the party who appeals the case, the losing party in the trial court, will usually be referred to as the appellant while the other party will be the appellee. In reading appellate court decisions, one must not assume that the first name in the case is the plaintiff because many appellate courts reverse the order of the names when the case is appealed. The case of Smith vs. Jones, for example, where Smith sued Jones in the trial court, might become Jones vs. Smith on appeal. The appellate court, as noted above, limits itself to a review of the law applied in the case and normally will not review the facts as determined by the judge or jury. In reviewing the case, the appellate court may affirm the trial court decision, modify or reverse the decision, or reverse and send the case back to the lower court for a new trial.

The final stage of the litigation process is collection of the judgment. The most common methods of collection are by writ of execution and by garnishment. A writ of execution entitles the plaintiff to have a local official seize the defendant's property and have the property sold to satisfy the judgment. A garnishment is an order to a third person who is indebted to the defendant to pay the debt directly to the plaintiff to satisfy the judgment. Often the third party is the employer of the defendant who will be ordered to pay a certain percentage of the defendant's wages directly to the plaintiff.[12]

12.  It should be noted that the procedure used in a criminal trial will differ in several respects from civil procedure. A detailed discussion of criminal procedure is beyond the scope of this book, it being the premise and hope of the author that persons in real estate will minimize their contact with the criminal justice system.

Chapter 2

# THE NATURE OF PROPERTY

I know of no country, indeed, where the love of money has taken stronger hold on the affections of men and where a profounder contempt is expressed for the theory of the permanent equality of property.

De Tocqueville, *Democracy in America*

## I. THE CONCEPT OF PROPERTY

Property is a complex term with meanings that vary depending on the context in which the word is used. In one sense, property means things—real or personal, corporeal or incorporeal, visible or invisible, and tangible or intangible. But the word is also used to describe characteristics; a desk, for example, has unique properties of color, shape, size, and surface. Finally, and most important in a legal sense, property describes the relationship between people and things, that is, the right of a person to possess, use, or own things.

The legal meaning of property was described by the English jurist Blackstone as "the free use, enjoyment, and disposal of all his acquisitions, without any control or diminution, save only by the laws of the land."[1] Furthermore, Blackstone observed that "there is nothing which so generally strikes the imagination, and engages the affections of mankind, as the right of property; or that sole and despotic dominion which one man claims and exercises over the external things of the world in total exclusion of the right of any other individual in the universe."[2] In Blackstone's definition, the concept of general property under the common law does not differ substantially from its meaning under Roman law: "Property in its nature is an unrestricted and exclusive right. Hence it comprises in itself the right to dispose of the substance of the thing in every legal way, to possess it, to use it, and to exclude every other person from interfering with it."[3]

Blackstone, however, raised a general question in his commentary on property. He noted that we are often afraid to look beyond our ownership of property to examine the reason or authority upon which the law is built. "We think it enough that our title is derived by grant of the former proprietor, by descent from our ancestors, or the last will and testament of the dying owner; not caring to reflect that  .  .  . there is no foundation in nature or in natural law why a set of words upon parchment should convey the dominion of land; why the son

1. 1 W. Blackstone, Commentaries *138.   3. Mackeldey, Roman Law § 265 (1883).

2. 2 W. Blackstone, Commentaries *2.

should have a right to exclude his fellow-creatures from a determined spot of ground, because his father had done so before him; or why the occupier of a particular field or of a jewel, when lying on his death bed and no longer able to maintain possession, should be entitled to tell the rest of the world which of them should enjoy it after him." [4]

This broader question relating to the natural origins of the concept of property has been the concern of legal philosophers for centuries. A nineteenth century British philosopher, Jeremy Bentham, viewed property as a "basis of expectation, the expectation of deriving certain advantages from a thing which we are said to possess, in consequence of the relation in which we stand towards it." [5] Viewed in this light, the law of property might be considered one of the keystones of civilized society, for the rights and duties imposed on modern man in defining his "basis of expectation" distinguish him from the savage who must use force to acquire and retain property. Bentham explained the law of property in this way: "The savage who has killed a deer may hope to keep it for himself, so long as his cave is undiscovered; so long as he watches to defend it, and is stronger than his rivals; but that is all. How miserable and precarious is such a possession! If we suppose the least agreement among savages to respect the acquisitions of each other, we see the introduction of a principle to which no name can be given but that of law. A feeble and momentary expectation may result from time to time from circumstances purely physical but a strong and permanent expectation can result only from law. That which, in the natural state, was an almost invisible thread, in the social state becomes a cable. Property and law are born together, and die together. Before laws were made there was no property; take away laws, and property ceases." [6]

In addition to its importance in legal philosophy, the concept of property is important in determining the outcome of specific legal disputes. See In re Marriage of Graham, infra.

## II.   REAL AND PERSONAL PROPERTY

It is possible to classify property in a variety of ways. For example, private property belongs to an individual who has the exclusive right of disposition, while public property includes those things owned by the public through a federal, state, or local governmental body. Literary property is the natural common law right of an author to the profits resulting from his composition, whereas theatrical property includes everything used in producing a play with the exception of the actors' costumes and painted scenery. In a legal sense, however, the most important classifications are real property and personal property.

4.  2 W. Blackstone, Commentaries *2.      6.  Id. at 112, 113.

5.  J. Bentham, Theory of Legislation
    111, 112 (1931).

Real property is property that is fixed, immovable, and permanent; it includes land, structures affixed to the land, property affixed to the structures, and in some cases, things growing on the land. Ownership of real property includes the right to the air space above the earth's surface and to the soil and minerals below. To describe these rights, courts often cite this rule: *cujus est solum ejus est usque ad coelum et ad inferos*, or "he who owns the soil owns also to the sky and to the depths." The implications of this rule will be examined in the following chapter.

Personal property includes everything that is not real property; its basic characteristic is its movability. It may be either tangible or intangible. Tangible property refers to things that can be touched, such as books, automobiles, or chairs, while intangible property includes property that has little or no value in itself but that represents something of value. For instance, if a corporation owns one asset, such as a one-hundred acre farm, and if all of the stock in the corporation is owned by Smith, Smith's interest would be classified as intangible personal property. The corporation, as a separate entity, owns the real estate and Smith's stock certificates represent only his interest in the corporation. The word "chattel" derived from the same Old French root as "cattle," is often used as a synonym for personal property.

## A. SOURCES OF LAW

One of the major reasons for distinguishing between real and personal property is that legal rules vary depending upon the nature of the property. If one were selling personal property, the law would be found in the Uniform Commercial Code, which has been enacted in all states but Louisiana. The Code has its origins in the law merchant, the law that developed in England for resolving disputes among traders and merchants. In 1942 preparation of the Code began, and in 1953 it was first adopted by Pennsylvania. Although a major goal of the Code is uniformity of commercial transactions, it is not uniform in fact, for by 1967 the various states that had enacted the Code had made approximately 775 separate amendments.[7] Citations to the Code below will refer to the 1972 Official Text, unless otherwise indicated.

Article 2 of the Code covers the sale of goods. The definition of goods here is identical to that of personal property: "all things  .   .   . which are movable at the time of identification to the contract for sale." Section 2–105. As noted in Chapter 1, the law relating to real property is derived mainly from case decisions and statutes rather than from the Code.

As one illustration of the difference between real and personal property law, we can assume that Jones enters into contracts with

7.  J. White & R. Summers, Uniform
Commercial Code 7 (1972).

Brown to sell his 1954 Rambler for $400 and to sell a small vacant lot in Arizona for another $400. Must these contracts be in writing to be enforceable? The answer is to be found in the Statute of Frauds, which lists those contracts that must be written. The Statute of Frauds section of the U.C.C. provides that only contracts for the sale of goods priced $500 or more must be in writing; however, the Code contains a number of exceptions to this requirement even in cases when the value exceeds $500. For example, if a party admits in court that an oral contract for more than $500 was made, the contract is enforceable. Under the general Statute of Frauds, however, any contract for the sale of land or of an interest in land must be written. Consequently, Jones' contract for the sale of the car can be oral, but the contract for the sale of the lot must be written.

## B. FORM OF TRANSFER

Another reason for distinguishing real and personal property concerns the requirements for transferring property. Ownership of real property is normally transferred by a deed, which must meet certain formal requirements. An interest in personal property may be transferred by a bill of sale, a document similar in form to a deed, although a bill of sale is usually neither required nor customary.

## C. TAXATION

There are also important tax considerations for distinguishing personal and real property. Personal property is generally not taxed at all, or it is taxed according to a rate structure different from that used for real property. For instance, in New York the real property tax law excludes personal property from taxation. A New York homeowner installed a swimming pool above ground, which cost around $5,000. The pool was not attached to the real estate and could be disassembled in a few hours and reassembled in a new location for less than $450. When the homeowner's real estate taxes were increased because of the pool, he filed suit to cancel the extra assessment. The court agreed with the homeowner that the pool had not become real estate and invalidated the assessment.[8]

## III. FIXTURES

Because Sally loved to shoot billiards, she installed a $5,000 slate-covered pool table in the basement of her home. The legs of the table were screwed to the floor, and she installed basement carpeting to match the felt on the table. Sometime after the table had been installed, Sally signed a contract to sell her house to Slim. Slim now claims that he purchased the pool table when he purchased Sally's real

8. Roberts v. Assessment Bd. of Review of the Town of New Windsor, 84 Misc. 2d 1017, 375 N.Y.S.2d 988 (1975).

estate. Sally claims that she can take the table with her. Who is correct?

The answer to this question depends on whether or not the table is considered a fixture. A fixture is a legal hybrid; it is a piece of personal property which has become affixed to real property in such a way that it becomes part of the real property. But as the court noted in the leading case of Teaff v. Hewitt, "In the great order of nature, when we compare a thing at the extremity of one class with a thing at the extremity of another, the difference is glaring; but when we approach the connecting link between the two divisions, it is often difficult to discover the precise point where the dividing line is drawn. . . . [T]he precise point in the connection with the realty, where the article loses the legal qualities of a chattel and acquires those of the realty, often presents a question of great nicety and sometimes difficult determination." [9]

## A. FIXTURE TESTS

In order to determine whether personal property has been transformed into a fixture, most American courts apply three tests: annexation, adaptation, and intention.

1. **Annexation.** The first test requires that the property be annexed to the real estate. As the *Teaff* court noted, "If there be any thing well settled in the doctrine of fixtures, it is this, that to constitute a fixture, it is an essential requisite that the article be actually affixed or annexed to the realty. The term itself imports this." [10]

Although the rule appears easy to apply, courts do not agree as to what constitutes annexation. For instance, in several cases they have decided that there is "constructive" annexation because of the relationship between the personal property and real estate, even when the personal property is not actually annexed to the real estate. Property which might be considered constructively annexed would include window screens, storm doors and windows that have been fitted for a house but are not yet in place, or devices such as garage door openers and television antenna dials.

The doctrine of constructive annexation also applies to cases where machinery is installed in industrial plants in such a way as to be considered a fixture. If the machinery itself is a fixture, then essential parts of the machinery are considered fixtures, although they may not be attached. At least one state, Pennsylvania, has gone a step further and adopted the "assembled industrial plant doctrine," which provides that even unattached machinery is to be considered a fixture if it is essential to the operation of the plant.[11]

9. Teaff v. Hewitt, 1 Ohio St. 511 (1853).

10. Id.

11. See W. Burby, Real Property 23, 24 (3rd ed. 1965).

In considering the annexation test, courts also attempt to determine if removal will damage the real estate, although they have not applied this doctrine uniformly. For example, one court concluded that a Murphy bed was not a fixture because it could be removed without damaging the real estate.[12] But in numerous other cases, items such as millstones, fences, doors, and windows have been considered fixtures even though their removal would not cause injury to the real estate.[13]

In some situations a court will decide that an article is a fixture even though the property is neither constructively annexed nor actually annexed by nails, bolts, screws, or glue. For instance, the weight of an object might lead a court to conclude that the annexation test has been met. In the case of Snedeker v. Warring, the court ruled that a three- or four-ton statue which was not cemented or clamped to the floor would be considered a fixture because "a thing may be as firmly affixed to the land by gravitation as by clamps or cement." [14]

Courts have also decided that a fixture will not become personal property if it was severed from the real estate for purposes of repair or severed by an act of God. In one case, a storm demolished a building and a dispute arose over the right to the ruins of the building. The court decided that even though the ruins had been detached from the real estate, "the act of God . . . shall prejudice no one." [15] Consequently, the court decided that the property was still classified as real, not personal, unless the owner himself had caused the severance.

2. **Adaptation.** A second test focuses on the question of whether an article is adapted to the use or purpose of the real estate. Although a few courts have made adaptation the sole test of a fixture, the test is too broad to be applied effectively. For instance, on this basis alone, fixtures could conceivably include implements on a farm [16] or furniture in an apartment. In applying the test, most courts attempt to determine whether the chattels are necessary or beneficial to the enjoyment of the real estate. Examples of such chattels include a furnace in a house, power equipment in a mill,[17] and computer systems in bank buildings. In Bank of America v. Los Angeles,[18] the plaintiff bank brought suit, seeking a refund of real estate taxes that had been levied on electronic computer systems installed in several buildings. The buildings had been especially designed for use as accounting centers:

12. Fisher v. Pennington, 116 Cal.App. 248, 2 P.2d 518 (1931).

13. Teaff v. Hewitt, 1 Ohio St. 511 (1853).

14. Snedeker v. Warring, 12 N.Y. 170 (1854).

15. Rogers v. Gilinger, 30 Pa. 185 (1858).

16. Teaff v. Hewitt, 1 Ohio St. 511 (1853).

17. Zangerle v. Ohio Oil Co., 144 Ohio St. 506, 60 N.E.2d 52, 30 O.O. 151 (1945).

18. 224 Cal.App.2d 108, 36 Cal.Rptr. 413 (1964).

they had fewer windows than ordinary commercial buildings; they were constructed near a constant electrical power source and away from prime military areas; and they contained an expensive raised floor to support the computer systems. The court decided that the systems were fixtures because they were "necessary or convenient to the use of a building for the purpose for which it is designed" and that they were properly taxed as real property.

3. **Intention.** According to modern courts, the controlling test of a fixture is the intention of the party who annexed the chattel to make the article a permanent part of the real estate. To determine intention, courts look to the actions, purpose, and relations of the parties. "The intention of the parties is not always governed by what is said by them, but the intention may be determined from the nature of the article, relations, and situation of the parties making the annexation, and the structure, use, and mode of annexation."[19] Even under the modern view, the tests of annexation and adaptation are important in determining intention.

It is often said that it is not the secret or hidden intention of the parties to the annexation that is important but the intention that can be deduced from the external facts.[20] In one case,[21] a person installed chandeliers that had been in the family for fifteen years in the dining room of his house. When he sold the house later, he took the chandeliers with him, even though the removal had never been discussed during negotiations. Deciding that the removal was wrongful because the chandeliers were fixtures, the court stressed its reasons for considering a party's subjective intention to be immaterial: "If a witness testifies that, when he put a chandelier in a house, he intended to take it out if he should ever sell the house, in what possible way can the evidence be disputed? . . . If it be held in this case that the secret intention of the defendant is determinative of the question whether or not the articles involved are fixtures, that holding will encourage and invite persons less honest than the respondents to attempt to remove from premises every at-all-movable article that can be disconnected without breakage."

Of the external facts examined by the courts, one of the most important is the relationship between the person who has annexed the chattel and the real estate. For instance, when the owner of real estate annexes personal property such as a heating system that is intended to benefit the general use and occupation of the real estate, the law presumes that he intended the property to become a fixture.

**19.** Citizens Bank of Greenfield v. Mergenthaler Linotype Co., 216 Ind. 573, 25 N.E.2d 444 (1940).

**20.** American Telephone and Telegraph Co. v. Muller, 299 F.Supp. 157 (D.S.C. 1968).

**21.** Strain v. Green, 25 Wash.2d 692, 172 P.2d 216 (1946).

See Premonstratensian Fathers v. Badger Mutual Ins. Co., and Paul v. National Bank, infra, for discussion of fixture tests.

4. **Special Tests.** Courts will often look to a statute to determine whether an article of personal property has become a fixture. The use of statutory guidelines is very common when a court must determine if an article is to be taxed as real property or if there has been a violation of a zoning ordinance. In one case,[22] a woman was convicted of unlawful habitation of a mobile home in violation of a zoning ordinance that permitted buildings but specifically excluded "all forms of vehicles even though immobilized." The tongue, axles, and wheels had been removed from the home in question. Furthermore, it rested on a foundation of concrete blocks and had been connected with a number of utilities. Guided by the statutory definition and ignoring the three traditional fixture tests, the court concluded that because the home was a building rather than an immobilized vehicle, the conviction should be reversed.

Special tests have also been developed to determine the status of two types of property vitally important to agriculture: things growing on land, and manure. Growing things commonly have been classified as *fructus naturales* or *fructus industriales*.

*Fructus naturales*—those things produced primarily by the powers of nature, such as trees and perennial bushes—are considered real property. *Fructus industriales*—those things produced primarily by the industry of man, such as crops or fruits of *fructus naturales* like blueberries—are considered personal property.

Traditionally, the distinction between *fructus naturales* and *fructus industriales* has been important in resolving two legal issues. The first issue is whether the law of real or of personal property governs when there is a separate sale of something growing on the land. This issue is now covered by the Uniform Commercial Code and will be discussed later in this chapter. The second issue involves the question of whether things growing on the land pass with the real estate when it is sold. Most states have adopted a "severance" test: growing things—whether *fructus naturales* or *fructus industriales*—pass to the buyer with the real estate if they have not been severed at the time of conveyance. However, a few states have decided that in certain circumstances *fructus industriales* will not pass to the buyer when the real estate is sold. One theory used to support this view is the "maturity" test, which holds that a mature crop does not draw sustenance and support from the soil and therefore should not pass with the soil.[23] In other states, statutes provide that "all crops, ma-

22. State v. Work, 75 Wash.2d 204, 449 P.2d 806 (1969).

23. See G. Dykstra & L. Dykstra, The Business Law of Real Estate 25 (1956).

tured or unmatured, shall be and the same hereby are declared to be personalty." [24]

Even when the majority rule is followed, it is possible for the vendor to reserve the right to remove things growing on the land. When he reserves the right to *fructus naturales,* the reservations should be in writing because he is reserving an interest in real estate that falls under the Statute of Frauds. But when the vendor reserves the right to *fructus industriales,* the reservation can be oral if the value is under $500. However, to be safe, all reservations should be written because of the parol evidence rule, a rule which provides that evidence of an oral side agreement cannot be proven when there is a complete written contract such as the contract for the conveyance of real estate in this case.[25]

The term "emblements" is often used as a synonym for *fructus industriales,* but the word is also used to describe the right of a tenant to remove, after the termination of the tenancy, the annual products of the land which have resulted from his own labor. In order to claim emblements, the tenant should prove: (1) existence of a tenancy of uncertain duration; (2) termination of the tenancy by the act of God or by the act of the lessor; and (3) proof that the crop was planted by the tenant, or someone working for him, during his right of occupancy.[26] The doctrine is based on fairness to the tenant who, holding the land for an uncertain time, would be reluctant to use the land productively without such a rule.

Although manure has lost much of its importance in our modern economy, disputes regarding its ownership have engaged a surprising number of courts. One of the earliest cases [27] involved a defendant who was sued for slander when he exclaimed, "Thou are a thief. Thou has stolen my dung." The defendant contended that the statement could not be slanderous because dung was not personal property and therefore could not be stolen. In discussing this defense, Justice Bacon observed that "dung is a chattel, and may be stolen." However, another justice responded that "dung may be a chattel, and it may not be a chattel; for a heap of dung is a chattel, but if it be spread upon the land it is not." After further discussion, the court concluded that regardless of whether or not the dung could be stolen, the words of the defendant were still "scandalous."

Most courts have decided that the purchaser of real estate acquires manure that was produced by food grown on the land, while manure that is produced from food brought from outside sources belongs to the seller of the real estate. In other words, that which is produced by the land remains with the land.

---

**24.** Chatham Chemical Co. v. Vidalia Chemical Co., 163 Ga. 276, 136 S.E. 62 (1926).

**25.** See W. Burby, supra note 11, at 17.

**26.** Miller v. Wohlford, 119 Ind. 305, 21 N.E. 894 (1889).

**27.** Carver v. Pierce, 23 Car.Banc.Reg.

## B.  FIXTURE DISPUTES

The law of fixtures becomes especially important when two or more persons claim ownership of the same article.  There are five types of transactions in which ownership disputes are especially common.

1.  **Transfer of Real Estate.**  A common legal dispute involving fixtures arises when a person sells real estate without realizing that certain articles in the home might legally be considered fixtures.  If they are fixtures, the general rule is that they pass to the buyer, whether they are actually or constructively annexed to the real estate.[28]

The major problem in these cases is determining whether the article is a fixture.  Here, as elsewhere, courts have adopted the three fixture tests, with emphasis on the intention of the parties.  For example, in one case a court held that an electric stove was not a fixture because it was "not convinced that the purchaser of a dwelling, knowing there is an electric range in it, thinks for a minute that he is buying the electric range when he buys the dwelling, unless he had some special arrangement whereby the title to the range is to pass with the building." [29]

The "unless" clause of this statement is an important exception to the general rule: the exception applies when the parties include provisions in their contract that determine whether personal property and fixtures remain with the seller or pass to the buyer.  Although an oral agreement might be enforceable, the agreement should be incorporated into the written real estate contract to avoid statute of frauds and parol evidence difficulties and to provide proof of the agreement should a dispute arise.

2.  **Transfer of Property Attached to Real Estate.**  Fixtures are frequently sold separately from the real estate, and their sale usually follows one of two patterns.  First, the fixture may be severed from the real estate and then sold.  For instance, a landowner may cut down several walnut trees and sell the logs.  Because the trees are personal property at the time of sale, personal property law will govern the sale.

Second, the landowner may sell articles affixed to real estate, such as the walnut tree, before severance; in this case it must be determined whether real property or personal property rules govern.  The answer to this problem may be found in Section 2–107 of the Uniform Commercial Code, which divides items attached to the land into two categories.  In the first category are those things which are attached to the real estate but can be severed without material harm

---

28.  Slater v. Dowd, 79 Ga.App. 272, 53 S.E.2d 598 (1949).

29.  Gas and Electric Shop, Inc. v. Corey—Scheffel Lumber Co., 227 Ky. 657, 13 S.W.2d 1009 (1929).

to the real estate. This category specifically includes timber to be cut and growing crops. In cases where things of this nature are sold while still attached to the land, the contract is considered to be a sale of goods governed by the Code. In the second category are things attached to the land which cannot be removed without material harm to the land, such as minerals and structures which are to be removed from the real estate.[30] If the contract of sale calls for these articles to be severed by the seller, the contract is still a sale of goods governed by the Code. If the buyer is to sever these goods, however, the contract is treated as a sale of real estate, and real estate principles govern. See Rosen v. Hummel, infra.

The above rules are subject to the rights of third persons under real estate law. For instance, the sale of a house to be severed from the real estate by the seller is a contract for the sale of goods; but if the seller sold the real estate to an innocent third party before severance, that party would be entitled to the house. To protect himself in this situation, the buyer should record the contract of sale.

3. **Tenant's Fixtures.** Frequently a person renting real estate installs fixtures on the property. A farmer renting real estate may install a corn crib on the land; a manufacturer renting a building may purchase and affix to the building thousands of dollars worth of equipment in order to carry on his business; and a person renting an apartment may attach a bookshelf to a wall or a lamp to the ceiling to make the apartment more comfortable. The legal issue in each instance is whether the tenant may remove the fixture at the termination of the tenancy.

In the older cases, courts emphasized the annexation test in deciding that anything the tenant had attached to the real estate could not be removed by the tenant at the end of the lease.[31] However, over time three exceptions have developed, and these are collectively referred to as tenant's fixtures. If one of these exceptions applies, the tenant may remove articles that he annexed to the real estate.

a. *Trade Fixtures*. These are defined as those articles placed on the premises by the tenant to carry on the trade or business for which he rents the premises. Courts have decided that trade fixtures include such articles as a tavern outbuilding, a kiln, a sawmill, an airplane hangar, a smokehouse, gasoline tanks and pumps, a furnace, machinery, railroad tracks, brass rails, bowling alleys, greenhouses, barber chairs, bars, a pipe organ, and a vault door.

b. *Agricultural Fixtures*. These are defined as articles annexed by the tenant for the purpose of farming and tilling the soil. Courts have determined that the following articles are agricultural fixtures:

---

30. In the 1962 Uniform Commercial Code, timber was included in the second category.

31. See G. Dykstra & L. Dykstra, supra note 23, at 53.

a milling plant, a cream separator, an irrigation plant, platform scales, a wooden silo, a brooder house, a hay carrier, a manure carrier, a hen house, a tool shed, and a maple sugar shed.

c.  *Domestic Fixtures.*  These are articles attached by the tenant to make his apartment more comfortable or convenient.  They include carpeting, screens, doors, windows, a toilet, a washing machine, a gas stove, an oil burner, and bookshelves.

Courts have developed the three exceptions to encourage a tenant to use the property beneficially.  The exceptions are further justified on the grounds that if a tenant makes an improvement to which the landlord has contributed nothing, the tenant intends to retain the improvement as his personal property.  As one court stated, "The right of the tenant to remove the erections made by him in furtherance of the purpose for which the premises were leased is one founded upon public policy and has its foundation in the interest which society has that every person shall be encouraged to make the most beneficial use of his property  .   .   .   .  The reason property of this kind is personal, rather than real, is based upon the rule the law implies an agreement that it shall remain personal property from the fact the lessor contributes nothing thereto and should not be enriched at the expense of his tenant  .   .   .  ." [32]

Nevertheless, the rules governing trade, agricultural, and domestic fixtures have been qualified in a number of ways.  First, the article annexed must fall within the exception.  It is possible that articles annexed by a tenant have not been installed for the purposes of carrying on a trade, farming, or making a house more livable.  If, for example, a court determines that a servant's room, drainage pipe, and cement walk do not fall within the definition of trade or domestic fixtures, the tenant has no right to remove them. [33]

Second, the tenant must be able to remove the fixture without causing substantial injury to the premises.  In Gordon v. Cohn, [34] for example, the tenant cemented fifty-two square yards of linoleum to the floor of the premises; to remove the linoleum, one-sixteenth inch of the floor surface would also have had to be removed.  The court held that the tenant had no right to remove the linoleum because the landlord is "not required to sacrifice any part of his building in an effort to restore it to its former use and attractiveness."

Third, the tenant must remove the articles before he turns over possession of the premises to the landlord.  The rule is designed to protect the landlord, who often will have leased the premises to another tenant, and it is based on the assumption that the tenant has abandoned the articles by failing to remove them at the time he left

32.  Cameron v. Oakland County Gas & Oil Co., 277 Mich. 442, 269 N.W. 227 (1936).

33.  Wright v. Du Bignon, 114 Ga. 765, 40 S.E. 747 (1902).

34.  220 Cal. 193, 30 P.2d 19 (1934).

the premises. However, if the landlord has evicted the tenant or if the lease is for an indefinite period, the tenant is given a reasonable time after leaving to remove the fixtures.[35]

If there is any doubt about a tenant's right to remove a fixture, the matter should be negotiated and an appropriate clause ought to be inserted in the lease. Landlords often include a clause to the ef-. fect that "all the improvements, alterations, repairs, and additions" must remain for the benefit of the landlord. However, in a number of decisions the courts have interpreted these terms strictly. For instance, in one case in which a lease contained the above clause, a landlord sued a tenant for damages after the tenant had removed an ornamental mahogany partition and a showcase. But the court held for the tenant on the grounds that terms such as "improvements" and "additions" normally refer to changes in the structure of the premises and not to trade fixtures that the tenant had installed.[36]

4. **The Use of Fixtures as Collateral.** A very common yet complex problem arises when fixtures are used as collateral to secure a loan. Here, three basic situations occur frequently. The first two cause little legal difficulty while the third situation is more complex.

a. *The Case of Mortgagor v. Mortgagee.* When Clyde decided to buy a house, he borrowed $30,000 from a local bank to finance his purchase and gave the bank a mortgage on the house. In legal terms, Clyde became a mortgagor and the bank a mortgagee. Shortly after Clyde moved into the house, he made a number of improvements, including the installation of built-in appliances, which under the state law were considered fixtures. But after one year Clyde defaulted on his mortgage payments and the mortgagee bank foreclosed. Does the mortgage cover not only the real estate as it existed when the mortgage was made, but also the fixtures added after execution of the mortgage? As a general rule, the mortgage covers later additions to the real estate.[37] This conclusion is often fortified by language in the mortgage declaring that all things annexed to the real estate at the time the mortgage is signed or annexed to the property afterward will be security for repayment of the loan.

b. *The Case of Owner v. Secured Party.* Mary owned her own home, which was not mortgaged. She decided to improve it by installing new kitchen cabinets, which were considered fixtures under state law. Mary borrowed money from the Friendly Finance Company to finance her purchase and gave the company a security interest in the cabinets. When she later defaulted in her loan payments, Friendly Finance claimed that it had the right to repossess the cabinets. Is repossession of fixtures allowed?

35. See G. Dykstra & L. Dykstra, supra note 23, at 58–60.

36. Smusch v. Kohn, 22 Misc. 344, 49 N.Y.S. 176 (1898).

37. Sequist v. Fabiano, 274 Mich. 643, 265 N.W. 488 (1936).

The answer requires an elementary understanding of the law of secured transactions, which is governed by Article 9 of the Uniform Commercial Code. The Code defines a security interest as "an interest in personal property or fixtures which secures payment or performance of an obligation." It includes the so-called "conditional sale," in which the seller delivers goods to a buyer but retains title until payment has been received. Section 1–201(37). If the seller takes a security interest in the goods being sold to secure payment of the price, or if any lender takes a security interest in goods which are purchased with the loan, the interest is a "purchase money security interest."

Two methods are used to obtain the security interest. First, the debtor may sign a written "security agreement" that contains a description of the collateral; if the interest covers crops, oil, gas, minerals to be extracted, or timber to be cut, a description of the real estate is also included. Second, the creditor may take possession of the goods. With either method, there must be an agreement between the debtor and the creditor, the creditor must give value, and the debtor must have rights in the collateral.

While the security interest gives the creditor rights against the debtor, the creditor should "perfect" the security interest in order to gain priority against third parties, such as other creditors or good faith purchasers of the goods. The creditor may perfect by taking possession of the collateral, but the more common method is to file a financing statement in a local office, such as the Register of Deeds, or in a state office, such as the Secretary of State. The reason for requiring possession or filing is to give public notice to third parties that the creditor is claiming a security interest in the collateral.

In Mary's case, whether or not the security interest has been perfected, the secured creditor would have the right to repossess the cabinets if we assume that other creditors claim no interest in them. The creditor's right to repossession is established by Mary's agreement to give the security interest.

c. *The Case of Secured Party v. Other Creditors.* The first two cases have involved the owner of real estate against either a mortgagee creditor or a secured party creditor. Now we will examine a situation involving a direct conflict between the secured party and the mortgagee. Assume that Sam, a dealer, sells an air conditioner to Pete on an installment basis and takes a security interest. The air conditioner, when placed in the home, becomes a fixture. What must Sam, the secured party, do to gain priority to the air conditioner over Pete's bank, which holds a mortgage on the property, or even to gain priority over a later purchaser of Pete's house who might also claim the air conditioner?

The answer can be found in Section 9–313 of the Uniform Commercial Code. This section defines fixtures as goods that have "become so related to particular real estate that an interest in them arises under real estate law." However, the section does not apply to ordinary building materials that have been incorporated into a structure, nor to other improvements on land.

Under Section 9–313, the secured party, Sam, has priority over mortgagees and other interests in four situations. (1) If Sam has a purchase money security interest and he perfects by a fixture filing within ten days after the goods become fixtures, he will prevail over existing mortgages.[38] A fixture filing is a filing of the financing statement in the same office where mortgages are recorded. This rule is qualified by the fact that a prior construction mortgage is given priority over the security interest if the goods become fixtures before construction is completed. A construction mortgage is given to secure a loan that is used to construct an improvement on the land. (2) A security interest that is perfected by a fixture filing has priority over interests recorded or acquired by legal proceedings at a later date. (3) If the fixtures are readily removable factory or office machines or replacements of appliances which are consumer goods, a security interest perfected before the goods become fixtures prevails over other interests. (4) Finally, a secured party will prevail in all cases over other interests if the person owning those interests consents in writing to the security interest.

5. **Wrongful or Mistaken Annexation.** The typical wrongful annexation case arises when the owner of a fixture wants to recover it because it has been affixed to someone else's real estate without his permission. In Eisenhauer v. Quinn,[39] Gerarci owned a house that was being removed to a new location. Smith stole the house, placed it on his own lot, and then sold the house and lot to an innocent third party, Eisenhauer. When Gerarci sued to recover the house, the court ruled that "one of the elementary rules of the law of fixtures is that a chattel, to become an irremovable fixture, must have been annexed to the realty by the owner of the fixture, or with his consent. . . . " The court held that Gerarci did not lose title to his property by Smith's devious actions. However, this rule is not followed in cases where personal property has lost its identity by incorporation, for example, when stolen brick or timber is used to build a house. In such a case it would be economically wasteful to allow the owner to destroy the house to recover the brick and timber. Consequently, the better rule would limit the owner to recovery of damages.[40]

A different situation arises when an innocent person mistakenly attaches his personal property to real estate owned by someone else.

---

38. In the 1962 Uniform Commercial Code, the secured party was given priority if the security interest attached to the goods before they became fixtures.

39. 36 Mont. 368, 93 P. 38 (1907).

40. See W. Burby, supra note 11, at 29.

The most expensive of these mistakes occurs when a person builds a house on the wrong lot. Courts have adopted a variety of approaches in these situations, but in the absence of a statute many courts would allow the innocent party to recover the value of the improvement to the real estate. In fact a number of states have enacted statutes that provide relief for the innocent party in certain situations. For instance, in Ohio a person who purchases property at an execution sale or a tax sale and who makes lasting improvements on it is entitled to reimbursement from a person who is able to prove better title.[41] See Ollig v. Eagles, infra.

# CASES

## IN RE MARRIAGE OF GRAHAM

Supreme Court of Colorado, 1978.
— Colo. —, 574 P.2d 75.

LEE, Justice. This case presents the novel question of whether in a marriage dissolution proceeding a master's degree in business administration (M.B.A.) constitutes marital property which is subject to division by the court. In its opinion in Graham v. Graham, Colo.App., 555 P.2d 527, the Colorado Court of Appeals held that it was not. We affirm the judgment.

The Uniform Dissolution of Marriage Act requires that a court shall divide marital property, without regard to marital misconduct, in such proportions as the court deems just after considering all relevant factors. The Act defines marital property as follows:

"For purposes of this article only, 'marital property' means all property acquired by either spouse subsequent to the marriage except:

'(a) Property acquired by gift, bequest, devise, or descent;

'(b) Property acquired in exchange for property acquired prior to the marriage or in exchange for property acquired by gift, bequest, devise, or descent;

'(c) Property acquired by a spouse after a decree of legal separation; and

'(d) Property excluded by valid agreement of the parties.' "

The parties to this proceeding were married on August 5, 1968, in Denver, Colorado. Throughout the six-year marriage, Anne P. Graham, wife and petitioner here, was employed full-time as an air-

41. Ohio Rev.Code § 5303.08.

line stewardess. She is still so employed. Her husband, Dennis J. Graham, respondent, worked parttime for most of the marriage, although his main pursuit was his education. He attended school for approximately three and one-half years of the marriage, acquiring both a bachelor of science degree in engineering physics and a master's degree in business administration at the University of Colorado. Following graduation, he obtained a job as an executive assistant with a large corporation at a starting salary of $14,000 per year.

The trial court determined that during the marriage petitioner contributed seventy percent of the financial support, which was used both for family expenses and for her husband's education. No marital assets were accumulated during the marriage. In addition, the Grahams together managed an apartment house and petitioner did the majority of housework and cooked most of the meals for the couple. No children were born during the marriage.

The parties jointly filed a petition for dissolution, on February 4, 1974, in the Boulder County District Court. Petitioner did not make a claim for maintenance or for attorney fees. After a hearing on October 24, 1974, the trial court found, as a matter of law, that an education obtained by one spouse during a marriage is jointly-owned property to which the other spouse has a property right. The future earnings value of the M.B.A. to respondent was evaluated at $82,836 and petitioner was awarded $33,134 of this amount, payable in monthly installments of $100.

The court of appeals reversed, holding that an education is not itself "property" subject to division under the Act, although it was one factor to be considered in determining maintenance or in arriving at an equitable property division.

\* \* \*

The legislature intended the term "property" to be broadly inclusive, as indicated by its use of the qualifying adjective "all" in section 14–10–113(2). Previous Colorado cases have given "property" a comprehensive meaning, as typified by the following definition: "In short it embraces anything and everything which may belong to a man and in the ownership of which he has a right to be protected by law."

Nonetheless, there are necessary limits upon what may be considered "property," and we do not find any indication in the Act that the concept as used by the legislature is other than that usually understood to be embodied within the term. One helpful definition is "everything that has an exchangeable value or which goes to make up wealth or estate." Black's Law Dictionary 1382 (rev. 4th ed. 1968). \* \* \*

An educational degree, such as an M.B.A., is simply not encompassed even by the broad views of the concept of "property." It does not have an exchange value or any objective transferable value on an open market. It is personal to the holder. It terminates on death of the holder and is not inheritable. It cannot be assigned, sold, transferred, conveyed, or pledged. An advanced degree is a cumulative product of many years of previous education, combined with diligence and hard work. It may not be acquired by the mere expenditure of money. It is simply an intellectual achievement that may potentially assist in the future acquisition of property. In our view, it has none of the attributes of property in the usual sense of that term.

Our interpretation is in accord with cases in other jurisdictions. We have been unable to find any decision, even in community property states, which appears to have held that an education of one spouse is marital property to be divided on dissolution. This contention was dismissed in Todd v. Todd, 272 Cal.App.2d 786, 78 Cal.Rptr. 131 (Ct. App.), where it was held that a law degree is not a community property asset capable of division, partly because it "cannot have monetary value placed upon it." Similarly, it has been recently held that a person's earning capacity, even where enhanced by a law degree financed by the other spouse, "should not be recognized as a separate, particular item of property." Stern v. Stern, 66 N.J. 340, 331 A.2d 257.

\* \* \*

A spouse who provides financial support while the other spouse acquires an education is not without a remedy. Where there is marital property to be divided, such contribution to the education of the other spouse may be taken into consideration by the court. Here, we again note that no marital property had been accumulated by the parties. Further, if maintenance is sought and a need is demonstrated, the trial court may make an award based on all relevant factors. Certainly, among the relevant factors to be considered is the contribution of the spouse seeking maintenance to the education of the other spouse from whom the maintenance is sought. Again, we note that in this case petitioner sought no maintenance from respondent.

The judgment is affirmed.

---

### PREMONSTRATENSIAN FATHERS v. BADGER MUTUAL INS. CO.

Supreme Court of Wisconsin, 1970.
46 Wis.2d 362, 175 N.W.2d 237.

This is an action to recover upon a fire insurance policy, the coverage clause of which provides:

> "When the insurance under this policy covers a building, such insurance shall cover on the building, \* \* \* all permanent fixtures, \* \* \*"

The Premonstratensian Fathers, called Fathers, are the owners of a one-story building, insured by the property insurance policy in question, which is used as a supermarket. * * *

* * * On March 7, 1960, Jacobs Brothers Stores, Inc. deeded, by warranty deed, the land and the improvements to the Fathers. On March 7, 1960, the Fathers leased the premises back to the Jacobs Brothers Stores, Inc. for a term of twenty years. The lease further provided that the lessee was to provide fire insurance on the building and the fixtures in the name of the lessor. Following this lease, the premises were operated in exactly the same manner as it had been since the initial construction. The lessee then provided the insurance which is the subject of the instant lawsuit.

On June 1, 1964, the building and improvements were severely damaged by a major fire. Following the fire, the building was replaced with a new building, and the interior of the building is substantially the same as that prior to the fire and is still run as a supermarket. The defendant-insurers paid to the plaintiff the sum of $83,-000 for the loss suffered to the building, but have refused to pay a claim in the amount of $23,551.62 for the destruction of five Hussman walk-in coolers which were situated in the building. The grounds upon which the insurers have refused to pay the claim of the Fathers, and upon which they relied in both the trial court and in this court are: (1) The coolers are not the property of the Fathers, and (2) even if the coolers are the property of the Fathers, they are not insured property. There is no issue as to the amount of the damages, or whether the policy was in full force and effect on the date of the fire. The trial court concluded that the coolers are insured property and granted judgment for the plaintiff.

The coolers which are the subject of this dispute are walk-in type coolers. There are five of these: two meat coolers, a deep-freeze, a produce cooler, and a dairy cooler. A further description of the coolers is set forth in the opinion.

CONNOR T. HANSEN, Justice.

Although the insurers have divided their argument into two sections, the basis of the entire appeal is a consideration of the legal status of the coolers. If the coolers are determined to be common-law fixtures, and were such at the time of the construction of the building and the installation of the coolers, then they would have passed to the Fathers under the warranty deed of March 7, 1960, and they would be insured under the terms of the policy. The issue then is whether these coolers constitute fixtures.

The rule which has developed in Wisconsin as to what constitues a fixture is not really a comprehensive definition, but rather a statement of the factors which are to be applied to the fact and circumstances of a particular case to determine whether or not the property in question does constitute a fixture:

> "* * * Whether articles of personal property are fixtures, i. e., real estate, is determined in this state, if not generally, by the following rules or tests: (1) Actual physical annexation to the real estate; (2) application or adaptation to the use or purpose to which the realty is devoted; and (3) an intention on the part of the person making the annexation to make a permanent accession to the freehold."
>
> * * *

## ANNEXATION.

Annexation refers to:

> "* * * the act of attaching or affixing personal property to real property and, as a general proposition, an object will not acquire the status of a fixture unless it is in some manner or means, albeit slight, attached or affixed, either actually or constructively, to the realty."

It has been held in Wisconsin that physical annexation, although a factor to be considered in the determination, is of relative unimportance:

> "* * * it has often been said by this court that the matter of physical annexation of the article to the freehold is relatively unimportant. * * *."

The trial court ably pointed out the physical facts which led to its conclusion that there is indeed annexation in this case. The more important of these are as follows: (1) The exterior walls of the cooler, in four instances, constituted the interior wall of another room. (2) In the two meat coolers, a meat hanging and tracking system was built into the coolers. These tracks were used to move large cuts of meats from the cooler area into the meat preparation areas, and were suspended from the steel girders of the building structure by means of large steel bolts. These bolts penetrated through the roof of the cooler supporting wooden beams, which, in turn, supported the tracking system. The tracking in the coolers was a part of a system of tracking throughout the rear portion of the supermarket. (3) The coolers were attached to hardwood plank which was, in turn, attached to the concrete floor of the supermarket. The attachment of the plank to the floor was accomplished through the use of a ramsetting gun. The planks were laid on the floor, and the bolts were driven through them into the concrete floor, where they then exploded, firmly fixing the coolers into place. There was a material placed on the planks which served both as an adhesive and as an insulation. (4) The floor of the coolers was specially sloped during the construction of the building so that the slope would carry drainage into a specially constructed drain in the concrete. In addition, four of the coolers were coated with a protective coating to seal the floors. In the freezer, a special concrete buildup was constructed in the nature of a trough, the purpose of which was to carry away moisture as frozen chickens melted. (5) A refrigeration unit was built into each cooler. The unit was suspended from the ceiling of the cooler, and tubing was run through the wall of the cooler to compressors located elsewhere in the store. (6) Electric lights and power receptacles were built into each cooler and were connected by electrical wiring through the walls and the ceiling of the cooler to the store's electrical power supply. (7) The walls of the cooler were interlocked, and set into the splines, the hardwood planks ramset into the concrete floor, in tongue and groove fashion.

These factors adequately support the conclusion that the coolers were indeed physically annexed to the premises. The insurers argue that the coolers were removable without material injury to the premises, which detracts from the annexation. * * * In any event, the element of removability without material damage to the building no longer enjoys the position of prominence in the law of fixtures which it once held. It is now only one of the factors which is to be considered by the trial court. Based on the evidence introduced, the finding of the trial court that the coolers were physically annexed to the premises is not contrary to the great weight and clear preponderance of the evidence.

## ADAPTATION.

Adaptation refers to the relationship between the chattel and the use which is made of the realty to which the chattel is annexed. The use of the realty was that of a retail grocery, commonly known as a supermarket. This was the intent of the parties at the time of the construction of the building, and the intent of the parties throughout the entire history of the business. The fact of operation has borne out this intent. In a business which carries fresh foods, frozen foods, produce, meats and butter, coolers used for storage and handling of these perishables are patently related to the use of the building. In fact, it would be hard to picture any equipment more closely related to the operation of a supermarket, where large quantities of perishables must, of necessity, be purchased for storage and processing.

The insurers raise a number of points to dispute this finding. They state: The coolers were not custom made; the coolers are useful not to the building, but to the use to which the building is put; the coolers could have been used anywhere; other coolers could have been used. There is no requirement that the coolers be custom made, but only that they be adapted to the use to which the building is put. The test here is not the adaptability to the building, but the adaptability to the use to which the building is put. The fact that other coolers could have been used, or that these coolers could have been used elsewhere, does not alter the fact that there was a close connection between these coolers and the retail grocery business conducted on the property. This finding of the trial court cannot be said to be against the great weight and clear preponderance of the evidence.

## INTENT.

This court has repeatedly held that intent is the primary determinant of whether a certain piece of property has become a fixture. The relevant intent is that of the party making the annexation.

\* \* \*

In its decision, the trial court found, as a reasonable and legitimate inference from all the facts and circumstances surrounding the placement of the coolers onto the realty, that there was an intention that the coolers became a permanent accession to the realty; that when Jacobs Realty Corporation conveyed the land together with all buildings and improvements thereon to Jacobs Brothers Stores, Inc., the intention still prevailed that the coolers were a permanent accession to the realty; and that the same intention still prevailed when Jacobs Brothers Stores, Inc., conveyed the building and improvements to the plaintiff, and when the plaintiff leased the premises (the land, with all buildings and improvements thereon) back to the corporation as lessee.

\* \* \*  It follows that the coolers were common-law fixtures from their installation. As this court has stated:

" \* \* \* Although it is true that, in applying that doctrine the question of whether such machines constitute fixtures is largely one of intent, that intent may be considered established conclusively by the fact that the machines in question were clearly adapted to, *and were in fact put by the owner of the realty and the machines to, the use to which he devoted the realty and the installed machines as an entirety.* \* \* \* " (Emphasis added.)

" \* \* \* But where property is adapted to the use to which the realty is devoted, [by the owner] the use thereof in such manner furnishes such strong evidence of intent to make it a part of the freehold as not to be overcome by bookkeeping practices. \* \* \* "

The coolers were fixtures when installed; passed to Jacobs Brothers Stores, Inc., through the warranty deed; subsequently passed to the Fathers through that warranty deed; and are in fact fixtures within the meaning of the coverage clause of the insurance policy in this case. The decision of the trial judge was not against the great weight and clear preponderance of the evidence.

## PAUL v. FIRST NAT. BANK OF CINCINNATI

Common Pleas Court of Ohio, Hamilton County, 1976.
52 Ohio Misc. 77, 369 N.E.2d 488.

BLACK, Judge. As the purchaser for $575,000 of an elegant residence known as Long Acres, located in Indian Hill, Hamilton County, plaintiff Lawrence M. Paul sues the defendants (1) for removing and converting from the buildings and grounds certain items of property, (2) for damages resulting from failure to maintain the estate prior to delivery of possession as required by the purchase contract, and (3) for punitive damages.

The following description from a sales brochure published and distributed by a real estate agent under contract with defendant The First National Bank of Cincinnati, as Executor of the Estate of Augustine J. Long, deceased, indicates the style and character of this transaction:

" 'Long Acres' is an estate of picturesque charm, styled after the stately manors of England during the Tudor period. Surrounding the 17-room stone house are 97 acres of beautiful, gently rolling terraces exquisitely landscaped to compliment the natural terrain. Although elegant in every manner, Long Acres is a marvelous family home.

"Magnificent carved doors welcome you into the main entrance or 'Great Hall', with its vaulted ceiling, medieval chandelier and stone stairways that wind majestically to the balcony. From either side of the Great Hall huge, hand-rubbed maple archways lead to the living quarters. To the left is the Elizabethan music living room, also with vaulted ceiling, marble fireplace and a pipe organ. Throughout the first floor there are pictorial, leaded glass windows."

On July 13, 1971, plaintiff entered into a purchase contract with the defendant Executor, which contained the following provisions, among others:

"1. *Purchase and Sale of Real Estate.* The Bank agrees to sell and Paul agrees to purchase certain residential real estate situated in the Village of Indian Hill, Hamilton County, Ohio, more particularly described on Exhibit 'A' attached hereto and made a part hereof, *improvements, fixtures, and appurtenances* being also described on Exhibit 'A', all of which is herein referred to as 'The Real Estate.' " (Emphasis added.)

\* \* \*

When possession was delivered to plaintiff on January 15, 1972, he noticed that a number of items were missing that had been on the property both before and after the date of the purchase contract. The defendants admit that these items had been removed by the individual defendants before surrendering possession.

\* \* \*

## DECISION

I.  The plaintiff is entitled to recover the following amounts from defendants Nancy L. Hogan, Dorothy L. Ward, Patricia L. Bonn and William A. Long, jointly and severally:

(A)  For conversion of property:

| | |
|---|---:|
| 4 Handmade lighting fixtures around swimming pool | $1,000 |
| Lighting fixture in living quarters of apartment over stable | 100 |
| 2 Lighting fixtures removed from chapel | 125 |
| Stair carpeting | 0 |
| 3 Metal cranes | 4,650 |
| Ornamental housing over well | 2,100 |
| Mercury statue | 800 |
| Range and oven | 0 |
| 4 Garden Statues | 500 |
| Walnut organ bench | 400 |
| Subtotal | $9,675 |

(B)  For punitive damages and attorney fees:

| | |
|---|---:|
| Punitive damages | $3,000 |
| Attorneys fees | 3,000 |
| Subtotal | $6,000 |
| TOTAL | $15,675 |

\*   \*   \*

## REASONING

### General

The court concludes that the pertinent contract (sometimes known as the $410,000 contract) was proved and is now before the court for interpretation.

### I(A)

The converted items must be considered in two groups, as follows:

(1) 4 Handmade lighting fixtures around swimming pool

Lighting fixture in living quarters of apartment over stable

2 Lighting fixtures removed from chapel

3 Metal cranes

4 Garden statues

(2) Ornamental housing over well

Mercury statue

Walnut organ bench

In the court's judgment, group (1) are legally classified as "fixtures," and group (2) are "appurtenances," under the intent and meaning of the purchase contract.  *  *  *

*  *  *

In Masheter v. Boehm (1974), 37 Ohio St.2d 68, 307 N.E.2d 533, the Supreme Court designated, in paragraph two of the syllabus, six "facts" to be considered in determining whether an item is a fixture:

(1) The nature of the property;

(2) The manner in which the property is annexed to the realty;

(3) The purpose for which the annexation is made;

(4) The intention of the annexing party to make the property a part of the realty;

(5) The degree of difficulty and extent of any loss involved in removing the property from the realty;  and

(6) The damage to the severed property which such removal would cause.

As the Supreme Court ruled, the expression of "a comprehensive and generally applicable rule of law" about fixtures has bedevilled the courts for years and is complicated by the need for different definitions in those situations where the relationship between the parties is different.  That case dealt with eminent domain (what comprises the "real estate" which was appropriated?), while the instant case deals with a buyer and a seller, and the distributees under a will. Nevertheless, the six considerations listed in Masheter v. Boehm, supra, are pertinent and applicable in the interpretation of "all fixtures relating to said real estate" in paragraph II of Exhibit "A" of the purchase contract.

Using the Supreme Court's considerations, the light "fixtures" (there is no other available word) from the swimming pool, the stable apartment and the chapel are clearly fixtures in contemplation of law. They meet the primitive tests of Teaff v. Hewitt (1853), 1 Ohio St. 511.  They are of a type universally recognized as fixtures.  This is true even though the pool "fixtures" were hung on brackets and could be unplugged and simply lifted off the brackets.  But they were designed and produced solely and only for the swimming pool, from the same design as was used for the light fixture in the porte cochere (which was not removed).  Further, the poles from which they were taken are barren and incomplete without them.

The three metal cranes and the four garden statues also meet five of the six criteria, in the judgment of the court.  The "nature"

of these items is that they were a part of the total elegance of Long
Acres.   They are not the type of fixture which would be commonly
found on other lawns or in other gardens in Hamilton County, but
they are an integral part of this sumptuous country estate.   The
cranes were "annexed" by being bolted or screwed into concrete
foundations in a manner similar to the annexation of the marble table
in the Great Hall, an item clearly admitted by all defendants to be a
fixture passing with the real estate.   The 4 garden statues (busts?)
were not simply placed on top of their columns, but were held in place
by 6-inch pipe protruding from the columns into the bases of the
statues.   The purpose of fixing these into position was to ensure their
presence and preservation as part and parcel of the landscape and approach to Long Acres.   These cranes and statues were not items
moved about at the whim of the owner or according to the seasons:
they were permanent implacements, intended to be part of the continuing visual effect of the estate.   While no great difficulty was encountered in removing any of them, their absence is a source of loss.
The cranes were prominent in the approach to the front door, and
that approach is damaged without them.   They are shown in several
photographs attached to the appraisal which was prepared by the
Cincinnati Real Estate Board and considered by plaintiff before entering into the purchase contract.   The removal of the statues leaves
the columns on which they stood barren and incomplete; the columns
appear to have been vandalized.

Group (2), being the ornamental well housing, the Mercury statue
and the organ bench, were not attached in a permanent way.   However, interpreting the contract from its four corners, in the light of
all the facts and circumstances in evidence, the Court concludes that
these items were "appurtenances" to the real estate, both in contemplation of law and in interpretation of this word as used in the
purchase contract.

The word "appurtenance" means more than rights of way or
other incorporeal rights:   it includes an article adapted to the use of
the property to which it is connected and which is intended to be a
permanent accession to the freehold.

All three items in group (2) form a part of the character of Long
Acres and enhance the style of its elegance.   They are appurtenant to
Long Acres in the sense that they are necessarily connected with the
use and enjoyment of this country estate.   They are incidental to the
total value of this estate.   The source of that value is not only the
grand design but also all of the details whereby that design is executed:   the location of the house on the property, the sweep of the
driveway as it approaches the porte cochere, the spread-out location
of the barns and other outbuildings, the majesty of the formal gardens, the spaciousness of the lawns on every side, and all the details
of the exterior and interior of the mansion itself.

To allow the heirs to walk off with an organ bench, leaving the built-in organ behind would be plainly ridiculous. You cannot play an organ while standing up, and no ordinary bench will do.

The Mercury statue is pictured in two photographs included in the appraisal of Long Acres which was considered by plaintiff before purchase. It may have been moved from the pedestal from time to time by the Long family, and it was not a "sun dial," despite this label in the appraisal. But interpreting the contract in the light of all facts and circumstances in evidence, the Court concludes that these items were appurtenances passing with the real estate.

\*   \*   \*

## I(B)

Punitive damages are awarded against the Long children with respect to the wrongful removal and conversion of the items comprising group (1), the amount being appropriate to the degree of malice in the judgment of the Court. \*   \*   \*

While there is no direct evidence of malice (in the form of personal hate or ill will) in this case, this element of plaintiff's case is inferred from defendants' conduct. Imputed malice is "that state of mind under which a person does a wrongful act purposely, without a reasonable or lawful excuse, to the injury of another."

Punitive damages can be awarded in an action for conversion where the proof shows fraud, malice, insult or wanton or reckless disregard of the legal rights of others. \*   \*   \*

\*   \*   \*

---

## ROSEN v. HUMMEL

Supreme Court, Appellate Division, 1975.
47 A.D.2d 782, 365 N.Y.S.2d 75.

Appeal from an order of the Supreme Court at Special Term, entered August 27, 1974 in Warren County, which granted a motion by defendant for summary judgment dismissing plaintiff's complaint, and from the judgment entered thereon.

Plaintiff alleges in his complaint that the parties hereto entered into an oral agreement whereby plaintiff agreed to pay defendants $500 in exchange for which plaintiff or his agents would be permitted to enter upon defendants' land for the purpose of dismantling and carrying off a structure. In his action for breach of contract following defendants' alleged refusal to permit plaintiff's agent to so enter, the court at Special Term found the contract to be unenforceable under the Statute of Frauds.

We begin with the general premise, too well settled to require citation of authority, that a building affixed to land constitutes realty, and, therefore, plaintiff's alleged contract would be one to purchase an "interest in real property * * * or in any manner relating thereto", requiring a signed writing to be enforceable (General Obligations Law, § 5–703, subd. [1]). Plaintiff contends, however, that under Cervadoro v. First Nat. Bank & Trust Co. of Hudson (267 App.Div. 314, 45 N.Y.S.2d 738), the parties are free to treat buildings attached to the land as personalty, "especially where the removal of the same was to be had immediately". The rationale of *Cervadoro* is not controlling, for that case was decided under former section 156 of the Personal Property Law, no longer in effect, which included in the definition of "goods", "things attached to * * * the land which are agreed to be severed before sale or under the contract of sale."

Rather, we are governed in this case by the distinction created by subdivision (1) of section 2–107 of the Uniform Commercial Code, which appears to have revived the common law rule, adverted to in *Cervadoro,* in effect prior to adoption of the Uniform Sales Act. Thus, a "contract for the sale of * * * a structure or its materials to be removed from realty is a contract for the sale of goods within this Article if they are to be severed by the seller but until severance a purported present sale thereof *which is not effective as a transfer of an interest in land* is only effective as a contract to sell" (Uniform Commercial Code, § 2–107, subd. [1]; emphasis supplied). Obviously, such a contract to sell refers to an interest in land as the Official Comment makes clear. Thus, in the case at bar, since the buyer rather than the seller was to sever the structure from the land, the Statute of Frauds is applicable and the alleged contract is unenforceable in the absence of a signed writing.

Plaintiff contends that even if the Statute of Frauds is applicable, there was part performance so as to entitle plaintiff to specific performance. The allegation of part performance is based on plaintiff's having entered into a contract with another to act as agent for plaintiff and remove the structure. We agree with Special Term that this is insufficient to take the case out of the Statute of Frauds. There was no actual performance under plaintiff's alleged contract with defendants.

Order and judgment affirmed, with costs.

———

## OLLIG v. EAGLES

Supreme Court of Michigan, 1956.
347 Mich. 49, 78 N.W.2d 553.

EDWARDS, Justice. This suit is a chancery action brought by a man who built a house on land he mistakenly believed to belong to his wife, but which, on her death, proved to belong to another. The latter, knowing he had title, had silently watched and even assisted in the building.

The builder seeks title or compensation. The owner contends that the law allows no recovery for such a mistake. The trial judge below denied relief, saying, this is "a strange case."

With this observation we can agree. Such mistakes have, however, tortured judges from the dawn of legal history. A Roman jurist, faced perhaps with a similar problem, gave us this adage: "For this by nature is equitable, that no one be made richer through another's loss." Combinations of human cupidity and stupidity have frequently confronted the courts with cases where strict application of legal rules would unjustly enrich one at the expense of another. Such cases gave rise to the rules of equity which we here seek to apply.

\* \* \* As we read this distinctly inadequate record it appears undisputed that plaintiff (with the assistance of his wife to an unascertained degree) built a house upon defendant's land. It appears undisputed that he did so in good faith and in reliance upon an assignment of a land contract to his wife and in complete ignorance of her unrecorded quit-claim deed back to the defendant. From this record it likewise appears that defendant, having full knowledge of his own legal title, stood by and watched and acquiesced fully in plaintiff's construction of the house without at any point asserting his claim of ownership thereto until long after the house was built and a year and a half after Mrs. Ollig's death. It even appears, as far as this record is concerned, that his silence on this point continued during this last period for a year and a half subsequent to his own recording of the quit-claim deed.

\* \* \*

Plaintiff's assertion that in building the house he mistakenly relied upon the belief that his wife had title to the land offers the only plausible common sense explanation of his actions and stands undisputed by any testimony to the contrary tendered by defendant at trial.

On appeal plaintiff urges upon this court a claim for "an equitable lien for the value of the improvements made in good faith by a party in possession under a mistaken claim of ownership where the true owner knew and consented to such improvements."

\* \* \*

This type of claim, where a party has placed improvements upon the land of another under mistaken belief as to title, has produced a vast amount of litigation in which courts have generally sought for equitable remedies without undue sacrifice of the statute of frauds.

And most states, including Michigan, have passed so-called "betterment" statutes giving the occupying claimant the right to compensation for the increased value resulting from his improvements where he held the property in good faith and under color of title and where the owner of the fee seeks to oust him in ejectment proceedings.

The present case cannot be disposed of under the general line of occupying claimant cases cited, nor under the Michigan statute, since it is distinguished therefrom in two ways. First, plaintiff here seeks affirmative relief in equity rather than the set-off of his claim in the fee owner's action. Second, plaintiff, under the facts above, cannot be held to have acted under color of title or with adverse possession.

The question, therefore, may be phrased as follows: when an occupying claimant in good faith, but mistakenly, relied upon the belief that his wife had title to land and built a house thereon with the full knowledge and silent acquiescence of the actual owner and upon discovery brings suit in equity for an accounting for the value of his improvements, is a chancery court powerless to grant relief?

Common sense and common justice answer strongly "No"; and Michigan case precedent does likewise.

\* \* \*

Our Court joined the minority amongst the 48 states on this issue in an opinion written by Mr. Justice Clark for a unanimous bench in Hardy v. Burroughs, 251 Mich. 578, on page 581, 232 N.W. 200, on page 201, which quoted Justice Story with approval:

> " 'To me it seems manifestly unjust and inequitable, thus to appropriate to one man the property and money of another, who is in no default. The argument, I am aware, is, that the moment the house is built, it belongs to the owner of the land by mere operation of law; and that he may certainly possess and enjoy his own. But this is merely stating the technical rule of law, by which the true owner seeks to hold, what, in a just sense, he never had the slightest title to, that is, the house. It is not answering the objection; but merely and dryly stating, that the law so holds. But, then, admitting this to be so, does it not furnish a strong ground why equity should interpose, and grant relief?' "
> \* \* \*

While citing and relying upon the Hardy case, supra, for its holding that in Michigan a plaintiff may seek affirmative equitable relief when mistakenly, but in good faith, he has improved the land of another to the unjust enrichment of the latter, we do not extend our present discussion beyond cases where the title owner had full knowledge of the improvement as it was being made.

\* \* \*

Finally in Seavey and Scott's Notes on Section 42 of The American Law Institute's Restatement of The Law of Restitution we find the following (p. 31):

> "If the owner of land remains silent although realizing that another is improving the land in the erroneous belief that it is his own, normally, it is held that the owner is estopped either to deny title or, more usually, to deny the improver the right to recover for the value added."

We hold that defendant appellee's silence as to his own title and his acquiescence and assistance in the plaintiff's construction of this house serve to estop him from asserting his legal defenses to this suit.

We hold further that plaintiff in his individual capacity is entitled upon this record to a decree awarding him the reasonable value of the improvements he made to this land, excluding any contribution to the above made by his wife and by defendant, and set off by the reasonable rental value of the unimproved land which he used for the years he occupied it.

We hold further that the court under the doctrine of an implied contract may grant a lien upon the property for the value of the improvements as determined above.

The decree of the lower court is affirmed in part and reversed in part, and the case is remanded for the taking of such additional testimony as is required for the computations referred to above and the entry of a decree consistent with this opinion.

Neither party having prevailed entirely, no costs are awarded.

## PROBLEMS

1. Clyde lived next door to a funeral parlor. The funeral parlor purchased and installed a large heavy pipe organ, but did not physically attach it to the building in any way. Clyde enjoyed listening to the organ music so much that he purchased and installed an identical organ in his house and bolted the organ to the floor. Are the two organs fixtures? Why?

2. Kloster purchased a piece of real estate; then he moved a barn onto the property and built a house which rested on blocks. Neither the barn nor the house had a foundation but Kloster never listed them as personal property for tax purposes. Later, the real estate was sold at a tax sale to Nelson, but now Kloster claims that he is entitled to both buildings because he never intended them to become fixtures. Is Kloster or Nelson entitled to the buildings? Why?

3. The Alaska Theater Company leased a movie theater and installed movie projectors, a screen, furnishings for the rest rooms, an electric sign,

a curtain, a pipe organ, and miscellaneous electrical fixtures. May the Alaska Theater Company remove those articles upon termination of the lease? Why?

4. In 1890 Abner leased a country inn for five years. In back of the inn he constructed a brick outhouse on a cement foundation. He also constructed a wooden storage shed on concrete blocks and nailed one side of the shed to the inn. One week before the lease ended, Abner removed both structures and restored the property to its original condition. When the landlord learned of Abner's actions, he sued Abner for the value of the buildings. Is Abner liable? Why?

5. Mr. and Mrs. Ott purchased a home in Phoenix that was equipped with a combination heating and cooling system. When they discovered that the system was defective, the Otts sued the builder, claiming a breach of implied warranty that the system was of good, average quality. However, under Arizona law, implied warranties are only given by the seller when personal property is sold; they do not apply to the sale of real estate. Will the Otts win? Why?

6. Savage leased a building to University State Bank for six years. When the bank left the premises it did not remove the vault, and Savage had it removed at a cost of over $1000. Is the bank liable for this amount? Why?

7. Smith purchased ranges and refrigerators from Friendly Appliance on a conditional sales contract. Friendly Appliance did everything necessary to create a valid security interest in the appliances. After the appliances were installed, Smith defaulted in his payments. Can Friendly Appliance recover the appliances? Why?

8. Tom built a new house and installed two four-foot by five-foot mirrors on the walls. The mirrors were hung from hooks and were bordered by molding, which was nailed to the wall. When Tom died he left his real estate to Dick and his personal property to Harry. Who is entitled to the mirrors? Why?

9. A construction company owned a lot on which stood a pile of topsoil twenty feet high and forty feet long. The company sold the lot to Simmons and the deed made no mention of the topsoil. Simmons spread the topsoil over his lot because the pile constituted a hazard to neighborhood children. The company then sued Simmons for the value of the topsoil, claiming that it had never been purchased by Simmons. Who wins? Why?

10. On January 2, 1980, Dick gave First Bank a mortgage on his twenty-year-old house, and the mortgage was recorded on January 3, 1980. On January 5, 1980, Dick contracted to buy a new furnace from Fancy Furnace Company for $500 down and $2,000 payable over three years. The $2,000 note was secured by a security interest in the furnace, which was installed on January 7, 1980. On January 28, 1980, Fancy Furnace made a "fixture filing." If the bank forecloses against Dick on January 30, 1980, who has prior rights to the furnace? Why?

# Chapter 3

## THE SCOPE OF REAL PROPERTY

All the rivers run into the sea; yet the sea is not full; unto the place from whence the rivers come, thither they return again.

Ecclesiastes 1:7.

The owner of the surface of real estate has property rights in the air above the surface and in the soil below. In the words of Lord Coke, *"cujus est solum ejus est usque ad coelum,"* a dictum still cited by modern courts. In Hannabalson v. Sessions, for example, the court noted that "the title of the owner of the soil extends not only downward to the centre of the earth, but upward *usque ad coelum,* although it is, perhaps, doubtful whether owners as quarrelsome as the parties in this case will ever enjoy . . . their property in the latter direction." [1]

Despite the apparent simplicity of the rule, a number of legal questions concerning the scope of real estate ownership have frequently been raised. For example, should limits be placed on the ownership of the air in order to accommodate air travel? Who owns minerals, such as gas and oil, that are capable of movement beneath the surface? What right does a landowner have in a body of water that adjoins his land? And may one person excavate his land when the excavation will cause his neighbor's property to subside? The focus of this chapter will be on these and related questions.

## I. RIGHTS TO THE SKY

### A. TRADITIONAL APPROACH

The ancient dictum of Lord Coke, which gave the owner of the surface the rights *ad coelum,* was uttered long before the development of air travel, and even today there is little difficulty in applying the rule in cases which do not involve the airplane. When a person invades the air space of another without permission, he has committed a trespass and under the common law would be liable for at least nominal damages even if no actual damages were proven. For instance, in Whittaker v. Stangvick,[2] the plaintiff owned a strip of land that formed a "duck pass" between two lakes. He alleged that the defendants were constructing duck blinds on one of the lakes and intended to shoot ducks and other water fowl that would be flying over the plaintiff's land. According to the testimony, a shotgun's range is 400 feet, and about half the shot from the blinds would drop on the

1. 116 Iowa 457, 90 N.W. 93 (1902).    2. 100 Minn. 386, 111 N.W. 295 (1907).

plaintiff's land and half would carry over the land. Although the appellate court sent the case back to the trial court for further hearings, it noted that on the basis of the facts presented there was a trespass, and "it is immaterial whether the quantum of harm suffered be great, little, or unappreciable." See Davies v. Bennison, infra.

## B.  AIR TRAVEL

In cases involving air travel, courts have had considerable difficulty in applying the *ad coelum* principle, because the rights of the surface owner must be balanced by the public necessity for air travel. Most state courts have used one of two theories in deciding cases involving aircraft. The first, the "technical trespass" theory adopted in Smith v. New England Aircraft Co.,[3] divides airspace into two zones. The landowner owns the lower zone, whose boundary is determined by the air that the owner "may reasonably expect to use or occupy," [4] and he may recover at least nominal damages for flights through this "zone of expected use." The second theory, often called the "nuisance rule," requires that the landowner prove actual damage to the property before recovery will be allowed.[5]

Burnham v. Beverly Airways [6] illustrates the choice faced by state courts: "Since the decision in the *Smith* case there has existed among legal writers on the subject and has been reflected in the few decisions as yet available made by courts of last resort a controversy as to whether the theory of technical trespass recognized in the *Smith* case has any proper application to invasions of unoccupied air space above the land of an owner. The opposing doctrine is not always expressed in the same form, but in general it maintains that by the common law, liberally interpreted in the light of modern conditions pertaining to an entirely new and highly important method of transportation, there exists a public right of aviation over the lands of all owners at any height which does not actually interfere in any manner with any existing use of the property. This theory has sometimes been referred to as the nuisance theory for the reason that it prefers not to recognize as a technical trespass the mere passage of aircraft without contact with anything connected with the land and tends to hold the aviator responsible only where, as in cases of nuisance, some harm has been done or some inconvenience caused.  .  .  .  In this case we have been invited to reconsider the theory upon which Smith v. New England Aircraft Co., Inc., rests in the light of the more recent discussion and decisions and to adopt in substance the 'nuisance' rule hereinbefore described, which is supposed to be somewhat more favorable to

---

3.  270 Mass. 511, 170 N.E. 385 (1930).

4.  Swetland v. Curtiss Airports Corp., 55 F.2d 201 (6th Cir. 1931).

5.  Hinman v. Pacific Air Transport, 84 F.2d 755 (9th Cir. 1936), cert. denied 300 U.S. 654, 57 S.Ct. 431, 81 L.Ed. 865.

6.  311 Mass. 628, 42 N.E.2d 575 (1942).

the aviator. We see no occasion to disturb the fundamental basis of the decision in the *Smith* case. That case was not a slavish application of the ancient maxim *cujus est solum ejus est usque ad coelum.* The just demands of modern progress were recognized, and room was left for their reasonable satisfaction, while at the same time protection was given to the landowner against that which he might naturally and justly regard as unwarranted intrusion." Most state court decisions, however, have adopted the nuisance approach.[7]

After state courts developed these theories, the Supreme Court considered similar issues in United States v. Causby.[8] The Causbys owned a 2.8-acre chicken farm near an airport outside Greensboro, North Carolina, which was used by military aircraft. One of the airport's runways ended approximately 2,200 feet from the farm's outbuildings, while the glide path for the aircraft passed 67 feet above the farm house and 63 feet above the outbuildings. Planes flying over the farm included U.S. bombers, transports, and freighters. According to the Court, these planes "come close enough at times to appear barely to miss the tops of the trees and at times so close to the tops of the trees as to blow the old leaves off. The noise is startling. And at night the glare from the planes brightly lights up the place. As a result of the noise, respondents had to give up their chicken business. As many as six to ten of their chickens were killed in one day by flying into the walls from fright. The total chickens lost in that manner was about 150. Production also fell off. . . . Respondents are frequently deprived of their sleep and the family has become nervous and frightened." As a result, Causby sued the government, claiming that there had been a "taking" of their property and that they should receive compensation for the "taking."

In its decision, the Supreme Court initially noted that under the Air Commerce Act of 1926, the United States has exclusive national sovereignty in the airspace over the country and any citizen has a public right to freedom of transit through the navigable airspace, that is, the airspace above the minimum safe altitudes prescribed by the Civil Aeronautics Authority. Thus the court concluded that the *ad coelum* doctrine "has no place in the modern world. . . . Were that not true, every transcontinental flight would subject the operator to countless trespass suits." However, the Court also noted that the minimum safe altitudes prescribed by the Civil Aeronautics Authority for flight ranged from 300 to 1,000 feet, depending on the type of aircraft, the time of day, and the terrain. In the *Causby* case, the government planes flew below this navigable airspace when they took off and landed. Having reached this conclusion, the Court was faced with determining the landowner's rights to the air below the navigable airspace. The court decided that "the landowner owns at least as

---

7. W. Prosser, Law of Torts 72, 73 (4th ed. 1971).

8. 328 U.S. 256, 66 S.Ct. 1062, 90 L.Ed. 1206 (1946).

much as he can occupy or use in connection with the land. The fact that he does not occupy it in a physical sense—by the erection of buildings and the like—is not material. . . . Flights over private land are not a taking, unless they are so low and so frequent as to be a direct and immediate interference with the enjoyment and use of the land." The Supreme Court then remanded the case to the Court of Claims for further hearings.

One question left unanswered by the Supreme Court was whether there can be liability for flights within the navigable airspace which interfere with the use of the land. In Griggs v. County of Allegheny,[9] the Court decided that there could be liability for such flights and also that the county should bear this liability, as the owner and lessor of the airport.

## C.  CLOUD SEEDING

In addition to the complications caused by air travel, the ancient *ad coelum* doctrine is being reexamined in an attempt to resolve another modern issue: does the owner of the surface have a property right in the clouds? There are several aspects to this issue. For instance, may a landowner seed clouds over his land in order to secure rain for himself if, by doing so, he deprives his neighbors of rain? This question often carries national and international implications. Israel, for example, has been accused of "rain rustling" by its neighbors, and the state of Washington was threatened with legal action by Idaho because of its cloud-seeding program to alleviate the effects of a prolonged drought. Another question raised by cloud seeding is: can a person seed clouds to prevent damage to his own land, even though the seeding deprives neighboring landowners of moisture? In 1973 two Central American countries accused the United States of stealing their rain by seeding hurricanes off the southern coast of Florida. In one of the few cases considering a similar question, a Texas court decided that seeding to prevent hail storms could be enjoined if the seeding activity takes place above the plaintiff's land. See Southwest Weather Research, Inc. v. Duncan, infra.

## D.  SALE OF AIR RIGHTS

Our discussion of air rights would not be complete without noting that the owner of these rights may sell them separately from the surface of the real estate. For example, the sale of a condominium usually involves the transfer of a unit of airspace, which may be described by these means: (1) the use of a subdivision plat of air lots, each of which is numbered; (2) a survey that shows the dimensions of each unit with reference to the boundaries of the land; or (3) a survey that utilizes a floor plan showing the location of each unit. Regardless

9.   369 U.S. 84, 82 S.Ct. 531, 7 L.Ed.2d 585 (1962).

of the method used to describe the air lots, one possibility should be dealt with in negotiations before construction begins: what are each owner's rights if a building settles and its air lots tilt into a neighbor's air space?[10]

## II.　RIGHTS TO THE DEPTHS

The corollary of the *ad coelum* doctrine is that the owner of real estate also has the right *ad inferos*, that is, to the depths. In contrast to the legal controversies over rights to the sky, there has been relatively little litigation involving the depths, primarily because underground travel has not enjoyed the popularity of air travel.

Courts generally agree that it is a trespass to enter another person's property beneath the surface, for example, to dig a mine under a neighbor's property; yet some courts have modified this approach when the trespass takes place at a great depth. Thus, in Boehringer v. Montalto,[11] the purchaser of real estate in Yonkers sued the vendor, claiming the vendor had warranted that the property was free from encumbrances when in fact there was a sewer running underneath it at a depth of over 150 feet. But the court decided that because of its depth the sewer was not an encumbrance: "Title above the surface of the ground is now limited to the extent to which the owner of the soil may reasonably make use thereof. By analogy, the title of an owner of the soil will not be extended to a depth below ground beyond which the owner may not reasonably make use thereof."

As with air rights, the rights to the depths may be sold apart from the surface of the real estate. When a sale of mineral rights takes place, for instance, the purchaser has the right to use the surface of the real estate and to tunnel below it to mine the minerals. However a number of older mineral deeds, written when coal was the primary concern, deed the coal "and other minerals" to the purchaser, thereby raising the question of whether oil, gas and other minerals have also been conveyed. In the leading case of Acker v. Guinn,[12] there had been a conveyance of rights to "oil, gas, and other minerals, in and under, and that may be produced from" a tract of land. The Court decided that the phrase, "other minerals," was not specific enough to include iron ore, especially since open pit or strip mining of the ore virtually destroys the surface estate. Careful drafting of the mineral deed can usually forestall this type of litigation.

The separate sale of oil and gas rights has created other unique legal problems. In some states like Texas and Pennsylvania, oil and gas are considered the property of the surface owner and can be sold

10.　R. Kratovil, Real Estate Law 385,　12.　464 S.W.2d 348 (Tex.1971).
　　386 (6th ed. 1974).

11.　142 Misc. 560, 254 N.Y.S. 276 (1931).

to third parties in the same manner as other minerals.  However, other states reject the "ownership" principle on the grounds that oil and gas are migratory and capable of movement across property lines.  These courts reason that oil and gas, like wild animals and other migratory things, cannot be owned until captured, although the owner of the surface can sell the "exclusive right" to extract them.  However, both "ownership" and "exclusive right" states recognize the migratory character of oil as embodied in the "capture" doctrine.  Under this doctrine a person may cause oil and gas to migrate across property lines by drilling a well and creating a low pressure area.  The driller thus acquires title to all oil and gas produced on his land, even though it migrated from his neighbor's property because of his drilling activity.[13]  The capture doctrine has lost much of its significance in recent years because states require that oil be divided among the owners in order to discourage wasteful drilling practices.

## III.  WATER RIGHTS

### A.  IMPORTANCE OF WATER RIGHTS

The right to use water has become a valuable part of real estate ownership in recent years for several reasons.  For one thing water has become increasingly important as a recreational resource since Americans continue to purchase vacation homes in unprecedented numbers on seashores, lakefronts, and riverfronts.  But more important still is the widespread awareness that the supply of water required for man's basic needs will be limited in the near future.  These limitations were recognized more than twenty years ago: "To most Americans today, pure palatable water in unlimited quantities is a kind of birthright, like citizenship, and not even the Supreme Court can ever take it away.  No following generation of Americans is ever likely to share this luxurious attitude.  We are rapidly running out of good water.  More than a thousand cities and towns already have been forced to curtail their water service.  Near Chicago, where artesian wells flowed under their own pressure a hundred years ago, new wells must go down 2,000 feet to reach the water table.  Dallas is already pumping the salt-tainted Red River into its mains, and New York faces the likelihood that eventually it will have to purify the polluted Hudson to slake its growing thirst.  In Mississippi, wells are now 400 feet deeper, on the average, than they were only ten years ago.  Denver, eager for new industry, has been turning away manufacturers whose production processes involve a heavy use of water."[14]

More recently, the West Coast has experienced its worst drought in over a century, while on the East Coast the balance between water

13.  Elliff v. Texon Drilling Co., 146 Tex. 575, 210 S.W.2d 558 (1948); E. Mitchell, U. S. Energy Policy: A Primer 29, 30 (1974).

14.  Rienow and Rienow, *The Day the Taps Run Dry*, Harper's Magazine 72 (October, 1958).

supply and water use remains critical. Following a study made in the mid-1970s, the U. S. Army Corps of Engineers reported that in Boston, New York, and Washington, D. C., "the gap between available supply and water use even in non-drought years is narrowing perceptibly . . . . Thus, the impact of the next drought . . . will be felt far more harshly than in the 1960s' drought. The cushion between safe yield and use was thin then; it is gone now." [15] There have been predictions that by the year 2,000 only New England, the Ohio River basin, and the Southeast will be able to live with their water supplies. Yet even in these areas purity will be a problem. Proposed solutions include towing icebergs from the Antarctic and piping water from Alaska.[16]

In addition to supplying man's daily needs and his vacation pleasures, water has gained international prominence in the last few years because of the mineral and edible resources it contains. In conferences on the law of the sea, nations continue their attempts to agree on the rights to minerals on the ocean floor, such as copper, nickel, cobalt, and manganese. Another concern has been the right to fish in waters off the coast of a country. In 1976, for example, the United States enacted legislation which changed the zone for fishing off the U. S. coast from 12 to 200 miles.

## B. NAVIGABLE WATER

It is sometimes difficult to perceive water as real estate; yet water, "like air, in its natural state is not a chattel. It is, for legal purposes, a part of the land over which it flows, and the rights, duties and privileges with respect to its use are those which pertain to property in land."[17] Among the important legal questions in the discussion of water rights are the following: Who owns the land under the water? Who has the right to use the surface of water? What use may be made of the water itself for business or domestic purposes? And what are the limitations in removing water beneath the surface of real estate?

Before these questions can be examined, however, it is important to understand the definition of navigable waters. Although the courts have not adopted any single precise definition, they agree that the waters must in fact be navigable. As the U. S. Supreme Court stated, "Those rivers must be regarded as public navigable rivers in law which are navigable in fact. And they are navigable in fact when they are used, or are susceptible of being used, in their ordinary condition, as highways for commerce, over which trade and travel are or may be

15. *Coast to Coast—Water Becomes a Big Worry*, U. S. News and World Report 27 (September 6, 1976).

16. *Is U. S. Running Out of Water*, U. S. News & World Report 33 (July 18, 1977).

17. Restatement of Torts, Scope Note §§ 850–857, at 348 (1939).

conducted in the customary modes of trade and travel on water." [18] When such water, by itself or by uniting with other bodies of water, forms a highway that may be used for commerce between or among states, it is said to be navigable water of the United States.[19]

State courts also require navigability in fact. In one case, a Florida court determined that a body of water was not navigable in fact because "one witness testified that it was so difficult to get a row boat over it that one had to 'push, cuss, and holler' at the same time to make it go. . . . From the pictures introduced in evidence one would designate it a cow pasture. Two or three small alligator lairs in the lap of a cow pasture could under no stretch of the imagination meet the test of navigability for useful public purposes."[20]

However, once the water has been found to be navigable in fact, states have used either of two basic approaches. One group of states has adopted the traditional "highway of commerce" rule stated above. But the more modern trend is to determine if the water may be put to public use, regardless of whether it can be used commercially. As the Ohio Supreme Court pointed out, the "increased recreational use of our waters has been accompanied by a corresponding lessening of their use for commerce. We are in accord with the modern view that navigation for pleasure and recreation is as important in the eyes of the law as navigation for a commercial purpose." [21]

## C.  OWNERSHIP OF LAND UNDER WATER

Samson has just purchased a cottage on a small tract of riverfront land in northern Minnesota. Does his real estate extend to the edge of the river, or does he also own part of the riverbed? The answer depends on whether the water is considered navigable or not. If the water is not navigable, the general rule is that the owner of the adjoining land owns the riverbed to the center of the river. But if the water is navigable, states disagree in their rulings, with most deciding that the state owns the bed to the high-water mark.[22]

If Samson had purchased an oceanfront lot, his ownership would extend to the high-tide mark, measured by averaging the tides over a period of eighteen years, although a few states extend ownership to the low-water mark. Generally, states own the shore, defined as the area between the average high tide and the average low tide, but allow the private owner to use the shore for access to the water. The area beyond the shore comes within U. S. jurisdiction.[23] Under the Sub-

18.  State of Oklahoma v. State of Texas, 258 U.S. 574, 42 S.Ct. 406, 66 L.Ed. 771 (1922).

19.  The Daniel Ball, 77 U.S. (10 Wall.) 557, 19 L.Ed. 999 (1871).

20.  Baker v. State, 87 So.2d 497 (Fla. 1956).

21.  Mentor Harbor Yachting Club v. Mentor Lagoons, Inc., 170 Ohio St. 193, 163 N.E.2d 373, 10 O.O.2d 131 (1959).

22.  78 Am.Jur.2d, *Waters* § 44 (1975).

23.  W. Burby, Real Property 46, 47 (3rd ed. 1965).

merged Lands Act passed by Congress in 1953, the United States relinquished to coastal states all rights to submerged lands within geographical limits not to exceed three marine leagues into the Gulf of Mexico or three miles into the Atlantic and Pacific Oceans.[24]

## D. USE AND CONTROL OF WATER

Determining rights to use and control water is complicated by the clause of the U. S. Constitution that gives Congress the power "to regulate commerce . . . among the several states." Article I, Section 8. This clause has been interpreted to mean that the United States has the right to control navigable waters which affect interstate commerce, even when the body of water lies within the boundaries of one state. If the waters are navigable but do not affect interstate commerce, the individual state has the right to their control. Nonnavigable waters are used and controlled by private owners.[25]

A recent Ohio decision illustrates the importance of determining navigability. The defendant concrete company owned land on the bank of the Little Miami River and on an island in the middle of the river. The company built a concrete causeway from the riverbank to the island so that its trucks could carry sand and gravel from the island. Water flowed under the causeway through three large concrete tubes. There was evidence that the causeway obstructed boat traffic, leading to the loss of business to an upstream canoe livery, and caused the drowning of a young man who was drawn into one of the tubes while wading near the causeway. As a result, the state of Ohio sought a judgment ordering the company to remove the causeway. In its decision, the court noted that the basic issue was whether or not the river was navigable, for "a division of watercourses into navigable and nonnavigable is merely a method of dividing them into public and private, which is the more natural classification." The court decided that the causeway had to be removed because the Little Miami River was a navigable and therefore a public watercourse.[26]

1. **Use of Surface.** Even in those cases involving nonnavigable water, questions often arise regarding the owner's use of the water's surface and regarding the use of the water itself for business or industrial purposes. Use of the water's surface may be approached in two ways. In most cases, the owner can use the full surface, subject to reasonable restrictions (see Florio v. State, infra); but in certain situations, a lot owner might be limited to using the water above the bed that he owns. For example, in Wickouski v. Swift[27] the plain-

24. United States v. Louisiana, 363 U.S. 1, 80 S.Ct. 961, 4 L.Ed.2d 1025 (1960).

25. 78 Am.Jur., *Waters* §§ 61, 75, 76, 230.

26. State ex rel. Brown v. Newport Concrete Co., 44 Ohio App.2d 121, 336 N.E.2d 453 (1975).

27. 203 Va. 467, 124 S.E.2d 892 (1962).

tiffs, who owned part of a thirty-acre pond, sought to enjoin the defendants from using the plaintiffs' part of the pond; they also asked the court's permission to fence in their section of the water. The court held for the plaintiffs on the ground that their claim to ownership of the bed was not based on their ownership of land adjacent to the pond, but on fee simple title to separate portions of the bed.

2. **Use of Water.** More important than use of the water surface, especially in light of present and future water shortages, are questions relating to the use of water itself for domestic or commercial purposes. In the United States a basic East-West dichotomy has developed over the right to use water. The eastern states have generally adopted the riparian rights theory, while western states have usually employed the prior appropriation theory.

a. *Riparian Rights Theory.* The riparian rights theory takes its meaning from the word "riparian": riparian land is land that either includes a part of the bed of a watercourse or borders on a public watercourse, the bed of which is in public ownership. A riparian owner is someone who owns such land. For example, if Brown owns a parcel of land on the east side of a private canal and his land includes part of the canal bed, and Blue owns land on the west side but his land does not include the canal bed, only Brown is a riparian owner.[28]

The use of water becomes controversial when two or more persons attempt to use the same limited supply of water. For instance, if Smith is the riparian owner of land on the Calahootchee River and Jones is a riparian owner downstream from Smith, the issue is whether Smith can use water from the Calahootchee in a way detrimental to Jones. This question was rarely subjected to litigation until the industrial revolution led to increased demands for water as well as increased water pollution.

Two theories of riparian rights have been adopted by eastern states in response to this question. Some have adopted the natural flow theory, which provides that each riparian owner is entitled to have the water maintained in its natural state. While each riparian owner may use the water for "natural" wants, such as drinking, washing and cleaning, "artificial" wants, which include agricultural and industrial purposes, are allowable only when they do not materially change the quality or quantity of the water. If the water is used continuously on nonriparian land, such use may be enjoined by a riparian owner even if he is not directly harmed.[29]

Other states have adopted the reasonable use theory, which allows each riparian owner to use the water beneficially so long as the use does not interfere unreasonably with the beneficial uses of other

28. Restatement of Torts §§ 843, 844 (1939).

29. Id., Scope Note §§ 850–857, at 342–344.

riparian owners.[30]  In determining whether a particular use of water is reasonable, courts attempt to balance the utility of the use against the gravity of the harm.[31]  They consider the following factors, among others, in determining the utility of a particular use of water:  (a) the social value of the use, (b) the suitability of the use to the watercourse, (c) the impracticability of avoiding or preventing harm, and (d) the classification of the use as riparian or nonriparian.[32]  To determine the gravity of the harm from the use of the water, courts take the following into consideration:  (a) the extent of the harm, (b) the social value of the use which has been harmed, (c) the suitability of the harmful use to the watercourse, (d) the burden of avoiding the harm, and (e) the classification of the use as riparian or nonriparian.[33]  See Hoover v. Crane, infra.

The balancing process may be illustrated if we apply it to the last and very important factor on both lists—classifying the use as riparian or nonriparian.  Assume that Jones, the lower riparian owner, diverts water from the river and sells it to nonriparian owners.  Then Smith, the upper riparian owner, builds a dairy on the river to take advantage of a convenient source of water.  Conflict arises when Smith pumps polluted water from his dairy into the river, contaminating Jones's water supply.  As a result, Jones can no longer sell his water.  In light of the last factor, riparian or nonriparian use, Smith's use is reasonable because the harm caused by his dairy only affects Jones's nonriparian use of the water.  However, if Smith intentionally polluted the river because he had a grudge against Jones, his use would be unreasonable.[34]

b.  *Prior Appropriation Theory.*  The prior appropriation theory has been adopted in one form or another in seventeen western states, where water is more scarce than in the East.  Unlike the riparian rights theory, prior appropriation is based not on equality of rights but on the principle of "first in time, first in right."  That is, the first person to appropriate the water, whether or not he owns land on the water, has priority over later users.  To establish his priority, a person must (1) intend to appropriate the water, (2) divert the water from the watercourse, and (3) use the water beneficially.[35]

For example, assume that Green owns a farm on a river in a state whose laws are based on prior appropriation, while Blue owns a farm twenty miles from the river.  There is enough water in the river to irrigate only one of the farms.  If Blue was the first person to use the water for irrigation, he becomes the prior appropriator and is entitled to use all of the water in the river.  Green, however, could use none of it, even though he was a riparian owner.[36]

**30.**  Id. at 344.

**31.**  Id. § 852.

**32.**  Id. § 853 (1939).

**33.**  Id. § 854 (1939).

**34.**  Id. § 855 (1939).

**35.**  C. Smith & R. Boyer, Survey of the Law of Property 189 (2nd ed. 1971).

**36.**  Id. at 188.

## E. PERCOLATING AND SURFACE WATER

While the above summary of water law has focused on water that flows or lies in a defined course, channel or bed, water often flows outside established channels. Two such forms of water are pertinent here: percolating water, which passes beneath the surface and apart from a definite channel, and surface waters which diffuse themselves over the earth's surface apart from a watercourse and are usually produced by heavy rains or melting snows.

In considering the right to use percolating water, courts have applied the reasonable use or prior appropriation theories discussed above. However, a few states follow the old common law rule— based upon the *ad inferos* principle—that declares the owner of the surface to be the absolute owner of the water beneath, which he may use as he pleases.

Diffuse surface water has been the subject of considerable litigation, as illustrated by the following example.[37] Assume that three lot owners, Able, Baker, and Chance, own homes on lots situated next to each other in a north-south direction of a hill. The highest and northernmost lot on the hill belongs to Able, the lot below is Baker's and the lot farthest down the hill belongs to Chance. Each spring melting snow causes a considerable amount of surface water to pass over the three lots. This surface water could raise three legal issues. First, may Baker build a wall on the north edge of his property to block the surface water and prevent it from passing over his property, even if by doing this he causes Able's property to be flooded? Most courts have adopted the common law approach, which is called the "common enemy" rule. Under this rule, the surface water is an enemy to every landowner, and each landowner is free to deal with it as he sees fit. Thus, Baker would be free to build the wall. Under another approach, the so-called civil law rule, a landowner like Baker cannot interfere with the natural flow of water over his land. A third view, the "reasonable conduct" doctrine, offers a compromise between the common law and the civil law rules and represents the current trend in decisions. To determine reasonable conduct, the court looks at all factors, especially the nature of the benefit to Baker and the harm to Able.

Second, may Baker build a dam on the southern edge of his property in order to create a lake, with the result that Chance has no opportunity to use the water? The general rule here is that the owner may use the surface water as he sees fit, although a few courts would require him to act reasonably.[38]

Finally, assume that Baker, instead of damming the water, constructs drains or ditches that cause the surface water to flow onto

---

37. Id. at 201.

38. Kinyon & McClure, *Interference with Surface Waters*, 24 Minn.L.R. 891, 914–915 (1940).

Chance's property and damage it. The well-settled rule is that Baker is not allowed to discharge the water by artificial means. For example, in E. J. Hollingsworth Co. v. Jardel Co.,[39] the plaintiff sought to enjoin the defendant from collecting and dumping surface waters onto his property by means of a storm sewer. The court determined that as a result of the defendant's development of his property, nine-tenths of the water falling on his land during a storm would reach the plaintiff's property, whereas in the past only two-tenths would flow off the defendant's property. The court issued a permanent injunction, concluding that "one may not in effect substantially enlarge or change a natural drainage easement by artificially collecting and casting the surface water on the lower owner to his substantial damage." See Burton v. Douglas County, infra.

## IV.  LATERAL SUPPORT

Increased demand for construction, coupled with a limited supply of land, has resulted in more concentrated land development than in the past; thus the rights of a landowner to support of his soil by his neighbors' land have become more important. If Able and Baker own adjoining parcels of real estate, the law is clear that Baker may not excavate and develop his property so as to cause Able's soil to subside. However, the extent of Able's right to support will depend on the nature of the land and the nature of Baker's excavation.

### A.  COMMON LAW

A lateral support case usually arises from one of four possible situations. First, assume that Baker was negligent in developing his property and Able's soil subsided as a result. Under traditional negligence principles, Baker would be liable for damage to the soil and for damage to any buildings on the soil. For instance, in S. H. Kress & Co., Inc. v. Reaves,[40] the court held that the failure of a developer to sample soil or to notify the adjoining owners before beginning to excavate was negligence: "One contemplating a project of this character owes the duty to an adjoining property owner of exercising at least ordinary care to ascertain the conditions under which the work would progress, and this includes some reasonable investigation as to the character of the soil to be excavated in making the proposed excavation. Failure to make such an investigation amounts to negligence and renders the one negligent in this respect liable for resulting damages."

Second, assume that Baker was not negligent and that Able's land was in its "natural state," that is, there were no buildings on it but Able's land still subsided as a result of Baker's excavations. In such cases, Able would still be allowed to recover because Baker

39.  40 Del.Ch. 196, 178 A.2d 307 (1962).  40.  85 F.2d 915 (2d Cir. 1936).

has an absolute duty to support his neighbor's property in its natural state.

Third, assume that Baker was not negligent, but that Able's land contained improvements, that the land and buildings were damaged by Baker's excavation, and that the land subsided because of the additional weight of the buildings. In such cases, courts generally agree that Able cannot recover damages either for the land or for the buildings.

Fourth, as in the third instance, assume that Baker was not negligent, that Able's land was improved, and that the land and buildings were damaged by the excavation. However, in this case, the land would have subsided even without the additional weight of the buildings. This is the most difficult of the four situations to resolve, and two divergent views have developed in the courts. In one view, Baker would be liable only for damages to the land. As one court stated, "To be liable in damages for injury to buildings, negligence must appear in the withdrawal of lateral support." Furthermore, the court noted that buildings are not to be considered part of the real estate in determining damages because of the differences between "the nature of soil and of material in a building, the flexibility of the one and the non-flexibility of the other in the movements of the earth. Soil easily accommodates itself to these movements, while a building, stiff and rigid, cracks."[41] However, most courts today hold a second view and will allow damages for both the land and the buildings; this view has been adopted in the Restatement of Torts, § 817 (1939).

## B.  STATUTORY APPROACH

In several states, the common law rules outlined above have been modified by statutes that apply to certain types of excavations. If the statute refers to a particular excavation, the common law rules would not be applied, and the rights and duties of the parties would be defined in the statute. In California, for example, the statute requires the person making the excavation to do the following: (1) give reasonable notice to adjoining owners stating how deep the excavation will be when excavation begins; (2) use ordinary care and skill and take reasonable precautions to sustain the adjoining land; and (3) allow adjoining owners thirty days to protect their structures if the excavation is to be deeper than the foundations of the adjoining buildings. Furthermore, if the excavation is to be nine feet or more and the foundations of adjoining buildings are at least nine feet, the person making the excavation must protect adjoining lands and buildings from damage at no cost to adjoining owners. If there is damage in such circumstances, the excavator will be liable.[42]

41.  Home Brewing Co. v. Thomas Colliery Co., 274 Pa. 56, 117 A. 542 (1922).

42.  West's Ann.Cal.Civ.Code § 832.

# CASES

## DAVIES v. BENNISON

22 Tasmania Law Rep. 52 (1927).

The CHIEF JUSTICE read the following judgment:—

The relevant facts in this case are that the defendant, while in his own yard fired a bullet from a small-bore rifle at, and killed, the plaintiff's cat, which was upon the roof of a shed in her yard.

The plaintiff claimed to be entitled to damages:—

(1) For illness caused by fright and shock, resulting from the firing of the bullet close to her.

(2) For the value of the cat and for illness resulting from the fright and shock of seeing it killed before her eyes.

(3) For trespass by firing the bullet into her land.

The defendant paid 2*l* into Court, as covering the value of the cat, but contended that he had committed no trespass to plaintiff's land and that the damage from the shock, etc., was too remote to be recoverable, even if proved.

The case was left by me to the jury to say:—

(1) Whether the amount paid in was sufficient as damages for the killing of the cat.

(2) Whether they found that plaintiff's illness was the result of the firing of the bullet, and, if it was, then to assess damages subject to a reserved nonsuit point.

(3) To assess damages for the trespass to land.

The jury found for the defendant on all the issues, evidently not realising that they had been directed to assess damages for the trespass to the land.

This is an application for a new trial as to

(1) The issue of trespass to land, upon the ground that the jury ignored the direction given from the bench.

(2) As to damages for shock, etc., upon the ground that the verdict was against the weight of evidence.

I left the whole of this latter matter to the jury, reserving defendant's application for a non-suit. The burden of proof was upon the plaintiff. There seemed to me to be little doubt that the illness of the plaintiff was caused by anger and agitation (at seeing her cat killed in her own yard) increasing an already disturbed condition of health, consisting of neurasthenia and long standing gastric trouble. Shock caused by seeing an injury occur to another human being is in law considered too remote from the original wrongful act of the defendant causing the injury to be a ground for damages, and it seems to me to be quite clear that a pet animal, however cherished, cannot be regarded as nearer and dearer than a child or other loved relative.

I do not think that there are grounds for a new trial on this issue.

The question of trespass to land is much more difficult. If it was a trespass, then it was committed in circumstances and in a manner which aggravated it. It is curious that the law as to trespass by missiles which do not touch the ground never has been authoritatively laid down in England nor (as far as I can discover) in the United States of America.

I have to make an original decision.

Trespass is actionable without pecuniary damage being proved, so that if this is a trespass it could be the subject of substantial damages if a jury were to take a serious view of the circumstances of aggravation.

Trespass is a breach of the negative duty, incumbent upon all, not to interfere directly and illegally with ownership.

Ownership, whether permanent or temporary, is a right *in rem,* a right to use, deal with and enjoy the thing owned to an indefinite and almost unlimited extent.

The ownership of land, part of the earth's surface, is necessarily different from that of moveables, and is generally described by the application of the maxim *"Cujus est solum ejus est usque ad coelum."*

A man who walks from his roof on to that of his neighbour is clearly guilty of trespass. The neighbour's house is part of his freehold. But when the intrusion consists of sending something such as a balloon, a bird, a kite, or a missile over another's land without touching it or anything built or growing upon it important fundamental and subtle questions arise. The only direct dictum upon the point is that of LORD ELLENBOROUGH in Pickering v. Rudd, 4 Campbell 219. LORD ELLENBOROUGH says: "I do not think it is a trespass to interfere with the column of air superincumbent on the close. I once had occasion to rule upon the circuit, that a man who, from the outside of a field, discharged a gun into it, so as that the shot must have struck the soil, was guilty of breaking and entering it. A very learned judge, who went the circuit with me, at first doubted the decision, but I believe he afterwards approved of it, and that it met with the general concurrence of those to whom it was mentioned. But I am by no means prepared to say, that firing across a field *in vacuo*, no part of the contents touching it, amounts to a *clausum fregit*. Nay, if this board overhanging the plaintiff's garden be a trespass, it would follow that an aeronaut is liable to an action of trespass *quare clausum fregit*, at the suit of the occupier of every field over which his balloon passes in the course of his voyage.

Whether the action may be maintained cannot depend upon the length of time for which the superincumbent air is invaded."

\*   \*   \*

It seems an absurdity to say that if I fire at another's animal on his land, hit it, kill it, and so leave the bullet in it, I have committed no trespass, and yet, if I miss the animal and so let the bullet fall into the ground, have committed a trespass. Such distinctions have no place in the science of the Common Law.

If the hovering aeroplane is perfected the logical outcome of LORD ELLENBOROUGH'S dictum would be that a man might hover as long as he pleased at a yard, or a foot, or an inch, above his neighbour's soil, and not be a trespasser, yet if he should touch it for one second he would be.

A man has the undoubted right to build a high tower on his land, and the space above the land is exclusively his for that purpose. Then why not for any other legal purpose? It seems to me that the only real difficulty is in saying (what I need not say here), viz., how far the rights of a landowner "*ad coelum*" will have to be reduced to permit the free use of beneficial inventions, such as flying machines, etc.

\*   \*   \*

Order:—New trial on issue of trespass to land.

———

## SOUTHWEST WEATHER RESEARCH, INC. v. DUNCAN

Court of Civil Appeals of Texas, 1958.
319 S.W.2d 940.

PER CURIAM. This is an appeal from a judgment of the Eighty-third District Court, Jeff Davis County, Texas, said judgment being in the form of an injunction commanding the appellants "to refrain from seeding the clouds by artificial nucleation or otherwise and from in any other manner or way interfering with the clouds and the natural condition of the air, sky, atmosphere and air space of plaintiffs' lands and in the area of plaintiff's lands to in any manner, degree or way affect, control or modify the weather conditions on or about said lands, pending final hearing and determination of this cause; and from further flying over the above-described lands of plaintiffs and discharging any chemicals or other matter or material into the clouds over said lands." Appellees are ranchmen residing in Jeff Davis County, and appellants are owners and operators of certain airplanes and equipment generally used in what they call a "weather modification program", and those who contracted and arranged for their services.

It is not disputed that appellants did operate their airplanes at various times over portions of lands belonging to the appellees, for the purpose of and while engaged in what is commonly called "cloud seeding." Appellants do not deny having done this, and testified through the president of the company that the operation would continue unless restrained. He stated, "We seeded the clouds to attempt to suppress the hail." The controversy is really over appellants' right to seed clouds or otherwise modify weather conditions over appellees' property; the manner of so doing; and the effects resulting therefrom. Appellants stoutly maintain that they can treat clouds in such manner as will prevent the clouds from precipitating hail, and that such operation does not and cannot decrease either the present or ultimate rainfall from any cloud or clouds so treated. Appellants were hired on a hail suppression program by a large number of farmers in and around Fort Stockton and other areas generally east, or easterly, of Jeff Davis County. It was developed that the farmers' land was frequently ravaged by damaging hail storms, which appellants claim originated in and over the Davis Mountains in the Jeff Davis County area.

The appellees' testimony, on the other hand, which was elicited from some eleven witnesses, was to the effect that this program of cloud seeding destroyed potential rain clouds over their property.

\* \* \*

So, summing up the fact situation or the evidence that was before the trial court, we find that the three appellees and other witnesses testified that they had visually observed the destruction of potential rain clouds over their own property by the equipment of the appellants. They testified that they had seen this happen more than once. The experts differed sharply in the probable effort of a hail suppression program accomplished by the cloud seeding methods used here. The trial court apparently, as reflected by his findings included in the judgment, believed the testimony of the lay witnesses and that part of the expert testimony in harmony with his judgment. This he had a right to do as the trier of facts.

\* \* \*

In Volume 34, Marquette Law Review, at Page 275, this is said:

"Considering the property right of every man to the use and enjoyment of his land, and considering the profound effect which natural rainfall has upon the realization of this right, it would appear that the benefits of natural rainfall should come within the scope of judicial protection, and a duty should be imposed on adjoining landowners not to interfere therewith."

In the Stanford Law Review, November 1948, Volume 1, in an article entitled, "Who Owns the Clouds?", the following statements occur:

"The landowner does have rights in the water in clouds, however. The basis for these rights is the common-law doctrine of natural rights. Literally, the term 'natural rights' is well chosen; these rights protect the landowner's use of his land in its natural condition." \* \* \*

"All forms of natural precipitation should be elements of the natural condition of the land. Precipitation, like air, oxygen, sunlight, and the soil itself, is an essential to many reasonable uses of the land. The plant and animal life on the land are both ultimately dependent upon rainfall. To the extent that rain is important to the use of land, the landowner should be entitled to the natural rainfall."

In California Law Review, December 1957, Volume 45, No. 5, in an article, "Weather Modification", are found the following statements:

"What are the rights of the landowner or public body to natural rainfall? It has been suggested that the right to receive rainfall is one of those 'natural rights' which is inherent in the full use of land from the fact of its natural contact with moisture in the air." \* \* \*

"Any use of such air or space by others which is injurious to his land, or which constitutes an actual interference with his possession or his beneficial use thereof, would be a trespass for which he would have remedy."
\* \* \*

We believe that under our system of government the landowner is entitled to such precipitation as Nature deigns to bestow. We believe that the landowner is entitled, therefore and thereby, to such rainfall as may come from clouds over his own property that Nature, in her caprice, may provide. It follows, therefore, that this enjoyment of or entitlement to the benefits of Nature should be protected by the courts if interfered with improperly and unlawfully. It must be noted that defendant's planes were based at Fort Stockton, in Pecos County, and had to fly many miles to seed clouds over defendants' lands in Jeff Davis County. We do not mean to say or imply at this time or under the conditions present in this particular case that the landowner has a right to prevent or control weather modification over land not his own. We do not pass upon that point here, and we do not intend any implication to that effect.

There is ample evidence here to sustain the fact findings of the trial court that clouds were destroyed over property of appellees by operations of the appellants. The trial court chose to believe the evidence to that effect, and we hold there was ample evidence to support him in so holding and finding. We further hold that the trial court was justified in restraining appellants from modifying or attempting to modify any clouds or weather over or in the air space over lands of the appellees.

However, we do find that the temporary injunction granted by the trial court was too broad in its terms, in that it purports to restrain appellants from any activity with reference to land in the area of "plaintiffs' lands". The trial court's injunction is, therefore, modified so as to restrain appellants from the activities therein described only as they apply to the lands of appellees.

————

## FLORIO v. STATE

Court of Appeals of Florida, 1960.
119 So.2d 305.

KANNER, Judge. The parties will be referred to as they appeared in the court below. The cause here on appeal was instituted by the state attorney of Hillsborough County under the provisions of sections 64.11, 823.01, and 823.05, Florida Statutes, F.S.A., upon the relation of certain complaining property owners. Finding that certain activities conducted and maintained from the place of business of the defendants constituted a nuisance in the community as denounced by the statutes, the court entered a decree permanently enjoining and restraining them from these pursuits at the place where they had been conducted.

\* \* \*

Factually, it appears that the complaining parties are riparian owners of property around and running into Egypt Lake, a lake of approximately 75 acres. The defendants, Robert and Fran Florio, own and operate as a public beach a 29 acre area on Egypt Lake known as Ralston Beach. The Florios lease a portion of this land to one of the defendants, McDonald, who for two years had been operating a water skiing school on Egypt Lake. Another defendant, the Tampa Ski Bees, is an unincorporated association having members who ski on the lake.

The plaintiffs as well as the defendants have engaged in water skiing on the lake. The plaintiffs objected to such things as noise, annoyance, and interference with the rights of residents of the community and their visitors in their use of the lake, erosion of the beaches, and domination of the lake by the defendants through the use of high powered tow boats and through negligent and reckless skiing to the extent that ordinary use and occupancy of the lake was rendered dangerous and unsafe for fishing, swimming, and skiing, thus resulting in a dangerous condition annoying and injuring the health of the community and physically jeopardizing plaintiffs and their children in use of their own property. They also objected to a forty-five minute ski show presented on Sunday afternoons by the Ski Bees for patrons of Ralston Beach. Thus, in this controversy, the interests of the plaintiffs as residents and riparian owners are opposed to the much more extensive and essentially commercialized interests of the defendants, although defendants assert that their interests are legitimate and good.

\* \* \*

The testimony clearly, convincingly, and satisfactorily established that the activities and conduct of the defendants resulted in physical dangers and hazards to the resident home owners and renters, their children and visitors, in the use of the lake; that there was usurpation, deprivation, and unreasonable interference with the use of the lake for fishing, swimming, skiing, and boating; that there were damages to the shores through erosion; that there were also debris, mud, and grass washed and thrown on the beaches; and that such conduct created and caused a continued annoyance and discomfort to the community around the lake. This is not a complaint between neighbor and neighbor but one created through wrongful conduct of the defendants that has seriously affected the entire lake community. As the chancellor succinctly commented, "the Court further finds that the organization, Tampa Ski-Bees and H. Stew McDonald, d/b/a Stew's Ski School, maintain an activity and project which are too big for Egypt Lake. * * *" Unquestionably the evidence sustains the findings of fact of the chancellor and his determination that a nuisance was created and maintained in violation of the statutes.

* * *

The rights of riparian proprietors to the use of waters in a non-navigable lake are equal, and each riparian owner has the right to use the water in the lake for lawful purposes, so long as his use is not detrimental to the rights of the other riparian owners. Except as to the supplying of natural wants, including the use of water for domestic purposes, it is immaterial what use is made if that use is lawful and reasonable. The use of lands which border on waters of a non-navigable lake for purposes of pleasure, recreation, and health is a use which requires a remedy on behalf of a riparian owner where there is unreasonable interference. One riparian owner is not entitled to use the lake to the exclusion of other riparian owners. Each owner of riparian rights is entitled to the reasonable use of the lake, and where an owner's lawful use is unreasonably interfered with, that owner is entitled to injunctive relief.

The parties recognize that water skiing is not a nuisance per se. Normally it is a legitimate and wholesome pursuit. The chancellor found it to be a nuisance here because of the extent to which it was pursued under the circumstances delineated and determined. However, the court's order was so broad as to prohibit all water skiing activities by the defendant, McDonald, doing business as Stew's Ski School, and to prohibit the leasing of property by defendants Florio to the other defendants for water skiing purposes, consequently amounting in effect to wrongful discrimination against the defendants.

An injunctive order should never be broader than is necessary to secure to the injured party, without injustice to the adversary, relief warranted by the circumstances of the particular case. An injunctive order should be adequately particularized, especially where some activities may be permissible and proper. Such an order should be confined within reasonable limitations and phrased in such language that it can with definiteness be complied with, and one against whom the order is directed should not be left in doubt as to what he is required to do.

Since the injunctive decree rendered by the chancellor was wrongfully discriminatory and too broad in scope, it is subject to being, and should be, modified so as to provide reasonable use by all parties of their riparian rights under appropriate regulations, to the end that the defendants are not deprived and excluded from reasonable legitimate use under the circumstances. Therefore the cause is affirmed as to the chancellor's determination of a nuisance, reversed as to the injunctive order against the Tampa Ski Bees, and further reversed as to restraining provisions of the order as applied to the other defendants. The cause is remanded to the court below for such further proceedings as are necessary in conformity with this opinion.

Affirmed in part and reversed in part.

---

## HOOVER v. CRANE

Supreme Court of Michigan, 1960.
362 Mich. 36, 106 N.W.2d 563.

EDWARDS, Justice. This appeal represents a controversy between plaintiff cottage and resort owners on an inland Michigan lake and defendant, a farmer with a fruit orchard, who was using the lake water for irrigation. The chancellor who heard the matter ruled that defendant had a right to reasonable use of lake water. The decree defined such reasonable use in terms which were unsatisfactory to plaintiffs who have appealed.

The testimony taken before the chancellor pertained to the situation at Hutchins lake, in Allegan county, during the summer of 1958. Defendant is a fruit farmer who owns a 180-acre farm abutting on the lake. Hutchins lake has an area of 350 acres in a normal season. Seventy-five cottages and several farms, including defendant's, abut on it. Defendant's frontage is approximately ¼ mile, or about 10% of the frontage of the lake.

Hutchins lake is spring fed. It has no inlet but does have an outlet which drains south. Frequently in the summertime the water level falls so that the flow at the outlet ceases.

All witnesses agreed that the summer of 1958 was exceedingly dry and plaintiffs' witnesses testified that Hutchins lake's level was the lowest it had ever been in their memory. Early in August, defendant began irrigation of his 50-acre pear orchard by pumping water out of Hutchins lake. During that month the lake level fell 6 to 8 inches—the water line receded 50 to 60 feet and cottagers experienced severe difficulties with boating and swimming.

\* \* \*

The tenor of plaintiffs' testimony was to attribute the 6- to 8-inch drop in the Hutchins lake level in that summer to defendant's irrigation activities. Defendant contended that the decrease was due to natural causes, that the irrigation was of great benefit to him and contributed only slightly to plaintiff's discomfiture. He suggests to us:

"One could fairly say that because plaintiffs couldn't grapple with the unknown causes that admittedly occasioned a greater part of the injury complained of, they chose to grapple mightily with the defendant because he is known and visible."

The circuit judge found it impossible to determine a normal lake level from the testimony, except that the normal summer level of the lake is lower than the level at which the lake ceases to drain into the outlet. He apparently felt that plaintiffs' problems were due much more to the abnormal weather conditions of the summer of 1958 than to defendant's irrigation activities.

\* \* \*

The decree entered provided:

"It is further Ordered, Adjudged and Decreed, that such use of water for the irrigation of said 45 acre pear orchard shall not be limited so long as water from Hutchins lake drains into the outlet thereof; that when the water from Hutchins lake no longer drains in the outlet, that defendant shall not be entitled to use more than $\frac{1}{4}$ inch of water from the area of Hutchins lake, which is established to be 352 acres; and that when the water of Hutchins lake no longer drains into the outlet, a meter shall be placed on the pump to determine the amount of water removed from Hutchins lake by the defendant.

"It is further Ordered, Adjudged and Decreed, that either the plaintiffs, or any of them, or the defendant may petition the court to take further proofs in this cause for other and additional relief if the circumstances or experience of the parties hereto indicate that the relief herein granted is unreasonable or inadequate."

Plaintiffs on appeal assert that any irrigation use when the lake level is below the outlet is unreasonable.

Michigan has adopted the reasonable-use rule in determining the conflicting rights of riparian owners to the use of lake water.

In 1874, Justice Cooley said:

"It is therefore not a diminution in the quantity of the water alone, or an alteration in its flow, or either or both of these circumstances combined with injury, that will give a right of action, if in view of all the circumstances, and having regard to equality of right in others, that which has been done and which causes the injury is not unreasonable. In other words, the injury that is incidental to a reasonable enjoyment of the common right can demand no redress."

\*  \*  \*

We interpret the circuit judge's decree as affording defendant the total metered equivalent in pumpage of ¼ inch of the content of Hutchins lake to be used in any dry period in between the cessation of flow from the outlet and the date when such flow recommences. Where the decree also provides for the case to be kept open for future petitions based on changed conditions, it would seem to afford as much protection for plaintiffs as to the future as this record warrants.

Both resort use and agricultural use of the lake are entirely legitimate purposes. Neither serves to remove water from the watershed. There is, however, no doubt that the irrigation use does occasion some water loss due to increased evaporation and absorption. Indeed, extensive irrigation might constitute a threat to the very existence of the lake in which all riparian owners have a stake; and at some point the use of the water which causes loss must yield to the common good.

The question on this appeal is, of course, whether the chancellor's determination of this point was unreasonable as to plaintiffs. On this record, we cannot overrule the circuit judge's view that most of plaintiffs' 1958 plight was due to natural causes. Nor can we say, if this be the only irrigation use intended and the only water diversion sought, that use of the amount provided in the decree during the dry season is unreasonable in respect to other riparian owners.

Affirmed. Costs to appellee.

---

## BURTON v. DOUGLAS COUNTY

Court of Appeals of Washington, 1975.
14 Wash.App. 151, 539 P.2d 97.

McINTURFF, Chief Judge. Plaintiff (Burton) appeals from a judgment entered on a jury verdict dismissing his action against the defendant (Douglas County). Burton seeks to recover for damage to his home caused by a road that concentrated and deposited surface waters in a volume on his property.

On June 9, 1972, an extremely heavy rainstorm occurred in the Wenatchee area. Burton's home was located adjacent to the Wenatchee Golf & Country Club, on the west side of Country Club Drive (see diagram).

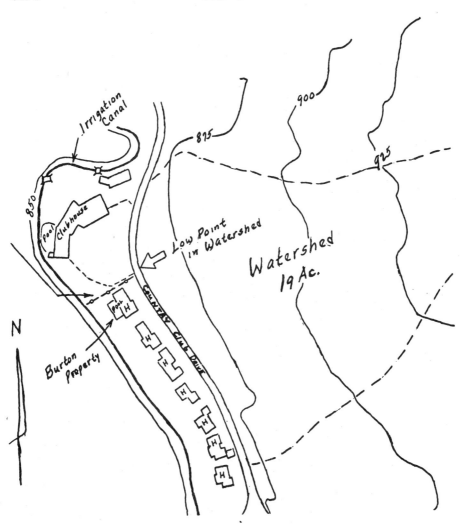

Country Club Drive had a slight crown in the center of the road that acted to collect and funnel surface waters draining in the watershed from the east to the west. Burton built his home at the low point in a natural drainage area of approximately 19 acres, east of Country Club Drive. On the day of the rainstorm—the severity of which would occur approximately every 25 years—the surface waters, draining from east to west, were funneled onto the Burton's property. Mud and water severely damaged his house, primarily the basement and its contents.

When Burton built his home in 1959 he installed six-inch drains on his property to drain away water which, particularly during the spring thaw, would be collected by the road and accumulate in front of his house. When sufficient water had collected at a point across from his home, the water would flow across the road and enter onto

Burton's property.   Until 1972 normal rainfall had created no problem, but prior to this time Mr. Burton had notified the Douglas County Commissioners that Country Club Drive was collecting runoff water and depositing it on his property.   The County Commissioners did not correct the drainage problem.

The primary issues to be answered are:  (1) does the road constitute an artificial drain or channel;  and (2) if so, is Douglas County liable whether or not the rainstorm constituted an act of God?   We answer both in the affirmative.

Burton contends that Douglas County—due to the presence of Country Club Drive—artificially channeled surface waters and deposited them on his property to his damage, citing Wilber Dev. Corp. v. Rowland Constr. Inc., 83 Wash.2d 871, 523 P.2d 186 (1974).   Douglas County contends it did not by "artificial means" convey outlaw waters and deposit them onto Burton's property.   Douglas County also urges that a municipality is not liable for injuries caused to private property as a result of the collection of surface waters on its streets, citing Wood v. Tacoma, 66 Wash. 266, 119 P. 859 (1911).   Douglas County emphasizes that it was not negligent in the performance of its road work;  thus, it cannot be held liable for the damage to Burton's property.

\*   \*   \*

A natural drain is defined as one formed by nature in which surface waters drain from higher to lower elevations naturally.   Country Club Drive acted as an artificial drain because the water draining from the east to the west, in the absence of the crown in the road, would have continued to run across the road instead of being channeled by it. Liability arises if surface water is artificially collected and discharged on surrounding properties in a manner different from the natural flow of water onto those properties.   Country Club Drive acted as an artificial drain, collecting, channeling, and depositing surface waters onto Burton's property to his damage.

Next we consider if the defendant is liable whether or not the rainstorm constituted an act of God.   The general rule regarding liability for artificially collecting the discharging surface water in a manner different from the natural flow concurring with an act of God was stated in Tope v. King County, 189 Wash. 463, 471–72, 65 P.2d 1283, 1287 (1937):

> When two causes combine to produce an injury, both of which are, in their nature, proximate and contributory to the injury, one being a culpable negligent act of the defendant, and the other being an act of God for which neither party is responsible, then the defendant is liable for such loss as is caused by his own act concurring with the act of God, provided the loss would not have been sustained by plaintiff but for such negligence of the defendant.

\*   \*   \*   Even if the jury deemed the rainstorm to be an act of God, Douglas County is, nevertheless, liable for the damage because the road's condition concurred with an act of God in producing the injury. But for the existence of the road, the surface waters would naturally have been dispersed instead of being collected, channeled and discharged upon Burton's property. Therefore, we find that Douglas County was liable for the injury whether the rainstorm was an ordinary freshet or an unprecedented flood.

\*   \*   \*

The judgment of the Superior Court dismissing Burton's action is reversed and the case is remanded to the Superior Court to determine the issue of damages only.

## PROBLEMS

1. In 1958, Congress expressly provided that navigable airspace includes "airspace needed to insure safety in takeoff and landing of aircraft." Federal Aviation Act of 1958, Section 101(24). What effect does this provision have on the *Causby* decision? Why?

2. "Red" Baron is planning to build a large airport near Ann Arbor. Five miles from the airport is a mink ranch. Minks are especially sensitive to noise—when they are caged in a noisy area the production of baby minks drops tremendously. Red now comes to Rocky Feller, his investment consultant, and asks whether he might be liable for damages for operating the airport near the mink ranch. Rocky tells Red that if he designs the airport in such a way that the planes never fly over the mink ranch, he will not be liable to the mink rancher. Is this good advice? Why?

3. Harold owns a piece of real estate. Underlying the surface of the real estate is a coal bed and a large pool of oil. Harold deeds the coal and oil to Maude—giving Maude a deed to the subsurface minerals. The state now sends Maude a real property tax bill claiming that she is the owner of the oil and coal. Maude claims that she owns neither the oil nor the coal until she removes them from the earth. Is Maude correct? Why?

4. Bonnie owns a recreational campsite, Brownacre. Clyde owns Greenacre, a crop farm that lies south of Brownacre in a valley. Bonnie recently constructed a large dam along the southern border of her property in order to create a reservoir for use by visiting campers. The dam deprived Clyde of water that had previously flowed from Brownacre to Greenacre and his crops die. Clyde sues Bonnie, asking the court to order her to destroy the dam. Who wins? Why?

5. The city of Medina, in need of additional water, purchased 130 acres of land three miles south of the city. The city hoped to use this land to build a large pumping station and to remove 4,000,000 gallons of percolating water from the ground daily. Rufus, a farmer who lived near the pumping station site, claims that the pumping operation will cause his well to go dry with the result that he will no longer be able to farm his 400 acre tract. If Rufus sues the city to restrain it from removing water, who will prevail? Why?

6.   Green and Blue both own homes and real estate on the Fox River. Green, whose property is upstream from Blue's, has used river water for several years for household purposes.  He also transports a large quantity of water to his farm, which is five miles from the river.  Green's use of the water lowers the water level significantly.  Blue now wants to use the water for farming his riverfront property but there is only enough water to service one farm.  Which farm is entitled to the water?  Why?

7.   Walter owned a house and lot in the city of Oakdale.  The city excavated a ditch, forty feet deep, near the sidewalk on Walter's lot.  When the ditch was near completion, the city encountered a pocket of quicksand, which extended from the ditch beneath Walter's lot.  When the city removed the quicksand, including quicksand that flowed from beneath Walter's lot, Walter's front yard began to sink.  As a result, Walter lost support for the front of his house, the plaster and ceiling in the house cracked, and the doors and windows could not be opened.  Assuming the city was not negligent and that there is no statute governing the situation, is the city liable?  Why?

8.   Pancho and Cisco owned adjoining property on Long Island Sound. During a hurricane, the tidewaters washed away part of Pancho's seawall and the land in back of it—to within three feet of Cisco's property.  Cisco demanded that Pancho rebuild the seawall and take other measures to prevent Cisco's soil from subsiding.  Pancho ignored Cisco's request and Cisco's land began to wash away.  Is Pancho liable to Cisco for failing to provide lateral support?  Why?

9.   In the *Causby* case which is summarized in the text, why did the Causbys sue the government on the theory that there had been a taking of their land by the government?  Since the Supreme Court analyzed the case in the terms of the tort concepts of trespass and nuisance, why did not the Causbys assert that the government was liable for committing a tort?  Was not the Causbys' claim also questionable because the government never commenced condemnation proceedings, which is the usual procedure when private property is taken?

10.   In the case involving Smith and Jones, discussed in the text in connection with the reasonable use theory of riparian rights, how should the court decide the case, taking into account all of the factors normally considered by courts?  Why?

Chapter 4

# RIGHTS IN LAND OF OTHERS

Persuade your neighbors to compromise whenever you can.
Point out to them how the nominal winner is often a real loser—
in fees, expenses, and waste of time.

Abraham Lincoln, July 1, 1850

One person frequently has the right to enter, use, or remove property from another person's real estate. In legal terminology, this
right may be classified as an easement, profit, or license.

## I. EASEMENTS

### A. DEFINITIONS AND CLASSIFICATIONS

An easement is an interest in land which gives the owner the right
to use real estate owned by another for a specified purpose. According to one court, it is "an interest in land created by grant or agreement, express or implied, which confers a right upon the owner thereof
to some profit, benefit, dominion or lawful use out of or over the estate
of another."[1] In the Restatement of the Law of Property, an easement is defined as an interest in land in the possession of another, and
it has the following specific characteristics: (a) the owner of the
easement is entitled to use and enjoy the land on a limited basis; (b)
he is entitled to protection from third parties in his use and enjoyment;
(c) the easement owner is not subject to the will of the possessor of
the land, as would be the case with a license; (d) an easement arises
from facts other than possession of land by its owner; and (e) the
easement is capable of conveyance.[2]

1. **Affirmative and Negative Easements.** Easements may be
either affirmative or negative. The owner of an affirmative easement
has the right to use the land that is subject to the easement, such as
the right to cross the land or tunnel under it. The easement owner
might also be allowed to perform acts on his own land which affect
the subject land, for example, polluting the air or water, or disturbing
his neighbors by making unreasonable noise. By contrast, a negative
easement enables its owner to prevent the person owning the subject
real estate from performing certain acts on it. For example, if Her-
cules buys a lot high on a hill overlooking San Francisco Bay, he
would be wise to obtain a negative easement from lot owners lower

---

1. Mosier v. Mead, 45 Cal.2d 629, 290
P.2d 495 (1955).

2. Restatement of Property § 450 (1944).
The discussion of easement definitions
and classifications is drawn generally
from the Restatement. See §§ 451–456,
487–493.

81

on the hill to prevent them from building high-rise structures on their lots which would obstruct his view of the bay. Negative easements have become increasingly important in recent years since the development of technology for heating and cooling buildings with solar energy. Before installing such heating and cooling devices, the landowner should obtain a negative easement from his neighbors guaranteeing that they will not erect buildings that would screen out the sunshine he needs to operate his solar equipment. See Fontainebleu H. Corp. v. Forty-Five Twenty-Five, Inc., infra.

2. **Easements Appurtenant and in Gross.** Easements may also be classified as "appurtenant" or "in gross." The former benefits the easement owner in using land that he possesses; that is, the easement is appurtenant to the land he owns. The land that is benefited is called the dominant tenement, while the land subject to the easement is the servient tenement. For example, assume the Squire owns Greenacre and Western owns neighboring Whiteacre. Squire grants to Western and his heirs "the privilege of laying a sewer line from Western's house across Greenacre to the main sewer line." Squire has thus granted Western an easement appurtenant to Whiteacre, with Whiteacre as the dominant tenement and Greenacre the servient tenement.

An easement in gross is granted to the owner independent of his ownership or possession of real estate. In this instance, there is a servient tenement but no dominant one. For example, if Farmer MacDonald grants to his neighbor Brown the right to use certain trails on MacDonald's property for riding snowmobiles, but he stipulates that the right is to be "personal to Brown and in no event is to be considered appurtenant to Brown's real estate," Brown owns an easement in gross and MacDonald's property is the servient tenement.

3. **Alienability and Apportionment.** The above forms of easement may also be distinguished from each other on the basis of their alienability and apportionment. Unless expressly limited, an easement appurtenant is alienable; that is, when the dominant estate is transferred, the buyer automatically becomes the owner of the easement. Furthermore, as discussed below, when the dominant estate is subdivided, the easement may be apportioned between the purchasers of each of the lots. But an easement appurtenant cannot be transferred separately from the dominant tenement.

The right to sell an easement in gross will depend on its classification as commercial or noncommercial. A commercial easement in gross, one which provides economic benefit rather than personal satisfaction, is alienable. Although many courts have decided that noncommercial easements in gross may not be transferred, such as the right to use the property for snowmobiling or water skiing, the preferred view would consider several factors in order to determine assignability. These factors include (a) the personal relation between the easement owner and the owner of the servient estate when the easement was created; (b) the probable increased burden on the servient estate which would result from allowing transfer; and (c) the consideration paid for the easement. For example, if Bill grants his brother Bob the lifetime right to fish in Bill's lake for $1 when the right could be worth $500 in other circumstances, a court would be likely to decide that Bob could not sell the right because of factors (a) and (c).

In Sandy Island Corp. v. T. S. Ragsdale,[3] the Williams Furniture Corporation, which owned extensive acreage on Sandy Island, deeded a 185-acre tract to T. S. Ragsdale but reserved for itself an easement over a road leading from a public road to the Great Pee Dee River. The easement was to "be for purposes of ingress and egress to said Great Pee Dee River . . . the said road to be used for transporting logs, forest products, etc., from the river bank out to the old 'River Road.'" Later, Williams sold about 8,000 acres on the island to the Sandy Island Corporation, along with the easement. But Ragsdale then built a gate across the easement, which he locked and refused to allow the plaintiff's employees access to the easement on the grounds that it was an easement in gross.

In its decision the court made the following distinction: "An easement is either appurtenant or in gross. An appendant or appurtenant easement must inhere in the land, concern the premises, have one terminus on the land of the party claiming it, and be essentially necessary to the enjoyment thereof. It attaches to, and passes with, the dominant tenement as an appurtenance thereof. An easement, or right-of-way, in gross is a mere personal privilege to the owner of the land and incapable of transfer by him, and is not, therefore assignable or inheritable." Although the court agreed with Ragsdale's contention that this easement was an easement in gross, it also noted: "An easement in gross is a right personal to the one to whom it is granted and ordinarily cannot be assigned by him to another. However, there is authority to the effect that the parties may make an easement in gross assignable by the terms of the instrument, particularly where the easement in gross is of a commercial character. Easements for pipe lines, telegraph and telephone lines, and railroad rights of way have been held assignable, although in gross. . . . An easement in gross is of a commercial character when the use authorized by it results primarily in economic benefit rather than personal satisfaction. Easements, if of a commercial character, are alienable." The court concluded that in this case Williams had reserved a commercial easement in gross which could validly be assigned to the Sandy Island Corporation.

If an easement in gross is declared transferable, the question often arises whether it may also be apportioned, or sold to more than one

---

3.   246 S.C. 414, 143 S.E.2d 803 (1965).

buyer. This will depend mainly upon the intention of the parties as inferred from the terms of the easement. For example, if Jupiter, the owner of Olympus, grants to Vulcan the exclusive right to mine copper on Olympus, Vulcan would be allowed to apportion his easement by selling the right to mine one half to Venus and the other half to Diana. Vulcan can divide his easement in this way because Jupiter, the owner of the servient tenement, granted him exclusive mining rights. Thus, Jupiter can neither mine copper on Olympus for himself nor be prejudiced by Vulcan's apportionment. However, had the grant been nonexclusive, the apportionment of the easement would not be allowed since it would be inconsistent with Jupiter's right.

Because of the restrictions on assignability and apportionment, courts attempt whenever possible to construe an easement as appurtenant rather than in gross. For instance, in De Shon v. Parker,[4] Carl De Shon granted to his son, the plaintiff, an "easement to use and maintain the leach bed heretofore installed upon the following described real estate  .  .  . and also the right of ingress and egress on and over said property to reconstruct, clean, repair and maintain the same." The easement was separated from the son's land by a thirty-foot right of way which was reserved for street purposes. Later, when the father sold his property to Parker, the defendant, a controversy developed over the transferability of the son's easement. The court held that the easement was transferable, citing the general rule that "an easement is never presumed to attach to the person of the grantee where it can fairly be construed as appurtenant to some other estate." See Shingleton v. State, infra.

## B.  CREATION OF EASEMENTS

An easement may be created by agreement of the parties or by operation of law. In most cases, its creation will fall within one of four categories.

1. **Express Conveyance.** An easement may be conveyed by a deed or by a will, but in either case the formal requirements for such instruments (which will be discussed in a later chapter) must be fulfilled. For example, the instrument must describe the real estate sufficiently so that the land may be identified, although language such as "the private driveway as presently located" has been held to be sufficient.[5] And an easement, like a deed, must be recorded under statutes that require recording of all interests in land. In a case in which the state of Indiana acquired easements for widening a highway but failed to record them, a later purchaser acquired the servient real estate free and clear of the easement.[6]

4.  49 Ohio App.2d 366, 361 N.E.2d 457, 3 O.O.3d 430 (1974).

5.  Champion v. Neason, 220 Ga. 15, 136 S.E.2d 718 (1964).

6.  State v. Anderson, 241 Ind. 364, 140 N.E.2d 812 (1960).

2. **Implied Easements.** Although careful legal planning would require that easements be expressly granted or reserved, there are several possible ways to create an easement by implication: (a) from a conveyance describing the premises as bounded by the easement or referring to a plat or map; (b) from prior use at the time that ownership of land is transferred; or (c) from necessity of use.[7]

a. *Reference to Easement or to Plat.* The first method is illustrated by the following two cases. In Hughes v. Lippincott,[8] the defendant claimed an easement in a private way known as Plaza Balentin; the claim was based on this description in her deed: "Beginning at an iron pipe set for the Southeast corner . . . thence S. 08° 38′ W. along the west side of Plaza Balentin 107.75 feet to the Southeast corner, the place and point of beginning. Bounded North by property of Mrs. K. M. Chapman; East by Plaza Balentin . . . ." The court decided that this description was sufficient to create an easement in Plaza Balentin because "it is the general rule and the rule followed in this state that where the description of property conveyed calls for a road or way as a boundary and the grantor owns the fee in said way, an easement in the way passes to the grantee and his heirs and assigns by implication of law." The court also noted that this rule applies whether or not the easement is necessary. In the second case, Hirlinger v. Stelzer,[9] the plaintiffs signed a lease for a cooperative apartment which referred to "appurtenances" and a "master plat of the entire project." The plaintiffs claimed that this language gave them the right to a recreation area that was part of the plat, and the court decided in their favor, noting that "an easement by implication . . . can be inferred from a construction of the terms and effect of the instrument involved."

b. *Implied Easements from Prior Use.* The second type of easement, an easement implied by prior use, can be illustrated with the following example. Lum owned a forty-acre estate on Tobacco Road. A farmhouse was located on the back twenty acres with a driveway connecting the house to the main road. Lum sold the house and back lot to Abner, but the deed did not mention an easement to use the driveway. Does Abner, who would otherwise be without access to the road, have an easement to cross Lum's property? In deciding whether Abner has an implied easement by prior use, courts refer to the driveway—before the sale to Abner—as a quasi-easement, while the front twenty acres would be the quasi-servient estate, and the back twenty acres the quasi-dominant estate. They are "quasi" because the definition of easements provides that an owner cannot have an easement in his own land.

---

7. Tratter v. Rausch, 154 Ohio St. 286,     9. 222 So.2d 237 (Fla.App.1969).
   95 N.E.2d 685, 43 O.O. 186 (1950).

8. 56 N.M. 473, 245 P.2d 390 (1952).

Four requirements must be met if the quasi-easement is to be considered an actual easement upon the sale to Abner. First, the prior use must be apparent at the time of the conveyance to Abner. Second, it must be continuous, thus indicating that the prior use was permanent, not temporary. Third, it must be reasonably necessary for the enjoyment of the quasi-dominant estate, a requirement that is met by showing that other means of access would be unreasonably expensive.[10] Finally, the owner of both the quasi-dominant and quasi-servient estates must originally have been one person, in our case, Lum.

Of the four elements, the first requirement has been the most troublesome to courts. In Van Sant v. Royster,[11] for example, the court held that an easement for a sewer line had been created even though the sewer was not visible. After noting that there is a split of authority over whether drain pipes and sewers fit the rule for apparent or visible easements, the court nevertheless took the position that "appearance and visibility are not synonymous, and that the fact that the pipe, sewer, or drain may be hidden underground does not negative its character as an apparent condition, at least where the appliances connected with and leading to it are obvious."

In the earlier, hypothetical case of Lum and Abner, the easement in question was considered an implied easement of grant, because, from Abner's point of view, Lum had granted him the right to use the driveway by implication when Lum sold him the back twenty acres. But suppose that Lum had sold Abner the front twenty acres instead, so that it is now Lum who is claiming the easement. In this situation, Lum is reserving the right to use the driveway himself, and the easement is considered an implied easement of reservation. In most courts, the rules governing implied easements of grant and by reservation are identical, but in a few courts an implied easement of reservation will not be allowed unless it is strictly necessary. These courts feel that grantors such as Lum should not be allowed to sell a tract of land and then later try to recover part of what had been granted originally.[12]

c. *Implied Easement of Necessity.* The third type of implied easement, that created by necessity, differs from an implied easement of prior use because necessity may exist even when there has been no prior use. Assume, for example that Lum had sold Abner a five-acre parcel in the center of his estate and that there was no existing right-of-way to the parcel, thus making it inaccessible from the main road. Obviously, the "implied easement of prior use" theory cannot be applied here since there was no prior use. However, the law presumes that Lum and Abner intended that Abner should have an easement of access over Lum's property and will grant Abner an implied easement

10. W. Burby, Real Property 73–74 (3rd ed. 1965).

11. 148 Kan. 495, 83 P.2d 698 (1938).

12. W. Burby, Real Property 74 (3rd ed. 1965).

of necessity if three requirements are met. First, as with the implied easement of prior use, there must be original common ownership in one person, in this case, Lum. Second, the necessity for an easement must exist when the common ownership is severed, that is, when Lum sold the parcel to Abner. Finally, the necessity must be great. Although some courts have determined that the necessity requirement has been met if it is impractical to use another means of ingress and egress, other courts have required proof of actual necessity.[13] In one case, for example, the court refused to declare an easement of implication because the plaintiff's property was accessible by water.[14] See Wagner v. Fairlamb, infra.

3. **Prescription.** It is possible to acquire title to land without paying for it by possessing it in a certain manner for a minimum period of time under what is called adverse possession. It is also possible for one person to acquire an easement to use another person's property by prescription. While in many instances the requirements for prescription are similar to those for adverse possession, they are sufficiently distinct to be discussed separately. (The specific requirements for adverse possession will be considered in Chapter 10.)

The Restatement of the Law of Property, § 457, declares that an easement is created by prescription if two requirements are met: (a) the use must be adverse; and (b) it must be continuous and uninterrupted for the period of prescription. Courts originally decided that the time period required to establish prescriptive rights was a period which extended longer than man could remember; it was based upon the fiction that the person claiming the easement must have received a grant which had been lost or forgotten. However, the presumption of a "lost grant" is no longer followed, and the period of prescription, which usually runs from ten to twenty years depending on the state, is now determined by statute.

a. *Adverse Use—Hostile.* The first requirement for prescription, adverse use, is actually a combination of separate requirements: the use must be hostile, and it must also be open and notorious. Hostile use means that the user must not recognize that the owner of the land has authority to prevent his use. For example, George crosses Ralph's yard on his way to work every day, but when Ralph asks him to stop using the yard George retorts, "Try to stop me." George's use would be considered hostile under this requirement.[15] See Shinn v. Rosenberger, infra.

If the use is not wrongful, it cannot be considered hostile. For instance Abbott builds a home which utilizes solar energy for its heating and cooling system, and he lives in it for fifteen years, which

---

13. Id. at 75.

14. Hildreth v. Googins, 91 Me. 227, 39 A. 550 (1898).

15. Restatement of Property § 458, Comment d (1944).

is the time required by statute in his state to create an easement of prescription.  During the sixteenth year, his neighbor Costello begins to build a high rise apartment that, when completed, will prevent sunshine from reaching Abbott's property.  Abbott, of course, would claim that Costello could not finish his apartment building because he, Abbott, had a negative easement by prescription.  Abbott's argument fails, however, because his use of the sunshine was never wrongful to Costello.[16]

It is sometimes stated that if the use is to be considered adverse, the person claiming the easement must use the property under a claim of right.  But this is simply another way of saying that the user is acting in a hostile manner by not recognizing the authority of the owner; it does not mean that the user feels his use of the property is legally justified.[17]

The hostile use requirement is illustrated by Plaza v. Flak.[18]  The plaintiff, Plaza, and the defendants, the Flaks, owned houses on adjoining lots in Passaic, New Jersey.  Between the adjoining lots was a five-foot-wide alleyway which was bisected by the lot line.  The owners used the alley until 1948, when the Flaks erected a fence on the boundary line in the center of the alley.  Plaza brought a suit to force the Flaks to remove the fence on the grounds that he had acquired an easement by prescription.  The Flaks, while admitting that other requirements for prescription had been met, claimed that Plaza's use of the property was not hostile.  However, the court decided that Plaza had an easement by prescription: "There was never any objection to the use, although it was not concealed; there was no reason to conceal it; there were no agreements concerning the use of the alleyway.  'There was no permission; we just used it.'  It is inescapable from a reading of the entire testimony before us that plaintiff's and his predecessor's use was under claim of right and with the intent to claim that right against the true owner, and that it was such use as should have warned defendants that plaintiff might acquire a prescriptive easement.  On the other hand, defendants make no proof concerning permissive use.  On the contrary they show no permission was asked or given.  It is suggested that their proofs tend to show permissive use in that the alleyway was paved by the joint owners at or near the time the dwellings were erected.  If a license to the occupants of either dwelling had been given by the former owners, such would have been revoked by the conveyance of the title to others and the continued use by the occupants of either dwelling would thereafter have been adverse to the owner of the fee of the other lands.  .   .   . "  It should be noted that other courts have treated the driveway easement as a special situation and will allow a prescriptive easement even when the use is permissive.[19]

16.  Restatement of Property § 458, Comment e (1944).

17.  Restatement of Property § 458, Comment d (1944).

18.  7 N.J. 215, 81 A.2d 137 (1951).

19.  See 27 A.L.R.2d 332 (1953).

b. *Adverse Use—Open and Notorious.* The second element of adverse use is that it must be open and notorious. The reasoning here is that, unless the use is open, the owner of the servient estate will have no notice of it and, without notice, will be unable to take action to prevent it. Under the rationale, a use might be open and notorious even when the user consciously attempts to conceal his use. For instance, if Hitchcock crosses Christie's land in order to visit a hidden cave and tries to keep his actions secret by crossing only after midnight, the use is considered open and notorious if Christie discovers it and thus has actual knowledge. On the other hand, Christie's actual knowledge is not necessary if the use is so open that it would be apparent from an ordinary inspection of the property. If Hitchcock had openly crossed Christie's land on a path to the cave that was clearly marked, the use would be open and notorious even if Christie lived in a foreign country and had no actual knowledge of Hitchcock's use.[20]

The case of Downie v. City of Renton [21] also illustrates the open and notorious requirement of adverse use. Once a year for more than twenty years, the city of Renton used an eighteen-foot natural gully on Downie's land to discharge forty thousand gallons of water in a two and one-half hour operation. But for twenty-one years Downie was not aware of how the city was using his land. In its decision, the court held that the city had not acquired an easement on Downie's land because its use was not open enough for Downie to know about it. Even if he had been present during the discharge each year, Downie would have had difficulty discovering the use because the gully was so deep and overgrown.

c. *Continuous Use.* In addition to being adverse—that is, hostile, open and notorious—the use must be continuous and uninterrupted in order to establish an easement by prescription. The continuity requirement does not mean that the use must be constant but instead refers to the intention of the user. For example, Orville flies model airplanes at low altitudes over his neighbor's property on irregular occasions, but never more than twice a month. His use, although not constant, is continuous and will remain so until he indicates through his actions or statements that his use is no longer adverse.[22]

d. *Uninterrupted Use.* In contrast to the continuous use requirement, which relates to the attitude of the user, the requirement that the use be uninterrupted relates to activities of the owner in obtaining a legal judgment or in taking action on his own to stop the use, for example, by placing a fence across a pathway.[23]

e. *Exclusive Use.* In addition to the Restatement requirements that the use be adverse (hostile, open and notorious) and continuous and uninterrupted, some courts also require that the use must be ex-

---

**20.** Restatement of Property § 458, Comment g, Illustration 9 (1944).

**21.** 167 Wash. 374, 9 P.2d 372 (1932).

**22.** Restatement of Property § 459 (1944).

**23.** Restatement of Property § 459, Comment c (1944).

clusive; in other words, the person making the claim must make a claim on his own that is not derived from the adverse use of another party. In Westfall v. Motors Ins. Corp.,[24] the defendants claimed that plaintiffs did not establish an exclusive use of a road on the defendants' property because it was also used by "the defendants and their predecessors in interest, and by persons owning irrigation ditches across the road in question, and also to some extent by persons going to and from pasture lands lying south of the plaintiff's land." The court rejected this defense on these grounds: "The rule that the user must be exclusive means no more, in the case of easement for a right of way, than that the right of the claimant must rest upon its own foundations and not depend upon a like right in any other person. It is not necessary under this rule that the person asserting a right of way by prescription should have been the only one who used the way, so long as he has exercised his right under a claim of right independently of others."

4. **Easements by Estoppel.** An easement may be created by estoppel when the owner of the servient estate allows the user to make improvements or expenditures in connection with the use; in such cases, the servient owner is estopped to deny the existence of the easement. In Monroe Bowling Lanes v. Woodsfield Livestock Sales,[25] the plaintiff Monroe had obtained permission from Woodsfield to use the latter's water line and, in relying on this permission, Monroe constructed costly bowling lanes and tapped into the water line. A controversy later ensued when Woodsfield used the bowling alley parking lot during its weekly livestock auction. The controversy culminated in 1967 when Woodsfield removed a section of the water line in order to stop water service to the bowling lanes. When Monroe sought an injunction to prevent the interference, the court initially determined that Woodsfield would prevail if the use was a mere license because "a parol license to use real estate is revocable at the will of the licensor." Furthermore, the court noted that the bowling lanes could not prevail on a theory of prescription because "permissive use by plaintiff, as in the instant case, cannot ripen into an easement by prescription no matter how long contained." Although these theories were inappropriate, the court decided that the injunction should be issued because of the estoppel doctrine. "Where an owner of land, without objection, permits another to expend money in reliance upon a supposed easement, when in justice and equity the former ought to have disclaimed his conflicting rights, he is estopped to deny the easement."

## C.  EXTENT OF THE EASEMENT

Once an easement has been created, a number of legal questions arise concerning the scope of its use. As a general rule, the scope will

---

**24.**  140 Mont. 564, 374 P.2d 96 (1962).   **25.**  17 Ohio App.2d 146, 244 N.E.2d 762, 46 O.O.2d 208 (1969).

be determined by the manner of creation. According to one court, "It is also established in the law that the process which creates an easement also fixes its extent. The extent of an easement created by prescription, for instance, is fixed by the use which created it. Likewise, the extent of an easement created by conveyance, as shown in the instant case, is fixed by the conveyance itself." [26]

To illustrate the extent of an easement by prescription, assume that Groucho walked to a store by crossing his neighbor Harpo's property for ten years, half of the period required to establish prescriptive rights. For the following ten-year period, Groucho continued to walk across Harpo's land, but also used the same path for riding his motorcycle early each morning. The extent of Groucho's rights is determined by his use during creation, and since he created the right to use the property only for walking to the store, he has no right to continue riding his motorcycle on his neighbor's property.[27] Once a prescriptive right has been established, some variations in use are allowed if they are close to the original use. In our example, if Groucho has walked across Harpo's property only in the evening during the twenty-year period, he would later be allowed to change the time of his walk to the morning. Additionally, as discussed below, if the easement is appurtenant to a dominant estate, its use may change to meet the needs which arise from the normal development of the dominant estate. However, the changed use must not create an unreasonable burden on the servient estate.[28]

The extent of an easement by implication will depend on the nature of the prior use or, if there was no prior use, on what is reasonably necessary in order to use the dominant estate.[29] If the easement was created by an express grant, the terms of the grant will govern the extent of the use, although where the words are ambiguous, "the way and manner in which the parties exercised their respective rights is legal evidence." [30]

1. **Development of the Dominant Tenement.** In determining the extent of an easement appurtenant courts assume "that the parties to the conveyance contemplated a normal development of the use of the dominant tenement." [31] What is normal development will depend on the facts in each case. In McDonnell v. Sheets,[32] the grant guaranteed to the owners of the dominant tenement the right to cross over the defendants' land with "team and wagon." The court, in deciding that

26. Hollosy v. Gershkowitz, 88 Ohio App. 198, 98 N.E.2d 314, 44 O.O. 221 (1950).

27. Restatement of Property § 477, Comment c (1944).

28. Restatement of Property § 478, Comment d, Illustrations (1944).

29. See G. Dykstra & L. Dykstra, The Business Law of Real Estate 541 (1956).

30. Rowell v. Doggett, 143 Mass. 483, 10 N.E. 182 (1887).

31. Restatement of Property § 484 (1944).

32. 234 Iowa 1148, 15 N.W.2d 252 (1944).

the grant did not amount to a restriction on the type of vehicle that could use the easement, stated the general rule that "where a right-of-way is granted it may be used for any purpose to which the land accommodated thereby may reasonably be devoted unless the grant contains specific limitations and the grantee can avail himself of modern inventions, if by so doing he can more fully exercise and enjoy or carry out the object for which the easement was granted." The court also emphasized the interpretation of the agreement by the parties, for the right-of-way had been used for over thirty years by all types of vehicles.

Questions about the use of an easement appurtenant frequently arise when the dominant estate is subdivided, with a resulting increase in the number of easement owners. In Crawford Realty Co. v. Ostrow,[33] complainant Crawford Realty purchased part of a large estate that had been owned originally by William Richmond and claimed the right to use an easement that was appurtenant to the Richmond estate. The court, in deciding for the complainant cited the following principles: "It is well settled that an easement appurtenant to land exists for the benefit of the dominant tenement as an entirety and not solely for any particular part thereof. The easement that was appurtenant to the land of William Richmond in 1795 clearly accrued to the benefit of that part of his land which is now owned by Crawford Realty Company. Once an easement appurtenant has been established it becomes an incident of possession of the dominant tenement and it passes automatically with any effective transfer of the land." The court also pointed out that "if a dominant tenement is subdivided between two or more owners, the easements appurtenant to it become subdivided and attach to each separate part of the subdivided dominant tenement unless this result is prohibited by the terms of its conveyance." Easements appurtenant are considered apportionable for two major reasons: first, because subdivision is so common that it is assumed that the parties are considering it as part of normal real estate development, and second, because the benefits to the dominant tenement generally outweigh the burden to the servient tenement.[34]

In contrast to the *McDonnell* and *Crawford* decisions is the California case of Wall v. Rudolph.[35] In this case, the dominant tenements originally had been used for growing citrus fruit, for grazing cattle, and for other rural activities; the easements appurtenant were used to transport ranch supplies, produce, and cattle, as well as for tradesmen's visits and social visits. However, with the development of the dominant tenements into dumping grounds for oil field wastes, the traffic became "terrific" in what had been a quiet rural area; 150 to 200 trucks used the easement each day, each one capable of carrying

33.  89 R.I. 12, 150 A.2d 5 (1959).

34.  C. Smith and R. Boyer, Survey of the Law of Property, 398 (2nd ed. 1971).

35.  198 Cal.App.2d 684, 18 Cal.Rptr. 123 (1961).

125 barrels of sludge. The court, which had to determine whether the use of the easement had become excessive, was guided by the following principles: "The grants here under consideration were made for road purposes in broad terms. It has been held that such phrasing creates 'a general right of way capable of use in connection with the dominant tenement for all reasonable purposes . . . limited only by the requirement that it be reasonably necessary and consistent with the purposes for which the easement was granted.' This reasonable contemplation presumptively includes normal future development within the scope of the basic purposes but not an abnormal development, one which actually increases the burden upon the servient tenement."

Applying these principles to the facts of the case, the court concluded that the use of the easements was unreasonable: "We are unable to endorse respondents' doctrine that development of an oil field is a reasonable use of a private road over a neighbor's property. It is not permissible to slant drill into his oil pools and we see no reason why one who drills for oil may convert his surface easement for ordinary rural purposes into a heavy traffic which is virtually a public use. . . . Not only do the trucks interfere with cultivation of plaintiff Wall's property but they also, as they pass each other on these narrow roads, pack down the soil; considerable dust is raised which settles on the citrus trees and damages them."

Courts agree that an easement appurtenant to one tract of land cannot be used on another tract, even if the tract adjoins the dominant tenement and is owned by the same person. For instance, in Miller v. Weingart,[36] the plaintiff established a subdivision of twenty-four lots and granted the purchasers of the lots an easement to use a driveway which connected with a public highway. The defendant, who owned a farm which adjoined the subdivision, purchased one of the lots which adjoined his farm and proceeded to use the easement to travel to and from the farm, to drive cattle, and to transport a concrete mixer to the farm. The court decided that the easement could not be used for these purposes: "The law is well settled that an easement that is appurtenant to one lot or tract cannot be used in connection with another lot or tract, although the other lot or tract belongs to the owner of the dominant estate to which the easement is appurtenant, and although the two tracts or lots join. The owner of the dominant estate cannot increase the burden imposed on the servient estate by the grant of the easement. This rule is applicable, whether the way was created by grant, reservation, prescription, or as a way of necessity. 'One having a right of way to his land, Blackacre, over the land of another, has no right to drive his cattle to Blackacre, and then to other land beyond it.'" See Penn Bowling Center v. Hot Shoppes, infra.

36. 317 Ill. 179, 147 N.E. 804 (1925).

2. **Use by Servient Owner; Repair of Easement.** Two final questions will conclude our review of the law governing the extent of an easement: who has the duty to repair the easement? and may the servient owner use the easement? The majority approach to both of these issues was taken in the old case of Durfee v. Garvey.[37] Plaintiff Durfee and defendant Garvey owned adjoining land in Los Angeles. Because Durfee's land was swampy it had to be drained before he could farm it, and for this purpose he acquired an easement across Garvey's land to a channel called the Arroyo Honda. In 1870 Durfee constructed a ditch on Garvey's property three feet deep and three feet wide; until 1882 he entered the property at least twice a year to clean the ditch. At that time, Garvey began to use his land for pasturing horses, mules and cattle, but, in feeding along the ditch, these animals filled it up and obstructed the flow of water. The court, in awarding damages to Durfee, stated first the rule governing use of the easement by the servient owner and then the rule governing repair of the easement: "The general rule is, that any man may use his own land in his own way, provided he does not use it negligently, so as to injure his neighbor. And the rule is, also, that where one man has an easement over the land of another, the duty of keeping the easement in repair rests upon its owner, and when repairs are necessary, he may enter on the servient tenement to make them."

## D. TERMINATION OF EASEMENTS

An easement may be terminated by many methods. The following is a list of the more common ones.

1. **Cessation of Purpose.** When an easement is created for a particular purpose, (for example, an easement used by a carting business),[38] it will terminate when that purpose no longer exists.

2. **Expiration of Period.** An easement granted for a specific period of time will, of course, terminate at the end of that period.

3. **Merger.** As noted earlier, an easement is an interest in land owned by another. If the owner of the easement acquires the servient estate, the easement is terminated because the land is no longer in another's possession.[39] In one case, a six-foot strip of land between two lots was used by the owners for a number of years.[40] In 1923, the Daskells acquired both lots, but eventually the lots came into the hands of Laboroff and Dimoff. Laboroff constructed a fence on the strip, Dimoff could no longer use it, and he started an action against Laboroff to have the fence removed. The court, however, determined

---

37. 78 Cal. 546, 21 P. 302 (1889).

38. Hohman v. Rochester Swiss Laundry Co., 125 Misc. 584, 211 N.Y.S. 217 (1925).

39. Restatement of Property §§ 497–499 (1944).

40. Dimoff v. Laboroff, 296 Mich. 325, 296 N.W. 275 (1941).

that the easement had been terminated when the Daskells acquired both lots, because "the union of dominant and servient estates in the same owner extinguishes prior easements. One cannot have an easement in one's own land."

4. **Abandonment.** An easement may be terminated if the owner relinquishes it intentionally, as indicated by his conduct.[41] The main issue is his intent as determined by the facts in each case, including his nonuse of the easement and his other activities.[42] An expression of intent to abandon, while relevent in determining intent, does not of itself result in abandonment unless it complies with the requirements for a release discussed below.

In Richardson v. Tumbridge,[43] although the defendant had an easement to construct a drain over the plaintiffs' property, he had never done so; instead, he excavated a stream bed to drain his land. After thirty-nine years, the plaintiffs sought a judgment that their land was no longer subject to the easement. The court applied the following rule: "Whether there has been an abandonment is a question of intention to be determined from all the surrounding circumstances, and is a question of fact and not of law. The proof must clearly indicate that it was the intention of the owner of the dominant estate to abandon the easement. Mere nonuse of an easement created by deed, however long continued, is insufficient to establish abandonment. . . . A right of way is not extinguished by the habitual use by its owner of another way, equally convenient, unless there has been an intentional abandonment of the former way. Such use of a different way, or as here, of a different method of drainage, may be under such circumstances as clearly to indicate an intention to abandon the right obtained by deed. An abandonment of an easement will be presumed when the owner of the right does or permits to be done some act inconsistent with its future enjoyment, or some other unequivocal act showing the intention permanently to abandon it." In applying these principles, the court decided that the defendant's acts did not indicate an intention to abandon the property, because even though he had dug out a stream bed to use as a drain, this "was not inconsistent with an intention, when occasion required, to exercise his right to build either a tile or stone drain, either in the bed of the stream or elsewhere. The clearing out of the bed of the stream in no way interfered with the building of a drain utilizing the flow of the stream."

5. **Destruction of the Servient Tenement.** If the servient tenement is destroyed through no fault of the servient owner, the easement is terminated even though the servient tenement is later rebuilt. In one case, the easement owner used a stairway inside a building for ac-

---

41. Restatement of Property § 504 (1944).

42. Charles C. Gardiner Lumber Co. v. Graves, 63 R.I. 345, 8 A.2d 862 (1939).

43. 111 Conn. 90, 149 A. 241 (1930).

cess to his own building. When the adjoining building, the servient tenement, was destroyed by fire through no fault of the servient owner, the easement was terminated. "It is the established doctrine that where a mere right to use a part of a building is granted, no proprietary interest in the land is conveyed. Upon this principle it has been held that a grant of the right to use the stairway of a building gives no interest in the soil which will survive the destruction of the building, and the right ceases whenever the building is destroyed *without the fault of the owner of the servient tenement*, and the owner of the right to use the stairway will not acquire any right in any new building which may be erected in the place of the one destroyed."[44]

6. **Estoppel.** When the servient owner takes action inconsistent with the rights of the easement owner, the easement is terminated if the following conditions are met: (1) the servient owner acts in reasonable reliance upon the conduct of the easement owner; (2) the servient owner's reliance was foreseeable by the easement owner; and (3) unreasonable harm would be caused the servient owner by allowing the easement to continue.[45] In one case, the servient owner fenced in the land that had been used as a pathway, constructed a large, valuable pond on it, and made other improvements in the area of the pathway. The court determined that the easement had been terminated because its owner seldom used it before the improvement, he lived near the easement and knew that improvements were being made but waited three years to advise the servient owner that he wanted to continue using it, and the reopening of the pathway would result in a $1,000 loss to the servient owner.[46]

7. **Prescription.** Just as an easement may be created by prescription, it can also be terminated by the servient owner's adverse, continuous, and uninterrupted use for the prescriptive period.

8. **Cessation of Necessity.** An easement implied by necessity will be terminated when the necessity ends. For example, when a previously landlocked dominant estate became accessible because of the relocation of a highway, an easement which had been implied from necessity was terminated.[47]

9. **Condemnation.** When the state, in exercising its sovereignty, acquires a servient estate or an interest in it that is inconsistent with the continuance of an easement, the easement is terminated.[48]

---

**44.** Muzio v. Erickson, 41 Cal.App. 413, 182 P. 974 (1919).

**45.** Restatement of Property § 505 (1944).

**46.** Trimble v. King, 131 Ky. 1, 114 S.W. 317 (1908).

**47.** Kux v. Chandler, 112 N.Y.S.2d 141 (1952).

**48.** Restatement of Property § 507 (1944).

10. **Release.** Just as the easement may be created by a deed or a will, it can be terminated by them as well. In either case, the instruments must be in a form required by law.[49]

## II. PROFITS

A profit *a prendre*, literally a profit "to take" but commonly called simply called a "profit," is a special type of easement which gives its owner the right to enter someone else's property in order to remove part of the land or a product of the land. A profit might include the right to take soil, gravel, seaweed, timber, wild animals, crops, or minerals. However, where there is an exclusive, unrestricted right to remove minerals, the person who acquires this right owns the minerals rather than a profit. Although older cases distinguished between easements and profits, the widely accepted modern view treats the profit as an easement. Like any other easement, it may be appurtenant or in gross. And in most cases the rules discussed above for easements also apply to the profit.

Most litigation involving profits arises when the owner of the profit attempts to sell it to a third party. The general rule—in the absence of an agreement to the contrary—is that profits may be sold, but whether or not they may be sold to more than one person depends upon whether the profit is appurtenant or in gross. A profit appurtenant, like the easement appurtenant, is divisible if the soil or its products is measurable with reference to the dominant estate. The divisibility of a profit in gross depends upon the intention of the parties, which is often determined by whether the profit is exclusive or nonexclusive. For instance, in Stanton v. Herbert & Sons,[50] the plaintiffs owned Hill's Island in the Cumberland river, about twenty miles from Nashville. At the time plaintiffs purchased the property, the grantors reserved "an easement, right, or privilege, to remove sand from said property for a period of ten years from the date of this conveyance." The grantors proceeded to sell their right to three separate building contractors in Nashville. The court determined that the sale should not be allowed because of the following principle: "If all the minerals are conveyed, or an exclusive right thereto, an interest in the land passes. This is a corporeal interest, which may be assigned, divided or dealt with as any other interest in land. If, under the grant, there passes only a right to remove minerals in common with the grantor, [it] . . . is assignable, it is not divisible." In this case, the reservation was determined to be nonexclusive, because "there is nothing in the language used in the deed to indicate that such right was intended to be exclusive. The right was described 'as an easement, right, or privilege.' The indefinite article 'an' was used, not 'the'. In addition to the right to remove sand, only such other rights and privi-

---

**49.** See Restatement of Property §§ 500–503 (1944).  **50.** 141 Tenn. 440, 211 S.W. 353 (1918).

leges were reserved as were necessary to effectuate the principal right. There is nothing to show an intention to deprive [the plaintiffs] of the right to remove sand themselves. Under the authorities, the presumption is against an exclusive grant or reservation of this nature."

Finally, the court explained the reason for limiting apportionment of profits: "The justice of the rule against the apportionment or division of an incorporeal hereditament, such as this, is strikingly illustrated in the case before us. The complainants here might very well have agreed that their immediate grantors, one of whom was a contractor, should reserve enough sand for use in their own business. The grantors, however, undertook to assign this right to three of the largest contractors in Nashville, who were engaged in the building of the largest plant in the United States—a plant demanded by the exigencies of the great war, and designed by the government to manufacture enough powder to supply the need of the United States and its Allies. To permit the grantor to apportion his right to sand among three such contractors engaged in such an enterprise would have required quantities of sand never dreamed of by the parties at the time this deed was made."

## III. LICENSE

A person with a license generally has personal, revocable, non-assignable permission to do one or more acts on another person's land. It differs from an easement in that the easement is an interest in land and normally must be created by a written instrument, while a license, not being an interest in land, may be created by any method that shows the assent of the owner of the land.[51] A license differs from a lease because a licensee never has possession of the land while a lessee always has the right to possession. And a license differs from a contract in that a contract requires consideration, whereas a license may or may not be based on consideration.[52]

Revocation of a license occurs when the licensor transfers the real estate, when he dies, or whenever he decides to exercise his right to revoke.[53] For instance, in Shubert v. Nixon Amusement Co.,[54] the plaintiff purchased four tickets to a play, but after he and his friends had entered the theater and were seated, they were thrown out. Shubert sued the theater, claiming that the theater "wrongfully and maliciously did . . . compel plaintiff and his guests to leave the theatre . . . [and that he] was also injured in his good name and credit, and did suffer great mortification and embarrassment of mind and feelings, and was subjected to the disdain and contempt of people."

51. Eastman v. Piper, 68 Cal.App. 554, 229 P. 1002 (1924).

52. C. Smith and R. Boyer, Survey of the Law of Property 418–419 (2nd ed. 1971).

53. Minnesota Valley Gun Club v. Northline Corp., 207 Minn. 126, 290 N.W. 222 (1940).

54. 83 N.J.L. 101, 83 A. 369 (1912).

The court, in citing an earlier decision, held that a plaintiff ejected from a theater might recover damages for breach of contract but could not recover in tort, because "a ticket confers a license essentially revocable; that the fact that a valuable consideration was paid makes no difference; for, if any action would lie, it would have to be founded on a breach of contract."

There are at least three well-recognized situations, however, when a license is considered irrevocable. Although courts refer to the right created in these situations as an irrevocable license, it is in fact an easement. First, a license is said to be irrevocable when the licensee has exercised the license by expending capital and labor in reliance on the licensor's promise. For instance in the Monroe Bowling Lanes v. Woodsfield Livestock Sales case discussed earlier, the court held that an easement had been created by the defendant's oral promise that the plaintiff could use a water line because the plaintiff relied on the promise when he built a bowling alley. Second, a license coupled with an interest is often irrevocable. The "interest" referred to is an interest in personal property located on the land of another. For instance, assume that Ernie sells his stereo to Bert, who lives in the apartment next to Ernie, and he tells Bert to pick up the stereo at any time. Bert thus has an irrevocable license to enter Ernie's apartment to get the stereo, although Ernie can limit the license to a reasonable time.[55] Third, some states have enacted statutes which specify that certain licenses are irrevocable. Under some statutes it is unlawful for a proprietor to refuse to admit ticketholders unless the person is "under the influence of liquor . . . guilty of boisterous conduct or . . . of lewd or immoral character."[56]

# CASES

---

## FONTAINEBLEAU H. CORP. v. FORTY–FIVE TWENTY–FIVE, INC.

Court of Appeal of Florida, 1959.
114 So.2d 357.

PER CURIAM. This is an interlocutory appeal from an order temporarily enjoining the appellants from continuing with the construction of a fourteen-story addition to the Fontainebleau Hotel, owned and operated by the appellants. Appellee, plaintiff below, owns

55. Restatement of Property §§ 513, 519 (1944).

56. For a discussion of one such statute by the U.S. Supreme Court see Western Turf Ass'n v. Greenberg, 204 U.S. 359, 27 S.Ct. 384, 51 L.Ed. 520 (1907).

the Eden Roc Hotel, which was constructed in 1955, about a year after the Fontainebleau, and adjoins the Fontainebleau on the north. Both are luxury hotels, facing the Atlantic Ocean. The proposed addition to the Fontainebleau is being constructed twenty feet from its north property line, 130 feet from the mean high water mark of the Atlantic Ocean, and 76 feet 8 inches from the ocean bulkhead line. The 14-story tower will extend 160 feet above grade in height and is 416 feet long from east to west. During the winter months, from around two o'clock in the afternoon for the remainder of the day, the shadow of the addition will extend over the cabana, swimming pool, and sunbathing areas of the Eden Roc, which are located in the southern portion of its property.

In this action, plaintiff-appellee sought to enjoin the defendants-appellants from proceeding with the construction of the addition to the Fontainebleau (it appears to have been roughly eight stories high at the time suit was filed), alleging that the construction would interfere with the light and air on the beach in front of the Eden Roc and cast a shadow of such size as to render the beach wholly unfitted for the use and enjoyment of its guests, to the irreparable injury of the plaintiff; further, that the construction of such addition on the north side of defendants' property, rather than the south side, was actuated by malice and ill will on the part of the defendants' president toward the plaintiff's president; and that the construction was in violation of a building ordinance requiring a 100-foot setback from the ocean. It was also alleged that the construction would interfere with the easements of light and air enjoyed by plaintiff and its predecessors in title for more than twenty years and "impliedly granted by virtue of the acts of the plaintiff's predecessors in title, as well as under the common law and the express recognition of such rights by virtue of Chapter 9837, Laws of Florida 1923 * * *." Some attempt was also made to allege an easement by implication in favor of the plaintiff's property, as the dominant, and against the defendants' property, as the servient, tenement.

\*   \*   \*

This is indeed a novel application of the maxim *sic utere tuo ut alienum non laedas*. This maxim does not mean that one must never use his own property in such a way as to do any injury to his neighbor. It means only that one must use his property so as not to injure the lawful *rights* of another. In Reaver v. Martin Theatres, Fla.1951, 52 So.2d 682, 683, 25 A.L.R.2d 1451, under this maxim, it was stated that "it is well settled that a property owner may put his own property to any reasonable and lawful use, so long as he does not thereby deprive the adjoining landowner of any right of enjoyment of his property *which is recognized and protected by law, and so long as his use is not such a one as the law will pronounce a nuisance*." [Emphasis supplied.]

No American decision has been cited, and independent research has revealed none, in which it has been held that—in the absence of some contractual or statutory obligation—a landowner has a legal right to the free flow of light and air across the adjoining land of his neighbor. Even at common law, the landowner had no legal right, in the absence of an easement or uninterrupted use and enjoyment for a period of 20 years, to unobstructed light and air from the adjoining land. And the English doctrine of "ancient lights" has been unanimously repudiated in this country.

There being, then, no legal right to the free flow of light and air from the adjoining land, it is universally held that where a structure serves a useful and beneficial purpose, it does not give rise to a cause of action, either for damages or for an injunction under the maxim *sic utere tuo ut alienum non laedas*, even though it causes injury to another by cutting off the light and air and interfering with the view that would otherwise be available over adjoining land in its natural state, regardless of the fact that the structure may have been erected partly for spite. * * *

Reversed with directions.

---

### SHINGLETON v. STATE

Supreme Court of North Carolina, 1963.
260 N.C. 451, 133 S.E.2d 183.

MOORE, Justice. The State of North Carolina owns a large body of land in Pender County, known as the Holly Shelter Wildlife Area. It is managed by the North Carolina Wildlife Resources Commission. No public roads or highways adjoin or cross any portion of the Wildlife Area involved in this action. The roads within the area are owned by defendants and used in connection with wildlife management.

There was a dispute between defendants and plaintiff Shingleton with respect to the ownership and location of certain lands within the boundaries of the Area. A suit was instituted, but before trial a compromise settlement was reached. Pursuant to the compromise agreement, plaintiff herein conveyed to the State a portion of the land in dispute and the State deeded to Shingleton a portion. * * *

The said conveyance by the State to plaintiff herein was by quitclaim deed. It conveyed to J. A. Shingleton and "his heirs and assigns" 110 acres situate in Topsail Township, Pender County. This land is described by metes and bounds, and lies entirely within, and a considerable distance from, the boundaries of the Wildlife Area. Immediately below the description are the following easement provisions:

"The party of the first part reserves from this conveyance the right to maintain and use the roads existing on the above described lands; and the said J. A. Shingleton is hereby granted the right to use the roads existing on other lands of the Wildlife Resources Commission for the purpose of ingress and egress to and from the above described lands by the most direct route."

The present controversy "arose when the plaintiff's (J. A. Shingleton's) brother and other kinsmen were attempting to go over (the) road in question which leads from the public road through the Wildlife Refuge of the defendants by the most direct route to the plaintiff's land and * * * defendants placed a locked gate at the entrance to the road in question and mounted armed guards to keep out all persons except plaintiff."

Plaintiff contends the right-of-way granted him by the State is an easement appurtenant. Defendants contend it is an easement in gross and may be used and enjoyed only by J. A. Shingleton personally. J. A. Shingleton instituted the present action to have determined his rights under the grant of easement, and makes allegations which, he contends, entitles him to injunctive relief.

Trial by jury was waived and the judge made findings of fact and conclusions of law and entered judgment. It was adjudged that the easement granted by the State to the plaintiff "is an unlimited easement appurtenant to plaintiff's land, given to plaintiff for his use and the use of his agents, servants, employees, licensees, and the public generally who have not been refused permission to use the easement by the plaintiff," and "that the defendants, their agents, servants and employees * * * are enjoined from interfering by gate or otherwise with the use of said easement or road as herein provided."

An appurtenant easement is one which is attached to and passes with the dominant tenement as an appurtenance thereof; it is owned in connection with other real estate and as an incident to such ownership. An easement in gross is not appurtenant to any estate in land or not belonging to any person by virtue of his ownership of an estate in other land, but is a mere personal interest in or right to use the land of another; it is purely personal and usually ends with the death of the grantee. An easement appurtenant is incapable of existence apart from the particular land to which it is annexed, it exists only if the same person has title to the easement and the dominant estate; it must bear some relation to the use of the dominant estate, and it must agree in nature and quality to the thing to which it is claimed to be appurtenant. An easement appurtenant is incident to an estate, and inheres in the land, concerns the premises, pertains to its enjoyment, and passes with the transfer of the title to the land, including transfer by descent. If an easement is in gross there is no dominant tenement; an easement is in gross and personal to the grantee because it is not appurtenant to other premises. An easement in gross attaches to the person and not to land.

* * * In the absence of express provision in the grant restricting the easement to the personal use of plaintiff, the presumption is that it is an easement appurtenant to plaintiff's 110-acre tract. Moreover, the situation of the property and the surrounding circumstances indicates beyond question that an easement appurtenant was intended. The original controversy, in the settlement of which the deed was given, arose from conflicting claims of rights and title to lands. The record does not disclose that plaintiff has ever claimed any personal rights, apart from land ownership, in the Wildlife Area. The deed conveys to plaintiff a tract of land which, without some adequate access over defendants' lands, would be completely cut off from any public or private road. The grant of easement was so clearly connected with the conveyance of the 110-acre tract that in the deed it follows immediately the description of the land. The words "ingress" and "egress" as used in the grant of easement show clearly it was intended that the easement is connected with and is to be used for the benefit of the land. The road in question is appurtenant to the land in fact, and leads from the land across the Wildlife Area to the public road beyond. Apart from the ownership of the 110-acre tract, the easement is worthless. If plaintiff did not own this land he would have no business or interest of any kind within the Wildlife Area. The land was conveyed to plaintiff in fee. It is not reasonable to conclude that the State would undertake to grant and plaintiff to accept a right of access to land which would end at the death of plaintiff and render the land thereafter inaccessible and worthless. Furthermore, it is not reasonable to suppose that plaintiff could, acting alone, cut and remove timber from his land or cultivate, harvest and remove crops, or make other beneficial use of the land. Certainly the parties did not intend that plaintiff's heirs, devisees or assigns should have no access to the property. We hold that the easement granted by the State to plaintiff is appurtenant to plaintiff's land described in the deed.

Modified and affirmed.

———

## WAGNER v. FAIRLAMB

Supreme Court of Colorado, 1963.
151 Colo. 481, 379 P.2d 165.

SUTTON, Justice. Defendants in error, who were plaintiffs in the trial court will be referred to as plaintiffs in this opinion. They alleged that they have a right-of-way for a recently constructed road to the south half of the Bradley claim across mining property owned by defendant. The issues were made by an amended complaint and the answer thereto. Trial was had to the court with an advisory jury, with the result that plaintiffs obtained judgment for the right-of-way claimed plus damages of $150.00. The judgment entered was based upon the existence of an implied easement, stemming from a common grantor, one A. E. Reynolds, who in 1919 had conveyed the north half of the Bradley claim to defendant's predecessor in title.

Plaintiffs' pleadings alleged several reasons why they were entitled to the claimed easement or right-of-way. The trial court narrowed the issues to those of whether a right-of-way had arisen by (1) implication or (2) by prescriptive use. The advisory jury found in the affirmative on both issues, but in its findings of fact the court concluded there was insufficient evidence to support the special verdict on adverse possession. It adopted, however, the jury's verdict as to a right-of-way by "implication" (meaning thereby one by pre-existing use).

\* \* \*

The evidence is that prior to 1919 Reynolds owned the entire Bradley claim; that at the time there was a public road which entered the west end of the Cimarron mill site and stopped about the middle of the site, and that this road continued on easterly as a private road across the mill site and the north half of the Bradley; further, that a mule pack or wagon trail at one time had served the south half of the Bradley and joined this road. Parts of this latter trail had long since become invisible through disuse and by the growth of bushes and other foliage. It also appears that the plaintiffs had bulldozed their truck road generally along the route of the old mule trail and in so doing had excavated across part of the defendant's dump. Shortly after defendant discovered plaintiffs' road she barricaded it and this lawsuit followed.

\* \* \*

The law has long recognized the interest in land known as an "easement" and that it can take several forms. One is the actual or express easement that appears in a deed or contract for the sale of land. This form is easy to recognize and usually not difficult to apply if fully described. A second type is the implied easement, which creates problems for both litigants and the courts. It is one not expressed by the parties in writing, but which arises out of the existence of certain facts implied from the transaction. Generally implied easements have not been looked upon with favor by the courts. Under some circumstances and facts, however, they are recognized.

\* \* \*

In 1 Thompson supra, § 396, at page 647, the necessary elements to prove an implied easement are set forth as:

"(1) Unity and subsequent separation of title; (2) obvious benefit to the dominant and burden to the servient tenement existing at the time of the conveyance; (3) use of the premises by the common owner in their altered condition long enough before the conveyance to show that the change was intended to be permanent; and (4) necessity for the easement."

It seems well to point out here that Thompson's four detailed requirements apply essentially to an implied easement by pre-existing use, for his third ground is not necessary for the existence of an implied easement by way of necessity as will more fully hereinafter appear. In any event an examination of this record reveals that the evidence does not support the trial court's finding of an implied easement by way *of a pre-existing use* since at best a terminated intermittent rather than a permanent use was shown. However, if the record discloses that that court arrived at the correct result for the wrong reason we will not set aside its judgment. Thus, we need to consider further the facts and the law applicable to this case.

\* \* \*

An implied way of necessity arises when the owner of a parcel of land conveys and grants part thereof to another, which leaves the remainder of the land without ingress or egress, except over the part conveyed. In such case reservation of a way of necessity is implied. The most common application of the doctrine occurs, however, when it is implied with the grant, i. e., where the lands conveyed are without ingress or egress except over lands retained. In such a case the lands retained are held to be subject to an easement in favor of the grantee.

It appears from the foregoing authorities that generally there are three requirements to be met before a way of necessity can be said to exist: The first requires that the original ownership of the entire tract be held by a single grantor prior to a division thereof. As previously noted, all of the Bradley claim originally was owned by A. E. Reynolds who conveyed away the north one-half thereof. The second requires that the necessity existed at the time of the severance. The evidence here indicates that in 1919, as at the present time, the south half of the Bradley was virtually inaccessible except by the route now in dispute. The third requirement is that the necessity for the particular right-of-way be great. Here the testimony of several residents of the Telluride area, as well as that of an expert witness (all borne out by the photographs in evidence), was to the effect that this is a very mountainous, rocky area with steep canyon walls, where roads at best are hazardous, expensive and dangerous to build. Documents in evidence support plaintiffs' contention that plaintiffs' road as now constructed is under all the circumstances the only practical method of affording ingress and egress for the purpose of mining or otherwise using the south half of the Bradley. And, based upon conflicting evidence and its view of the area during the course of the trial, the trial court found that this road was necessary and that the necessity existed in 1919 as well as today. In this connection we take cognizance of the fact that some authorities have held that a way of necessity cannot exist merely because the land is too steep or too narrow for a reasonable route. We hold that the rule as applied to property like this means a practical inability to have access any other way than by a way of necessity.

\*   \*   \*

The judgment is affirmed.

———

## SHINN v. ROSENBERGER

Supreme Court of Pennsylvania, 1943.
347 Pa. 504, 32 A.2d 747.

PATTERSON, Justice. This appeal arises out of a controversy over the use of a non-navigable lake for the purpose of boating, fishing and swimming.

Arthur T. Shinn and Lawrence D. Shinn are owners of a tract of land, comprising about 600 acres, in Middle Smithfield Township, Monroe County. This tract, on which is located thirty-nine fortieths of an entirely non-navigable lake, formerly known as "Seely's Pond," later as "Echo Lake," has been operated by the Shinn family as a summer resort or bungalow colony continuously since 1909 or 1910. The remaining one-fortieth of the lake is included within the lines of a tract of about 150 acres formerly owned by M. D. Turn and used by him in the operation of a summer boarding-house or hotel. Following the death of M. D. Turn, on December 11, 1920, operation of the boarding-house was continued by the Turn heirs until August 30, 1937 when they entered into articles of agreement for the sale of the property to Albert Rosenberger and Elsie C. Rosenberger, his wife. Pursuant to the articles of agreement the Rosenbergers entered into possession of the Turn property early in 1938 and they are in possession, as equitable owners, at the present time.

In 1935, following a dispute with the Turn heirs, the Shinns erected a fence or boom across the lake entirely on their own side of the division line. Before executing the agreement of sale Rosenberger informed the Shinns of his intention to purchase the Turn property and he requested that they remove the boom, thereby making the entire lake available for use by himself and his boarders. This request was refused. In 1939 Rosenberger consulted counsel with reference to his rights in the lake and was advised there was a "fifty-fifty chance" he might be successful in asserting a claim to use of the entire lake for boating, fishing and swimming purposes based upon the theory of a prescriptive right. Accordingly, during the summer of 1940 Rosenberger informed his boarders that they might cross over the boom onto the Shinn portion of the lake, if they so desired, and he directed that if the Shinns or their employees attempted to interfere they should be told to "go to hell." Some of the boarders did as directed and the Shinns thereupon instituted this suit in equity asking for an injunction.

At the hearing in the court below the parties entered into a stipulation as follows: "It is stipulated and agreed between counsel for plaintiffs and counsel for defendants that the following facts may be deemed and taken to be established with the same force and effect as though proven by testimony of witnesses from the stand, viz: That for a period of more than twenty-one years prior to the year 1935 boarders from the property owned at various times by M. D. Turn, later by his son, E. B. Turn, and daughter, Philura Turn, used the waters of Echo Lake for the purpose of pleasure boating in boats belonging to the Turns and for swimming; that the persons using said boats did in fact row over all portions of the lake, and that the swimmers did in fact bathe on any portion of the lake, even though it was beyond the boundaries of the Turn property * * *. Such use by strangers to the title occurred practically every year and was practiced continuously every year for such portions of said years as is commonly recognized as the 'summer season' in Monroe County, counsel for plaintiffs reserving the right at all stages of this case to contend that such use was merely permissive and not in any sense hostile or adverse, and counsel for defendants reserving the right at all stages of this case to contend that such use was hostile and adverse." The chancellor filed an adjudication in which he rejected the claim of the Rosenbergers to a prescriptive right and entered a decree nisi granting a perpetual injunction. The Rosenbergers filed exceptions, all of which were dismissed, and a final decree was entered from which they have appealed.

We all agree that the result reached by the court below was the proper one under the evidence. Title by prescription has its foundation in the presumption of a grant arising from the long continued use or possession of some right of common or other profit or benefit to be taken from or upon the land of another. Accordingly, the use must be such as to indicate that it is claimed as a right and is not the effect of indulgence or anything short of a grant. Mere user, no matter how long continued, will not give title. In order to give title the right must not only have been enjoyed without interruption for twenty-one years, but the enjoyment must have been adverse to the rights of the owner of the land. Open, notorious and uninterrupted user for a period of twenty-one years will be presumed to have been in pursuance of a full and unqualified grant, in the absence of evidence of some license, indulgence or some special contract inconsistent with the right claimed. But where the evidence produced by the claimant in support of his alleged right to an easement fully explains the manner in which the enjoyment began and is not sufficient to warrant a finding that the owner knew or ought to have known that the use was under a claim of right, the presumption of a grant does not arise.

Clarence Van Allen, a witness for appellants, testified on cross examination as follows:

"Q.  Now, these people were neighbors living within a few hundred yards of each other, were they not?  A.  Yes.

"Q.  Each one of them was accustomed to row all over that lake, wasn't he?  A.  Yes  *  *  *

"Q.  This use which was made of the lake  *  *  *  for pleasure boating and swimming and that sort of thing, was all done by permission of these adjoining owners, was it not?  A. Yes.

"Q.  Just nothing but a neighborly accommodation, you might say—it was done as a matter of neighborly accommodation, was it not?  A.  Yes."  This and similar evidence given by the other witnesses for appellants—Clinton Warner, caretaker of the Shinn property for many years, his son, Wilmer Warner and daughter-in-law, Ruth Warner—fully justifies the finding of the court below that "the use made of plaintiff's thirty-nine fortieths of this pond or lake by M. D. Turn was a permissive use and, therefore, could not ripen into a right by prescription." * * *

Decree affirmed at the cost of appellants.

---

## PENN BOWLING RECREATION CENTER
### v. HOT SHOPPES

United States Court of Appeals, 1949.
179 F.2d 64.

McALLISTER, Circuit Judge.  In 1938, the Norment Estate conveyed a portion of its real property to appellee, Hot Shoppes, Inc., and subjected a part thereof to a sixteen-foot right of way for ingress and egress.  This resulted in an easement for the benefit of the balance of the unconveyed property, adjacent thereto, which was retained by the Estate, and which, by virtue of the easement, became the dominant tenement.  A part of this dominant estate came into ownership of appellant, Penn Bowling Recreation Center, Inc., by mesne conveyances, in 1940, two years after the creation of the right of way.

On February 5, 1948, appellee, Hot Shoppes, erected a barrier of iron posts and cement concrete blocks within the right of way and alongside of it, interfering with the full enjoyment of the easement by Penn Bowling;  and shortly thereafter, appellant filed its complaint to enjoin appellee from maintaining the structure within the right of way and interfering with the use thereof. * * * The district court granted appellee's motion for summary judgment as prayed; and from such judgment, the Penn Bowling Recreation Center appeals.

The arguments that appellee addressed to the district court on the hearing on the motion for summary judgment embraced the contentions that appellant, as owner of the dominant tenement, had forfeited and extinguished the right of way by abandonment, as the result of subjecting the servient tenement to an additional and enlarged use or servitude in connection with other premises to which the easement was not appurtenant; that it had been guilty of the misuse of the easement of the right of way by reason of having used it for the parking of motor vehicles; and that, by certain masonry constructions, appellant had, in any event, made it impossible to use the right of way for egress and ingress.

With regard to the claim that appellant had subjected the servient tenement to a burden in excess of that imposed by the original easement, it appears that after the creation of the right of way for the benefit of the dominant tenement, appellant purchased not only that tenement but other real property adjacent thereto, the latter property not being entitled to the enjoyment of the easement. Appellant then constructed a building occupying a part of the dominant tenement, as well as the additional property adjacent thereto. Not all of the dominant tenement is occupied by the building. In fact, the total of the area of that portion of the dominant tenement, together with the non-dominant property over which the building is constructed, is a smaller area than the area of the original dominant tenement. The building, thus constructed, houses a large bowling alley and restaurant. Appellant in the past has been using the right of way to bring fuel oil, food, equipment, and supplies to the building, and removing trash, garbage, and other material therefrom.

It is contended by appellant that since the area of the dominant and non-dominant land served by the easement is less than the original area of the dominant tenement, the use made by appellant of the right of way to serve the building located on the lesser area is not materially increased or excessive. It is true that where the nature and extent of the use of an easement is, by its terms, unrestricted, the use by the dominant tenement may be increased or enlarged. But the owner of the dominant tenement may not subject the servient tenement to use or servitude in connection with other premises to which the easement is not appurtenant. And when an easement is being used in such a manner, an injunction will be issued to prevent such use. Appellant, therefore, may not use the easement to serve both the dominant and non-dominant property, even though the area thereof is less than the original area of the dominant tenement.

The disposition of the foregoing issue brings us to the principal legal question in the case: whether appellant's use of the right of way resulted in the forfeiture and extinguishment of the easement by abandonment, and thereby entitled appellee, on a motion for summary judgment, to a decree permanently enjoining appellant from using the right of way.

Misuse of an easement right is not sufficient to constitute a forfeiture, waiver, or abandonment of such right. The right to an easement is not lost by using it in an unauthorized manner or to an unauthorized extent, unless it is impossible to sever the increased burden so as to preserve to the owner of the dominant tenement that to which he is entitled, and impose on the servient tenement only that burden which was originally imposed upon it.

From the record before us, we are unable to ascertain what the total additional burden is that has been cast upon the servient tenement as the result of appellant's use of the right of way for ingress to, and egress from, the building which was located on part of the dominant and the non-dominant property.  *  *  *

*  *  *

Appellee claims that appellant itself has made the use of the right of way for ingress and egress impossible, by constructing adjacent to its building a wall and loading platform which occupies the space between the building and the right of way, and that, therefore, appellant can not get onto its premises from the right of way but can only come up to them.  To this contention, appellant replies that the platform, which occupies a space ten feet wide, can easily be demolished and leveled off even with the right of way, and thus afford ample space for any of its trucks to park on appellant's own land for purposes of loading or unloading.  If the loading dock were removed so as to permit the use of the right of way for the dominant estate, appellee's contention that appellant has made it impossible to use the easement for ingress or egress could not be sustained. This is a question, however, to be determined by the trial court after the taking of proofs in regard thereto.

*  *  *

Appellee further complains that appellant misused the easement by parking motor vehicles on the right of way. The use of the easement for purposes of ingress and egress does not include its use for parking purposes and an injunction may issue to prevent such a use. However, it is to be said that appellant is entitled to a reasonable use and enjoyment of the easement for purposes of ingress and egress.  In determining what is a reasonable use, the easement is to be construed in the light of the situation of the property and the surrounding circumstances for the purpose of giving effect to the intention of the parties.  The long continued use of the right of way for the purpose of loading or unloading supplies at appellant's premises may indicate an intention of the parties that the easement might be used for that purpose. \* \* \*

In accordance with the foregoing, the judgment is set aside and the case remanded to the district court for further proceedings consonant with this opinion, with the reservation of right to the appellee to apply for a temporary injunction pending final decision of the court.

## PROBLEMS

1. Romeo owned a house that was heated and cooled with solar energy. Before building the house, Romeo had entered into a written agreement with his neighbor, Juliet, providing that she would not build within thirty feet of Romeo's lot. Romeo later sold his house and lot to Mercutio. After the sale, Juliet started to build a high-rise apartment within five feet of Mercutio's lot. Mercutio brought suit, asking the court to "enjoin Juliet from building on or making use of her real estate" within thirty feet of Mercutio's lot. Should the court issue the injunction? Why?

2. Petruchio and Katherina owned adjoining tracts of real estate in a residential area. There was no water on Katherina's property. There was, however, a deep well on Petruchio's lot and he gave Katherina written permission to enter his property and to remove water for use on her lot. After the agreement was signed, Katherina converted her house into a thirty-room hotel. Petruchio claims that she cannot use the water for hotel purposes. Is he correct? Why?

3. Toby works for Olivia Enterprises. He has decided to purchase the back 100 acres of Sebastian's 200-acre farm for his company, which plans to construct a large warehouse on the property. The front parcel, which Sebastian will retain, lies along a major highway but the back parcel is landlocked. What legal issues relating to easements should be resolved by Toby and Sebastian before the purchase is completed? Why?

4. Constance purchased a general admission football ticket to the Soup Bowl. Halfway through the game an usher, for no reason, told Constance to "get out of here before I throw you out." Constance left the stadium and now sues the organization that runs the Soup Bowl for damages, alleging that she had (1) an easement, (2) a lease, (3) a contract, and (4) a license. Will Constance prevail on these theories? Why?

5. Warwick and Salisbury owned neighboring estates. In 1978, because of energy shortages resulting from a tremendous rise in coal prices, Salisbury began to mine and remove coal openly and continuously from Warwick's property, without Warwick's permission. From 1978 until 1989, Salisbury removed 15 million tons per year. From 1989 until 1995, he removed 20 million tons a year. Warwick now sues Salisbury, asking the court (1) to enjoin further removal of coal and (2) for damages for the coal already removed. The period of time necessary to establish an easement by prescription is 15 years, while the statute of limitations for tort actions is 2 years. Decide the case.

6. Helen and Alex owned adjoining lots. In 1915 Helen granted to Alex "the right to pass through my land." Alex drove his horse-drawn

wagon over the right-of-way for the next ten years. In 1925, however, Alex purchased an automobile and now wants to use it on the right-of-way. May he? Why?

7. Duncan and Malcolm owned adjoining lots. In 1923 Malcolm began using a common driveway that was bisected by the lot lines. In 1945, Malcolm sold his lot to Angus, who continued to use the driveway. In 1951, Angus and Duncan blacktopped the driveway, each paying one-half the cost. In 1960, Duncan decided to build a carport on his half of the driveway. Angus sued Duncan, asking the court to enjoin the construction of the carport. At the trial, Malcolm was called to testify, and the following exchange was reported: "Q. So I understand you never at any time were using it contrary to the wishes of Duncan? A. Absolutely not. Everything was all right." If we assume that the time period for prescription is twenty-one years, will Angus win? Why?

8. In 1932 Hamlet, without permission, erected two billboards on Gert's property at the intersection of two highways. The billboards were used for advertising a business owned by Hamlet. Gert's property was undeveloped woodland and Gert lived in another state. Hamlet used the billboards for twenty-five years; he occasionally entered the property to cut down brush and weeds, to repair the billboards, and to replace them when they were blown down by storms. May Gert now force Hamlet to cease making use of her property? Why?

9. Oswald owned a large apartment building. He leased an apartment on the tenth floor to Lear under a two-year, written lease. Lear can reach his apartment by using a stairway or elevator, which was not mentioned in the lease. When Lear used the elevator for the first time, Oswald told him that if he continued to use it his rent would be raised $500 per month. May Lear use the elevator without paying additional rent? Why?

10. Henry and Isabel owned adjoining farms. Henry ran a lumber mill on his farm while Isabel's farm was heavily forested. Isabel sold Henry the right to enter her farm and to cut down and remove timber. Henry later sold the north half of his farm to York, along with a non-exclusive right to remove timber from Isabel's farm. Henry retained the south half of his farm. When both Henry and York attempted to remove timber, Isabel refused to allow them onto her property. May Isabel refuse them entry to her property? Why?

## Part Two

# THE TRANSFER OF REAL ESTATE

---

## Chapter 5

### TYPES OF OWNERSHIP

Forrester pulled the microphone over. "As was recommended, Mr. Dow, Mr. Wasnak and I consulted an attorney about this whole matter. . . . He states that constant changes are being made in the law, to protect the condominium dweller, and that though many of these may not stand up in court if tested, most of them will. He said that it would not be possible to do exactly what was done to us, if this project were just starting at this time."

John D. MacDonald, *Condominium*

In Part One, the nature and scope of interests in real property, including fixture law, the implications of the *ad coelum* doctrine, water rights, and rights in real estate owned by others, have been examined. Part Two focuses on legal problems that arise when a person attempts to buy or sell the bundle of rights reviewed in Part One. The chapters in Part Two cover each step in the typical real estate transaction.

The real estate transaction normally begins with the search for the real estate (Chapter 6) and the search will culminate in the signing of a real estate contract (Chapter 7). After the contract is signed, the vendor's title must be examined (Chapter 8) and in most cases the buyer must arrange for financing (Chapter 9). When these matters have been completed, the contract will be performed at the closing (Chapter 10). Alternative methods of real estate transfer or acquisition will also be examined in Chapter 10, including adverse possession and transfer at death.

Before the real estate transaction commences, however, the person who deals in real estate must resolve two preliminary questions: What type of estate should be bought or sold? And should the real estate be placed in single ownership, joint ownership or a type of business ownership? This chapter will examine these problems.

## I. ESTATES IN LAND

"Estate" is a word of many meanings. In medieval Europe, a person was classified by his estate, the usual estates being the clergy, nobility and commoners. In modern times, estate is used to describe all the real and personal property that a person owns. For instance, a person might develop an estate plan, serve as the executor in the probate of a deceased relative's estate, or attempt to minimize the estate tax that will be paid on his death. The word is also used to describe real property. For example, a large parcel of land might be referred to as "the Turner estate."

In legal terms, however, estate also describes the nature, quality, and quantity of a person's interest in real property—an interest that might vary from absolute ownership to naked possession.[1] Legally, estates fall into two categories: (1) freehold estates, which are estates in fee or for life and are characterized by their uncertain duration, and (2) nonfreehold or leasehold estates, which are considered to be personal property and which may be of definite duration. Leasehold estates will be covered in Part Four under Landlord and Tenant Law. This chapter examines four types of freehold estates: the fee simple absolute, the qualified fee simple, the fee tail, and the life estate.

### A. THE FEE SIMPLE ABSOLUTE

The fee simple absolute, often called the fee simple or the fee, is the greatest estate possible; it corrsponds to what the average person thinks of as ownership. A fee simple estate is not subject to special limitations and is absolutely controlled by its owner, subject of course to governmental regulations and duties which arise under tort law. "The grant of a fee in land conveys to the grantee complete ownership, immediately and forever, with the right of possession from boundary to boundary and from the center of the earth to the sky, together with all the lawful uses thereof."[2]

Statutory law is often important in determining the scope of fee simple ownership. A Georgia statute provides the following definition: "An absolute or fee simple estate is one in which the owner is entitled to the entire property, with unconditional powers of disposition during his life, and which descends to his heirs and legal representatives upon his death intestate."[3] In most states[4] there are statutes providing that, unless a conveyance expressly states an intent to create another type of estate, a fee simple absolute is created. For instance, a will that grants a farm "to Jones" gives Jones a fee simple absolute.

1. Black's Law Dictionary 643 (4th ed. 1951).

2. Magnolia Petroleum Co. v. Thompson, 106 F.2d 217 (8th Cir. 1939).

3. Ga.Code Ann. § 85–501.

4. See Restatement of Property § 39 (1944) for a list of such states.

## B.　FEE SIMPLE DEFEASIBLE

In many cases, a fee simple is qualified by language that will cause the fee simple to end when a certain event occurs.　In such a case a fee simple defeasible is created.　There are three common types of such fees.　First, a conveyance of a tract of land might read: "To McGuffey for the purpose of operating a school and for no other purpose.　This conveyance shall be good so long as there is a schoolhouse kept on the property."　This is called a fee simple determinable because, while it may exist forever, the estate may also end if the special limitation is not followed.　If, at a future date, a schoolhouse were not kept on the property, McGuffey's interest would cease immediately, without action by the grantor.　The grantor's interest is called a "possibility of reverter."[5]　Alternatively, the grantor could have provided that if a schoolhouse was not kept on the premises, the estate would automatically pass to a third party.　This is called a fee simple subject to an executory limitation.　A third type of fee simple defeasible might read as follows: "To McGuffey provided that if the property be used for other than a school, Grantor shall have the right to re-enter the property and cause McGuffey to forfeit the estate."　A close reading of this language reveals that, unlike the fee simple determinable, the grantor in this case must take action by physically retaking the property or by going to court.　In this situation, the technical name for McGuffey's estate is a fee simple subject to a condition subsequent, and the grantor is considered to have a right of entry.

In creating a fee simple defeasible or any other limited property interest, a grantor will often be limited by a number of technical social restrictions, such as the rule against perpetuities, the rule in Shelley's case, the doctrine of worthier title, and restraints on alienation.　While application of these restrictions is best left to professional counsel and lies outside the scope of this book, restraints on alienation will be discussed below in order to illustrate the nature of the problem.

Restraints on alienation are the oldest of social restrictions, restrictions that limit individual liberty for the general benefit.[6]　The rationale for restricting the grantor's power to place restraints on alienation by the grantee has been stated as follows: "The underlying principle which operates throughout the field of property law is that freedom to alienate property interests which one may own is essential to the welfare of society. . . . [This is a freedom] found to rest in part upon the necessity of maintaining a society controlled primarily by its living members, in part upon the social desirability of facilitating the utilization of wealth, and in part upon the social desirability of keeping property responsive to the current exigencies of its current beneficial owners."[7]

5.　Lynch v. Bunting, 42 Del. 171, 29 A. 2d 155 (1942).

6.　4 Restatement of Property, Introductory Note 2119 (1944).

7.　4 Restatement of Property, Introductory Note 2379 (1944).

A restraint on alienation—an attempt by the grantor to restrict the grantee's ability to transfer the real estate—is in direct conflict with these socially desirable policies and might be invalid, depending on the extent of the restriction.  In determining whether the restraint is valid, courts consider whether the grantee is permitted to sell the property and whether the restraint is generally reasonable.[8]  For instance, assume that Able conveys his real estate, which is only suitable for coal mining purposes, "to Baker and his heirs, but if Baker or his heirs ever convey said real estate to Chance (Able's brother), Able and his heirs have the right to reenter and terminate the estate."  This restraint is reasonable because only one person, Chance, is excluded.  However, if the conveyance was made "to Baker and his heirs, but if Baker or his heirs ever convey said real estate to any coal company, Able or his heirs shall have a right to reenter and terminate the estate," a later conveyance to a coal company would be valid because the restraint unreasonably includes the only parties that would be interested in the land.[9]

## C.  FEE TAIL

A fee tail estate is one in which the grantor conveys real estate "to Doe and the heirs of his body."  At one time, the consequences of such a conveyance were that Doe could only use the land during his lifetime; he could not convey the real estate outside the family since it had to pass to his male children and grandchildren; and if Doe died without heirs, the property would revert to the grantor.  In modern times, this severe restraint on Doe's ability to alienate his property has been prohibited by thirty-three states, while in other states the effect of the fee tail is limited.[10]

## D.  CONVENTIONAL LIFE ESTATES

A life estate is an estate whose duration is measured by the life of a person.  A conventional life estate is created by the act of the parties whereas a legal life estate is created by operation of law.  Legal life estates—dower, curtesy and homestead—will be defined and discussed in Chapter 10.  A life estate may be measured by the life of the grantee or by the life of a third party, in which case it is an estate *pur autre vie*.  For example, the owner may convey his property "to Abbott for life" or "to Abbott for the life of Costello."  The owner may also create a life estate measured by more than one life: "to Able for the life of the survivor of Baker and Chance."

In each of the above illustrations, the property will revert to the owner at the termination of the life estate, thereby giving the owner a reversion.  However, it is also possible for the owner to provide

---

**8.**　Restatement of Property § 406 (1944).

**9.**　Id.

**10.**　C. Smith and R. Boyer, Survey of the Law of Property 13, 39 (2nd ed. 1971).

that the property will pass to a third party, giving the third party what is called a vested remainder interest: "to Abbott for life and then to Costello." Costello's remainder interest is said to be vested because it is certain that the property will pass to Costello on Abbott's death. Remainders are classified as contingent when they depend upon the occurrence of an uncertain event. Costello's remainder would be contingent if the grant read: "to Abbott for life and then to Costello if Costello marries before Abbott's death."[11]

The life estate—like the fee simple absolute, the fee simple defeasible and the fee tail—is considered to be a present estate; that is, the owner has an immediate right to possess and enjoy the property. Reversions and remainders (such as possibilities of reverter, rights of reentry and executory interests) are future interests because enjoyment or possession must be postponed until a future date.[12]

After the creation of a life estate, disputes often arise between the owners of the present and the future interests as the following example illustrates. Owner owns a large wheat farm, part of which is used as a coal mine. Owner deeds the farm "to Clyde for life" but keeps a reversionary interest. Shortly after Clyde has moved to the farm, a conflict arises between Clyde and Owner over Clyde's duties to make insurance, tax and mortgage payments, his duty to make repairs, and his right to use the property for farming and mining purposes. The following rules have been developed by the courts to resolve such disputes.

1. **Taxes and Interest.** The well-established rule states that the life tenant must pay all annual taxes and interest on debts on the land to the extent that he has received profits, rents, or income from the property. For instance, assume that Clyde earns $5,000 per year from the farm for three years and pays taxes and interest of $3,000 each year. During the fourth year, Clyde has no earnings from the farm, yet he still must pay the interest and taxes because of his earnings in prior years.[13]

The above rule does not apply to special taxes or assessments. Assume that the county installs a new sewer, which passes through Owner's farm, and Owner receives a sewer assessment for $10,000, with $1,000 to be paid each year for ten years. Since the sewer is a permanent public improvement that increases the value of the reversion, most courts would prorate the assessment in proportion to the benefits Owner and Clyde receive from the sewer. A court might conclude that Clyde ought to pay interest on the assessment and that Owner would be liable for the principal.[14] On the other hand, a court might figure the life tenant's share of a special tax by dividing

11. C. Smith and R. Boyer, Survey of the Law of Property 80 (2nd ed. 1971).

12. Id. at 3, 67.

13. Restatement of Property §§ 129, 130 (1944).

14. Cooper v. Barton, 208 Iowa 447, 226 N.W. 70 (1929).

the present value of the life estate by the present value of a life estate which would last as long as the improvement. For instance, we might assume that Clyde is sixty-three years old and his life estate is valued at $5,000. If the present value of a life estate lasting fifty years (the life of the sewer system) is $20,000, Clyde might be asked to pay $\frac{\$5,000}{\$20,000}$ or 25 percent of the $10,000 assessment. If the special tax was for an improvement that would not reasonably be expected to last beyond the life estate, the life tenant would be responsible for the full amount of the special tax.[15]

2. **Insurance.** If there were a farmhouse and a number of buildings on Owner's farm, two major questions would arise: Who has the duty to insure these buildings? And who is entitled to the insurance proceeds if the buildings are destroyed? The general rule is that neither the life tenant nor the remainderman has a duty to insure the buildings, but if either does insure them, the distribution of the proceeds will depend on the facts of each case. For example, if Owner purchased insurance before the life estate was created and the property is destroyed thereafter, the life tenant is given a life estate in the proceeds of the policy.[16] If an insurance policy is taken out solely by the life tenant or by the remainderman after creation of the life estate, as a general rule the party that has taken out the insurance is entitled to the full proceeds of the policy. Even if the value of the proceeds exceeds the insured's interest in the property, the insured will receive the full amount on the theory that an insurance policy is a personal contract between the insured and the company. Whenever possible, however, courts attempt to find an intention that the policy was taken out for the benefit of both the life tenant and the remainderman.[17]

In Morris v. Morris,[18] a woman held a life estate in a farm and her son was the remainderman. The mother purchased a $15,000 fire policy insuring the farmhouse and, in 1973, the farmhouse was totally destroyed. After the insurance company paid the mother, she was sued by her son who claimed that he was entitled to part of the proceeds. The court, deciding that the son had no right to the proceeds, noted the general rule that "a life tenant is entitled to all the proceeds for a loss if the life tenant has procured the insurance policy in his own name and for his own benefit and has paid the premium from his own funds. The general rule is not changed by the fact that the insurance is for the full value of the property rather than only for the value of the life tenant's interest in the property."

---

15. Restatement of Property § 133 (1944).

16. R. Keeton, Insurance Law—Basic Text 210 (1971).

17. W. Vance, Insurance 783, 784 (1951).

18. 274 Or. 127, 544 P.2d 1034 (1976).

3. **Repairs.** When a life estate is created, there is considerable potential for controversy over the life tenant's duty to keep the property in repair. If the farmhouse needs painting, the roof needs repair, windows must be replaced, or if the farmhouse is totally destroyed, must the life tenant repair or rebuild the house? The answer will depend on whether the repairs are considered to be ordinary or extraordinary. The life tenant who receives income, rents, or profits from the real estate has a duty to make ordinary repairs—for example, painting, window replacement, or roof repairs. If the repairs are extraordinary, however, the life tenant will not be responsible. In one case, a court held that a life tenant was not responsible for installing a new furnace because the old furnace was already old and rusted when she took possession. Furthermore, she was not responsible for replacing gutters that had reached a stage at which patching was not beneficial.[19]

It is possible that a tenant might voluntarily go beyond making ordinary repairs and actually make improvements on the property. For example, Clyde might decide to add a new room onto the farmhouse. If the improvements are considered to be fixtures, then they may be removed within a reasonable time after the termination of the life estate. However, if the improvement is attached and considered an integral part of the premises, it cannot be removed at the termination of the life estate, and the tenant is not entitled to reimbursement from the remainderman.

4. **Tenant's Use of Property.** How a life tenant may use the property often leads to thorny legal questions. For example, may Clyde farm and mine the land and keep all the profits from these activities? May he cut down timber from the farm and sell it? May he tear down the farmhouse and other buildings? As a general rule, a life tenant may act as the fee simple owner would if he were on the land,[20] but he is limited in his ability to use the land in such a way as to diminish the market value of the remainder.[21]

In applying this test, courts have decided that the life tenant may keep all the rents and profits that he produces. As noted by one court: "It is a general rule, well established in this and other jurisdictions of this country that . . . a life tenant is entitled to everything in the nature of revenue or income produced by the property during his tenancy."[22] Furthermore, the life tenant may sell whatever interest he has in the land to a third party although, if the tenant attempts to

19. Saving Investment & Trust Co. v. Little, 135 N.J.Eq. 546, 39 A.2d 392 (1944).

20. C. Smith and R. Boyer, Survey of the Law of Property 237 (2nd ed. 1971).

21. Restatement of Property §§ 119, 138 (1944).

22. Medlin v. Medlin, 203 S.W.2d 635 (Tex.Civ.App.1947).

sell more than the life estate, the purchaser only obtains the rights of the life tenant.[23]

Although the life tenant may not diminish the market value of the remainder interest, he is entitled to cut timber as needed for repair of structures, fences, or fuel under what is called the right of "estovers." In a recent Florida decision, the court concluded that the life tenant had no right to cut and sell timber because "an ordinary tenant may cut timber and not be liable for waste if he uses the timber for fuel; for repairing fences and building on the estate; for fitting the land for cultivation; or for use as a pasture if the inheritance is not damaged and the acts are conformable to good husbandry; and for thinning or other purposes which are necessary for the enjoyment of the estate and are in conformity with good husbandry. . . . An ordinary life tenant has no right to cut the timber from an estate for purely commercial reasons and so to do is tortious conduct for which the remainderman may sue immediately." [24]

In addition to the right of estovers, the tenant may continue profitable operations such as mining, drilling, or the removal of timber for sale if the land was used for such operations before the life estate was created. As one court observed, "The most obvious inference would seem to be that when a man devises land with an open mine upon it, to a person for life, he intended the devisee to derive profit from the mine, as well as from the surface of the land." [25]

In using the land, the life tenant is limited by the general rule that he is not allowed to commit waste. Waste is generally defined as destruction of property by the life tenant to the harm of the reversion or remainder. In Beliveau v. Beliveau,[26] the defendant, sixty-six years old at the time of trial, was the life tenant on a 320-acre farm. She failed to repair buildings and fences on the farm, allowed "foul weeds" to infest and depreciate the farm, failed to pay taxes, and became involved in serious lawsuits relating to management of the farm. The court, in deciding to appoint a receiver to manage the farm, made this observation: "It was the duty of appellant as a life tenant not to permit waste, to make necessary and reasonable repairs, to pay current taxes, to pay the interest on the mortgage, and not to permit noxious weeds to infest the lands to the injury of the freehold. . . . Her failure to pay the taxes and make necessary and reasonable repairs of the building and fences constituted waste. While there is some conflict among the authorities we think the better rule is that a life tenant commits waste by permitting farm lands to become infested with noxious weeds which do injury to the freehold. Such acts not only constitute ill husbandry but also injury to the land itself."

23. Restatement of Property § 124 (1944).

24. Sauls v. Crosby, 258 So.2d 326 (Fla. App.1972).

25. Neel v. Neel, 19 Pa. 323 (1852).

26. 217 Minn. 225, 14 N.W.2d 360 (1944).

A difficult question arises when the life tenant decides to commit waste but, in so doing, actually increases the value of the real estate. The old English rule provided that anything that changed the nature of the real estate, even if it were an improvement, would be considered waste. This rule has not been followed by modern courts, which will allow basic changes in the property to reflect a general change in the neighborhood or in society in general. In one case a widow who lived on a plantation allowed barns and outbuildings to decay. The court held that her failure to keep up these buildings was not necessarily waste because the buildings had been erected before the Civil War when the plantation was operated by slaves. The court felt that it was for a jury to decide whether she was justified in allowing the buildings to remain in disrepair after emancipation, when the plantation could no longer be run at a profit.[27] See Melms v. Pabst Brewing Co., infra.

5. **Estate Planning.** The creation of a life estate as part of an estate plan often creates unforeseen complications. For example, assume that an elderly widow, Clarissa, hopes to avoid the expense of probate court by deeding her house to "my son Clyde, a married man, and my daughter Bonnie, excepting and reserving a life estate in Clarissa." Before deciding to use this device, Clarissa and the children should reach an agreement regarding insurance, mortgage payments, taxes, and general use of the property. Furthermore, Clarissa must remember that if she ever decides to sell or mortgage more than her life estate, she will need the permission of Clyde, Bonnie, and Clyde's wife, who has a dower interest. And if one of these parties should become incapacitated, a legal proceeding would probably be necessary in order to complete the sale.

## II. GENERAL FORMS OF OWNERSHIP

In the first half of this chapter we have examined four types of freehold estates—those interests in land measured in terms of duration. Interests in land are also classified by the form of ownership. It is, of course, possible for one person to own an interest in land—the so-called owner in severalty. However, because of marriage relationships or the expense of purchasing real estate, it is more common for two or more persons to purchase real estate together. In this section we will examine several forms of concurrent ownership, forms which can be used in purchasing real estate for personal or investment purposes. The chapter will conclude with a review of a number of ownership vehicles used primarily for real estate investment purposes.

### A. JOINT TENANCY

The most important characteristic of the joint tenancy is the right of survivorship. If X sells real estate "to A and B as joint ten-

27. Sherrill v. Connor, 107 N.C. 630, 12 S.E. 588 (1890).

ants and not as tenants in common," upon the death of either A or B the survivor becomes the sole owner of the real estate. If A and B died under circumstances in which it cannot be determined who died first, the Uniform Simultaneous Death Act states that each estate would receive one-half of the property.

A joint tenancy is created by use of a deed or a will. Regardless of the method, however, the common law requires four unities—time, title, interest and possession—in order to create a valid joint tenancy. Unity of time requires that the interests of the joint owners begin (vest) at the same time. Unity of title means that the parties must acquire their interest in the same conveyance. Unity of interest requires that each tenant have an equal interest; for instance, one cannot have a life estate and the other a fee simple estate. Finally, unity of possession has been interpreted to mean that all parties have an equal right to take possession of the real estate. According to Blackstone, joint tenants must "have one and the same interest, accruing by one and the same conveyance, commencing at one and the same time, and held by one and the same possession." [28]

In Deslauriers v. Senesac [29] the court applied the common law rule. Ida Boudreau acquired a parcel of real estate in Kankakee, Illinois, in 1903. She later married Homer Deslauriers and, in 1911, Ida and Homer deeded the real estate to themselves as joint tenants and not as tenants in common. The deed also noted that "said grantors intend and declare that their title shall and does hereby pass to grantees not in tenancy in common but in joint tenancy." Ida died in 1918 and a question arose whether Homer was the sole owner of the property or only the holder of a one-half interest as a tenant in common. The court admitted that "it was clearly the intention of the grantors to convey an estate in joint tenancy." However the court concluded that Homer was a tenant in common because two of the four unities were missing. "Hence the interest of Ida Deslauriers and her husband were neither acquired by one and the same conveyance, nor did they vest at one and the same time. Two of the essential properties of a joint estate—the unity of title and the unity of time— were therefore lacking. Where two or more persons acquire individual interests in a parcel of property by different conveyances and at different times, there is neither unity of title nor unity of time, and in such a situation a tenancy in common, and not a joint tenancy, is created."

Ida and Homer could have avoided this decision by use of a "straw party" transaction where they would deed the real estate to a third party and the third party would immediately deed it back to them. However, the modern view, adopted in a majority of states either by statute or court decision, is that a direct conveyance from the owner to himself and the joint tenants is valid despite the four unities.

28.   Cleaver v. Long, 69 Ohio L.Abs. 488,     29.   331 Ill. 437, 163 N.E. 327 (1928).
      126 N.E.2d 479 (1955).

One court, following the modern view, gave the following opinion: "Some courts hold that an owner may not convey directly to himself and another to create a joint tenancy, but may do so with the intervention of a trustee. In effect this is merely saying that it is entirely proper and legal to do indirectly that which 'the rules of law' prohibit doing directly. In reaching just conclusions to carry out the intention of persons, where no statute or public policy is violated, courts today are disregarding fictions and technical niceties and distinctions of the common law. The writer of this opinion cannot escape wondering why the courts have dwelt at great pains on the 'four unities' of the old common law joint tenancy when the incident of survivorship is expressly provided for as the clear intention in a deed. Although some courts over the United States have taken the technical view, I believe the weight of authority is that such a view must yield to the intention of the parties. The right of survivorship is from the viewpoint of a layman the principal characteristic of a joint tenancy." [30]

A joint tenancy will be terminated whenever one of the four unities is destroyed. Although states are not in agreement on the time of destruction, the general rule is that a voluntary or involuntary conveyance destroys the unities of title and interest, thereby converting the ownership into a tenancy in common. For instance, if Burns and Allen own a farm as joint tenants and Allen sells her interest to Benny, Burns and Benny now own the land as tenants in common. The result would be identical if Allen's conveyance were involuntary, that is, if a sheriff were to sell the real estate to satisfy a judgment against Allen. Other methods of severance include partition, which is a voluntary or court-ordered division of the real estate among the joint tenants. In some states a divorce decree will sever a joint tenancy, while in other states the decree must specifically refer to the joint tenancy if it is to be severed. [31] A mortgage taken out by only one of two joint tenants severs the joint tenancy, at least under the title theory to be discussed in a later chapter. [32]

The effect of murder of one joint tenant by another has been especially troublesome to courts. In Abbey v. Lord, [33] for instance, Mr. and Mrs. Lord as joint tenants owned 500 shares of telephone stock worth $5,000. After an argument over his wife's refusal to sign a check, Mr. Lord killed his wife with a butcher knife. He was charged with murder, but later he entered a plea of guilty to manslaughter and was ordered to serve one year in the county jail. When a dispute arose concerning ownership of the telephone stock the court decided that the husband's act of killing his wife terminated the joint tenancy and converted it into a tenancy in common, with the heirs of the

30. Cleaver v. Long, 29 Ohio L.Abs. 488, 126 N.E.2d 479 (1955).

31. See R. Kratovil, Real Estate Law 194 (6th ed. 1974).

32. Van Antwerp v. Horan, 390 Ill. 449, 61 N.E.2d 358 (1945).

33. 168 Cal.2d 499, 336 P.2d 226 (1959).

victim taking one-half the property. While several states follow the *Abbey* approach, some other courts have held that the murderer is entitled to the entire property as a surviving joint tenant. Yet other courts take the opposite extreme and completely divest the killer of the estate. See Bradley v. Fox, infra.

In most cases, courts will attempt to find severance whenever possible because of judicial bias against joint tenancy. "[J]oint tenancies are not favored and can only be created by clear and definite language not reasonably capable of a different construction." [34] It should be kept in mind, however, that there is one common situation in which courts uniformly deny claims of severance—when a person makes a will. If two bachelors, Sam and Joe, purchase real estate as joint tenants and later Joe marries Betty Sue and executes a will leaving his interest in the real estate to her, Betty Sue inherits none of the property on Joe's death. In the words of one court, "As to property held in joint tenancy, there is nothing to inherit from the one dying first." [35]

## B. TENANCY BY THE ENTIRETY

In approximately half of the states, it is possible for two persons to hold real estate as tenants by the entirety. Ohio was the most recent state to authorize estates by the entirety; a 1972 statute provides that an estate by the entirety is created when a deed conveys real estate to "husband and wife, for their joint lives, remainder to the survivor of them." The Ohio statute also adopted the modern view, permitting such an estate to be created by one or both of the parties without using a straw person.[36]

A tenancy by the entirety is identical to a joint tenancy, with three major qualifications. First, tenancy by the entirety can only be created between husband and wife. Thus a fifth unity, unity of person (husband and wife), is added to the four unities of joint tenancy. Courts generally presume that when a husband and wife purchase property jointly and the words of conveyance do not indicate otherwise, a tenancy by the entirety is created.[37] If two unmarried parties purchase property as tenants by the entirety, their ownership will be considered a joint tenancy or tenancy in common.

In Lopez v. Lopez,[38] Alejo, while already married to Soledad, married Helen. He and Helen purchased real estate as "tenants by the entireties." Later Alejo and Soledad were divorced and Alejo married Helen again. When Alejo was killed in an accident, the

34. Short v. Milby, 31 Del.Ch. 49, 64 A.2d 36 (1949).

35. Draughon v. Wright, 200 Okl. 198, 191 P.2d 921 (1948).

36. Ohio Rev.Code Ann. § 5302.17.

37. Hardin v. Chapman, 36 Tenn.App. 343, 255 S.W.2d 707 (1953).

38. 250 Md. 491, 243 A.2d 588 (1968).

question arose of Helen's interest in the real estate. The court's opinion was as follows: "Helen, while admitting that tenancies by the entirety were not created, contends that an intent to create rights of survivorship has been shown, sufficient to vest title in Helen, as the survivor of Alejo. In our view, Helen must prevail. We are here dealing with deeds which convey property to the grantees as husband and wife. Had they been validly married, a tenancy by the entirety would have been created. . . . However, a tenancy by the entirety can only be created when the parties stand in relationship of husband and wife at the time of the grant to them . . .. Absent such a relationship, the attempt to create a tenancy by the entirety fails. Generally, in the case of a deed conveying property to grantees as husband and wife who are in fact not married, there is a presumption favoring tenancies in common, but this presumption will yield to the showing of a contrary intent. . . . In the instant case, we regard Alejo's attempt to take title as tenants by the entirety as a sufficient showing of his intention to create a right of survivorship, and the presumption favoring a tenancy in common must yield to a joint tenancy." See Thurmond v. McGrath, infra.

The second and most important distinction between a joint tenancy and tenancy by the entirety is that the latter can only be terminated by the joint action of the husband and wife, while the former can be terminated by one party's actions. For example, if Husband and Wife own property as tenants by the entirety, Husband cannot sell or lease his estate without the consent of Wife. Furthermore, a creditor of Husband alone may not take or sell Husband's interest in the property, although the property could be taken by creditors if the debt were owed by both Husband and Wife. One court, in deciding that a wife who was separated from her husband could not lease the property, defined the situation in these terms: "Neither spouse may separately dispose of any part so as to work a severance of the estate, nor encumber the property in any way. Neither spouse may convey an interest in the estate without the other's authority or consent, nor perform any act or make any contract respecting the property which would prejudicially affect the other, for it belongs to both, and each has a joint right with the other to its possession, use and enjoyment during the existence of the marriage. As a corollary of these principles it follows that a lease of the property can be made only by the act of both parties joining therein, and this, of course, is especially true if it purports to be for a term extending beyond the lifetime of the spouse who executes it. Since a judgment creditor of either spouse cannot sell or execute on his debtor's interest in an estate by the entireties, and a purchaser at a sheriff's sale thereunder would not acquire any right to possession, it is obvious that neither husband nor wife can voluntarily put a stranger, even though a creditor, into possession, and thereby infringe the co-tenant's rights."[39]

39. Schweitzer v. Evans, 360 Pa. 552, 63 A.2d 39 (1949).

Finally, in a few states, the tenancy by the entirety is unique because the husband is given exclusive right to possession and control of the property.  In these states' view, the husband has the right to use the property, lease it to a third party and even exclude the wife from the real estate.  See D'Ercole v. D'Ercole, infra.

## C.  TENANCY IN COMMON

A tenancy in common results when the tenants have unity of possession, with each entitled to occupy the property.  Although the unities of time, title and interest may be present, they are not required to establish a tenancy in common.

Unlike the joint tenancy or the tenancy by the entirety, a tenancy in common may be created not only by the acts of the parties through a deed or a will but also by law when a property owner dies without leaving a will and his property passes to more than one person.  Also, under the common law or under many state statutes, courts generally presume that a tenancy in common was created if the intention of the parties is not clear.  For instance, if real estate is conveyed "to Smith and Wesson," in most states it is presumed that a tenancy in common has been created.  When Smith dies, his undivided one-half interest will pass to his heirs rather than to the survivor, Wesson.  Thus if Smith died without a will and left two sons, A and B, they would each receive one-half interest as tenants in common.

A tenant in common may sell, lease, or mortgage his undivided interest as he pleases.[40]  In addition the tenant, or a purchaser of the tenant's interest, may seek a partition either by agreement with the other joint tenants or by judicial proceedings.  A partition does not create a new title, for the parties have already established title through ownership as tenants in common.  However, the partition does have the effect of severing the unity of possession, thereby terminating the tenancy in common.

## D.  RIGHTS OF CONCURRENT OWNERS

The rights of a joint tenant stem from the one unity that is common to the three types of concurrent ownership—the unity of possession.  This means that each tenant has the right to use the real estate as if he were the sole owner, except that "he has no right to exclude his co-owners, or to appropriate to his sole use any particular portion thereof.  The tenants out of possession may at any time assert their right to share in the possession, or they may have the property partitioned by a division, each taking a distinct part according to the extent of his interest."[41]  Although normally the tenants will share profits from the land, a tenant in sole possession is entitled to

---

**40.**  Stevahn v. Meidinger, 79 N.D. 323, 57 N.W.2d 1 (1952).

**41.**  Massman v. Duffy, 333 Ill.App. 30, 76 N.E.2d 547 (1947).

keep the profits resulting from his own use and is not required to pay rent to the other tenants.

In Black v. Black,[42] a father and three sons owned a citrus grove as joint tenants, and the father operated the grove. After the father's death, the sons sued their stepmother, claiming that she must turn over revenues received from her deceased husband. The court decided that she could keep the revenues for the following reasons: "A joint tenant in the sole and exclusive occupancy of the land is not required to account to his cotenant for any portion of the revenues derived therefrom so long as they are the fruitage of his own capital, labor and skill. The risks incurred by the occupier of the land (held jointly) in the cultivation of crops are his as are also the profits he may enjoy or the losses he may sustain in producing crops by his industry. In taking all the fruits grown upon the land, decedent herein received no more than his just share inasmuch as it is no more than the reward for his own labor and capital to no part of which is cotenant entitled."

In certain circumstances, however, the tenant in sole possession will have certain duties to his co-tenants. For instance, he must make tax and mortgage payments and keep the property in repair— expenses which would normally be shared by all tenants. Furthermore, the tenant in possession must account to his co-tenants in cases when he refuses to allow them onto the property [43] or when he rents the property to a third party.

A difficult situation arises when one tenant decides to expend money to repair or improve the property. Assume that Gert and Amos jointly own a vacant lot worth $50,000. Amos decides to build a large apartment house on the lot and asks Gert to contribute half the cost. When Gert refuses, Amos proceeds to build the structure at a cost of $150,000. In such a case, the law is clear: Amos cannot force Gert to contribute for either repairs or improvements. However, he could seek relief in the form of a partition action brought in a court of equity. In this case the court would probably not physically divide the property (a partition in kind), even though such partitions are favored in the law,[44] because of the nature of the property. Consequently, the court would order a partition by sale. If the property were sold for $200,000, Amos would receive $175,000, the cost of his improvement plus half of the remaining proceeds, and Gert would receive $25,000.[45] However, if the value of the property increased by more than the improvement cost, some courts would limit Amos to recovery of the cost of the improvement while other courts would also

**42.** 91 Cal.App.2d 328, 204 P.2d 950 (1949).

**43.** Murphy v. Regan, 8 N.J.Super. 44, 73 A.2d 191 (1950).

**44.** Formosa Corp. v. Rogers, 108 Cal. App.2d 397, 239 P.2d 88 (1952).

**45.** C. Smith and R. Boyer, Survey of the Law of Property 58, 59 (2nd ed. 1971).

allow him to recover the amount the value of the land increased because of his improvements.[46]

## E.  JOINT OWNERSHIP AND ESTATE PLANNING

In an attempt to avoid the expense and delay inherent in probate proceedings, married couples frequently place all their property in joint ownership.  In many cases assets can be transferred to joint ownership without gift tax consequences.  Under the Tax Reform Act of 1976, gifts less than $3,000 per year to any person are tax free, there is a lifetime $100,000 marital deduction for gifts to a spouse, and one-half of lifetime gifts to a spouse in excess of $200,000 are not taxed.  However, while joint ownership is a useful device in estate planning, the dangers of relying solely on joint ownership to transfer an estate are illustrated by the following two examples.

First, assume that a young married couple, Tom and Mary, have two young children.  Tom and Mary own a $50,000 house as tenants by the entirety, jointly own two automobiles worth a total of $10,000, and have $10,000 in a joint bank account.  If their goal is to avoid probate, Tom and Mary have succeeded admirably, for on the death of one spouse, the survivor automatically becomes the sole owner of the property.  Furthermore, their estate is exempt from federal estate and gift tax because of a liberal tax credit provided under the Tax Reform Act of 1976.  However, what will happen to the estate if Tom and Mary die together in an automobile accident or if Mary dies a few years after John?  If the couple had no will to complement their use of joint ownership, probate proceedings would be necessary and the property would pass under the state laws of intestacy, to be discussed in Chapter 10.  Also, in the absence of a will, the probate judge would appoint an administrator to supervise the probate proceedings and a guardian, who would not only control the assets for the children until they reach the age of majority but would also have physical custody of the children.  The appointment of a guardian often leads to a contest in probate court between relatives who hope to be named guardian.  To avoid potential problems, John and Mary should execute wills specifying the persons who are to receive the property at their death, naming an executor to handle probate of the estate and naming a guardian for the children and their estate.  In addition, John and Mary might consider a trust agreement, possibly with a local bank, providing that if they both should die, the property will pass to the trustee who will distribute it to the children when they reach the ages specified by the parents in the agreement.

Second, assume that Tom and Mary accumulate substantial assets through the years and that their children are grown.  Tom and Mary now own a house worth $100,000 as tenants by the entirety, have

---

**46.**  Buschmeyer v. Eikermann, 378 S.W.
2d 468 (Mo.1964).

$50,000 in a joint bank account, and jointly own a $50,000 cottage and $200,000 in securities. Once more they have succeeded in avoiding probate, for on the death of either John or Mary, the survivor would become sole owner of their property. And with grown children, they are no longer concerned with the appointment of a guardian. However even in this situation it is necessary for John and Mary to establish a more detailed estate plan. If they should die in a common accident, probate proceedings would again be necessary, and the property would pass by the laws of intestacy in the absence of a will. More important, federal estate tax has now become a consideration with the increased size of their estate. For example, we might assume that John passes away first. Federal estate taxes would be insignificant at his death because the estate subject to taxation would be reduced by the substantial marital deduction that is available when property passes to a spouse. However, Mary would now own the entire estate, which will be taxable in full at her death since her estate could not claim a marital deduction. The estate tax on Mary's estate could be reduced by tens of thousands of dollars if John and Mary sever their ownership of the jointly held property and establish an estate plan whereby, on the death of one spouse, only half of their total property would pass to the survivor. The other half would go into a trust which could be used for the benefit of the survivor but would not be subject to estate tax on the survivor's death.

## F. CONCURRENT OWNERSHIP—MODERN APPLICATIONS

A number of new housing arrangements have been developed that utilize shared facilities to make better use of our limited supply of real estate. The planned unit development and the condominium have been the most popular of these developments.

Typically, a planned unit development consists of a concentrated area of homes or townhouses and a common area that is used for recreational purposes. A buyer acquires a home or a townhouse in a planned unit development by means of traditional forms of ownership, such as the joint tenancy, although townhouse ownership is often complicated by the extensive use of easements to establish rights to use utilities, party walls, parking areas or walkways. The common area in a planned unit development, on the other hand, is usually owned by a homeowner's association, a nonprofit corporation. The homeowners are the shareholders in the association and acquire their shares at the time they buy the home. Each homeowner has the right to use the common areas, subject to the restrictions set forth in the association agreement, and each homeowner must pay a reasonable share of the association's expense for maintaining the common areas.[47]

47. See A. Grezzo, Condominiums: Their Development and Management 17 (1972).

The word condominium is derived from the Latin word meaning joint ownership or control. Condominiums have been popular throughout history whenever land has been costly and limited in supply. For example, condominiums were popular in ancient Rome, especially near the Forum where real estate was scarce and expensive, and in the walled cities of medieval Europe.[48] Although condominiums first appeared in the United States in the late 1940s, condominium ownership became popular in the 1960s and 1970s. From 1970 to 1975, the number of condominium units increased from 85,000 to 1,-250,000, and it is estimated that one-half the population in the United States will live in condominium housing by 1995.

The purchase of a condominium involves two forms of ownership. First, the buyer owns the condominium unit—the living space—in any of the traditional forms of ownership. Second, the condominium purchaser, as a tenant in common, also buys an interest in the common areas of the condominium, such as the swimming pool, tennis courts, the space between units, the roof, and the land under the structure. The condominium owner cannot sell his interest in the common area separately from his unit. A recent Florida decision stated that "the undivided share in the common elements appurtenant to each unit shall not be separated from the unit; that a share in the common elements cannot be conveyed or encumbered except together with the unit; and that the shares in the common elements appurtenant to units shall remain undivided and not subject to action for partition. . . . [O]ne must reach the inescapable conclusion that all condominium units have an undivided share of the common elements and neither can exist separately from the other." [49]

In purchasing a condominium, there are two documents that are especially important to the buyer. The most important document is the master deed, also known as the enabling declaration or the declaration of conditions. In most cases, the master deed (1) authorizes a board of directors to administer the condominium affairs in line with the bylaws and to assess the owners for adequate maintenance of the condominium; (2) describes the condominium units and the common areas and any restrictions on their use; and (3) establishes the undivided interest percentage, which is the ratio of one unit to the total number of units as determined by original value, living area or market price. In some cases, all units are given an equal share. The undivided interest percentage is used to determine the owner's interest in the common area, the owner's number of votes in meetings of the owners' association, and the owner's share of maintenance and operating expenses. In order to change the provisions of the master deed, it is usually required that every owner consent to the change.[50]

---

**48.** Id. at 1–3.

**49.** Daytona Development Corp. v. Bergquist, 308 So.2d 548 (Fla.App.1975).

**50.** See Questions About Condominiums 27–31 (HUD, 1974).

The other important document contains the bylaws, which generally govern the internal affairs of the condominium in the same manner that bylaws govern the internal operations of a corporation. Condominium bylaws usually establish the responsibilities of the owners' association, the voting procedures to be used at association meetings, the qualifications, powers, and duties of the board of directors, the powers and duties of the officers, and the obligations of the owners in regard to assessments, maintenance, and use of the units and common areas.[51] One important difference between the bylaws and the master deed is that the bylaws usually may be amended by a majority vote instead of a unanimous vote.

In examining condominium documents, the purchaser should be aware of a number of potential legal problems. First, the monthly assessment fee should be closely analyzed. Disreputable developers have been known to engage in "lowballing" practices whereby they initially establish a low monthly assessment to encourage buyers, but later when all the units are sold, they increase the monthly assessment drastically. The buyer should determine whether the maintenance costs are realistic. In addition, if the condominium has been in existence for several years or is a converted rental property such as an apartment house, the purchaser must consider the cost of repairing common elements such as the roof, wiring, and plumbing.

Second, the purchaser should review the provisions that have been made for insurance. The need for liability insurance is illustrated by White v. Cox, infra, where the court held that even a member of the owners' association may sue the association for negligence in maintaining common areas. In such cases, most state laws provide that a condominium owner is liable only for his proportionate share of the damages, although a Mississippi statute declares that individual owners have no personal liability for damages resulting from use of the common area.[52] In any event, sufficient insurance should be purchased by the association to cover potential liability. The Urban Land Institute recommends a minimum of $1 million in liability insurance for an association and $5 million for larger developments. Owners also might consider incorporating the association, if state law allows this. In addition to liability insurance, the association should purchase errors and omissions coverage for the association officers and directors, worker's compensation insurance to cover employees, and fire insurance for the common areas. And the owners, of course, must maintain their own insurance coverage for the individual units.

Third, a purchaser must consider possible restrictions on the right to rent or resell the condominium unit. If owners are given an unlimited right to rent, the purchaser should realize that renters

---

51.  Id. at 31–33.

52.  White v. Cox, 17 Cal.App.3d 824, 95 Cal.Rptr. 259 (1971).

may not maintain the property as well as an owner would. Of course, if a condominium is purchased in a resort area for vacation purposes, the purchaser usually intends to rent his own unit most of the year. Restraints upon alienation—for instance, a requirement that the association approve a prospective purchaser or a right of first refusal by the association—are permitted by many condominium statutes as long as they are not used to discriminate on the basis of race, creed, color, or national origin.[53]

Finally, prospective purchasers of condominium units should determine who owns the common areas. Some condominium developers retain ownership of the common areas, lease the common areas to the association for ninety-nine years, and then proceed to charge exorbitant rent to the association. In Wechsler v. Goldman,[54] a group of owners brought an action against certain developers to cancel or modify the terms of several ninety-nine-year leases. The court, in upholding the leases, came to these conclusions: "The principal question here relates to the validity of a lease which the promoters (through corporations owned or controlled by them) made to the condominium associations for use of the recreation area. In making that lease the promoters, in effect, were dealing with themselves. It is disclosed that the rental which they thus imposed on the condominium associations for use of the represented recreational area was exorbitant, amounting to more per year than the assessed value of the property leased; and that thereby the promoters acquired for themselves an excessive profit at the ultimate expense of the purchaser-members of the condominium association . . . . . The individual plaintiffs sought to cancel the lease. The plaintiff condominium associations sought to have the rental revised to a realistic and reasonable amount. The rights of the individual plaintiff members are affected by the fact that they acquired knowledge of the lease at the time they closed their purchase contracts and by their express acceptance of the lease in their closing contracts notwithstanding the fact that they were not advised of the lease earlier when they were solicited as purchasers and signed preliminary contracts. It is not without some reluctance that we hold the plaintiff condominium associations do not have a cause for relief against the claimed exorbitant lease rental obligation imposed on them while both lessor and lessee were owned or controlled by the promoters."

## G. COMMUNITY PROPERTY

In eight states in the South and West—Arizona, California, Idaho, Louisiana, Nevada, New Mexico, Texas, and Washington—certain property owned by husband and wife is designated as community property. The concept of community property is derived

53. Powell on Real Property § 633.36(5)   54. 214 So.2d 741 (Fla.App.1968).
  (b) (1969).

mainly from French and Spanish law, although community property was first used by Germanic tribes in the seventh century.[55]

Community property is property acquired during a marriage through the efforts of either the husband or wife or both. All other property—acquired before marriage or acquired by the husband or wife as a gift or through inheritance—is separate property. Courts do disagree over the classification of rents and profits derived from separate property. Some states follow the old civil law rule that such rents and profits are considered to be community property but an equal number of states have adopted statutes classifying them as separate property. Even in states adopting the latter approach, earnings from separate property will be considered community property when they result from the efforts of one or both of the parties. In one case, a husband owned two restaurants as separate property. At the husband's death, the court held that income from the restaurants would be considered community property because it resulted mainly from the husband's efforts.[56]

Property classified as community property is, in several states, managed and controlled by the husband, although the husband has no control over the wife's personal earnings and he may not sell community real property unless the wife signs the deed. In the case of Fairchild v. Wiggins,[57] a husband sold timber without his wife's signature on the bill of sale. The court declared the sale void because the timber was considered community real estate and state law contained the following provisions: "The husband has the management and control of the community property, except the earnings of the wife for her personal services and the rents and profits of her separate estate. But he cannot sell, convey or encumber the community real estate unless the wife joins him in executing and acknowledging the deed or other instrument of conveyance, by which the real estate is sold, conveyed or encumbered."

In most states, the husband and wife may change the status of their property by agreement. For instance, they may agree to purchase real estate with community property in a joint tenancy form of ownership. Or the parties may partition community property by entering into a property settlement agreement in divorce proceedings. In the absence of a property settlement agreement, some state statutes provide that community property is to be divided equally in a divorce action, while other statutes allow the court to exercise its discretion in dividing property. In a state that has not adopted a no-fault divorce statute, the court is authorized by some statutes to consider adultery or extreme cruelty in dividing the property.[58]

---

**55.** W. Burby, Real Property 236, 237 (3rd ed. 1965).

**56.** Steward v. Torrey, 54 Ariz. 369, 95 P.2d 990 (1939).

**57.** 85 Idaho 402, 380 P.2d 6 (1963).

**58.** W. Burby, Real Property 249, 261 (3rd ed. 1965).

Upon the death of the husband or wife, the survivor retains an interest in one-half of the property while the other half passes according to the will of the deceased person. If there is no will, the one-half interest will pass according to the laws of intestate succession.[59]

## III.  FORMS OF OWNERSHIP FOR INVESTMENT PURPOSES

The general forms of ownership discussed above may be used in purchasing real estate for either personal or business reasons. However, the general forms—especially the joint tenancy and the tenancy by the entireties—are often inadequate for business and investment purposes because most investors do not want their interest to pass to surviving investors at death. Consequently, investors often utilize one of the four following types of ownership for investment purposes: partnerships, limited partnerships, corporations, and business trusts.

### A.  PARTNERSHIPS

The source of partnership law in the United States is the Uniform Partnership Act, which has been adopted in forty-seven states. In Section 6 of the Uniform Partnership Act, a partnership is defined as "an association of two or more persons to carry on as co-owners a business for profit." A person who shares in the profits of a business will usually be considered a partner because the receipt of profits is prima facie evidence that a partnership exists.[60]

Since co-ownership is included in the definition of a partnership, are persons who purchase property in one of the forms of joint ownership discussed previously considered to be partners? Two friends who purchase a cottage as tenants in common are co-owners, but are they also partners? The answer can be found in Section 7(2) of the Act: "Joint tenancy, tenancy in common; tenancy of the entireties, joint property, common property, or part ownership does not of itself establish a partnership, whether such owners do or do not share profits made by use of the property." The key factor that is necessary to establish a partnership is co-ownership of a business, defined in the Act as "every trade, occupation or profession." [61]

Two partnership rules relate specifically to real estate ownership. First, under the common law, a partnership could not buy or sell real estate because it was not a legal entity. However, the modern rule adopted by the Uniform Partnership Act regards as valid a conveyance to the partnership in the partnership name. Furthermore, real estate may be conveyed by the partnership either in the name of the partnership or in the name of a partner.[62]

59.  Id. at 663 (3rd ed. 1965).          61.  Id. § 2.

60.  Uniform Partnership Act § 7(4).          62.  Id. §§ 8(4), 10.

Second, the classifications of partnership real estate and other specific property has been a long-standing problem in several jurisdictions. The modern approach, in Section 25 of the Uniform Partnership Act, is that each partner is a co-owner with his partners of specific partnership property and holds such property as a tenant in partnership. The incidents of a tenancy in partnership are the following: (1) subject to an agreement to the contrary, each partner has an equal right to possession of partnership property; (2) the interest in specific partnership property is not assignable by an individual partner; (3) a partner's right in specific property is not subject to attachment or execution; (4) partners cannot claim a homestead or other exemption when partnership property is attached for partnership debts; (5) on the death of a partner, his interest passes to the surviving partner; and (6) a partner's right in specific property is not subject to dower, curtesy, or allowance to widows, heirs or next of kin. Having a tenancy in partnership in specific property, such as the land, structure, equipment, and inventory, allows the partnership to continue business when one partner goes into debt or dies. Despite the tenancy in partnership, however, each partner retains an interest in the partnership, defined as his share of profits and surplus, that passes to his heirs as personal property and is subject to individual creditors' claims.[63]

The partnership, as a real estate investment vehicle, carries a number of benefits and burdens. On the benefit side, the partnership is easy to form; it is even possible for two parties to form a partnership unknowingly by sharing profits from a business enterprise. There are potential tax benefits from the partnership form, to be discussed below. And the right to share control is an important factor, for each partner has equal right to manage the partnership business unless the partnership agreement provides otherwise. On the other hand, the major drawback to the partnership form is potential unlimited personal liability for each partner. This would include liability for contracts made by other partners who had been authorized to do so, and for any wrongful act of other partners acting within the ordinary course of business.

## B. LIMITED PARTNERSHIPS

A limited partnership differs from a partnership in two major respects. First, in order to form a limited partnership, two or more persons must execute a certificate of limited partnership and file the certificate in the appropriate office.[64] Second, the limited partnership includes one or more general partners and one or more limited partners. The liability of the limited partners is limited to their capital contributions; they are not personally liable for partnership contracts or torts.

---

63. Id. §§ 26, 28.

64. Uniform Limited Partnership Act § 2.

Three actions, however, might make a limited partner subject to the same liability as a general partner. First, a limited partner is liable as a general partner if he takes part in the control of the business. However, some courts have held that a limited partner may give advice. In Trans-Am. Builders, Inc. v. Woods Mill, Ltd.,[65] when the limited partnership encountered financial difficulties, the limited partners visited a construction site and made suggestions as to possible courses of action. The court held that the advice did not make them liable as general partners because it is unreasonable that a "limited partner may not advise the general partnership and visit the partnership business, particularly when the project is confronted with severe financial crisis." Second, if a limited partner allows his surname to be used in the partnership name, he is liable to creditors who extend credit without knowledge that he is only a limited partner. Third, if false statements were made in the limited partnership certificate, anyone who suffers a loss by relying on the statements may hold the limited partner liable if the limited partner knew the statements were false.

The limited partnership is an especially important real estate investment vehicle because it combines the tax advantages of the partnership with the limited liability of the corporation. When the term "tax shelter" is used, the shelter is often provided by a limited partnership. A report prepared for the House Ways and Means Committee in 1975 included the following illustration of the benefits resulting from a limited partnership.[66] A limited partnership is formed to purchase real estate and to construct an $800,000 building on the land. The partners invest a total of $250,000 and borrow $800,000 to finance the project. After the building has been completed, the building is leased and the rental income is used to pay (a) operating expenses, real estate taxes, and mortgage payments, and (b) an annual $10,000 distribution to the partners. The building is depreciated over 25 years using the double declining balance method and each partner receives a depreciation deduction from his personal income. If we assume that the partners are in the 60 percent tax bracket and that they invest their tax savings and cash distributions in 7 percent tax-exempt bonds, the $250,000 investment will have resulted in cash benefits totalling $429,936 at the end of ten years. After twenty years, the cumulative cash benefits would be $745,559. And, in the meantime, the value of the land and the building will normally increase significantly in value. Although the Tax Reform Act of 1976 curtailed the tax advantages of limited partnerships, the act specifically provided that the limitations do not apply to partnerships that invest principally in real property.[67]

65.  133 Ga.App. 411, 210 S.E.2d 866
     (1974).

66.  Tax Shelters: Real Estate (Committee on Ways and Means, 1975).

67.  I.R.C. § 704(d).

## C.  CORPORATIONS

The use of a corporation for real estate investment purposes is disadvantageous because the corporation is more difficult to form than the partnership, and corporate earnings are often subject to double taxation.  Forming a corporation involves filing articles of incorporation with the Secretary of State and obtaining a corporate charter.  After the charter is issued, the business must be conducted using corporate procedures:  the shareholders and directors should hold annual meetings, financial reports must be filed with the state, personal assets and corporate assets must not be commingled, and the corporation should have adequate capital.  If the business is not conducted according to normal corporate procedures, a court might "pierce the corporate veil" and hold the shareholders liable as individuals.  Double taxation occurs when the corporation is first taxed on its earnings and then the earnings are taxed again when they are received by shareholders as dividends.  Furthermore, shareholders may not deduct corporate expenses and losses from their individual taxable income.  These disadvantages are often balanced by the major advantage of the corporation form:  the limited liability of the shareholders.  The corporation, as a separate legal entity, absorbs liability for contracts made with third parties and for personal injuries committed by company employees.

It is possible to combine the liability advantages of the corporation with the tax advantages of the partnership by creating a Subchapter S corporation.  Subchapter S, a subdivision of the Internal Revenue Code of 1954, was enacted in 1958 in order to allow closely held corporations some of the tax advantages of the partnership.  To qualify for Subchapter S tax treatment, a corporation must comply with the following requirements:  (1) it may have no more than fifteen shareholders;  (2) the stock must be owned by individuals who are citizens or residents of the United States, estates, or trusts;  (3) it must be a domestic corporation;  (4) the corporation is allowed to have only one class of stock issued and outstanding;  and (5) no more than 80 percent of the corporation's gross receipts may come from sources outside the United States and no more than 20 percent may come from interest, dividends, rents, royalties, annuities, and gains from sale or exchange of securities.[68]  Subchapter S corporations have not been popular with real estate investors because of the last requirement.

## D.  BUSINESS TRUSTS

Business trusts were originally developed to avoid the state regulations on corporations.  In establishing a business trust, the trust

---

68.  See Byerhof & Lanuza, *Partnership or Subchapter S Corporation?*  62 A.B. A.J. 505 (1976).

beneficiaries transfer property to the trustees, who hold legal title. The trustees then issue transferable trust certificates to the benficiaries. The trustees hold and manage trust property and are personally liable for the trust's contractual obligations.

Real estate investment trusts (REITs) became popular with the passage, in 1960, of the Real Estate Investment Trust Act, which exempted them from income tax if they met certain requirements. These requirements include the following attributes: (1) one or more trustees, who hold legal title to the trust property, must have the exclusive authority to manage and conduct the affairs of the trust; (2) the interest of the beneficiaries must be evidenced by transferable shares or certificates; (3) the trust must have the attributes of a domestic corporation; (4) the trust cannot hold property primarily for sale in the ordinary course of business; (5) there must be at least one hundred or more beneficiaries; (6) five or fewer individuals may not own 50 percent of the value of the trust stock; (7) at least 75 percent of the trust's income must come from rents, mortgage interest, gains from the sale of real estate, dividends from shares in other REITs, or real estate tax refunds; and (8) at least 90 percent of the trust income must be distributed to the beneficiaries.[69]

In practice, there are two basic types of REITs, both of which must meet the eight requirements just listed. With equity REITs, the investors' capital is used to purchase interest in real estate. Although equity REITs often borrow money to finance real estate purchases, the loans are secured by long-term mortgages and are paid from income derived from the real estate. Mortgage REITs, on the other hand, are engaged in financing real estate developments. Typically, the mortgage REITs borrow money from lenders and then loan this money, along with investors' capital, to builders and developers, some of whom are unable to obtain other financing. A number of mortgage REITs encountered financial difficulties in the recession of the early 1970s when builders and developers defaulted on their loans.[70]

# CASES

---

## MELMS v. PABST BREWING CO.

Supreme Court of Wisconsin, 1899.
104 Wis. 7, 79 N.W. 738.

This is an action for waste, brought by reversioners against the defendant, which is the owner of an estate for the life of another

---

69. 34 Am.Jur. *Federal Taxation* § 7860.　　70. Wall St.J., Aug. 27, 1976 at 1, col. 6.

in a quarter of an acre of land in the city of Milwaukee. The waste claimed is the destruction of a dwelling house upon the land, and the grading of the same down to the level of the street. The complaint demands double damages, under section 3176, Rev.St.1898. The quarter of an acre of land in question is situated upon Virginia street, in the city of Milwaukee, and was the homestead of one Charles T. Melms, deceased. The house thereon was a large brick building, built by Melms in the year 1864, and cost more than $20,000. At the time of the building of the house, Melms owned the adjoining real estate, and also owned a brewery upon a part of the premises. Charles T. Melms died in the year 1869, leaving his estate involved in financial difficulties. After his decease, both the brewery and the homestead were sold and conveyed to the Pabst Brewing Company, but it was held in the action of Melms v. Brewing Co., 93 Wis. 140, 66 N.W. 244, that the brewing company only acquired Mrs. Melms' life estate in the homestead, and that the plaintiffs in this action were the owners of the fee, subject to such life estate. As to the brewery property, it was held in an action under the same title, decided at the same time, and reported in 93 Wis. 153, 66 N.W. 518, that the brewing company acquired the full title in fee. The homestead consists of a piece of land 90 feet square, in the center of which the aforesaid dwelling house stood; and this parcel is connected with Virginia street on the south by a strip 45 feet wide and 60 feet long, making an exact quarter of an acre. It clearly appears by the evidence that after the purchase of this land by the brewing company the general character of real estate upon Virginia street about the homestead rapidly changed, so that soon after the year 1890 it became wholly undesirable and unprofitable as residence property. Factories and railway tracks increased in the vicinity, and the balance of the property was built up with brewing buildings, until the quarter of an acre homestead in question became an isolated lot and building, standing from 20 to 30 feet above the level of the street, the balance of the property having been graded down in order to fit it for business purposes. The evidence shows without material dispute that, owing to these circumstances, the residence, which was at one time a handsome and desirable one, became of no practical value, and would not rent for enough to pay taxes and insurance thereon; whereas, if the property were cut down to the level of the street, so that it was capable of being used as business property, it would again be useful, and its value would be largely enhanced. Under these circumstances, and prior to the judgment in the former action, the defendant removed the building, and graded down the property to about the level of the street, and these are the acts which it is claimed constitute waste. The action was tried before the court without a jury, and the court found, in addition to the facts above stated, that the removal of the building and grading down of the earth was done by the defendant in 1891 and 1892, believing itself to be the owner in fee simple of the property, and that by said acts the estate of the plaintiffs in the property was substantially increased, and that the plaintiffs have been in no way injured thereby.

WINSLOW, J. (after stating the facts).  Our statutes recognize waste, and provide a remedy by action, and the recovery of double damages therefor (Rev.St.1898, § 3170 et seq.); but they do not define it.  It may be either voluntary or permissive, and may be of houses, gardens, orchards, lands, or woods (Id. § 3171); but, in order to ascertain whether a given act constitutes waste or not, recourse must be had to the common law as expounded by the text-books and decisions.  In the present case a large dwelling house, expensive when constructed, has been destroyed, and the ground has been graded down, by the owner of the life estate, in order to make the property serve business purposes.  That these acts would constitute waste under ordinary circumstances cannot be doubted.  It is not necessary to delve deeply into the Year Books, or philosophize extensively as to the meaning of early judicial utterances, in order to arrive at this conclusion.  The following definition of "waste" was approved by this court in Bandlow v. Thieme, 53 Wis. 57, 9 N.W. 920: "It may be defined to be any act or omission of duty by a tenant of land which does a lasting injury to the freehold, tends to the permanent loss of the owner of the fee, or to destroy or lessen the value of the inheritance, or to destroy the identity of the property, or impair the evidence of title."  *  *  *  Again, and in accordance with this same principle, the rule that any change in a building upon the premises constitutes waste has been greatly modified, even in England; and it is now well settled that, while such change may constitute technical waste, still it will not be enjoined in equity when it clearly appears that the change will be, in effect, a meliorating change, which rather improves the inheritance than injures it.  *  *  *  [T]he law upon the subject of waste is not an unchanging and unchangeable code, which was crystallized for all time in the days of feudal tenures, but that it is subject to such reasonable modifications as may be demanded by the growth of civilization and varying conditions.  And so it is now laid down that the same act may be waste in one part of the country while in another it is a legitimate use of the land, and that the usages and customs of each community enter largely into the settlement of the question.  This is entirely consistent with, and in fact springs from, the central idea upon which the disability of waste is now, and always has been, founded, namely, the preservation of the property for the benefit of the owner of the future estate without permanent injury to it.  This element will be found in all the definitions of waste, namely, that it must be an act resulting in permanent injury to the inheritance or future estate.  It has been frequently said that this injury may consist either in diminishing the value of the inheritance, or increasing its burdens, or in destroying the identity of the property, or impairing the evidence of title.  The last element of injury so enumerated, while a cogent and persuasive one in former times, has lost most, if not all, of its force, at the present time. * * *

There are no contract relations in the present case. The defendants are the grantees of a life estate, and their rights may continue for a number of years. The evidence shows that the property became valueless for the purpose of residence property as the result of the growth and development of a great city. Business and manufacturing interests advanced and surrounded the once elegant mansion, until it stood isolated and alone, standing upon just enough ground to support it, and surrounded by factories and railway tracks, absolutely undesirable as a residence, and incapable of any use as business property. Here was a complete change of conditions, not produced by the tenant, but resulting from causes which none could control. Can it be reasonably or logically said that this entire change of condition is to be completely ignored, and the ironclad rule applied that the tenant can make no change in the uses of the property because he will destroy its identity? Must the tenant stand by, and preserve the useless dwelling house, so that he may at some future time turn it over to the reversioner, equally useless? Certainly, all the analogies are to the contrary. As we have before seen, the cutting of timber, which in England was considered waste, has become in this country an act which may be waste or not, according to the surrounding conditions and the rules of good husbandry; and the same rule applies to the change of a meadow to arable land. The changes of conditions which justify these departures from early inflexible rules are no more marked nor complete than is the change of conditions which destroys the value of residence property as such, and renders it only useful for business purposes. Suppose the house in question had been so situated that it could have been remodeled into business property; would any court of equity have enjoined such remodeling under the circumstances here shown, or ought any court to render a judgment for damages for such an act? Clearly, we think not. Again, suppose an orchard to have become permanently unproductive through disease or death of the trees, and the land to have become far more valuable, by reason of new conditions, as a vegetable garden or wheat field, is the life tenant to be compelled to preserve or renew the useless orchard, and forego the advantages to be derived from a different use? Or suppose a farm to have become absolutely unprofitable by reason of change of market conditions as a grain farm, but very valuable as a tobacco plantation, would it be waste for the life tenant to change the use accordingly, and remodel a now useless barn or granary into a tobacco shed? All these questions naturally suggest their own answer, and it is certainly difficult to see why, if change of conditions is so potent in the case of timber, orchards, or kind of crops, it should be of no effect in the case of buildings similarly affected. * * *

\* \* \* Under all ordinary circumstances the landlord or reversioner, even in the absence of any contract, is entitled to receive the property at the close of the tenancy substantially in the condition in which it was when the tenant received it; but when, as here, there has occurred a complete and permanent change of surrounding conditions, which has deprived the property of its value and usefulness as previously used, the question whether a life tenant, not bound by contract to restore the property in the same condition in which he received it, has been guilty of waste in making changes necessary to make the property useful, is a question of fact for the jury under proper instructions, or for the court, where, as in the present case, the question is tried by the court. Judgment affirmed.

---

## BRADLEY v. FOX

Supreme Court of Illinois, 1955.
7 Ill.App.2d 106, 129 N.E.2d 699.

DAVIS, Justice.

Plaintiffs Rolland L. Bradley, administrator of the estate of Matilda Fox, deceased, and Alice E. Bradley, daughter of the decedent, have appealed directly to this court from a judgment of the circuit court of Winnebago County, dismissing their claims for damages for the unlawful killing of Matilda Fox by her husband, defendant Lawrence Fox, and for the imposition of a constructive trust on property formerly held in joint tenancy by the decedent and defendant Lawrence Fox.

The cause presents the issues of whether the daughter of a woman murdered by her husband can sue the latter for damages under the wrongful death statute, and whether a constructive trust can be imposed upon property formerly held in joint tenancy by a husband and wife where the husband killed his wife and then conveyed the property in trust to the attorney who defended him on the murder charge, as security for attorney's fees.

The operative facts are not in dispute. It appears from the pleadings that Lawrence Fox and Matilda Fox were married on May 6, 1949, and resided near Rockford, in Winnebago County. On April 18, 1950, they purchased with their individual funds the property in controversy, which they held in joint tenancy. Lawrence Fox murdered his wife on September 14, 1954, and three days later conveyed the premises, then valued at $20,000, to his attorney. Fox was convicted of murder on November 26, 1954, and sentenced to the State Penitentiary.

It further appears that at the time of her death, and for many years prior thereto, Matilda Fox had operated a beauty shop, and from those earnings contributed substantially to the support of plaintiff Alice E. Bradley, a daughter by a former marriage. For loss of this support, and for damages for the wrongful death of her mother, proceedings were instituted by plaintiff Alice E. Bradley, and plaintiff Rolland L. Bradley, as administrator of the estate of Matilda Fox. Plaintiffs also sought to establish a trust in the property formerly held in joint tenancy by Lawrence and Matilda Fox, and asserted a further claim for damages for breach of the implied contract between the joint tenants that neither would act to jeopardize the interest of the other.

The circuit court of Winnebago County allowed defendants' motion to dismiss the entire complaint, and rendered judgment against plaintiffs, from which they have appealed directly to this court, since a freehold is involved.

\* \* \*

The issue of whether a murderer may acquire or increase his property rights by the fruits of his crime is not a novel legal question. It has arisen in three principal categories of cases: where the beneficiary or heir under a life insurance policy murders the assured to acquire the proceeds of the policy; or where a devisee or distributee feloniously kills the testator or intestate ancestor; and, as in the instant case, where one joint tenant murders the other and thus creates survivorship rights.

In the insurance cases the courts, practically with unanimity, construe the insurance policy in the light of the fundamental common-law maxim originating in English law that no man shall profit by his own wrong, and follow the approach of the early United States Supreme Court case of New York Mut. Life Ins. Co. v. Armstrong, 117 U.S. 591, 6 S.Ct. 877, 881, 29 L.Ed. 997, which held that a person who procured a policy upon the life of another, payable to himself, and then murdered the assured could not recover thereon. Mr. Justice Field stated: "It would be a reproach to the jurisprudence of the country if one could recover insurance money payable on the death of a party whose life he had feloniously taken." \* \* \*

There has not been the same unanimity in the case law, however, with reference to the right of a devisee or distributee who feloniously kills his ancestor to inherit from the decedent in the absence of a statute. \* \* \*

From the foregoing analysis of the entire issue as considered in the related insurance policy and descent cases, and in the analogous joint tenancy cases, as well as by legal scholars and lawmakers, certain conclusions follow. Contracts and other instruments creating rights should properly be construed in the light of prevailing public policy evidenced in the statutes. The Illinois statute prohibiting the devolution of property to a convicted murderer from his victim, while not determinative of the rights of the parties in this situation, does evince a legislative policy to deny the convicted murderer the fruits of his crime. That policy would be thwarted by a blind adherence to the legal fiction that a joint tenant holds the entire property at the date of the original conveyance, and acquires no additional interest by virtue of the felonious death of his cotenant, since that rationale sanctions in effect the enhancement of property rights through murder. For legal fictions cannot obscure the fact that before the murder defendant, as a joint tenant, had to share the profits of the property, and his right to complete ownership, unfettered by the interests of a joint tenant, was contingent upon surviving his wife; whereas, after, and because of, his felonious act that contingency was removed, and he became the sole owner of the property, no longer sharing the profits with any one nor fearing the loss of his interest.

\* \* \*

In joint tenancy the contract that the survivors will take the whole necessarily presupposes that the death of either will be in the natural course of events and that it will not be generated by either tenant murdering the other. One of the implied conditions of the contract is that neither party will acquire the interest of the other by murder. It is fundamental that four coexisting unities are necessary and requisite to the creation and continuance of a joint tenancy; namely, unity of interest, unity of title, unity of time, and unity of possession. Any act of a joint tenant which destroys any of these unities operates as a severance of the joint tenancy and extinguishes the right of survivorship. It is our opinion, therefore, that it would be unconscionable for defendant Fox, as murderer of his joint tenant, and for defendant Downey, as transferee with full knowledge of how Fox acquired the sole legal title to the property and of the fact that the conveyance was in fraud of creditors' claims, to retain and enjoy the beneficial interest in the property. It is our conclusion that Fox by his felonious act, destroyed all rights of survivorship and lawfully retained only the title to his undivided one-half interest in the property in dispute as a tenant in common with the heir-at-law of Matilda Fox, deceased.

\* \* \*

In so construing the rights of the parties to deny a murderer the fruits of his crime, this court is functioning, not as a "theological institution," as suggested in the Ohio case cited by defendants, but as a tribunal dedicated to the adjudication of law, for effecting justice is not a novel role for the courts, nor one transcending the sphere of other institutions.

On the basis of our analysis, the judgment of the circuit court dismissing plaintiffs' complaint was in error, and the cause will be remanded with directions to reinstate the complaint and enter a judgment in conformity with the views expressed herein.

Reversed and remanded, with directions.

---

## THURMOND v. McGRATH

Supreme Court of New York, Richmond County, 1972.
70 Misc.2d 849, 334 N.Y.S.2d 917.

VITO J. TITONE, Justice.

This is a classic case of why people should get title insurance when they buy a home. The facts were stipulated at a trial before the Court.

On February 15, 1954, Mirosol Homes Inc. delivered its deed to the one-family house located at 250 Gansevoort Boulevard to Charles V. Scaramutz and Julia Zabicki Scaramutz, as husband and wife and the deed was recorded on February 16, 1954 in Liber 1269 page 54. Simultaneously, Charles and Julia gave their bond and mortgage to the Citizens Bank of Brooklyn for the sum of $9,700.00 which mortgage was recorded in Liber 1125 page 293. Julia died intestate on February 10, 1969 and her death certificate gave her name as Julia M. Scaramutz; her address as 250 Gansevoort Boulevard; leaving a surviving spouse, Charles; and her occupation was given as a housewife. By deed dated March 27, 1970, Charles Scaramutz conveyed the property to the defendant Martin J. McGrath, which was recorded on April 2, 1970 in Liber 1897 page 339. Simultaneously, McGrath gave a mortgage to the Union Mortgage Corp. for the sum of $25,000.00 dated March 27, 1970 which was recorded April 2, 1970 in Liber 1815 page 228, and thereafter the mortgage was assigned to the defendant, Federal National Mortgage Association which assignment was recorded on April 21, 1970 in Liber 1817 page 96.

Julia and Charles were never in fact married, and the plaintiffs, Julia's three sisters, claim that as her sole distributees (EPTL Sec. 4–1.1(a)(7)) they are entitled to one-half the property. They rely on the settled principle that where a tenancy by the entirety fails for lack of a marriage, a tenancy in common is created.   *   *   *

   *   *   *

Charles V. Scaramutz, of course, perpetrated a blatant fraud against the defendants; he actually executed and delivered an affidavit at the closing which affirmatively stated: "That my wife [Julia] died 2/10/69 while married to me." This was false. He had never married Julia, and as a matter of fact his real wife, whom he married many years before and whom he never divorced, was alive at the time and is alive to this day. As to Julia's interest, Charles had no more right to convey this than a thief, which in substance he was. The defendants do have a remedy against Charles; they can sue him for fraud. Also, title insurance is available to purchasers of real estate which protects them against situations such as this one.

To summarize, the law is that when a tenancy by the entirety fails because the grantees were unmarried a tenancy in common is created, and that the distributees of one who holds real estate as a tenant in common inherits that person's interest upon his death intestate. If there is to be any change in these concepts it should come from the appellate Courts or the Legislature. Perhaps some thought should be given, with due regard to a widow's right of election, to declaring that such a deed creates a joint tenancy rather than a tenancy in common; then the survivor could validly convey the entire fee. However, it is not the province of trial courts to make such changes in the law.

On the basis of the foregoing, the Court finds and concludes that the plaintiffs by reason of the death intestate of their sister Julia Zabicki Scaramutz on February 10, 1969, are the owners of one-half of the real property known as 250 Gansevoort Boulevard, Richmond County (as more particularly described in the complaint), and that they hold same as tenants in common with the defendant Martin J. McGrath, owner of the other one-half interest. * * *

---

## D'ERCOLE v. D'ERCOLE

United States District Court of Massachusetts, 1976.
407 F.Supp. 1377.

TAURO, District Judge.

* * *

Basically, plaintiff's complaint states that the common law concept of tenancy by the entirety, as formulated and enforced by case law, and as recognized by the statutes of the Commonwealth of Massachusetts, deprives her of due process and equal protection of the law in that it gives the defendant, her husband, the right of possession and control during his lifetime of their home, owned by them as tenants by the entirety. Defendant's position is that plaintiff's complaint fails to state a claim upon which relief can be granted.

The plaintiff and the defendant have been married for some thirty five years. In November of 1962 they bought a residence at 61 Stone Road, Waltham, Massachusetts, for $20,000. The percentage of down payment provided by each party for the home is disputed. Plaintiff used her own funds to purchase some $3500 in new furnishings for the home at the time of purchase. She has been steadily employed during the entire thirty five years of her marriage and, by agreement with the defendant, assumed financial responsibility for all household expenses, except for mortgage payments and real property taxes. Defendant further concedes that plaintiff has paid for all the preparatory and college expenses of her son.

In 1971, the plaintiff and defendant determined they could no longer live together. When the defendant refused to leave the marital home, plaintiff departed, moving to a relative's home where she still resides.

Proceedings for legal separation and for divorce are now pending in the Middlesex County Probate Court. The defendant husband is seeking a divorce. The plaintiff wife is seeking a separation and is vehemently opposing the divorce on factual issues and because of religious beliefs.

Defendant has refused to share the marital home with plaintiff by allowing her sole occupancy for part of the year, by selling the house and dividing the proceeds, by paying plaintiff her share in the equity of the house, or by renting the premises and dividing the proceeds. In support of his position, defendant points out that the property in question is held under a tenancy by the entirety, which gives both him and the plaintiff an indefeasible right of survivorship, but gives him exclusive right to possession and control in his lifetime. He has stated that he will grant plaintiff one-half the equity in the house if she will grant him an uncontested divorce.

When two or more persons wish to hold property together in Massachusetts they may select one of three common law forms of ownership: the tenancy in common, joint tenancy or tenancy by the entirety.

The tenancy in common is the holding of land "by several and distinct titles."

> Each tenant owns an undivided fraction, being entitled to an interest in every inch of the property. With respect to third persons the entire tenancy constitutes a single entity. There is no right of survivorship as between tenants in common. Upon the death of a tenant in common his undivided interest in the property is transferred to his heirs or devisees, subject to liens, claims and dower.

There is a presumption in favor of the tenancy in common over the joint tenancy as a matter of construction in Massachusetts. Each tenant in common has a right to free usage of the whole parcel and may freely convey out his share of the property to a third party, who then becomes a tenant in common in relation to the remaining cotenants.

The joint tenancy is "a single estate in property owned by two or more persons under one instrument or act."

> A joint tenancy is similar to a tenancy in common in that all tenants have an equal right to possession, but the joint tenants hold the property by one joint title and in one right, whereas the tenants in common hold by several titles or by one title and several rights.
>
> The joint tenancy differs also in that there is a right of survivorship in a joint tenancy but not in a tenancy in common. On

the death of one of the joint tenants his interest does not descend to his heirs or pass under his will as in a tenancy in common * * *. The widow of the deceased tenant has no dower rights and his creditors have no claim against the enlarged interest of the surviving tenants.

A joint tenant may convey out his share in the property via a legal partition.

The tenancy by the entirety is designed particularly for married couples and may be employed only by them. Until 1973 unless there was clear language to the contrary a conveyance to a married couple was presumed to create a tenancy by the entirety. This form of property ownership differs from the joint tenancy in two respects. First, each tenant has an indefeasible right of survivorship in the *entire* tenancy, which cannot be defeated by any act taken individually by either spouse during his or her lifetime. There can be no partition. Second, the spouses do not have an equal right to control and possession of the property. The husband during his lifetime has paramount rights in the property. In the event of divorce the tenancy by the entirety becomes a tenancy in common unless the divorce decree reflects that a joint tenancy is intended.

* * *

As was conceded in *Klein*, the common law concept of tenancy by the entirety is male oriented.

It is true that the only Massachusetts tenancy tailored exclusively for married persons appears to be balanced in favor of males. There is no equivalent female-biased tenancy, nor is there a "neutral" married persons' tenancy providing for indefeasible survivorship but not vesting paramount lifetime rights in the male. Married couples may, it is true, elect a joint tenancy, a tenancy in common, or a sole tenancy. However, the survivorship feature of a joint tenancy may be destroyed by partition. A wife who wants the security of indefeasible survivorship can achieve it only by means of a male-dominated tenancy.

But, the dispositive issue is not merely whether the tenancy by the entirety favors males. Rather, the issue is whether it does so in a manner that creates a constitutionally impermissible classification. On the specific facts of this case, this court holds that tenancy by the entirety, being but one option open to married persons seeking to take title in real estate, is constitutionally permissible.

It may be possible in some future case for a plaintiff wife to demonstrate factually that a selection of tenancy by the entirety was made through coercion, ignorance or misrepresentation. But no such facts were presented here, nor does plaintiff advance such a theory. Rather, this record makes almost inescapable the conclusion that plaintiff freely entered into a contract along with her husband in 1961, selecting one among several options open to her. Events have not transpired as she expected and now she seeks to revise the terms of her contract, because she now feels that her husband got the better end of the bargain.

Without greater justification than plaintiff's unsubstantiated allegations of prejudice, this court will not declare unconstitutional a form of property ownership selected by and presently relied upon by thousands of Massachusetts residents, including this plaintiff and defendant. As was noted in *Klein,*

> [t]he state does not compel husbands and wives to hold their property as tenants by the entirety. Undoubtedly, that choice is knowingly made in many instances despite or even, perhaps, because of its male oriented aspects. The choice would have been the same whether or not alternatives were available.

\* \* \*

This court is sympathetic with plaintiff's concern that the tenancy by the entirety is to some degree a legal artifact, formerly justified by the presumed incompetence of women to manage property. But this decision is not based on such an archaic and patently invalid stereotype. Rather, the fact is that, regardless of its roots, the tenancy by the entirety exists today as one of several options open to married persons seeking to purchase real estate. Its existence constitutes a matter of choice not discrimination. If there is a classification, it is one selected by the plaintiff, not one imposed by the Commonwealth. She is entitled to the benefit of her bargain, no more and no less. There being no evidence that the plaintiff in this case made her choice among then existing options other than freely, this court will not step in to re-write the agreement between her and her husband.

The court orders entry of judgment for the defendant.

---

## WHITE v. COX

California Court of Appeals, Second Dist., 1971.
17 Cal.App.3d 824, 95 Cal.Rptr. 259.

FLEMING, Associate Justice.

Plaintiff White owns a condominium in the Merrywood condominium project and is a member of Merrywood Apartments, a nonprofit unincorporated association which maintains the common areas of Merrywood. In his complaint against Merrywood Apartments for damages for personal injuries White avers he tripped and fell over a water sprinkler negligently maintained by Merrywood Apartments in the common area of Merrywood. The trial court sustained Merrywood's demurrer without leave to amend and entered judgment of dismissal. White appeals.

The question here is whether a member of an unincorporated association of condominium owners may bring an action against the association for damages caused by negligent maintenance of the common areas in the condominium project. In contesting the propriety of such an action defendant association argues that because it is a joint enterprise each member is both principal and agent for every other member, and consequently the negligence of each member must be imputed to every other member. Hence, its argument goes, a member may not maintain an action for negligence against the association because the member himself shares responsibility as a principal for the negligence of which he complains.

        *   *   *

Since 1962 the trend of case law has flowed toward full recognition of the unincorporated association as a separate legal entity. A member of an unincorporated association does not incur liability for acts of the association or acts of its members which he did not authorize or perform.   *   *   *

In view of these developments over the past decade we conclude that unincorporated associations are now entitled to general recognition as separate legal entities and that as a consequence a member of an unincorporated association may maintain a tort action against his association.

Does this general rule of tort liability of an unincorporated association to its members apply in the specific instance of a condominium? A brief review of the statutory provisions which sanction and regulate the condominium form of ownership will clarify the nature of what we are dealing with. A *condominium* is an estate in real property consisting of an undivided interest in common in a portion of a parcel of real property together with a separate interest in another portion of the same parcel. A *project* is the entire parcel of property, a *unit* is the separate interest, and the *common areas* are the entire project except for the units. Transfer of a unit, unless otherwise provided, is presumed to transfer the entire condominium. Ownership is usually limited to the interior surfaces of the unit, a cotenancy in the common areas, and nonexclusive easements for ingress, egress, and support. Typically, a condominium consists of an apartment house in which the units consist of individual apartments and the common areas consist of the remainder of the building and the grounds. Individual owners maintain their own apartments, and an association of apartment owners maintains the common areas. The association obtains funds for the care of the common areas by charging dues and levying assessments on each apartment owner.

The original project owner must record a condominium *plan* (Civ.Code, § 1351), and restrictions in the plan become enforcible as equitable servitudes (Civ.Code, § 1355). The plan may provide for management of the project by the condominium owners, by a board of governors elected by the owners, or by an elected or appointed agent. Management may acquire property, enforce restrictions, maintain the common areas, insure the owners, and make reasonable assessments. Only under exceptional circumstances may the condominium project be partitioned. Zoning ordinances must be construed to treat condominiums in like manner as similar structures, lots, or parcels. Condominium projects with five or more condominiums are subject to rules regulating subdivided lands and subdivisions. Individual condominiums are separately assessed and taxed. Savings and loan associations may lend money on the security of condominium real property.

California's condominium legislation parallels that of other jurisdictions (see Law of Condominium, Ferrer & Stecher (1957)), and a review of this legislation brings out the two different aspects of the typical condominium scheme. (1) Operations. These are normally conducted by a management association created to run the common affairs of the condominium owners. The association functions in a manner comparable to other unincorporated associations in that it is controlled by a governing body, acts through designated agents, and functions under the authority of bylaws, etc. (the plan). In this aspect of the condominium scheme the management association of condominium owners functions as a distinct and separate personality from the owners themselves. (2) Ownership. In its system of tenure for real property the condominium draws elements both from tenancy in common and from separate ownership. Tenancy in common has also been brought into the structure of the management association, for under Civil Code section 1358 the management association holds personal property in common for the benefit of the condominium owners. In a formal sense, therefore, the condominium owners are tenants in common of the common areas and the personal property held by the management association, and they are owners in fee of separate units, which are not separate in fact. It is apparent that in its legal structure the condominium first combines elements from several concepts—unincorporated association, separate property, and tenancy in common—and then seeks to delineate separate privileges and responsibilities on the one hand from common privileges and responsibilities on the other. At this juncture we return to the tests used in *Marshall* to determine the tort liability of an association to its members and pose two questions. Does the condominium association possess a separate existence from its members? Do the members retain direct control over the operations of the association?

\* \* \* A condominium, like a labor union, has a separate existence from its members. Control of a condominium, like control of a labor union, is normally vested in a management body over which the individual member has no direct control. We conclude, therefore, that a condominium possesses sufficient aspects of an unincorporated association to make it liable in tort to its members. The condominium and the condominium association may be sued in the condominium name under authority of section 388 of the Code of Civil Procedure. The condominium and the condominium association may be served in the statutory manner provided for service on an unincorporated association (Corp.Code, §§ 24003–24007), and individual unit owners need not be named or served as parties in a negligence action against the condominium and the condominium association.

We conclude (1) the condominium association may be sued for negligence in its common name, (2) by a member of the association, (3) who may obtain a judgment against the condominium and the condominium association.

The judgment of dismissal is reversed.

## PROBLEMS

1. Cicero grants Homer a life estate in Cicero's farm and the property is to return to Cicero at Homer's death. Which of the following acts is considered waste? Why?

    a. Homer removes timber from the property for the purpose of using the land to grow crops. He sells the timber for $50,000.

    b. Homer tears down the house on the farm.

    c. Homer drills a new oil well and removes oil from the land.

    d. Homer removes timber from a part of the farm that is unfit for agricultural purposes and uses the timber to repair a fence on the farm.

2. Bob and Carol, husband and wife, owned a farm as joint tenants. Marital problems developed and Bob and Carol separated. While they were separated, Bob deeded his interest in the farm to a friend, Alice. Later Bob and Carol were reconciled and Bob signed a will leaving the farm to Carol. At Bob's death, who owns the farm? Why?

3. Adam had two sons, Cain and Abel. Adam wanted to deed a valuable farm to his sons as joint tenants but he liked Abel nine times more than he liked Cain. Consequently, Adam worded the deed: "To Cain, a one-tenth interest, and to Abel, a nine-tenths interest, as joint tenants with rights of survivorship." Abel later died of natural causes. Who now owns the real estate? Why?

4. Harry and Wilda, husband and wife, owned a car and a house. The title to the car was in Wilda's name and the house was owned by Harry and Wilda as tenants by the entirety. One day, while driving to the grocery store, Harry caused an automobile accident and seriously injured Macbeth. Macbeth sued Harry and Wilda for $100,000 and claimed that he could take their house if they failed to pay the damage award. Is Macbeth correct? Why?

5. Two brothers, Barry and Harry, owned a farm as joint tenants. They farmed the land together for thirty years. On Barry's death Harry took his deed to an attorney to have the title changed to his name alone. The attorney advised Harry that there had been a mistake on the original deed and that Barry and Harry had owned the land as tenants in common rather than as joint tenants. Barry left no will and his only heirs were

Harry and two sisters, Lettie and Betty. There was a long-standing feud between the brothers and sisters and they had not spoken to each other for years. Who now owns the farm?

6. Karen and Tim, husband and wife, own a farm as tenants in common. Karen dies and, under her will, her interest passes to Kevin. Tim sells one-half of his interest "to Laurie for life, remainder to Garfunkel." Kevin takes possession of the farm and refuses to pay farm taxes and to allow anyone else to enter. Describe the present ownership of the farm (including the percentage owned by each party). Who is entitled to possession? Who must pay taxes?

7. Tex owned an apartment building and a blueberry farm. At Tex's death, the apartment and farm passed to Sheryl and Kim, as tenants in common. Sheryl and Kim shared equally the rent from the apartment and the profits from the blueberry farm. One evening, while driving to the farm to water the blueberries, Kim negligently struck Denny with her car. Is Sheryl liable for Denny's injuries? Why?

8. Hilda, a widow, lives on a 500-acre farm worth $500,000. She has one son, Clyde. In order to avoid probate, Hilda has decided to deed the farm "to Hilda and Clyde, as joint tenants with rights of survivorship and not as tenants in common." What potential problems might arise from this arrangement? Why?

9. Pancho and Cisco, roommates at Big U, decide to build and run a large racquetball club after graduation. In starting this business, they consider the following forms: (1) corporation; (2) Subchapter S corporation; (3) partnership; (4) limited partnership; and (5) real estate investment trust. Which form would you recommend? What are the major problems with each form in this situation?

10. George Babbitt was a real estate developer. Whenever George started a new project, he formed one corporation to handle construction and another corporation that owned the project. Beyond the development itself, each corporation had little or no assets. A creditor who is owed $100,000 by one of George's corporations now sues George as an individual for the debt. On what theory would the suit be brought? How can George best defend the suit?

# Chapter 6

## THE SEARCH FOR REAL ESTATE

> The average American moves about fourteen times in his lifetime. . . . At least a fifth of all Americans move one or more times each year; and the pace of the movement of Americans is still increasing.
>
> Vance Packard, *A Nation of Strangers*

The typical real estate transaction involves a series of five major contracts: (1) the seller's contract with the broker; (2) the purchase agreement between seller and buyer; (3) a contract with the party who provides evidence of title; (4) the buyer's contract for fire insurance; and (5) the buyer's contract with a lender for financing.

In the following chapters these five contracts will be considered in chronological order. Throughout the study of these contracts, keep in mind that while the purchase and sale of real estate is usually the most important financial transaction in a person's lifetime, real estate contracts are usually negotiated without the assistance of an attorney. According to an American Bar Association report, "it is probably safe to say that in a high percentage of cases the seller is unrepresented and signs the contracts of brokerage and sale on the basis of his faith in the broker. The buyer does not employ a lawyer. He signs the contract of sale without reading it and, once financing has been obtained, leaves all the details of title search and closing to the lender or broker. The lender or broker may employ an attorney but, where title insurance is furnished by a company maintaining its own title plant, it is possible that no lawyer, not even house counsel will appear."[1] Consequently, the discussions in the following chapters are especially important for the average person, who often will be acting as his own attorney.

The major emphasis in this chapter will be on the seller's relationship with the broker and on the problems involved in the search for real estate. The chapter includes an examination of the licensing requirements for brokers, the types of listing agreements, and the duties of the broker as an agent once the contract is made. Beyond the contract with the broker, the search for real estate raises special issues regarding interstate land sales and discrimination in selling real estate, which will be considered near the end of this chapter.

1. The Proper Role of the Lawyer in Residential Real Estate Transactions 13 (American Bar Association, 1976).

## I.  THE REAL ESTATE AGENT

### A.  LICENSING REQUIREMENTS

A real estate broker is a person who is hired to negotiate the sale or purchase of real estate for a commission.  All states require real estate brokers to be licensed.  State licensing laws normally require that the broker pass an examination.  The examination covers the principles of real estate practice (including a knowledge of the broker's duties), real estate transactions, instruments used in the transactions, and the canons of ethics relating to brokers.  In addition, several states require an applicant to have been associated with a real estate broker as a salesman for one or two years, and to have completed a specified number of courses in real estate practice, law, appraisal and finance.[2]  In these states imposing additional requirements, a person must pass a special examination in order to be licensed as a salesman.

Licensing requirements are established by statute, and the statutes usually give a state real estate commission the duty of establishing rules and regulations to carry out the statutory requirements.  These rules often cover details about applications to take the examinations and ethical standards governing real estate practice.[3]  See Cochrane v. Wittbold, infra.

### B.  PENALTIES FOR ACTING WITHOUT A LICENSE

In many states, a person who violates the brokers' licensing statutes faces criminal penalties in the form of a possible fine and imprisonment, and under many statutes he faces the added penalty of not being allowed to collect a commission from his client.  Even where a statute is silent with regard to civil penalties, courts have uniformly decided that to allow an unlicensed broker to collect a commission violates public policy.  The broker's license is considered to be a regulatory license; that is, the statute regulates licensing of brokers in order to protect the public from unscrupulous brokers who lack knowledge of real estate transactions.  Denying the unlicensed broker a commission helps serve the public purpose of protecting consumers.

The same public policy applies in cases where a licensed broker deals in real estate transactions outside the state in which he was licensed.  For instance, in one case[4] a broker licensed in Illinois was promised a fee of $17,000 for selling a parcel of Illinois real estate, but the listing agreement was signed in New York where he was not licensed.  The court decided that he could not collect the fee.  "The

2.  See Ohio Rev.Code Ann. § 4735.07.

3.  See Ohio Rev.Code Ann. § 4735.10.

4.  Frankel v. Allied Mills, Inc., 369 Ill. 578, 17 N.E.2d 570 (1938).

rule is that when a statute declares that it shall be unlawful to perform an act, and imposes a penalty for its violation, contracts for the performance of such acts are void and incapable of enforcement. . . . The object of the statute is to promote the public welfare by permitting only persons with the necessary qualifications to act as real estate brokers and salesmen. The location of land outside the State of New York does not affect the policy of the statute, since it is the vendor and the purchaser who are sought to be protected. The statute does not in any way seek to regulate the sale of Illinois real estate, but operates only on the brokerage contract."

In some cases, an unlicensed broker may be entitled to a commission if he can prove that he only acted as a "finder," a person who brings the buyer and seller together but who does not take part in contract negotiations. "One who merely procures does not act as an agent in the consummation of the sale, or have anything to do with the fixing of the price, or the terms of the sale. The principals negotiate the terms between themselves. All the finder is required to do is to bring the seller to the attention of the purchaser." [5] However, many licensing statutes prohibit unlicensed persons from engaging in any act relating to the purchase and sale of real estate, even if the act is only an incidental part of the transaction. Under such statutes, a finder will not be allowed to collect a fee.[6]

## II.   THE LISTING AGREEMENT

### A.   STATUTE OF FRAUDS

Whenever a broker is hired, the broker and client should enter into an agreement covering details such as the term of the employment, the amount of commission, and the duties of the broker. Normally brokers are hired by persons wishing to sell real estate and the contract between seller and broker is called a listing agreement.

The listing agreement should be in writing, in case a dispute arises later. In approximately twenty states, the contract is included within the Statute of Frauds and therefore must be in writing. In states where the agreement must be in writing, most courts require that details such as the amount of commission and an exact description of the real estate be included in the contract.

### B.   TYPES OF LISTING AGREEMENTS

Lynn listed his house with a broker, Marilyn, and signed a listing agreement. Lynn found a buyer without Marilyn's assistance and another broker, Adam, brought a second buyer to Lynn. Now Lynn questions whether he will be liable for a commission to Marilyn if he

5. Bittner v. American-Marietta Co., 162 F.Supp. 486 (E.D.Ill.1958).

6. Zalis v. Blumenthal, 254 Md. 265, 254 A.2d 692 (1969).

sells the house to either buyer. The answer will depend on which of the following types of listing agreements he has signed with Marilyn.

1. **Exclusive Right to Sell.** The following language in a listing agreement could give a broker the exclusive right to sell the real estate: "Should I [the seller], or anyone acting for me, including my heirs, sell, lease, transfer or otherwise dispose of said property within the time herein fixed for the continuance of the agency, you [the broker] shall be entitled nevertheless to your commission as herein set out." [7] If the broker has an exclusive right to sell, the broker is entitled to a commission even when the owner or another broker locates a buyer.

2. **Exclusive Agency.** An exclusive agency is created when the listing agreement uses language similar to the following: "A commission is to be paid the broker whether the purchaser is secured by the broker or by any person other than the seller." While such an agreement makes the broker an exclusive agent, the principal (owner) can find his own buyer without incurring liability for the commission.

In many cases, the listing agreement uses language such as: "The broker has the exclusive right to sell said property." Does this mean that the broker has the exclusive right to sell in the legal sense, or does the language designate the broker as the exclusive agent? The courts are split on this question, but the usual rule is that where a contract is ambiguous, the ambiguity is interpreted against the person who drafted the agreement, in this case the broker. If this approach is used here, the broker would become the exclusive agent. To avoid this, the broker should use language similar to the above listing agreement that created an exclusive right to sell.

3. **Open Listing.** Occasionally a listing agreement is signed that merely authorizes "the broker to act as agent in securing a purchaser for my property." This language creates an open listing agreement whereby the broker is not entitled to a commission if the purchaser is secured by another broker or by the seller.

## C.  PROCURING CAUSE OF SALE

In cases where an exclusive agency or open listing agreement is used, a dispute often arises between two or more brokers or between the broker and seller, each of whom claims that the buyer was procured through his efforts. For example, assume that Lynn signed open listing agreements with two brokers, Adam and Corey. Adam finds a prospective buyer, Graham, who wants to buy the property if some details, such as the closing date and proration of taxes, can be worked out. Without Adam's knowledge, Corey then steps in, negotiates the

7. West v. Barnes, 351 S.W.2d 615 (Tex. Civ.App.1961).

details with Graham, and persuades him to sign the contract. In this case the general rule would entitle Adam only to a commission. "If a broker sets in motion machinery by which a sale is made, which without break in its continuity was procuring cause of sale, he is entitled to commission although he does not conduct all negotiations." [8] Stated another way, he "who sows the seed and tills the crop is entitled to reap the harvest—rather than one who volunteers to assist in tilling a crop, the seed for which he has not sown." [9]

On the other hand, if the broker finds a potential buyer but later ceases negotiations with the person, another broker who then persuades the buyer to sign a contract is entitled to a commission. In Vreeland v. Vetterlein,[10] the plaintiff broker opened negotiations with a prospective buyer, Henderson, but could not persuade him to buy the property for $20,000. Later, Henderson learned that a public sewer was being constructed near the property, went to another broker, Garrabrants, and agreed to buy the property for $20,500. The court decided that the plaintiff broker was not entitled to a commission because "where the property is openly put in the hands of more than one broker, each of such agents is aware that he is subject to the arts and chances of competition. If he finds a person who is likely to buy, and quits him without having effected a sale he is aware that he runs the risk of such person falling under the influence of his competitor—and in such case, he may lose his labor. This is a part of the inevitable risk of the business he has undertaken."

If an owner negotiates and signs a contract with a buyer who has been sent by a broker, the owner must pay a commission. This rule applies even though the owner was not aware that the buyer had been procured by the broker. See Mehlberg v. Redlin, infra.

## D. BROKER'S COMMISSION

Most disputes between a seller and a broker relate to the amount of commission due the broker. The commission should be agreed upon when the broker is hired. If the broker's commission is not agreed upon in advance, courts will allow the broker a reasonable commission based on the fees charged by other brokers in the area unless state law requires the commission to be stated in writing, in which case the broker will recover nothing.

The broker's commission is based on the gross sales price unless the listing agreement states otherwise. For example, if an owner listed his $40,000 home with a broker who charged a seven percent commission and the house was subject to a $35,000 mortgage, at the

8. Averill v. Hart and O'Farrell, 101 W.Va. 411, 132 S.E. 870 (1926).

9. Julius Haller Realty Co. v. Jefferson-Gravois Bank, 161 Mo.App. 472, 144 S.W.2d 174 (1940).

10. 33 N.J.L. 247 (1869).

closing the bank would receive $35,000, the broker, $2,800 and the owner, $2,200. Instead of using a percentage of the gross price, the broker might use a net listing whereby the owner will receive a certain amount (for example, $40,000) and the broker keeps everything above that amount as commission. In a few states net listings are illegal.

## E. PERFORMANCE OF THE LISTING AGREEMENT

The broker earns the agreed-upon commission whenever he procures a buyer who is "ready, willing and able" to purchase the real estate. This is true even when the owner refuses to sign a contract with the buyer. When the purchase agreement is signed by the buyer and seller, the buyer has shown that he is ready and willing and the seller has indicated that he thinks the buyer is able. Thus even if the contract is never performed, the broker is entitled to a commission.

In Kruger v. Wesner,[11] the defendants hired a real estate broker to sell their property for at least $30,000 and promised him a commission of 10 percent. The broker found a buyer who signed an offer to purchase the real estate for $40,000 while he was apparently under the influence of liquor. Later the same purchaser signed another offer to buy at the same price, and this offer was accepted by the defendants. The buyer afterward refused to perform the contract, but the broker claimed a commission of $4,000. The court decided that the broker should receive his fee: "It may be generally stated that when a real estate broker procures a purchaser who is accepted by the owner, and a valid contract is drawn up between them, the commission for finding such purchaser is earned, although the purchaser later defaults for no known reason, or because the purchaser deliberately refuses to consummate the contract, or because of financial inability of purchaser to comply with the contract. The courts are practically unanimous in holding that a broker employed to sell or exchange lands earns his commission, unless the contract of employment contains a stipulation to the contrary, when a customer and the employer enter into a valid and binding contract for the sale or exchange of lands."

Courts have reached the same result in cases where the buyer signs a contract but is unable to obtain financing to complete the purchase. In Retterer v. Bender,[12] a broker located buyers who signed a purchase agreement for the owners' real estate, but the sale was not consummated, apparently because the buyers could not obtain financing. The court decided that the broker is entitled to a commission when he "makes a contract with the owner to find a purchaser for his real estate at a commission for his services and

11. 274 Wis. 40, 79 N.W.2d 354 (1957).    12. 106 Ohio App. 369, 154 N.E.2d 827, 7 O.O.2d 105 (1958).

pursuant thereto performs such services by producing a purchaser, and the owner enters into a written contract of sale with such purchaser . . . . In such case, the broker is not required to prove that the buyer was ready, willing and able to consummate the transactions." Yet the *Retterer* decision has been considered too favorable for the broker by some courts, and there is a recent trend toward holding for the owner. See Seidel v. Walker and Ellsworth Dobbs, Inc. v. Johnson, infra.

The results in *Kruger* and *Retterer*, representing the approach taken by most courts, can be avoided by using a "no deal, no commission" clause in the listing agreement so that if the deal is not closed, the broker is not entitled to a commission. Using another approach, the owner might require the buyer to make a down payment of "earnest" money large enough to cover the broker's commission. The specific problem in the *Retterer* case might also be avoided by including in the purchase agreement a clause which makes the agreement—and therefore the broker's commission—contingent on the buyer's ability to obtain financing.

## F. MULTI–LISTING

It is common for real estate brokers to belong to associations or boards at the local, state and/or national level. Many local boards operate multi-listing services that permit properties listed with one board member to be sold by any member of the board. If the original realtor sells the property, he will receive the full commission; if another board member procures the buyer, the commission will be split between the original realtor and the other realtor.

Realtor boards occasionally engage in practices such as suggesting the rate of commission which each member should charge and restricting membership on the board. These practices raise antitrust questions, especially under Section One of the Sherman Antitrust Act which provides: "Every contract, combination in the form of trust or otherwise or conspiracy, in restraint of trade or commerce among the several states, or with foreign nations, is declared to be illegal." If a real estate board, as a result of its activities, were charged with conspiracy under the Antitrust Act, two major issues would have to be resolved.

First, is the board's activity a "restraint of trade?" Some activities, such as price fixing, are considered to be *per se* violations of the Sherman Act, while other activities, such as limiting membership on the boards, would be considered under a "rule of reason" approach where proof of economic harm is required to prove a violation of the Act. In a leading case, Goldfarb v. Virginia State Bar,[13] the Goldfarbs needed a title examination before they could purchase a house

13. 421 U.S. 773, 95 S.Ct. 2004, 44 L.
Ed.2d 572 (1975).

in Virginia. They contacted nineteen attorneys, and each attorney stated the same fee, which was prescribed by the bar association minimum fee schedule. When the Goldfarbs brought suit claiming a violation of the Sherman Act, the Supreme Court decided that the fee schedule amounted to price fixing because the schedule was not merely advisory, but amounted to a "fixed, rigid price floor" that was enforced through the possibility of professional discipline by the state bar association.

In a case directly relevant to the real estate profession, U. S. v. National Ass'n of Real Estate Boards,[14] the Supreme Court held that the National Association of Real Estate Board's provision that brokers should not use rates lower than those adopted by a board constituted illegal price fixing. The Court declared the guideline violated Section Three of the Sherman Act relating to antitrust activities in the District of Columbia. In reaching this decision, the Supreme Court decided that real estate brokers are engaged in a trade, not a profession that might be exempted from the Act.

The second question is more difficult to resolve: Does real estate brokerage involve interstate commerce as required by the Sherman Act? As a general rule a transaction will meet this requirement even where no state lines are crossed if the transaction has a "substantial effect" on interstate commerce. Applying this test to the purchase of real estate in *Goldfarb*, the Supreme Court noted that a significant portion of the funds necessary for purchasing real estate in Virginia came from outside the state. The Court concluded: "Given the substantial volume of commerce involved and the inseparability of this particular legal title search from the interstate aspects of real estate transactions we conclude that interstate commerce has been sufficiently affected." In addition, the facts that the buyer and seller are often from different states and that real estate firms often advertise in more than one state support the view that real estate brokerage involves interstate commerce.

The counter-argument maintains that a court should focus on the object of the transaction—real estate, which is within one state. For example, in Marston v. Ann Arbor Property Managers Ass'n,[15] the plaintiff tenants brought a class action against the defendant association that they claimed controlled a major portion of the housing surrounding a university campus. The plaintiffs sought damages from alleged violations of the Sherman Act, and claimed specifically that the defendants conspired to fix the price levels of rental apartments and to control the supply of new apartments on the market. The court dismissed the complaint on the grounds that the defendants' business was not interstate in character. "The complexity of modern business leaves little room for contracts, or business transactions,

14. 339 U.S. 485, 70 S.Ct. 711, 94 L.Ed. 1007 (1950).

15. 302 F.Supp. 1276 (D.C.Mich.1969).

which cannot be said in some degree to affect interstate commerce. However, in the case at bar, the court is unable to classify or look upon plaintiffs as being a part of interstate commerce. The fact that an individual attends a university in a state other than his own and is regarded as being part of interstate commerce is beyond the comprehension of this court. It is this court's view there is presently no way that plaintiffs, as individuals or students, may come within the definition of interstate commerce. The actions of defendants are purely local in nature, restricted to the Ann Arbor area. Any effect their actions would have on interstate commerce is remote and inconsequential. There is not evidence of an intent to restrain interstate commerce, or a substantial and actual restraint of interstate commerce. Any conspiracy which only indirectly or incidentally affects and restrains interstate commerce is not within the purview of Section 1 of the Sherman Act. If the court were to assume that defendants' actions, indirect and remote as they may be to interstate commerce, were to affect interstate commerce, it would follow that all such acts, remote to the main stream of interstate commerce, are subject to the federal antitrust laws, no matter how local may be their operations."

Even if a court determines that the activity is interstate in character, many states have enacted their own antitrust legislation, known as "little Sherman acts," which cover many activities beyond price fixing. For instance, when the State of Ohio sued the Cleveland Area Board of Realtors, alleging violations of the Ohio antitrust law, the Board agreed to a consent judgment under which the Board was enjoined from "(1) restricting the offering of real estate training services by members; (2) restricting broker-members as to their recommendations of applicants for salesmen's licenses; (3) restricting broker-members in their selection of salesmen; (4) requiring licensed salesmen working with broker-members to join the Board; and (5) restricting or attempting to restrict salesmen working with broker-members in selecting educational services, materials, or facilities." [16]

## G. CANCELLATION OF THE LISTING AGREEMENT

Harry has listed his house with a broker. Shortly after signing the listing agreement, Harry decides that he wants to revoke the agreement. May he? Several different analyses of this question are possible, depending on the facts of the case.

First, in any case, Harry may not revoke the agreement in bad faith or after the broker has made considerable expenditures of his own. For instance, Harry, knowing that the broker is negotiating with a buyer, may not cancel the agreement and then conclude negotiations on his own with the buyer.[17] Second, subject to these qualifica-

16. *Brokers: Here's an Antitrust Red Flag for Real Estate Boards and Multiple Listing Exchanges*, 5 Real Estate Law Report 1 (No. 7) (1975).

17. Alexander v. Smith, 180 Ala. 541, 61 So. 68 (1912).

tions, Harry may revoke the agreement if the agreement does not specify a time period. In such cases if a reasonable time passes, the agreement will automatically expire. Third, if the agreement does specify a time period, the owner's right to revoke depends on whether the contract is considered to be unilateral or bilateral. A unilateral contract is formed when a promise, the owner's promise to pay the broker's commission, is exchanged for an act, the broker's efforts to find a ready, willing and able buyer. Thus if the contract is considered to be unilateral, most courts conclude that the contract is formed when the broker advertises and shows the house to prospective buyers; after that time, the offer cannot be revoked. A bilateral contract is formed when the owner's promise is exchanged for a promise by the broker. For example, in the agreement the broker might promise to use his best efforts to find a purchaser and, if a purchaser is found, to take responsibility for supervising the closing. If the broker has made such promises, the contract is formed when the listing agreement is signed and cannot be revoked for the specified time period.

## III. THE DUTIES OF THE BROKER

### A. AUTHORITY OF THE BROKER

Although it is common to speak of a broker as a real estate agent, the broker is not a general agent with broad authority to act in place of owner, the principal. Instead, the broker is a special agent with authority limited to the instructions given by the principal. This authority might be expressed, implied or apparent.

For example, Claude, the owner, hires a broker to sell his real estate. The broker finds a buyer, Marcus, who signs a purchase agreement and gives the broker a down payment of $10,000. If the broker absconds with the $10,000, does the loss fall on Claude, because the broker was his agent, or on Marcus? If Claude gave the broker express authority to accept the down payment for him, Claude would bear the responsibility for the acts of his agent and consequently would bear the loss. If Claude did not give the broker express authority to accept the down payment, Marcus might still argue that such authority would be implied by the fact that Claude hired the broker as his agent. However, a broker hired merely to find a buyer has no implied authority to accept money from a buyer: "Unless specially authorized the broker has no authority other than to state the asking price and to point out the land as described by the owner. He has no authority to represent the condition of the property. He has no authority to receive all or part of the purchase price or to represent to a buyer who makes a deposit that the deposit will be returned if the buyer cannot obtain a mortgage. He is an agent, but with an authority to speak for the principal almost at the vanishing point." [18] If the broker is expressly authorized to sign the real estate contract, however, he has the implied authority to make representations concerning the property, to give the usual warranties of title and to receive the down payment. And if the broker is expressly authorized to sign the deed, he is implicitly authorized to receive the full purchase price for the seller.

Even in the absence of express or implied authority, the owner, Claude, might be liable if the broker had apparent authority. In Parsley Brothers Constr. Co. v. Humphrey,[19] the plaintiff buyer, after initially making a down payment, paid the balance of the purchase price to a broker. When the broker absconded with the money, the court determined that the loss must fall on the seller. The court initially determined that real estate brokers usually have no authority to receive payments on behalf of the principal. However in this case the agent was determined to have apparent authority, which was defined by the court: "Apparent authority is that which the principal knowingly permits his agent to assume, or which a principal by his actions or words holds the agent out as possessing. Apparent authority is grounded on the estoppel doctrine which embraces generally the elements of (1) a representation by the principal, (2) reliance on that representation by a third party, and, (3) a change of position by the third party in reliance upon such representation. . . . It is readily discernible that Roberts had operated on a former occasion in the same manner as he had done in the present case. . . . The record bears out the conclusion that the agent, Roberts, was permitted to act on behalf of the owners over and above his otherwise limited authority. When one of two innocent persons must suffer for the wrongful act of a third person, the loss should fall upon the one who by reasonable diligence or care could have protected himself."

## B. THE SECRET AGENT

As a general rule, an agent will not be held personally liable for contracts negotiated on behalf of a principal. A major exception to this rule arises in real estate transactions. Often major developers attempt to accquire large tracts of real estate by using secret agents because, if the identity of the principal was discovered before acquisition, the price of the real estate would escalate rapidly. Once a contract with a secret agent is signed, the seller is bound to the contract unless the agent falsely represents that he is acting for himself and not for the principal. The buyer, as undisclosed principal, is also bound to the contract and, after disclosure has been made, the seller may elect to hold either the agent or the principal to the contract, but not both.

18. W. Seavey, Law of Agency § 28 (1964).     19. 136 So.2d 257 (Fla.App.1961).

## C.  THE BROKER'S FIDUCIARY DUTY

The real estate broker owes a fiduciary duty, a duty of the highest loyalty and trust, to the principal who engaged him.  Because of this duty, the broker cannot purchase the principal's real estate for himself or for his associates without full disclosure to the principal.  "The broker was and is looked upon as a fiduciary and is required to exercise fidelity, good faith, and primary devotion to the interests of his principal.  .  .  .  It is a corollary of the principle discussed above that the failure of the broker to inform the principal that the purchaser is an *alter ego* of the broker or a relative or partner renders the transaction voidable at the option of the principal." [20]

Furthermore, even when the purchaser is not associated with the broker, the broker must always put the interest of the principal first.  According to the court in Haymes v. Rogers,[21] "A real estate agent owes the duty of utmost good faith and loyalty to his principal.  The immediate problem here is whether the above proposition is applicable to the facts in this instance.  The question is, is it a breach of a fiduciary duty and a betrayal of loyalty for a real estate broker to inform a prospective purchaser that a piece of realty may be purchased for less than the list price?  We believe that such conduct is a breach of faith and contrary to the interest of his principal, and therefore, is a violation of the fiduciary relationship existing between agent and principal which will preclude the agent from recovering a commission therefrom."

An agent breaches his fiduciary duty when he secretly receives a commission from the prospective buyer, even though he has performed the contract as promised for the principal.  In Spratlin, Harrington & Thomas, Inc. v. Hawn,[22] the agent, a mortgage banking firm, was engaged by the principal for a promised $50,000 commission to obtain a $10,000,000 loan commitment.  After the agent obtained a commitment from the American National Insurance Company, the principal refused to pay the commission on the grounds that the agent received a finder's fee and a servicing fee from the insurance company without telling the principal.  The court, in relying on earlier cases, decided that the principal did not have to pay the commission: "The first duty of an agent is that of loyalty to his trust.  He must not put himself in relations which are antagonistic to that of his principal.  His duty and interest must not be allowed to conflict.  He cannot deal in the business within the scope of his own benefit  .  .  .  nor is he permitted to compromise himself by attempting to serve two masters having a contrary interest unless it be that such contracts

20.  Thompson v. Hoagland, 100 N.J. Super. 478, 242 A.2d 642 (1968).

21.  70 Ariz. 257, 219 P.2d 339 (1950), modified 70 Ariz. 408, 222 P.2d 789 (1950).

22.  116 Ga.App. 175, 156 S.E.2d 402 (1967).

of dual agency are known to each of the principals. . . . Simply stated, the Biblical expression . . . is apt: 'No man can serve two masters; for either he will hate the one and love the other, or else he will hold to the one and despise the other.' "

The *Spratlin* court did note that an exception to the rule would be a case where the agent's acts for each party did not conflict with duties owed the other party, for instance, when the agent acts only as a middleman and does not participate in the negotiations or when an agent performs ministerial acts for one party even though he is the agent for the other. However, the court concluded that the plaintiff was much more than a middleman and therefore this case did not fall within the exceptions. Furthermore, the court noted in the *Spratlin* case that if the agent makes full disclosure to both parties, he will be entitled to a commission. But if the broker makes disclosure to only one of the principals, the fiduciary duty is interpreted so strictly that he will not be allowed to recover a commission—even from the party to whom disclosure was made.[23]

## D.  THE BROKER'S UNAUTHORIZED PRACTICE OF LAW

Often a broker's work borders upon the practice of law, although the courts are generally divided on the question of what constitutes unauthorized practice of law. Most courts have decided that a broker's law-related activities must be limited to filling in blanks in standard printed forms if this service is incidental to the real estate transaction and if the broker makes no separate charge for the service. As a general rule, the broker may not draft the forms himself and may not give legal advice.

## IV.  LAND SALES ACTS

### A.  INTERSTATE LAND SALES ACT

Elmer had worked his entire life in a factory in a midwestern state. As he approached retirement, he considered purchasing real estate in a warm climate, where he hoped to relocate after retirement. One day Elmer was contacted by Slick Development Corporation. A representative of Slick invited Elmer to a local restaurant for a free steak dinner and a slide show describing real estate investments in Arizona. Elmer accepted the invitation and, at the restaurant, the representative used a combination of cajolery and threats to persuade Elmer to purchase a lot in a new development with his life's savings. A few years later Elmer retired and traveled to Arizona to inspect his lot for the first time. After much searching he found the lot—in the middle of a desert, miles away from utilities, roads, and civilization.

23.  Hughes v. Robbins, 164 N.E.2d 469,
12 O.O.2d 319 (1959).

Because of cases such as Elmer's, Congress enacted legislation in 1968 to protect buyers in interstate land sales or leases. The Interstate Land Sales Full Disclosure Act applies to sellers who offer for sale or lease fifty or more unimproved lots in another state. Certain transactions are exempt from the act, such as (a) the sale or lease of lots in a subdivision when all of the lots are five acres or more, (b) the sale or lease of cemetery lots, (c) the sale of securities by a real estate investment trust, (d) the sale or lease of real estate to a person engaged in the business of developing or reselling such lots, (e) the lease of lots for less than five years, and (f) the sale or lease of lots for less than $100. Also exempt from the Interstate Land Sale Act are transactions in which the purchaser has personally inspected the real estate before signing a contract, if the property is free of liens, encumbrances, and other adverse claims.

If an interstate sale is not exempt, the act imposes two major requirements on developers. First, developers must file a statement of record with the Department of Housing and Urban Development before offering the unimproved lots for sale or lease. Second, a property report must be given to buyers before a contract is signed. This report is a summary of the statement of record and includes such information as the existence of liens on the property, the availability of sewer and water service, the type of title the buyer will receive and the distance by road to nearby communities.

A seller who fails to comply with the act is subject to both civil and criminal penalties. The civil penalties include the right of the buyer to cancel the contract and obtain a refund of payment if a property report was not furnished, and the right to recover damages if the seller has not complied with the law. The maximum criminal penalties for violation of the act are a fine of $5,000, five years imprisonment, or both.

## B. STATE LAND SALES ACTS

The federal interstate land sales law has been complemented in most states by land sales regulations. In some states, regulations are similar to the federal requirements. The most comprehensive state legislation, the Michigan Land Sales Act of 1972, regulates the sale or lease of lots within subdivisions of twenty-five or more lots. As under the federal law, there are exemptions under the Michigan statute and the Michigan law requires both registration with the state and distribution of a property report to purchasers. The penalties for violation of the Michigan act are up to $25,000 fine and 10 years imprisonment for certain violations.

## V.  DISCRIMINATION IN SELLING OR LEASING REAL ESTATE

Archie has decided to sell his home without using a broker and without advertising in the local newspaper.  Archie refuses to sell to the first prospective buyer visiting his home because the buyer is black.  Archie refuses to sell to the next prospective buyer, an unmarried woman, because he dislikes women.  He finally sells his home to a third prospect, a white male.  May Archie legally engage in such discrimination in selling his home?

### A.  CIVIL RIGHTS ACT OF 1866

The answer is to be found in two civil rights acts:  the Civil Rights Act of 1866, and Title VIII (the Fair Housing Law) of the Civil Rights Act of 1968.  The 1866 Act, the current version of which is 42 U.S.C.A. § 1982, states that "all citizens of the United States shall have the same right in every State and Territory, as is enjoyed by white citizens thereof to inherit, purchase, lease, sell, hold and convey real and personal property."  In the leading decision of Jones v. Alfred H. Mayer Co.,[24] the Supreme Court held that this statute was valid under the Thirteenth Amendment, which prohibits slavery and involuntary servitude.  In the words of the Court, the act prohibits "all racial discrimination, private as well as public, in the sale or rental of property."  A victim of discrimination on racial grounds may take the case to federal court and the court may award damages, prevent the sale of the house to someone else, or force the seller to transfer the property to the plaintiff.  See Walker v. Pointer, infra.

### B.  THE 1968 FAIR HOUSING ACT

The 1968 Fair Housing Act is more comprehensive than the 1866 act in terms of the types of discrimination prohibited.  The 1968 act prohibits discrimination on the grounds of race, color, religion, sex or national origin by means of the following actions:  (1) refusing to sell to, rent to, deal or negotiate with any person;  (2) manifesting discrimination in the terms or conditions for buying or renting housing;  (3) discriminating by advertising that housing is available only to persons of a certain race, color, religion, or national origin;  (4) denying that housing is available for inspection, sale, or rent when it really is available;  (5) persuading owners to sell or rent housing by telling them minority groups are moving into the neighborhood, i. e. "blockbusting";  (6) denying or establishing different terms for home loans by commercial lenders;  and (7) denying someone the use of real estate services.[25]

24.  392 U.S. 409, 88 S.Ct. 2186, 20 L.Ed. 2d 1189 (1968).

25.  Fair Housing U.S.A. (Department of Housing and Urban Development, 1973).

Although the 1968 act prohibits several types of discrimination, it does not cover all types of housing. For example, the act does not cover the sale or rental of a single-family house owned by a private individual who owns less than four such houses if (a) a broker is not used, (b) discriminatory advertising is not used, and (c) no more than one house in which the owner was not the most recent resident is sold within a two-year period. The 1968 act also does not apply to (1) rentals in owner-occupied apartment buildings that house less than five families as long as discriminatory advertising is not used, (2) religious organizations which limit the sale or rental of noncommercial dwellings to persons of the same religion, if the religion is not restricted on the basis of race, color or national origin, and (3) a private club that limits rental of its noncommercial property to its members.[26]

The 1968 Civil Rights Act provides for three methods of enforcement. First, a person claiming injury under the act may file a complaint with the Department of Housing and Urban Development (HUD), although the complaint must be filed within 180 days after the alleged discriminatory conduct. HUD will then investigate the complaint and, if necessary, attempt to resolve the complaint by informal methods; or it might refer the complaint to a state or local agency that administers a law substantially equivalent to the 1968 act. However, if the state or local agency does not proceed with the case in a timely manner, the case will be returned to HUD.

Second, whether or not a complaint has been filed with HUD, a person may file suit in federal or state court within 180 days of the alleged discrimination. If a complaint has been filed with HUD, the state or federal suit must be filed within 31 to 60 days after the HUD complaint was filed or after the case was returned to HUD from a state or local agency. The courts are authorized to grant a temporary or permanent injunction or a temporary restraining order, and they may award the plaintiff actual damages, punitive damages up to $1,000, court costs, and attorney fees.

Third, the United States Attorney may commence a civil action to enforce the act if he has cause to believe that there is a pattern or practice of resistance to the rights granted by the act. The 1968 act also provides for criminal penalties in certain cases where there is interference with the rights or with the enforcement of remedies provided by the act.

The net result of the two civil rights acts is that discrimination on the basis of race or color is never allowed, while other types of discrimination covered in the 1968 act are not allowed unless one of the exemptions applies. As the Supreme Court noted in comparing the 1866 act (42 U.S.C.A. § 1982) with the 1968 act: "Whatever else it may be, 42 U.S.C.A. § 1982 is not a comprehensive open housing law.

**26.** Id.

In sharp contrast to the Fair Housing Titl⌐ (Title VIII) of the Civil Rights Act of 1968, . . . the statute in this case deals only with racial discrimination and does not address itself to discrimination on grounds of religion or national origin. It does not deal specifically with discrimination in the provision of services or facilities in connection with the sale or rental of a dwelling. It does not prohibit advertising or other representations that indicate discriminatory preferences. It does not refer explicitly to discrimination in financing arrangements or in the provision of brokerage services. It does not empower a federal administrative agency to assist aggrieved persons. It makes no provision for interventions by the Attorney General. And, although it can be enforced by injunction, it contains no provision expressly authorizing a federal court to order the payment of damages. . . . [There are] vast differences between, on the one hand, a general statute applicable only to racial discrimination in the rental and sale of property and enforceable only by private parties acting on their own initiative, and, on the other hand, a detailed housing law, applicable to a broad range of discriminatory practices and enforceable by a complete arsenal of federal authority." [27]

## C.  STATE AND LOCAL LAWS

In addition to the federal laws, there are a number of state and local "open housing" or "fair housing" laws directed at private discrimination in housing. Some of these statutes go further than the federal laws because they prohibit discrimination on the basis of age or handicap. For instance, in an opinion regarding the Michigan statute that prohibits age discrimination, the Michigan Attorney-General noted that the refusal of a landlord to rent to a tenant on the grounds that the tenant has children constitutes age discrimination.[28]

The Supreme Court has dealt with two issues relating to state and local ordinances. First, must a fair housing ordinance be specially approved by local voters? For example, in 1964 the city of Akron, Ohio, enacted a fair housing ordinance, based on the premise that society incurs social and economic losses from substandard ghetto housing and from discrimination and segregation. Nellie Hunter filed a complaint under this ordinance that she had talked with a real estate agent but the agent said that none of the listed houses could be shown "because all of the owners had specified they did not wish their houses shown to Negroes." Despite the apparent discrimination in this instance, Mrs. Hunter could not use the Akron ordinance because a later city charter amendment stated that any ordinance regulating the sale or lease of real estate on the basis of race, color, religion, national origin, or ancestry had to be approved by a majority of voters. Mrs. Hunter challenged this city charter amendment, and the Su-

27.  Jones v. Alfred H. Mayer Co., 392 U.S. 409, 88 S.Ct. 2186, 20 L.Ed.2d 1189 (1968).

28.  Mich.Att'y Gen.Op. No. 4953, April 21, 1976.

preme Court held that the amendment constituted a denial of equal protection under the Fourteenth Amendment. The Court found the Akron amendment treated racial housing matters differently from other housing matters and made it more difficult to enact fair housing ordinances than to enact other types of ordinances.[29]

The second question considered by the Supreme Court was whether a township may attempt to stem the flight of white houseowners from a racially integrated community by enacting an ordinance prohibiting the posting of "For Sale" and "Sold" signs. The population growth of Willingboro, New Jersey, located near two military bases and several national corporation offices, slowed to 3 percent between 1970 and 1973 after a decade of rapid growth. During the three years, the white population declined by 5 percent while the nonwhite population increased by 60 percent. In order to reduce panic selling, the town council passed an ordinance prohibiting "For Sale" and "Sold" signs except on model homes. When this ordinance was challenged by a property owner and a realtor, the Supreme Court unanimously decided that the ordinance was unconstitutional because it violated the First Amendment. The court noted that alternative methods of communications, such as newspaper advertising, are often more costly and less effective than the use of signs. Furthermore, the Court felt that the ordinance was not needed to promote the government's objective of stable, integrated housing and that in any event this objective could not be achieved in a manner which impaired the flow of legitimate commercial information. "If dissemination of this information can be restricted, then every locality in the country can suppress any facts that reflect poorly on the locality, so long as a plausible claim can be made that disclosure would cause the recipient of the information to act 'irrationally.' " [30]

# CASES

---

## COCHRANE v. WITTBOLD

Supreme Court of Michigan, 1960.
359 Mich. 402, 102 N.W.2d 459.

EDWARDS, Justice.

This is a libel suit by a real estate saleswoman, Marilyn Cochrane, against her former employer, Wittbold & Company, and its president, Robert Wittbold, a real estate broker. At the trial of the case in Wayne county circuit court, a jury awarded plaintiff $7,500, and the

29. Hunter v. Erickson, 393 U.S. 385, 89 S.Ct. 557, 21 L.Ed.2d 616 (1969).

30. Linmark Associates, Inc. v. Township of Willingboro, 431 U.S. 85, 97 S.Ct. 1614, 52 L.Ed.2d 155 (1977).

circuit judge denied a motion *non obstante veredicto* and entered judgment.

\* \* \*

The charges with which we deal are contained in a statement to the Michigan corporation and securities commission written by Wittbold on a commission form provided for applying for a salesman's transfer to another broker and in a letter which he sent the commission. Plaintiff had asked defendants to fill out the form for her transfer, at which point they discharged her and sent the statement and letter which follow:

(on reverse side)

"I have discharged Marilyn H. Cochrane for what I consider to be a direct violation of the rules and regulations of the Michigan securities commission. The particular rule that has been violated is a rule which prohibits real estate people from purchasing for their own account listings without revealing to the seller that they are purchasing for their own account. This salesman asked me about the propriety of buying a piece of property which we had listed, and I informed her that it was O.K. provided the seller knew full well that she was a purchaser and was no longer acting as the seller's agent. Salesman proceeded to purchase the property, but instead of buying it in her own name, she had her parents buy it and she received a commission from the seller. Some time later it was pointed out to me that she had executed a conveyance as the owner of the property to a third party on the day that the deal had been closed. After finding this out, I talked to the original owners of the property and they feel as I do that acts of this kind should not be condoned. I asked the salesman to pay over to the original owners any profits she may have made on the transaction, but this she refused to do. If you want further details as to this case or should you care to investigate further, I shall be pleased to forward such details and documents as you may request."

"Gentlemen:

"I wish to cancel the application for the renewal of salesman's license of Marilyn H. Cochrane, as I have this day discharged her for what I consider to be a direct violation of the rules and regulations of the Michigan corporation and securities commission.

\* \* \* \*

"This salesman has asked for the transfer of her license to another broker and I have refused, as I will not take the responsibility for helping to allow a person who has committed such acts as described above, from continuing in the real estate business.

"Very truly yours,

"Wittbold & Co.

"/s/ Robert L. Wittbold"

The undisputed evidence, including plaintiff's own testimony, shows the following regarding the transaction:

On March 19, 1955, a Mr. and Mrs. Dowling listed 6½ acres on Gross Ile for sale with the Wittbold firm. Plaintiff, as a Wittbold saleswoman, presented an offer of $1,000 an acre from a Mr. and Mrs. Mitchell which the Dowlings accepted on April 16. Mr. and Mrs. Mitchell were actually plaintiff's father and mother who were buying the property for plaintiff. Plaintiff discussed the situation with Wittbold who told her that she could buy the property if she made full disclosure to the sellers.

On May 21, 1955, the transaction was closed. On the way to the closing, Mrs. Cochrane for the first time told Mrs. Dowling that the purchasers were relatives of hers. The closing statement included the language, "Seller has full knowledge that the salesman is related to the purchaser."

Mrs. Cochrane could not remember at trial whether or not the Dowlings were told that her mother and father were purchasing the property. Mrs. Dowling testified that they were not told.

It appears that as of May 21, when such disclosure as is shown by this record was made, 3 important facts were not revealed:

(1) The purchasers were not only related, but were in fact plaintiff's mother and father;

(2) The purchase was being made by them for plaintiff;

(3) Plaintiff already had a binding agreement with a Mr. Anthony for her to sell him the property concerned at a price of $1,200 per acre.

As to these matters, plaintiff testified at cross-examination:

"Q. You purchased this property for your own account? A. No.

"Q. You did not? A. No. Indirectly yes, but actually no.

"Q. Indirectly you purchased it for your own account? A. Yes. I mean I asked my parents to purchase it.

"Q. In other words, you knew of the entire deal beforehand? In other words, before May 21st, you had this all set up, is that correct? That you were going to buy it and that you could make a profit and the commission on it? A. I had knowledge of it, yes.

"Q. Did you reveal to Mrs. Dowling that you were buying for your own account? A. No."

Within 2 days after the Dowling-Mitchell closing, the Mitchells assigned the land contract to plaintiff and plaintiff in turn assigned it to Anthony.

The Dowlings were charged the regular commission on their sale and plaintiff made an individual profit of $1,196 on the Anthony transaction.

Wittbold's uncontradicted testimony is that he first knew all these facts as a result of checking into a report to him made 2 or 3 months later by another real estate broker who had found the recording of the assignment to plaintiff.

Wittbold thereupon discussed the matter with plaintiff and with the Dowlings. He did not, however, discharge plaintiff until March of 1956 when plaintiff presented him with the application form for transfer to another real estate broker.

As a result of the communication previously quoted, plaintiff's license was suspended and a hearing was held before a deputy commissioner on a charge of violation of Rule 6 of the rules and regulations of the Michigan corporation and securities commission:

> "A broker shall not buy for himself either directly or indirectly property listed with him, nor shall he acquire any interest therein either directly or indirectly, without first making his true position clearly known to the listing owner."

Wittbold, though notified, did not appear or testify, and the complaint was dismissed and plaintiff's license restored.

Subsequently the instant suit for libel was started.

At trial, the judge instructed the jury that the only communications of the alleged libel proved were those to the corporation and securities commission. Plaintiff offered no request for instruction on this point and, when afforded an opportunity to object to the charge, specifically indicated no objection. The judge also instructed the jury that the communications to the corporation and securities commission were qualifiedly privileged and, hence, that both their falsity and defendants' malice must be found antecedent to recovery.

\* \* \*

The claim of falsity really is addressed to defendants' stated conclusion that these acts represented a violation of the rules of the corporation and securities commission. As to this, the jury may well have been led, by the restoration of plaintiff's license, to conclude that the decision of the deputy commissioner was a determination of the falsity of the violation charge, and that the determination was binding on them.

Whatever the proofs may have shown at the license hearing, we believe that the acts of plaintiff, which are established beyond dispute by this record, represent both a violation of the corporation and secu-

rities commission rule, and a violation of the public policy of this
State.

Common law establishes the principle upon which Rule 6 is
based, that an agent may not serve himself while purporting to serve
and accepting a fee from his principal without the fullest and most
complete disclosure to the principal.

Justice Cardozo, while on the New York bench, put the matter
this way:

> "If dual interests are to be served, the disclosure to be effec-
> tive must lay bare the truth, without ambiguity or reservation, in
> all its stark significance (Dunne v. English, L.R. 18 Eq. 524;
> Imperial Merc. Credit Assn. v. Coleman, L.R. 6 H.L. 189)."

There are in this record facts to support a finding of malice on
the part of defendants. The jury finding on this point may have
rested on the unexplained delay in defendants' indignation about this
deal and the coincidence of their complaints and plaintiff's statement
of intention to leave their employment.

Nonetheless, the damaging statements contained in the publications were true when compared to plaintiff's own testimony.

Recovery in a libel action cannot be predicated upon defamatory
charges which are proven to be true.

The motion for verdict *non obstante* should have been granted.

Reversed. Costs to appellants.

---

### MEHLBERG v. REDLIN

Supreme Court of South Dakota, 1959.
77 S.D. 586, 96 N.W.2d 399.

SMITH, Judge.

This action was brought by plaintiff to recover judgment against
defendants for a broker's commission for services rendered at the
specific request of defendants in the sale of a Watertown residential
property. A general denial was interposed by defendants. The jury
returned a verdict for plaintiff as prayed in her complaint. The defendants have appealed and, predicated upon grounds stated in their
motions for a directed verdict, and for judgment n. o. v., assert that
the evidence is insufficient to support the verdict in several particulars.

In the spring of 1957 the defendants were engaged in building
homes at Watertown, South Dakota, for sale. In late April defendant
Redlin called at plaintiff's real estate office in Watertown and offered
to list two of their new properties for sale. According to Redlin's
version of their negotiations, the property of present concern was
listed at $15,500 net to defendants; all to be received above that

amount to constitute plaintiff's commission.  According to plaintiff, she having refused to serve defendants on the basis suggested, Redlin finally agreed that she would be allowed a commission at that price of 5% on the first $5,000 and 2½% on the remainder, and told her to go ahead and sell it.  It was understood that defendants reserved the right to sell the property if they found a purchaser.

A synod of the Evangelical Lutheran Church had an established church in Watertown.  A Rev. Schumann was pastor of that church. A second church was in process of organization in the spring of 1957. A plan was afoot to build a parsonage for the new pastor and an apartment had been rented for his use until a new home could be erected.  Actual construction of the new dwelling had not commenced.  On Friday, April 26th of that year Rev. Kell arrived to take over the new pastorate.  On the same day his furniture arrived in a van.  It was determined that the rented apartment was wholly inadequate and Rev. Schumann undertook to assist in finding suitable quarters for rent.  He called plaintiff for a list of rental properties. She gave him the addresses of two properties she had for rent, and in addition she told him of the two new properties of defendants she had for sale.  During the afternoon of that day Schumann, Kell and an officer of the synod viewed defendants' property from the outside. Thereafter they went to the office of defendant Redlin at his lumberyard.  They inquired as to whether he would rent the dwelling and received a negative answer.  When asked if he said anything to them about selling the house, he replied, "Yes, I made them an offer.  The committee knew already what I wanted, it was $15,500."  He accompanied them to and into the property.  While they were in the house Rev. Schumann mentioned to Redlin that they had received the listing from plaintiff.  Schumann testified, "He did not reply.  Mr. Redlin is hard of hearing and I would not be willing to say that he heard me."  Redlin was then wearing a hearing aid.  When inquiry was made as to whether Schumann had told him they had received the listing from plaintiff, he first replied, "I don't remember that.  There was a lot of fellows talking, everyone was excited because the load was loaded and he wanted to move in an hour, the sun was pretty near down."  Thereafter he testified, "There was nothing said, no" * * *.  "No.  I didn't know nothing about it."

Within a brief time the committee returned to Mr. Redlin's office and told him they would buy the property.  He suggested the formal contract could wait until the first of the next week.  Rev. Kell moved in that evening.  The contract to purchase for $15,500 was executed at a local bank on the following Tuesday.

About a week or ten days after the sale was made Redlin called at plaintiff's office and told her she need not sell the property as it was sold.  Upon inquiry he informed her that it had been sold to the church. She then asked for her commission, and he answered she "didn't do anything toward the sale." This litigation resulted.

\*   \*   \*

In the absence of a special contract, to earn a commission a broker must be the "procuring cause" of a sale consummated by his principal. This universally accepted principle was recently reiterated by this court in Dobson v. Wolff, 74 S.D. 493, 54 N.W.2d 469.

A number of the cases digested in 34 Words & Phrases, phrase the definition of "procuring cause" substantially in terms as one originating a series of events which, without break in their continuity, result in the accomplishment of the prime object of the broker's employment.

The Restatement employs the phrase "effective cause" and states, "An agent is an 'effective cause,' as that phrase is used in this Section, when his efforts have been sufficiently important in achieving a result for the accomplishment of which the principal has promised to pay him, so that it is just that the principal should pay the promised compensation to him." Restatement of Agency 2d, § 448, Comment a.

\*   \*   \*

Although plaintiff did no more than to initiate the negotiations which were consummated by defendants, because of the potency which her suggestions gained from the existing peculiar circumstances we have outlined, we are persuaded that reasonable minds, acting reasonably, could conclude that her mere introduction of the synod to defendants' property was the procuring or efficient cause of its sale.

We concur in the view expressed in Mechem, Agency, 2d Ed., § 2435, p. 2011, in these words: "His efforts, it is said, may have been slight, but if they brought about the desired result, no more could be asked; \*   \*   \*."

The foregoing view gains support from Langford v. Issenhuth, 28 S.D. 451, 134 N.W. 889 and Dobson v. Wolff, supra. In those decisions it was declared that a personal introduction of purchaser to the principal is not essential, if through the efforts of the broker the parties are brought together.

Elsewhere it is written, "If a person employs only one broker to procure a customer, the broker is ordinarily entitled to his commission, under the rule stated in this Section, if he causes a customer to negotiate with the principal and the customer makes a purchase without a substantial break in the ensuing negotiations. It is not necessary that the broker conduct the negotiation or even be an influential factor in persuading the customer to accept the terms; nor is it necessary that the broker should personally introduce the customer or bring the principal to his attention; he introduces the customer if, through any means which he uses to attract attention, the purchaser is led to the principal." Restatement of Agency, 2d, § 448, Comment d.

\* \* \*

\* \* \* The contract of plaintiff must be interpreted as requiring her to produce a purchaser ready, able and willing to buy for $15,500. The defendant Redlin took over and sold to the customer with whom plaintiff had opened negotiations, at the price at which the property was listed with plaintiff. Thus, even if it be assumed that Redlin failed to hear the statement made to him by Rev. Schumann, the very object of the listing was accomplished, and defendants were placed at no disadvantage by reason of a lack of notice. In that circumstance, if the broker is the procuring cause of the sale, he is entitled to his commission. In Rounds v. Allee, 116 Iowa 345, 89 N. W. 1098, Justice Ladd wrote:

> "The fact that defendant did not know Gravesen had been sent to him by plaintiff is not controlling. It was no part of the contract. All he was to do was to find a purchaser who was ready, able, and willing to buy, or would in fact buy; and if he did this the contract was fulfilled, regardless of defendant's information of what he had done."

Such is the weight of authority.

For all of the foregoing reasons we conclude the trial court did not err in refusing to direct a verdict for defendants.

The judgment of the trial court is affirmed.

--------

## SEIDEL v. WALKER

Court of Appeals of Texas, 1915.
173 S.W. 1170.

CARL, J. On September 9, 1913, appellant, Albin Seidel, through appellee, his agent, made a contract with Frank Bushick, whereby he agreed to sell Bushick 52 acres of land near the city of San Antonio for the sum of $5,000, to be paid $2,000 in cash and three notes each for $1,000. The contract provided that, if the purchaser failed to comply, the seller had the option of taking a small forfeit which was put up, or of pursuing an action for specific performance. This contract was delivered to appellant at the time, together with the forfeit check. It was an absolute binding contract to purchase, in so far as Bushick was concerned; the only means of his escape being failure of title or defective title, etc., and he was given the right of an action for specific performance. Seidel knew the purchaser, accepted the contract and money, and, about two days before the time to close up, the purchaser notified him that he would be unable to complete the purchase. Appellant thereupon forfeited and retained the money put up. Under the terms of the contract, appellant had the right to do either as he did, or to hold Bushick to a specific performance of the contract.

This is not a case involving the question as to whether the agent presented a customer ready, willing, and able to buy, as is ordinarily the duty of an agent before he may be entitled to a commission; but it is a case where the agent produces a customer with whom the seller is satisfied and a contract is made. In this last event, the agent is not concerned as to the ability of the purchaser to buy, for the seller relieves him of any further duty in that respect when he accepts the purchaser as satisfactory and a binding contract is made.

It may be unfortunate that appellant accepted a contract wherein he was not adequately protected: First, as to his ability to have the same performed by the purchaser; and, second, which did not protect him against the payment of a commission in such case as this happened to be. But he acted for himself in accepting and retaining the contract as written, and no fraud is pleaded or proved on part of the agent in the procurement of his acceptance. This court, however, does not make contracts for parties, but only passes upon them after they are made. In the absence of fraud, mistake, or some special reason which does not here exist, "as parties bind themselves, so shall they be bound." A binding contract was made for the sale of the land which was susceptible of specific performance, and that appellant made a mistake as to the purchaser's ability to perform is such an error of judgment as any man may make; but for that mistake he, and he alone, is responsible.

The judgment is in all things affirmed.

---

### ELLSWORTH DOBBS, INC. v. JOHNSON

Supreme Court of New Jersey, 1967.
50 N.J. 528, 236 A.2d 843.

FRANCIS, J.

Plaintiff Ellsworth Dobbs, Inc., a real estate broker, sued John R. Johnson and Adelaide P. Johnson, his wife, and Joseph Iarussi for commissions allegedly earned in a real estate transaction. The Johnsons, as owners of certain acreage in Bernards Township, New Jersey, and Iarussi as purchaser, entered into a written agreement, the former to sell and the latter to buy the property. There is no doubt that Dobbs brought the parties together, and into the signed contract of sale. Title did not close, however, because of Iarussi's inability to obtain financial backing for his intended development of the property. * * * Dobbs then brought this action charging the Johnsons with breach of an express agreement to pay a commission due for bringing about the contract of sale, and charging Iarussi with breach of an implied agreement to pay the commission if he failed to complete the purchase and thus deprived the broker of commission from the seller. The trial judge held, as a matter of law, that Dobbs' commission claim against the Johnsons vested upon execution of the contract of sale with Iarussi, and that the right to commission was not dependent upon the closing of title. Consequently, he declined to submit that issue to the jury for determination. Instead he instructed them that plaintiff was entitled to a commission against the Johnsons, and limited their function to a determination of the amount due. The jury found for Dobbs in the amount of $15,000.

As to the defendant Iarussi, the trial judge submitted this issue to the jury: Did the facts as they found them show by a preponderance of the evidence that Iarussi impliedly agreed with Dobbs' representative that if the representative located property satisfactory to Iarussi for residential development purposes, and the owner entered into a contract with Iarussi to sell the property on terms mutually agreeable, Iarussi would perform the contract and thus enable the broker to earn a commission from the owner? The jury found that there was such an implied agreement; further, that the implied agreement was breached by Iarussi's failure to perform his contract to buy the Johnsons' property. Therefore he became liable to the broker for payment of the commission. Since the jury had been charged that the amount of the verdict against Iarussi would have to be the same as that returned against the Johnsons, he was assessed $15,000.

On appeal the Appellate Division, 92 N.J.Super. 271, 223 A.2d 199, reversed the judgment against the Johnsons, holding that there was a jury question as to their liability to pay the commission to the plaintiff, and a new trial was ordered on this phase of the case. The judgment against Iarussi was reversed also, on the ground that the evidence was insufficient to show a contract, express or implied, under which Iarussi made himself liable to pay the commission Dobbs would have received from the Johnsons if Iarussi had performed his agreement to buy their property. On plaintiff's application, this Court granted certification.

\*    \*    \*

### The sellers' liability to the broker.

Corbin notes that there has been an immense amount of litigation over the years with respect to the commissions of land brokers. 1 Corbin on Contracts § 50 (1963). Almost a century ago, the former Supreme Court ruled that when a broker who had been duly authorized by the owner to find a buyer for his property produced a willing and able purchaser who entered into a contract to buy on terms agreeable to the owner, the broker had fulfilled his undertaking and his right to commission from the owner was complete.

Hinds v. Henry, 36 N.J.L. 328 (Sup.Ct.1873). The doctrine has been with us ever since.

\*    \*    \*

A new and more realistic approach to the problem is necessary.

There can be no doubt that ordinarily when an owner of property lists it with a broker for sale, his expectation is that the money for the payment of commission will come out of the proceeds of the sale. He expects that if the broker produces a buyer to whom the owner's terms of sale are satisfactory, and a contract embodying those terms is executed, the buyer will perform, i. e. he will pay the consideration and accept the deed at the time agreed upon. Considering the realities of the relationship created between owner and broker, that expectation of the owner is a reasonable one, and, in our view, entirely consistent with what should be the expectation of a conscientious broker as to the kind of ready, willing and able purchaser his engagement calls upon him to tender to the owner.

The present New Jersey rule as exemplified by the cases cited above is deficient as an instrument of justice. It permits a broker to satisfy his obligation to the owner simply by tendering a human being who is physically and mentally capable of agreeing to buy the property on mutually satisfactory terms, so long as the owner enters into a sale contract with such person. The implication of the rule is that the owner has the burden of satisfying himself as to the prospective purchaser's ability, financial or otherwise, to complete the transaction; he cannot rely at all on the fact that the purchaser was produced in good faith by the broker as a person willing and able to buy the property. Once he enters into a contract of sale with the broker's customer, he is considered to have accepted the purchaser as fully capable of the ultimate performance agreed upon. If it later appears that the purchaser is not financially able to close the title, or even that he never did have the means to do so, the owner must pay the broker his commission, so long as he acted in good faith. Such a rule, considered in the context of the real relationship between broker and owner, empties the word "able" of substantially all of its significant content and imposes an unjust burden on vendors of property. It seems to us that fairness requires that the arrangement between broker and owner be interpreted to mean that the owner hires the broker with the expectation of becoming liable for a commission only in the event a sale of the property is consummated, unless the title does not pass because of the owner's improper or frustrating conduct.

The principle that binds the seller to pay commission if he signs a contract of sale with the broker's customer, regardless of the customer's financial ability, puts the burden on the wrong shoulders. Since the broker's duty to the owner is to produce a prospective buyer who is financially able to pay the purchase price and take title, a right in the owner to assume such capacity when the broker presents his purchaser ought to be recognized.  It follows that the obligation to inquire into the prospect's financial status and to establish his adequacy to fulfill the monetary conditions of the purchase must be regarded logically and sensibly as resting with the broker.  Thus when the broker produces his customer, it is only reasonable to hold that the owner may accept him without being obliged to make an independent inquiry into his financial capacity.  That right ought not to be taken away from him, nor should he be estopped to assert it, simply because he "accepted" the buyer, i. e., agreed to convey to him if and when he paid the purchase price according to the terms of the contract.  In reason and in justice it must be said that the duty to produce a purchaser able in the financial sense to complete the purchase at the time fixed is an incident of the broker's business; so too, with regard to any other material condition of the agreement to purchase which is to be performed at the closing.  In a practical world, the true test of a willing buyer is not met when he signs an agreement to purchase; it is demonstrated at the time of closing of title, and if he unjustifiably refuses or is unable financially to perform *then*, the broker has not produced a willing buyer.

\* \* \*

We come now to another aspect of the over-all problem.  To what extent may the broker, by special contract, thwart the general rules now declared to control the usual relationship between him and an owner who engages him to find a purchaser?  \* \* \*

The record in the present case contains samples of standardized printed forms of special agreements, used by brokers and real estate boards, which are presented to intending sellers for signature when a broker is retained.  They are designed to impose on the owner liability for commissions immediately upon execution of a contract to sell to a customer produced by the broker, irrespective of whether the buyer proves unable financially or unwilling for some other unjustifiable reason to complete the sale.  Two examples of such agreements are as follows:

> "Commission or commissions shall be earned when the agreement of sale is executed by the buyer and seller, and both the agent and his cooperating broker are authorized to deduct all or part of their commissions from the initial deposit at the time of signing of the sales agreement, provided however, that the initial deposit shall be at least double the amount of the commissions deducted."

> "The owner or owners of property or properties to be sold or exchanged hereunder hereby recognize(s)                        as the broker negotiating this agreement of sale and hereby agree(s) to pay said broker, for services rendered, a commission as now established by the real estate board in whose territory the above property is situated, namely ———% of the within-

mentioned selling price; same to be paid upon the execution of this agreement. It is the intention of the parties hereto that this provision of this agreement is made for the benefit of said broker."

The rules which we have set down above to govern dealings, rights, and duties between brokers and owners are necessary for the protection of property owners, and constitute the public policy of our State. Whenever there is substantial inequality of bargaining power, position or advantage between the broker and the other party involved, any form of agreement designed to create liability on the part of the owner for commission upon the signing of a contract to sell to a prospective buyer, brought forward by the broker, even though consummation of the sale is frustrated by the inability or the unwillingness of the buyer to pay the purchase money and close the title, we regard as so contrary to the common understanding of men, and also so contrary to common fairness, as to require a court to condemn it as unconscionable.

\*   \*   \*

### Liability of the buyer to the broker.

\*   \*   \*

This Court has held that when a prospective buyer solicits a broker to find or to show him property which he might be interested in buying, and the broker finds property satisfactory to him which the owner agrees to sell at the price offered, and the buyer knows the broker will earn commission for the sale from the owner, the law will imply a promise on the part of the buyer to complete the transaction with the owner. If he fails or refuses to do so without valid reason, and thus prevents the broker from earning the commission from the owner, he becomes liable to the broker for breach of the implied promise.

\*   \*   \*

For the reasons outlined, the judgment against the Johnsons in the trial court, as well as the reversal of that judgment by the Appellate Division and the ordering of a new trial are reversed, and judgment is entered in their favor and against the plaintiff Dobbs.

Further, the judgment in the trial court against Iarussi, as well as that of the Appellate Division directing entry of judgment in his favor as a matter of law, are reversed, and the cause is remanded for a new trial against Iarussi on the theory explained herein.

———

## WALKER v. POINTER

United States District Court of Texas, Dallas Div., 1969.
304 F.Supp. 56.

HUGHES, District Judge.

This case involves the scope of 42 U.S.C. section 1982 which provides that:

> "All citizens of the United States shall have the same right, in every State and Territory, as is enjoyed by white citizens thereof to inherit, purchase, lease, sell, hold, and convey real and personal property."

Plaintiffs, Cheryl Walker and her brother, James E. Walker, filed a complaint in this court on December 26, 1968, alleging that on October 7, 1968 they rented an apartment from defendant, G. M. Pointer and signed a one year lease. The apartment was in a complex of several buildings at 14230 Heritage Circle in the City of Farmers Branch in Dallas County, Texas. Defendant F. R. Branscome was the manager. The lease provided for rental payments to be made on the first and fifteenth of each month. At the time of the lease Cheryl Walker was 20 years old and James Walker was 19. About noon on Saturday, December 14, 1968, a written notice signed by F. R. Branscome was delivered to James Walker in the apartment stating that suit would be filed in the Justice Court to evict them unless he and his sister surrendered possession of the apartment by 4:00 o'clock of that day.

Plaintiffs further alleged that on December 16, 1968, at about 1:30 P.M. when neither of the plaintiffs were present, Branscome entered the apartment with three employees, who put their clothes and possessions in boxes and sheets and hauled them away in a truck. These facts are admitted by defendants.

Plaintiffs and defendants belong to the white race. At the time of this occurrence Cheryl Walker was employed in a racially integrated business and James was a student at North Texas State University, a predominantly white institution, attended also by a number of Negro students. Both had black friends who visited in the apartment on several occasions. It is the contention of plaintiffs that they were evicted because they had Negro guests and that such eviction was a violation of 42 U.S.C.A. § 1982.

The defendants deny that the Walkers were evicted because they entertained blacks as guests. The contention of defendants is that the eviction was caused by the failure of the Walkers to pay the rent on time and by complaints from tenants of noise and disturbance in the apartment.

\* \* \*

There are few cases construing section 1982, but one case, Jones v. Alfred H. Mayer Co., 392 U.S. 409, 88 S.Ct. 2186, 20 L.Ed.2d 1189 (1968), is of major importance in discussing the statute. In that case plaintiffs alleged that defendants had refused to sell them a home for the sole reason one of the plaintiffs was a Negro. The Supreme Court held that section 1982 applies to all discriminations against Negroes whether from private or public sources in the sale or rental of property. There is no doubt that if the plaintiffs in this case had been Negroes, the statute would apply. The fact that they are white distinguishes this case and makes it in part one of first impression.

Section 1982 in its original form was part of section 1 of the Civil Rights Act of 1866. The history of this Act, as outlined in *Jones*, reveals that it was passed to implement the Thirteenth Amendment which provides as follows:

> "Neither slavery nor involuntary servitude, except as a punishment for crime whereof the party shall have been duly convicted, shall exist within the United States, or any place subject to their jurisdiction."

The discussion of the Court in *Jones* indicates that the institution of slavery prompting the Thirteenth Amendment was ordinarily associated with the black man. Yet whites too have historically been susceptible to enslavement in many countries throughout the centuries. In this country white slavery was known to exist during the antebellum period in the South. Current statutes punishing practices relating to slavery continually refer to the victimization of "any person." 18 U.S.C.A. §§ 1581–1588. The bar against involuntary servitude has been invoked by the courts in numerous contexts where race is immaterial.

The first six words of section 1982 appear to lead inescapably to the conclusion that the statute contemplates a reach as broad as the amendment upon which it is based. "All citizens of the United States" are to be protected. The inclusiveness of these words is reinforced by the *Jones* opinion which states that the rights granted in 1982 are granted "to all citizens without regard to race or color."
\*   \*   \*

     \*   \*   \*

It is the conclusion of this Court that the plaintiffs are within the jurisdictional scope of section 1982 in their own right—even though they are not Negro persons and irrespective of whatever harm might have befallen Negro persons as a result of the alleged interruption of the Walker leasehold by defendants.

     \*   \*   \*

Section 1982 establishes for Negro persons, *inter alia*, the right to "hold \*   \*   \* real and personal property". It is alleged that defendants evicted the Walkers in retaliation for the appearance of Negro guests on or about the Walker premises and in order to prevent a recurrence of such visits in the future. In light of the decision of the Supreme Court in *Jones* it is reasonable to characterize the freedom of Negro persons to come and go at the invitation of one lawfully in control of the premises as sufficiently pertaining to a condition of property to be a right to "hold" under section 1982. In *Jones* the Court cites with approval of the "great fundamental rights" sought to be preserved by the Civil Rights Act of 1866:

> the right to acquire property, the right to go and come at pleasure, the right to enforce rights in the courts, to make contracts, and to inherit and dispose of property.

\*     \*     \*

The evidence thus establishes that the reason for the eviction and the termination of the lease was a policy of racial discrimination implemented by Branscome. The racially motivated termination of the lease violated section 1982 which expressly protects the right to "lease" real property. The evidence shows that as a result of this violation the Walkers suffered damages. Their clothing and other possessions were retained for almost three months and some were never returned. Others were returned in damaged condition. Branscome was employed by Pointer to manage the apartments. Pointer testified that Branscome had authority to ask tenants to move. Hence he as well as Branscome is liable for actual damages resulting from the eviction.

With regard to the claim for exemplary damages there is abundant evidence that Branscome acted with malice. There is credible testimony that on the day of eviction, Monday, December 16th, Branscome had James' car, which was legally parked next to the apartment building, backed into a lane and pushed 300 yards to a thoroughfare where it was left on the highway six feet from its edge. While James went after the car, Branscome with 3 employees entered the apartment with boxes, dumped all their clothes and food from the refrigerator into boxes and sheets from the bed and carried them away in a truck without advising either James or Cheryl, who had arrived while the eviction was taking place, where their belongings were to be taken. When James attempted to use the telephone, Branscome pulled the telephone out of the wall and threw it at James. When plaintiffs asked to be allowed to spend the night, Branscome said they could stay without heat and pulled the thermostat from the wall. Branscome had taken no action in the Justice Court to evict plaintiffs as he had said he would do in his notice of December 14th. The malice with which Branscome acted entitles plaintiffs to exemplary damages.

## PROBLEMS

1.　Myrtle hired two real estate agents to sell a large tract of land. Her contract with the agents provided that (1) the agents would pay all expenses incurred in getting the property ready to sell; (2) the agents would have the property surveyed and divided into town lots and would have the streets graded; and (3) the agents would use their best efforts to sell the property and would not be paid for expenses incurred except for a specified share of the sale proceeds. The contract did not specify a time limit for performance. After the agents had performed their part of the agreement and had found buyers for several of the lots, Myrtle attempted to terminate the agreement for no apparent cause. May she cancel the agreement? Why?

2.　A Missouri statute provides that a broker is not entitled to a commission unless he was licensed "at the time when the alleged cause of action arose." A Missouri broker was promised a $34,500 commission for negotiating the sale of property. The sellers paid the broker only $7,500 and he sued for the balance. Before trial the sellers learned that the broker did not have a license at the time he was hired, although he did obtain a license one month prior to the closing. Is the broker entitled to the remainder of the commission? Why?

3.　Green owned a house worth $15,000 that was subject to a $5,000 mortgage. In response to a newspaper advertisement, Green called Trusty Realty to make arrangements for the sale of his house. A salesperson for Trusty persuaded Green to exchange his house for a new $20,000 house owned by Trusty and to assume a mortgage on the new house in the amount of $15,000. Trusty agreed to assume the mortgage on the old house. No other payments were to be made. After Green's house was transferred, Green sued Trusty for actual and punitive damages. Should Green win? Why?

4.　Cecil wanted to sell his farm for $60,000, and he signed open listing agreements with two realtors, Blue and Black. Blue found a potential purchaser, McKinney, who offered $60,000 to Cecil at 10:00 a. m. on March 2. The offer was accepted by Cecil. Later in the day, before details such as the amount of down payment and the date of possession were settled by Cecil and McKinney, Black produced a potential purchaser, Brinkman, who offered $63,000 for the farm. Cecil accepted the offer and sold the farm to Brinkman. Does Cecil owe a commission to Blue? Why?

5.　Cleon listed his business property with Chumney, a real estate broker. The listing agreement included the following provision: "During the life of this contract if you find a buyer who is ready, able and willing to buy, lease or exchange said property, . . . , or if I agree to an exchange of said property, or any part thereof, or if said property or any part thereof is sold, leased or exchanged during said term by myself or any other person, firm, or corporation, I agree to pay you the 6% commission." The agreement covered the period from June 8, 1960 to December 8, 1960. On August 2, 1960, Cleon sold the property to Super Tire Mart, which had in no way dealt with Chumney, for $120,000. Before the sale, Chumney had shown the property to several prospective buyers, had placed a "For Sale" sign on the property, and had advertised in the newspaper. Chumney's expenses totalled $73. Is Cleon liable to Chumney for damages? Why? If your answer is yes, what would be the amount of damages?

6. Quincy owned a large parcel of real estate. A local congregation of Jehovah's Witnesses wanted to purchase Quincy's lot but was afraid that he would refuse to sell to a religious group. Consequently, the church hired a broker who agreed to purchase the real estate in his own name and then transfer it to the church. The broker contacted Quincy, and a sales contract was signed after Quincy was led to believe that the land was being purchased for a single man. Later, when the check for the purchase price was delivered to Quincy, he discovered the true motive for the purchase. To be safe, Quincy cashed the check, but he also attempted to cancel his contract. However, Quincy took no further action for three months, thinking that the church would not obtain approval from the zoning board for a proposed church. Much to Quincy's surprise, the church was approved. He immediately filed suit to revoke the contract because of fraud. Will he win? Why?

7. Phyllis entered into an exclusive sales agreement with Florence, a real estate agent. The agreement read: "June 16, 1947, Exclusive sale of property. #26 Prospect Street, West Bridgewater, Mass., to my agent Florence. We are asking $12,000 (will take as low as $11,000). She is to have exclusive sale of same—for 90 days. Phyllis." Florence advertised the property, discussed the sale with many prospective buyers, and also kept a key to the house. During the listing period, however, Florence had to leave town for a week; when she returned, she discovered that Phyllis had sold the property to a relative for $10,000. Florence sued Phyllis for her commission. Will Florence win? Why?

8. The Marin County Board of Realtors consists of three-fourths of the brokers actively engaged in selling residential real property in Marin County, California. The board provides a number of benefits to its members, of which the most important is the only multiple listing service for residential property operating exclusively in Marin County. Multiple listing is a system of pooling each member's listings in a central registry. This service is available only to board members, who are prohibited by the board's bylaws from disseminating published listings to nonmembers. Palsson, a licensed real estate salesman, applied to the board for membership after obtaining employment with an active member. His application was denied because the board found that, as an airline flight engineer, he did not meet the requirements of one of the board's bylaws—a member must be "primarily engaged in the real estate business." This provision was enforced through sanctions against active members who shared offices with or employed a person who had been denied membership in the board. Thus, a salesman denied membership was also denied employment with 75 percent of the residential brokers in Marin County. Are the board's actions legal? Why?

9. The Schepers owned a quarter section of land in Merrick County. They entered into a real estate listing contract with Lautenschlager, a real estate broker. Lautenschlager was instructed by the Schepers to secure the best price he could for the property, but under no circumstances to

take less than $150 an acre. Lautenschlager was contacted by two prospective purchasers. One purchaser was Lautenschlager's uncle, who offered $150 an acre, and the other was Yost, who offered $200 an acre. Lautenschlager informed the Schepers only of his uncle's offer, which they accepted, and a purchase agreement was signed. Subsequently, Lautenschlager and his uncle as joint owners transferred the same property for $200 an acre to Yost. When the Schepers learned of the sale to Yost, they sued Lautenschlager for the profits of the second sale as well as for the commission previously paid to Lautenschlager, $1,200. Will they win? Why?

10. Russ signed a sales agreement giving Larsen the exclusive right to sell his house. The agreement provided that Larsen could sign a sales agreement for Russ and could receive from the buyer a cash deposit ("earnest" money) to be held for Russ. The Gerigs agreed to purchase the house for $21,000 and made a $500 cash deposit, which was delivered by Larsen to Russ. They also paid $11,500 to Larsen over the next few months, although this money was never given to Russ. Russ now demands payment of the balance due. How much do the Gerigs owe Russ? Why?

Chapter 7

# THE REAL ESTATE CONTRACT

"My idea of an agreeable person," said Hugo Bohum, "is a person who agrees with me."

Disraeli, *Lothair*

A study of the principles of contract law as they apply to real estate is especially important to a nonlawyer for two reasons. First, in many cases a person will sign a preprinted "offer to purchase" without realizing that it is a legal commitment to purchase real estate. Second, even when the form clearly states that it is a contract, many purchasers do not consult an attorney before signing. There is a common belief that an attorney should only be consulted, if at all, to handle the closing. However, if the purchaser has already signed a contract, there is often little the attorney can do at the closing to extricate the buyer from his commitment.

As we discuss the law relating to real estate contracts, it is important to keep in mind the distinction between contract *formation* and contract *performance*. In many of our day-to-day transactions, contracts are formed and performed at the same time. For example, when you purchased this book, the contract was formed and performed (you took possession of the book and paid for it) at the same time. The typical real estate contract, however, is rarely formed and performed at the same time; in most cases a gap of a few weeks between formation and performance allows the buyer to examine the title and purchase insurance (Chapter 8) and obtain financing (Chapter 9). When these matters have been completed, final performance of the real estate contract will take place at the closing (Chapter 10).

In this chapter we will first examine the legal requirements if the real estate contract is to be binding. We will then look at a number of provisions that, although not required by law, should be included in the contract to protect the seller and the buyer. Finally, we discuss methods of avoiding the contract.

## I.  REQUIRED PROVISIONS

### A.  STATUTE OF FRAUDS

Hatfield and McCoy were attending a party when Hatfield offered to purchase McCoy's farm for $90,000. McCoy accepted the offer and they proceeded to discuss details of the purchase. When they concluded their negotiations, they announced their agreement in detail to the persons present at the party and sealed their agreement with a handshake. Is the agreement binding?

Prior to 1677, Hatfield and McCoy would be held to their agreement, which could be proven through the testimony of the witnesses. However, this approach led to certain types of fraud. For example, if Hatfield wanted McCoy's real estate but McCoy refused to sell, Hatfield might pay witnesses to testify that McCoy had orally agreed to sell the real estate when in fact no agreement had been made. To prevent such fraud, a 1677 English law, the Statute of Frauds, required certain contracts such as the sale of real estate to be in writing. "No action shall be brought upon any contract or sale of lands, tenements, or hereditaments, or any interest in or concerning them . . . unless the agreement upon which such action shall be brought, or some memorandum or note thereof, shall be in writing, and signed by the person to be charged therewith or some other person thereunto by him lawfully authorized."

While the Statute of Frauds was designed to prevent fraud, in some cases the strict application of the statute would require an unfair result. Suppose that McCoy really did agree orally to sell his farm, and Hatfield moved onto the farm and rebuilt the farmhouse. When Hatfield finished improving the property, could McCoy force him to leave because the agreement was not in writing? If the court strictly followed the Statute of Frauds, this would be the result. In many states, however, an exception to the statute has been developed to prevent such unfairness when there has been "part performance" of the contract. Although courts differ on the requirements for part performance, one statement of the rule is as follows: "Where, acting under an oral contract for the transfer of an interest in land, the purchaser with the assent of the vendor (a) makes valuable improvements on the land, or (b) takes possession thereof or retains a possession thereof existing at the time of the bargain, and also pays a portion or all of the purchase price, the purchaser or the vendor may specifically enforce the contract." [1]

## B. REQUIRED TERMS IN THE WRITING

1. **Names of Buyer and Seller.** The contract must, at a minimum, contain the names of both the buyer and seller. However, the names do not have to be included within the body of the agreement; the signatures of the parties are sufficient.

1. Restatement of Contracts § 197 (1932). The Restatement, Second, of Contracts (Tent. Draft 1973) provides: "A contract for the transfer of an interest in land may be specifically enforced notwithstanding failure to comply with the Statute of Frauds if it is established that the party seeking enforcement, in reasonable reliance on the contract and on the continuing assent of the party against whom enforcement is sought, has so changed his position that injustice can be avoided only by specific enforcement."

2. **Description of the Real Estate.** The contract must include a description of the real estate detailed enough that a court could identify the real estate without considering evidence outside the contract. For example, if the real estate was described as "811 Lindenwood Lane, County of Medina, Ohio," a court would have to look outside the agreement to determine which city in Medina County has a Lindenwood Lane.

3. **Price.** The agreement must state the price in terms clear and definite enough for a court to enforce. Real estate contracts often lack such precision. Cash sale contracts are rarely disputed, for even when the contract merely states the price, it is assumed that a cash sale was intended and that the payment is due at closing. But errors occur even with simple cash sales. In Marsico v. Kessler,[2] the defendants agreed to sell real estate located in Stanford, Connecticut to the plaintiff for $30,000. The written contract provided that $500 was to be paid when the contract was signed, and $25,000 paid when the deed was delivered. The defendants later claimed that the agreement was not enforceable because it did not meet the requirements of the Statute of Frauds. The court agreed, on the grounds that the agreement failed to specify how the remaining $4,500 was to be paid. The presumption that a cash sale was intended did not apply, the court noted, because "the presumption rests upon the failure to agree rather than upon a failure to state what was agreed. It has no application here, since the sum payable in cash is definitely specified." The court also concluded it was irrelevant that the plaintiff was ready and willing to pay the full $30,000 in cash, since the agreement was not enforceable under the Statute of Frauds.

Details of the price are most likely to lack clarity and completeness in contracts that call for the buyer to make deferred payments, usually on an installment basis over a period of time. In Montanaro v. Pandolfini,[3] the contract stated that the buyer was to give a "purchase money mortgage to seller in the amount of eighteen thousand dollars ($18,000) payable monthly for 15 years at 5%." The seller later refused to perform the contract and, when sued by the buyer, claimed the price terms were not specific enough. The court agreed with the seller, citing the following rule: "We have uniformly held that such an agreement must state the contract with such certainty that its essentials can be known from the memorandum itself, without the aid of parol proof, or from a reference contained therein to some other writing or thing certain; and these essentials must at least consist of the subject of the sale, the terms of it and the parties to it, so as to furnish evidence of a complete agreement."

In applying the rule here, the court could not determine the amount of the monthly payment. The parties might have intended

2. 149 Conn. 236, 178 A.2d 154 (1962).   3. 148 Conn. 153, 168 A.2d 550 (1961).

equal monthly payments, much like mortgage payments to a bank. Or the parties might have intended steady principal payments, with varying total monthly payments depending on the interest due. Or the parties might even have intended the buyer to make whatever monthly payments he could. Whatever the intention, it was not specified in the contract. Furthermore, the agreement was defective in failing to state when the monthly payments would begin.

4. **Signatures of the Parties.** The written purchase agreement should be signed by both the seller and the buyer. However, the rule only requires the signature of the person against whom enforcement of the contract may be sought. For example, John and Mary enter into a written agreement whereby Mary agrees to purchase John's house but only Mary signs the agreement. If Mary later refuses to perform the contract, she is liable on the contract because she signed. However, if John refused to turn the house over to her, Mary could not enforce the agreement against him in the absence of his signature.

Often the contract is signed by an agent of the seller or purchaser. Many states require not only that the agent sign the purchase agreement but also that the authorization given the agent by the seller or purchaser be in writing.

If the four essential terms are included in the written agreement, the contract will be enforceable even when the terms are written informally, such as on a receipt, on the back of a matchbook cover or in the margin of a textbook. Courts are unconcerned with the length of the agreement so long as the essentials are present. In Lucy v. Zehmer,[4] the court held that the following agreement was binding on the persons who signed it, A. H. and Ida Zehmer: "We hereby agree to sell to W. O. Lucy the Ferguson Farm complete for $50,000, title satisfactory to buyer." The Zehmers had claimed that the agreement was signed as a joke and Mr. Zehmer claimed he had been drinking and "was high as a Georgia pine." The court, however, concluded that Zehmer was not too drunk to make a valid contract and that he never told the other party that he was joking.

## C. OTHER CONTRACTUAL REQUIREMENTS

Although most real estate contracts founder on the writing requirements, other principles of contract law are applicable to the real estate contract. It is beyond the scope of this chapter to review contract law in detail, but the following points are typical of contract issues that arise in the context of a real estate transaction.

1. **Offer and Acceptance.** A contract represents mutual agreement between the parties, which usually takes the form of an offer by one party and an acceptance by the other. In most real estate

---

4. 196 Va. 493, 84 S.E.2d 516 (1954).

transactions, a seller hires a broker (see Chapter 6) to find a prospective purchaser who will make an offer which is then accepted by the seller. The purchaser can revoke the offer any time before it is accepted by the seller, even when his offer states that it will be held open for a specified time.

A major exception to the revocation rule is the option contract. In the real estate setting, a buyer persuades a seller to offer his real estate for sale at a specified price, e. g. $100,000. However, the buyer might not want to accept the offer immediately because of certain contingencies; for example, he first might want to secure other options to purchase real estate in the same area. Consequently, the parties might enter into an option contract in which the buyer pays the seller a specified sum, say $10,000, in return for the seller's promise to hold his offer to the buyer open for a certain time period, such as six months. Often the option contract states that if the holder of the option decides to buy the property, the $10,000 will be applied toward the purchase price. But whether or not the offer is accepted, the seller receives the $10,000 in exchange for giving up the right to revoke the offer.

An offer is accepted when the seller signs the agreement and communicates his acceptance to the buyer. In face-to-face transactions, communication is no problem because the buyer is present and can observe the seller signing the agreement. If contracts are negotiated over long distances, a "mail box" rule has been developed to determine the moment the acceptance goes into effect. To illustrate, in Morrison v. Thoelke,[5] a real estate purchaser, signed and sent a contract to the sellers, who were in Texas, on November 26, 1957. On November 27, the sellers signed and mailed the contract to the purchaser's attorney in Florida. Before the contract arrived, however, the sellers called the attorney and cancelled the acceptance. The court decided that the sellers had made a binding acceptance when the contract was mailed and cited the following authority: "A second leading treatise on the law of contracts, Corbin, Contracts §§ 78 and 80 (1950 Supp.1961), also devotes some discussion to the rule urged by appellants. Corbin writes: 'Where the parties are negotiating at a distance from each other, the most common method of making an offer is by sending it by mail; and more often than not the offeror has specified no particular mode of acceptance. In such a case, it is now the prevailing rule that the offeree has power to accept and close the contract by mailing a letter of acceptance, properly stamped and addressed, within a reasonable time. The contract is regarded as made at the time and place that the letter of acceptance is put into the possession of the post office department.' "

In accepting the buyer's offer, the seller is bound by the "mirror-image" rule of contract law: the acceptance must be on the terms

5. 155 So.2d 889 (Fla.App.1963).

stated in, or must "mirror," the offer. If the seller changes one of the terms of the offer before signing (the date of closing, for example), the seller has not accepted the offer but instead has made a counter-offer to the buyer that may or may not be accepted by the buyer. Furthermore, a counter-offer kills the original offer so the seller cannot thereafter accept that offer. This point is especially important to keep in mind when negotiating a real estate transaction. A possible solution is offered in the following example from a case: [6] "It is the law that when A offers B to enter into a contract on certain terms, and B declines to accept those terms but offers a counter-proposition, the original offer loses its effect, and is thereafter only open to acceptance by B when renewed by A. In the other hand, if A makes an offer which is unconditionally accepted by B, the fact that B, after such acceptance, proposes a modification of the original contract, which is declined by A, does not affect the validity of the original contract." See Pravorne v. McLeod, infra.

2. **Consideration.** Stated in general terms, the law requires that if one party is to be held to a contractual promise, the other party must give something in exchange, in consideration, for the promise. Thus, if Tom promises to transfer his real estate to Mary, Mary must give up something in exchange, usually her promise to pay for the real estate. So long as something is promised, no matter what its value, the contract will be enforced. In the early Virginia case of Hale v. Wilkinson,[7] Hale agreed to sell his house and fourteen acres to Wilkinson in 1863 for $10,000, payable on an installment basis in Confederate money. Wilkinson made the payments, but Hale refused to execute a deed; Hale claimed the price was inadequate since the currency was worthless after the defeat of the Confederacy. The court, in holding for Wilkinson, cited the rule that inadequacy of consideration is no defense in the absence of fraud.

3. **Parol Evidence Rule.** The parol evidence rule provides that if the parties have put their contract in writing and intend the writing to be their final agreement, evidence of prior or contemporaneous agreements reached during negotiations may not be used in court to vary or contradict the written agreement. For instance, in Mitchell v. Lath,[8] the Laths, in negotiating the sale of their farm to Mrs. Mitchell, promised to remove a nearby ice house which Mrs. Mitchell found objectionable. Relying on their promise, Mrs. Mitchell signed a written contract to purchase the farm for $8,400. However, the final contract did not include the Laths' promise to remove the ice house and, when the Laths later refused to remove the ice house, the court held that the Laths would not be held to their promise. According to the court, the promise to move the ice house did not constitute a sep-

---

6. Hargrave v. Heard Inv. Co., 56 Ariz. 77, 105 P.2d 520 (1940).

7. 62 Va. (21 Grat.) 75 (1871).

8. 247 N.Y. 377, 160 N.E. 646 (1928).

arate contract but was merely part of the principal real estate transaction. And the real estate contract represented the final agreement describing the rights and duties of the parties. In the words of the court, "an inspection of this contract shows a full and complete agreement, setting forth in detail the obligations of each party. On reading it one would conclude that the reciprocal obligations of the parties were fully detailed."

The practical implications of the parol evidence rule are obvious: when you put your agreement in writing, include all the terms in the agreement, remembering that side agreements not in writing may not be proven in court.

## II. ADDITIONAL CONTRACT PROVISIONS

In discussing the Statute of Frauds, we noted the provisions that must be included in the writing. Additional provisions, although not required by law, should be negotiated and included in the writing in order to avoid harsh results for either the seller or the buyer. We will begin by considering two important real estate concepts: marketable title and equitable conversion.

## A. MARKETABLE TITLE

The term marketable title is synonymous with good, clear or perfect title. In Siedel v. Snider,[9] the court noted that "such a title is one that can again be sold to a reasonable purchaser, a title that a man of reasonable prudence, familiar with the facts and apprized of the questions of law involved, would in the ordinary course of business accept."

The general rule is that if the contract is silent, the law presumes the vendor is to convey a marketable title clear of restrictions. Since the law assumes marketable title, why should the parties state otherwise in their contract? To illustrate the reasons for making specific reference to marketable title, let us examine three common types of problems.

1. **Easements and Restrictive Covenants.** Most real estate is subject to easements (see Chapter 4) and/or restrictive covenants (see Chapter 13) and these make the title unmarketable. Consequently, if the seller promises to convey marketable title, he will be unable to perform the contract if a utility company has a recorded easement running through the center of the property. To avoid this result, the agreement should state that the property is "subject to easements and restrictions of record."

While this language solves the seller's problem—the buyer having agreed to purchase the property subject to the recorded utility

9. 241 Iowa 1227, 44 N.W.2d 687 (1950).

easement—the language might cause problems for the buyer. Most buyers sign real estate contracts without first examining the public records to determine what easements are on record. This is a dangerous practice. If the buyer does not check records or require the seller to list the easements to which the sale is subject, he runs the risk that there might be easements crossing the property that make the real estate unusable.

2. **Zoning and Building Code Restrictions.** In most cases, real estate is subject to both zoning and building code restrictions. For instance, Ralph agrees in writing to sell a parcel of real estate to Waldo, who wants to build a restaurant on the property. After the contract is signed, Waldo learns that the property is zoned for residential use only; furthermore, he could not build the restaurant he had planned anyway because of building code restrictions. May Waldo back out of the contract by claiming that the title is unmarketable? According to the general rule, such restrictions do not make the title unmarketable. The buyer must either determine the nature of such restrictions before signing the purchase agreement or make the contract contingent on the approval of the appropriate local government agency. However, if the seller is using the property in violation of zoning or building ordinances, this use does make the title unmarketable and the buyer could back out of the contract.

3. **Mortgages and Other Liens.** Let us assume that when Ralph signed the contract to sell his real estate to Waldo, the real estate was subject to a mortgage that Ralph had taken out, or to another type of lien such as a tax lien or mechanic's lien. May Waldo avoid the contract because of the lien, even if Ralph promises he will pay off the lien at the closing when Waldo pays for the property? In many states, the title will still be considered marketable if the mortgagee or lienholder is ready and willing to release the lien after receiving payment at the closing.

In other states, a lien on the property makes the title unmarketable unless there is an agreement to the contrary. In Johnson v. Malone,[10] Johnson agreed to purchase property from the Tuckers, and he paid 20 percent of the purchase price as earnest money. Under the terms of the sale, if Johnson defaulted, he would forfeit the earnest money unless the title was proven to be unmarketable. Johnson later refused to perform the contract because the property was subject to a $19,100 mortgage to C. E. Poole, and Johnson sued to recover his earnest money. The Tuckers claimed that the title was marketable because the purchase money would be used to satisfy the Poole mortgage. The court decided in favor of Johnson, citing the rule "that to comply with the contract to furnish a marketable title and an abstract exemplifying the same, as a condition precedent to the

---

10.   252 Ala. 609, 42 So.2d 505 (1949).

vendee paying the purchase price, time being of the essence, the vendor must furnish a title free from encumbrances . . . by the date set for closing." The court concluded that this was not a harsh rule, since the contract could have declared that title would be marketable despite the mortgage if the buyer received evidence the lien had been cleared at the time of closing.

4. **Marketable Title Acts.** Given the usual requirement that the seller must provide marketable title, a purchaser, aided by a knowledgeable attorney, can easily claim that a title is unmarketable. We might assume that the property Ralph is selling Waldo was originally granted by President John Quincy Adams to a pioneer family in 1825, and that the property had changed hands fifteen t'mes between 1825 and 1975, when Ralph acquired it. If Waldo wanted to avoid the contract, his attorney would "flyspeck" the title. That is, the attorney would examine each of the fifteen conveyances closely to determine whether something might make the title unmarketable. He might discover, for example, that the wife of a previous grantor had not signed the deed, that an agent signed the deed for a vendor but no written authorization was recorded, or that an executor of the estate of a deceased party sold the property but that there was no proof on record that he had authority to make the sale.

To alleviate the problem of proving marketable title in these circumstances, especially when the alleged defect occurred so many years ago that it is difficult for the seller to correct or disprove it, many states have enacted Marketable Record Title Acts. If there are no defects in the title over a certain time span (usually the preceding forty-year period), the Marketable Record Title Acts consider the title marketable. Each act contains certain exceptions, such as the rights of persons who are in hostile possession of the real estate, easements which are clearly observable by examining the property, and rights of the state. While it allows for such exceptions, the act simplifies and facilitates clearing titles by allowing purchasers to rely on the record title for the forty-year period.

5. **When Marketable.** The seller must provide marketable title at the time of closing rather than on the date the contract is signed. Most contracts specify that the seller must pay for and provide evidence of title, usually in the form of an abstract of title or title insurance policy. If the contract is silent, the buyer must secure his own evidence of title.

If, at the closing, the seller cannot provide marketable title but the purchaser decides to complete the transaction anyway, the purchaser loses his right to object thereafter to the conditions which make the property unmarketable. In such a case it is said that the contract is merged with the deed, with the result that the rights of the parties will be defined after the closing by the deed rather than by the contract.

There is an important exception to the merger rule, illustrated by Lipson v. Southgate Park Corp.[11] The plaintiff entered into a contract with the defendant on October 3, 1957, under which the defendant was to transfer a parcel of land and to construct a house in accordance with detailed plans and specifications. On January 20, 1958, after the house was built, the plaintiff paid the purchase price and the defendant delivered a deed to the land. The plaintiff later sued the defendant for damages, claiming that the building was erected in an unskillful manner, the plans and specifications were not followed and that the wrong building materials were used. The defendant conceded that the plaintiff was correct but claimed that the plaintiff could not collect because of the merger rule. The court cited the general rule and the exception from an earlier case: "In Pybus v. Grasso, we stated the rule to be that: 'The acceptance of a deed of conveyance of land from one who has previously contracted to sell it, discharges the contractual duties of the seller to the party so accepting except such as are embodied in the deed  . . . .' We went on, however, to say that: 'To the general rule as stated above there is an exception to the effect that promises in the original agreement which are additional or collateral to the main promise to convey the land and are not inconsistent with the deed as given are not necessarily merged in the deed, but may survive it and be enforced after the deed is given.' "

Applying the rule here, the court decided that the promise to construct the house was collateral to the promise to convey the land and consequently survived the deed: "A provision in a contract as to title and possession will usually be merged in an accepted deed. However, the provisions imposing an obligation upon the defendant to erect a dwelling were so far collateral to the undertaking relating to title and possession, as to indicate that the omission of these provisions from the deed was without an intent to preclude their survival."

## B.  EQUITABLE CONVERSION

The doctrine of equitable conversion developed from a principle of equity, "That which ought to be done is regarded as done." Once a real estate contract is signed, what "ought to be done" is that the purchaser should acquire the real estate and the seller should receive the purchase price. Equity regards this "as done" by theoretically converting the seller's interest in the purchase price into personal property, even though the seller retains legal title to the real property, which serves as security before the purchase price is paid. The purchaser's interest is theoretically converted into real property.

There are several consequences of treating the seller's interest as personal property and the buyer's interest as real property for the interval between signing the contract and the closing. For example, if

11.  345 Mass. 621, 189 N.E.2d 191 (1963).

the seller dies before the closing, the purchase price will pass to the representative of his estate as personal property while if the buyer dies, his interest will pass to his heirs as real property. Another consequence is that increases in the land's value go to the buyer but, as a corollary, the buyer also bears losses that result from natural causes or the acts of third parties. Let us suppose that on May 15, 1980, Ralph entered into a written agreement to sell his $100,000 house to Waldo and that the closing was scheduled for June 15, 1980. On June 1, the house was struck by lightning and burned to the ground. Under the equitable conversion rule just cited, the loss would fall on Waldo, and he would have to pay $100,000 to Ralph for the charred remains of the house.

In many cases this is a harsh rule because most buyers do not purchase property insurance until the closing, thinking that they are not the legal owners until that date. To avoid this result, a number of states have enacted the Uniform Vendor and Purchaser Risk Act, which provides that unless the contract specifies otherwise, the risk of loss shall remain with the vendor unless legal title or possession has been transferred to the purchaser or unless the purchaser causes the loss. Whether or not a state has enacted the Uniform Risk Act, it is recommended that the contract specify who is to bear the risk of loss, so that the person may acquire appropriate insurance coverage.

## C. MISCELLANEOUS CONTRACT PROVISIONS

In addition to the problems related to marketable title and equitable conversion, other matters should be negotiated by the parties and included in the purchase agreement.

1. **Earnest Money.** The vendor usually has substantial expenses after the contract is signed and before closing, including the cost of proving title and paying the broker's commission—even when the buyer refuses to perform the contract. For protection from the buyer's default, the vendor should require the buyer to make a down payment of earnest money when the contract is signed that is large enough to cover expenses.

The buyer should keep in mind that the earnest money will be forfeited if he breaches the contract. In Ottenstein v. Western Reserve Academy,[12] Ottenstein entered into a contract to purchase ten lots in Hudson, Ohio, from Western Reserve Academy for approximately $185,340. The plaintiff paid $5,000 in earnest money when the contract was signed, but he never paid the balance. Finally the Academy sold the lots to another party and the plaintiff brought suit to recover the earnest money. The court, in following the majority

12.  54 Ohio App.2d 1, 374 N.E.2d 427, 8 O.O.3d 22 (1977).

rule, declared that the earnest money is forfeited even when the contract does not mention forfeiture.

2. **Fixtures.** As discussed in Chapter 2, the contract should specify which fixtures, if any, will be retained by the seller.

3. **Contingencies.** Performance of a real estate contract is commonly made contingent on the happening of a certain event, such as a change in the zoning law, the sale of the buyer's present house, or the buyer's obtaining a loan at a specified interest rate. Contingencies are placed in the contract for the protection of one of the parties, but that party may choose to waive the contingency. For instance, the contract could be made subject to the buyer's obtaining a loan at an interest rate of below 9 percent; yet if he cannot obtain a loan for less than 9½ percent, he may waive the condition and hold the seller to the contract.

Contingencies are especially important in construction contracts. When these contingencies are explicit, they will be enforced as agreed on by the parties. Thus, if an owner hires an architect to prepare plans for a new home but the plans are "subject to the owner's satisfaction," the architect will not be paid if the owner is honestly dissatisfied. The condition has not been met. In many construction contracts, certain conditions are implied. The most important of these relates to the owner's duty to pay the contractor. It is implied that this duty is conditional on the contractor's completing the structure exactly as promised. If the contractor does not complete his part of the agreement, the condition has not been met and the owner does not have to pay.

This implied condition would often lead to an unfair result if it were applied strictly by the court. For example, Ethel hired a contractor, Fred, to build a $100,000 house. After Fred completed the house, Ethel discovered that the bathroom tile was the wrong color and refused to pay Fred anything since he had not met the condition of completing the building as promised. Most courts, realizing that this result would be unfair to Fred, would apply the "substantial performance" doctrine. Under this rule, if Fred has substantially performed the contract, which is a question of fact that must be determined on a case-by-case basis, he is entitled to his payment minus deductions to compensate Ethel for his failure to perform the contract exactly. In this case, assuming that Fred's performance was considered to be substantial, Fred would be entitled to $100,000 less the cost of replacing the tile. If Fred's performance was not considered substantial enough, for example if he used the wrong set of plans in building the house, he would receive nothing. In some states, however, if Ethel lived in or otherwise used a house that had not been substantially completed as promised, she would enjoy an unjust windfall unless Fred received payment equivalent to the value of the house.

4. **Easements.** If the seller grants ar easement to the buyer or if he reserves an easement for himself, this should be spelled out in the contract.

5. **Time for Performance.** Bonnie signed a purchase agreement on May 5, offering to buy Clyde's house for $50,000. She heard nothing from Clyde, so on May 25 she signed a contract to purchase a house from Sam. On May 26, she received Clyde's acceptance of her offer in the mail. Is she liable on both contracts?

The answer to this surprisingly common dilemma depends on whether or not the court feels a reasonable time passed between the time Bonnie made her offer and the time Clyde accepted it. If a reasonably long time has passed, then the offer would be considered cancelled. To avoid this problem, a buyer signing a purchase agreement should state in the offer that the seller's acceptance must be received within a certain period, for example, five days. This provision forces sellers like Clyde to act promptly; it also avoids claims that the seller accepted under the mail box rule in cases where the agreement did not arrive until several days later.

Several other time provisions should be inserted into the agreement to avoid unnecessary delay by one of the parties. Each of these provisions should state that "time is of the essence," which means that a party who fails to meet a time deadline is in breach of contract. Times should be established for the following: (1) the seller's delivery of the evidence of title; (2) the buyer's review of the evidence of title; (3) correction of title defects by the seller; (4) closing date; and (5) possession by the buyer.

Although these times should be included in the contract, the contract is still enforceable without them. In Buehring v. Hudson,[13] Hudson entered into a written contract to sell his house to Buehring. Hudson later sold the house to other persons and, when sued by Buehring, he claimed the contract was unenforceable because the date for closing was not stated. The court, in holding for Buehring, concluded that "The fact that the contract of sale fixed no time for its performance did not evidence that the minds of the parties had not met with respect to an essential element of the contract. When a contract of sale fixes no time for performance, the law allows a reasonable time. In other words, if the parties do not agree upon the time, an agreement for performance within a reasonable time will be implied."

6. **Proration.** Ordinarily, the vendor in a real estate transaction has made certain advance payments for taxes, insurance, fuel oil, and other expenses of home ownership. The buyer will benefit from these advance payments unless the contract provides that the payments are to be prorated; that is, the buyer is to reimburse the ven-

---

13.  219 S.W.2d 810 (Tex.Civ.App.1949).

dor for advance payments which cover any period of time after the buyer takes possession.  If the contract does not contain a proration provision, a court will not force proration, although some states have statutes that require proration of taxes in the absence of a contrary agreement.

7.  **Type of Deed and Estate.**  Unless the contract states otherwise, the vendor must transfer to the vendee a fee simple estate, but he is only required to give a quitclaim deed.  Consequently, for reasons to be discussed in Chapter 10, the contract should state that the vendor is to deliver a warranty deed.

## D.  WARRANTIES

Cicero recently purchased his first house.  Within one year after moving in, sewage from the septic tank backed three inches deep into his basement.  The smell eventually became so bad that the septic tank system, which had been negligently designed, had to be rebuilt at a cost of some $2,000.  Can Cicero recover this amount from the vendor?  The decision will differ depending on which of four possible factual variations applies to the case.

1.  **Express Warranties.**  The first question to be examined is, did the vendor expressly promise or warrant the condition of the septic tank system?  In addition to a warranty given directly by the vendor, warranty insurance arrangements have developed in recent years.  For instance, many purchasers of new homes and condominiums are now covered by the Home Owners Warranty (HOW) plan developed by the National Association of Home Builders.  Under this plan, based on a British home warranty insurance program that began in 1936, a buyer is covered for defects in plumbing, cooling, heating, and electrical systems for two years and for major structural defects for ten years.  The coverage extends to anyone who purchases the home within the ten-year period.  Buyers of used homes may also acquire warranty coverage from private companies.  In Cicero's case, if an express warranty exists on the new or used home, the seller or insurer would be obligated to pay the cost of repairing the septic tank system.  In the remaining three examples, we shall assume that no express warranties have been given.

2.  **Contract with Builder.**  If Cicero had contracted with a builder who was to build the house according to certain specifications, it is implied, even when the contract is silent, that the builder gives Cicero warranties that the job will be completed in a workmanlike manner and that the house will be habitable.  The defective septic system represents a breach of these warranties for which the builder would be liable.

3.  **Purchase of New Home.**  If, instead of hiring a builder to build the house, Cicero purchased a home that the contractor had

just completed, should the result be different from the above example? The traditional approach, based on *caveat emptor* or "let the buyer beware," has been that no implied warranties should pass with the sale of an existing new home. The rationale for this approach, still followed in many states, is that in purchasing a completed house the buyer has a chance to inspect the builder's work before entering into the contract.

However, in recent years most courts have become critical of this rationale. The typical buyer is not a professional, like the seller-builder, and is not able to spot defects. Furthermore many defects do not become apparent until the house settles and is used for two or three years. The modern trend, therefore, is to give the person who purchases a new, completed home from a builder implied warranties that the house is habitable and that the builder has completed the house in a workmanlike manner. The facts in Cicero's case are based on Tavares v. Horstman,[14] in which the Wyoming court adopted the modern approach in deciding that the vendor-builder breached an implied warranty in designing and constructing the septic system. The rationale for this decision, as stated by another court,[15] is that "The old rule of caveat emptor does not satisfy the demands of justice in such cases. The purchase of a home is not an everyday transaction for the average family, and is in many instances the most important transaction of a lifetime. To apply the rule of caveat emptor to an inexperienced buyer, and in favor of the builder who is daily engaged in the business of building and selling houses, is manifestly a denial of justice."

The *Tavares* approach is still relatively new and represents a radical departure from *caveat emptor*. Most courts following this approach have decided that the implied warranties pass only from a builder-vendor to the first purchaser of the home, who has dealt directly or is in "privity of contract" with the builder. See House v. Thornton, infra. However, there are indications that the rule requiring privity of contract is being abandoned, and that the warranties will be extended to a later purchaser who is the first occupant of the house. For example, in Utz v. Moss,[16] the court held that when a builder constructed a house for a realtor, the builder's implied warranties passed to a person who purchased the house from the realtor and was the first occupant.

4. **Purchase of Used Home.** In the sale of a used home, the traditional *caveat emptor* rule still applies and no warranties are implied. Thus, if Cicero had purchased a used home, he would have to bear the cost of rebuilding the defective septic tank system.

---

14.  542 P.2d 1275 (Wyo.1976).

15.  Padula v. J. J. Deb-Cin Homes, Inc., 111 R.I. 29, 298 A.2d 529 (1973).

16.  31 Colo.App. 475, 503 P.2d 365 (1972).

However, a 1976 Indiana case, Barnes v. Mac Brown & Co., Inc.,[17] is a logical extension of a case such as *Utz* and may well represent the beginning of a new trend. In the late 1960s, Mac Brown built and sold a house to the Shipmans, who resold the house to Barnes in 1971. Barnes later discovered that the basement walls were cracked and the basement leaked. The Indiana Supreme Court decided that implied warranties could pass from the builder to Barnes as the purchaser of the used house. "The logic which compelled this change in the law of personal property is equally persuasive in the area of real property. Our society is an increasingly mobile one. Our technology is increasingly complex. The traditional requirement of privity between a builder-vendor and a purchaser is an outmoded one."

5. **Builder's Tort Liability.** In addition to the warranty liability for structural defects discussed above, a contractor will also be liable when the purchaser or a third person is injured by a defect which was a hidden, dangerous condition known to the builder, or by a defect resulting from the builder's negligence.[18]

In a few states, builders have also been held liable under a strict liability theory, which declares a seller in the business of selling products is liable for damages resulting from the sale of an unreasonably dangerous, defective product. This development is especially significant because a builder may be held liable even though he "has exercised all possible care in the preparation and sale of his product," according to Section 402A of the Second Restatement of Torts. Furthermore, privity is not an issue under the strict liability rule; Section 402A applies the rule even when the user or consumer has not contracted with the seller.

As an illustration of the strict liability principle, in Schipper v. Levitt & Sons, Inc.,[19] the defendant builder was a well-known, mass-developer of houses including houses in Willingboro (Levittown), New Jersey. One of the houses was sold to the Kreitzers, who were advised in a Homeowner's Guide that "you will find the hot water in your Levittown house much hotter than that to which you are accustomed." The Kreitzers were burned on several occasions by the hot water and complained to Levitt, but nothing was done. Later the Kreitzers leased the house to Schipper, who noticed that the water was extremely hot and warned his wife and children to be careful until he could discover how to regulate it. Shortly thereafter, Schipper's sixteen-month-old son was scalded by hot water from a bathroom sink. The son was hospitalized four times, including one stay of seventy-four days, and had to undergo two skin grafting operations. The court decided that even though there was no privity of

17.  264 Ind. 227, 342 N.E.2d 619 (1976).     19.  44 N.J. 70, 207 A.2d 314 (1965).

18.  W. Prosser, Law of Torts § 104, at
     681 (4th ed. 1971).

contract between Schipper and Levitt, Levitt should be liable for the injuries under the strict liability principle if the hot water system was proven to be unreasonably dangerous.

In remanding the case for further trial, the court observed: "The law should be based on current concepts of what is right and just and the judiciary should be alert to the never-ending need for keeping its common law principles abreast of the times. Ancient distinctions which make no sense in today's society and tend to discredit the law should be readily rejected as they were step by step in *Henningsen* and *Santor*. We consider that there are no meaningful distinctions between Levitt's mass production and sale of homes and the mass production and sales of automobiles and that the pertinent overriding policy considerations are the same. That being so, the warranty or strict liability principles of *Henningsen* and *Santor* should be carried over into the realty field, at least in the aspect dealt with here. Incidentally, recent reference to the sweep of Levitt's mass production approach may be found in the July 1963 issue of American Builder, at pages 42–45 where the president of Levitt, in response to an inquiry as to whether its policy of 'no changes' would be applied in the building of its more expensive homes at Long Island, had this to say: 'We intend to hold to our mass production approach in Long Island. People buy Cadillacs, don't they, and they're mass produced.' "

The strict liability rule is not limited to mass producers of homes nor to personal injury actions. In Patitucci v. Drelich,[20] the defendant builder constructed and sold the plaintiffs a four-bedroom house. Shortly after the plaintiffs and their six children moved into the house, the sewage system overflowed, damaging the house and their personal property. When the plaintiffs brought suit under a strict liability theory, the court refused to dismiss the case, noting that strict liability applies to any builder, regardless of the size of the business, and further noting that the home was in a defective, dangerous condition.

## III.   AVOIDING THE CONTRACT

In the following situations, courts may allow a person to avoid performance of a real estate contract.

## A.   MISTAKE

If one party to a contract makes a mistake, for example by offering to sell a farm for $790 per acre instead of an intended $970 per acre, that party cannot use the mistake as an excuse for refusing to perform the contract. The law applies an objective standard: a par-

---

20.   153 N.J.Super. 177, 379 A.2d 297 (1977).

ty will be held to his expressed agreement regardless of what he was thinking. However, mutual mistake, a mistake by both parties, will be grounds for avoiding the contract.

In Berard v. Dolan,[21] the plaintiff entered into a written contract to purchase the defendant's store. The defendant told the plaintiff that the property was subject to a $6,000 mortgage that could be assumed by the plaintiff, and the plaintiff indicated that he would have to assume the mortgage in order to finance the purchase. After the contract was signed, the parties discovered that the mortgage in fact covered other property as well as the store and the plaintiff could not assume the mortgage by purchasing the store alone. Because of this mutual mistake, the plaintiff was allowed to avoid the contract and recover his down payment. But the court also noted that, if only the plaintiff had been mistaken, there could be no rescission. "The defendant testified that when he talked with the plaintiff about the sale of the property and the subject of mortgages he knew that the only mortgage on it also covered other property. If the jury believed this statement there was no mutual mistake and they were required under the charge of the court to return a verdict for the defendant. Their verdict shows that they did not believe this testimony but found that the defendant was mistaken as to what property was covered by the mortgage and mistakenly believed before the payment was made that only the store property was covered."

## B.  MINORITY

It is the policy in most states to protect minors by allowing them to avoid liability under contracts to sell real estate within a reasonable time after reaching the age of majority, which in most states is eighteen. In Spencer v. Lyman Falls Power Co.,[22] the plaintiff sold his real estate on November 30, 1918 and did not reach the age of majority until April 5, 1919. The property was later resold and the new purchaser made improvements on the property totaling $93,000. On September 8, 1936, the plaintiff filed suit, claiming that he wished to avoid the contract. The court noted that courts disagree about how long a time the minor has to disaffirm a contract after he reaches the age of majority. In a few states, the minor may disaffirm the contract any time after becoming an adult unless he has ratified the contract. This court, however, adopted the majority rule that the minor must disaffirm the contract within a reasonable time after reaching the age of majority. The court held that the minor here could not disaffirm the contract because seventeen years was well beyond a reasonable time. The court also noted that the minor would be held to the contract even under the other approach, because, in standing by and allowing the purchaser to make large expenditures, his ratification would be implied.

21.  118 Vt. 116, 100 A.2d 581 (1953).　　22.  109 Vt. 294, 196 A. 276 (1938).

## C.  DURESS

If a person enters into a contract as the result of wrongful force or a threat that prevents his exercise of free will, he may avoid the contract.  To determine whether a person was placed in such fear that he was acting against his free will, the courts apply a subjective test.  For instance, in a Missouri case, a son-in-law threatened to make it "hotter than hell" for his deceased wife's parents until they deeded certain real estate to him.  The parents were suffering from typhoid fever at the time, and they thought he was threatening to burn down their house with them in it.  Applying the subjective test, a court cancelled the deed.[23]

## D.  UNDUE INFLUENCE

If one person, in a dominant position, persuades another person to sell real estate or enter into any other contract under circumstances in which it appears the second party was not acting of his own free will, the contract may be avoided.  For example, a seventy-six-year-old patient who was an alcoholic, chronically ill, and in great pain, signed a contract to sell valuable real estate to his physician, who had been treating him at least once daily.  Under the contract, the physician was given the right to purchase 20 acres, with a market value of $1,200 an acre, in exchange for $4,000 and a new Cadillac.  When the physician later brought suit to enforce the contract, the court denied him recovery, noting that on the basis of the inadequacy of the purchase price and the confidential relationship between the parties, there was a presumption that the physician had taken advantage of the patient.[24]

## E.  FRAUD

Fraud is the most common claim raised by the purchaser of real estate.  Often the vendor, either directly or through a broker,[25] makes exaggerated claims about the property.  An examination of real estate advertisements in any newspaper will offer ready illustrations: "Victorian house updated for 20th century living," "immaculate house—the best value in town," or "mechanically fit, on a quiet court."

23.  See L. Smith & G. Roberson, Business Law 86 (3rd ed. 1971).

24.  Hodge v. Shea, 252 S.C. 601, 168 S.E.2d 82 (1969).

25.  In most real estate transactions, the broker is a special agent hired to find a purchaser and with no authority to make statements on behalf of the vendors.  Consequently, the vendor will not be liable for the statements of the agent unless the statements were specifically authorized.  However, the vendee will be allowed to rescind a transaction resulting from a misrepresentation because the vendor will not be allowed to retain the proceeds of a fraud committed for his benefit.  W. Seavey, Law of Agency § 28 at 50, § 92 at 164 (1964).

Courts face the problem of distinguishing between mere sales talk, to be regarded with skepticism by the purchaser, and fraudulent statements, entitling the purchaser to avoid the contract. Fraud is defined as the false representation of a material fact which is relied on by the other party to the contract. Many cases turn on whether a statement was one of fact or opinion. In Cannaday v. Cossey,[26] the Cannadays purchased a house from Cossey who, during the negotiation, told them it was a "good house." Cossey also told the Cannadays that he had seen flying ants around the premises for about forty years. After moving in, the Cannadays discovered that the house was seriously damaged by termites. The court refused to allow rescission, finding that Cossey was unaware of the termites and his statement that the house was in "good condition" was a statement of opinion. "A general statement of this kind amounts only to an expression of opinion and cannot be relied on by the purchaser as an assurance against the various defects that are apt to be found in a twenty-eight-year-old dwelling."

Even when a party deliberately lies about a material fact, most courts will not allow the other party to avoid the contract if the fact could have been verified. For example, if the seller deliberately lies in telling the purchaser that the taxes on the property are $1,500 a year when in fact they are $2,500 a year, the purchaser will not be allowed to back out of the contract on the basis of fraud, because the actual amount of tax could easily have been checked by calling the local taxing authority. The same principle holds true when the seller makes a statement of law such as, "Under the zoning law covering this property, you can build a racquetball club." Every person is presumed to know the law, and the purchaser can make his own investigation to determine if, in fact, the zoning laws allow such use. In recent years, however, there is a trend to protect the innocent party by avoiding application of these rules when possible. See Bobak v. Mackey, infra.

Perhaps the toughest question is, Can fraud be proven when the seller is silent? Many courts have concluded that fraud exists, even in the absence of a statement, in order to prevent an unfair or harsh result. In several of these cases, however, the seller has done or said something that is very close to a false representation of fact. For instance, if the plumbing in a house is in bad condition and the seller paints over water stains caused by leakage, this concealment has been considered equal to a false representation. Also, statements by the seller that are true as stated but that require clarification have been treated as fraudulent. See Ikeda v. Curtis, infra.

In other cases, however, courts have decided that fraud exists when the property contains a serious hidden defect, even if no con-

26.   228 Ark. 1119, 312 S.W.2d 442 (1958).

cealment or misleading statements were made. In Obde v. Schlemeyer,[27] Schlemeyer sold an apartment house to Obde that he knew was infested with termites. The court, in allowing Obde to recover damages for fraudulent representation, decided that in such cases the vendor has a duty to inform the vendee of the termites. The court indicated that such a duty exists when the vendor knows of concealed defects that are dangerous to the property, health, or life of the purchaser.

Finally, whether the fraud is based on an actual statement or on silence, the innocent party may forfeit a remedy if he does not take prompt action. In Morse v. Kogle,[28] the Morses relied upon alleged misrepresentations of the vendor in entering into a contract to purchase a residence on March 21, 1946. On March 25, the Morses told a real estate agent of the misrepresentation but, because they saw "no use having any arguments about it," asked him to resell the property. The property was not resold, and on April 18 the Morses brought suit, claiming rescission on the basis of fraud. The court refused to allow rescission because, in offering the house for resale, the Morses had acted as if they were the owners and therefore had ratified the contract. The court cited the following rule from an earlier case: "If, after discovery or knowledge of facts which would entitle a party to rescind, he treats the contract as a subsisting obligation and leads the other party to believe that the contract is still in effect, he will have waived his right to rescind. Prompt action is essential when one believes himself entitled to such relief." Although not discussed in the *Morse* case, it is still possible for a party who has ratified the contract to recover damages resulting from the fraud.

## IV.  NEW TRENDS

To perceive new trends in real estate law, it is often instructive to examine the law relating to the sale of goods, embodied in the Uniform Commercial Code. For example, the recent trend to abolish the privity requirement in real estate warranty cases originated in cases involving the sale of goods. In the Uniform Land Transactions Act now being developed by the National Conference of Commissioners on Uniform State Laws, there are a number of provisions which are derived from the Code. Among these provisions are (1) a section that defines the defense of unconscionability; (2) a statute of frauds provision that allows oral real estate contracts to be enforced in certain instances—for example, when a party admits the contract in court; and (3) limitations on the seller's ability to disclaim warranties.

27.  52 Wash.2d 449, 353 P.2d 672 (1960).  28.  162 Kan. 558, 178 P.2d 275 (1947).

# CASES

### PRAVORNE v. McLEOD

Supreme Court of Nevada, 1963.
79 Nev. 341, 383 P.2d 855.

BADT, Chief Justice

The question here involved for determination is whether the instrument herein referred to as a contract of purchase and sale was a completed contract, or whether it was merely an offer made by the McLeods to Pravorne to enter into a contract, which offer was rejected by Pravorne and a counteroffer made by him, which in turn was not accepted by the McLeods.

\*   \*   \*

The parties had been negotiating with respect to a proposed purchase of real property by Pravorne from McLeod. Pravorne had the Nevada Title Insurance Company prepare escrow instructions. They were mailed to McLeod but were unsatisfactory to him, so he had his attorney draft a complete new contract entitled "Agreement for Sale of Realty," which in turn contained escrow instructions. McLeod then mailed this agreement to Pravorne's real estate broker, with a letter addressed to the broker and signed by McLeod, reading as follows:

"Dear Mr. Bell:

"Upon reviewing your Escrow Instructions which were prepared by Nevada Title Insurance Company, I took them to my attorney, Mead Dixon, for his approval.

"Obviously, we decided to prepare our own Agreement of Sale and I am sending it for the examination and approval of your buyer. There is no change in any of the conditions of our telephone agreement, but merely that the conditions are set forth more clearly.

"I am sending two copies of this Agreement to Nevada Title Insurance Company. If the Agreement is acceptable to your buyer, please have him sign and return two copies as soon as possible. We will then sign one and return it to Nevada Title Company immediately.

"If these papers are in order and acceptable to your buyer, we are going to be very anxious to close this matter as soon as possible.

"Sincerely yours,
"Wayne McLeod

"cc: Nevada Title Insurance Company

"118 South Fourth Street

"Las Vegas, Nevada

"ATTENTION: Evelyn Wilson"

Two unsigned copies of the agreement were enclosed.   *   *   *
*   *   *

Pravorne signed the contract of purchase and sale in duplicate and delivered the copies to the title insurance company.  The title insurance company mailed the signed agreement to McLeod, but stapled to the agreement were three sheets of paper.  For the most part these comprised the regular printed form used by the escrow holder, listing some 20 items concerning escrow instruments with a space to be filled by a checkmark if any of these items were required.  On the first page there was typed the following: "Mr. Gordon Bell asked us to prepare an amendment pertaining to Release clause on the deed of trust to be submitted for your approval and signature."   *   *   *
*   *   *

The case turns upon the question whether the title company's return to the sellers of the signed contract, accompanied by the notation that Mr. Bell, the buyer's broker, asked the title company to prepare an amendment relating to the release clause "on the deed of trust to be submitted for your approval and signature" constituted a conditional acceptance, in effect, a rejection of the offer and the submission of a counteroffer; or whether the signing and returning of the contract was an unconditional acceptance, resulting in a binding contract between the parties, with a request for an amendment by the insertion of the release clauses in the deed of trust being merely a request for an additional provision for the convenience of the buyer, if approved by the seller, the buyer's acceptance of the signed contract not being dependent thereon.

"An acceptance which requests a change or addition to the terms of the offer is not thereby invalidated unless the acceptance is made to depend on an assent to the changed or added terms."  Restatement, Contracts § 62.

In Foster v. West Pub. Co., 77 Okl. 114, 186 P. 1083, 1084, the court said: "In the case of Bleecker v. Miller et al., 40 Okl. 374, 138 P. 809, the acceptance was held to be absolute and unqualified, notwithstanding the accepting party objected to certain provisions of the offer and expressed the opinion that the offerer should not ask such conditions.  This objection and request was held to be no part of the contract but a favor asked of the seller, to be granted or withheld at his option, and in no way invalidating the acceptance.  In the case of

Kaw City Mill & Ele. Co. v. Purcell Mill & Ele. Co., 19 Okl. 357, 91 P. 1022, it was said:

> " 'An offer of sale of personal property and its acceptance must receive a reasonable construction, and the proposer is bound by its acceptance in that sense. Immaterial variances between the offer and its acceptance will be disregarded.' " It further quoted with approval 6 R.C.L. 609, as follows: " 'From the rule that the acceptance must be unconditional it must not be inferred that the mere mention in a letter of acceptance of matters upon which the acceptance of the proposition does not depend prevents the contract from being completed. There is authority to the effect that, though an acceptance which introduces a new term as part of the proposed contract is insufficient, the mere addition to the acceptance of a collateral or immaterial requisition not warranted by the terms of the offer does not prevent the contract from being completed. Although a request for a change or modification of a proposed contract made before an acceptance thereof amounts to a rejection of it, a mere inquiry as to whether one proposing a contract will alter or modify its terms, made before acceptance or rejection does not amount to a rejection. * * * ' "

For additional authorities see 1 Williston, Contracts § 79, and cases cited therein.

We are of the opinion that when appellant signed and returned the agreement he made an unconditional acceptance which was not made to depend upon McLeod's assent to the proposed amendment, which was simply a request for an additional benefit which was not an essential term or condition of his acceptance.

         * * *

Judgment reversed with costs, and remanded with instructions for entry of judgment not inconsistent with the foregoing opinion.

---

### HOUSE v. THORNTON

Supreme Court of Washington, 1969.
76 Wash.2d 428, 457 P.2d 199.

HALE, Judge.

Fraud is so easy to claim that the law makes it hard to prove. When the basement, walls, floors and foundation of a house plaintiffs had bought from defendants slipped and cracked and the supporting terrain slid away from the foundation, plaintiffs brought this suit to rescind the sale. Plaintiffs Homer and Noreen House charged the sellers with overt false misrepresentations and deceit but the court granted the rescission although expressly finding that these allegations were not clearly, cogently and convincingly proved. Defendant sellers appeal, and we perceive the major issue to be whether, in the sale of a brand-new house to its first buyer and occupant, the law impresses the transaction with a warranty that the foundation is firm and secure.

\* \* \*

Homer and Noreen House, plaintiffs, first saw the house in August, 1964. At the time, it was virtually complete and the upstairs was ready for occupancy but some partitions and plasterboard had yet to be installed in the basement. Landscaping was largely uncompleted. Plaintiffs noticed ruts and crevices in the rockery and ditches in the backyard apparently caused by erosion. A few weeks later, in September, 1964, they bought the house and lot 9 plus an adjoining 10 feet on lot 10 for $32,583.38, making a down payment of $12,583.38 and financing the $20,000 balance through a mortgage with the University Federal Savings and Loan Association.

About 3 months later, in December, 1964, following a period of heavy rains, the Houses observed a three-eighths inch crack open up in the earth outside of but running the length of and parallel to the east wall of the house and on into the adjacent lot. Water accumulated in the yard, and Mr. House, on the advice of Mr. Thornton, the builder, dug a trench to drain it. In digging this trench, Mr. House first discovered the existence of the old foundation.

During the following winter, 1965, another crack in the yard opened up and Mr. House dug another trench to drain the water away from it and found that the earth beneath it settled for about 3 inches near the north end of the house. Then the steps and basement wall separated, and the seam between the chimney and house opened so that daylight showed through it into the living room. Earth supporting the end of the concrete patio dropped 4 to 6 inches and the walkway to the patio separated 4 to 5 inches for a distance of 20 feet. Mr. Thornton brought in a machine, cracked up and removed the patio, and discovered that the east wall of the basement had bulged. A crack developed in the basement floor running up into a section of the concrete basement wall. The floor of the basement dropped about 6 inches and another crack opened up in the basement wall.

Nearly all of the doors in the house settled and had to be planed but finally the shifting of the house made the planing futile. Cracks developed in the plasterboard of the kitchen, hallway, stairwell and bedroom. Thornton, the builder, treated the yard soil and rockery with plastic sheeting to reduce moisture content of the subsoil, separated the drain tile from the downspouts, and connected fire hose to lead the water away from the basement.

But the crack in the yard running parallel to the east side of the house widened to 4 to 6 inches and deepened to nearly 3 feet in places. Cracks in the basement walls continued to widen and deepen, and at one place near a basement window a wide, jagged, open crack appeared which would leave doubts that the house was safe for occupancy. Pictures of the place showed long, jagged cracks in the yard, and the earth sluffing away from under the foundation. Cracks appeared in the concrete basement walls which formed part of the foundation. There was little doubt among the parties that, after 23 months of occupancy and continuous efforts to remedy the slipping and cracking, the house was untenable and unfit for further occupancy as a dwelling.

Plaintiffs brought this suit for rescission. The trial court granted a decree rescinding the sale on tender of a deed by plaintiffs to the defendants, awarded plaintiffs judgment in the sum of $11,685.69, and ordered the defendants to hold plaintiffs harmless from any further liability on the mortgage. In allowing plaintiffs rescission and arriving at damages of $11,685.69 for moneys paid in and expended by them, the court deducted from their award a reasonable rental for their occupancy fixed at $200 per month for 39 months, or a total reduction in the judgment of $7,800.

\* \* \*

Although the court found that the defendants were free of fraud and misrepresentation, and there was no proof that the defendants failed to properly design and erect the building, or that they used defective materials or in any respect did an unworkmanlike job, and that they were innocent of any intentional wrong, the fact remains that they sold and turned over to plaintiffs a brand-new $32,000 residence which turned out to be unfit for occupancy. As between vendor and purchaser, the builder-vendors, even though exercising reasonable care to construct a sound building, had by far the better opportunity to examine the stability of the site and to determine the kind of foundation to install. Although hindsight, it is frequently said, is 20–20 and defendants used reasonable prudence in selecting the site and designing and constructing the building, their position throughout the process of selection, planning and construction was markedly superior to that of their first purchaser-occupant. To borrow an idea from equity, of the innocent parties who suffered, it was the builder-vendor who made the harm possible. If there is a comparative standard of innocence, as well as of culpability, the defendants who built and sold the house were less innocent and more culpable than the wholly innocent and unsuspecting buyer. Thus, the old rule of caveat emptor has little relevance to the sale of a brand-new house by a vendor-builder to a first buyer for purposes of occupancy.

We apprehend it to be the rule that, when a vendor-builder sells a new house to its first intended occupant, he impliedly warrants that the foundations supporting it are firm and secure and that the house is structurally safe for the buyer's intended purpose of living in it. Current literature on the subject overwhelmingly supports this idea of an implied warranty of fitness in the sale of new houses.

Other jurisdictions have imposed an implied warranty of fitness upon the vendor-builder of a new house.

Affirmed.

---

## BOBAK v. MACKEY

California Court of Appeal, Second District, 1951.
107 Cal.App.2d 55, 236 P.2d 626.

HANSON, Justice pro tem.

The only question presented by appellant is whether the complaint of the respondent vendee states a cause of action in deceit against appellant as his vendor. The appellant as defendant below did not demur to the complaint nor did he in his answer aver by way of defense that the complaint did not state a cause of action. At the conclusion of the trial upon the issues which had been joined the trial court entered a judgment for damages based upon findings that the defendant had made certain misrepresentations of fact upon which the plaintiff had relied in the purchase of the real estate which gave rise to the lawsuit. The defendant below is here with an appeal based alone on the judgment roll.

The complaint alleged that plaintiff informed the defendant that he was looking for a piece of property suitable for a dwelling and with separate facilities wherein he could also carry on his business of manufacturing and selling a malted food drink powder. It was further alleged that the defendant falsely represented to the plaintiff as matters of fact:

(1) That the plaintiff could lawfully carry on his business of manufacturing and selling a malted food drink powder on said premises,

(2) That said premises were as a matter of fact located in a City of Los Angeles C-2 zone, in which type of zone light manufacturing activities could be lawfully carried on, including the plaintiff's business of manufacturing and selling a malted food drink powder.

And it was alleged:

(3) That said representations were false and fraudulent in that said premises were located in a City of Los Angeles R-3 zone, in which type of zone manufacturing of any sort whatsoever was unlawful.

(4) That the defendant knew that the representations were false, that they were made for the purpose of inducing the plaintiff to purchase the property, and that the plaintiff purchased the property in reliance on said misrepresentations.

Appellant contends that the misrepresentations charged against him in the complaint, which we have briefly summarized above, are at most representations of law and not of fact and hence no cause of action was stated upon which a judgment could legally have been rendered. For reasons presently to be stated we see no merit in the contention.

The complaint alleges that the premises which were the subject of a purchase and sales agreement between the parties were represented to the plaintiff by the defendant as being located within a certain territory of the City of Los Angeles which the City had zoned as C-2 when in fact the premises were located in a territory of the city which had been zoned not as C-2, but as R-3, in which type of zone the plaintiff, as defendant well knew, could not use the premises for the purpose for which alone he purchased them.

Such a statement, if made, and relied upon by the purchaser is as much a representation of fact as would be a statement that the premises involved were within the corporate limits of Los Angeles, when they were not, or that they abutted on a certain named thoroughfare in Los Angeles, when they did not. In each of these examples the facts represented come about by reason of law. But the facts as stated are not for that reason misrepresentations of law, but on the contrary of facts. The same is true here. The territory in which the premises were located was by reason of law classified as being in zone R-3, rather than in zone C-2. For aught that appears the law could have classified the premises as C-2 rather than R-3, but it did not do so.

The representation was not a mere misrepresentation of law, i. e., the classification made by the law, but of the fact that the property lay within a zone of a particular character, i. e., which the law had classified as R-3 rather than C-2. Manifestly, the representation was of a fact and not merely one of law. In the Seeger case the court said with respect to a representation which had been made in that case as follows: "The representation that a levy of execution and sale of the property had occurred was a false statement of fact and is not rendered less actionable because it also contained legal conclusions."

Without detailing further the additional allegations of the complaint, it suffices to say that it stated a cause of action and consequently there is not the slightest merit in the appeal.

The judgment is affirmed.

---

## IKEDA v. CURTIS

Supreme Court of Washington, 1953.
43 Wash.2d 449, 261 P.2d 684.

SCHWELLENBACH, Justice.

This is an appeal from a judgment for damages for fraud in the sale of a hotel property.

George S. Ikeda and his wife are Japanese. He has spent most of his life doing farming and farm labor in Salinas and San Jose, California. They have seven children, five of whom are living with them. They came to Seattle in November, 1950. At first they lived with his brother-in-law, Tom Funamori, who operated the American Hotel in Seattle. Ikeda did janitor work and operated the elevator. In June, 1951, they purchased the Strand Hotel, located at 2212½ First Avenue.

August 26, 1951, Frank Yamashita, a real estate salesman representing the Alberg Realty Company, obtained a fifteen day exclusive listing from Nellie Curtis for the sale of the LaSalle Hotel, located at First and Pike Place Market. The sale price was to be $25,000. The proposed sale included good will, licenses, lease, furniture and equipment. The hotel consisted of fifty-seven rooms, fifty-three of which were rentable. Yamashita contacted the Ikedas, who were interested in the purchase. September 15, 1951, an earnest money receipt was signed by the Ikedas, in which they offered to pay $17,500; $7,500 on the closing of the deal (including $1,000 which they put up as earnest money); and the balance of $10,000 at the rate of $200 per month. Yamashita reported to Mrs. Curtis, who stated that she would have to see her attorney before anything final was done. Yamashita contacted her several times without result, and finally returned the $1,000 to the Ikedas, telling them that the deal was off.

Shortly thereafter, George D. Tucker, representing the Grace Ruud Realty Company, contacted the Ikedas with regard to the sale of the same property. Ikeda went to the hotel once with Yamashita and twice with Tucker, but did not see Mrs. Curtis until October 9th. He was always told that she was too ill to see anyone. (During all of this time she was working from 8 p. m. to 8 a. m. as night clerk at the hotel.) Gladys Westbrooke, a colored day clerk, was at the desk during the times Ikeda visited the hotel. There was a card rack at the desk and she stated, upon inquiry by Ikeda, that there were thirty-four or thirty-five permanent guests. When asked about transient guests she stated that there were two or three vacancies during the week, but that they were filled up on week-ends.

October 6, 1951, an earnest money receipt and agreement was signed which was practically identical with the one signed September 15th, except that the latter one provided for a down payment of $10,000. The Ikedas testified that when they saw Mrs. Curtis she told them that the monthly income was from $1,900 to $2,200. When the lease, prepared by the owner, Pike Place Investment Company, was presented by Tucker, Ikeda refused to sign it, because of three clauses which his attorney had advised him should be eliminated. This took a few days of negotiating. Finally, in the afternoon of October 16th, Tucker came back with the word that everything was agreeable. He then asked for a check for the $9,000 balance of the down payment. Ikeda postdated the check to the 17th because that was the day he was to execute the lease.

Ikeda took over the hotel at about 10 o'clock in the morning of October 18th. He there met Tucker and Mrs. Curtis, who remained about fifteen minutes and then left. Mrs. Curtis handed him a memorandum of advance rental collections. He counted the rentals and learned that there were only twelve permanent tenants listed. He testified that he was surprised and asked Mrs. Curtis if that were all, and that she replied, "That is right."

Ikeda testified that while he was working at the desk the first day, several men came in and asked for girls. In response to a question as to the number, he testified:

"A. About eighteen; seventeen or eighteen men during the daytime while I was at the desk. They come up to ask about the girls and I told them it was under new hand and I don't have any girls and he said: 'You don't have to be scared, I am seaman.' And he pulled out their identification cards and everything, but I say 'I am sorry, I don't have any girls here, see.' And they said 'Where is Mrs. Curtis; where is Gladys?' and I told them 'I don't know, they left no forwarding address; I don't know how to locate them.' That was the same day, you know, but a couple of days later some men came up there and say 'Give me room' and alright I give him room and he went up to room and he called me and he say 'I want a girl,' and I say 'I am sorry, I don't have any girls' and he just took off."

Ikeda's son, Bob, a pre-law student at the University of Washington, clerked the Saturday and Sunday night shifts from October 26th to November 17th. He testified that, during that time from thirty to fifty men would come each night and ask for girls.

Concerning this situation, Ikeda testified, "I feel ashamed my standing over the desk and answer the same old question all day long. I really feel ashamed of myself." He called his attorney the first day and in a couple of days put out a sign reading, "No Girls". He testified that the transient trade was one or two tenants a day.

This action was commenced, alleging that the defendant represented that the monthly gross income during the several years she operated the hotel, was from $1,900 to $2,000; that such representations were false and known to be false and were made with intent to induce the plaintiffs to purchase the property; and that the plaintiffs relied upon such misrepresentations to their damage.  *  *  *

The ledger book for the LaSalle Hotel, kept from September, 1946, until the day of sale, was admitted in evidence. The left hand sheet shows the income (Mrs. Curtis testified that the book reflects all the income which she received from the hotel) and the right hand sheet shows the expenses. However, the sheet showing the income has two rows of figures. For example, the income sheet for September, 1951, shows:

LaSalle Hotel
83 Pike Street                                            September 1, 1951

| Date | | | | |
|------|------|------|------|------|
| 1 | $37 | | $50 | Extra $172 |
| 2 | 10 | | 49.50 | |
| 3 | 12 | | 40 | |
| 4 | 30 | | 45 | |
| 5 | 78 | 312 5 wks rent | 32.50 | |
| | | 405 2 wks rent | | |
| 6 | 16 | 401 2 wks rent | 27.57 | |
| 7 | 20 | | 41 | |
| 8 | 18 | | 35 | |
| 9 | 10 | | 49.50 | |
| 10 | 18 | | 25 | |
| 11 | 26 | | 40 | |
| 12 | 40.50 | | 35 | |
| 13 | 12 | | 53 | |
| 14 | 42 | | 45 | |
| 15 | 28 | | 45 | |
| 16 | 12 | | 32 | |
| 17 | 40 | | 45 | |
| 18 | 24 | | 62 | |
| 19 | 18 | | 40 | |
| 20 | 40 | rentals | 41.50 | |
| 21 | 45 | " | 35 | |
| 22 | 47 | | 47.50 | |
| 23 | 12 | | 61 | |
| 24 | 20 | | 50 | |
| 25 | 14 | | 53.50 | |
| 26 | 28 | | 37.50 | |
| 27 | 40 | | 63 | |
| 28 | 52 | | 67.50 | |
| 29 | 16 | | 60 | |
| 30 | 6 | | 45 | |

With reference to the September, 1951 income, she testified:

"Q. Isn't it a fact, Mrs. Curtis, the two columns on the left hand side of the page, that the left hand column represents the income from roomers and the right hand column represents income from the whore house business? * * * A. I refuse to answer.

"Q. Mrs. Curtis, do you also refuse to answer with respect to the month of October, 1946 on the same ground? A. Yes, all through the book.

"Q. And on the ground of self-incrimination, is that correct? A. Yes."

* * *

Was there a duty to disclose the source of income? The rule is stated in Restatement of the Law under the heading, Deceit: Business Transactions, p. 116, § 550:

"One party to a business transaction who by concealment or other action intentionally prevents the other from acquiring material information is subject to the same liability to the other as though he had stated the nonexistence of the matter which the other was thus prevented from discovering," and § 551:

"(1) One who fails to disclose to another a thing which he knows may justifiably induce the other to act or refrain from acting in a business transaction is subject to the same liability to the other as though he had represented the nonexistence of the matter which he has failed to disclose, if, but only if, he is under a duty to the other to exercise reasonable care to disclose the matter in question.

"(2) One party to a business transaction is under a duty to exercise reasonable care to disclose to the other before the transaction is consummated

"(a) such matters as the other is entitled to know because of a fiduciary or other similar relation of trust and confidence between them."

We held in Perkins v. Marsh, 179 Wash. 362, 37 P.2d 689, 690, that, under certain circumstances, there is a duty to disclose a material fact even where there was no fiduciary relationship, saying:

"It is true that, in the absence of a duty to speak, silence as to a material fact does not of itself constitute fraud. However, the concealment by one party to a transaction of a material fact within his own knowledge, which it is his duty to disclose, is actual fraud. If appellants intentionally concealed some fact known to them, which it was material for respondents to know, that constituted a fraudulent concealment; that is, the concealment of a fact which one is bound to disclose is the equivalent of an indirect representation that such fact does not exist, and differs from a direct false statement only in the mode by which it is made."

Fraudulent misrepresentation may be effected by half truths calculated to deceive. A representation literally true is actionable if used to create an impression substantially false.

In the case at bar there was no misrepresentation as to the *amount* of the income. The court correctly found that the *amount* of the income was larger than that represented by appellant. The only representation as to the *source* of the income was that it came from permanent and transient guests. Nothing was said or shown to respondents which would put them on notice concerning the source of the income. They were buying the good will, furniture and equipment of the hotel. They naturally felt that they were buying a legitimate business. Appellant deceived them to their damage, by failing to reveal the source of the income. Under the peculiar circumstances of this case, it was the duty of appellant to reveal the source of her income to respondents.

\* \* \*

The judgment is affirmed.

## PROBLEMS

1. The Farringtons entered into a signed agreement to sell their farm to the Tucsons. The price was stated in the agreement as follows: "Sum of fifty thousand dollars ($50,000). Approximately one third down, the balance to be paid over a period of 10 years at 7% interest. This option to expire in 30 days. One hundred dollars ($100.00) to be paid at time of agreement with said amount to be applied on purchase price." Is this an enforceable agreement? Why?

2. Miller leased certain premises from Bloomberg in Bloomingdale, Illinois. The lease contained a clause which stated that "at any time during the original term of this lease or any extension thereof or any tenancy thereafter, lessee shall have the option to purchase the premises for the then prevailing market price." A few years after the lease had been signed, Miller notified Bloomberg of his intention to purchase the property at the prevailing market price but Bloomberg claimed that their agreement was not enforceable. Is Bloomberg correct? Why?

3. Bert orally promised Ernie that if Ernie would quit his job to care for Bert, who was elderly and ill, Ernie would receive Bert's real estate at Bert's death. Ernie quit his job and cared for Bert until Bert died two years later. No will or deed was found. Is Ernie entitled to Bert's real estate? Why?

4. The Lowerys owned a farm consisting of 365 acres. They arranged to sell the farm by public auction; bids were to be given orally. The sale was to be for cash with a 10% down payment at the auction and the balance upon transfer of the deed. Couture was the highest bidder at the auction. Since the auction was on a Saturday, he orally sought and was granted permission by the Lowerys to deliver the down payment on

Monday after his bank opened. On Monday Couture presented the Lowerys with the down payment, but they refused to accept it. May Couture enforce their agreement? Why?

5. Eric acquired a parcel of land through a gift from his parents. Shortly thereafter, he entered an agreement to sell the land to the Muellers. The Muellers took possession of the land on March 15. On April 26, a transcript of a judgment entered several years before against Eric was recorded in the county where the property was situated. On April 30, the sheriff of the county levied execution on the property which had been sold to the Muellers. The Muellers received a deed to the property on June 3. May the Muellers stop the execution sale? Why?

6. Schaeffler hired Newcomb to build a house and promised to pay Newcomb the cost of materials and an agreed profit. Schaeffler was to provide Newcomb with the drawings and specifications to erect the residence. Work was commenced in July and continued until September, when Newcomb reported to Schaeffler that cracks had developed in the foundation and walls of the structure. The damage was partially due to a soil defect and partially due to Newcomb's deviation from specifications that had been submitted to him. Schaeffler personally paid to correct the soil condition and sought recovery of his cost from Newcomb. Newcomb claims he substantially performed the contract and Schaeffler owes him the balance of his profit due on the job. Decide.

7. Hartley purchased a new house from Ballou, the builder. Hartley inspected and obtained possession of the house shortly after the closing. On several occasions, the basement of Hartley's new home became flooded after rain storms. Hartley informed Ballou of the problem and Ballou attempted to rectify the problem, but to no avail. Hartley sued Ballou for breach of the implied warranty that the house was fit and suitable for its intended purpose as a residence. What defenses should Ballou assert? Who will win? Why?

8. Bassford, who was seeking a home in the Denver area, was shown a new house owned by Cook and while inspecting the house he observed substantial cracks in the interior walls of the house. Cook informed Bassford that an engineer had determined the cracks were the result of the settling of the house. Cook stated that corrective action was being taken and also informed Bassford that there were minor soil conditions which required keeping water away from the foundation. Bassford purchased the house from Cook; then several months later additional and more severe cracking occurred. Bassford now seeks to rescind the contract for fraud. May he? Why?

9. Johnson purchased a house and lot from Lina Olsen. During negotiations for the sale, Lina represented the lot width to be 60 feet when in fact it was only 50 feet. There were no physical boundaries which made the lot's width easily discernible by the naked eye. Johnson, upon discovery of the true width of the lot, promptly brought action for rescission of the sale on the grounds of fraud. Will he win? Why?

10. Able decided to sell his hotel. Able told Baker, a potential purchaser, that the hotel was in "A–1 condition." In fact, unknown to Able or Baker, the walls of the hotel were structurally defective and ready to collapse. Baker relied upon Able's statement and bought the hotel. When he learned of the defective walls, Baker sued to rescind the sale. Able claimed his statements were innocently made and therefore Baker is not entitled to rescission. Who is correct? Why?

# Chapter 8

## TITLE AND INSURANCE

What do they know of the law of insurance contract, who only the law of contract know?

Woodruff, *Cases on Insurance*

During the interval between the signing of a real estate contract and the closing, three important activities take place: (1) the seller must prove that he has title to the real estate; (2) the buyer makes arrangements for property insurance; and (3) the buyer borrows money to finance the purchase. In this and the following chapter we will examine these transactions.

## I. TITLE

The seller has three methods available to prove that he has good title, that is, the right to possess the real estate as evidenced by a historical record: abstract and opinion, title insurance, and the Torrens system. To understand these methods, however, we must first consider the legal framework upon which the methods are based—the recording statutes.

### A. RECORDING STATUTES

As an illustration of how the recording statutes operate, let us assume that Owen owned Whitecaps Cottage. On June 10, 1980, Owen deeded Whitecaps to Abby, who paid Owen $40,000. On June 20 Owen deeded the same property to Bo, who also paid $40,000 for the property without realizing the property had already been sold to Abby. As one might expect, on June 21 Owen left the country for Costa Rica with his $80,000 and was never seen again. Who now owns Whitecaps, Abby or Bo?

Before recording statutes were enacted, the common law rule was simple and easy to apply: the first deed prevails over later deeds. Thus in our example, Abby would own Whitecaps and Bo's only recourse would be against Owen, the person who fraudulently sold the real estate.

1. **Recording Defined.** The common law priority is often reversed under recording statutes. Recording is the process whereby the purchaser of real estate takes the deed to a county office, often called the Recorder's Office or Register of Deeds, to have the deed placed on the public record. Recording gives notice to the rest of the world that the property has been conveyed to a new owner. A deed

that has not been recorded is still valid between the seller and the purchaser; however, if the deed is not recorded, third parties may acquire better rights to the property than the purchaser. See Campbell v. Storer, infra.

Certain requirements must be met before an instrument can be recorded. A deed, for example, must meet the usual requirements for a valid deed—this will be discussed in Chapter 10. If a major error exists in the deed, then the recording does not protect the purchaser who has recorded the deed. In Saxon v. Saxon,[1] a deed was executed, delivered to the purchaser, and recorded. However, the court held that the deed did not give notice to later purchasers because the description in the deed did not include the section number, Section 13: "The registration of an instrument is constructive notice to the world of the contents of the paper there recorded or intended to be recorded, and of its particular contents only, and it will have no operation or effect unless the original instrument correctly and sufficiently describes the premises which are to be affected."

In addition to the usual deed requirements, many states impose special requirements for recording purposes only. One such requirement is that the grantor must acknowledge the instrument before a public official, such as a notary public. Another special requirement is that all real estate taxes must be paid before the instrument is recorded. And under the case law in some states, the deed must be in English. For example, one court held that a deed executed partly in Polish was not entitled to be recorded; the purpose of recording is to give notice, and this purpose would be defeated if deeds were executed and recorded in foreign languages.[2]

2. **Types of Statutes.** Three types of recording statutes have been enacted by various states. To illustrate them, let us take our original example and assume that Abby recorded her deed of June 10 on July 1 and that Bo recorded his deed of June 20 on July 5. The first and most common type of statute is the *notice* statute, under which an unrecorded conveyance is not valid against later bona fide purchasers. Thus if Bo is a bona fide purchaser, his deed will prevail over Abby's because hers was not recorded until after the June 20 conveyance to Bo.

A second statute, almost as common as the notice statute, is the *notice-race* statute. Under this statute, a later purchaser must not only be bona fide but must also record the deed before other purchasers do. In other words, the later purchaser must race to the Register of Deeds before earlier purchasers get there. Under this statute, Abby would have title to the property because she recorded her deed first.

1. 242 Miss. 491, 136 So.2d 210 (1962).    2. Moroz v. Ransom, 158 Misc. 443, 285 N.Y.S. 846 (1932).

The third type of statute, a rather uncommon one, is the *race* statute. Under this type of statute, later purchasers do not have to be bona fide; the only question is who recorded first. Under the race statute Abby would win, since she raced to the deed office to record her deed before Bo.

Under the two common statutes, the notice and the notice-race, the first purchaser will lose only to a bona fide purchaser. A bona fide purchaser is one who (1) pays a valuable consideration for the property or, in the case of a mortgage, lends money to the owner; (2) buys in good faith; and (3) has no notice of the earlier sale. Notice may be either actual (the later purchaser might be told by a friend that the property has already been sold) or constructive (for example, the purchaser should have known that the property has been sold because the earlier purchaser is living on the property). The earlier purchaser's recording of a deed is constructive notice to all later purchasers or mortgagees of the sale, and this recording will defeat later parties whether or not they actually check the public records.

3. **Chain of Title.** Title to real estate is not based upon an absolute or natural right to the property but instead is derived from a historical record consisting of recorded deeds. The record of deeds links the deeds to one piece of property from early times to the present, and it is called the chain of title. To create a chain, a person must engage in some detective work, aided by one of two indices. The tract index in the county office indexes each tract of land separately and lists all prior conveyances. The tract index makes it easy to create a chain of title because the conveyancer need only obtain a correct legal description of the property and then find where that description is indexed.

The other, more common index lists the names of all grantors and all grantees alphabetically in annual volumes. Most marketable title legislation requires the conveyancer to review the index for the preceding forty years in order to create a chain of title. For instance, if Woody wants to purchase property from Diane and needs to determine whether she has title, his first question would be, Did Diane ever purchase the property? To answer this, he would review the grantee indices until he found that she purchased the real estate (or was grantee) from Warren in 1972. Then Woody might wonder whether Diane had already conveyed the property to someone else after she acquired the land in 1972. To answer this question, he would review the grantor indices from 1972 to the present. Next, Woody should follow the same process to determine the date that Warren acquired the real estate and whether, after his acquisition and before conveying the land to Diane, he had sold it to a third party. Woody would then continue the process for Warren's grantor and for previous owners over the forty year period.

## B.  PROOF OF TITLE

In the example above, it would be possible for Woody to create his own chain of title by visiting the local deeds office and investigating the appropriate indices.   However, this would be a time-consuming process, and even if Woody created an accurate chain of title, questions would still arise about the legal validity of the instruments on record.   Consequently, most purchasers hire professionals to determine whether the sellers have good title.   The three following methods are used to make this determination.

1.  **Abstract and Opinion.**   The first method combines the use of an abstract of title and a legal opinion.   An abstract of title is a summary of the chain of title, usually prepared by a title company or an attorney, listing all recorded instruments including deeds, mortgages, mortgage discharges, and tax liens.   A complete short abstract follows the cases at the end of the chapter.   The abstract itself is of little value to the purchaser; although it lists and summarizes instruments, it does not indicate if they are legally valid.   Consequently, the abstract should be reviewed by an attorney who will render a title opinion.   In some areas it is common practice for an attorney to render an opinion, called a certificate of title, based upon his own review of the recorded instruments rather than upon a review of an abstract of title.

There are problems inherent in using this method to prove title. One major problem is that the opinion or certificate covers only the title as it is established by instruments on record.   But in many cases an instrument that appears to be valid may contain hidden defects. For example, Tom, age 17, conveys a parcel of real estate to Dick. Dick records his deed from Tom and shortly thereafter signs a contract to sell the real estate to Harry.   If Harry hired a title company to prepare an abstract and an attorney to review the abstract, the record would show that Dick had good title.   In fact Dick has voidable title because a minor can avoid a contract and recover the real estate by disaffirming the contract before or within a reasonable time after reaching the age of majority.   Similar hidden problems could arise if the recorded deed was signed by an incompetent person, if a deed stated that the grantor was single when in fact he was married and his wife refused to sign away her dower rights, if the signature on a deed was forged, or if a deed was never legally delivered to the grantee.   In all of these examples, the abstract and the attorney's opinion would show good title, but in fact the purchaser would receive voidable or void title.   And in each case the purchaser would not have recourse against the title company or the attorney because abstracts and opinions are expressly limited to matters on the public record. Even if the defect appears on the public record, the attorney preparing the opinion might not be liable for failure to point out the defect. Negligence or malpractice can be difficult to prove when the title opinion involves questions of interpretation of deeds, wills, and other documents.

2. **Title Insurance.** As an alternative method of securing title, title insurance is free of the above problems. Title insurance is issued by a title insurance company after it reviews the recorded instruments in the same manner an attorney would review them in preparing an abstract and opinion. If the company is satisfied that title is good, it issues a policy covering the purchaser and his heirs for as long as they own the property. Only one premium is paid at the time the policy is purchased, and the amount of the premium varies depending on the locale. For example, if a purchaser bought a $50,000 house with a $40,000 mortgage, the premiums for policies covering the purchaser and the mortgagee-lender could range from approximately $250 to $550. These rates are often reduced significantly if the purchaser sells the insured property and the policy is reissued to a new purchaser within a certain period. An owner may also obtain an inflation rider to increase the amount of coverage over time as the value of the real estate increases.

The two most common types of policies are those issued to the owner and to the mortgagee-lender. Nearly all lenders require protection in the form of title insurance. Purchasers pay for the lender's title policy and often believe mistakenly that they are protected by this policy. However, the lender's policy only provides coverage for the lender in the amount of the mortgage loan and for risks that affect the security interest of the lender. Furthermore, if the title company is forced to pay the lender, it takes the lender's right to collect the loan from the owner. For complete protection, then, the purchaser should acquire a separate owner's title policy.

Two common types of owners' policies have been developed by the American Land Title Association and are used by most title insurance companies. Under Form A, the title company insures against losses that may occur if (1) title belongs to someone else; (2) title is subject to a lien, encumbrance, or other defect; or (3) the owner lacks a right of access to and from the land. Thus the policy owner would be protected from losses caused by forgery and minority as discussed above. Form B, the preferred form, also insures the owner against losses that result from an unmarketable title. To illustrate, in 1978 Mark entered into a contract to purchase real estate from Rosy, who was supposed to produce marketable title. Before closing it was discovered that the title was unmarketable, but because a title insurance company was willing to issue a policy, Mark decided to purchase the property anyway. If Mark tries to sell the property later but a prospective purchaser refuses to complete the transaction because of the unmarketable title, he might sustain a loss. With Form B, Mark would be covered for the loss.

Both Form A and Form B provide the owner with another advantage that the abstract and opinion lack: if there is litigation involving the status of title, the title company is required to bear the costs and attorneys' fees. Should the company refuse, the penalties can be severe. For instance, in Fohn v. Title Ins. Corp. of St. Louis,[3] the plaintiffs purchased twenty-five acres of land for $6,400. Realizing that the land was worth much more, they purchased title insurance from the defendant in the amount of $20,000. As the plaintiffs were constructing a shopping center on the land, they discovered a sign advertising a cave and learned that the one-half acre of the property around the sign was claimed by someone else. The title insurance company refused to participate in later litigation, and the plaintiffs eventually lost the half acre. They then sued the title company and recovered $20,000 in actual damages, $6,200 in attorney's fees, and $2,000 in punitive damages. The court felt that damages should be based on the difference in value with and without the disputed segment. In this case the one-half acre contributed significantly to the total value of the plaintiff's property because it included extensive highway frontage. The attorney's fees and punitive damages were awarded because of the company's wrongful refusal to participate in the original suit to determine title.

Forms A and B contain several exclusions and exceptions that the owner should review carefully before purchasing a policy. Three general types of exclusions are common in these standard policies. First, governmental laws may restrict or regulate the occupation, use, enjoyment, or development of the real estate. Second, there may be governmental rights to take and control the land under eminent domain or police power. For instance, if you purchase a parcel of real estate to build a restaurant but the zoning laws limit the area to residential use, you will have no coverage under your title policy for any resulting losses. Third, the title insurance company does not provide coverage for defects, liens, claims and other matters (a) created or agreed to by the insured, (b) known by the insured but not by the company, (c) resulting in no loss to the insured, or (d) created after the policy was issued. To illustrate, in the *Fohn* case above, the title company claimed it was not liable because the insured parties knew of the sign advertising the cave and did not disclose this to the company when the policy was issued. The court, however, felt that the insureds' discovery of the sign did not mean that they knew the surrounding property was owned by another party.

In addition to the above general exclusions, individual companies have developed their own general exclusions that often cover rights which have not been recorded. Examples of these exclusions include the right of a person claiming the land by adverse possession, mechanics' liens, easements, and matters that would be disclosed by an accurate survey of the premises.

---

3.   529 S.W.2d 1 (Mo.1975).

Title insurance companies often make specific exceptions in addition to their general exclusions. For example, title coverage might expressly exclude public utility easements or building and use restrictions. Certain exceptions such as unpaid taxes will be listed in the title company's commitment to insure the property, which is given to the purchaser before closing, but will not be excepted from the final coverage if taxes are paid on or before closing.

Despite the exclusions and exceptions, title insurance is the most effective—and popular—method of proving title. However, the use of title insurance is subject to potential abuse, which has caused Iowa to forbid its use. See Chicago Title Ins. Co. v. Huff, infra.

3. **Torrens System.** Ten states use the Torrens System for establishing title to real estate, although these states use the recordation system in most transactions. The Torrens System was developed in Australia by Robert Torrens and was modeled on English shipping law, under which ownership of ships was recorded in an official register and the owner received a copy of the registry page as a certificate of title. When the owner sold the ship, the old certificate was surrendered, the new sale was registered, and the purchaser received a new certificate of title. Under the system Torrens developed for real estate transactions, the Register of Titles issues a "Torrens" certificate to a purchaser whenever property is transferred, after first cancelling the seller's certificate.[4] Unlike the recording system, in which the recorded instruments are merely evidence of title that must be verified by creating a chain of title, the "Torrens" certificate is itself the title, and a chain of title is not prepared before property is conveyed. Distinctions between the recording system and the Torrens system are discussed in People v. Mortenson, infra, while the importance of the Torrens certificate is illustrated by Eliason v. Wilborn, infra.

In order to bring real estate under the Torrens system, the title must first be registered. Registration begins when an owner applies to the appropriate local court, and the court investigates the title and related matters, such as whether the land is occupied. Next, the court notifies all persons who claim an interest in the real estate and schedules a trial to determine whether the applicant is really the owner. If the applicant has good title, the court orders the title to be registered; from that point on, title passes with the issuance of a Torrens certificate, free of all encumbrances except those noted on the certificate.[5]

4. 1 American Land Title Association, The Title Industry: White Papers, Ch. 5, 2–5 (1976).

5. State v. Westfall, 85 Minn. 437, 89 N.W. 175 (1902).

## II.  HOMEOWNER'S INSURANCE

In addition to obtaining proof of title, the real estate purchaser at some point before closing will acquire an insurance policy covering the property.  The effective date of the coverage should coincide with the assumption of the risk of loss by the purchaser.  As noted in Chapter 7, most states declare that the risk of loss falls on the purchaser at the time the contract is signed if the contract is silent.[6]  However, in practice contracts usually state that the risk remains with the seller until closing or until the buyer takes possession.

To acquire insurance coverage, the vendee may purchase a new policy, or alternatively the vendor may assign his insurance coverage to the vendee.  However, since the insurance contract is a personal one between the vendor and the company, the company must approve the assignment.  This is often a trap for the unwary purchaser.  For instance, in many cases the vendor will give the vendee a written assignment of the policy at the closing, and this assignment will be forwarded to the insurance company for approval, which normally takes one to two weeks.  During the period before approval, the vendee has no coverage and must personally bear any losses resulting from damage to the premises.  In the following discussion we will assume that a home has been sold and that the buyer is purchasing a new homeowner's policy, although many of the legal principles also apply to other types of property insurance.

### A.  PROPERTY COVERAGE

Most homeowner's insurance policies today cover two types of losses:  (1) losses resulting from damage to property and (2) losses arising when the owner injures another person.  Property damage provisions under a standard homeowner's policy cover the dwelling, appurtenant structures such as a garage or a gazebo, and personal property incidental to the occupancy of the dwelling—even when the loss of the owner's personal property occurs at another location.  The amount of coverage on the dwelling determines the coverage on the other property.  For instance, appurtenant structures are usually insured for 10 percent of the coverage on the dwelling, and personal property is insured for 50 percent of that amount.  A homeowner is also covered for "additional living expense"—up to 20 percent of the value of the dwelling—for expenditures incurred when the owner cannot occupy the house because of damage.

A homeowner usually chooses one of three common forms of homeowner's policies, depending on the number and type of perils against which he wishes to insure the property.  Under the Basic

---

6. Although the authorities are split, in most states the vendor's insurance will protect the vendee.  W. Vance, Law of Insurance § 131 (3rd ed. 1951).

Form (HO-1), there is coverage for eleven perils: fire or lightning, loss of property removed from endangered premises (for example, property removed from a house that is threatened by a fire next door), windstorm or hail, explosion, riot or civil commotion, aircraft, vehicles, smoke, vandalism and malicious mischief, theft, and breakage of glass that is part of the building. The most popular form, the Broad Form (HO-2), adds seven additional perils: falling objects; weight of ice, snow, and sleet; collapse of building; accidental damage involving steam or hot water heating systems or appliances for heating water; accidental discharges of water or steam from a plumbing, heating, or air conditioning system or appliance; freezing of plumbing, heating, air-conditioning systems and appliances; and accidental injuries involving certain electrical equipment. The Comprehensive Form (HO-5) is often called the "all risk" form because all perils are covered, with specified exceptions for events such as flood, earthquake, landslide, tidal waves, war, and nuclear attack.

Regardless of the form the homeowner selects, each policy's coverage contains a number of exclusions that should be reviewed carefully. For instance, the coverage for specified personal property normally excludes animals, birds, fish, motorized vehicles, aircraft, and other items. And even where an exclusion is not specifically stated, courts have developed certain implied exceptions. See Youse v. Employers Fire Ins. Co., infra.

The maximum amount of coverage is set forth in the policy declarations; as noted above, the coverage for appurtenant structures, unscheduled personal property, and additional living expense is a specified percentage of the coverage for the dwelling. An owner cannot recover more than the maximum specified in the declaration, and there are many cases in which the owner will recover less than the maximum coverage—even when damage is greater than that amount. Why would this be the case? As one example, standard policies state that coverage is limited to the interest of the insured. Thus if Charley and Joan purchase a $50,000 building as tenants in common with equal interests and Charley takes out a $50,000 policy in his name alone, he can recover only $25,000, the value of his interest in the event the building is completely destroyed.

Another common limitation is a form of coinsurance clause included in insurance policies. Although these clauses are not uniform,[7] a typical clause in a homeowner's policy provides that if the building is insured for 80 percent or more of the full replacement cost, the coverage will include the full cost of repair or replacement up to the policy limits. However, if the amount of insurance is less than 80 percent of the full replacement cost, the coverage will not exceed the larger

---

7. See Keeton, Insurance Law § 3.7 (1971), for a discussion of the New York Standard Coinsurance Clause.

of (a) the actual cash value of the part of the building damaged or destroyed, or (b) the proportion of the replacement cost of the damaged structure which the full amount of insurance applicable to the building bears to 80 percent of the full replacement cost of the building. For example, Clyde purchased a large Victorian home for $60,000 which, because of its intricate and detailed construction, would cost $80,000 to replace. He wished to save insurance premiums and, reasoning that buildings are seldom completely destroyed, he purchased only $40,000 coverage. Later a fire destroyed the roof, which had an actual value of $500 but would cost $2,000 to replace. Since Clyde's coverage was less than 80 percent of the full replacement cost, he is not entitled to the full cost of repair or replacement up to policy limits. Instead, recovery is limited to the larger of (a) the actual cash value of the part of the building damaged or destroyed (in this case $500) or (b) the proportion of the replacement cost of the damage ($2,000) which the total amount of insurance ($40,000) bears to 80 percent of the full replacement cost of the building: 80 percent of $80,000 is $64,000 and thus this proportion is $\frac{40,000}{64,000} = \frac{5}{8}$ and $\frac{5}{8}$ of $2,000 is $1,250. Consequently, the company will pay only $1,250 of Clyde's $2,000 loss even though Clyde had $40,000 worth of coverage; Clyde must bear the remaining loss; that is, he becomes the coinsurer and pays $750.

Obviously, to receive protection up to policy limits, owners should insure at least for the percentage specified in the policy (in Clyde's case, 80 percent). Many homeowners are underinsured because home replacement costs rise even faster than the rate of inflation, and insurance coverage quickly falls below the required percentage. As an added measure of protection, companies offer an "inflation guard" endorsement that raises policy coverages automatically at periodic intervals.

## B. LIABILITY COVERAGE

Most homeowner policies include liability provisions to cover the insured for damages that the insured is legally obligated to pay as the result of an accident caused by the insured, as well as for the costs of defending against lawsuits. Policies cover accidents both on or away from the insured premises. For instance, a homeowner would usually be covered for damages if a guest slipped on a tool that the owner left on the sidewalk, or for damages caused when the insured hit a golf ball and injured another golfer. However, the liability coverage does not apply to damages claimed by an employee, such as a maid, under worker's compensation law; specific coverage should be purchased to cover such losses. Also excluded are injuries resulting from the use of motor vehicles and from business pursuits. For example, an owner covered for an accidental injury to a customer at a garage sale would lose his coverage if he holds regular garage sales for profit because this would constitute a business pursuit.

## C. INSURABLE INTEREST

The insured must have an insurable interest to collect on a policy; that is, he must have an interest in the property such that he will suffer a loss if the property is damaged or destroyed. In the absence of an insurable interest, the insurance contract would be nothing more than a wager, which is illegal in most states. And with property insurance, unlike life insurance, the insurable interest must exist at the time of the loss. See Westfall v. American States Ins. Co., infra.

## D. MORTGAGE INSURANCE

As Chapter 9 will explain in detail, a mortgagee has a legal interest in the mortgaged real estate and consequently has an insurable interest up to the amount of the debt. Since the mortgagor, as owner, also has an insurable interest, it is possible for the mortgagee and the mortgagor to obtain separate policies covering the same property. If the property is damaged or destroyed, each party could collect on its own policy and would have no rights in the proceeds of the other policy. Since the insurance company that pays on a mortgagee's policy may step into the mortgagee's shoes and collect the balance of the debt from the mortgagor, it is especially important that the mortgagor purchase separate coverage.

The situation changes if the mortgage requires the mortgagor to acquire insurance for the benefit of the mortgagee, as is commonly the case. This requirement means that the proceeds of the insurance policy will be applied for the benefit of the mortgagee, even when the mortgagee is not named in the policy. Furthermore, if the mortgagor refuses to purchase the required coverage, the mortgagee may obtain its own coverage and charge the premiums to the mortgagor. If the mortgagee collects on such a policy, the mortgagor's debt is discharged up to the amount of the proceeds.

To meet the mortgage requirement to provide insurance on the property for the mortgagee, mortgagors usually purchase a policy with a clause stipulating that, in the event of a loss, the mortgagee will be paid up to the amount of its interest. Under an older type of clause called the "loss payable clause," the mortgagee's rights were derived from those of the mortgagor; thus if the mortgagor could not collect neither could the mortgagee. Under the modern mortgagee loss clause now in common use, the mortgagee's insurance will not be invalidated by an act which would cancel the coverage of the mortgagor-owner. For example, if the mortgagor intentionally destroyed the property by arson, the company would still be liable to the mortgagee. In such cases, the company would pay the claim but would then step into the shoes of the mortgagee to collect the debt from the mortgagor.

Although insurance coverage under the mortgagee loss clause is not cancelled by the acts of the mortgagor, in certain cases the mortgagee will be unable to collect because of its own carelessness. For example, the mortgagee must notify the insurance company of any change in ownership or increase of hazard of which the mortgagee is aware. Or if the mortgagor fails to pay the insurance premium, it must be paid by the mortgagee after the insurance company demands payment. The mortgagee is also bound by basic coverage provisions such as the policy limits stated in the declaration and coinsurance provisions.

# CASES

---

## CAMPBELL v. STORER

Court of Appeals of Ohio, Lucas County, 1975.
52 Ohio App.2d 103; 368 N.E.2d 301, 6 O.O.3d 68.

POTTER, J. Appellants purchased real property from appellees on or about December 2, 1965. A warranty deed was given to appellants but was not recorded. Thereafter, in 1970, appellees conveyed, in a larger parcel to another purchaser, the same parcel they had previously conveyed to appellants. Subsequently, the latter purchaser's grantees filed an action in ejectment against appellants. That cause was settled.

The case *sub judice* is one for damages against the original grantor by the original grantees. In this case, appellees, the original grantors, filed their motion for summary judgment. The motion was granted, the cause was dismissed, and this appeal followed.

\* \* \*

Appellees urge here, and did so successfully in the trial court, that the neglect and failure of appellants and/or their counsel to record the general warranty deed delivered to them in December of 1965 prohibited the plaintiffs from acquiring legal title.

We hold that this conclusion is untenable and the mere failure of the grantees to record a deed without more is no defense to a grantee's action against his grantor for the grantor's act of conveying the identical property a second time.

Appellees cannot rely on R.C. 5301.25(A). R.C. 5301.25(A) affords protection to a subsequent bona fide purchaser, but affords no protection to the original but forgetful or fraudulent grantor in a suit by the original grantee. A requirement that the deed must be recorded before a grantor is deemed to have notice of his own act would lead, as the case of Wayne Bldg. & Loan Co. v. Yarborough (1967), 11 Ohio St.2d 195, at 212, suggests, to absurd results.

Between the original grantors and grantees, title to the real property passed upon delivery and acceptance of the deeds.

We hold that the granting of appellees' motion on the premise asserted by appellees in the trial court was error and appellants' assignment of error is, therefore, well taken.

The judgment of the Court of Common Pleas of Lucas County is reversed.

---

## CHICAGO TITLE INS. CO. v. HUFF

Supreme Court of Iowa, 1977.
256 N.W.2d 17.

RAWLINGS, Justice.

Equity action by plaintiff seeking to enjoin enforcement by defendant of Section 515.48(10), The Code 1973, which prohibits corporations doing business in this jurisdiction from insuring titles to real estate, resulted in adjudication adverse to plaintiff and it appeals. We affirm.

Plaintiff, Chicago Title Insurance Company (Chicago Title), is a foreign corporation. May 29, 1972, it duly caused to be filed in the office of defendant, William H. Huff III, Iowa Insurance Commissioner, an application for authority to operate as an insurer of real estate titles in this jurisdiction. August 8, this application was denied because of the aforesaid statutory enactment which provides:

"Any company organized under this chapter or authorized to do business in this state may:

"Insure any additional risk not specifically included within any of the foregoing classes, which is a proper subject for insurance, is not prohibited by law or contrary to sound public policy, and which, after public notice and hearing, is specifically approved by the commissioner of insurance, *except title insurance or insurance against loss or damage by reason of defective title, encumbrances or otherwise.* When such additional kind of insurance is approved by the commissioner he shall designate within which classification of risks provided for in Section 515.49 it shall fall." (emphasis supplied).

\* \* \*

Now to the fundamental issues presently entertained.

As aforesaid, Chicago Title maintains the statute in question essentially denies it a property right without due process and equal protection of the law, under both federal and state constitutions.

The substance of Chicago Title's argument is that because the legislatures of some states have permitted title insurance to be written, then by the same process, Chicago Title is endowed with a property right to initiate and conduct a similar business in Iowa. But no such property right exists. At cost of repetition, we must again be mindful of the fact that ours is a federal system, and the Iowa mode of barring title insurance operations simply precludes creation of the very property right which Chicago Title asserts is denied. In the same vein, we are not here concerned with property rights, if any, which Chicago Title might have had were its business operable in Iowa, then banned.

Obviously the due process problem posed is whether the present prohibition has a definite and reasonable relationship to legitimate state goals. And the equal protection question put is whether the involved classification bears a fair and substantial relation to the same state interests. Thus, an equal protection vis-a-vis due process analysis may be said to here merge.

## DUE PROCESS

A variety of reasons have been urged in support of legislation prohibiting the insuring in Iowa of loss or damage arising from defective land titles. A discussion of all these supportive arguments will serve no useful purpose. Rather, in order to sustain the statute presently under consideration we need only consider the abuses which may arise when title insurance is written.

A plaintiff-called witness admitted it was Chicago Title's intent to "convert" the present Iowa abstract-attorney's opinion system to title insurance as the norm for locally determining marketability of titles. Plaintiff also conceded that over a given five-year period it collected approximately $370,000 in title "insurance" premiums, written outside the state for the insuring of Iowa titles, and from these premiums paid out nothing in claims. Obviously, a loss ratio of zero per cent presents a potentially lucrative source of revenue to an insurer of titles and this court cannot say the general assembly overstepped its power in barring a costly form of "insurance" for which plaintiff's own testimony demonstrates there is little need.

Even more potent is the trial court testimony of an intervenor-called Iowa attorney specializing in land titles. This witness opined that in some cases mortgagees receive commissions or rebates from title insurance companies, thus implying like practices may make such insurance a virtual requirement if made available in this state. Also, as previously indicated, real concern in this area has been noted in other proceedings. It can hardly be disputed the general assembly could have reasonably concluded the statute in question was necessary for the accomplishment of a general welfare goal—to avoid those exploitive marketing activities which would be inimical to public good and welfare. In other words, it cannot be gainsaid the involved statutory restriction was adopted in order to avoid needless consumer costs and impede the machinations which would otherwise become prevalent between Iowa lenders and title insurance companies, all to public detriment.

Again mentioned is Chicago Title's misconceived reliance on the fact that Iowa is the only state which prohibits local insuring of real estate titles. Conceding Iowa so stands—its uniqueness does not make the Act vulnerable to constitutional attack.

Clearly Chicago Title has not negated every reasonable basis which supports the involved statute.

Plaintiff's contention that § 515.48(10) deprives it of property without due process of law is without merit.

## EQUAL PROTECTION

It is also to us evident the involved statutory prohibition does not deny plaintiff equal protection of the law. As noted above, if a state legislative enactment classifies commercial enterprises for purpose of regulation and such classification, as here, is neither premised upon a suspect criteria nor infringes a fundamental right, a presumption of constitutionality attaches and the statute will be set aside as violative of due process or equal protection only if it is arbitrary and without foundation in public policy, its means are unrelated to objectives, or the distinction drawn is invidious and lacks a rational basis incapable of justification under any conceivable set of facts.

As heretofore revealed the legislature is accorded wide discretion in defining classes when a statute involves a categorization of persons or things. If a classification is reasonable and operates equally upon all within the class, it is not subject to constitutional attack.

\* \* \*

Unquestionably, classification must be based upon some apparent difference in situation or circumstance of the subjects placed within one class or the other which establishes the necessity or propriety of distinction between them. And discrimination is unreasonable only if the classification lacks rational relationship to a legitimate state purpose.

On this subject, Chicago Title asserts § 515.48(10) stands as unconstitutional class legislation in any one of three ways. It supportively argues (1) there is no basis for dissimilar treatment between all corporate entities qualified to do business in the state and title insurance companies; (2) the legislature improperly created a separate classification for title insurance, while insurance against all other insurable risks—other than life—are statutorily placed in a general classification; therefore (3) all forms of title protection (insurance, registration and attorney opinions based upon abstract examinations) should be placed in the same classification. We are not so persuaded.

In connection with the first above stated argument, this court has long recognized the insurance business is peculiarly subject to special supervision and control.

Turning next to above noted second averment, title insurance has several characteristics which distinguish it from other forms of similar coverage. As summarized in 22 Drake L.Rev. at 714–715:

"Title insurance is directed at loss prevention—similar to boiler insurance. Most property and casualty insurance, on the other hand, is concerned to a greater extent with risk assumption and distribution. * * *

"Another significant difference is that title insurance insures against loss resulting from occurrences which have taken place in the past. Most forms of insurance obviously insure against future events. Also, title insurance requires the payment of only one premium, and the policy remains in effect until the property in question is sold by the owner who purchased the policy. The reason for this is that the event which may cause the loss insured against has already occurred at the time of issuance, so the premium actually covers the past, not the future."

Thus it cannot be said the instantly applied distinction between types of insurance is invidious or arbitrary and capricious. Noticeably, application of the term "insurance" to a form of contract which, over a five-year period, produced no loss to the insurer, is a strained interpretation of the term.

* * * *

All issues here raised by Chicago Title Insurance Company, whether or not discussed above, have been considered and found to be without merit.

Affirmed.

---

## PEOPLE v. MORTENSON

Supreme Court of Illinois, 1949.
404 Ill. 107, 88 N.E.2d 35.

GUNN, Justice.

On April 6, 1946, [a] public sale was held, and the appellant, who was not one of the owners of the property, bid at said sale the sum of $3700 and the property was sold to him. Thereafter a report of the sale was duly made, showing payment of the bid, and a decree entered confirming the report, and a certificate of purchase delivered to appellant. Appellant complied with the provisions of the Revenue Act by serving the necessary notices and paying subsequent taxes, and on May 10, 1948, filed his petition, praying for the issuance of a deed to the premises sold. Demand was made upon the county clerk for the issuance of the deed, and the certificate of purchase was delivered to the county clerk, who refused to issue a deed on the ground that the appellant had not complied with the provisions of section 82 of the Torrens Act, which provides as follows: "The holder of any certificate of sale of registered land or any estate, or interest therein for any tax, assessment or imposition shall  *  *  *   within one year from the date of any such sale  *  *  *   present the same or a sworn copy thereof to the registrar, who shall thereupon enter on the register of the land a memorial thereof, stating the day of sale and the date of presentation, and shall also note upon the certificate of sale the date of presentation and the book and page of the register, where the memorial is entered. The holder of such certificate shall also within the same time mail to each of the persons who appear by the register to have any interest in the land, a notice of the registration of such certificate. Unless such certificate is presented and registered, and notice given as herein provided within the time above mentioned, the land shall be forever released from the effect of such sale, and no deed shall be issued in pursuance of such certificate." This section makes other provisions as to certificates of purchase relating to municipalities not relevant to this case.

The appellant, as holder of the certificate of purchase, did not present and register said certificate of purchase within the time provided in said statute, and the county clerk thereupon refused to issue and deliver a deed for said property, pursuant to the certificate of purchase.

      *   *   *

      *   *   *   The Torrens Act differs in many material respects from the usual method of transferring title and the requirement for recording instruments affecting title. In respect to property not registered under the Torrens Act, title is transferred by the delivery of a deed from the owner to the grantee. The recording of such instrument is not necessary to the validity of the transfer. The instrument when recorded serves as notice to other persons dealing with the title to such property. Instruments affecting title to land not registered under the Torrens system will be recorded by the recorder without passing upon their validity or effect, and the extent to which such instruments affect title is left to the judgment of persons examining the record of such instruments.

The general purpose of the Torrens Act is to provide an independent system of registration, whereby an intending purchaser of land can determine from the register the condition of the title. Under the ordinary system of recording, evidences of title are placed of record, while under the Torrens system the title itself is registered. And one of the objects of the Torrens system is to create a system of registration of land titles where all instruments affecting any title shall be filed and registered in one department and no other.

There are several fundamental differences in effect between registration of title under the Torrens Act and the ordinary recording of documents affecting land. Under the Torrens Act an instrument, such as a deed or mortgage, does not directly affect the title to registered land, but affects it only by way of contract between the parties constituting authority to the registrar to register the transfer or mortgage, and on completion of the registration the land, estate, or interests, shall become transferred or mortgaged in accordance with the purport of the deed, mortgage, or other instrument.

When title is registered under the Torrens system in the name of one person, it cannot again be registered in another's name, until the duplicate certificate is surrendered to the registrar. One of the many differences is illustrated by the fact that after land is registered under the Torrens system no title thereto, adverse or in derogation to the title of the registered owner, can be acquired by any length of possession. When a transfer is to be made under the provisions of the Torrens Act, the registrar of titles, unlike the recorder of deeds, investigates to determine the validity of the transfer, and the registrar will not issue his certificate of title without proof that the instrument is valid, and that the grantee is the owner. In fact, under the Torrens system an innocent purchaser may acquire a good title if a certificate of title is issued to him, notwithstanding the fact that a prior purported transfer was a forgery, of which the registrar was unaware. And when land is registered under the Torrens Act, purchasers of such land are presumed to know the terms of the Torrens Act, and are bound by its terms.

\* \* \*

It is the contention of the appellant in this case that the procedure set forth in the Revenue Act of 1939, in regard to tax foreclosure proceedings, is a complete procedure, and that compliance with the provisions of section 82 of the Torrens Act is unnecessary. We cannot agree with the contention of appellant in this respect. There can be no question but that the Torrens Act controls the transfer of title, whether such title is transferred by deed, judicial proceeding, tax sale, tax or other foreclosure, the law of descent, or otherwise. In fact, there can be no question but that if appellant were to receive a tax deed, the real estate in question and the title thereto would be controlled by the provisions of the Torrens Act, and the appellant would have to comply with that act in order to secure a transfer of the title to himself.

———

## ELIASON v. WILBORN

Supreme Court of the United States, 1930.
281 U.S. 457, 50 S.Ct. 382, 74 L.Ed.2d 962.

Mr. Justice HOLMES delivered the opinion of the Court.

The appellants had been holders of a certificate of title under the Torrens Act of Illinois. As a result of negotiations they entrusted this certificate to one Napletone, who is alleged to have presented it together with a forged conveyance to himself to the Registrar and by those means to have obtained from the Registrar a new certificate of title in Napletone, on May 19, 1926. Napletone a few days later sold and conveyed to the Wilborns, appellees, whose good faith is not questioned. After the Wilborns had bought but before a new certificate was issued to them, they had notice of the appellants' claim and the appellants notified the Registrar of the forgery and demanded a cancellation of the deeds and certificates to Napletone and the Wilborns and the issue of a certificate to themselves. The Registrar refused and this petition is brought to compel him to do what the appellants demand. It was dismissed on demurrer by the Circuit Court of the State, and the judgment was affirmed by the Supreme Court. The Supreme Court construed the statutes as giving title to the Wilborns, who purchased in reliance upon the certificate held by Napletone. Whether we are bound to or not we accept that construction and its result. The petitioners appealed to this Court on the ground that the statute, construed as it was construed below, deprived the appellants of their property without due process of law contrary to the Constitution of the United States, by making the certificate of title issued by the Registrar upon a forged deed without notice to them conclusive against them.

\*    \*    \*

The appellants seem to claim a constitutional right to buy land that has been brought under the Torrens Act free from the restrictions that that Act imposes. But they have no right of any kind to buy it unless the present owner assents, and if, as in this case, the owner from whom the appellants bought, offered and sold nothing except a Torrens title we do not perceive how they can complain that that is all that they got. Even if the restrictions were of a kind that was open to constitutional objection the appellants bought knowing them and got what they paid for, and knew that they were liable to lose their title without having parted with it and without being heard. Even if they had been the original holders under the Torrens Act and had attempted to save their supposed rights by protest the answer would be that they were under no compulsion when they came into the system, that an elaborate plan was offered of which the provisions objected to were an important part, and that they could take it as it was or let it alone. There are plenty of cases in which a man may lose his title when he does not mean to. If he entrusts a check indorsed in blank to a servant or friend he takes his chance. So when he entrusts goods to a bailee under some factors' acts that are well known. So, more analogous to the present case, a man may be deprived of a title by one who has none; as when an owner who has conveyed his property by a deed not yet recorded executes a second deed to another person who takes and records the later deed without notice of the former. There are few constitutional rights that may not be waived.

But there is a narrower ground on which the appellants must be denied their demand. The statute requires the production of the outstanding certificate, as a condition to the issue of a new one. The appellants saw fit to entrust it to Napletone and they took the risk. They say that according to the construction of the act adopted the Registrar's certificate would have had the same effect even if the old certificate had not been produced. But that, if correct, is no answer. Presumably the Registrar will do his duty, and if he does he will require the old certificate to be handed in. It does not justify the omission of a precaution that probably would be sufficient, to point out that a dishonest official could get around it. There is not the slightest reason to suppose that Napletone would have got a certificate on which the Wilborns could rely without the delivery of the old one by the appellants. As between two innocent persons one of whom must suffer the consequence of a breach of trust the one who made it possible by his act of confidence must bear the loss.

Decree affirmed.

---

### YOUSE v. EMPLOYERS FIRE INS. CO., BOSTON, MASS.

Supreme Court of Kansas, 1951.
172 Kan. 111, 238 P.2d 472.

PRICE, Justice.

This was an action to recover for the loss and damage to a star sapphire ring caused by fire. Plaintiff insured prevailed in the court below and defendant company has appealed.

For convenience, the parties will be referred to as the insured and the company.

Both parties state the sole question for determination to be: "Is the loss resulting from damage to jewelry, by a fire intentionally kindled in and confined to a place where fire was intended to be, insured against under the terms of the fire insurance policy in question?"

The facts, which are not in dispute, are as follows:

On an occasion while the policy in question was in force the wife of insured was carrying her ring wrapped in a handkerchief in her purse. Upon arriving at her home she placed the handkerchief, together with some paper cleansing tissues (Kleenex), on the dresser in her bedroom. Later her maid, in cleaning the room, inadvertently picked up the handkerchief containing the ring, together with the cleansing tissues, and threw them into a wastebasket. Still later, another servant emptied the contents of the wastebasket, along with other trash, into a trash burner at the rear of the premises and proceeded to burn the trash so deposited. The trash burner was intended for that purpose, the fire was intentionally lighted by the servant, and was confined to the trash burner. About a week later the ring was found in the trash burner. It had been damaged to the extent of $900.

The policy, a standard form, insured household goods and personal property, usual or incidental to the occupancy of the premises as a dwelling, belonging to insured or a member of his family while contained on the premises, "*   *   * against all direct loss or damage by fire, except as hereinafter provided,   *   *   *" in an amount not exceeding $2,000. The parties agree that the "exceptions" contained in the policy are immaterial to the issues in this case.

　　*　*　*

The company contends here, as it did in the court below, that the quoted insuring clause of the policy, "against all direct loss or damage by fire" covers only loss or damage resulting from a "hostile" fire as distinguished from a "friendly" fire; that here, the fire being intentionally lighted in and confined to a place or receptacle where it was intended to be, was not a hostile fire within the usual and well-established meaning of the term and therefore no recovery can be had.

The insured argues that he purchased and paid for *fire insurance* —not just for fire insurance to cover loss resulting only from so-called "hostile" fires; that the direct loss and damage to the ring by fire is undisputed; that the company would have the court write into the policy an unauthorized and unreasonable restriction; that there is no ambiguity in the terms of the policy and therefore it should be enforced according to its literal terms; and that even though there were some uncertainty as to its meaning the court is bound to construe the policy strictly against the company and favorably to the insured.

Although courts of other jurisdictions and text writers on the subject have had occasion to distinguish between so-called "friendly" and "hostile" fires in connection with loss or damage due to fire, it appears that the precise question before us is one of first impression in this state.

　　*　*　*

In C.J.S. Insurance § 809, pp. 861, 862, the rule is stated:

"Recovery usually may be had for loss or damage of whatever character, which proximately resulted from an actual hostile fire. The liability of an insurance company under a policy of fire insurance ordinarily is measured by the terms of the policy. Although it has been held that an insurance against loss or damage by fire is broad enough to include all fires, however originating, and all damages therefrom of whatever character, as a general rule, to constitute a 'direct loss or damage by fire,' within the usual terms of a policy, there must be an actual fire in the proper sense of that term, from which the loss or damage results, * * *.

"While there seems to be authority to the contrary, it must be a hostile fire, that is, one which becomes uncontrollable or breaks out from where it was intended to be, and becomes a hostile element, * * *.

"Where the fire is a friendly one, * * * it is not a fire within the usual terms of a policy, and recovery cannot be had for loss or damage caused thereby, * * *."

* * *

From the foregoing authorities, as well as from numerous others which we have examined, the very great weight of authority appears to be that "fires," within the meaning of standard insuring clauses in fire insurance policies, are classified as friendly or hostile in nature, notwithstanding that such distinction is not made in the language of the policy itself.

A friendly fire is defined as being a fire lighted and contained in a usual place for fire, such as a furnace, stove, incinerator, and the like, and used for the purposes of heating, cooking, manufacturing, or other common and usual everyday purposes.

A hostile fire is defined as being a fire unexpected, unintended, not anticipated, in a place not intended for it to be and where fire is not ordinarily maintained, or as one which has escaped in the usual and ordinary sense of the word. A fire originally friendly, by escaping, becomes hostile, and ordinarily recovery may be had for loss or damage resulting thereby.

The rule is well stated in Progress Laundry & Cleaning Co. v. Reciprocal Exchange, Tex.Civ.App., 109 S.W.2d 226, 227: "In determining the liability of the insurers for the damage sustained, we deem it advisable to note the distinction between fires that are hostile and those that are friendly. We think the overwhelming weight of authorities is that, so long as a fire burns in a place where it was intended to burn and ought to be, it is to be regarded as an agency for the accomplishment of some intended purpose, although damages may have resulted where none were intended, thus such fire is a 'friendly fire' and insurers are not liable for damages flowing therefrom; but, where a friendly fire escapes from the place where it ought to be to some place where it ought not to be, resulting in damages, such fire becomes a hostile peril for which the insurers are liable."

Words employed in contracts of insurance are to be construed according to the meaning of the terms used, and are to be taken and understood in their plain, ordinary and peculiar sense, so as to give effect to the intention of the parties. In applying the rule the test is not what the insurer intended the words to mean but what a reasonable person in the position of an insured would have understood them to mean.

We think it cannot be denied that in common parlance and everyday usage one has not "had a fire" so long as it has burned only in the place where it was intended to burn, and where fire ordinarily is maintained. By way of illustration, when a person maintains a fire in his furnace, cookstove or fireplace, or when he burns trash in his incinerator, he has not "had a fire" in the ordinary, common acceptation of the term. On the other hand, if a fire on the roof results from sparks from fire in the furnace, cookstove or fireplace, if sparks from the latter should burn a rug or furniture or if the fire in the trash burner escapes therefrom and sets fire to the garage or fence, such person has "had a fire" for which recovery can be had, notwithstanding the fire was originally friendly.

We think it is quite true to say that when one purchases standard fire insurance he does so with the idea in mind of protecting himself from loss or damage resulting from what the law defines as a "hostile" fire, and that the word "fire," as used in fire insurance policies, has, in common parlance, such well-understood meaning. In the Mode case, supra, it was stated: "The meaning of the term 'loss by fire' as being a 'hostile' and not a 'friendly fire' has been so extensively and long recognized that reasonably we must consider, even under liberal interpretation that both insured and insurer contracted with such definition in mind, determinative of what losses were covered."

\* \* \*

It follows that the court erred in overruling the demurrer to the evidence and in rendering judgment in favor of insured. The judgment of the lower court is therefore reversed.

———

## WESTFALL v. AMERICAN STATES INS. CO.

Court of Appeals of Ohio, 1974.
43 Ohio App.2d 176, 334 N.E.2d 523, 72 O.O.2d 400.

JACKSON, Judge.

This is an appeal from a judgment entered by the Common Pleas Court of Cuyahoga County, sitting without a jury, in favor of plaintiffs appellees, John C. Westfall, et al., and against defendant appellant, The American States Insurance Company.

Appellees were the owners of certain premises on Franklin Boulevard, in Cleveland, Ohio. These premises consisted of a lot with two frame buildings, one behind the other.

On April 22, 1970, appellant issued a fire insurance policy to the appellees, insuring these two frame buildings. The pertinent clause of this policy provided:

"* * * this company * * * to an amount not exceeding * * * [$9,000] * * * does insure the insured named above * * * to the extent of the actual cash value of the property at the time of loss, but not exceeding the amount it would cost to repair or replace the property with materials of like kind and quality * * * nor in any event for more than the interest of the insured * * * against all direct loss by fire * * *."

On March 26, 1971, the appellees contracted to sell the premises on Franklin Boulevard, including the two buildings, for a total consideration of $8,000. A clause in this contract provided: "Buildings on premises to be razed by purchaser."

On April 17, 1971, the rear building was damaged by fire. Subsequent to this fire, on June 11, 1971, title to the premises was transferred to the new owners and the appellees received the full consideration of $8,000.

Appellees sued appellants for the full amount of the insurance coverage. The trial court awarded the appellees $8,373, plus interest. Appellant assigns three errors for review by this court.

Appellant contends that the trial court erred in holding that the sellers of a building had an insurable interest and could recover under their insurance policy for a fire loss to the building when the sales contract, entered into prior to the loss, required the purchasers to demolish the building. We find merit in this assignment of error.

A long-standing axiom of insurance law is that an insured must have an insurable interest in the property before he can recover on a policy insuring against damages to the property.

Neither party disputes the proposition that a vendor of real property retains his insurable interest until title is transferred. The narrow issue presented by this case is whether the contractual provision in the purchase agreement that the buildings on the premises were to be "razed by the purchaser" eliminated appellees' insurable interest in these buildings. This issue has apparently not been previously resolved in a reported opinion from this state.

After considering economic realities rather than merely examining the state of legal title, we conclude that the appellees did not retain an insurable interest in the building which they had contracted to sell and have destroyed by the purchaser.

The rationale for the rule that an insured party must have an insurable interest in the insured property stems from the public policy against "wager policies." A "wager policy" is one in which the insured has interest only in the loss or destruction of the property. Having contracted to sell the premises and have the building "razed by the purchaser," the appellees would gain no profit or advantage from the continued existence of the building. Appellees have failed to demonstrate that they were in any way injured by the destruction of the building. They suffered no economic disadvantage from the fire, as they were paid the full contract price for the premises by the purchasers. Under these circumstances, a conclusion that the appellees retained no insurable interest is mandated by the spirit and purpose of the rule prohibiting wagering policies, as well as fundamental fairness.

\*    \*    \*

Judgment reversed.

## ABSTRACT OF TITLE[8]

### 1.  CAPTION

Situated in the Township of Audrain, in the County of Dore and in the State of Ohio, and Being the Northwest quarter of the Southeast quarter, and the North half of the Southeast fraction of the Southwest quarter of Section 34, Township one South, of Range five East, containing 83 acres of land, more or less.

**1–A–Plat.**

Section 34 Tp. 1 South R. 5 East

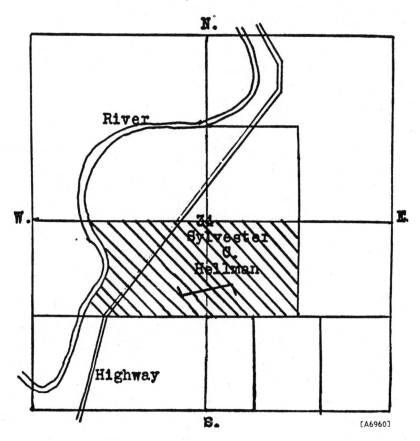

[A6960]

8.  This short, though complete, abstract is reprinted with permission from Flick, Abstract and Title Practice, Vol. 1, pp. 22–40 (2d ed. 1958).  Copyright, 1958, West Publishing Company.

2.

### STATE DEED

The State of Ohio

TO

John Glander

Date of Instrument?    August 5, 1835

Filed: December 16, 1842

Recorded in Volume 12, Page 236 of the Record of Deeds of Dore County, Ohio

Consideration $132.33

Estate conveyed:

What if any defect in instrument? None.

Description: The Southeast fraction of the West half of Section No. 34, Township one South of Range five East within the land and containing 105 acres of land, more or less.

Regularly signed, sealed, witnessed and acknowledged.

3.

### WARRANTY DEED

John Glander and Elizabeth Glander, his wife

TO

Henry Joseph Boehmer

Date of Instrument?   September 4, 1847

Filed: June 4, 1848

Recorded in Volume 2, Page 315 of the Record of Deeds of Dore County, Ohio

Consideration $390.00

Estate conveyed: Fee simple

What if any defect in instrument? None.

Description: Situated in the County of Dore and State of Ohio and bounded and described as follows. to-wit: The Southeast fraction of the West half of Section No. 34, Township one South, Range five East, containing 105.86 acres, more or less.

Also, the Northeast fraction of Section No. 34, Township one South, Range five East, containing 71.51 acres of land, more or less.

Regularly signed, sealed, witnessed and acknowledged.

4.

### WARRANTY DEED

Henry Joseph Boehmer and Mary Boehmer, his wife

TO

Mathias Hellman

Date of Instrument?    January 29, 1848

Filed: November 28, 1848

Recorded in Volume 2, Page 405 of the Record of Deeds of Dore County, Ohio

Consideration $155.00

Estate conveyed: Fee simple

What if any defect in instrument? None.

Description: Situated in the County of Dore and State of Ohio and bounded and described as follows, to-wit: The Northeast fraction of the Southwest quarter of Section 34, Township one South, Range five East, containing 43.20 acres of land, more or less.

Regularly signed, sealed, witnessed and acknowledged.

### 5.

|  |  |
|---|---|
| The State of Ohio | **STATE DEED** |
|  | Date of Instrument?  September 16, 1853 |
| TO | Filed:  January 7, 1854 at 12:30 P.M. |
| J. C. McCowen | Recorded in Volume 87, Page 93 of the Record of Deeds of Dore County, Ohio |
|  | Consideration $160.00 |
|  | Estate conveyed: |
|  | What if any defect in instrument? None. |

Description: The Southeast quarter of Section No. 34, Township one South, Range five East, containing 160 acres of land.

Regularly signed, sealed, witnessed and acknowledged.

### 6.

|  |  |
|---|---|
| John McCowen and Drucilla McCowen, his wife | **WARRANTY DEED** |
|  | Date of instrument?  August 10, 1854 |
|  | Filed: November 9, 1854 |
| TO | Recorded in Volume 11, Page 164 of the Record of Deeds of Dore County, Ohio |
| Mathias Hellman | Consideration $120.00 |
|  | Estate conveyed: Fee simple |
|  | Defects: None. |

Description: The West half of the Northwest quarter of the Southeast quarter of Section 34, Twp 1 S of R 5 E, in the county of Dore, Ohio, containing 20 acres of land.

Regularly signed, sealed, witnessed and acknowledged.

### 7.

|  |  |
|---|---|
| John McCowen and Drucilla McCowen, his wife | **WARRANTY DEED** |
|  | Date of instrument?  January 14, 1860 |
|  | Filed: September 12, 1860 |
| TO | Recorded in Volume 14, Page 221 of the Record of Deeds of Dore County, Ohio |
| Mathias Hellman |  |

Consideration $140
Estate conveyed: Fee simple
What if any defect in instrument?
None.

Description: Situated in the County of Dore in the State of Ohio and in _____ and bounded and described as follows: Being the East half of the Northwest quarter of Section 34, Township one South, Range five East, containing 20 acres of land in the County of Dore, Ohio.

Regularly signed, sealed, witnessed and acknowledged.

8.

### WARRANTY DEED

Mathias Hellman

TO

Joseph Hellman

Date of instrument?  April 2, 1883
Filed: May 11, 1883
Recorded in Volume 42, Page 426 of the Record of Deeds of Dore County, Ohio
Consideration $3500.00
Estate conveyed: Fee simple
What if any defect in instrument?
None.

Description: Situated in the Township of Audrain, in the County of Dore and State of Ohio and being the Northeast fraction of the Southwest fractional quarter, and the Northwest quarter of the Southeast quarter of Section 34, Township one South of Range five East, containing 80 acres of land, more or less.

Regularly signed, sealed, witnessed and acknowledged.

9.

### WARRANTY DEED

Joseph Hellman and
Bernadina Hellman,
husband and wife

TO

Sylvester C. Hellman

Date of instrument?  October 17, 1929
Filed: April 28, 1930 at 4:15 P.M.
Recorded in Volume 139, Page 398 of the Record of Deeds of Dore County, Ohio
Consideration $1.00
Estate conveyed: Fee simple
What if any defect in instrument?
None.

Description: Situated in the Township of Audrain, County of Dore and State of Ohio, and being the Northeast fraction of the Southwest fractional quarter, and the Northwest quarter of the Southeast quarter of Section 34, Township one South, of Range five East, and containing 80 acres of land, more or less.

Regularly signed, sealed, witnessed and acknowledged.

## 10.

### CERTIFICATE TO RECORDER
### REAL ESTATE DEVISED BY WILL

Probate Court, Dore County, Ohio

To the County Recorder of said County:

I the undersigned, Probate Judge of said County, do hereby certify that on the 18th day of March, A.D. 1930, the Last Will and Testament of Joseph Hellmann, late of said County, was duly admitted to probate in this Court, and the same has been duly recorded in Volume P Page 159 of the Records of Wills in this office.

That by the terms of said Will certain real estate was devised to Bernadina Hellmann and Sylvester Hellman.

That the following is a description of said real estate as is contained in the Will, to-wit:

Second: I give, devise and bequeath to my beloved wife, Bernadina, the farm on which we now reside together with all chattel property I may have at the time of my decease. She to have full possession of same during her natural life. After the death of my beloved wife, I give to my son, Sylvester, the aforementioned farm located in Section 34, Audrain Township, Dore County, Ohio, containing 83 acres of land, together with all chattels. He, however, must pay all funeral expenses and debts contracted by my said wife. Also to pay my following named children within three years after the death of my said wife as follows:

Witness my signature and the seal of said Court, this 6th day of January, 1931.

W. M. Bunge,
*Probate Judge*
By Mary McLeasure,
*Deputy Clerk*

[*Seal*]
Recorded in Vol. 141, Page 191
Record of Deeds of said County

## 11.

### APPLICATION FOR PROBATE OF WILL

Dore County, Ohio
Probate Court,

In the Matter of
  The Last Will and Testament
of Joseph Hellmann,

Application To Admit To Probate

_____

Deceased.

To the Probate Court of said County:

Your petitioner respectfully represents that Joseph Hellmann, late a resident of the Township of Audrain in said County, died on or about the 4th day of March, A.D., 1930, leaving an instrument in writing, herewith produced, purporting to be his last Will and Testament;

That the said Joseph Hellmann died leaving Bernadina Hellmann, widow, who resides at Fort Audrain, Ohio, and the following named persons his only next of kin, to-wit:

| Name | Degree of Kinship | P. O. Address |
| --- | --- | --- |
| Mathias Hellmann | Son | Fort Audrain, Ohio |
| Otto Hellmann | " | Delton, Ohio |
| Christina Brinkman | Daughter | Fort Audrain, O. |
| Bernadina Beining | " | Fort Audrain, " |
| Mary Hellmann | " | " " " |
| Sylvester Hellman | Son | " " " |

Your petitioner offers said Will for Probate and prays that a time may be fixed for the proving of the same, and that said above named persons resident in this State may be notified according to law of the pendency of said proceedings.

Sylvester Hellmann,<br>
*Petitioner*

Properly verified.

12.

LAST WILL AND TESTAMENT

In the Name of the Benevolent Father of All: Amen.

I, Joseph Hellmann, of the Township of Audrain, County of Dore and State of Ohio, being about 70 years of age and of sound and disposing mind and memory, do make, publish and declare this my last will and testament, hereby revoking and annulling any and all will or wills by me made heretofore:

First: My will is that all my just debts and funeral expenses be paid out of my estate as soon after my decease as shall be found convenient.

Second: I give, devise and bequeath to my beloved wife Bernadina the farm on which we now reside together with all chattel property I may have at the time of my decease. She to have full possession of same during her natural life. After the death of my beloved wife I give to my son Sylvester the aforementioned farm located in Section thirty-four, Audrain Township, Dore County, Ohio, containing eighty-three (83) acres of land together with all chattels. He, however, must pay all funeral expenses and debts contracted by my said wife. Also to pay my following named children within three years after the death of my said wife as follows:

Item 3. My son Mathias to get Seven Hundred ($700.00) Dollars, I having paid him Eight Hundred ($800.00) Dollars.

Item 4.  My son Otto to get Fifteen Hundred ($1500.00) Dollars.

Item 5.  My daughter Christina Brinkman to get Fourteen Hundred ($1400.00) Dollars.  She having been paid One Hundred ($100.-00) Dollars.

Item 6.  My daughter Bernadina Beining to get Fourteen Hundred ($1400.00) Dollars.  She having been paid One Hundred ($100.-00) Dollars.

Item 7.  My daughter Mary to get Eighteen Hundred ($1800.00) Dollars and the privilege of remaining and living on said farm with my son Sylvester, as long as she lives, and to occupy the East upstairs room.  However in case Sylvester is forced to sell, then my daughter may so give up the aforesaid privileges.

Item 8.  I desire that there be no appraisement of my property and ask that the court omit the same.

Item 9.  I hereby revoke any and all wills formerly made by me.

In Testimony Whereof, I have set my hand to this my last will and testament at Fort Audrain, Ohio, this 8th day of April in the year of our Lord one thousand nine hundred and twenty-four.

Joseph Hellmann

The foregoing instrument was signed by the said Joseph Hellmann in our presence, and by him published and declared as and for his last will and testament and at his request, and in his presence, and in the presence of each other, we hereunto subscribe our names as attesting witnesses, at Fort Audrain, Ohio, this 8th day of April, A.D., 1924.

Anton J. Berelman        resides at Fort Audrain, Ohio
Rudolph Rasbe        resides at Fort Audrain, Ohio

Filed March 18, 1930

13.

NOTE:  The order for hearing, the admission to probate and record, the waiver of notice and consent to probate, the testimony of witnesses to the will, the application for letters, the issuance of letters;  the order for bond;  and the proof of publication of notice to creditors are all regular and complete and are not set out.

14.

JOURNAL ENTRY

IN  PROBATE  COURT<br>Dore County, Ohio<br>May 13, 1930

In the matter of the Estate of
    Joseph Hellman,
        Deceased.          Estate Not Subject to Tax

Determination of Inheritance Tax

Sylvester C. Hellman as Administrator of the estate of Joseph Hellman, deceased, having filed an application duly verified, for a finding and order that said estate and the successions therein are exempt from any inheritance tax under the laws of Ohio, the same came on for hearing.

And the Court being fully advised in the premises, finds and determines that the gross value of said estate is $885.86; the debts and costs of administration are $585.00, and the net actual market value thereof is $300.86, (a) Said decedent died leaving three sons and three daughters, and that as a result said estate and the successions therein are exempt from such inheritance tax.

It is ordered that the court costs on this proceeding taxed at $3.00 be certified to the County Auditor to be paid and credited in the manner provided by law.

W. M. Bunge, Probate Judge

Filed May 13, 1930.

15.

| In the Matter of the Estate of | IN PROBATE COURT |
|---|---|
| <u>Joseph Hellman,</u> | Dore County, Ohio |
| Deceased. | Saturday May 2, 1931. |

The first and final account of Sylvester Hellman, Administrator with will annexed of the estate of Joseph Hellman, deceased, herein filed on the 23rd day of March, A.D., 1931, came in this day for hearing and settlement, due notice thereof having been published according to law. No exceptions having been filed thereto, and no one now appearing to except or object to the same; and the Court having carefully examined said account and the vouchers therewith and all matters pertaining thereto, and being fully advised in the premises, finds the same to be in all respects just and correct and in conformity to law.

It is ordered that the same be and hereby is approved, allowed and confirmed.

The Court further finds said Administrator with will annexed chargeable with the assets of the estate of said Joseph Hellman to the amount of $929.11 and that he is entitled to the credits in the sum of $929.11 and that there is no balance due to said estate.

And the Court further finding that said estate has been duly and fully settled, it is ordered that said Administrator with will annexed be discharged and his bond released from further liability. It is ordered that said account and the proceedings herein be recorded in the records of this office, and that said Administrator with will annexed pay the costs herein taxed at $5.00.

W. M. Bunge, Probate Judge

Filed May 2, 1931.

16.

EASEMENT

Sylvester Hellman

TO

The General Utilities Co.
of Deshler, Ohio

Date of Instrument. April 22, 1933

Recorded May 17, 1933 in Volume
143 at Page 596

No defects in instrument

Grants the right to construct, operate and maintain its lines through and along the following described property: The Northeast 43.1 acres of the Southwest quarter of section 34, Township one South, Range five East.

17.

TAX STATEMENT

The tax duplicates of the Treasurer's Office and the records of the Auditor's Office and Surveyor's Office of Dore County, Ohio, show the following in connection with the taxes levied against caption lands:

Amount of Special Assessments and Terms:
No specials
Description of Land as it Appears on the Duplicates:

| | |
|---|---|
| Sec. 34 NW¼ SE¼ | 40A |
| Sec. "N½ SE fr. SW¼ | 43.10A |
| Assessed Value of | |
| Land | $4390.00 |
| Buildings | $2340.00 |
| | |
| Total | $6730.00 |

Current Taxes:

Paid    Taxes for the first half of the year 1937, due and payable in December 1937 .................. $33.65

Unpaid    Taxes for the last half of the year 1937, due and payable in June 1938 ....................... $33.65

18.

State of Ohio, County of Dore

I hereby certify that the annexed abstract, which is furnished ————, as prospective mortgagee for use in passing on the title to premises covered thereby, is a correct abstract of the title to the land described in the caption thereof, to-wit:

CAPTION LANDS

in the said county and state: that said abstract correctly shows all matters affecting or relating to the said title which are of record or on file in said county, including conveyances, deeds, trust deeds, land

and other liens, attachments and foreign or domestic executions in the hands of the sheriff, certificates of authority to pay taxes, suits pending by or against owners of record within the last two years or against Sylvester Hellman, notices of Federal liens, tax sales, tax deeds, probate proceedings, special proceedings, and unsatisfied judgments and transcripts of judgments from United States and State courts against owners of record or against Sylvester Hellman, notices of liens on bail bonds or recognizances filed against said premises, or against owners of record on or since April 1, 1929, or against Sylvester Hellman, under chapter 14, section 13435–5, of laws of Ohio of 1929; that said abstract also shows all bankruptcy proceedings and certified copies of orders of adjudication and orders approving bonds of trustee in bankruptcy proceedings by or against any party who, within three years past, has been an owner of record of said land or against Sylvester Hellman on file or of record in said county; that all taxes and special assessments against said premises are paid in full to and including the first instalment of the taxes for the year 1937 and that there are no outstanding instalments of special assessments to become due in the future.

Dated at _____, Ohio this 2nd day of May, A.D. 19__, at 10:00 o'clock A.M.

C. W. McLain
*Abstracter*

Continued to this date and recertified as above, this _____ day of _____, A.D. 19__, at _____ o'clock __.M.

## PROBLEMS

1.  Siedel lived in a state that has a "notice" recording statute. On August 1, 1980, he deeded his real estate to Alpha, the deed providing that "Seidel conveys and warrants Sunnybrook Farm to Alpha." On November 1, 1980, Siedel deeded the same real estate to Beta, the deed providing that "Siedel conveys and warrants Sunnybrook Farm to Beta." Both Alpha and Beta recorded their deeds on the date of purchase. Who is now the owner of Sunnybrook? Why?

2.  Jones deeded his real estate to Hamilton on April 24, 1979, although Jones continued to live on the property. Jones deeded the same real estate to Randall on June 29, 1979. Randall, who had no knowledge of the prior sale, immediately took possession of the property. Hamilton recorded his deed on August 5, 1979, and Randall recorded his deed on August 20, 1979. A state statute provides that a deed is not valid against later purchasers without notice of the deed if the later purchase was made before the deed was recorded. Who is entitled to the real estate— Jones, Hamilton, or Randall? Why?

3.  Shifty sold his farm to Leroy on November 1, 1975, for $75,000. Leroy immediately recorded his deed and took possession of the farm. On December 1, 1975, Shifty sold the farm for $5.00 to his brother-in-law, Crafty, who recorded his deed on that date. A dispute over ownership of the farm later developed between Leroy and Crafty. Assuming the

state has a "notice" recording statute, list all arguments that Leroy should raise to prove that he is entitled to ownership.

4. Holt borrowed the sum of $400 from Andrew County and executed a mortgage to the county on a lot owned by him in the city of Savannah. The mortgage was promptly recorded, but the recorder mistakenly listed the debt on the record as $200 instead of $400. Holt then sought to obtain a loan from Terrell. After examining the county records, which showed a mortgage of only $200, Terrell decided to lend Holt the funds he sought and take a junior mortgage. Later Andrew County sought to foreclose its mortgage. Terrell claimed that his junior mortgage gave him priority to proceeds from the foreclosure sale above $200. Is he correct? Why?

5. The cost and complexity of real estate title transfers has been subject to a great deal of criticism (see the quotation at the beginning of Chapter 10). Which method of proving title will you use when you purchase a house? How can the proof of real estate titles be simplified without sacrificing the interests of the purchaser?

6. Review the abstract at the end of the chapter. If you were purchasing this property, would you be satisfied that the seller has good title? What potential problems appear on the abstract?

7. Hall owned a parcel of land which he mortgaged to Morse on August 8, 1872. Hall also mortgaged the same land to Clark, who had notice of the earlier mortgage, on September 7, 1875. The mortgage to Clark was recorded on January 31, 1876 and the mortgage to Morse was recorded September 8, 1877. On October 4, 1881, Clark assigned his mortgage to Curtis, who had no actual notice of the mortgage to Morse. Under a "notice" recording statute, does the Morse mortgage or the Curtis mortgage have priority? Why?

8. Dorothy and John, husband and wife, owned certain property as joint tenants. In October, 1957, Dorothy separated from John and went to Nevada, where she obtained a divorce on November 13. However, they continued to own the property as joint tenants. John lived on the property and obtained fire insurance as the sole insured to cover improvements he had made on the land. Dorothy had no knowledge of the improvements or the fire insurance. Fire later destroyed the improvements and, when John died, Dorothy became sole owner of the property. She claimed that she is entitled to the fire insurance proceeds which were paid into John's estate. Does she have a valid claim? Why?

9. Pratz purchased a home in the city of St. Louis. The home was mortgaged to the Pulaski Saving and Loan Association (Pulaski), which obtained fire insurance from United States Fidelity and Guaranty Company. The standard mortgage clause in the policy provided that "loss or damage, if any, under this policy, shall be payable to the mortgagee . . . and this . . . interest . . . shall not be invalidated . . . by any change in the title ownership of the property . . . .. The mortgagee . . . shall notify this Company of any change of ownership or occupancy or increase of hazard which shall come to the knowledge of said mortgagee; . . . otherwise this policy shall be null and void." On September 14, 1971, Pratz sold the property to Magee, but Magee's deed was not recorded until July 19, 1972. Pulaski had no actual knowledge of the sale but was given the impression that Pratz was contemplating a

sale. When the property was partially destroyed by fire, Pulaski sought to recover under the fire policy. United States Fidelity argued that Pulaski cannot recover because it violated the standard mortgage clause by not giving notice of the change of ownership. Decide.

10. Slate purchased a tract of land in Columbia, Missouri. At the request of the sellers, the Boone County Abstract Company (Boone) certified and delivered to Slate an abstract of title. The abstract did not mention a utility easement on the property. Slate did not learn of the easement until after he purchased the land and now seeks damages from Boone on a negligence theory. Boone argues that, since its contract was with the seller, it is not liable to Slate. Is this a good defense? Why?

## Chapter 9

## FINANCING THE REAL ESTATE PURCHASE

> For which of you, intending to build a tower, sitteth not down
> first, and counteth the cost, whether he have sufficient to finish
> it? Lest haply, after he hath laid the foundation, and is not able
> to finish it, all that behold it begin to mock him.
>
> St. Luke 14: 28–9

Once a real estate contract has been signed and the seller has
proven marketable title, it would be possible for the purchaser to
close the transaction immediately by writing a check for the purchase price. However, the purchase of real estate represents the
largest financial investment of a lifetime for most purchasers; they
usually cannot afford to pay cash but, instead, must obtain financing
to complete the purchase. The most common method of financing is
to borrow money and to give the lender some form of security in case
the borrower defaults on the loan.

Three types of security arrangements are frequently used either
separately or concurrently. First, the creditor might ask for security
in the form of personal property, for example, an automobile owned
by the debtor. As discussed in Chapter 2, the creditor's acquisition
of a security interest in personal property is governed by the law of
secured transactions. Second, the creditor might ask the debtor to
find another person with a good credit record who will agree to become liable along with the debtor on the loan. The third party is
called a surety, and the transaction is governed by the law of suretyship. Finally, the creditor might ask for security in the form of real
estate, in which case the debtor will give the creditor a mortgage covering the real estate. This chapter will focus on the rights and duties
of the lender and borrower when a real estate mortgage is given to
secure the loan.

The law of mortgages is very complex; its origins date back to
early Saxon law and there are many variations from state to state.
In order to simplify our presentation and to make mortgage law more
manageable, we will first define essential mortgage terms and then
cover a typical mortgage transaction in chronological order, from the
loan application through foreclosure. After discussing mortgage law,
we will examine an alternative method of financing, the installment
or land contract, and conclude the chapter with a review of other interests, such as a mechanic's lien, which might impair the value of
the mortgage.

## I.  DEFINITIONS

When a person who borrows money, a debtor, gives an interest in real estate as security for the debt, he becomes a mortgagor.  The party who lends money, the creditor, becomes a mortgagee when he takes an interest in real estate as security for the loan.  Any individual may lend money and become a mortgagee, although in many cases mortgagees are professional lenders such as savings and loan associations, commercial banks, mortgage banks and insurance companies.  In the following discussion of a typical mortgage transaction, we will assume that the purchaser is borrowing money from a savings and loan institution or a commercial bank.

The mortgage itself was considered under the common law to be a transfer of title to the real estate from the mortgagor to the mortgagee, with the transfer to become void if the mortgagor paid the debt as promised.  The modern view, however, is that the mortgage represents merely a lien, that is, a type of security which gives the creditor the right to have property sold and to be paid from the proceeds, rather than a transfer of title.  While most states follow the lien theory, a few states still consider mortgages to be title transfers, at least in regard to the form of the transaction.  However, apart from a few exceptions to be noted later, the rights and duties of the mortgagor and mortgagee are now identical under both the title and lien theories.

The conventional mortgage, sometimes called a regular mortgage, will be used in our example of the typical mortgage transaction.  In some cases the transaction may take a different form even though the legal effect is similar to that of the conventional mortgage.  One common variation is the deed of trust.  Under this arrangement, the trustor (debtor) deeds property to an independent third party (trustee) to hold for the beneficiary (creditor) as security for the loan.  If the debt is repaid, the property will be deeded back to the debtor; if the debtor defaults, the trustee will foreclose on behalf of the beneficiary in a proceeding that is often less expensive and less time-consuming than a conventional mortgage foreclosure.  In a corporate setting, the deed of trust may be used when a corporation, wanting to borrow money, sells bonds and deeds property to a trustee to secure the debt represented by the bonds.

A second possible variation is the purchase money mortgage.  Although technically a purchase money mortgage results whenever the borrowed money is used to purchase the real estate that is given as security, in many cases the term is limited to transactions where the vendor deeds property to the vendee and takes a mortgage from the vendee to secure any part of the purchase price that has not yet been paid.

Another variation is the creation of a mortgage that is second or even third, fourth and so on, to a first mortgage. Although a few states forbid or limit them, secondary mortgages have become popular in recent years with the dramatic increase in homeowners' equity brought on by inflation. In many cases second mortgage loans are preferred by borrowers over consumer installment loans because interest rates are lower, the repayment period is longer (five to ten years) and a larger amount can be borrowed. For example, if a homeowner owes $30,000 on his first mortgage and his house is valued at $50,000, lenders usually will lend the difference between 80 percent of the value of the home ($40,000) and the amount of the first mortgage. There are, however, drawbacks to second mortgage financing. The interest rates normally run 3 to 6 percent above those for first mortgages. And, in the event of default and foreclosure of the first mortgage, the first mortgage will be paid off, followed by the second mortgage, with anything remaining going to the owner. If the second mortgage alone is foreclosed, the rights of the first mortgagee are not impaired and a purchaser at the foreclosure sale takes title subject to the first mortgage.

A final variation of the conventional mortgage is the equitable mortgage. In many cases a court in equity will treat a transaction as a mortgage even though the documents do not meet the legal requirements (to be discussed below); such a mortgage is called an equitable mortgage. Often a court will create an equitable mortgage to protect a creditor. For example, if a note signed by the debtor states that the note is secured by a real estate mortgage but no real estate mortgage is formally drawn up, a court will hold that an equitable mortgage has been created because of the intention of the parties expressed in the note.[1]

In other cases an equitable mortgage will be declared for the protection of the debtor. This happens most frequently when a debtor deeds his real estate to a creditor with no mention in the deed that the conveyance is intended only as security on the loan. If a court determines that, in fact, the parties intended the deed as security, the creditor's interest will only be that of a mortgagee and the debtor will be allowed to recover the property by paying off the debt. In determining the intention of the parties, courts focus on three factors. First, did the grantor owe money to the grantee at the time of conveyance and thereafter? Second, is the land worth considerably more than the amount of the loan given in payment for the land? For instance, in Leathers v. Peterson,[2] the grantor, who could not obtain a loan elsewhere because of his drinking and spending habits, borrowed between $10,000 and $24,000 from a friend who was also his accountant. When the grantor deeded property worth $40,000 to

1.　Trustees of Zion Methodist Church v. Smith, 335 Ill.App. 233, 81 N.E.2d 649 (1948).

2.　195 Or. 62, 244 P.2d 619 (1952).

his friend, the court held that the deed was really a mortgage because of the disparity between the amount of the advance and the value of the property. Third, did the grantor continue to act as owner after the conveyance? To answer this question courts stress the grantor's continued possession of the property, and his payment of taxes and insurance premiums.[3] See McCool v. Ayres, infra.

## II.  LOAN APPLICATION AND COMMITMENT

Although there are the variations noted above, most mortgages are conventional in form. The conventional mortgage transaction begins with a loan application to the creditor, in this example, a bank. If the bank is satisfied with the applicant's credit rating and is convinced that the real estate offers sufficient security, the bank will send the applicant a commitment which sets forth the terms of the loan and the conditions that must be met before closing. In some states the commitment is regarded as the bank's acceptance of the applicant's offer to borrow money, with the result that the applicant owes the commitment fee, which is usually charged by the bank for holding the mortgage funds, from that date. In other states the commitment is viewed as an offer by the bank that must be accepted by the applicant within a certain time period, for example, ten days. If the applicant accepts, the bank will hold the funds for the borrower for a specified time, such as three months, in exchange for the commitment fee, which is due whether or not a loan is eventually made. For instance, in Weiner v. Salem Five Cents Sav. Bank,[4] the defendant banks committed themselves to lend a developer a specified sum in exchange for a commitment fee of $54,000. When, through no fault of the banks, the loan was never made, the banks were allowed to retain the fee.

In deciding whether to make a loan commitment, lenders must consider an expanding body of recent legislation and regulations often promulgated in the interest of consumers. The following are four prominent examples of such legislation.

### A.  TRUTH IN LENDING

Pursuant to the Truth in Lending Act, the Board of Governors of the Federal Reserve System drafted Regulation Z. The purpose of Regulation Z is to require lenders to make full disclosure when advertising the terms of a loan and when advising individual borrowers of loan costs. Regulation Z applies to consumer loans, not to business or commercial credit transactions.

Two special provisions under Regulation Z apply to real estate transactions. First, although the lender must disclose the annual

3. Alber v. Bradley, 321 Mich. 255, 32     4. — Mass. —, 360 N.E.2d 306 (1977).
N.W.2d 454 (1948).

percentage rate (APR), which is higher than the interest rate alone because the APR includes discount points, fees, and other charges, the lender is not required to disclose to the borrower the total dollar amount of the finance charge. Second, the lender must notify the borrower who uses his residence as security that he has three business days to cancel the credit arrangement, unless the residence secures a purchase money first mortgage.

## B.  EQUAL CREDIT OPPORTUNITY ACT

The Equal Credit Opportunity Act, which became effective in 1975, provides that a lender may not refuse a loan on the grounds of a person's sex or marital status if the person is eligible for credit in all other respects. This means that lenders can no longer question applicants about their plans to have children in the future; neither can creditors require additional cosigners because the applicant is a single woman, nor refuse to put an account in the names of both husband and wife. Under a 1977 amendment to the act, discrimination is also prohibited on the basis of race, color, national origin, age, and receipt of welfare.

## C.  REDLINING

"Redlining" occurs when lenders refuse to make mortgage loans or impose stricter mortgage terms in certain neighborhoods. The term originates from the alleged practice of some lenders and insurance firms of mapping out risky areas with boundaries of red ink. Critics of redlining claim that this practice discriminates on the basis of race and contributes to the decline of inner cities. While many lending institutions deny that redlining is practiced, the argument made in support of redlining is that lending institutions should have the right to select their customers on the basis of traditional credit standards and should not be forced to accept real estate as security which does not meet those standards.

Although resolution of the redlining issue is largely a political question which will in all likelihood be settled by Congress, there has been significant legislative, regulatory, and judicial activity to date. Several states have enacted legislation that prohibits redlining. A Michigan statute effective in 1978, for instance, prohibits redlining on the basis of ethnic or racial characteristics, prohibits denial of a loan because of the age of a building, and requires lenders to disclose where their loans are made.[5]  On the administrative level, the Federal Home Loan Bank Board approved regulations in 1978 that prohibit savings and loan institutions from "arbitrary refusals" to make loans

5.  Mich. Comp. Laws Ann. § 445.1601. See also the Community Reinvestment Act, 12 U.S.C.A. §§ 2901–2905, which provides that "regulated financial institutions have a continuing and affirmative obligation to help meet the credit needs of the local communities in which they are chartered."

on property that is old or in an area the loan institution assumes is declining.  The rules also require lenders to give copies of their loan underwriting standards to customers upon request and to provide loan applicants with a copy of the property appraisal if the application is turned down because the appraised value of the property is too low to provide adequate security.  Judicial activity relating to redlining has resulted from lawsuits brought under the Fair Housing Act. For instance, in Harrison v. Otto G. Heinzeroth Mortgage Co.,[6] the court awarded damages to a home mortgage applicant when it was shown that the lender violated the Fair Housing Act by discriminating on the basis of the racial composition of the neighborhood.  The lender had required a 50 percent down payment on a home in a neighborhood that was changing from white to black, and had offered the borrower better terms on property in other neighborhoods.

## D.  REAL ESTATE SETTLEMENT PROCEDURES ACT

The Real Estate Settlement Procedures Act of 1974 (RESPA) was the result of a 1972 study by the Department of Housing and Urban Development.  The study concluded that, on a national level, settlement costs for purchasing a home worth $20,000 to $24,000 ranged from $50 to $2,000.  The study also discovered that kickbacks and undisclosed commissions were paid to professionals involved in real estate closings.  On the basis of the study, Congress found, in Section 2 of the act, "that significant reforms in the real estate settlement process are needed to insure that consumers throughout the nation are provided with greater and more timely information on the nature and costs of the settlement process and are protected from unnecessarily high settlement charges caused by certain abusive practices that have developed in some areas of the country."  Several reforms to achieve these goals are included in the act, which covers first mortgage loans secured by 1-to-4-family residential properties and given by a federally regulated or insured lender.  First, in order to provide more effective advance disclosure of settlement costs, the act requires the lender to give a copy of a HUD guide to settlement costs to the borrower at the time the loan application is submitted.  This booklet provides advice on how to shop for professional services, and on homebuyers' rights and obligations.  At the same time, the lender is required to provide the applicant with a good faith estimate of settlement service charges and, one business day before closing, the applicant has the right to inspect a Uniform Settlement Statement that itemizes the service fees charged by the lender.  Second, the act states that persons who give or accept kickbacks or referral fees shall be liable for civil damages and subject to maximum criminal penalties of one year in prison and a $10,000 fine.  Also, a seller cannot require the buyer to purchase insurance from a particular company.

6.   430 F.Supp. 893 (N.D.Ohio 1977).

Third, most lenders require borrowers to deposit funds in a reserve or escrow account to cover future insurance and tax charges the lender pays on the property.  These funds are deposited monthly with the mortgage payment, each monthly escrow payment representing approximately one-twelfth of the annual charges.  Under RESPA, the amount the borrower pays into the escrow account at closing is limited to a sum sufficient to make required payments due by the date of the first mortgage payment plus an extra "cushion" not to exceed two monthly escrow payments.  Although not required by RESPA, a few states require lenders to pay interest on funds deposited in escrow accounts.

### III.  THE MORTGAGE CLOSING

The closing of the mortgage transaction usually is accomplished concurrently with the closing of the real estate transaction.  At the closing the mortgagee will disburse the loan, less the mortgage closing costs, and the loan will be used by the borrower to complete the purchase.  The HUD booklet lists the following closing costs related to the mortgage:  (1) a loan origination fee, often a percentage of the loan charged to cover administrative costs in processing the loan;  (2) a loan discount or "points," used to offset restrictions on yield imposed by government regulation, each point being equal to 1 percent of the mortgage amount;  (3) an appraisal fee paid to an independent appraiser who has prepared an appraisal that the lender uses to determine the value of the security;  (4) a credit report fee to cover the cost of a report on the borrower's credit history;  (5) a lender's inspection fee in cases where the lender inspects a building that has recently been constructed;  (6) a mortgage insurance premium for private mortgage insurance, which is required on certain loans to protect the lender against loss if the borrower defaults;  (7) attorney's fees for services provided to the lender in connection with the settlement;  (8) a premium for lender's title insurance;  and (9) a charge for a survey, which a lender may require to determine the location of a building, easements, and lot lines.  It is important to remember that, although these charges are paid by the borrower and deducted from the amount of the loan, they are incurred to protect the lender;  to completely protect his own interest, the borrower should hire an attorney and purchase owner's title insurance.  In addition to these closing charges, the lender will also deduct certain items such as interest, insurance premiums, and tax payments that are required to be paid in advance or that are placed in escrow accounts.

### A.  THE NOTE

Two instruments, the note and the mortgage, are signed by the debtor at the mortgage closing.  In the note the mortgagor promises to pay a specified principal amount plus interest on or before a certain date. In most cases a mortgage without a note is worthless because it would secure nothing, but a note without a mortgage is valid and remains the personal obligation of the debtor.

Notes may be divided into two broad categories: negotiable and non-negotiable. A negotiable note is one which meets the requirements of Section 3–104 (1) of the Uniform Commercial Code: "Any writing to be a negotiable instrument within this Article must (a) be signed by the maker or drawer; and (b) contain an unconditional promise or order to pay a sum certain in money and no other promise, order, obligation or power given by the maker or drawer except as authorized by this Article; and (c) be payable on demand or at a definite time; and (d) be payable to order or to bearer." If any of these requirements is missing, the note is considered to be non-negotiable. A non-negotiable note can still be sold or assigned by the lender; however, as discussed below, such notes are more difficult to sell because the purchaser's rights are limited. Consequently, from the lender's viewpoint, it is important that all notes meet the U.C.C. requirements for negotiability.

While it is beyond the scope of this book to review each of the requirements in detail, one example will illustrate the type of issue raised under Section 3–104(1). In Holly Hill Acres, Ltd. v. Charter Bank of Gainesville,[7] the maker of a note was sued by a bank that had purchased the note from the payees, Rogers and Blythe. The main legal issue in the case was whether the note was negotiable since it included the following language: "This note with interest is secured by a mortgage on real estate, of even date herewith, made by the maker hereof in favor of the said payee, and shall be construed and enforced according to the laws of the State of Florida. The terms of said mortgage are by this reference made a part hereof." The court concluded that the note was not negotiable because it did not contain an unconditional promise to pay but instead was conditioned on the terms of the mortgage. The court distinguished another case, holding that a note was negotiable when it read "this note secured by mortgage," on the grounds that the language merely referred to the mortgage but was not conditioned on the mortgage.

1. **Acceleration Clause.** In addition to negotiability, the lender faces two major legal concerns in accepting notes. First, the note— and the mortgage itself—should contain an acceleration clause stating that if the debtor defaults in any one payment, the entire principal and interest will become due immediately at the lender's option. Without an acceleration clause, the lender could not foreclose the entire mortgage until the end of the term of the note; instead, his only recourse would be to foreclose on each individual overdue payment.

7. 314 So.2d 209 (Fla.App.1975).

An acceleration clause will not be enforced unless the mortgagee acts in an equitable and fair manner. For instance, in Harrell v. Perkins,[8] the note and mortgage contained the following acceleration clause: "If default be made at any time in payment of any of said installments for a period of 60 days, all of the remaining installments not then due shall at the option of the holder at once become due and payable, for the purpose of foreclosure." The mortgagee, who lived next door to the mortgaged property, persuaded the mortgagor to obtain an FHA loan in order to pay off the mortgage at a discount. While the FHA loan was in process, and after the mortgagor had made over $11,000 in improvements to meet FHA requirements, the mortgagee told the mortgagor that she need not make further monthly payments until she received the FHA loan. However, the mortgagee later changed his mind, refused to accept the defaulted monthly payments, and brought foreclosure proceedings. The court denied foreclosure on the grounds that "equity will relieve against acceleration when the creditor's conduct has been responsible for the debtor's default." See Graf v. Hope Bldg. Corp., infra.

A special type of acceleration clause has been litigated frequently in recent years. This kind of clause specifies that if the mortgagor sells the mortgaged real estate, the entire principal and interest will become due immediately, thus requiring the purchaser to obtain a new mortgage or to renegotiate the existing mortgage with the lender, often at a higher interest rate. A growing number of courts have refused to honor these "due on sale" clauses. In one such case,[9] a mortgage agreement provided that "the mortgage shall become due and payable forthwith at the option of the mortgagee if there shall be any change in ownership of the mortgaged property." When the mortgagor sold the property on a land contract without the approval of the bank, the bank commenced foreclosure proceedings and the mortgagor brought suit to enjoin the foreclosure. The court held for the mortgagor on the grounds that the clause constituted an unreasonable restraint on alienation because the bank's only interest in enforcing the clause was "in maintaining its portfolio at current interest rates." However the court noted that such clauses might be enforceable if the bank could show that the property would decline in value because of the transfer or that the purchaser was not a good credit risk.

2. **Usury Laws.** The other major concern of lenders is the effect of relevant state usury laws on the transaction. Usury laws set a maximum amount of interest that can be charged on a loan. Usury law is especially complex because of variations among states and because, within each state, the law is subject to a number of exceptions. For example, in some states certain lenders, such as building and loan

8. 216 Ark. 579, 226 S.W.2d 803 (1950).  9. Nichols v. Ann Arbor Federal Sav. & Loan Ass'n, 73 Mich.App. 163, 250 N.W.2d 804 (1977).

associations, might be exempt from the law; or loans to certain borrowers, often businesses, might be exempt. In many states, certain transactions might be exempt, including real estate loans and credit arrangements made by the seller as part of a sale. Finally, certain payments to the lenders are exempt, such as appraisal fees and credit reports, because they represent fees for services rendered rather than compensation paid for the use of money.

If none of the exemptions applies, the penalties imposed for charging a usurious rate of interest are also subject to much variation. In some states, the creditor forfeits both principal and interest while in other states only part or all of the interest is forfeited. In a few states, the creditor will forfeit a multiple of the interest. For instance, in Davenport v. Unicapital Corp.,[10] the plaintiffs borrowed $2,360, which was payable in 84 monthly installments of $54.96. This produced a 14 percent interest rate, while the maximum lawful rate was 7 percent. The court decided that the mortgage should be cancelled and that the plaintiffs were entitled to recover twice the amount of usurious interest.

The complexity of the usury law has been compounded in recent years by the development of several new types of mortgage loans. Under the traditional fixed payment mortgage, the mortgage interest and payments remain fixed over the life of the loan and, as the years pass, a larger portion of the monthly payment is used to pay the principal, since the interest portion of the payment is based upon the principal balance and decreases with that balance. A recent development that alters the traditional approach is the graduated payment mortgage, under which mortgage payments are small at first and then increase every year for five to ten years until they reach a fixed amount, which is higher than under a conventional mortgage. For example, instead of paying $241 per month on a conventional $30,000 30-year mortgage at 9 percent interest, the monthly rate might begin at $190 and, after a few years, level off at $270 a month. This arrangement presumably would allow first-time home buyers, who expect higher earnings in the future, a better opportunity to obtain financing. While not yet litigated, there is a potential usury problem with this plan because if the monthly payments are not large enough in the early years to cover fully the interest due, the extra interest is added to the principal. This means that the borrower will later be paying interest on interest—which is illegal under the usury laws in most states.

Another recent development is the variable rate mortgage, under which the interest rate rises and falls on the basis of a specified index such as the interest paid on savings deposits. When the rate rises, the debtor may be given the option of making the same monthly payments while extending the maturity date, or paying at a higher

10.  267 S.C. 691, 230 S.E.2d 905 (1976).

monthly rate. The variable rate mortgage is subject to potential legal attack on two grounds. First, there is the danger that interest rates will rise above the limits established by the state usury law. Second, the mortgage note probably will not be considered negotiable under the Uniform Commercial Code because both the amount and the time for payment can vary.[11]

3. **Early Payment Clause.** While the lender is concerned primarily with negotiability, the acceleration clause, and the impact of usury laws, the borrower is especially concerned with one aspect of the note: the note should contain an "on or before" clause that allows the borrower to pay off the mortgage in full on or before the due date. This clause would allow the mortgagor to obtain refinancing if interest rates drop significantly. If a $30,000 mortgage for 25 years was taken out at the rate of 9.5 percent annual interest, the interest cost alone over the 25 years would be $48,660; yet if the same loan could be refinanced immediately at 8 percent annual interest, the total interest cost would drop to $39,480, a significant saving. Lenders, of course, are wary of early payments because of the interest they will lose, so it is common for lenders to charge a prepayment penalty if the mortgage is paid off in the early years of the loan. Instead of paying off the full amount early, some mortgagors make extra monthly payments early in the loan period, thus reducing the total amount of interest paid on the loan. If the mortgagor in these cases is unable to make his monthly payments at a later date because of financial hardships or other reasons, the additional early payments cannot be used to cover the defaulted payments, although there is some case authority to the contrary.

## B. THE MORTGAGE

1. **Form.** The second instrument signed by the borrower at the closing, the mortgage, includes many of the provisions found in a deed (which will be discussed in the following chapter). For instance, the mortgage must be in writing and should name the parties, describe the property subject to the mortgage, and include any warranties given by the mortgagor. Like the deed, the mortgage should include words granting the mortgagee an interest in the property. In title states these words are "convey and warrant," while in lien states the phrase "mortgage and warrant" is used. Finally, like a deed, the mortgage should be in the form required for recording, that is, it should be acknowledged and witnessed where required by state law.

In most states an unrecorded mortgage, like an unrecorded deed, will be subject to the rights of a later bona fide purchaser or mortgagee. In one situation, however, the usual priority rules under the re-

---

11. Baker, *Adjustable Interest Rates in Home Mortgages: A Reconsideration,* 1975 Wis.L.Rev. 742.

cording statutes are not followed. When the purchaser of real estate gives a purchase money mortgage to acquire the property and he uses the entire loan to pay for the real estate, the purchase money mortgage is given priority over any earlier claims against the mortgagor, even though they may have been recorded. The reason for this rule is that before the purchase, the mortgagor has no interest against which the earlier claims can be applied and, at the time of purchase, the mortgagor receives property title that is instantaneously subject to the purchase money mortgage. To illustrate the application of this rule, in Fecteau v. Fries,[12] Fries decided to purchase several lots and on August 6, 1926, borrowed $7,500 from Patterson, $5,000 of which was used to make the purchase; he executed a note and mortgage to Patterson. On August 11, 1926, the vendor, Fecteau, delivered a deed to Fries, and Fries gave Fecteau a purchase money mortgage for $24,000 on the same property covered by the Patterson mortgage. In a later foreclosure proceeding, the court was asked to decide which mortgage had priority—Patterson's mortgage, which was recorded first, or Fecteau's mortgage. The court decided that Fecteau's purchase money mortgage had priority, citing earlier authority to the effect that the deed and the Fecteau mortgage "executed at the same time are to be construed together as one instrument. They constitute an indivisible act." The court further noted that there was never a moment between Fries' taking title and giving the Fecteau mortgage in which Fries could have encumbered the title.

2. **Consideration.** In addition to the usual requirements for executing and recording a deed, certain provisions are unique to the mortgage.[13] For example, the mortgage will often include the terms of the debt and the mortgagor's duties with regard to taxes, insurance, and repairs, to be discussed in greater detail below. One of the most important provisions in the mortgage is the clause that states the consideration received by the mortgagor—the amount of the debt. A statement of consideration in a deed is not required in all states and, even where required, is often stated in terms such as "$1 and other valuable consideration." With a mortgage, however, concealing the exact amount of the debt is a dangerous practice because innocent third parties will rely on the stated amount to determine the value of the lien. Consequently, both the amount of the debt and a description of the note should be included in the mortgage. In Bull-

---

12. 253 Mich. 51, 234 N.W. 113 (1931).

13. In some transactions these provisions might appear in the note instead of the mortgage, while the note provisions discussed earlier might appear in the mortgage. For example, the mortgagor's promise to keep the property in good repair might appear in the note, in the mortgage or in both. Probably the more conservative approach would be to include essential provisions in the mortgage itself in order to make those terms part of the public record or, at least, to incorporate by reference the note into the mortgage.

ock v. Battenhousen,[14] the mortgage stated the maturity date and rate of interest for a debt but did not specify the amount, $6,000. When the mortgagor later sold the property to an innocent purchaser, he fraudulently told the purchaser that the mortgage debt had been paid. The court, in holding that the purchaser took the property free of the mortgage, observed: "The spirit of our recording system requires that the record of a mortgage should disclose, with as much certainty as the nature of the case will admit, the real state of the incumbrance. If a mortgage is given to secure an ascertained debt, the amount of that debt should be stated, and if it is intended to secure a debt not ascertained, such data should be given respecting it as will put any one interested in the inquiry upon the track leading to a discovery."

3. **Future Advance Clause.** The statement of consideration, and its effect on later purchasers, becomes more complicated when the mortgage is given to secure a future advance. To illustrate, on June 1, Igor mortgaged his property to First Bank. The mortgage was to secure a loan of $45,000 that was to be paid to Igor in $15,000 installments on September 1, October 1, and November 1. First Bank made the three payments but on September 15, before the last two payments were made, Second Bank lent Igor $30,000 and took a mortgage on the same property. Each mortgage was recorded on the day it was executed. Now Igor is in default on both mortgages, the two banks each foreclose, and the property is worth a total of $60,000. How should the $60,000 be divided?

The critical legal issue in answering this question is whether First Bank was obligated to make the future advances on the promised dates. If the advances were obligatory, the rule is simple and easy to apply: the mortgagee who is obligated to make future advances has priority over later mortgagees and purchasers. This is fair to First Bank, of course, because of its binding obligation, and it is fair to Second Bank, which could ascertain from the mortgage on record and from related documents that First Bank's loan was obligatory. Obligatory future advance loans are especially common in the construction industry, where advances are made as various stages of construction are completed. In our case, if its payments were obligatory, First Bank would be paid in full while Second Bank would receive the remaining $15,000.

If the advances of First Bank were not obligatory but were to be made at the bank's option, the rule followed in most states is that the optional advance under the prior mortgage has priority unless the prior mortgagee, First Bank, had actual notice of the intervening claim. A common optional advance arrangement is the open-ended mortgage under which the mortgage secures an original loan and any future loans the mortgagee chooses to make. In our case, if First

14. 108 Ill. 28 (1883).

Bank had no actual notice, the results would be the same as above. If, however, Second Bank has given notice of its loan on September 15, First Bank would have priority for its loan of September 1 ($15,000), Second Bank for its loan of September 15 ($30,000) and First Bank would then receive the remaining $15,000. This is fair because First Bank, after receiving notice, has the option of refusing to make additional loans. In four states—Illinois, Michigan, Ohio, and Pennsylvania—recording Second Bank's intervening mortgage constitutes constructive notice to First Bank and has the same effect as actual notice. In these states a lender such as First Bank must search the records for intervening claims before making the optional advance.

## IV.  RIGHTS AND DUTIES AFTER CLOSING

The mortgage instrument may (and usually does) spell out the duties of the mortgagor and mortgagee with regard to the mortgaged premises. In the absence of an agreement, the following rules have been developed by the courts.

### A.  POSSESSION

In theory, the right to possession should pass with the title to the real estate, with the result that in title states the mortgagee would be entitled to possession; in lien states the possession would remain with the mortgagor until foreclosure. In practice, however, possession remains with the mortgagor in virtually every transaction, even in title states, pursuant to state statutes providing that the mortgagor is entitled to possession until default, or under provisions in the mortgage instrument. The law favors possession by the mortgagor so strongly that in some lien states it is against public policy for the mortgagor to give up possession through a provision in the mortgage.[15]

When the mortgagee does take possession, for example, after default, he must manage the property with the same care a prudent owner would provide, and he is liable for the reasonable rental value of the property, which is deducted from the debt. Furthermore, in most states the mortgagee is not entitled to payment for services in managing the property unless the mortgage stipulates a fee.

### B.  RENTS AND PROFITS

It is possible, especially when commercial and industrial real estate is mortgaged, that the property will produce valuable rents and profits. Rentals may come from a lease executed before the mort-

---

15.  Kratovil, Modern Mortgage Law and
Practice § 294 (1972).

gage, in which case foreclosure of the mortgage would not terminate the lease; a lease to rent made after the mortgage would be subject to the mortgage and terminated by foreclosure.

The right to rents and profits provided by real estate belongs to the person in possession, in most cases the mortgagor. Allowing the mortgagor to retain rents and profits is in accord with the intention of the parties, for mortgages usually state that only the land is to be security, not the profits from the land. However, in two instances a court in equity will order the rents and profits to be collected for the benefit of the mortgagee, who must deduct them from the amount of the debt. In the first situation, the mortgagee must prove that the mortgagor is insolvent or otherwise uncollectable and that the mortgagee's security in the property is insufficient to cover the debt. One court made the following statement: "The right to appropriate the rent and profits which equity gives the mortgagee, where a receiver is appointed at his instance, does not result from any specific pledge of such rents contained in the mortgage. Equity makes the mortgage, as between mortgagor and mortgagee, a charge upon the rents and profits whenever the mortgagor is insolvent and the security is inadequate." [16] In the second situation, the mortgagor has assigned the rents and profits to the mortgagee as additional security. Courts have interpreted such assignments to be valid, but only after the mortgagee has taken possession of the real estate.

## C. REPAIRS AND IMPROVEMENTS

As a general rule, a mortgagor has no duty to repair the mortgaged property if it has been damaged through no fault of his own. As a corollary, when the mortgagor does make repairs or improvements, their cost cannot be deducted from the debt even though they benefit the mortgagee by increasing the value of the security. There are, however, two major qualifications to these rules. First, the mortgagor in possession is not allowed to commit waste, which occurs when the value of the secured real estate decreases through the action or inaction of the mortgagor. For example, waste is committed when the mortgagor mortgages the property and then begins to run a strip mining operation that impairs the value of the land.

Second, when the mortgagee is in possession, he has the duty to make reasonable and necessary repairs and can add these to the mortgagor's debt. In Wise v. Layman,[17] where the mortgagee was allowed to recover the cost of wallpaper, plumbing, window shades, screens, and sodding a yard, the court observed that "what are reasonable and necessary repairs depends upon the particular circumstances of each case. The said expenditures made by appellee, in our

---

16. Carolina Portland Cement Co. v. Baumgartner, 99 Fla. 987, 128 So. 241 (1931).

17. 197 Ind. 393, 150 N.E. 368 (1920).

opinion, were for reasonable and necessary repairs to keep the property from deterioration and to maintain same in rental condition." However, if the expenditure is considered to constitute an improvement rather than a repair, the mortgagee is not entitled to reimbursement. Not only is this consistent with the rule that mortgagors cannot deduct the cost of improvements from the mortgage debt, but it also prevents an injustice to the mortgagor. "A contrary holding under such circumstances would mean that at his discretion a mortgagee can put improvements upon real estate to such an extent as to render it impossible for the mortgagor to redeem. His additions might vastly enlarge the value of the land, but prevent redemption by the mortgagor for the want of funds to meet the increase though he might be able to pay the original debt. It would practically destroy the debtor's right of redemption but leave intact the creditor's right to foreclose." [18]

## D.  TAXES

The mortgagor, as the owner of the land, has the duty to pay taxes. This duty is usually reinforced by a clause in the mortgage specifying that the mortgagor has this duty and that failure to pay is one of the acts of default that will trigger the acceleration clause.

# V.  MORTGAGE TERMINATION BY PAYMENT OR TRANSFER

The relationship between the mortgagor and mortgagee may terminate at the time the mortgage is paid in full by the mortgagor, assigned by one of the parties, or upon foreclosure by the mortgagee.

## A.  MORTGAGE PAYMENT

A mortgagor may discharge the mortgage through periodic payments over the life of the mortgage or in a lump sum payment before the due date through agreement of the parties. In most cases, payment is made when the mortgaged property is sold; the purchaser usually obtains his own mortgage that will cover the seller's equity and pay off the seller's mortgage.

If the mortgagor makes an offer to pay the mortgage in full—a tender of payment—on the due date (or earlier if allowed by the mortgage) and the mortgagee refuses to accept payment, the mortgage is cancelled and no additional interest is due on the loan. The tender, of course, must be at a proper time and place. For instance, in one case [19] the mortgagors made tender payment to the president of the mortgagee bank in the middle of a street when the bank presi-

---

18.  Caro v. Wollenberg, 83 Or. 311, 163 P. 94 (1917).

19.  Waldron v. Murphy, 40 Mich. 668 (1879).

dent was going to visit a neighbor. When the bank president told the mortgagors to make payment at the bank on the following morning, they refused to do so; later they argued that their tender discharged the mortgage. The court disagreed, deciding that the time and place of tender were not reasonable.

If payment in full is accepted by the mortgagee, it is important that the mortgagor demand the note and a mortgage discharge in return. The discharge should be recorded immediately; in the absence of a discharge the mortgage will continue to cloud the title, thus making it unmarketable.

## B.  TRANSFER BY MORTGAGOR

1.  **Sale Subject to Mortgage.**  When the mortgagor sells the mortgaged property to a purchaser, the purchaser may pay the full purchase price and the mortgagor may pay off the mortgage at closing, or the parties may use two alternative arrangements. To illustrate the alternatives, Mary owns a house worth $45,000 which she has mortgaged to First Bank for $35,000. She now sells her house to Nick, who pays $45,000 in cash at the closing. Under the terms of their agreement, Mary, instead of discharging the mortgage at the closing when she is paid by Nick, promises to discharge the mortgage at a future date because she wants to use the purchase price for other purposes. The deed to Nick in this situation would state that the conveyance is "subject to" the mortgage to First Bank. A sale subject to an existing mortgage has the following legal consequences: (1) the mortgagor, Mary, remains personally liable for the mortgage loan; (2) the purchaser, Nick, is not personally liable to First Bank; (3) the house is still subject to the mortgage, which may be foreclosed by First Bank on Mary's default; and (4) if Nick loses the property on foreclosure, he may recover damages from Mary on the basis of their agreement.[20]

Another example of a "subject to" sale is the case where Nick pays Mary $10,000, promises he will pay the remaining $35,000 directly to First Bank under the terms specified in the mortgage, and the contract states that Nick is purchasing the house "subject to but not assuming" the mortgage. The legal effect would be the same as the first example, except that under (4) Nick would have no recourse against Mary because he agreed to pay the mortgage.

2.  **Mortgage Assumption.**  The alternative to the "subject to" sale is the mortgage assumption: Nick pays Mary $10,000 at closing and assumes and agrees to pay the $35,000 mortgage to First Bank. Such an arrangement, like the second "subject to" arrangement above, has advantages for Nick because the interest rates on older

20.  If the deed had not contained the "subject to" clause, Nick could also have recovered on the theory that the warranty against encumbrances was breached.

mortgages such as Mary's are usually lower and the mortgage closing costs for an assumption are minimal. The major distinction between the "subject to" sale and the assumption is that when the purchaser, Nick, assumes personal liability to First Bank, he must make up the deficit if a foreclosure sale does not cover the amount of debt on the mortgage. In case Nick has not expressly assumed the mortgage, his assumption will be implied if he has deducted the amount of the mortgage debt from the purchase price paid to Mary—unless the agreement states otherwise. One court explained the principle in this way: "Having accepted land subject to mortgage and kept back enough of the vendor's money to pay it, it is only common honesty that he should be required either to pay the mortgage or stand primarily liable for it. His retention of the vendor's money for the payment of the mortgage, imposes upon him the duty of protecting the vendor against the mortgage debt. This must be so even according to the lowest notions of justice." [21]

3. **Novation.** Many mortgagors mistakenly believe that because the purchaser has assumed and agreed to pay the mortgage, they are no longer liable. A mortgagor does, in fact, remain liable as a surety, a person equally liable with the principal debtor; if the purchaser defaults, the mortgagee can collect from the mortgagor. To eliminate this liability, the mortgagor should obtain a release from the mortgagee when the property is sold. This arrangement, under which the purchaser is substituted for the mortgagor, is called a novation.

## C. TRANSFER BY MORTGAGEE

1. **Method and Effect of Transfer.** The mortgagee, like the mortgagor, may assign its interest to a third party. We might assume that Darcy has mortgaged her property to First Bank and that First Bank now wants to sell the mortgage to Second Bank. To accomplish this, First Bank will negotiate Darcy's note to Second Bank —by delivery alone if the note is a bearer instrument, or by properly endorsing it if the note is payable to the order of First Bank—and will also give Second Bank an assignment of the mortgage, which should be recorded. However, even if the mortgage is not assigned, it passes automatically to the purchaser because it is the security for the note. An assignment of the mortgage alone, however, gives the purchaser nothing, since the mortgage serves only as security for the note.

The legal effect of the note transfer is determined by the nature of the note. If the note is non-negotiable, that is, if it does not meet the requirements of U.C.C. Section 3–104(1), the purchaser, Second Bank, acquires only the interest of First Bank subject to any defenses

21. Heid v. Vreeland, 30 N.J.Eq. 591 (1879).

that Darcy has against First Bank. For instance, if Darcy had been defrauded by First Bank when the loan was made, she could raise fraud as a defense even against Second Bank.

On the other hand, if the note is negotiable and it is sold to a holder in due course, the holder in due course takes the note free of most defenses. A holder in due course is a person who has purchased the note in good faith, for value and without notice of defenses. To illustrate, in Burchett v. Allied Concord Financial Corp.,[22] an aluminum siding salesman visited a couple at their home and offered them what amounted to free aluminum siding on their home if they would allow the house to be used as a show house to promote sales. The couple accepted the offer and immediately signed various forms. Later the couple discovered that the salesman committed a fraud because the contract clearly stated that the salesman had no authority to promise a free aluminum siding job. Furthermore, the forms they had signed were a note and mortgage, which the aluminum siding company later sold to a holder in due course. Although the court recognized that the couple had been defrauded, it refused to cancel the note and mortgage because they were owned by a holder in due course.

The same result might occur with a non-negotiable note if the mortgagor signed a "waiver of defense" agreement, giving up the right to assert defenses. In mortgage transactions this agreement usually takes the form of an estoppel certificate under which the mortgagor in our earlier example, Darcy, would state to the purchaser, Second Bank, that she has no defense.

2. **Real Defenses.** Even when a negotiable note is transferred or a waiver of defense clause is used, there are certain defenses, most of which are called "real" defenses, that could still be raised by the mortgagor when sued on the debt by the holder in due course. These defenses include (1) minority of the mortgagor; (2) void transactions such as a note and mortgage given to pay an illegal gambling debt; (3) fraud in the execution, where the mortgagee was tricked into executing documents that he had no reason to believe were a note and mortgage; (4) bankruptcy of the mortgagor; (5) forgery of the mortgagor's name on the note; and (6) an unauthorized alteration of the note. In addition to these defenses, the Federal Trade Commission has ruled that, as of May 14, 1976, consumer purchasers and borrowers can raise any available defenses against a holder in due course. However, the FTC rule only applies when consumers acquire goods or services for personal, family, or household use.

3. **Notice of Transfer.** Another problem is that the sale of Darcy's note and mortgage to Second Bank might cause Darcy to pay the wrong creditor if she has not been notified. In some states, at

22.  74 N.M. 575, 396 P.2d 186 (1965).

least when the note is non-negotiable, the assignee has a duty to inform the mortgagor of the assignment and, in the absence of notice, payment by the mortgagor to the first mortgagee cancels the debt. When the note is negotiable or, in some states, even when the note is non-negotiable, notice of the assignment is not required and the mortgagor must demand to see the note or run the risk of paying twice. In Kraemer v. Leber,[23] the Kraemers, as mortgagors, executed negotiable notes and a mortgage, in the form of a trust deed, to Pickles, who later assigned them to Leber. Leber did not notify the Kraemers of the assignment and they continued to make payments to Pickles, who remitted the interest to Leber but wrongfully kept the principal. When Pickles died and his activities were discovered, the court decided that although the Kraemers did not have to make interest payments again since Pickles was Leber's agent for purposes of collecting interest, they did have to pay again over $700 in principal. "The $4,500 note was a negotiable instrument of such a character that plaintiffs were bound to have known that it could and probably would be negotiated and passed into the hands of a third party. As a consequence plaintiffs in making payments on this note should have ascertained that the person to whom payment was made either owned the note or had possession thereof for the purpose of collection. When the maker pays money on a note to one who does not have the note in his possession he pays at his peril and at the risk of being required to show that the payee was authorized to collect the payment as the agent of the owner. Plaintiffs, in making payments on the principal note, in order to fully protect their own interests, were obliged to see to it that endorsements of the payments were made thereon and could not rely on a receipt from Pickles for credit on the amounts thus paid without laying themselves open to the charge of negligence should he fail to remit faithfully to the owner of the note." In other cases the courts have decided that the agency covers both principal and interest. See Steele v. Seaton, infra.

## VI.    MORTGAGE TERMINATION BY FORECLOSURE

### A.    THE FORECLOSURE PROCESS

The final method of terminating the relationship between the mortgagor and mortgagee is foreclosure. Foreclosure involves a chronological sequence of four events that are best understood by referring to the history of mortgage law, which represents centuries of struggle between lenders and borrowers.[24] Historically, the mortgage was regarded as a conveyance of title to the mortgagee, subject to the condition that, if the mortgage were paid on the due date, the conveyance would be void. The mortgagor thus had a legal right of

23.  267 S.W.2d 333 (Mo.1954).

24.  Kratovil, Modern Mortgage Law and Practice §§ 2–7 (1972).

redemption on the due date, but if he failed to exercise this right (for example, if his carriage broke down on the way to the bank and his payment was one day late), the right was lost and the property belonged to the mortgagee. Today, the failure to pay on the due date, the default, is the first event leading to foreclosure.

The legal rule was often unjust, especially in cases such as the one noted in which the mortgagor failed to pay because of circumstances beyond his control. To provide relief, courts in equity began to allow mortgagors an additional time for redemption in cases of hardship and, by the 17th century this right, known as the equity of redemption, was given to all mortgagors. Today, the second event in a foreclosure is the running of the time period in which a mortgagor may exercise the equity of redemption. This right is considered so important that courts will not allow a mortgagor to waive the right. Furthermore, the right has become synonymous with the mortgagor's interest in the property above the mortgage debt, the owner's "equity." According to one court, " 'Equity of redemption' is a term used in the law of mortgages to describe either (1) the right in equity of the mortgagor to redeem after default in the performance of the conditions in the mortgage, (2) the estate which remains in the mortgagor after the execution of the mortgage." [25]

The response of lenders to the creation of the equity of redemption was to file suit to cut off or foreclose the equity. Foreclosure, the third event in the foreclosure process, might result in the lender's taking possession or in sale of the property, both of which will be discussed below.

Finally in approximately one-half the states, it is felt that mortgagors should have an additional time period after a foreclosure sale to redeem the property, and statutes have been enacted to give the mortgagor a redemption period, usually running six months or a year. The running of the statutory redemption period is the last event in the foreclosure process.

## B.  FORECLOSURE BY SALE

Of the above four events, the foreclosure is the most complicated. Lenders have two options to foreclose by sale, and two options if they want to foreclose the mortgage and take possession of the premises without sale. First, foreclosure by sale may be accomplished by a sale ordered by a court, after giving notice to all parties with an interest in the property and after a hearing. In order to avoid the time and expense of a judicial sale, many lenders prefer the alternative: sale pursuant to a "power of sale" clause in the mortgage, whereby the mortgagor authorizes the mortgagee to sell the property after default at a public sale without court proceedings.

25.  Reitman v. Whitaker, 74 N.D. 504,
23 N.W.2d 393 (1946).

With both the judicial sale and the exercise of a power of sale, statute and/or custom dictate that notice of the sale be published in a local newspaper and posted on the property, and that the sale be conducted by a public official such as a sheriff. Often the only bidder at the sale is the mortgagee, who can bid up to the amount of the debt without paying cash, although the mortgagee's right to bid should be specified in a mortgage containing a power of sale clause. At the conclusion of the sale a deed will be executed by the person conducting the sale, although the mortgagor holds the right to redeem the property by paying the purchase price within the statutory redemption period. If the sale proceeds exceed the debt, the mortgagor or junior mortgagees are entitled to the excess. If the proceeds are less than the amount of the debt, the mortgagee is entitled to recover the deficiency from the mortgagor. However, when the mortgagee purchases the property at the sale at a price below the market value, and if the market value exceeds the debt, courts will not hold the mortgagor liable for a deficiency. In a few states deficiency judgments have been completely abolished by statute.

Although there are several similarities between judicial foreclosure and the exercise of a power of sale, there is one difference that has often been litigated in recent years. With a judicial foreclosure, the property is sold only after the debtor has had an opportunity to be heard in court, but this right has been waived under a power of sale clause. The procedural due process requirements of the Constitution require that the owner is entitled to notice and to an opportunity for a hearing before property is taken. These requirements, however, only apply to state action. The legal issue thus becomes: Does the exercise of a power of sale clause involve sufficient state action to require a court hearing despite the power of sale clause? In recent years there has been a split of opinion on this question; Northrip v. Federal Nat. Mortgage Ass'n, infra, represents the dominant view.

## C.  FORECLOSURE BY POSSESSION

The other two methods of foreclosure, which allow the lender to take possession of the property, are rarely used. One of these is strict foreclosure, under which a lender who already has title to the property obtains a court order foreclosing the equity of redemption. Under the other method, foreclosure by entry and possession, the mortgagee actually takes possession of the mortgaged property either with the permission of the debtor, or without permission if entry can be made peaceably, or under a court order. After the mortgagee has been in possession for a specified period, the mortgagor's right of redemption is automatically foreclosed. Entry and possession is used only in a few New England states.

In concluding our discussion of mortgage law, it should be noted that statutes of limitation in each state bar suits on mortgage notes after a specified time period. Furthermore, many states have special statutes declaring that a mortgage will operate as a lien on the real estate only for a certain time after the note has matured. As a result of the latter statutes, a creditor who still might be able to collect on the note would be unable to foreclose the mortgage.

## VII.  INSTALLMENT CONTRACTS

As an alternative to mortgage financing, an installment or land contract is used in many cases. Under this arrangement the purchaser takes possession of the real estate and makes installment payments to the seller over a number of years, until the purchase price is paid or until the purchaser is able to obtain a conventional mortgage. With the cash sale contract we noted that there is a gap of several weeks between the signing of the contract and the closing that enables the purchaser to obtain financing and check title. With an installment contract the gap will last for years because the contract is the method of financing. Installment contracts are especially popular at times when loans are unavailable from mortgage lenders, since installment contract sellers are often willing to accept a lower down payment and a lower interest rate.

The installment contract is in many respects a blend of a cash sales contract and a mortgage. Like the cash sales contract, the installment sales contract should contain provisions covering such matters as the type of title, the method of proving title, the times for performance, and the type of deed to be delivered at closing. Like the mortgage, the installment sales contract will include provisions covering the terms of payment, the purchaser's duty to pay taxes and insure the premises, the seller's right to accelerate payment of future installments on the purchaser's default, and the purchaser's duty not to commit waste. The reader should refer to the above review of mortgage law and to Chapter 7 on the sales contract for discussion of the legal effect of these provisions. In addition, the following provisions may be of some concern in executing an installment contract.

### A.  INTEREST OF PARTIES

John and Mary, husband and wife, have decided to purchase a house as tenants by the entireties. In signing a cash sale contract, buyers such as John and Mary often neglect to specify the form of ownership in the contract, although the deed will state the nature of their interests. With an installment contract, however, it is especially important for them to state their ownership interests and survivorship rights because, with the installment contract in effect over several years, there is a greater likelihood that one of the parties will die before the contract is completely performed. Furthermore, if John and Mary decide to sell the property as tenants by the entireties or joint tenants, the need for clearly stating survivorship rights is even greater; in the event of the death of one of the parties, some courts have decided that the sales proceeds are held in a tenancy in common—the survivor would receive one-half of the proceeds and the estate would receive the other half.

## B.  PROOF OF TITLE

The purchaser in a land contract faces two special concerns regarding title.  First, does the seller actually have title when the contract is signed?  To answer this question the buyer should require an abstract of title, title insurance policy, or other proof of title when the contract is signed.  But even this proof of title does not fully protect the buyer, who might discover after making payments for fifteen years that the seller had conveyed the property to an innocent third party after the contract was signed and before closing.  To prevent this possibility, the purchaser should either live on the premises or record the installment contract; either of these actions would be constructive notice to third parties of the purchaser's interest.

## C.  REMEDIES ON DEFAULT

When the purchaser defaults on an installment contract, the seller has available, in addition to a full range of contract remedies, the remedy of foreclosure discussed above.  Most installment contracts also stipulate that if the purchaser defaults, the property, improvements on the property, and all payments which have been made are forfeited to the seller.  In some cases this is a harsh penalty—for instance, if a purchaser has made payments over several years and then is late on one payment.  To alleviate this problem, there are statutes in several states that grant the purchaser a certain period, perhaps six months, to make the overdue payments.  Furthermore, according to judicial interpretation, a seller who elects to exercise his rights under the forfeiture clause may not recover under other remedies for breach of contract.

## VIII.  STATUTORY LIENS

A lien is the right of a creditor to have the debtor's property sold and to be paid from the proceeds.  A creditor may obtain a lien as a result of a contract with the debtor; for example, the debtor may give the creditor a mortgage on real estate or a security interest in personal property.  A creditor may also obtain a lien without the contractual agreement of the debtor by following the requirements specified in certain statutes.  Statutory liens are especially important to mortgagees because, in many cases, they will be given priority over a contractual lien and thus lessen the value of the creditor's security.

## A. MECHANICS' LIENS

Mechanics' liens are given to persons who furnish labor, services or materials in connection with the improvement of real estate. We must review mechanics' lien law in general terms because state statutes are not uniform in nature and are exceedingly complex. For instance, the first sentence of the Michigan mechanics' lien law is over two pages long. The most important legal issues raised in connection with mechanics' lien law are the following: (1) When does the owner of real estate subject his interest to a possible mechanic's lien? (2) Who is entitled to a lien? (3) What type of work is covered? (4) What is the procedure for claiming a lien? and (5) What are the priorities among lienholders? We will consider these issues in order.

1. **Owner's Contract or Consent.** The states are not in agreement as to what the owner must do to subject his interest to a possible mechanic's lien. It would obviously be unfair to allow a contractor to construct a building secretly on the owner's property and then to claim a lien for the value of the building. It should be just as obvious that if an owner has contracted for the construction of a building, the contractor should be entitled to a lien to secure the owner's payment. Problems arise when a case falls between these extremes. For example, what if the owner did not contract directly with the builder but did consent to the construction under a contract between the builder and an installment contract purchaser or a tenant? Or what if the owner did not consent but knew of the construction? In general terms, in order for a mechanic's lien to attach to the owner's interest, some states require a contract by the owner, others require only the consent of the owner, and still others hold that the owner's knowledge alone is enough, unless he makes it known immediately that he will not be responsible for the work. In addition, specific rules sometimes allow a lien if a tenant makes improvements required by the lease.

Once the legal rule for the particular state is determined, whether or not there was a contract, consent, or knowledge becomes a question of fact. In Fetters, Love and Sieben, Inc. v. Simon,[26] a tenant hired a plumbing firm to install nine bathrooms in the leased building. While the bathrooms were being installed, the husband of the owner of the building visited the tenant and observed the work in progress. Later, when the tenant failed to pay, the plumbing firm filed a mechanic's lien. The court refused to enforce the lien: "The foundation of a mechanic's lien is the contract with the owner of the

26. 46 Ill.App.2d 232, 196 N.E.2d 700 (1964).

land for the improvement thereof and the furnishing of material and labor according to the contract, in connection with the statute giving the lien.  .  .  . The contract for the improvements must either have been made with the owner or with one whom the owner has authorized or knowingly permitted to have done the work for him. The defendant in the present case did not enter into any contract, either express or implied, with the plaintiffs nor did she perform any acts which would indicate that she gave her husband authority to act for her as her agent. She cannot be said to have knowingly permitted the alterations to be made on the premises since there was no evidence that she knew the work was being undertaken nor did she acquiesce in accepting the alleged benefits."

2. **Persons Entitled to Lien.** Statutes in each state determine the persons entitled to a lien, and the statutes usually include anyone —whether a general contractor or a subcontractor—who furnishes labor or materials for the improvement of the real estate. In many instances the statutory language requires interpretation by a court. For instance, may a company that leases earth-moving equipment to a subcontractor claim a mechanic's lien for the rental payments? It might be argued that the equipment constitutes materials or that it constitutes labor since it is a modern substitute for manual labor. Courts, however, have interpreted the lien law more narrowly and they refuse to allow such liens.[27]

Additional problems are created by allowing liens to subcontractors, who contract with the general contractor rather than with the owner. If the owner pays the general contractor the full contract price and the general contractor fails to pay the subcontractor, must the owner pay the subcontractors to avoid a lien? Two approaches have been developed to resolve this problem. Several states maintain that the total of all liens cannot exceed the contract price; so if the owner pays the general contractor when he has no notice of other claims, he will be discharged up to the amount of the payments. The second approach requires the subcontractor to notify the owner within a specified time period of his intention to claim a lien so that the owner can hold back payments to the general contractor until he is assured that the subcontractors are being paid. For additional protection, the owner should obtain a sworn statement listing the subcontractors from the general contractor; and he should then obtain a waiver of lien rights from each subcontractor on the list as the claims are paid.

3. **Work Covered.** Mechanics' liens are available only when the work results in a permanent improvement of the real estate. As an illustration, a tenant who leased a store entered into a contract for

---

27. Lembke Constr. Co. v. J. D. Coggins
Co., 72 N.M. 259, 382 P.2d 983 (1963).

the installation of shelving, with the consent of his landlord. In order to prevent the shelves from falling, the tenant had them attached to a plywood strip on the wall, but they could be removed without seriously harming the building. When the lumber company that supplied the lumber for the shelves filed a lien on the property, the court refused enforcement because the removable shelving was not a permanent improvement. The court also decided that the landlord was not liable for the materials since the only recourse against him in this case was under the lien statute.[28]

4. **Procedure For Claiming a Lien.** In addition to any notices required of subcontractors, every lien claimant must record a lien statement specifying the amount due and the nature of the improvement within a certain period (often ninety days) after the work is completed. After recording the lien the claimant must commence an action to enforce the lien within a limited time period, usually one year. If the court decides that the lien is valid, the property will be sold to satisfy the debt.

5. **Priority.** The priority given a lien claimant varies considerably from state to state. To illustrate this, we might assume that on April 15, the owner of a vacant lot hires a contractor to build a house. Work begins on May 15 and the house is completed on August 15. On September 15, the owner sells the house to a young couple, and they finance the purchase with a mortgage to Last Bank, which recorded the mortgage on that date. However, the seller does not pay the contractor. In this state the contractor has ninety days to file a lien after completing the work, and he records a lien on November 2. Mechanics' liens, in most states, are not given priority on the basis of the time of recording; instead, priority usually dates from another event. In many states the event is the date work commences, in this case May 15. In other states, the event is the date of the contract, April 15. Only in a few states does priority date from recording, November 2. Thus, under the first two approaches, the lien would have priority over the interests of later mortgagees and purchasers. In our case, unless the bank or the purchasers paid the contractor, the property could be sold to satisfy the contractor's lien. The bank or the purchaser would have recourse against the seller—if he could be found and if he was not bankrupt. To avoid losses from mechanics' liens that have not yet been recorded, purchasers should investigate the property for signs of recent improvements and, if there have been improvements, hold back part of the purchase price or place the purchase price in escrow until the period for recording liens has expired.

28. Broadmoor Lumber Co. v. Liberto,
162 So.2d 800 (La.App.1964).

## B. OTHER STATUTORY LIENS

Several other statutory liens might be filed against real estate and other property. An attachment lien is often used to prevent a defendant from hiding or selling his property before the conclusion of a lawsuit. In most cases, if the court decides that there is cause to believe the defendant will secrete his property, the plaintiff will post a bond and a writ of attachment will be issued, directing the sheriff to levy or seize the property in question. If the property is real estate, the attachment is recorded to give notice to prospective purchasers. If attachment is ordered and if the plaintiff ultimately wins the case, a writ of execution will be issued, which authorizes the sheriff to sell the attached property to satisfy the judgment.

If an attachment lien is not used, the plaintiff may enforce a judgment through a judgment lien or execution lien. In some states the plaintiff is given a judgment lien either automatically when the judgment is rendered or when the judgment is recorded. In either event, the lien is enforced by issuing a writ of execution. Some states do not provide for judgment liens but do allow execution liens. The legal effect of enforcing a judgment under a judgment lien or under an execution lien is generally the same: the lien on the property, which is seized by the sheriff, has priority over later liens and, if the judgment is not paid after demand by the sheriff, the property will be sold to satisfy the judgment.

Finally, it is possible that all other liens, contractual or statutory, will be subordinate to a tax lien. As a general rule, local real estate tax liens have priority over all other liens, even when those liens are recorded first. A lien resulting from refusal to pay federal taxes arises when a tax assessment is made. However, to be valid against the interest of a purchaser of the property or the holder of a competing lien, the federal tax lien must be recorded in the appropriate local county office and must be indexed in the Internal Revenue Service office for the district in which the land is located.

# CASES

---

## McCOOL v. AYRES

Appellate Court of Indiana, 1963.
136 Ind.App. 72, 192 N.E.2d 636.

KELLEY, Judge.

\* \* \*

For clarity and understanding, it seems proper to set forth the pertinent material parts of the findings and conclusions. Parts thereof not necessary for elucidation of the factual basis of this decision are omitted.

## "FINDINGS OF FACT."

"1. That The Little Company of Mary Hospital & Home for Chronically Ill, Inc., hereinafter called 'Hospital' was prior to 1956 and still is engaged in the operation of a hospital and home for chronically ill persons at San Pierre, Indiana.

"2. On September 26, 1956, John F. McCool was admitted to the Hospital and was a patient there until 8:30 A.M., September 21, 1959.

"3. At the time of his admission to the Hospital John F. McCool was 80 years old. He was suffering from diabetes, which required daily injections of insulin. He was a double amputee of the legs and required the use of a wheel chair to move about.

\* \* \*

"5. When John F. McCool became a patient at the Hospital on September 26, 1956, he was, and had been for many years prior thereto, the owner of the following described real estate in Pulaski County, Indiana:

"Northwest quarter of the Northwest quarter;

"Southeast quarter of the Southwest quarter;

"Southwest quarter of the Northwest quarter;

"Northwest quarter of the Southwest quarter;

"Southeast quarter of the Northwest quarter;

"Southwest quarter of the Southwest quarter; all in Section Seventeen (17), Township Thirty (30) North, Range Four (4) West, containing 240 acres, more or less.

Such real estate is herein referred to as the 'Farm'.

"7. On April 29, 1959, John F. McCool was unmarried, and was 83 years of age.

"8. On April 29, 1959, John F. McCool and the Hospital entered into an agreement in writing, which was duly acknowledged by an officer authorized to administer oaths, and which said agreement is attached to this Finding of Facts, made a part thereof and marked Exhibit 'A'. Concurrently with the execution of said contract, and on April 29, 1959, the said John F. McCool executed and delivered to the Hospital, his Warranty Deed, which said deed was duly recorded by the Hospital on April 30, 1959, in Deed Record 120, page 347 in the office of the County Recorder of Pulaski County, Indiana. By said deed he conveyed to the said Hospital his 240 acres of real estate. * * *

* * *

The vital and determinative questions on this appeal are whether or not the aforementioned deed was, in fact, an equitable mortgage and, consequently, whether or not the said real estate constituted an asset of the decedent's estate.

A careful examination and analyzation of the special findings made by the court seems to clearly demonstrate that the Warranty Deed given by decedent to the Home, pursuant to the provisions of the written agreement of the parties, both of which were executed as a part of the one transaction, was, in fact, an equitable mortgage, notwithstanding its caption. Apropos, is the statement made in Kerfoot v. Kessener (1949), 227 Ind. 58, 84 N.E.2d 190:

" '* * * The form and names of the instruments are not of controlling effect, for the law looks through form to substance and will give effect to the real and dominant intention of the parties when definitely ascertained. * * *' "

Hereinafter referred to are some of the facts and factors appearing in the record herein, and in the findings of the court, which seem to clearly and definitely lead to the conclusion that the decedent and the Home, at the time the contract was made and the deed given, intended the creation of an equitable mortgage as security for a continuing indebtedness running from the decedent to the Home; and that initially it was so recognized by several of the parties hereto who are most vitally affected by the construction of the arrangement entered into by the decedent.

It is noted that the involved written agreement, in the latter part of the WHEREAS clause, provides for a fixed "flat" monthly rate of Two Hundred Dollars ($200) for the care of decedent to start from the date of execution of the agreement, thus establishing a constant rate of indebtedness to the Home which continued on to the time of decedent's death. It is held that when a deed is given in securance of an existing indebtedness, it will be held to be a mortgage.

A rather conclusive indication that the parties intended the deed as a mortgage and that the Home intended to hold the real estate as security for decedent's indebtedness, is the provision in the next to last paragraph of the contract that "if" the conditions thereof are carried out and fulfilled by both parties and "there is no redemption" within two years of decedent's death, the Home "shall be the absolute owner, in fee simple" of the real estate. Now, if the parties had intended the deed as a present conveyance of the title to the Home, said provision, as worded, would have been wholly unnecessary and, in fact, without legal application. The stated provision definitely withheld the vesting of any fee title to the real estate in the Home until the accomplishment of the expressed precedents. In other words, under the provision referred to, if the debt was not paid within the time allowed, then, and then only, was the fee title to the real estate to vest in the Home as against the appellant, William S. McCool, and the appellee, Martha Ayres.  *  *  *

The contract contains a specific provision for "the right to redeem the lands" within a certain time after decedent's death.  Such a provision is indicative that a mortgage was intended.

The agreement was dated April 29, 1959.  It appears that the decedent, by and through his son, the appellant, William S. McCool, retained possession of the real estate and occupied one of the two dwellings located thereon since the date of the deed, without the payment of any rent therefor.  This fact of free occupancy by the said appellant is found as a fact by the court in its special finding number 11.  Our court has expressed that the retention of the possession of the land, rent free, is indicative of an intention to mortgage the property.

The agreement provides that the redemptioners of the real estate shall pay interest at the rate of four (4%) per cent on the monies expended by the Home "on behalf" of the decedent after one year from the date of decedent's death.  Such provision further substantiates the view that a mortgage was intended.

It appears from the stipulation of the parties and the special findings of fact by the court that the Home reduced the contract obligation of the decedent by crediting him with the "landlord's" share of all crops received by it from the real estate.  Thereby, we think that the parties evinced a clear intention and understanding that the deed did not and was not intended to operate as a discharge of the decedent's existing obligation.  *  *  *

[The judgment appealed from is reversed.]

------

### GRAF v. HOPE BLDG. CORP.

Court of Appeals of New York, 1930.
254 N.Y. 1, 171 N.E. 884.

O'BRIEN, J.

Plaintiffs, as executors of Joseph L. Graf, are the holders of two consolidated mortgages forming a single lien on real property the title to which is vested in defendant Hope Building Corporation.  According to the terms of the agreement consolidating the mortgages the principal sum is made payable January 1, 1935.  Nevertheless, a clause provides that the whole shall become due after default for twenty days in the payment of any installment of interest.  David Herstein is the controlling stockholder and also president and treasurer of defendant.  He alone was authorized to sign checks in its behalf.  Early in June, 1927, he went to Europe.  Before his departure a clerical assistant who was also the nominal secretary of the corporation computed the interest due July 1, and through an error in arithmetic incorrectly calculated it. Mr. Herstein signed the check for the erroneous amount, but before the date upon which the interest became due, the secretary discovered the error, notified the mortgagee of the shortage of $401.87, stated that on the president's return from Europe the balance would be paid, and on June 30 forwarded to the mortgagee the check as drawn. It was deposited by the mortgagee and paid by defendant. On July 5, Mr. Herstein returned, but, through an omission in his office, he was not informed of the default in the payment of interest. At the expiration of twenty-one days this action of foreclosure was begun. Defendant made tender of the deficiency, but the mortgagee, strictly insisting on his contract rights, refused the tender and elected to assert the power created by the acceleration clause in the consolidation agreement.

On the undisputed facts as found, we are unable to perceive any defense to the action, and are therefore constrained to reverse the judgment dismissing the complaint. Plaintiffs may be ungenerous, but generosity is a voluntary attribute and cannot be enforced even by a chancellor. Forbearance is a quality under which the circumstances of this case is likewise free from coercion. Here there is no penalty, no forfeiture, nothing except a covenant fair on its face to which both parties willingly consented. It is neither oppressive nor unconscionable. In the absence of some act by the mortgagee which a court of equity would be justified in considering unconscionable he is entitled to the benefit of the covenant. The contract is definite and no reason appears for its reformation by the courts. We are not at liberty to revise while professing to construe. Defendant's mishap, caused by a succession of its errors and negligent omissions, is not of the nature requiring relief from its default. Rejection of plaintiffs' legal right could rest only on compassion for defendant's negligence. Such a tender emotion must be exerted, if at all, by the parties rather than by the court. Our guide must be the precedents prevailing since courts of equity were established in this state. Stability of contract obligations must not be undermined by judicial sympathy.   *   *   *

The judgment of the Appellate Division and that of the Special Term should be reversed, and judgment ordered in favor of plaintiff for the relief demanded in the complaint, with costs in all courts.

---

## STEELE v. SEATON

Kansas City Court of Appeals, Missouri, 1952.
248 S.W.2d 81.

BROADDUS, Presiding Judge.

This is a suit for cancellation of a promissory note and deed of trust securing it, both of which were executed by plaintiff, Edeth L.

Steele. The court below found in plaintiff's favor and defendants appeal.

Briefly, the facts are: On May 8, 1944, plaintiff, a widow, purchased the residence known as 3221 Olive Street, in Kansas City, Missouri. The purchase price was $5500, of which Mrs. Steele paid $1100 in cash and gave her note, secured by the deed of trust, for the balance of $4400. The payee in the note and the beneficiary in the deed of trust was Ida E. Leach. She was merely a "straw" and the real owner of the note was one T. J. Clark. It was out of the latter's criminal acts that the present controversy arose.

\* \* \*

T. J. Clark, the original owner of the note signed by plaintiff, Mrs. Steele, was the president, principal stockholder and moving force of the Pioneer National Corporation.

On July 20, 1945, Mrs. Steele's note, with others, was purchased by defendant Victory State Bank from Pioneer National Corporation through defendant, Ferd C. Mueller, acting then as a broker.

On July 16, 1945, four days prior to the transfer of said notes, defendant, Victory State Bank, entered into a "Service Agreement" with Pioneer National Corporation (Clark's company), by the terms of which Pioneer was to act as "Servicer" for all of the notes purchased by the defendant, Victory State Bank from Pioneer.

Paragraph 4 of that contract provided that: "The Servicer (Clark's company) agrees that it will maintain facilities for the collection of all sums payable by any mortgagor \* \* \*". In paragraph 5 "The Servicer agrees to remit to the Purchaser, (Victory State Bank) the principal and interest collected by it from such mortgages \* \* \*." And in paragraph 6: "The Servicer hereby agrees to keep complete and accurate account of, and to properly apply, all sums paid to it by any mortgagor under any loan covered by the contract."

Mrs. Steele, the plaintiff, made the regular payments of $50 each until March 3, 1947. On that date she cashed some bonds which she owned and purchased a cashier's check for $2550. This she endorsed and delivered to Clark. Afterwards, in her desire "to get the obligation paid off as quick as possible" she made payments ranging from $100 to $200 to Clark. Finally, on April 3, 1948, she paid the balance due on her note. At that time, Clark endorsed on Mrs. Steele's receipt book "received payment in full." He likewise endorsed on her copy of the note the same notation. Although Clark admittedly received these payments, he did not remit the entire amounts collected by him to defendant, Victory State Bank. Rather, he deposited the payments made by Mrs. Steele to his own account and remitted to defendant, Victory State Bank, only $50 each month.

Mrs. Steele testified that she never at any time received notice, written or otherwise, that defendant, Victory State Bank, was the owner of the note here involved.

In May of 1948, Clark's license as a real-estate broker, was revoked. At that time, and, apparently for that reason, defendant, Victory State Bank, revoked the Pioneer servicing agency and transferred the same to defendant Mueller. In August of 1948, Mueller came to see plaintiff relative to payments on her note. Mrs. Steele told him that she had paid the note in full in the preceding April and referred him to Clark. Thus it was not until August, 1948, that either Mrs. Steele, Mueller, or Victory State Bank discovered the facts cerning Clark's embezzlement.

The sole question before us is whether the payments made by Mrs. Steele to Clark were payments made to an agent authorized to collect same for defendant, Victory State Bank. In our opinion the question is answered by the plain terms of the written contract entered into between defendant, Victory State Bank, and Clark. By that "Service Agreement" the "Servicer" (Clark, in fact) was authorized to collect "*principal* and interest" payable by any mortgagor. The note gave Mrs. Steele a prepayment privilege. When defendant, Victory State Bank, made Clark its agent to handle these collections, it knew or should have known that sums in excess of the minimum monthly payments might and would likely be received by its agent. To us it is clear that Mrs. Steele had the right to make the payments to Clark and he had authority to receive them.

\*    \*    \*

Defendants claim that Mrs. Steele made these excess principal payments at her peril and was negligent, and, inasmuch as said payments were not received by the Victory State Bank, she was not entitled to credit therefor. In their brief, defendants discuss five cases in support of their position. Those cases hold that the obligor in a negotiable note cannot assume continuing ownership by the original payee, for the obligor is on notice that the note may be negotiated at any time. They say that the obligor must satisfy himself that the person to whom he pays is still in possession of the note, *or* he must assume the obligation of proving that the one to whom he did pay the money was an agent authorized to accept on behalf of the holder of the note. Thus, those cases make it clear that even if the obligor does not demand production of the note and endorsement of payment thereon, nevertheless he is entitled to the benefit of the payment if he can show that the one to whom he paid stood in the position of agent to the rightful owner of the note. Showing this is true, we quote from the first case discussed by defendants, that of McDonald v. Smith, 201 Mo.App. 78, 206 S.W. 591, 592, as follows:

> "The law has often been stated that when a debtor owes a negotiable note, and pays money thereon to another as agent, it

is his duty at his peril to ascertain that the person thus paid is in possession of such note; *and, if not in such possession, the debtor must then show that the person he pays has express or implied authority to collect the note not in his possession.*" (Italics ours.)

\* \* \*

It follows that the judgment directing the cancellation of the note and deed of trust should be affirmed. It is so ordered.

All concur.

---

## NORTHRIP v. FEDERAL NAT. MTG. ASS'N

United States Circuit Court of Appeals, Sixth Circuit, 1975.
527 F.2d 23.

McCREE, Circuit Judge.

This is an appeal and cross-appeal from a judgment of the district court setting aside a mortgage foreclosure made pursuant to a Michigan statute regulating foreclosure of mortgages by advertisement. The district court held the foreclosure proceeding violative of the due process clause of the Fourteenth Amendment of the United States Constitution and Article I, Section 17 of the Michigan Constitution of 1963. Because we find no significant state involvement in the foreclosure proceedings assailed here, we reverse the judgment of the district court.

Northrip brought this action in Michigan Circuit Court and defendant Federal National Mortgage Association (FNMA) removed it to the U.S. District Court for the Eastern District of Michigan. Jurisdiction was asserted on diversity of citizenship and the existence of a question arising under the Constitution and laws of the United States. 28 U.S.C.A. §§ 1331 and 1332. Northrip sought injunctive relief to set aside the mortgage foreclosure proceedings taken pursuant to the Michigan statute regulating the foreclosure of mortgages by advertisement, Mich.Comp.Laws Ann. § 600.3201 et seq., on the grounds that the procedure deprived her of property without notice and a prior hearing as required by the Fourteenth Amendment.

On July 28, 1970, Northrip signed a mortgage note and mortgage acknowledging a debt in the principal amount of $11,000 owed to Auer Mortgage Company. The funds acquired by Northrip in the transaction were paid to a home repair company for work performed on Northrip's home. Auer later assigned the mortgage to FNMA.

The parties stipulated that Northrip made her last payment on the mortgage on April 6, 1972, because of her dissatisfaction with the home repairs. FNMA began foreclosure proceedings shortly after the default, and, on October 19, 1972, purchased the property at a sheriff's sale for $11,476.68, the accelerated balance due on the mortgage note. Six months later, the statutory period for redemption expired and appellant's title to the property became final.

Chapter 32 of the Revised Judicature Act of the Compiled Laws of Michigan sets forth the requirements necessary to foreclose a real estate mortgage by advertisement: the mortgage must contain a power of sale; a default must have occurred in a condition of the mortgage by which the power to sell becomes operative; no suit or proceeding to recover the debt secured by the mortgage can have been instituted and remained pending; and the mortgage itself and its assignments must have been recorded. A notice that the mortgage will be foreclosed by sale must be printed in a newspaper published in the county where the property is located for at least four successive weeks at least once in each week. Within 15 days after the first publication, a true copy of the notice must be posted in a conspicuous place on the premises. The notice must specify the mortgage, the mortgagee, the assignees, the date of execution and recording of the mortgage, the amount claimed to be due at the date of notice, a description of the property, the date, time, and place of the sale and the length of the redemption period. The mortgagee may appoint a person to conduct the sale or the sheriff of a county may conduct it. A deed by the officer or person conducting the sale must be prepared and recorded. The mortgagor or persons claiming under him have six months after the sale within which to redeem residential property not exceeding four (housing) units if less than one-third of the debt has been paid and one year for such redemption if more than one-third of the debt has been paid. The record indicates that FNMA foreclosed in strict compliance with the requirements of the statute.

The district court, in its opinion reported at 372 F.Supp. 594 (1974), correctly observed that a predicate to finding a due process violation is a finding of state action. The district court considered several theories advanced by Northrip upon which a finding of state action might be based and expressly rejected all but one. The court held that the involvement of the sheriff and register of deeds in the foreclosure proceedings did not constitute state action; that the statute authorizing mortgage foreclosure by advertisement did not authorize a private party to perform a government function and therefore did not constitute state action; and that the statutory scheme regulating mortgage foreclosure did not so pervasively govern FNMA's conduct that private action became state action. The court, however, accepted plaintiff's theory "that state action exists because the statute encourages mortgagees to seek foreclosure by advertisement, rather than by judicial process," relying on Reitman v. Mulkey, 387 U.S. 369, 87 S.Ct. 1627, 18 L.Ed.2d 830 (1967), and Bond v. Dentzer, 362 F.Supp. 1373 (N.D.N.Y.1973), rev'd, 494 F.2d 302 (2d Cir. 1974). Proceeding then to the question whether the foreclosure procedures followed by FNMA complied with the requirements of due process, the district court determined that they did not because Northrip was not afforded a hearing prior to foreclosure.

\* \* \*

Michigan recognizes that the power of sale is an incident of the private right to contract. A power of sale remedy in a mortgage was recognized by Michigan courts as a part of common law even before the first statute dealing with the subject was enacted. \* \* \*

Therefore, it is clear that the statute under attack here did not create the power of sale foreclosure. Instead, the state, by enacting this statute, acted to regulate and standardize a recognized practice. If anything, the statute made foreclosure more difficult for the mortgagee because he was required to comply with its provisions.

\* \* \*

We also reject cross-appellant's arguments that state action exists because of the involvement of a state official in the foreclosure process and because the mortgagee is engaged in a traditional state function. The cross-appellant contends that state action may be found because the sheriff conducted the foreclosure sale pursuant to Mich.Comp.Laws Ann. § 600.3216 and because the register of deeds was involved in transferring the title.

We observe at the outset that although a deputy sheriff conducted the foreclosure sale in this case, Michigan law permits the parties to agree that another person will conduct the sale. In fact, in Watson v. Lynch, 127 Mich. 365, 86 N.W. 807 (1901), the Michigan Supreme Court held in a case where the sale was advertised to be made by the mortgagee, the sheriff was not authorized to conduct the sale unless so instructed by the mortgagee.

Appellee cites Sniadach v. Family Finance Corp., 395 U.S. 337, 89 S.Ct. 1820, 23 L.Ed.2d 349 (1969) and Fuentes v. Shevin, 407 U.S. 67, 92 S.Ct. 1983, 32 L.Ed.2d 556 (1972) as examples of cases where state action was present because state officers acted to deprive persons of property. The garnishment (in *Sniadach*) and replevin (in *Fuentes*) did not depend upon a contractual power granted to the creditor as is the case here. Instead, any person could invoke the aid of the state with no more than a bare assertion that money was owed him. A state officer then directed the debtor's employer to withhold wages (in *Sniadich*) or physically removed personal property from the premises (in *Fuentes*). In this case, the sheriff's presence was only incidental, and not essential, to the employment of a remedy entered into privately by the mortgagee and mortgagor.

With respect to the register of deeds, it appears that he is required to do no more than to record the deed and indicate whether a redemption takes place. As one court has observed: There is "little significance in the fact that a clerk may perform the ministerial act of recording the deed under power evidencing sale or that courts of the State of Georgia may enforce the agreement the parties have made. Were those factors considered determinative, every private agreement between citizens would be imbued with state action."

Thus, we do not believe the presence of the sheriff and register of deeds in this procedure constitutes state action under the Fourteenth Amendment. * * *

The judgment of the district court is reversed.

* * *

## PROBLEMS

1. Abraham owned a parcel of real estate. Six days before Abraham's death his son Tobias mortgaged the real estate to Avon State Bank, the mortgage providing that Tobias was the heir-at-law of the estate of his deceased father. What interest did Avon State Bank have in the property before Abraham's death? After his death? Why?

2. Kolker was the holder of a second mortgage, dated September 10, 1932, given by the Kleimans to secure an $8,000 loan. It was payable in three annual installments beginning on September 10, 1933. The mortgage contained the following covenant: "In case of any default being made in the payment of the aforesaid mortgage debt, principal or interest in whole or in part, at the time or times limited and mentioned for the payment of the same, as aforesaid, or in case of any default being made in any covenant or condition of this mortgage, then the whole mortgage debt hereby intended to be secured shall be deemed due and payable and the sale of said mortgaged property may be made." The only amount paid on the mortgage was $1,586.28, which represented the surplus from the foreclosure sale on the first mortgage paid on March 9, 1939. On September 10, 1946, Kolker instituted suit against the Kleimans to collect the balance due. They argued that the entire amount became due when they failed to make the first installment payment and Kolker is now prevented from recovery by the 12-year Statute of Limitations. Are they correct? Why?

3. Henry decided to borrow $40,000 from First Bank in order to purchase a house. The mortgage closing has been scheduled for April 30, 1980, and Henry's first mortgage payment is due on June 1, 1980. Under their agreement, First Bank is to collect $30 each month to be placed in an escrow account for the payment of real estate taxes. The annual taxes of $360 are due on December 1 each year. What is the maximum amount which the bank can collect from Henry at the closing to place in the escrow account? Why?

4. In problem 3, assume that Henry agreed to pay First Bank 10 percent interest annually, which was the maximum interest allowed by law, on the $40,000 loan. The bank also charged Henry for a credit report, a survey, a lender's title insurance policy, attorney's fees payable to the bank's attorney, an appraisal fee and a fee for preparation of legal documents used in the mortgage closing. These charges, and a bank commission of $1,000, were deducted from the amount of the loan, and the remainder distributed to Henry. Is the loan usurious? Why?

5.   Under New York law, a married woman's dower rights could not be asserted against the holder of a purchase money mortgage.  Walter and his wife Virginia, a minor, borrowed $3,000 from the Syracuse Savings and Loan in order to purchase a lot.  The lot was mortgaged to the bank and both Walter and Virginia signed the mortgage.  They used $2,900 of the loan to build a house on the lot; the remaining $100 was applied to the purchase price of the lot.  Later, when the couple defaulted on the mortgage, the bank commenced a foreclosure action.  Virginia argued that the purchaser at a foreclosure sale would take the property subject to her dower rights.  The bank claimed that (1) Virginia signed away her dower rights by signing the mortgage and (2) her dower rights cannot be asserted because the bank has a purchase money mortgage.  Is the bank correct?  Why?

6.   On January 6, 1971, Tex borrowed $20,000 from First Bank and gave First Bank an open-ended mortgage on his house.  On February 20, 1972, First Bank advanced an additional $5,000, which was secured by the mortgage.  On March 3, 1973, Tex borrowed $20,000 from Second Bank and gave Second Bank a mortgage on the same house.  Second Bank recorded the mortgage but did not notify First Bank of its loan.  On April 5, 1974, First Bank advanced another $5,000 under the original mortgage and recorded the mortgage.  If both mortgages are foreclosed and Tex's house is sold for $30,000, how much would each bank receive from the proceeds?  Why?

7.   Grafton Bank held a first mortgage and Ohan held a second mortgage on a house that was damaged by a hurricane.  The first mortgage contained a standard clause stating that the mortgagors agreed not to commit waste.  Since the mortgagors were financially unable to pay for needed repairs, Grafton paid the $970 for the repair work.  After the repairs were completed, the mortgagors defaulted on their payments to Grafton and the first mortgage was foreclosed.  The proceeds from the foreclosure sale, after the first mortgage was paid in full, totalled $1,075.  Grafton claims that it is entitled to $970 of this amount as reimbursement for the repair work.  Ohan claims that the full amount must be used to pay the second mortgage.  Who is correct?  Why?

8.   Merchants Nat. Bldg. Corp. borrowed $135,000 from the Metropolitan Life Insurance Co. and gave Metropolitan a mortgage on property Merchants owned in Chicago.  As an inducement for the loan, Merchants had stated on its loan application that the premises were leased to W. T. Grant Co. for a term of 30 years at annual rentals gradually to rise from $15,000 to $22,000.  Later the property was sold to the W. T. Grant Co. and the sale was made subject to the mortgage.  However after Grant received a deed, it cancelled the lease, claiming that the lease was merged into its fee simple estate.  Metropolitan objects and instituted a foreclosure action claiming the lease payments were collateral for its loan because without them the property had a net value of only $50,000.  Metropolitan also argued that the mortgage lien on the rents was an intervening lien which prevented a merger of the leasehold estate into the reversion.  Is Metropolitan correct?  Why?

9.   Agnes borrowed money from National Savings Bank and signed a mortgage agreement whereby she agreed to pay the maximum rate of

interest allowed by law. The mortgage agreement did not allow Agnes to prepay the mortgage in full. Agnes later decided to prepay the mortgage and she offered to pay the bank a prepayment penalty of 3% of the original amount of the mortgage debt. If you worked for National as a loan officer, what legal question would you want to resolve before accepting Agnes's offer? Why?

10. On February 4, Stewart gave Hughes a mortgage to secure a debt of $10,000. Hughes was obligated to advance $5,500 of this amount in the future. The mortgage was recorded on February 7 and the $5,500 was advanced in April, May, July and August. However, on November 6, Ashdown Hardware acquired a mechanic's lien for materials furnished to improve the mortgaged property. The lien was effective from the date materials were originally furnished—February 21. Does the Hughes mortgage or the Ashdown lien have priority if the property is sold? Why?

# Chapter 10

## THE REAL ESTATE CLOSING

[T]he basic system of real estate titles and transfers—and the related matters concerning financing and purchase of homes— cries out for re-examination and simplification. In a country that transfers not only expensive automobiles but multimillion dollar airplanes with a few relatively simple papers, I believe that if American lawyers will put their ingenuity and inventiveness to work on this subject they will be able to devise simpler methods than we have now.

*Chief Justice Warren E. Burger, 1974*

The real estate closing represents the final performance of a real estate contract. At the closing the purchaser first settles the mortgage transaction and then pays the seller, who delivers a deed to the purchaser. The deed is the key to a successful closing and this chapter will emphasize the form of the deed and its delivery. Other aspects of the closing process will also be summarized, including the law of taxation as it affects the acquisition of real estate.

Chapters 6 through the present one have dealt with acquiring real estate by purchase, but two other methods of acquiring real property will be discussed at the end of this chapter: (1) transfer of real estate at the death of the owner and (2) adverse possession.

## I. DEEDS

A deed is a written instrument used to convey real estate from one party to another. A deed is distinguished from a contract to sell real estate in that the contract represents a promise to convey the real estate whereas a deed is the actual conveyance of the real estate or execution of the contract. A practical consequence of this distinction is that a deed, unlike an executory contract, will be valid even in the absence of consideration.

### A. TYPES OF DEEDS

Two major types of deeds are commonly used in real estate transactions: the warranty deed and the quitclaim deed. Real estate contracts usually specify that a warranty deed is to be delivered by the grantor; in the absence of a contract provision, the grantor may give a quitclaim deed.

1. **Warranty Deed.** There are two classes of warranty deeds. Under the general warranty deed, usually required by a real estate contract, the grantor gives three warranties: (1) the covenant of

seisin, a warranty that he has good title to the real estate; (2) the covenant against encumbrances, a warranty that the title is not encumbered by interests such as a lien or an easement unless the deed states otherwise; and (3) the covenant of quiet enjoyment, a warranty that the property will not be taken by someone with a better title. If these warranties are breached, the grantor will be liable for damages.

A "special warranty" deed may be given, in which case the grantor does not give warranties for title defects created before he acquired title but, instead, only for claims that arise "under, by or through" the grantor. To illustrate, Louise deeded a parcel of land to Tom which was subject to a mortgage given to Last Bank by the person who sold Louise the property. The deed did not state that title was subject to the mortgage, and Last Bank later foreclosed. If Louise had given a general warranty deed, she would be liable for damages resulting from the foreclosure even though the encumbrance, the mortgage, arose before she acquired the real estate. But if she had given a special warranty deed, she would not be liable for preexisting mortgages but only for mortgages and other defects that she created.

2. **Quitclaim Deed.** Under a quitclaim deed, the grantor makes no warranties but only transfers whatever title or interest he has to the grantee. The quitclaim deed entails a greater risk for the purchaser because if the grantor has no right, title, or interest in the land, the grantee receives none and has no recourse against the grantor. Quitclaim deeds are often used to remove a cloud on the title; the grantor simply deeds whatever interest he has to the grantee.

## B. FORMAL REQUIREMENTS

A deed, whether written in longhand in everyday language or on preprinted forms, must be in writing and must meet the following minimal requirements.

1. **Grantor.** Deeds should and usually do begin with the name of the grantor. Although it is sound practice to name the grantor, other designations that identify the grantor are sufficient. For example, if the deed states that the conveyance is by "We the heirs of Whitmill Stephens" and is signed by the heirs, the designation is sufficient for identification.[1] Furthermore, the name may suffice even if the grantor's name is misspelled, when a middle initial is not used, when the name in the body of the deed (Henry S. Woodworth)[2] is different from the signature (Harry S. Woodworth), and even if a fictitious name is used—so long as in each case the grantor may be easily identified.

1. Stephens v. Perkins, 209 Ky. 651, 273 S.W. 545 (1925).

2. Woodward v. McCollum, 16 N.D. 42, 111 N.W. 623 (1907).

Although the form of the deed may be correct, the deed will be voidable if the grantor lacks capacity. For individuals, capacity means that the grantor must not only be of full age, which in most states is eighteen, but also must be of sound mind: the grantor must be capable of reasonable understanding of the nature and effect of the conveyance. Old age, sickness, or extreme physical disability are irrelevant as long as mental capacity is present. See Heiligenstein v. Schlotterbeck, infra.

For corporations, capacity means that the grantor must be legally in existence and that the conveyance is properly authorized. To illustrate, a corporate law rule states that when a corporation sells substantially all of its assets, the sale must be approved by both the board of directors and a majority of the shareholders. Consequently, a person purchasing substantially all of the real estate from a corporate grantor should find answers to the following questions before closing: (1) Does the corporation legally exist under state law? (2) Was the sale approved by the board of directors and a majority of shareholders? (3) Does the corporate officer who will sign the deed on behalf of the corporation have the authority to do so under the by-laws or pursuant to a corporate resolution?

If the property is owned by more than one party, all of the joint owners should sign the deed as grantors. Further, if the property is conveyed by a married person, the spouse should be named as a grantor and should sign the deed too—even though the spouse is not an owner—to remove dower, curtesy, and homestead claims. If property is deeded by a single person, the deed should state this fact to avoid possible confusion when title is examined in the future.

2. **Grantee.** A deed must name the grantee clearly enough to identify him. For example, the grantee's name may be sufficient even though it is misspelled ("David Kessler" when his name was "David Kesler" [3]), part of the name is omitted, the grantee is not identified by name ("William Farley and wife" [4] or "Hannah Simshouser and her children" [5]), or a fictitious name is used.

A deed naming a grantee not legally in existence (for example, a deceased person or a corporation that has not been formed under state law) does not operate as a conveyance because it is impossible to deliver the deed. However if the corporation were to come into existence later and delivery were made, the conveyance would be valid.[6] The same general approach is used with deeds that omit the name of the grantee: the deeds are invalid while blank, but when the grantee's name is added by someone with authority to do so, the deed

3. Langley v. Kesler, 57 Or. 281, 110 P. 401 (1910).

4. Ballard v. Farley, 143 Tenn. 161, 226 S.W. 544 (1920).

5. Faloon v. Simshauser, 130 Ill. 649, 22 N.E. 835 (1889).

6. Zulver Realty Co. v. Snyder, 191 Md. 374, 62 A.2d 276 (1948).

is valid. In some states, however, this authority to act as an agent must be written. In Green v. MacAdam,[7] MacAdam served as Green's attorney and advised his client to sign several deeds to her property in blank. MacAdam later filled in one of the deeds, naming his secretary as grantee, sold part of the property to a third party, and kept the proceeds. A court held that the deed to the secretary was void: "Though the decisions of other jurisdictions are not in entire harmony upon the question, it has been definitely decided in this state that under our statute of frauds the name of the grantor or the grantee or the description of the property cannot be inserted by an agent of the grantor, in the absence of the latter, unless the agent's authority be in writing. If the authority of the agent be not in writing, his insertion of the name of the grantor or grantee or description of the property does not pass title."

At one time it was required that the name of the grantee be followed by "and his heirs" in order to grant a fee simple estate. Today these words of inheritance are not required, but it is still important that the deed clearly specify the interests of the parties. For instance, if property is deeded to "Francis Lucas, a single man, and Joseph Lucas and Matilda Lucas, his wife," what are the interests of the parties? Do each of the parties have a one-third interest as tenants in common? Or does Francis have a one-half interest as a tenant in common with Joseph and Matilda, who hold their one-half interest as tenants by the entireties? Or does Francis have a one-third interest as tenant in common, with Joseph and Matilda holding the remaining two-thirds interest as tenants by the entireties? In this case, although the court eventually adopted the second construction,[8] a great deal of time, expense and uncertainty could have been avoided by clearly stating the intention in the deed.

3. **Addresses.** It is common practice to include the address of the parties in the deed. Although a deed without addresses will be valid, in some states it will not be eligible for recording.

4. **Words of Conveyance.** A deed must show a present intention on the part of the grantor to transfer his interest to the grantee. A warranty deed uses the words "convey and warrant" to transfer title. Although older deed forms often list the warranties that are given by the grantor, modern statutes provide that the warranties are given, listed or not, when the above words are used. In a quitclaim deed, the words "convey and quitclaim" are used to transfer the grantor's interest. Both types of deeds sometimes use the words "bargain and sell" in place of "convey."

---

7. 175 Cal.App.2d 481, 346 P.2d 474 (1959). In some states a description of the property cannot be filled in even by an authorized agent. Barth v. Barth, 19 Wash.2d 543, 143 P.2d 542 (1943).

8. Heatter v. Lucas, 367 Pa. 296, 80 A. 2d 749 (1951).

5. **Description.** One of the most important—and complex—requisites for a valid real estate contract or deed is an accurate description of the land being conveyed. As a general rule, the description must be clear enough so that the land can be identified without the aid of outside evidence. In the words of one court, "In construing a deed in order to ascertain the specific property that is conveyed, it is sufficient if the description of the land affords the means of identification. Generally it may be said that the test is whether a surveyor with the deed before him and with or without the aid of extrinsic evidence can locate the land and establish the boundaries." [9] Most deeds contain one of four types of descriptions.

a. *Government Survey.* The U.S. Government Survey was developed after the Revolutionary War to survey the Northwest Territory (Illinois, Indiana, Ohio, Michigan, and Wisconsin) so that the land could be sold to pay war debts. The Government Survey is also used in Alabama, Florida, Mississippi and west of the Mississippi River with the exception of Texas; [10] where it is available, it offers the simplest method of survey. The key to the Government Survey is the township which, in theory, is a square tract, six miles to a side. In actuality, of course, townships cannot be perfectly square because square townships cannot fit into a circle, in this case the earth, especially when the township lines converge as they approach the north pole. To compensate for this convergence, there are odd lots, called fractional forties or eighties, or government lots, along the north and west sides of each township.

To illustrate the government survey methods of identifying real estate, we will use the following description from a deed: "The East ½ of the West ½ of the Southwest ¼ of the Southeast ¼, Section 22, T1S–R2E." With a Government Survey description, the property is located by reading the description from back to front. We begin by locating the township, T1S–R2E. Government surveying begins with two reference lines: a principal meridian line running north and south and a base line running east and west. Once we find the intersection of these two lines, it is easy to locate the township. In our case the "T1S" means that the township is in the first row of townships—that is, in the first Township Line—running in an east-west direction south of the base line while the "R2E" means that the township lies in the second row of townships—that is, the second Range—running in a north-south direction east of the principal meridian. This township, like all others, is divided into thirty-six sections, each of which is 640 acres. The sections are numbered as follows.

---

9. Mitchell v. Nicholson, 71 N.D. 521, 3 N.W.2d 83 (1942).

10. R. Kratovil, Real Estate Law § 49 (6th ed. 1974).

| 6 | 5 | 4 | 3 | 2 | 1 |
|---|---|---|---|---|---|
| 7 | 8 | 9 | 10 | 11 | 12 |
| 18 | 17 | 16 | 15 | 14 | 13 |
| 19 | 20 | 21 | 22 | 23 | 24 |
| 30 | 29 | 28 | 27 | 26 | 25 |
| 31 | 32 | 33 | 34 | 35 | 36 |

After locating Section 22, we then find the southeast quarter of the section, then the southwest quarter of that quarter, then the west half of that quarter, and finally the east half of that half.

### SECTION 22

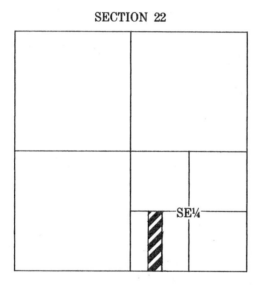

b. *Metes and Bounds.* The second and oldest method of description is by metes and bounds. With this method, the survey begins at a designated point called a monument, which might be a tree or a rock, and then proceeds to define the boundary in terms of angles and distances until returning to the monument. The property is located by reading the description from beginning to end. "Commencing at the iron pipe marking the south west corner of the east half of the south west quarter of section twenty seven; thence north on the west line of said east half of the south west quarter of section twenty seven, 521.76 feet to the center line of Geddes Road; thence deflecting 118 degrees eighteen minutes to the right 126.03 feet along the center line of Geddes Road to an iron pipe; thence south deflecting sixty one degrees forty eight minutes thirty seconds to the right 324.82 feet to an iron pipe and brick monument, thence southerly deflecting five degrees and three minutes to the right 136.16 feet to an iron pipe; thence west deflecting 83 degrees fifty five minutes to the right 98.13 feet to the place of beginning."

c. *Plats.* A plat is a map of a parcel of real estate which has been divided into lots, each of which is numbered. Once a plat has been recorded, a description is sufficient if it refers to the plat and lot number, for instance, "Lot 9, Vinewood Subdivision, recorded in Liber 6 of Plats, page 30, Washtenaw County Records."

d. *Informal Description.* It is recommended that one of the above methods be used whenever property is conveyed. However, occasionally an informal description will be sufficient to pass title if, following the general rule, the property can be identified with certainty. For instance, references to property by its popular name ("Commencement Plantation, consisting of 1330 acres") [11] or by street numbers ("my property at 91 and 95 East Webster Avenue, Muskegon, Michigan") [12] have been judged sufficient to identify the property.

Even when the description is uncertain on its face, courts have developed rules that may be applied to interpret and clarify the language. To illustrate, in January 1784, the owners of Pennsylvania, John Penn and John Penn, Jr., contracted to sell a parcel of land in the "manor of Pittsburgh, lying and being in a point formed by the junction of the two rivers Monongahela and Allegheny; bounded on two sides by the rivers aforesaid, on a third side by the top or ditch of Fort Pitt." The deed given pursuant to the contract stated that the two rivers were the boundaries of the real estate, but the deed also referred to a plat of the real estate which showed open spaces for Water Street and Duquesne Way between the real estate and the river. In interpreting this deed a century later, a court noted the obvious ambiguity between the general description and the plat description and, citing rules of interpretation from earlier cases, decided that the precise and accurate description in the plat governed the more general language in the deed. "The precise and accurate description and location of the lots, furnished by the plan given in evidence by plaintiff herself, cannot be controlled by the general language of the deed calling for the rivers as boundaries of the respective blocks of lots. The plan, which was incorporated with the deed for the very purpose of definitely fixing the location of lots, clearly shows that they did not extend to the water line on either river, nor include any of the land in controversy. The parties to the deed never intended that they should; nor is there any evidence that would justify a jury in finding that they did. Those who were concerned in laying out the town, that was destined soon to become a great city, never dreamed that the lots, accurately described on the plan, embraced any portion

11. Vaughn v. Swayzie, 56 Miss. 704 (1879).

12. Stamp v. Steele, 209 Mich. 205, 176 N.W. 464 (1920).

of the narrow, open space on each river, evidently intended as a means of public access to and along the rivers." [13]

In cases involving boundary line disputes, courts will also look beyond the description in a deed. For example, Rowan and Martin are neighboring farmers. The monuments used to identify the boundary line between the farms have been removed, and the neighbors do not know where the boundary should be. Consequently, they orally agree to establish a new boundary and mark it with a fence or other permanent monument. A court will enforce an oral agreement in this situation, even though it violates the Statute of Frauds, on the grounds that the acts of the parties may be used to interpret the description of the land in each owner's deed.

Although courts attempt to clarify language whenever possible, in some cases the description of the real estate is so indefinite that the deed must fail. In Miller v. Best,[14] the court was asked to interpret three deeds which contained descriptions such as "Thirty acres in the northern part of Spanish Grant No. 2425 and West and adjoining the ten acre tract known as the Will Lemon's Tract." The court concluded: "It is settled that 'part' descriptions such as these are void for indefiniteness. . . . Although a surveyor testified that he was able to locate the tracts from the descriptions we have quoted, he must have relied upon physical evidence such as fences, for the language of the deed supplies no clue that could lead to an identification of the property. The rule is that the conveyance itself must furnish that clue."

6. **Exceptions and Reservations.** The description of the real estate will often be followed by clauses under which the grantor creates and reserves a new right out of the estate granted, termed a reservation, or excepts a part of the estate that is already in existence, called an exception. For example, if a grantor sells a part of his farm which has an access drive running through it, he would incorporate a reservation of an easement for himself; but if he had already sold the remainder of the farm and the easement to a third party, he would make an exception for the easement in the deed. Although the terms are theoretically distinct, there is a tendency to use the words exception and reservation synonymously in deeds: "While there is a distinct difference between an exception and a reservation, the words are often used interchangeably. A reservation is something taken back from the grant while an exception is some part of the estate described in general terms in the deed which is not granted." [15]

Reservations and exceptions cannot be used to deed property to persons not a party to the deed. In Stetson v. Nelson,[16] Kistler con-

13. Schenley v. City of Pittsburgh, 104 Pa. 472 (1883).

14. 235 Ark. 737, 361 S.W.2d 737 (1962).

15. Murphy v. Sunset Hills Ass'n, 243 Wis. 139, 9 N.W.2d 613 (1943).

16. 118 N.W.2d 685 (N.D.1962).

veyed property to Iverson, "excepting and reserving to said L. G. Marcus," a stranger to the deed, a portion of the oil, gas, and mineral rights. The court followed the rule that "a reservation, to be valid, must be to the grantor" and declared the reservation invalid; it decided that the reserved interest remained the property of Kistler. "Generally a grantor who makes a reservation or exception to his grant, does not part with his full title to the grantee. Therefore, where such reservation is not effective, such interest remains in the grantor."

7. **Statement of Consideration.** Consideration is the payment received by the grantor in exchange for the real estate. While consideration is necessary to enforce an executory real estate contract (a contract not yet performed), it is not required that a grantor receive consideration for a deed. In other words, it is the grantor's prerogative to give away his property. However, most states require by statute that some consideration must be stated in the deed, whether the conveyance is a gift or another type of transaction. Even in the absence of a statute, it is customary to state a consideration. In the words of one court, "It is true that a deed without any consideration is good as between the parties or their heirs. However, it is a simpler, and a usual and sound conveyancing practice to recite at least a nominal consideration, so that a stated consideration will appear on the face of the deed. We have held that any . . . stated sum of money in excess of one cent, one dime, or one dollar which are the technical words used to express nominal considerations, is a valuable consideration within the meaning of the law of conveyancing." [17] While it is not required that the true consideration be stated on the deed, taxes will be based on the actual consideration paid to the grantor.

In cases where the grantor is to receive payment, courts are not concerned with whether the consideration is adequate payment for the land: as long as some consideration is given, it will be considered legally sufficient. However, this rule does not apply if the inadequacy is so great as to be unconscionable or to amount to fraud. A seventy-year-old woman deeded property worth $14,000 to a close friend, a young woman, for one dollar (which was never paid); the court cancelled the deed when the two parties later quarreled. "The general rule is that mere inadequacy of price or consideration is no ground for claiming the rescission of a contract in equity. . . . Equity does not undertake to act as the guardian of mankind. It does not aid people who make foolish bargains. But there are exceptions to the rule, which apply with peculiar force, where the parties do not stand in equal positions, do not possess equal knowledge, and where there are circumstances of fraud and oppression, on the one part, and of distress and submission, on the other." [18]

17. Brown v. Weare, 348 Mo. 135, 152 S.W.2d 649 (1941).

18. Frey v. Onstott, 357 Mo. 721, 210 S.W.2d 87 (1948).

Support deeds are governed by a special consideration rule whereby, if the grantee has promised to support the grantor and fails to do so, the deed will be cancelled. See Lewelling v. McElroy, infra.

8. **Date.** Although most deeds are dated as a matter of custom, a deed without a date is still valid.

9. **Execution.** A deed will conclude with the signatures of the grantor and witnesses and an acknowledgment of the signatures by a notary public. The deed must be signed by the grantor or a person authorized by the grantor pursuant to an instrument known as a "power of attorney," which should be recorded with the deed. The attestation and acknowledgment are not generally required in order to make a deed valid; however, they are required in most states in order to make the deed eligible for recording.

## C. DELIVERY

There is a popular misconception that a conveyance of real estate will be effective if there is a deed that meets the above requirements. The misconception is illustrated by the all too common "safety deposit box" case. For instance, in Allenbach v. Ridenour,[19] Ridenour deeded property to his son but did not tell his son of the deed; he continued to pay taxes on the real estate and even leased it. Shortly after Ridenour's death the deed was found in his safety deposit box along with a will, executed the same day as the deed, which referred to the deed and noted that the deed would be placed in escrow with a bank. The court held that the deed was invalid because there had been no legal delivery. Delivery usually requires (1) a physical delivery to the grantee, (2) an intention on the part of the grantor to convey title, and (3) acceptance of title by the grantee. Delivery must take place during the lifetime of the grantor; after death the transfer is made by means of a will.

The third requirement, acceptance by the grantee, is rarely litigated because the acceptance is presumed, even when the grantee dies before being advised of the deed, unless the facts clearly indicate otherwise. The first two requirements have been subject to a great deal of litigation, and most cases fall into one of four categories.

1. **Delivery to Grantee without Conditions.** In the typical case where the grantee takes physical possession of the deed at the closing, there is a presumption that legal delivery has been made, although this presumption can be rebutted by other evidence. In Keesee v. Collum,[20] a father called his four children to his bedside three days before his death, opened a tin box and removed $2,630, which he

**19.** 51 Nev. 437, 279 P. 32 (1929). Apparently the result would be the same if the grantor had told the grantee or third parties of the deed. Orris v. Whipple, 224 Iowa 1157, 280 N.W. 617 (1938).

**20.** 208 Ga. 382, 67 S.E.2d 120 (1951).

divided into four shares. He also removed a deed that named one daughter as grantee and laid it beside his cot. The daughter picked it up, looked at it, and placed it with the other papers. The father kept the deed and the money, stating "I will fix the rest tomorrow, I have got to lay down," but he died before taking further action. The court held that there was no delivery on these facts: "Even though the evidence authorized a finding that at the time the grantor was preparing a division of his property, and Mrs. Keesee at one time had physical possession of the deed to her for a few minutes, the jury, under the facts and circumstances appearing, were authorized to find that the maker did not intend to surrender dominion over the deed. Apparently all the children felt that the grantor had not completed delivery of the money or the deeds, because when he instructed his son to put the papers up, all the money and the deeds were returned to the grantor's trunk. The delivery of a deed is complete as against the maker only when it is in the hands of or in the power of the grantee or some one authorized to act for him, with the consent of the grantor, and with intention that the grantee hold it as a muniment of title. But a mere manual delivery to the grantee is not sufficient, where the intention of the grantor to surrender the dominion is not present."

If the grantor retains physical possession of the deed, a presumption exists that delivery was not intended, although this presumption may also be rebutted. For example, a valid delivery occurs when the grantor retains the deed but records it.[21] The presumption was also rebutted in Shaver v. Canfield.[22] Willis, a widower, delivered three deeds to his daughter, Nettie. After reading them and thanking her father, Nettie gave them back to him for safekeeping in his little tin box. Willis continued to collect and keep rent from the property, and he later mortgaged the property. He also remarried, and after his death his second wife claimed that the deeds to Nettie were invalid. The court disagreed with the widow: "Where a deed has been delivered the fact that the grantee allows it to remain in the custody of the grantor will not invalidate it. A deed may be returned after delivery to the grantor, so as to insure that it would not be placed on the record without affecting the delivery. The fact that Mr. Canfield collected the rents or a greater portion of them, and used them for himself and mortgaged the property without the knowledge of the grantee, did not affect the delivery. . . . The fact that after the delivery of the deeds they were placed in a tin box in the grantor's room would not affect the legality of the delivery."

2. **Delivery to Grantee on Oral Condition.** Wilfred attended Eastern State University. One year he decided to travel across the state to watch the annual football game between his university and

21. Tackaberry v. Monteith, 295 Mich. 487, 295 N.W. 236 (1940).

22. 21 Cal.App.2d 734, 70 P.2d 507 (1937).

its archrival, Western State University. Because he considered this a dangerous mission, he deeded all of his real estate to his roommate and handed the deed to the roommate saying, "I want you to have this property if I do not return alive." When Wilfred returned, he discovered that his roommate had recorded the deed and refused to deed the property back to Wilfred. May the deed be cancelled? Although all decisions are not in agreement, most courts would decide that the roommate now owns the property for the reason that the intention of the grantor should be evidenced only by the writing in the deed, not by oral statements that may or may not have actually been made. See Takacs v. Takacs, infra.

3. **Delivery to a Third Party Agent.** When a deed is delivered to a third party instead of the grantee, the major legal issue is whether the third party was acting as the agent of the grantor or the grantee. A delivery to the grantor's agent is not legally valid because, since the agent by definition is controlled by the grantor, the deed could be revoked at the grantor's discretion. A delivery to the grantee's agent, however, is legally valid.

4. **Delivery to an Independent Third Party with Conditions.** A grantor will often deliver a deed to an independent third party, who is to hold the deed until certain conditions have been met. For example, a grantor may deliver a deed to an independent third party and state that, after his death, the deed is to be transferred to the grantee. In this case the grantee immediately acquires an interest in the real estate, although enjoyment of that interest is deferred until the condition, the grantor's death, is met. However, delivery is not effective if the contingency is within the control of the grantor or if there are no instructions to deliver the deed to the grantee on certain conditions. In Fiore v. Fiore,[23] John executed a deed to his wife Antoinette in 1940 and gave it to his attorney without telling her of its existence. John died in 1942. The attorney misplaced the deed, discovered it in 1957, notified Antoinette, and had it recorded. Antoinette's son, who had maintained the property and removed clouds from the title over the years, then sued his mother, claiming that the deed should be nullified. The court decided in favor of the son on the grounds that "in order for the delivery to be effectual and to result in a cumulation of the transition of the title, there must be an express and definite instruction that the deed is to be given to the grantee then or at some future time."

The most common instance of delivery to a third party is the commercial escrow. To illustrate this method, we might assume that Cedric has contracted to purchase a new house from Rowena for $100,000. He does not want to pay her $100,000 at the closing in return for the deed because he is fearful that he would have to pay any

---

23. 405 Pa. 303, 174 A.2d 858 (1961).

mechanics' liens that might be filed after the closing if Rowena were not collectable. Rowena, however, refuses to deliver the deed until she receives her money. This impasse could be solved if Rowena delivered the deed to a third party escrowee, such as a title company or bank, which will in turn deliver the deed to Cedric when the condition—payment—is met. Cedric would deliver the $100,000 to the escrowee at the closing on the condition that the money would be paid if no liens were filed within the time period allowed by law.

If an escrow arrangement is used, the legal delivery date will be the date when the conditions are met; however, to avoid injustice in certain cases, a court might relate the title back to the date the grantor delivered to the escrowee. In the above case, for example, if Rowena died between the time she delivered the deed to the escrowee and the date the conditions were met, most courts would consider the first date as the delivery date to avoid claims to the property made by Rowena's heirs.

## II.   THE CLOSING PROCESS

Closing a real estate transaction raises no unique legal issues in addition to those already discussed, yet the settlement process is extremely confusing to most sellers and purchasers. The confusion is understandable because the mortgage transaction and the real estate contract are closed simultaneously, and a large number of documents and checks change hands in a very short time. It is hoped that the following summary will alleviate much of the confusion. In reviewing the closing, it helps to visualize the participants. On one side of the table sit the seller and his "seconds"—his attorney, his mortgagee, and his real estate broker. The purchaser and his "seconds"—his mortgagee and his attorney—are seated across the table.

### A.   FLOW OF MONEY

Money begins to change hands as the purchaser turns to his mortgagee to close his mortgage. The purchaser signs the note and mortgage, and he receives in return a check for the amount of the loan less itemized closing costs, prepayment of interest, and funds to be placed in escrow. The prudent purchaser will have reviewed these items the day before closing, at which time the statement must be furnished under the Real Estate Settlement Procedures Act.

Next the purchaser pays the seller the purchase price, using his own funds plus the borrowed money. In most transactions, various adjustments must be made to the purchase price. First, certain items charged to the purchaser should be added to the price, such as taxes and insurance premiums that have been prepaid by the seller. Items charged to the seller must be subtracted from this new figure, such as the amount of the purchaser's downpayment when the contract was signed, any unpaid utility bills, and state transfer taxes. After these adjustments have been made, the purchaser writes a check to the seller for the net amount. The purchaser then writes a check to his attorney to cover her fees and the cost of recording the deed.

Now it is the seller's turn to write checks. The seller first turns to his mortgagee and writes a check for the principal and interest due on this mortgage. The seller will then turn to the real estate broker and pay a commission based upon the gross sales price, not on the amount the seller actually receives. The broker will also be paid for expenses incurred on behalf of the seller, including the cost of the title insurance policy. Finally the seller pays the attorney for his assistance, which includes preparation of the contract and the deed.

## B. FLOW OF DOCUMENTS

Both the seller and the purchaser should receive an itemized closing statement listing the above charges. In addition, the purchaser should receive the following: (1) from the seller, a deed, title insurance policy, receipt for payment, copy of the seller's mortgage discharge, a bill of sale if personal property is being sold, the seller's homeowner's insurance policy if it has been assigned, and receipts for payment of last utility bills and taxes; (2) from his mortgagee, copies of the note, mortgage, and other mortgage closing documents. The seller should receive the mortgage note and the mortgage discharge from his mortgagee.

Amid the bustle and confusion of the closing, three important matters must not be overlooked. First, the abstract of title or title insurance policy is often certified for a date two or three weeks prior to closing and should be brought up to date to insure that there have been no last-minute liens or transfers. Second, the legal documents (deed, buyer's mortgage and seller's mortgage discharge) should be recorded immediately after the closing to avoid later transfers to good faith purchasers. Finally the buyer should ask for the keys to the house to avoid being locked out of the newly purchased home, as the author was on his return from the closing.

## III. TAXATION OF REAL ESTATE

### A. TAXATION OF SELLER

The transfer of real estate has important tax consequences for both seller and buyer. In most cases, the sale of real estate will result in a profit to the seller. Let us assume that Sam has just sold a parcel of real estate to Pete for $70,000 which he purchased for

$50,000, thereby receiving a profit of $20,000.[24] If Sam is in a 50 percent tax bracket and if the $20,000 profit is considered to be ordinary income, Sam will receive a net of $10,000, the other $10,000 going to the government. However, Sam might use one of three methods to reduce this heavy tax burden.

First, if the profit is considered to be a long-term capital gain, the Revenue Act of 1978 provides that only 40 percent of the gain is taxed as ordinary income; the rest passes tax-free to the taxpayer. To qualify for capital gains treatment, a sale of real estate must meet two major requirements. The first requirement is that the real estate must be a capital asset, that is, property held for personal or investment purposes. Profits from the sale of property that does not qualify as a capital asset (for example, real property sold by an owner whose business is buying and selling such property), will be taxed as ordinary income. The second requisite is that the capital asset must have been owned by the seller for at least one year to qualify as a "long-term" capital gain. Profits from the sale of property held for less than one year are considered short-term capital gains and are taxed as ordinary income.

Sam may use two other methods to reduce his tax burden in conjunction with the capital gains treatment. First, it is often advantageous for a seller to receive the purchase price in installments, for instance, under a land contract or by taking a purchase money mortgage from the buyer. By spreading the gain over several years, the seller might avoid the higher tax rate which would result if the entire gain were taxed in one year. To elect the installment method, the seller must not receive over 30 percent of the selling price in the year of sale. To figure the capital gain on each installment payment, the seller will first determine what percentage of the contract price is profit and then multiply that percentage times each installment payment.

Second, it is possible for Sam to defer the tax or even avoid it completely if he is selling his principal residence. The tax deferral results whenever a principal residence is sold and a more expensive principal residence that has already been built is purchased and occupied within eighteen months before or eighteen months after the sale. If a taxpayer is constructing a new residence, the construction must begin no later than eighteen months after the sale of the old residence and must be occupied and used as a principal residence not lat-

---

24. Although in the discussion of tax liabilities we will determine profit by subtracting the purchase price from the sale price, in most cases various adjustments must be made to these prices. For instance, the purchase price (or "basis") will be increased by permanent improvements and other capital expenditures and reduced by depreciation claimed by the taxpayer. The sales price is reduced by selling expenses and certain "fixing up" expenses incurred to make a residence more salable.

er than two years after the sale.  A principal residence may be a co-operative apartment, a condominium, or even a houseboat.

To illustrate the tax deferral in Sam's case, let us assume that after selling his $70,000 home for a gain of $20,000, he purchased and occupied a new $85,000 home within eighteen months.  Sam must report the sale to the Internal Revenue Service, but he must defer payment of tax on the $20,000 gain.  If Sam later sells his new home and decides not to purchase another residence, he must then pay tax on the $20,000 plus any additional gain from the sale of the replacement residence.  However, if Sam purchases another residence within eighteen months after selling the replacement residence, he must continue to defer paying taxes on the gains from both sales.  On the other hand, if the replacement residence costs less than the sales price of the old residence, Sam would pay tax on the difference between the sales price and the purchase price up to the amount of the gain.  Assume Sam purchased the new residence for $65,000;  he would then pay tax on $5,000 of the gain, and taxes on the remaining $15,000 would be deferred.

If Sam is aged 55 or over, he may elect to exclude from his income up to $100,000 of the gain from the sale of his principal residence.  In order to make this election, which is allowed only once in a lifetime, the owner must have occupied the property as a principal residence for three of the five years preceding the sale.

## B.  TAXATION OF PURCHASER

The acquisition of real estate will bring both tax burdens and tax benefits to the purchaser.  The major tax burden is the real property tax which is levied by local governments.  Over 80 percent of the tax revenue used to support local governments is derived from the property tax, and most of this revenue is used to support school systems. Property taxes vary greatly from one area to another;  for instance, the annual property tax on a house with a market value of $100,000 would be around $8,400 in Boston and approximately $400 in New Orleans.  The variation is caused by two factors.  First, property taxes are based on the assessed value of a house, but the methods of assessment vary from state to state.  In some states, homes are assessed at 100 percent of market value, while in other states the assessment might be based on only 25 or 30 percent of market value. Second, the tax rate is subject to a great deal of variation.  To illustrate one method of taxing property, let us assume that Kathy has just purchased a used home in Ann Arbor, Michigan.  In 1978 the average home in Ann Arbor sold for approximately $60,000.  Under Michigan law, all property must be assessed at 50 percent of market value, in this case, $30,000.  The annual tax rate in Ann Arbor is 70 mills.  One mill is equal to 1/1000 of a dollar or, stated another way, each mill is the equivalent of $1 per thousand dollars of the property's assessed value.   In Kathy's case the tax bill would be $70 for each $1000 of assessed valuation, or $2100.

The tremendous rise in property taxes in recent years, as the value of real estate has increased even faster than the rate of inflation, has given impetus to tax reform.   In one notable example, California voters passed a proposal in 1978 which lowered property taxes by an estimated $7 billion.   The proposal, known as Proposition 13 or the Jarvis-Gann constitutional amendment, set a 1 percent tax limit on real estate assessments, rolled back property taxes to 1976 levels, and provided that two-thirds of the state legislature must approve new taxes.

Reform of real property taxation is also being forced on states as the result of litigation involving school financing.   Because schools rely heavily on property taxes, the claim has been made that schools in poor districts have less to spend on education, with the result that students in those districts are deprived of equal educational opportunities.   The proposed solution would be to move from the system of local financing of education to state financing, under which the expenditure for students throughout the state would be equalized.   The tax consequence would probably be a reduction in local property tax and an increase in state income tax.

Reform of school financing was considered by the Supreme Court in San Antonio Independent School Dist. v. Rodriguez,[25] where the Texas system of financing schools was challenged in a class action brought on behalf of school children who are members of minority groups or who reside in areas with a low tax base.   The Texas system, which relies on local property taxes that are supplemented by state and federal contributions, resulted in discrepancies in expenditures per student.   For example, in the affluent Alamo Heights school district with less than 20 percent minority enrollment, the land tax in 1967–68 yielded $333 per pupil which, with state and federal supplements, was increased to $594 per pupil.   Meanwhile in the least affluent district in San Antonio, with more than 96 percent minority enrollment, the local tax yielded $26 per pupil and, as supplemented, totaled $356.

The Supreme Court, in a five to four decision, concluded that the Texas system did not result in a denial of equal protection under the Constitution.   The Court initially observed that the case did not involve a suspect classification, such as one based on race, or a fundamental right which would require that the legislation meet stricter standards.   The justices reached this conclusion because it had not been shown that poor families were clustered in districts with low property tax bases.   The court cited a Connecticut study that indicated poor people tend to live in industrial areas which provide a superi-

25.   411 U.S. 1, 93 S.Ct. 1278, 36 L.Ed.
2d 16 (1973).

or property tax base. Furthermore, the court noted that education was not among the rights explicitly protected by the Constitution. The court decided that the Texas system met less strict constitutional tests: "Apart from the unsettled and disputed question whether the quality of education may be determined by the amount of money expended for it, a sufficient answer to appellees' argument is that at least where wealth is involved the Equal Protection Clause does not require absolute equality or precisely equal advantages. . . . In sum, to the extent that the Texas system of school finance results in unequal expenditure between children who happen to reside in different districts, we cannot say that such disparities are the product of a system that is so irrational as to be invidiously discriminatory. In its essential characteristics the Texas plan for financing public education reflects what many educators for a half century have thought was an enlightened approach to a problem for which there is no perfect solution."

Despite the Supreme Court decision, judicial reform of school financing is still available under state constitutional provisions. A few states have rejected reform for reasons similar to those expressed by the Supreme Court; other states have ordered reform on the basis of constitutional provisions requiring equal protection and a public education for all children.

With the burdens of real property ownership come a number of tax benefits for the purchaser. Most notably, property taxes and mortgage interest payments may be deducted for federal income tax purposes. Furthermore, a depreciation deduction may be taken for wear and tear or obsolescence of property held for the production of income or used in a trade or business. However, the Tax Reform Act of 1976 curtailed such deductions for vacation homes used for rental income and business use of homes. A taxpayer who uses a vacation home during a tax year for more than fourteen days or 10 percent of the number of days the property is rented must allocate expenses between personal and rental use, and rental expenses are deductible only to the extent of rental income. A deduction for the business use of a home, such as a home office, is allowed only when a portion of the home is used regularly and exclusively as the taxpayer's principal place of business, or as a place of business used to meet patients, customers, or clients in the normal course of business, or as a separate structure used in the business. Deductions for these uses are limited to the amount of income resulting from the business use of the home.

## IV. OTHER METHODS OF REAL ESTATE ACQUISITION

### A. DEATH

On the death of the owner, title or interests in real estate may pass to persons designated in the decedent's will; in the absence of a will, state statutes will determine ownership.

1. **Wills.** Transfer of property by will differs from transfer by deed: under a will no interest passes until the person executing the will, the testator, dies; a deed gives a present interest to the grantee upon delivery. The will, unlike a deed, is revocable during the life-time of the testator because it is not effective until his death. Fur-thermore, unlike a deed, a will may pass title to personal property.

In some states oral (or nuncupative) wills are valid, at least to transfer personal property, if made shortly before death and proved by a specified number of witnesses. In most cases, however, the will must be in writing and must meet certain requirements. These re-quirements are determined by reference to the law of the state where the decedent's real estate is located or, if personal property is in ques-tion, the state of the decedent's residence. In most states the formal requirements are simple and easy to meet: the will must be signed by the testator and witnessed by two or in some states three witnesses who will also sign the will. Even a holographic or handwritten will is valid if these requirements are met.

However, in virtually every state, there are also certain mental requirements. The testator must have the intention to make a will, which is usually determined by the language in the will. The testa-tor must have the capacity to make a will, which means that he must have reached the age of majority (in most states age eighteen) and must be of sound mind. Finally, the will is invalid if it was executed as the result of fraud, undue influence, or mistake.

As an illustration of the nature of the mental requirements, in one case [26] a sixty-five-year-old woman, shortly before her death, exe-cuted a will under which her property was to pass to relatives who had died before her. When the will was challenged, there was testi-mony that at the time she wrote the will the woman screamed at all hours, cursed the brother who helped her with household tasks, rare-ly bathed or groomed herself, and often wore little clothing, thus in-decently exposing herself. The court, in considering these idiosyncra-sies, concluded that the will was valid: "The rule is that even though a testator does suffer from delusions or hallucinations, unless the will itself was a creature or product of such delusions or hallucinations, it

26. In re Stitt's Estate, 93 Ariz. 302, 380 P.2d 601 (1963).

is not invalid. While in the instant case the contestants have put on much testimony of what they might consider delusions or hallucinations, they have not put on any testimony that the will was a creature or a product of the supposed delusions or hallucinations."

Although it is not required by law, most wills follow a standard format and include the following provisions: (1) publication clause, which is a statement of the testator's name, his capacity ("being of sound mind") and intention to make a will; (2) revocation clause, stating that all earlier wills are revoked; (3) burial instructions; (4) payment of debts, specifying which property is to be used to pay the decedent's debts; (5) bequests, or gifts of personal property by will; (6) devises, which are gifts of real property by will; (7) residuary clause, governing disposition of all property not covered by a specific bequest or devise; (8) penalty clause, which penalizes a party named in the will who contests the will; (9) name of guardian of minor children; and (10) name of executor. These provisions will be followed by the required signatures of the testator and witnesses.

The executor should be a responsible person because he or she is charged with performing the will. The will must first be filed in a probate court, where it will be reviewed to determine whether formal requirements have been met. The executor will then, under probate supervision, assemble and manage the decedent's assets, pay taxes and other claims, distribute the assets according to the directions in the will, and render a final accounting to the probate court.

Because a will by its very nature is effective only at death, the will must be revised occasionally to reflect the changing circumstances of the testator. The revision can be accomplished by means of a supplement to the will, known as a codicil, or through a complete revision of the will. The following questions are important in determining whether a revision is necessary: Has the testator moved to another state where the formal requirements for a will are different? Has one of the beneficiaries died? Has the testator purchased real estate in another state? Have assets declined in value or been sold? Has the executor or guardian died or moved away? Has property been purchased jointly? Has there been a change in the law, especially the law relating to taxation of estates? See Ford Will, App. B.

2. **Intestacy.** Each state has adopted a statute governing the descent and distribution of property for persons who die without leaving a will, that is, who die intestate. The statutes might also govern a part of the estate in cases where the will is incomplete. Under these statutes, title to real property descends to heirs designated by the law of the state in which the property is located. Distribution of personal property is governed by the law of the state in which the decedent was domiciled.

Three examples illustrate the descent and distribution of property under a typical statute if the decedent did not leave a will. First, let us assume that Harry is unmarried and dies intestate. Both his real and personal property will pass to his parents, or if his parents are not living, to his brothers and sisters. If the brothers and sisters are not living, the property passes to their children; but if there are no nieces and nephews, the property goes to the next of kin beginning with the grandparents. Second, if Harry is married but dies intestate leaving no children, one-half of his real and personal property passes to his widow and one-half to his parents. If his parents are dead, their share passes to Harry's brothers and sisters or, if they are deceased, to their children. If Harry has no surviving nieces and nephews, his widow receives the remaining one-half of the estate. Finally, if Harry is married and has one child when he dies intestate, one-third of his real estate will pass to his widow and two-thirds to the child, while the widow and child will each receive one-half of the personal property.

3. **Dower and Homestead.** In many states the property share passing to the widow on the death of her husband will be determined by (1) the will, if there is one; (2) the statute of descent and distribution, if the decedent died intestate; or (3) the widow's share under dower and homestead laws if the widow elects this option in place of (1) or (2).

Dower originated in the Middle Ages when the legal existence of a woman ended at marriage; consequently, a widow was often left with no property on the death of her husband. However, the prevailing attitude of that period was that the widow should receive a better fate.[27] Sir Joseph Jeckyl expressed the more benevolent attitude in this way: "The relation of husband and wife, as it is the nearest, so it is the earliest, and therefore the wife is the proper object of the care and kindness of the husband; the husband is bound by the law of God and man, to provide for her during his life, and after his death, the moral obligation is not at an end, but he ought to take care of her provision during her own life." [28]

The solution at common law was to give the widow a dower right in the decedent's real estate. The dower right gave the widow a life estate in one-third of the inheritable land owned by the husband during the marriage. This definition excludes a woman who was divorced when the decedent died, for she would no longer be a widow. It also excludes property held in joint tenancy, for this property is not inheritable since it passes to the surviving joint owner rather than to the estate. But if the husband held property as a tenant in common, his share would be inheritable, thus giving the widow a dower interest in that share.

27. Petzke, *A Short Essay On Dower's Eroding Foundation,* 4 Mich.Real Prop.Rev. 2 (1977).

28. Banks v. Sutton, 2 P. Williams 700 (1732).

Today approximately one-third of the states give the widow a dower right, and almost as many states give a widower a right similar to dower called curtesy. In some states the common law definition of dower has been modified by statute. Under both common law and statutory dower, a wife may sign away her dower rights; the most common method is to sign the deed whenever her husband conveys property.

A homestead is the family home and the land surrounding it. In some states the homestead is limited in terms of acres; for instance, in Kansas a rural homestead is limited to 160 acres and an urban homestead to one acre. In other states the homestead is limited to a dollar amount (for example, $4,000). The homestead laws are designed to protect the family from eviction by creditors and from the whims of an improvident husband. As one method of protection, the widow is given or may elect the right to retain the homestead on the death of the husband.

Two other methods are used to protect the homestead even when the husband is alive: the homestead is exempt from sale by creditors, and the homestead cannot be sold by the husband unless the wife agrees to the sale. In Stolldorf v. Stolldorf,[29] Howard and Otie Stolldorf were married in 1918 and lived together in Nebraska until separating in 1930, when Howard moved to Wyoming. In 1942 Howard purchased a house in Cheyenne, and shortly before his death in 1960, he deeded the home to a third party. After Howard's death, Otie claimed the deed was invalid under Article 19, Section 9 of the Wyoming Constitution: "A homestead as provided by law shall be exempt from forced sale under any process of law, and shall not be alienated without the joint consent of husband and wife, when that relation exists." The Wyoming statutes further provided that the homestead might consist of a house and lot of any size but the value of the right could not exceed $4,000. The court decided that Otie could claim a homestead right because the parties had never been divorced, and it gave the person who purchased the property from Howard three options: (1) pay Otie $4,000; (2) sell the house and give Otie $4,000 of the proceeds; or (3) if the house could not be sold for over $4,000, give Otie full title to the property.

## B.  ADVERSE POSSESSION

It is possible for a person to obtain ownership of real estate or an easement at no cost if certain requirements are met. Adverse possession is the method of acquiring ownership, and prescription is the method of acquiring an easement. Five tests must be met if a person is to acquire ownership by adverse possession; these requirements are in many respects similar to the requirements for an easement by prescription, which was discussed in Chapter 4. As summa-

29.  384 P.2d 969 (Wyo.1963).

rized by a New York court,[30] "the essential elements of adverse possession are as follows: (1) possession must be hostile and under claim of right, (2) it must be actual, (3) it must be open and notorious, (4) it must be continuous, and (5) it must be exclusive."

1.  **Hostile Possession.**  A person claiming real estate by adverse possession must take possession of the land in a manner that is hostile to the interests of the owner.  Hostility does not mean that he must be personally hostile or offensive to the owner as an individual, but it does require that the possessor occupy the land without the owner's permission and with the intention of claiming ownership.  In discussing the hostile requirement, courts sometimes state that the possession must be under a "claim of right," which is simply another way of saying that the possessor intends to claim ownership.  To illustrate the hostile test, in Dimmick v. Dimmick,[31] two brothers owned a ranch, which they farmed together.  In 1937 one of the brothers told the other that he was not going to continue in the farming operations.  The other brother continued to farm, paid off the mortgage, paid the taxes, and made a number of improvements on the ranch without any financial assistance from his brother.  After several years the brother in possession brought suit claiming that he had acquired title by adverse possession.  The court held that there was no adverse possession because the possession was permissive rather than hostile.  Citing earlier cases, the court noted that "the exclusive occupancy of a cotenant is deemed permissive; it does not become adverse until the tenant out of possession has had either actual or constructive notice that the possession of the cotenant is hostile to him."

A common adverse possession case is the boundary line dispute, and often the outcome turns on the hostile requirement.  For example, Waldo and Rufus own adjoining farms which are separated by a fence that Rufus built thirty years ago.  Rufus now discovers that he built the fence on Waldo's property, fifty feet beyond the true boundary line.  When Waldo orders Rufus to remove the fence, Rufus refuses on the ground that he owns the property by adverse possession.  Waldo claims that Rufus cannot prove that the possession was hostile since Rufus admittedly built the fence and used the strip as the result of an innocent mistake.

In most states, courts have decided that Rufus's actual possession of the strip meets the hostile test even though he never intended to take his neighbor's property.  Under this view, Rufus would win even if he testified that "I do not want anything not belonging to me" and "I did not do it deliberately."[32]  In other states, following the more traditional view, Rufus's intention will determine the outcome.  Thus

30.  Evans v. Francis, 101 N.Y.S.2d 716 (1951).

31.  58 Cal.2d 417, 24 Cal.Rptr. 856, 374 P.2d 824 (1962).

32.  Flynn v. Korsack, 343 Mass. 15, 175 N.E.2d 397 (1961).

if Rufus testifies that he actually intended to claim all land within the fence, he will win. But if he testifies that he only intended to claim to the true boundary line, his actions will not be considered hostile and he will lose the case.

2. **Actual Possession.** In order to claim ownership by adverse possession, the possessor must enter the land and make actual use of it in a manner appropriate to the nature of the land and the locality. In some states the type of possession required is defined by statute. For example, under the California statute, possession occurs only if the property is protected by a substantial enclosure or if it has been cultivated or improved.[33] But in most states, the courts must determine what constitutes actual possession on a case by case basis. For example, in one case [34] the court decided that a party had acquired title by adverse possession through his use of the land for grazing from April to November each year for over twenty years. The court cited the rule in the American Law of Property that "possession may exist in a person who uses the land in the way in which an average owner of the particular type of property would use it though he does not reside on it and his use involves considerable intervals in which the land is not actually used at all."

There is one situation where only constructive, not actual, possession of the real estate is required: if the person entering the land has a deed that appears to give him title to the land, but for some reason the deed is invalid. It is often said that the person has "color of title" through the defective deed as opposed to actual title. The deed might be invalid for any number of reasons, such as the fact that the grantor had no title or because the grantor, unknown to the grantee, was insane. If the grantee has color of title under such a deed, the amount of land claimed by adverse possession is measured by the description in the deed rather than by the land actually possessed by the grantee. Furthermore, the period of time necessary to establish adverse possession is often reduced substantially.

3. **Open and Notorious Possession.** The actual use of the land by the adverse possessor must be open enough that the owner, visiting the land, would know that his land is being claimed, and the use must be notorious enough that it would be generally known by people living in the vicinity. In the words of one court, citing earlier authority, the adverse possessor "must unfurl his flag on the land, and keep it flying so that the owner may see, if he will, that an enemy has invaded his domains, and planted the standard of conquest." [35]

In Marengo Cave Co. v. Ross,[36] a cave company used a cave, which extended beneath the adjoining owner's property for a number

**33.** Hayes v. Mitchell, 184 Cal.App.2d 301, 7 Cal.Rptr. 364 (1960).

**34.** Springer v. Durette, 217 Or. 196, 342 P.2d 132 (1959).

**35.** Robin v. Brown, 308 Pa. 123, 162 A. 161 (1932).

**36.** 212 Ind. 624, 10 N.E.2d 917 (1937).

of years.  The court concluded that adverse possession had not been established: "Here the possession of appellant was not visible.  No one could see below the earth's surface and determine that appellant was trespassing upon appellee's land.  . . .  We cannot assent to the doctrine that would enable one to trespass upon another's property through a subterranean passage and under such circumstances that the owner does not know, or by the exercise of reasonable care could not know, of such secret occupancy, for 20 years or more and by so doing obtained a fee simple title as against the holder of the legal title."

4.  **Continuous Possession.**  An adverse possessor must use the land for a specified period in a manner that is appropriate to the nature of the land.  For example, in Turnipseed v. Mosely,[37] Turnipseed claimed by adverse possession thirty-nine acres of wooded swampland on the basis of his occasional cutting and selling of timber from the land over a twenty-year period.  The court held that his use was not continuous: "Such intermittent acts evidencing possession are regarded as merely transitory trespasses without legal right."  See Hardy v. Bumpstead, infra.

Although the time varies from state to state, the continuous possession usually must last a period of twenty years.  When the adverse possessor sells his interest before the required time or when the property passes to his heirs at death, the periods of successive possession may be "tacked" together.  Thus when property passed from Eli to his son-in-law Bill, then to Bill's heirs, and then to D. J. Jacobs, the possession of all parties could be tacked together to meet the twenty-year requirement.[38]  The sale of the property by the owner of record will not interrupt the accumulation of the time needed to prove continuous possession.  However, if the owner of record is under a disability such as insanity or minority, the owner will have an additional period after the disability has been removed to evict the possessor.

5.  **Exclusive Possession.**  The possessor must have exclusive possession.  This means that he cannot share possession and use of the land with the owner or other parties.  For example, a person claimed adverse possession of a lot overlooking the ocean on the basis of her weekly visits to picnic and enjoy the view.[39]  The court held that this was not actual possession, and furthermore, "there was nothing  . . .  to indicate exclusive ownership or possession.  It was no more than other persons residing in the city might have done and probably did."

6.  **Government Land.**  If the five tests are met, a claimant will become the owner of the real estate even though his interest is not

37.  248 Ala. 340, 27 So.2d 483 (1946).

38.  International Paper Co. v. Jacobs, 258 N.C. 439, 128 S.E.2d 818 (1963).

39.  Hart v. All Persons, 26 Cal.App. 664, 148 P. 236 (1915).

written in a deed or recorded on the public record. A purchaser from the prior owner—the record owner—will acquire no rights. However, even when the requirements have been met, a person cannot claim government property by adverse possession unless the government is using the land for a proprietary activity, one designed to make a profit. Although at one time government land could be acquired by homesteading, the Homestead Act, passed in 1862 to encourage settlement of the frontier, was repealed in 1976.

# CASES

---

### HEILIGENSTEIN v. SCHLOTTERBECK

Supreme Court of Illinois, 1921.
300 Ill. 206, 133 N.E. 188.

THOMPSON, J. August 25, 1919, Josephine Wittmeier died intestate, leaving two brothers, Gus Heiligenstein and Jo Heiligenstein, and three sisters, Mary Hahn, Adeline Schlotterbeck, and Lena Holmes as her only heirs. August 21, 1919, she executed a deed to her sister Adeline Schlotterbeck for the consideration of $1 and love and affection, conveying two and one-half lots in Altamont, together with personal property on said premises, reserving a life estate in the realty and providing that the personalty should be the absolute property of the grantee from the date of the delivery of the deed. On the same day she executed a deed to her niece, Maggie Heiligenstein Schott, for a consideration of $1 and love and affection, conveying two lots in Altamont, reserving a life estate. The next day she executed a deed for the consideration of $1 and the stipulations contained in a trust agreement of even date, conveying to William H. Engbring 120 acres of farm lands. * * * On the same day she executed a deed for the consideration of $1 to St. Clare's Roman Catholic Church of Altamont, conveying a 60-acre farm and part of two lots in Altamont. This deed provided, among other things, that it was made on condition that the east 20 acres should be used by said church forever as a memorial park, to be known and called Wittmeier Park, the premises to be planted with trees and the ground laid out in flower beds and shrubs, so as to be fit for a park and pleasure ground for social gatherings for the congregation and their friends. The church was given authority to sell the west 40 acres of said tract for not less than $150 an acre, and was required to pay to Charles Wittmeier the sum of $50 a month, beginning one month after grantor's death, for and during his life, pay his doctor and hospital bills, provide him a Christian burial, pay his funeral expenses, and inter his body on the lot owned by the grantor in the cemetery at Altamont.

* * *

Deceased was 61 years old at the time of her death. She owned the property described in the deeds above mentioned, and it was worth approximately $25,000. She was married in 1880 to Charles Wittmeier. They lived together until 1895, when they separated on account of his drunkenness, and at that time he conveyed to her practically all his property. The property she owned at her death was the property he had conveyed to her, with the exception of two of the city properties, which she purchased from her mother's estate for $2,700, with the proceeds received by her from the sale of 40 acres additional lands which her husband had conveyed to her. In 1916 she procured a divorce from her husband in order that she might sell some of the property. She was a member of the Catholic church, and very devout in her belief. She never had any children. An adopted daughter, Leonella, died in 1906 at the age of 21 years. She had been very fond of this child, and many of the witnesses stated that the death of the child had a profound influence over her, and that they noticed a change in her mental attitude after that time. She was a woman of high temper, and frequently engaged in quarrels and disputes as a result of misunderstanding with her neighbors and friends. She was naturally of a suspicious nature, and had trouble with her tenants over trivial matters, and was very exacting in reference to her demands, which were often unreasonable. She became angry at her sister Adeline Schlotterbeck, and refused to speak to her for seven or eight years. In 1907 her mother died, and she presented a claim for $29 against the estate, and two days later swore to a claim for $529. On a trial of the claim she was defeated, and this made her angry at her brothers and sisters who opposed her, and she did not speak to them for several years. One time she left her purse at the baker's, and forgetting about it she accused a neighbor lady of stealing it, but afterwards found it and apologized for her accusation, saying that she was forgetful. On one occasion she had trouble with her washerwoman over her pay, claiming that she had paid her, and afterwards found on the clock shelf the money she had intended for her and acknowledged her mistake in reference to it. She gave her brother Gus a receipt for rent and signed her name Mrs. J. M. Heiligenstein. She received an unsigned letter through the mail warning her to make peace with her God, the Catholic church, and her divorced husband, because her relatives were waiting to get what she had. This letter worried her, and she made inquiry from several sources trying to find who wrote it, and claimed that she found the authors, Mrs. Schoening, and Mrs. Cable, but they testified denying the authorship. She suffered from cancer of the stomach, from which she finally died. She went to the hospital at Effingham the latter part of July, and died at the hospital August 25, 1919. She weighed about 185 pounds when in health, but lost weight until she weighed less than 100 pounds. Her sickness made her very weak, both physically and mentally, and at times she did not recognize acquaintances, and called them by the wrong names. She made statements to different witnesses relative to the disposition she intended to make of her property which are in accord with the disposition she made of it in the deeds in question. The evidence relative to her condition during the last week she was in the hospital is very conflicting.

The witnesses are about equally divided as to number and credibility, but considering the interest of the witnesses we agree with the chancellor that the weight of the evidence shows that deceased was competent mentally to execute the deeds and understand the disposition of the property she made. The test of mental capacity necessary to make a valid deed is that the grantor is capable of understanding in a reasonable manner the nature and effect of the act in which he is engaged. There is practically an entire failure of evidence on the issue of undue influence. On the contrary, complainants' evidence shows that she was a strong-willed woman, hard to influence, and they showed nothing that would make a case of undue influence. The chancellor heard the witnesses testify, and was in a much better position to judge their credibility than we are. Under such conditions the court will not disturb the findings of the chancellor unless it is apparent that a clear and palpable error has been committed.

It is claimed that the deed to Engbring and the trust agreement when construed together, show that the instruments are testamentary in character. When an instrument is testamentary it is ambulatory, like a will. A will is ambulatory for the reason that it does not take effect until the death of the testator, and may be changed by the testator any time before death. If a deed lacks delivery—i. e., if the intended disposition is not to take effect in the lifetime of the grantor, but is ambulatory, changeable until the death of the grantor—such disposition is not operative unless executed in writing in conformity with the statute of wills. With deeds that have been delivered it is different. A deed signed, sealed, and delivered becomes at once binding and effective, and from thenceforth it is irrevocable and unchangeable. If not delivered it is not effective and is not a deed. The delivery is as necessary to make it a deed as the signing and sealing. In order that a writing in form a deed may be held to be testamentary, it must lack delivery. If the instrument in form a deed is delivered it at once becomes binding and effective, and cannot thereafter be revoked or changed. Such an instrument is not testamentary in character.

It is further contended that the deeds in question were not delivered. These deeds were voluntary settlements without consideration, and the presumption of law in such case is in favor of the delivery, and the burden of proof is on complainants to show clearly that there was no delivery.

The evidence shows that the deeds executed August 21 were delivered to Adeline Schlotterbeck, and the deeds executed August 22, naming Engbring grantee, were delivered to Engbring. This constituted a good delivery. An acceptance of the deeds would be presumed.

Complainants contend that the deed made to St. Clare's Roman Catholic Church of Altamont is void because it is an attempt to convey to a religious corporation land exceeding in quantity 20 acres, in violation of section 42 of the act concerning corporations (Hurd's Rev.St.1917, c. 32). Defendants claim that the church is not a corporation, but that it is a mere voluntary religious organization, and that the restrictions of the statute have no application. We do not find it necessary to determine whether St. Clare's Roman Catholic Church of Altamont is a corporation, because this deed is void regardless of our conclusion on that point. If the church is a corporation the deed is void because the conveyance is in violation of the statute. If the church is a mere voluntary association of individuals for religious purposes, it is not a person, natural or artificial, nor is it any other entity that may be the owner of property. In Alden v. St. Peter's Parish, 158 Ill. 631, 42 N.E. 392, 30 L.R.A. 232, the grantors conveyed to "the rector, church wardens, and vestrymen of St. Peter's parish, in the city of Sycamore and the diocese of Illinois," certain real estate, and it was held that the officers of the church took the property in trust for a designated charitable and pious use, and that the deed was not void for want of a grantee capable of taking by deed. In the instant case the conveyance is not to the officers of the church, but it is to a religious society claimed by defendants to be unincorporated, and if this claim is sustained it is to a grantee incapable, in law, of taking by deed. It follows that the chancellor erred in confirming title in St. Clare's Roman Catholic Church of Altamont.

&ast; &ast; &ast;

The decree with respect to the deed to St. Clare's Roman Catholic Church of Altamont is reversed, and the cause is remanded to the circuit court of Effingham county, for further proceedings in accordance with the views herein expressed. In all other respects the decree is affirmed.

Reversed in part and remanded.

---

### LEWELLING v. McELROY

Supreme Court of Nebraska, 1947.
148 Neb. 369, 27 N.W.2d 268.

SIMMONS, Chief Justice.

This is an action to cancel a deed to real estate on the ground that the consideration therefor was a promise to care for the grantor during her lifetime. The grantee died before the grantor. The trial court canceled the deed on condition. We affirm the judgment of the trial court.

     \*   \*   \*

The grantor pleaded that the grantee and his wife promised that if grantor would convey the property to them, they would remain in the home and care for her as long as she lived, and that, relying on the promise and without any other consideration, she made the conveyance; and that they had not cared for her since the execution of the deed. She further alleged that the promise was made without any intention of complying therewith. The defendants deny the promise and necessarily the intent not to perform.

The property involved in this action is a tract of land of about six acres, improved by a house and outbuildings, and located at the outskirts of Western, Nebraska. It had been the home of the grantor for half a century. The grantor had been a widow for many years. She was 86 years of age when the deed was given. The grantor received a pension as a soldier's widow. She was thrifty and lived within her income. In 1926, she bought and thereafter rented another property of a value of about $1,500 or $2,000 in Western.

The grantee was a favored nephew of grantor, and not in good health. On June 16, 1943, he and his wife moved from Omaha to Western and lived with the grantor. The grantee secured employment at Western. On July 21, 1943, the grantor and the grantee went to a notary public in Western and the deed in question was executed and delivered. It was a deed of general warranty, reciting a consideration of $1,000. It was delivered on the date of its execution, and was filed for record and recorded on July 28, 1943. It bore revenue stamps canceled as of that date.

The grantor, the grantee, and his wife lived in the premises until November 24, 1943, when the grantee died. A week later the widow moved from the premises to Omaha, and did not thereafter live there. In February 1944, the widow leased the premises. On February 25, 1944, the widow wrote the grantor asking for possession by April 1, 1944. This lease later was surrendered when the grantor refused to vacate the premises.

The notary testified that he made out the deed at the request of the grantor, and delivered the deed to the grantee at the grantor's direction and in her presence. The grantor directed that the consideration be recited as $1,000. The notary testified that to the best of his knowledge no consideration ever was paid. There is some testimony that about that time the grantor paid a judgment of less than $1,000 to the notary, but that the consideration recited in the deed had nothing to do with the judgment. The widow, called as a witness by the plaintiff, testified that the grantor was offered $1 for the deed and refused it, and that so far as she knew neither she nor the grantee paid anything to the grantor. The grantor testified that she was not paid a cent for the property. Defendants moved to strike this testimony as improper under section 25–1202, R.S.1943. The motion to strike was overruled. Defendants assign this as error. We need not determine this question. There is ample evidence that there was no money consideration. Defendants plead that the conveyance was a gift. If error, it was error without prejudice.

What, if anything, was the consideration for the deed?

The grantor offered the testimony of three witnesses. The first was a neighbor woman and a friend of the grantor, who had lived nearby since 1941. She testified that shortly after the deed was delivered the grantee told her of it, and that he was supposed to take care of the grantor for the rest of her life. About the same time the grantor told the witness "they was supposed to take care of her." A doctor, who was the grantee's physician, testified that in September 1943, the grantee told him, "I have taken over Aunt Anna's property and I am to take care of her so long as she lives"; and that on the evening before the grantee died, when the grantee thought he was going to die, the grantee again made that statement to the doctor. The grantee's employer at Western testified that he took the grantee to Wilber to record the deed, and that on the trip over the grantee told the witness that "Aunt Anna had given the deed for taking care of her the rest of her life."

\* \* \*

We are convinced, as was the trial court, that the promise was made by the grantee; that the widow knew of it; and that it was the sole and only consideration for the deed.

During the life of the grantee the three people lived together in the home, the women doing the housework together. Some of the bills for running expenses were paid by each. During this period of time the grantor was taking pills for a heart ailment, but was not ill enough to need a doctor and was never down in bed. After the death of the grantee, and after the widow removed to Omaha, the grantor's health failed; she required and employed the neighbor lady to do her housework and care for her, and later required attendance both day and night at her home, which she secured and for which she paid.

Was there a failure of the consideration? What did the grantor contract to receive and the grantee to furnish?

The grantor had a home, a rental property, and her pension. These obviously were sufficient to furnish food and clothing and shelter. Just as obviously, she contracted to receive that attention and care that an old lady desired over and above physical wants. The care was to continue during the lifetime of the grantor. That she did not receive. There is no evidence that the grantee furnished it during his lifetime. The widow and defendants, who seek to retain the benefit of the transaction, failed to furnish it after the grantee's death.

As we view these facts, they result in a failure to perform the consideration for the deed.

We have repeatedly held that where a grantor conveys land in consideration of an agreement of the grantee to support, maintain, and care for the grantor during his lifetime, and the grantee neglects or refuses to comply with the contract, the deed may be set aside and the title quieted in the grantor.

\*    \*    \*

The judgment of the trial court affirmed.

Affirmed.

----

### TAKACS v. TAKACS

Supreme Court of Michigan, 1947.
317 Mich. 72, 26 N.W.2d 712.

CARR, Chief Justice.

This suit was started in the circuit court to set aside a deed executed by plaintiff to his son and his daughter-in-law, the defendant herein. The material facts leading to the giving of the instrument in question are not in dispute. Plaintiff came to the United States from Hungary in 1922, leaving his wife and son in that country. Approximately 14 years later plaintiff forwarded to his son Stephen Takacs, Jr., money for transportation to Detroit. The young man arrived there in October, 1936. Both plaintiff and the son were employed by the Ford Motor Company.

In March, 1937, Stephen Takacs, Jr., married the defendant in this case. At that time she was 15 years of age. The young couple desired a home and apparently plaintiff was anxious to assist them. As a result a lot was purchased, the conveyance being executed to plaintiff and the son as tenants in common. Thereafter arrangements were made with a contractor to build a house, the construction being financed from the proceeds of a mortgage placed upon the property. Following the completion of the house in June 1941, plaintiff and the young couple lived therein together until February, 1943, when plaintiff left the premises. During the time that plaintiff remained with his son and daughter-in-law he paid them, at first, $40 per month for his board and room, and thereafter, $45 per month. It appears further that he voluntarily contributed to certain improvements, principally a garage and a fence. Including the amount contributed by him towards the initial price of the lot, plaintiff contributed approximately $1,250 to the home and its improvement.

In February, 1942, while the parties were living together in the home, plaintiff, accompanied by his son and daughter-in-law, went to the office of an attorney, Miss Suzanne Popp, for the purpose of having an instrument drawn and executed that would insure the passing of plaintiff's interest in the property, on his death, to the young couple. The attorney in question, who was a witness on the trial of the case in the circuit court, spoke the Hungarian language, and it appears from the record that she discussed the matter with plaintiff at some length. The preparation of a will was suggested, but plaintiff indicated quite positively that he did not want a will because his son would have to go to court in connection with it and he wished to avoid the necessity for such action. As a result of the conversation and in accordance with plaintiff's desires, a quitclaim deed was prepared conveying plaintiff's interest in the property in question to "Stephen Takacs, Jr., and Mabel R. Takacs, his wife," the instrument being signed by plaintiff and witnessed. The proofs indicate that at that time there was an understanding among the parties that the deed would become effective on the death of plaintiff, and that it was not to be recorded during his lifetime. Following the transaction, and while the parties were still in the attorney's office, the deed was delivered to Stephen Takacs, Jr. It does not appear that thereafter plaintiff had the instrument in his possession at any time, or that he made any attempt to obtain it. No claim is made that he reserved the right, conditional or otherwise, to recall the conveyance.

After plaintiff left the home of his son in February, 1943, defendant caused the deed to be recorded. On December 15, following, Stephen Takacs, Jr., died. Plaintiff claims that thereafter he learned for the first time that the deed had been recorded. He also learned that defendant was trying to sell the property. * * *

＊　＊　＊

It is clearly apparent from the evidence in the case that plaintiff did not wish to execute a will. It was his desire that on his death his son and daughter-in-law should take his interest in the property, without the necessity of any court procedure. He might have delivered the instrument, following its execution, to a third person with directions to deliver it to the grantees following plaintiff's death. Instead of following this course plaintiff turned the instrument over to the grantees without any reservation as to its recall. It remained thereafter in the possession of the grantees. * * *

＊　＊　＊

The general rule on the question in issue is summarized in C.J.S. Deeds, § 48, pp. 251, 252, as follows: "As a general rule, a delivery of a deed must be absolute and unconditional, unless it is in escrow. Further, as appears in [30] C.J.S. title Escrows § 7, also 21 C.J. p. 873 note 96–p. 878 note 31, a delivery in escrow may be made only to a third person not a party to the transaction, and there can be no such delivery to the grantee upon a condition not expressed in the instrument. Accordingly, while there is some authority to the contrary, it is generally held that the delivery to the grantee of a deed absolute on its face will pass complete title to him regardless of any condition or contingency on which its operative effect is made to depend, provided, of course, there is otherwise a sufficient delivery under the rules stated supra §§ 41–47, without reservation of control or dominion over the deed by the grantor. To thus vest complete title in the grantee, however, it is essential that it shall be the intention of the grantor that the instrument shall become operative, without further act upon his part, upon performance of the condition, and the rule applies only to those deeds which are upon their face complete contracts requiring nothing but delivery to make them perfect, and does not apply to those which upon their face import that something besides delivery is necessary to be done in order to make them complete."

The decisions of this court above referred to are controlling on the question as to the effectiveness of the delivery of the deed in the instant case. In accordance therewith we hold that the delivery was sufficient to pass title to the grantees, that the terms of the conveyance may not be altered by parol, and that the attempted verbal stipulation as to when the conveyance should become operative was ineffective.

It is further contended on behalf of appellee that the deed should be set aside because it was executed without consideration. The instrument recited a consideration of "One ($1.00) Dollar and other valuable considerations." It is conceded, however, that the grantees made no payment of any kind to plaintiff, nor was there any agreement on their part to support him in the future, or otherwise to do anything for his benefit. Unquestionably plaintiff executed the conveyance because of his affection for his son, which prompted his desire to assist him and to save him any inconvenience incident to the probating of a will. Under the circumstances a pecuniary consideration was not essential to the validity of the conveyance. A somewhat similar situation was presented in Flood v. Flood, 295 Mich. 366, 294 N.W. 714, 715, where it was said: "The deeds, intended by the father to vest title to the property in his son as a voluntary gift, required no pecuniary consideration."

\* \* \*

The claim that defendant acted fraudulently in placing the deed on record does not require extended consideration. Such act on her part was in violation of the verbal agreement between the parties, but under the circumstances presented by the record it did not operate to the injury of the plaintiff. In view of the fact that title to the property passed as the result of the delivery of the deed to the grantees, the right to have such conveyance placed on record may well be regarded as a resulting legal incident, nothwithstanding the attempted oral stipulation on plaintiff's part. In any event plaintiff is not in position to seek relief on the theory that he was injured by defendant's act in causing the deed to be recorded.

For the reasons indicated the decree of the trial court is vacated, and a decree will enter in this court in conformity with the foregoing opinion, with costs to appellant.

————

## HARDY v. BUMPSTEAD

Commission of Appeals of Texas, 1931.
41 S.W.2d 226.

LEDDY, J.

Plaintiffs in error are the record owners of the land in controversy and entitled to recover the same unless defendant in error has title under the ten-year statute of limitation.

In order to justify the conclusion that title has been perfected by defendant in error under the provisions of the ten-year statute (Rev. St.1925, art. 5510), it must appear his possession and use of the land has been continuous and uninterrupted for the required period of time. If there is a break in the continuity of his possession, it devolves upon him to show that it only existed for a reasonable period.

A careful consideration of the facts shown by this record convinces us that the continuity of defendant in error's possession was broken in 1925 for a period of more than eight months, an unreasonable length of time under the existing circumstances; hence he has failed to show the required continuous and unbroken possession of the premises in controversy for the complete statutory period.

The evidence discloses that defendant in error, with his family, consisting of a daughter and two minor sons, went upon this 106-acre tract of land in 1917. At the time he moved on the place, there was a small shack or building located thereon which he floored and moved into. He cleared and inclosed a tract of about two acres near the house and built a small chicken house and smokehouse, these buildings being eight by ten feet in size, and constructed of pine slabs. The small tract of land inclosed was gradually enlarged by clearing from year to year up to 1922, when it embraced about five acres within the inclosure. There was no enlargement of the inclosed portion after that time. It appears defendant in error raised crops upon the five-acre tract each year, with the exception of 1925, which consisted of corn, potatoes, and vegetables. At different times he had some hogs and chickens upon the place. His daughter married and left the place in 1920, the two sons remaining with him until 1924, when one of them moved to the state of Arkansas. In 1922, the dwelling was destroyed by fire, and defendant in error moved into a little crib and smokehouse on the place, and remained there, making a crop within the small inclosure during that year. In 1924, he built a one-room house out of lumber cut from the premises, and lived in this house with his son. In 1925, no crop or garden was cultivated on the place. During that year, defendant in error and his son moved to other premises two and a half miles from the land in question and resided on what was known as the Daniels place, where they cut railroad ties on their own account. They cultivated no crop on the premises in question, and made no other use of the land during the year 1925, except the son occupied the house during the trapping season, which terminated about the first of March, 1925. From that date until 1926, the place was not used or cultivated in any manner, outside of occasional visits to the house by the father and son, who stayed all night there perhaps once or twice a week. It was in evidence that, when defendant in error and his son moved to the Daniels place in 1925, they took with them a part of the household goods and left a portion, as well as some plow tools. The record is silent as to what household goods remained in the house or the condition thereof, nor does it disclose the number or character of plow tools left on the place. It was not shown whether the house was locked so as to prevent its use by strangers during the time defendant in error resided at the Daniels place.

Does the evidence, when considered in the most favorable light to defendant in error, show that there was such a break in the continuity of his possession in 1925 as to prevent the perfection of title under the ten-year statute of limitation? We think it does.

To constitute adverse possession, the party occupying the land must in some way appropriate the same to some purpose to which it is adapted. While actual residence on the land is not essential to constitute adverse possession (Cantagrel v. Von Lupin, 58 Tex. 570), it has been determined that the possession referred to by the statute means an actual residence on the land, or such continuous and uninterrupted cultivation, use, and enjoyment of same as to be visible, notorious acts of ownership sufficient in character to give notice to the owner that his land is being adversely claimed by another.

Nor is the mere fencing of the land or erection of other improvements thereon sufficient to constitute adverse possession, unless accompanied by actual occupation or open use.

\*   \*   \*

The gap in defendant in error's possession was not merely an interval between the harvesting of one crop and the preparation for another, as it is undisputed no crop of any character was made on the land during the year 1925, nor was the place used for any other purpose for which it was adapted. No livestock or fowls were kept on the place nor any timber cut therefrom during said year. The only occupancy during this period was the occasional visits of the father and son, at most once or twice a week, to stay all night in the house on the premises. We do not think that such use of the place was sufficient to constitute notice to the owners during the year 1925 of an existing intention of defendant in error to claim ownership of the land.

The owners of this land could have visited it every day during the daytime for a period of eight months without discovering that it was being used for any of the purposes to which it was adapted, or that the house was actually occupied by any one asserting a claim to the land. Certainly plaintiffs in error were not required to use the extraordinary degree of diligence necessary to discover defendant in error's nocturnal visits to this property. The fact that the land appeared to have been previously used and occupied was not notice to the owners of an existing intent of the former occupant to appropriate the land. On the contrary, all the appearances during 1925 indicated an abandonment of any such purpose.

It is true defendant in error offered proof tending to show that during the time he was away from the place in 1925 he continuously claimed it as his own. In order to perfect title by limitation, it is essential that more than a mere claim to the land must be shown. The claimant is required to establish continuous and uninterrupted cultivation, use, and enjoyment thereof.

*   *   *

We conclude that as the defendant in error's use and enjoyment of the premises during the year 1925 was insufficient to constitute the character of adverse possession required by the statute, plaintiffs in error's requested peremptory instruction should have been given.

We recommend the judgments of the trial court, and the Court of Civil Appeals be reversed, and that judgment be here rendered for plaintiffs in error.

## PROBLEMS

1. Parks and Miller agreed to deed tracts of real estate to Hamilton. Shortly after Hamilton's death, Parks executed a deed to Hamilton, and Miller executed a deed to the "estate of James L. Hamilton, deceased." Hamilton's widow and ten children now claim title to the property under these deeds. Do they have title? Why?

2. Julius went to his banker, Armstrong, and asked him to prepare deeds conveying two eight-acre tracts of land. Armstrong prepared the deeds, but the names of the grantees were not included because Julius could not remember the names of his grandchildren, who were to receive the land. After Julius died, Armstrong discovered the names of the grandchildren, added their names to the deeds and delivered the deeds to them. Are these valid deeds? Why?

3. Fenwick, a Roman Catholic bishop, acquired certain land from a fellow bishop. Bishop Fenwick later attempted to convey the property to Eliza Ann Scanlon. Eliza Ann, a minor, was married to Thomas Scanlon. The marriage was unknown to Bishop Fenwick, and in the deed he used Eliza Ann's maiden name, Eliza Ann Castin. Does Eliza Ann have title to the property? Why?

4. A small tract of land, on which a home was located, and a larger tract used for farming, were both called the "Jim Smith Tract". The

owner deeded the "Jim Smith Tract" to Sam, but after the owner's death, his heirs claimed that the deed was invalid because the description was defective. Are the heirs correct? Why?

5. Charlie lived on a 110-acre farm with his daughter Maggie. Charlie had a deed prepared that conveyed 65 acres of the farm to Maggie and handed the deed to her. Maggie and Charlie then placed the deed in a dresser drawer where they kept their personal papers. When Charlie died several years later, Maggie recorded the deed. Maggie's sister now claims that the conveyance was invalid because there was no effective delivery. Is the sister correct? Why?

6. Mahala inherited a small tract of land from her father. She divided the land between her two sons, Emzy and Benton, and executed and delivered to them separate deeds of conveyance. Afterwards, when Mahala's two daughters voiced their displeasure over the conveyances, the two sons voluntarily surrendered the deeds (which were not recorded), and the deeds were destroyed. New deeds were then executed and delivered to the sons requiring them to pay each daughter $300. Sometime later Mahala, dissatisfied with the new deeds, entered her sons' home during their absence and destroyed the deeds. When the sons threatened to prosecute Mahala for housebreaking, she executed and delivered new deeds to them. She then claimed that the deeds were invalid and that she still owns the real estate. Is she correct? Why?

7. Jones owned two adjoining lots. One lot was conveyed to Miller, who operated a gristmill on the property. The second lot was conveyed to the East Fork Baptist Church. Later, because of bad business conditions, Miller removed his machinery and gristmill from the lot. The members of the congregation cleaned up Miller's lot and occasionally trimmed the small shade trees growing on the lot. Now and then, when the weather permitted, Sunday school services were held on the lot, dinners were served under the shade trees during all-day meetings, and the lot served as a parking area for churchgoers. After these activities had taken place for around forty years, the church leased both lots to an oil company. Miller claims that the company cannot drill for oil on his lot. Is he correct? Why?

8. Isabel recently acquired title to land that was wild, undeveloped, and not suitable for farming, but it was suitable for hunting, fishing, and recreational purposes. Prior to Isabel's acquisition, Edwin had made use of the land for over twenty years. He had built a hunting cabin on the land, cleared portions of the land, and used the land every year for hunting, fishing, and vacations. He also paid taxes on the property for a period of twenty-five years. Isabel now seeks to evict Edwin, who claims title by adverse possession. Isabel claims that Edwin cannot establish adverse possession because he never fenced, posted, or lived continuously on the property. Is she correct? Why?

9. James owned real estate in the city of New Haven. James executed a quitclaim deed purporting to give his son, James Jr., an undivided two-thirds interest and his brother John an undivided one-third interest in the property. An attorney prepared and kept the deed with the understanding it was to go to John and James Jr. when James died. James continued in possession of the property until his death. After James's

death, the attorney showed the deed to James Jr. and John, who had it recorded. Now, James's widow, Elizabeth, claims that the quitclaim deed is null and void because delivery was not made during her husband's life. Is she correct? Why?

10. Tilley acquired property fronting on Conesus Lake. In constructing a cement wall to serve as a breakwater, Tilley mistakenly enclosed a parcel of land belonging to West. Tilley later built a shuffleboard and planted shrubs and grass on West's property. When West sought to evict him, Tilley claimed title to the land by adverse possession. West argued that Tilley could not establish adverse possession because Tilley's use of the land resulted from a mistake rather than an intention to claim ownership. Is West correct? Why?

———————

# Part Three

# LAND USE AND REGULATION

---

## Chapter 11

## RIGHTS OF LAND OWNERS AND OCCUPANTS

The house of everyone is to him as his castle and fortress, as well
for his defence against injury and violence as for his repose.

Sir Edward Coke

Acquiring real estate through purchase, lease, death, or adverse
possession brings the owner a bundle of rights and duties that affect
his ability to develop and use the property.  In this and the following
chapter, the rights and duties arising under tort law will be considered;  later chapters emphasize private control of land use by contract, and public control of land use through zoning and environmental legislation.

## I.  TORT LAW

A tort is a wrongful act which injures another person's body,
property or reputation.  Torts commonly fall within one of three categories: negligence, intentional torts, and strict liability.  The key to
a negligence action is a duty owed by the person committing the tort
to the injured party.  Once the duty has been established, for example, the duty of an automobile driver to operate the automobile in a
reasonable manner, the victim must prove that the duty has been
breached and that the breach caused injury to the victim.  Even if
negligence has been established, however, the victim might not be allowed to recover damages if his own negligence contributed to the
loss; such a situation comes under the doctrine of contributory negligence.  In recent years many courts have shifted from the contributory negligence approach to a comparative negligence theory, whereby the victim who is also negligent may recover damages, although
the damages will be reduced in proportion to his negligence.

The intentional tort, as the name implies, requires proof that the
wrongful act was intentional and that the act caused an injury.  For
instance, if an automobile driver intentionally hits a pedestrian he
would be liable for the intentional tort of battery, which is defined as
a harmful or offensive touching of another person without consent.
In addition to the tort of trespass, which is discussed below, other intentional torts include:  (1) assault, an attempted or threatened bat-

341

tery; (2) false imprisonment, the unlawful detention of another person; and (3) conversion, the unjustified taking or detention of another person's property. In many cases the commission of an intentional tort also constitutes a criminal act.

Strict liability is liability imposed on a party even though the party has not been negligent and has not intentionally caused injury. Strict liability often results when a person is engaged in dangerous or abnormal activities, such as blasting operations. In recent years, the most common example of strict liability is the liability imposed upon a business person who sells a defective product. Section 402A of the Restatement, Second, Torts, imposes strict liability on the seller even though "the seller has exercised all possible care in the preparation and sale of his product."

## II.   TRESPASS TO LAND

### A.   ELEMENTS

A trespass occurs when a person physically enters another person's land. At one time a person who entered another person's land was strictly liable, even though the entry was not intentional and not negligent. However, the modern view is that a person will not be held liable for trespass unless it is proven that he intentionally or negligently entered the land of another.[1] According to Section 166 of the Restatement, Second, Torts, "except where the actor is engaged in an abnormally dangerous activity, an unintentional and non-negligent entry on land" does not result in liability. For example, in Parrott v. Wells Fargo & Co.,[2] the employees of a freight carrier, Wells Fargo, used a hammer to open a box containing nitroglycerine, causing an explosion that damaged the plaintiff's property. The Supreme Court decided that the carrier should not be held liable for causing a trespass since it was not proven that the employees were negligent.

Once the required act is shown, courts next require proof of a physical invasion of the land. For example, a blasting operation that is carried on at all hours of the night and that causes extreme discomfort to persons living in the neighborhood will not result in liability, because noise alone does not constitute a physical invasion. However, if heavy objects or even dust and particles too small to be observed by the human eye are deposited on the neighboring premises, these would result in liability for trespass. As discussed in Chapter 3, the trespass might be below the surface or above the surface. In Butler v. Frontier Telephone Co.,[3] the plaintiff brought an

---

1. W. Prosser, The Law of Torts § 13    3. 186 N.Y. 486, 79 N.E. 716 (1906).
   at 64, 65 (4th ed. 1971).

2. 82 U.S. (15 Wall.) 524, 21 L.Ed. 206
   (1872).

ejectment action against a telephone company that had run a telephone wire over his property, thirty feet above the land. The court decided that there had been a physical invasion of the plaintiff's interest in the land on the following grounds: "According to the fundamental principles and within the limitation mentioned, space above land is real estate the same as the land itself. The law regards the empty space as if it were a solid, inseparable from the soil, and protects it from hostile occupation accordingly. . . . [A]n owner is entitled to the absolute and undisturbed possession of every part of his premises, including the space above as much as a mine beneath."

Finally, the plaintiff in a trespass action must prove that he has the right to possession of the real estate. If the land owner leases his property to a tenant, the tenant has the exclusive right of possession; consequently, the landlord would not be allowed to recover for a trespass. However, if the trespasser causes injury to the reversionary interest of the landlord, the landlord may recover damages, although not on the basis of trespass.[4]

## B.  DAMAGES

A trespasser faces liability for four possible types of damages. First, in any case the trespasser will be liable for at least nominal damages because "it is an elementary principle that every unauthorized, and therefore unlawful entry, into the close of another, is a trespass. From every such entry against the will of the possessor, the law infers some damage; if nothing more, the treading down the grass or the herbage, or as here, the shubbery."[5]  For example, in a case where the defendant's employee removed "about forty canoe loads of sand" from the plaintiff's beach, no actual damages were proven and the court awarded nominal damages of one dollar.[6]

Second, compensatory damages will be awarded in cases where harm is proven. In many cases, the plaintiff may recover the lesser of (1) the depreciation in the value of the land as a result of the trespass or (2) the cost of restoring the land.[7] See Kopplin v. Quade, infra, for a lighthearted discussion of damages.

Third, if the trespasser has acted willfully, entering the land knowing that he is wrong, a court might award punitive damages. In Elliott v. Sherman,[8] the plaintiffs owned two summer estates between a summer hotel and the sea. The defendant ordered employees of the hotel to cut down trees on the summer estates, which had

---

4. Walden v. Conn, 84 Ky. 312, 1 S.W. 537 (1886).

5. Dougherty v. Stepp, 18 N.C. 371 (1835).

6. Hahn v. Hemenway, 96 N.H. 214, 72 A.2d 463 (1950).

7. Welker v. Pankey, 225 S.W.2d 505 (Mo.App.1949).

8. 147 Me. 317, 87 A.2d 504 (1952).

beautified and sheltered the estates from onlookers, so that there would be a direct view from the hotel to the sea. The court, in awarding $16,000 in damages to the plaintiffs, noted that "there was credible evidence from which the jury could find that the trespasses were committed at the direction of the defendant, that his action in this respect was willful, and knowingly taken in total disregard of the plaintiffs' property rights  . . . . The attitude of the defendant is well shown by the uncontradicted testimony of a witness who testified that the defendant stated, prior to the cutting of the trees on the Collins property and upon being told they would make trouble: 'To hell with them. Let them sue me. All they can get is the cost of the trees.' "

Finally, several states have statutes that allow a landowner to recover double or triple damages in cases of willful trespass. For example, the Michigan statute (M.C.L.A. § 600.2919) provides that "any person who (a) cuts down or carries off any wood, underwood, trees, or timber or despoils or injures any trees on another's lands, or (b) digs up or carries away stone, ore, gravel, clay, sand, turf, or mould or any root, fruit, or plant from another's lands, or (c) cuts down or carries away any grass, hay, or any kind of grain from another's lands without permission of the owner of the lands, or on the lands or commons of any city, township, village, or other public corporation without license to do so, is liable to the owner of the land or the public corporation for 3 times the amount of actual damages."

## C.  PRIVILEGED TRESPASS

In many cases, a landowner will be unable to recover damages from a trespasser because the trespass is privileged. As a general rule, privileges are based upon the social value of the act in question; as the social purpose of the act becomes greater, the trespasser achieves broader protection. There are six privileges which are especially relevant to trespass.[9]

1.  **Consent.** A landowner who has consented to another person's entry on his land may not recover on a trespass theory. Although consent is often referred to as a privilege, as Mr. Justice Holmes noted in discussing assault, "the absence of lawful consent is part of the definition." [10] In Plate v. Southern Bell Telephone & Telegraph Co.,[11] the plaintiff sued the defendant telephone company for willful trespass when the company entered his apartment to remove his telephone. The removal took place after the plaintiff had failed to pay his telephone bill for three months. The employee of the company who removed the telephone gained entrance to the apartment with the assistance of a person who had a master key to all of the apart-

9. W. Prosser, supra note 1, § 16 at 98.    11. 98 F.Supp. 355 (E.D.S.C.1951).

10. Ford v. Ford, 143 Mass. 577, 10 N.E.
    474 (1887).

ments in the building. The court, in deciding that the company had not committed a trespass, noted that the plaintiff had agreed to the telephone company's regulations when he applied for telephone service, and one of the regulations provided that "the Company's employees and agents may enter said premises at any reasonable hour, . . . upon termination or cancellation of the service, to remove such instruments and lines." This agreement gave the company the privilege to enter the property subject only to the condition that the company not commit a breach of peace, an exception which was not applicable to this case.

2. **Reclamation of Personal Property.** There are three common situations where one person will attempt to reclaim his personal property by entering the land of another. First, the personal property might be on the land as a result of the landowner's wrongful act. In such cases the owner of the personal property is entitled to enter the land in order to remove the property, although he must act in a reasonable manner and must first request that the landowner return the goods.

Second, if the personal property is on the land of another because of an act of God, the owner of the personal property may enter the land to remove the property, although he will be liable for damage caused during the removal. For instance, if a gazebo is blown onto a neighbor's property during a tornado, the owner of the gazebo may retrieve it but must pay for the shrubbery he ruins in the process of removal.

Finally, if the personal property is on someone else's land through the fault of the personal property owner, there is no right of entry. For example, if the owner of an animal allows the animal to run onto a neighbor's land, he does not have the right to enter the land to retrieve the animal. Furthermore, the owner of a trespassing animal will be liable for damages caused by the animal even when the animal's owner is unaware of the trespass. An exception has been created, however, for dogs and cats. In Bishop v. Plescia,[12] the plaintiff left his registered schnauzer, Fifi, who was in heat, in his fenced-in back yard while he answered the telephone. When he returned, he discovered Fifi in a misalliance with a nonpedigreed mongrel by the name of Sneaker. After separating the dogs, Fifi's owner asked a veterinarian to administer shots to avoid conception but, as a result of the shots, Fifi developed an infection and could no longer be bred. When the plaintiff sued Sneaker's owner for damages, the court decided for the defendant on the grounds that Sneaker did not exhibit vicious propensities but was merely following his natural instincts.

---

12. Civil Court of the City of New York (December 2, 1975), reported in 62 A.B.A.J. 370 (1976).

3. **Necessity.** In certain instances, when it is necessary to save life or property, a person is privileged to enter the land of another. Some cases involve public necessity, as when one person enters another's land to dynamite a building in order to stop a fire which threatens a town.[13] In cases of public necessity, the owner of the real estate is not entitled to compensation from the trespasser because "the 'champion of the public' is not required to pay out of his own pocket for the general salvation."[14]

In cases of private necessity, which results when a person acts to protect himself or his property, the trespasser will be liable for actual damages. If, for example, a person ties his boat to someone else's dock during a storm, he must pay for any resulting damages to the dock.[15]

4. **Operation of Law.** A public officer is privileged to enter the land of another to execute legal process, for example, to seize property under a writ of execution or to arrest a person under a warrant. The privilege extends to cases where an arrest may be made without a warrant. In one case, a California ranch owner sued agents of the U.S. Immigration Service, alleging a trespass on his land when agents entered without a warrant to arrest Mexican laborers who were in the United States illegally. The court decided in favor of the agents and observed that the agents had the right to make an arrest without a warrant in cases in which they had reason to believe that a felony was being committed.[16]

5. **Forcible Entry.** A landowner is privileged to enter his land to remove a person who is living there without permission. For instance, if a tenant remains in his apartment after the period of the lease, the landlord is technically not committing a trespass when he physically removes the tenant. However, because of the potential for harm when a person uses force, most states have made forcible entry by the owner a criminal offense; furthermore, the person evicted will be allowed to recover damages for assault and battery. Consequently, the dispossessed landowner would do best to start a civil action in the courts, where possession can often be recovered within a matter of days.[17]

6. **Abatement of Nuisance.** A person injured by a nuisance is privileged to enter the land of another person to abate the nuisance. However, the injured party must act within a reasonable time after

13. Surocco v. Geary, 3 Cal. 69 (1853).

14. W. Prosser, supra note 1, § 24 at 126.

15. Vincent v. Lake Erie Transportation Co., 109 Minn. 456, 124 N.W. 221 (1910).

16. Taylor v. Fine, 115 F.Supp. 68 (S.D. Cal.1953).

17. W. Prosser, supra note 1, § 23 at 123.

discovering the nuisance; if a reasonable time has already passed, most courts will decide that he should have commenced an action in court rather than used self-help. In most states the injured party must also notify the landowner, when possible, that he intends to enter the property to abate the nuisance. If these requirements are met, the injured person may use reasonable force to terminate the nuisance and may even go so far as to destroy property such as a dam, a telephone pole, a barge or a dog, when they are nuisances.[18] We will now examine more specifically what constitutes a nuisance.

## III. NUISANCE

The law of nuisance has confused lawyers and laymen for centuries. In the words of Professor William Prosser, "there is perhaps no more impenetrable jungle in the entire law than that which surrounds the word 'nuisance.' It has meant all things to all men, and has been applied indiscriminately to everything from an alarming advertisement to a cockroach baked in a pie. There is general agreement that it is incapable of any exact or comprehensible definition." [19]

### A. NUISANCE DEFINED

1. **Private Nuisance.** Although the term "nuisance" cannot be precisely defined, the general character of private and public nuisances may be distinguished. A private nuisance results when there is interference with the use and enjoyment of one's land. As one court noted, "every person is bound to make a reasonable use of his property so as to occasion no unnecessary damage or annoyance to his neighbor. If he makes an unreasonable, unwarrantable or unlawful use of it, so as to produce a material annoyance, inconvenience, discomfort, or hurt to his neighbor, he will be guilty of a nuisance to his neighbor." [20] We will focus primarily on the law of private nuisance because of its impact on the rights of a landowner.

2. **Public Nuisance.** A public nuisance is one which damages the rights of the public in general. Creating a public nuisance is a criminal act, and public nuisances are generally defined by statutes such as the following: "Any building, vehicle, boat, aircraft or place used for the purpose of lewdness, assignation or prostitution or gambling, or used by, or kept for the use of prostitutes or other disorderly persons, or used for the unlawful manufacture, storing, possessing, transporting, sale, keeping for sale, giving away, bartering, furnishing or otherwise disposing of any narcotic and/or hypnotic drug as

18. Id. § 90 at 606.

19. Id. § 86 at 571. In addition to the distinction between public and private nuisance, discussed below, a few courts have classified some activities as nuisances "per se." This means only that the nuisance did not arise out of negligent conduct. Id. § 87 at 582.

20. Canfield v. Quayle, 170 Misc. 621, 10 N.Y.S.2d 781 (1939).

defined by law or of any vinous, malt, brewed, fermented, spirituous or intoxicating liquors or any mixed liquors or beverages, any part of which is intoxicating, is hereby declared a nuisance." (Michigan Compiled Laws Annotated § 600.3801). Under this statute the attorney general, a prosecuting attorney, or any citizen may bring an action for an injunction to stop the nuisance. If the court issues an injunction and the injunction is violated, the offender may be fined up to $1,000 and imprisoned for as long as six months.

It is possible that even a lawful business will be considered a public nuisance because of the manner in which it is operated. In State v. Turner the court held that a dance hall was a public nuisance: "Although the defendants may have a license for the sale of wine and beer, and the drinking of it on the premises violates no statutory law, they have no right to habitually allow the assembling in and around the Circle Bar of noisy, drunken, boisterous crowds, whose noise and profanity disturb the peace and quiet of the public coming within the range of its influence. One who knowingly suffers or permits such conduct commits a public nuisance." [21]

In some instances, a public nuisance might also be a private nuisance; however, individuals are allowed to recover damages only when the individual injury differs in kind from the injury to the public. For example, a house of prostitution might be considered a public nuisance because of its effect on public morals, and the house might also be a private nuisance if the late night activities disturb neighboring landowners' sleep.

## B.  ELEMENTS OF PRIVATE NUISANCE

1.  **Act.** A nuisance is caused by an act of the defendant that may be either intentional (which is usually the case) or negligent. In a few cases a defendant will be held strictly liable under nuisance theory, especially when he has engaged in a dangerous activity such as running a blasting operation. In discussing the type of act which may result in nuisance liability, one court observed: "Much confusion exists in respect to the legal basis of liability in the law of private nuisance because of the deplorable tendency of the courts to call everything a nuisance, and let it go at that. . . . The confusion on this score vanishes in large part, however, when proper heed is paid to the sound propositions that private nuisance is a field of tort liability rather than a single type of tortious conduct; that the feature which gives unity to this field of tort liability is the interest invaded, namely, the interest in the use and enjoyment of land; that any substantial non-trespassory invasion of another's interest in the private use and enjoyment of land by any type of liability forming conduct is a private nuisance; that the invasion which subjects a person to liability for private nuisance may be either intentional or unintentional;

21.  198 S.C. 487, 18 S.E.2d 372 (1942).

that a person is subject to liability for an intentional invasion when his conduct is unreasonable under the circumstances of the particular case; and that a person is subject to liability for an unintentional invasion when his conduct is negligent, reckless or ultrahazardous."[22]

2. **Interference with Property Rights.** Because, by definition, a private nuisance is an interference with the use of one's land, the plaintiff in a nuisance action must prove that he has a property interest in the affected land and that there was interference with this interest. The interference with the land normally does not involve a physical invasion of the land, which would be grounds for a trespass action, although it is possible for one activity to create both trespass and nuisance liability. For instance, a blasting operation might cause a trespass by throwing debris on neighboring land and might also create a nuisance because of the noise created.

3. **Substantial Harm.** The plaintiff in a nuisance action must prove that the harm is substantial. Courts often state that substantial harm must be of a permanent rather than temporary nature. While permanency might be a requirement if the plaintiff were seeking an injunction to prevent harm in the future, there have been many cases where courts have found that a nuisance resulted from a single activity by the defendant. The burial of a dead cow or a factory's release of gases into the air after a fan broke down [23] are examples of such cases.

More important than permanency is the question of whether a reasonable person would object to the harm. In Rogers v. Elliott,[24] the plaintiff earlier had suffered a sunstroke and, as a result, was subject to convulsions when he heard loud noises. The plaintiff's father asked Father Elliott, the priest in charge of a Catholic church across the street from the plaintiff's house, not to ring the church bell one Sunday because of the plaintiff's illness. The priest ignored the request and rang the bell as usual, with the result that plaintiff suffered convulsions. The court decided that the bell ringing was not a nuisance because it did not affect ordinary persons. Other activities determined by the courts not to be nuisances have ranged from playing croquet [25] to digging worms.[26]

However, nuisances have been found where the defendant's factory produced odors and soot which caused the plaintiffs to have nausea, vomiting, and headaches; [27] where the defendants manufactured

22. Morgan v. High Penn Oil Co., 238 N.C. 185, 77 S.E.2d 682 (1953).

23. Rauh & Sons Fertilizer Co. v. Shreffler, 139 F.2d 38 (6th Cir. 1943).

24. 146 Mass. 349, 15 N.E. 768 (1888).

25. Akers v. Marsh, 19 App.D.C. 28 (1901).

26. Hobson v. Walker, 41 So.2d 789 (La. App.1949).

27. People v. Detroit White Lead Works, 82 Mich. 471, 46 N.W. 735 (1890).

jewelry by using a 500 pound drop hammer, causing the plaintiff's house to tremble and his newspaper to shake as he was reading it; [28] and where the operation of a factory interfered with the sleep of the plaintiff.[29]

4. **Unreasonable Harm.** The last element necessary to prove the existence of a nuisance, unreasonable harm, is more complex than the other elements because courts examine all factors in the case to determine reasonableness. Courts have traditionally attempted to balance the interests of both parties in nuisance cases because of the two competing principles present in every case: "The principle that every person is entitled to use his property for any purpose that he sees fit, and the opposing principle that everyone is bound to use his property in such a manner as not to injure the property or rights of his neighbor. For generations courts, in their task of judging, have ruled on these extremes according to the wisdom of the day, and many have recognized that the contemporary view of public policy shifts from generation to generation." [30]

Closely related to the question of reasonableness is trying to determine an appropriate remedy. In most cases the court must decide whether to grant damages or to use injunctive relief in order to abate the nuisance. An award of damages is always the preferred remedy because injunctive relief often will put the defendant out of business and because, throughout history, courts have refused to grant equitable relief if the legal remedy, damages, is adequate.

In determining whether or not an activity is reasonable and whether the plaintiff should be awarded damages or injunctive relief, courts commonly consider six factors. First, courts often consider the value to society of the activity in question. In Bartel v. Ridgefield Lumber Co.,[31] smoke, sawdust, and burned lumber blew from the defendant's sawmill onto the plaintiff's land and damaged clothing hung in the yard, vegetables, and fruits. While the court held the defendant liable for damages, it refused to enjoin the activity: "Here the plaintiff's property is of comparatively small value and importance. That of the respondent is of great value. If we held that defendant must not, under any circumstances, cast sawdust, smoke and cinders on plaintiff's property, then we, in effect, forever close the mill. This, under the circumstances, we will not do. The manufacture of lumber is the most important business of western Washington, and no unnecessary interference therein will be permitted. . . . Apparently defendant is solvent and capable of responding to such damages as the plaintiffs may suffer. It is infinitely more

---

**28.** Blomen v. N. Barstow Co., 35 R.I. 198, 85 A. 924 (1913).

**29.** Frank v. Cossitt Cement Products, Inc., 277 Misc. 670, 97 N.Y.S.2d 337 (1950).

**30.** Antonik v. Chamberlain, 81 Ohio App. 465, 78 N.E.2d 752, 37 O.O. 305 (1947).

**31.** 131 Wash. 183, 229 P. 306 (1924).

equitable, under all the circumstances, to require them to enforce payment of their damages than to force the closing of this manufacturing plant." The court thus echoed the philosophy of Lord Justice James in an earlier English case: "If some picturesque haven opens its arms to invite the commerce of the world, it is not for this court to forbid the embrace, although the fruit of it should be the sights, the sounds, and smells of a common seaport and shipbuilding town, which would drive the Dryads and their masters from their ancient solitudes." [32]

The *Bartel* case also raised a second factor considered by the courts: Did the plaintiff move near an existing nuisance? In *Bartel,* the court followed the approach used by most courts in awarding the plaintiff damages even though the sawmill was in operation when the plaintiff purchased the neighboring farm. Another example is Mahone v. Autrey,[33] in which the court held that the defendant's operation of riding stables was a nuisance even though there were no residences near the stable when it was established and the area became residential only after a number of years.

Just as the plaintiff who comes to the nuisance will normally be allowed to prevail, the plaintiff who does nothing to prevent the establishment of a nuisance will later be allowed relief. For instance, in a case where the plaintiff knew that his neighbor was constructing a baseball diamond but did not object until a year later, the court noted that "if plaintiff had attempted to prevent construction of the diamond or playing of games before they were so conducted as to be a nuisance in fact he would have been met with the rule that a threatened or anticipated nuisance will not be enjoined unless it clearly appears a nuisance will necessarily result from the act it is sought to enjoin. Relief will usually be denied until a nuisance has been committed where the thing sought to be enjoined may or may not become such, depending on its use or other circumstances. . . . Knowledge or acquiesence in the erection of a structure will not estop one from suing to abate it as a nuisance because of the manner of its operation. Plaintiff was not required to anticipate that the diamond would be so used as to become a nuisance." [34]

A third factor important to the courts is the hardship to the plaintiff suffering the nuisance compared to the hardship to the defendant if the nuisance were abated. In Harrisonville v. Dickey Clay Co.,[35] the small town of Harrisonville, Missouri, built a sewage disposal plant at a cost of $60,000. The operation of the plant polluted a small stream that ran through the plaintiff's stock farm, and the

32. Salvin v. North Brancepeth Coal Co., 9 Ch.App. 705 (1874).

33. 55 N.M. 111, 227 P.2d 623 (1951).

34. Amdor v. Cooney, 241 Iowa 777, 43 N.W.2d 136 (1950).

35. 289 U.S. 334, 53 S.Ct. 602, 77 L.Ed. 1208 (1933).

plaintiff asked the court to close the plant. The court decided that since the plaintiff's injuries amounted to only $500, an award of damages would be more appropriate than injunctive relief: "Where substantial redress can be afforded by the payment of money and the issuance of an injunction would subject the defendant to grossly disproportionate hardship, equitable relief may be denied although the nuisance is undisputable."

Fourth, courts often consider the location of the activity that has created the alleged nuisance. In one case,[36] for example, the defendant raised ducks, sometimes as many as 1,000 in number, on his farm, which was in a rural farming area. The plaintiff, who lived across the road from the defendant, complained that the ducks created a nuisance because their quacking kept her awake all night. The court disagreed, noting that raising ducks was a proper pursuit in this location and that a person must suffer discomfort resulting from the "circumstances of the place and the usual business carried on in the vicinity." In many cases the question of whether an activity is proper for a given area is determined by a zoning ordinance. However, even where an activity is allowed by a zoning ordinance, the activity must be conducted in a reasonable manner. See Jack v. Torrant, infra.

A fifth factor considered by the courts, especially when they are faced with the question of closing down a business completely, is whether the damage can be prevented. In Mitchell v. Hines,[37] the defendant raised 400 pigs in his piggery and fed them by dumping garbage in open fields, plowing under any uneaten garbage. The piggery created a revolting odor, especially during warm weather, and the plaintiffs asked the court to close it down. The court reluctantly did so, noting that the odor could not otherwise be avoided. "To so conduct a piggery on a large scale is difficult, if not impossible, even when great care is taken and the most advanced methods are used in disposing of the remainder of the garbage. . . . We have a case where for some years the piggery was conducted on a small scale and was not objectionable. Then, either the increased size of the piggery or the condition of the fields through the continued dumping of garbage thereon, or both, created such odors that this suit resulted. . . . The court of equity is reluctant to bar the operation of a lawful business and will not do so if a remedy may be applied to the nuisance incidental thereto. However, tests do not show any satisfactory means of carrying on a large-scale garbage-feeding piggery. No method of feeding garbage to pigs on a commercial scale, as is here the case, in a manner that will not constitute a nuisance has been disclosed by the proof."

Finally, courts consider the motive of the defendant in determining the existence of a nuisance. The general rule is that if the de-

36. DeAlbert v. Novak, 78 Ohio App. 80, 69 N.E.2d 73, 33 O.O. 425 (1946).    37. 305 Mich. 296, 9 N.W.2d 547 (1943).

fendant is motivated only by malice or spite, the activity will be enjoined. For instance, in Burke v. Smith,[38] two neighbors started to quarrel and one of them, the defendant, erected wooden screens on his own property which shut out the light and view from the plaintiff's windows. At trial it was shown that the screens had no necessary, useful, or ornamental purpose. The court ordered the defendant to remove the screens. "It must be remembered that no man has a legal right to make a malicious use of his property, not for any benefit or advantage to himself, but for the avowed purpose of damaging his neighbor. To hold otherwise would make the law a convenient engine, in cases like the present, to injure and destroy the peace and comfort, and to damage the property of one's neighbor for no other than a wicked purpose, which in itself is, or ought to be unlawful. . . . What right has the defendant, in the light of the just and beneficent principles of equity, to shut out God's free air and sunlight from the windows of his neighbor, not for any benefit or advantage to himself, or profit to his land, but simply to gratify his own wicked malice against his neighbor? None whatever." Several state statutes have been enacted dealing with the erection of spite fences. Typically, these statutes prohibit the malicious erection of a fence at a specified height (for example, six feet) for the purpose of annoying neighbors.

See Spur Industries, Inc. v. Del E. Webb Development Co., infra.


# IV. INVASION OF PRIVACY

## A. TORT RIGHT TO PRIVACY

The complexity of modern society, coupled with an increasing population and an aggressive press, has resulted in greater judicial respect for a "right to be let alone," that is, a right of privacy. The impetus for the recognition of this right was an article entitled "The Right to Privacy," published in 1890 in the *Harvard Law Review* by Samuel D. Warren and Louis D. Brandeis. In the article, the authors observed, "The press is overstepping in every direction the obvious bounds of propriety and of decency. Gossip is no longer the resource of the idle and of the vicious, but has become a trade, which is pursued with industry as well as effrontery. To satisfy a prurient taste the details of sexual relations are spread broadcast in the columns of the daily papers. To occupy the indolent, column upon column is filled with idle gossip, which can only be procured by intrusion upon the domestic circle. The intensity and complexity of life, attendant upon advancing civilization, have rendered necessary some retreat from the world, and man, under the refining influence of culture, has become more sensitive to publicity, so that solitude and pri-

---

38. 69 Mich. 830, 37 N.W. 838 (1888).

vacy have become more essential to the individual; but modern enterprise and invention have, through invasions upon his privacy, subjected him to mental pain and distress, far greater than could be inflicted by mere bodily injury."

Four types of invasion of privacy actions have developed since 1890.[39]  First, in many states a person may recover damages if his name or picture is used to advertise a product without permission. Second, a person may recover damages when there is objectionable publicity of private information, as when a commercial motion picture dealt with a famous murder trial and disclosed the present identity of the defendant in the trial, a reformed prostitute.[40]  Third, it is wrong to put a person in a false light in the public eye.  Under this principle, Lord Byron was able to prevent the circulation of a poem which had been falsely attributed to him.[41]

The fourth type of invasion of privacy is one directly related to the rights of a property owner:  the wrongful intrusion into the plaintiff's physical privacy.  Examples include making an illegal search of a home, using electronic eavesdropping equipment, making unwanted telephone calls, and a physician's allowing a friend to observe a home birth.  See Dietemann v. Time, Inc., infra.

## B.  CONSTITUTIONAL RIGHT TO PRIVACY

Beginning with the case of Griswold v. Connecticut [42] in 1965, the Supreme Court has articulated a constitutional right to privacy that also affects the rights of landowners.  In *Griswold,* the defendants, officers of the Planned Parenthood League, advised married couples on methods of preventing conception.  They were convicted as accessories under a Connecticut statute making it a criminal offense to use "any drug, medicinal article or instrument for the purpose of preventing conception."  In reversing the convictions, Mr. Justice Douglas, writing the opinion for the Court, observed that "specific guarantees in the Bill of Rights have penumbras, formed by emanations from those guarantees that help give them life and substance.  Various guarantees create zones of privacy.  The right of association contained in the penumbra of the First Amendment is one, as we have seen.  The Third Amendment in its prohibition against the quartering of soldiers 'in any house' in time of peace without the consent of the owner is another facet of that privacy.  The Fourth Amendment explicitly affirms the 'right of the people to be secure in their persons, houses, papers, and effects, against unreasonable searches and seizures.'  The Fifth Amendment in its Self-Incrimina-

---

39.  W. Prosser, supra note 1, § 117 at 804.

40.  Melvin v. Reid, 112 Cal.App. 285, 297 P. 91 (1931).

41.  Lord Byron v. Johnston, 2 Mer. 29, 35 Eng.Rep. 851 (1816).

42.  381 U.S. 479, 85 S.Ct. 1678, 14 L.Ed. 2d 510 (1965).

tion Clause enables the citizen to create a zone of privacy which government may not force him to surrender to his detriment. The Ninth Amendment provides: 'The enumeration in the Constitution, of certain rights, shall not be construed to deny or disparage others retained by the people.' . . . We deal with a right of privacy older than the Bill of Rights—older than our political parties, older than our school system. Marriage is a coming together for better or for worse, hopefully enduring, and intimate to the degree of being sacred. It is an association that promotes a way of life, not causes; a harmony in living, not political faiths; a bilateral loyalty, not commercial or social projects. Yet it is an association for as noble a purpose as any involved in our prior decisions."

In a decision following *Griswold,* Stanley v. Georgia,[43] the Supreme Court decided that a person has the right to engage in certain criminal activities in the privacy of his own home. The defendant in that case was investigated by the police for alleged bookmaking activities. During the course of the investigation, state and federal agents entered Stanley's home with a search warrant but found little evidence of bookmaking activity, although they did discover three reels of film. Using a projector they found in the home, they viewed the film, concluded it was obscene, and arrested Stanley on charges of possession of obscene matter. Stanley was convicted by a jury; however, the Supreme Court reversed the conviction on appeal: "This right to receive information and ideas, regardless of their social worth, is fundamental to our free society. Moreover, in the context of this case—a prosecution for mere possession of printed or filmed matter in the privacy of a person's home—that right takes on an added dimension. For also fundamental is the right to be free, except in very limited circumstances, from unwanted governmental intrusions into one's privacy. . . . [W]hatever may be the justifications for other statutes regulating obscenity, we do not think they reach into the privacy of one's own home. If the First Amendment means anything, it means that a State has no business telling a man, sitting alone in his own house, what books he may read or what films he may watch. Our whole constitutional heritage rebels at the thought of giving government the power to control men's minds."

Given the *Stanley* decision, courts now face the question of whether other types of activities should also be privileged within the home. The most far-reaching opinion in this regard is Ravin v. State,[44] in which the Alaskan supreme court ruled unanimously that possession of marijuana by adults at home for personal use is constitutionally protected. According to the court, "We conclude that no adequate justification for the state's intrusion into the citizen's right to privacy by its prohibition of possession of marijuana by an adult

---

43. 394 U.S. 557, 89 S.Ct. 1243, 22 L.Ed. 2d 542 (1969).　44. 537 P.2d 494 (Alaska, 1975).

for personal consumption in the home has been shown. The privacy of the individual's home cannot be breached absent a persuasive showing of a close and substantial relationship of the intrusion to a legitimate governmental interest. Here, mere scientific doubts will not suffice. The state must demonstrate a need based on proof that the public health or welfare will in fact suffer if the controls are not applied."

## V.   LOST AND MISPLACED PROPERTY

When a person misplaces or loses personal property, the finder of the property usually may keep it against all but the rightful owner. In the leading case of Armory v. Delamirie,[45] the plaintiff, a chimney sweep, found a piece of jewelry and took it to the defendant, a goldsmith, for appraisal. An employee of the goldsmith removed the jewels and the goldsmith refused to return them. The court decided that the finder, the chimney sweep, was entitled to the jewels subject only to the rights of the original owner, who was not a party to the case.

The rights of the finder, however, are often subordinate to those of the owner of the *locus in quo,* that is, the owner of the "place in which" the personal propery is found. If the owner of the real estate can prove any one of five elements, many courts will decide that he has both the superior right to possession and, if the true owner never appears, the right to keep the goods.

First, many courts will decide for the owner of the *locus* if the personal property has been discovered in a private rather than a semi-public place; "if the premises on which the property is discovered are private it is deemed that the property discovered thereon is and always has been in the constructive possession of the owner of said premises and in a legal sense the property can be neither mislaid nor lost." [46]   Thus, if property is discovered in a bank lobby, a semi-public area, the finder would be entitled to possession; but if it is discovered in a safe deposit room, a private area, the bank may keep the property.

Second, courts also make a distinction between lost and mislaid property. Lost property is property with which the owner has parted through carelessness; for example, a glove might fall out of the owner's pocket. Mislaid property is property that the owner has intentionally laid down and then forgotten where it was laid; for instance, the owner may place his gloves on a hat rack in a restaurant and leave without them.[47]   The finder is entitled to possession of lost property, whereas the owner of the *locus* can keep mislaid property

---

**45.**  1 Strange 505, 93 Eng.Rep. 664 (1722).

**46.**  Bishop v. Ellsworth, 91 Ill.App.2d 386, 234 N.E.2d 49 (1968).

**47.**  Jackson v. Steinberg, 186 Or. 129, 200 P.2d 376 (1948).

since the owner is likely to return; if he does, the owner of the *locus* will be holding the property for him.

Third, some courts have held that if the goods are discovered by an employee, the employee has the duty to turn the goods over to the employer. In one case, a chambermaid in defendant's hotel discovered eight one-hundred-dollar bills in the dresser drawer of a room she was cleaning. The court decided that the hotel owner was entitled to the money: "The decisive feature of the present case is the fact that plaintiff was an employee or servant of the owner or occupant of the premises, and that, in discovering the bills and turning them over to her employer, she was simply performing the duties of her employment." [48]

Fourth, if the property is found buried in the ground, the owner of the *locus* is entitled to possession. Thus, in a case of the finders' discovering a prehistoric Indian canoe embedded in the soil, the court decided that the owner of the *locus* was entitled to possession.[49] However, a few courts, following the English approach, will hold for the finder if the buried property is considered treasure trove: gold, silver, money, or coin.

Finally, the owner of the *locus in quo* will prevail if the finder was a trespasser on the property. In Bishop v. Ellsworth,[50] the defendants, three small boys, discovered a bottle containing $12,590.00 in the plaintiff's salvage yard. When the plaintiff sued the boys to determine ownership of the money, the trial court dismissed the complaint on the grounds that the plaintiff had not stated a cause of action. The appellate court reversed the trial court and remanded the case for trial, noting that "if the discoverer is a trespasser such trespasser can have no claim to possession of such property even if it might otherwise be considered lost."

# CASES

---

## KOPPLIN v. QUADE

Supreme Court of Wisconsin, 1911.
145 Wis. 454, 130 N.W. 511.

BARNES, J. On September 14, 1907, the plaintiff was the owner of a thoroughbred Holstein-Friesian heifer, which was born on January 8, 1906, and had been thereafter duly christened "Martha

---

**48.** Id.

**49.** Allred v. Biegel, 240 Mo.App. 818, 219 S.W.2d 665 (1949).

**50.** 91 Ill.App.2d 386, 234 N.E.2d 49 (1968).

Pietertje Pauline." The name is neither euphonious nor musical but there is not much in a name anyway. Notwithstanding any handicap she may have had in the way of a cognomen, Martha Pietertje Pauline was a genuine "highbrow" having a pedigree as long and at least as well authenticated as that of the ordinary scion of effete European nobility who breaks into this land of democracy and equality and offers his title to the highest bidder at the matrimonial bargain counter. The defendant was the owner of a bull about one year old, lowly born and nameless as far as the record discloses. This plebeian, having aspirations beyond his humble station in life wandered beyond the confines of his own pastures, and sought the society of the adolescent and unsophisticated Martha, contrary to the provisions of section 1482, St.1898, as amended by chapter 14, Laws 1903. As a result of this somewhat morganatic mesalliance, a calf was born July 5, 1908. Plaintiff brought this action to recover resulting damages and secured a verdict for $75, upon which judgment was entered, and defendant appeals therefrom.

\* \* \*

If on the evidence before the court the plaintiff was entitled to recover any amount, then the court properly denied the motion. The plaintiff offered testimony tending to show that he kept and intended to keep Martha for breeding purposes and for the milk which she might produce, and not for sale. It also showed that plaintiff was the owner of a blue blooded bull of the Holstein-Friesian variety, to which he intended to breed Martha some three months later than the date of the unfortunate occurrence related. There was evidence tending to show that a thoroughbred calf would be worth all the way from $22.50 to $150, depending on its sex, markings, and other characteristics. Its sinister birth disqualified the hybrid calf born from becoming a candidate for pink ribbons at county fairs, and it was sold to a Chicago butcher for $7, and was probably served up as pressed chicken to the epicures in some Chicago boarding house.

Numerous witnesses testified that a thoroughbred calf had a much greater value than a grade calf, and this evidence is not contradicted in any way. True, the witnesses vary widely as to the amount of such difference in value, but the matter of arriving at an exact amount of compensation in most tort actions is involved in uncertainty and difficulty, and it was for the jury to say on all the testimony what sum would reasonably compensate the plaintiff. This element of damages was direct and proximate and the objection to it on the ground of remoteness is not well taken.

The true measure of damages was the difference between the value of the heifer to the plaintiff before and after the trespass, in view of the uses which the plaintiff intended to make of the heifer. Such a rule furnishes compensation, and this is what the law aims at. There was no direct question asked of any witness as to what such difference would be, but the line of examination pursued elicited at least some if not all of the items or elements of damages that a witness would consider in answering such a question if it were asked. One of those elements would be the difference between the value of the calf dropped and the value of a calf from the heifer if bred to a registered Holstein-Friesian bull. It is apparent, therefore, that there was some competent evidence before the jury from which it might properly return a verdict for substantial damages, and that, therefore, the motion to direct a verdict was properly denied. Indeed, this result might well follow if the plaintiff were entitled to recover nominal damages only.

Judgment affirmed.

---

## JACK v. TORRANT

Supreme Court of Errors of Connecticut, 1950.
136 Conn. 414, 71 A.2d 705.

BROWN, Judge.

\* \* \*

An undertaking establishment is not a nuisance per se. Whether it constitutes a nuisance depends upon the facts in the particular case. These consist of the manner in which it is operated and the situation in which it is placed. Since the finding is that this establishment was conducted in a proper manner, the decisive issue concerns its location under the existing circumstances. A study of the cases has satisfied us that "The greater weight of recent authority is to the effect that the establishment and operation of an undertaking business in a purely residential section, under circumstances which would cause a depressed feeling to the families in the immediate neighborhood, and a constant reminder of death, appreciably impairing their happiness, or weakening their power to resist disease, and depreciating the value of their property, constitutes a nuisance."

\* \* \*

The trial court has made an extensive and detailed finding of the subordinate facts upon which it rests its conclusion that the conduct of the undertaking business upon the defendants' property constituted a nuisance in fact. As already stated, the defendants' property is located on the west side of North Street and is bounded on the south by the Fisher property and on the north by the Jack property. A seven-foot sidewalk with a forty-four-foot green area between the walk and the street extends in front of all three properties. The defendants' house is 158 feet from the Fisher house and 88.3 feet from the Jack house. North Street is one-third of a mile long, is of ample width, with a double row of large trees on each side, and is part of through highway. It is within the borough of Litchfield, which, except for a small compact business area a short distance south of North Street, is almost exclusively residential in character. Within the borough are numerous very old houses of architectural beauty and historical interest, giving the community an atmosphere which makes it unique. North Street is one of its most charming residential streets, and along both sides of it are many large and valuable houses of great age and historical interest. The Jack home is a large dwelling surrounded by spacious and beautifully landscaped grounds, and the Fisher home is one of the historical and architectural treasures of the community.

The ancient Litchfield jail stands on the west side of North Street at its extreme southerly end facing the Litchfield green, and directly north of it is a building in which are two banks. Next north of this building is a residence, and next beyond that is a house used as a convalescent home, with a sign "Rose Haven" on the front. Between this and the Fisher property are two dwellings. Diagonally across the street from the defendants' property is the residence of Dr. Warner, in which he maintains his office. On the south side of the house on the eighth property north of the Warner house is a kennel in which a number of dogs are kept. In the residence next north of this the owner maintains his law office, and in the most northerly house on the west side of the street the doctor who owns it maintains his office. Except as stated above, North Street is, throughout its extent, devoted exclusively to residential uses and has been for a number of years. These facts warrant the court's further finding that until the intrusion of the defendants' business there was no use on the North Street inconsistent with the exclusively residential character of the neighborhood.

The defendant Francis L. Torrant purchased his property with the purpose of extending his existing undertaking and embalming business to Litchfield. The house was a large eighteen-room dwelling. He made alterations to provide for the conduct of the funeral business and also for three living apartments. In connection with the former, he transformed a small basement kitchen with windows facing the Jack property into a room for the embalming of human bodies at any time of the day or night, and equipped it with embalming facilities and instruments for use in the business, including the performance of autopsies. A large front room facing toward the Fisher property was prepared for and frequently used for funeral services. Other rooms back of it were used for the display and sale of caskets and for the storage of caskets and other equipment in connection with the business. After the place was licensed as a funeral establishment on November 1, 1946, a twelve by eighteen inch sign, "Francis L. Torrant Mortician," was placed on the front of the house, and the establishment for undertaking and embalming was advertised in the newspaper. Prior to the court's temporary injunction of June 23, 1947, a number of bodies were embalmed and funerals held on the premises. A hearse was used in connection with the business and at times remained parked on or in front of the premises. In his role as undertaker and embalmer, the defendant Francis L. Torrant conducted the business in a proper manner, and there was no testimony that any smoke, odor or spread of disease was caused thereby on the property of the plaintiffs. The business was, however, especially harmful to the other properties on North Street, because a funeral business with its morgue, funeral processions and attendant activities is a particularly undesirable business, and in the invasion of the neighborhood by it would adversely affect and ultimately destroy the privacy, seclusion and quiet so characteristic of this residential community and therefore would substantially reduce the market value of its residential property. The undertaking occupation as conducted by the defendant Francis was and is a business and not a profession. The defendant Mary H. Torrant had full knowledge of and acquiesced in all that her husband did in carrying on the business.

As a result of the operation of this funeral business, the surrounding properties and their occupants suffered a direct and immediate adverse effect. The consciousness of the plaintiff Jack and his household of the use made of the basement room as a morgue and the transportation of human bodies over the defendants' adjacent driveway by night and by day had an immediate and continuing depressing effect upon them which substantially decreased their quiet and peaceful enjoyment of their home. The presence of the funeral business in such close proximity to the home of this plaintiff substantially decreased the market value of his property. The conduct of the funeral business as referred to, including the parking of long lines of cars of mourners in front of the plaintiffs' homes, had a like effect upon the plaintiff Fisher and her household and upon the value of her property, for similar reasons. On one occasion, by mistake, an attempt was made to deliver a load of coffins to the Fisher home. On another, a prospective patron of the funeral home called at the Fisher home through error. At different times, a member of the Fisher household observed embalmed human bodies laid out in caskets in the defendants' first-floor room. These incidents served to accentuate the effect upon the Fishers already recited. This effect was experienced not only by them as persons of normal sensitivity but likewise by others in the neighborhood, and the property values of the latter were similarly depreciated. The trial court viewed the entire North Street area and found that it appeared therefrom that the defendants' funeral business is wholly unsuited to the residential character of the remainder of the neighborhood in which it is located. It was warranted in concluding, upon this view and the facts found, that the use of the defendants' property for an undertaking and embalming establishment constituted a nuisance in fact, and that under the principles discussed above the plaintiffs are entitled to injunctive relief.

The fact that the defendants expended a substantial amount in adapting the premises for use as such an establishment cannot avail to defeat the plaintiffs' right to an injunction, since the finding is conclusive that they were seasonably and amply warned that they had no right to use the premises for this purpose and that the plaintiffs would resist their effort to do so by every lawful means; notwithstanding, they ignored all warnings and persisted in their course. Only one other contention of the defendants requires mention. The witness Fisher was permitted, over their objection, to testify to his reaction and feelings, as "a normal person," to the establishment of the funeral home on the defendants' adjoining property. As sufficiently appears from the authorities we have discussed, such a reaction was a fact directly in issue, and the court properly allowed the question.

In sustaining the court's judgment granting this injunction, we would emphasize that our decision is predicated upon the correctness of the court's conclusion upon the particular facts found. Had the defendants established and maintained this funeral home for a substantial period without objection, a very different question might be involved in determining whether the plaintiffs could obtain injunctive relief.

*    *    *

---

## SPUR INDUSTRIES, INC. v. DEL E. WEBB DEVELOPMENT CO.

Supreme Court of Arizona, 1972.
108 Ariz. 178, 494 P.2d 700.

CAMERON, Vice Chief Justice.

From a judgment permanently enjoining the defendant, Spur Industries, Inc., from operating a cattle feedlot near the plaintiff Del E. Webb Development Company's Sun City, Spur appeals. Webb cross-appeals. Although numerous issues are raised, we feel that it is necessary to answer only two questions. They are:

1. Where the operation of a business, such as a cattle feedlot is lawful in the first instance, but becomes a nuisance by reason of a nearby residential area, may the feedlot operation be enjoined in an action brought by the developer of the residential area?

2. Assuming that the nuisance may be enjoined, may the developer of a completely new town or urban area in a previously agricultural area be required to indemnify the operator of the feedlot who must move or cease operation because of the presence of the residential area created by the developer?

*    *    *

Del Webb's suit complained that the Spur feeding operation was a public nuisance because of the flies and the odor which were drifting or being blown by the prevailing south to north wind over the southern portion of Sun City. At the time of the suit, Spur was feeding between 20,000 and 30,000 head of cattle, and the facts amply support the finding of the trial court that the feed pens had become a nuisance to the people who resided in the southern part of Del Webb's development. The testimony indicated that cattle in a commercial feedlot will produce 35 to 40 pounds of wet manure per day, per head, or over a million pounds of wet manure per day for 30,000 head of cattle, and that despite the admittedly good feedlot management and good housekeeping practices by Spur, the resulting odor and flies produced an annoying if not unhealthy situation as far as the senior citizens of southern Sun City were concerned. There is no doubt that some of the citizens of Sun City were unable to enjoy the outdoor living which Del Webb had advertised and that Del Webb was faced with sales resistance from prospective purchasers as well as strong and persistent complaints from the people who had purchased homes in that area.

        \*     \*     \*

### MAY SPUR BE ENJOINED?

The difference between a private nuisance and a public nuisance is generally one of degree. A private nuisance is one affecting a single individual or a definite small number of persons in the enjoyment of private rights not common to the public, while a public nuisance is one affecting the rights enjoyed by citizens as a part of the public. To constitute a public nuisance, the nuisance must affect a considerable number of people or an entire community or neighborhood.

Where the injury is slight, the remedy for minor inconveniences lies in an action for damages rather than in one for an injunction. Moreover, some courts have held, in the "balancing of conveniences" cases, that damages may be the sole remedy.

        \*     \*     \*

We have no difficulty, however, in agreeing with the conclusion of the trial court that Spur's operation was an enjoinable public nuisance as far as the people in the southern portion of Del Webb's Sun City were concerned.

§ 36–601, subsec. A reads as follows:

"§ 36–601. Public nuisances dangerous to public health

"A. The following conditions are specifically declared public nuisances dangerous to the public health:

"1. Any condition or place in populous areas which constitutes a breeding place for flies, rodents, mosquitoes and other insects which are capable of carrying and transmitting disease-causing organisms to any person or persons."

By this statute, before an otherwise lawful (and necessary) business may be declared a public nuisance, there must be a "populous" area in which people are injured.   *   *   *

It is clear that as to the citizens of Sun City, the operation of Spur's feedlot was both a public and a private nuisance. They could have successfully maintained an action to abate the nuisance. Del Webb, having shown a special injury in the loss of sales, had a standing to bring suit to enjoin the nuisance. The judgment of the trial court permanently enjoining the operation of the feedlot is affirmed.

## MUST DEL WEBB INDEMNIFY SPUR?

A suit to enjoin a nuisance sounds in equity and the courts have long recognized a special responsibility to the public when acting as a court of equity:

§ 104.   Where public interest is involved.

"Courts of equity may, and frequently do, go much further both to give and withhold relief in furtherance of the public interest than they are accustomed to go when only private interests are involved. Accordingly, the granting or withholding of relief may properly be dependent upon considerations of public interest.   *   *   *

In addition to protecting the public interest, however, courts of equity are concerned with protecting the operator of a lawfully, albeit noxious, business from the result of a knowing and willful encroachment by others near his business.

*   *   *

There was no indication in the instant case at the time Spur and its predecessors located in western Maricopa County that a new city would spring up, full-blown, alongside the feeding operation and that the developer of that city would ask the court to order Spur to move because of the new city. Spur is required to move not because of any wrongdoing on the part of Spur, but because of a proper and legitimate regard of the courts for the rights and interests of the public.

Del Webb, on the other hand, is entitled to the relief prayed for (a permanent injunction), not because Webb is blameless, but because of the damage to the people who have been encouraged to purchase homes in Sun City. It does not equitably or legally follow, however, that Webb, being entitled to the injunction, is then free of any liability to Spur if Webb has in fact been the cause of the damage Spur has sustained. It does not seem harsh to require a developer, who has taken advantage of the lesser land values in a rural area as well as the availability of large tracts of land on which to build and develop a new town or city in the area, to indemnify those who are forced to leave as a result.

Having brought people to the nuisance to the foreseeable detriment of Spur, Webb must indemnify Spur for a reasonable amount of the cost of moving or shutting down. It should be noted that this relief to Spur is limited to a case wherein a developer has, with foreseeability, brought into a previously agricultural or industrial area the population which makes necessary the granting of an injunction against a lawful business and for which the business has no adequate relief.

It is therefore the decision of this court that the matter be remanded to the trial court for a hearing upon the damages sustained by the defendant Spur as a reasonable and direct result of the granting of the permanent injunction. Since the result of the appeal may appear novel and both sides have obtained a measure of relief, it is ordered that each side will bear its own costs.

Affirmed in part, reversed in part, and remanded for further proceedings consistent with this opinion.

----

## DIETEMANN v. TIME, INC.

United States Dist. Court, C.D.Calif., 1968.
284 F.Supp. 925.

### OPINION

CARR, District Judge.

This is a diversity suit for invasion of privacy seeking $100,000.00 general damages and $200,000.00 exemplary damages. Plaintiff, a disabled veteran with little education, was engaged in the practice of healing with clay, minerals, and herbs—as practiced, simple quackery.

Defendant, Time, Incorporated, a New York corporation, publishes Life Magazine. Its November 1, 1963 edition carried an article entitled "Crackdown on Quackery." The article depicted plaintiff as a quack and included two pictures of him. One picture was taken at plaintiff's home on September 20, 1963, previous to his arrest on a charge of practicing medicine without a license, and the other taken at the time of his arrest.

Life Magazine entered into an arrangement with the District Attorney's Office of Los Angeles County whereby Life's employees would visit plaintiff and obtain facts and pictures concerning his activities. Two employees of Life, Mrs. Jackie Metcalf and Mr. William Ray, went to plaintiff's home on September 20, 1963. When they arrived at a locked gate, they rang a bell and plaintiff came out of his house and was told by Mrs. Metcalf and Ray that they had been sent there by a friend, a Mr. Johnson. The use of Johnson's name was a ruse to gain entrance. Plaintiff admitted them and all three went into the house and into plaintiff's den.

The plaintiff had some equipment which could at best be described as gadgets, not equipment which had anything to do with the practice of medicine. Plaintiff, while examining Mrs. Metcalf, was photographed by Ray with a hidden camera without the consent of plaintiff. One of the pictures taken by him appeared in Life Magazine showing plaintiff with his hand on the upper portion of Mrs. Metcalf's breast while he was looking at some gadgets and holding what appeared to be a wand in his right hand. Mrs. Metcalf had told plaintiff that she had a lump in her breast. Plaintiff concluded that she had eaten some rancid butter 11 years, 9 months, and 7 days prior to that time. Other persons were seated in the room during this time.

The conversation between Mrs. Metcalf and plaintiff was transmitted by radio transmitter hidden in Mrs. Metcalf's purse to a tape recorder in a parked automobile occupied by Joseph Bride, Life employee, John Miner of the District Attorney's Office, and Grant Leake, an investigator of the State Department of Public Health. While the recorded conversation was not quoted in the article in Life, it was mentioned that Life correspondent Bride was making notes of what was being received via the radio transmitter, and such information was at least referred to in the article.

The foregoing events were photographed and recorded by an arrangement among Miner of the District Attorney's Office, Leake of the State Department of Public Health, and Bride, a representative of Life. It had been agreed that Life would obtain pictures and information for use as evidence, and later could be used by Life for publication.

\*    \*    \*

Plaintiff contends that under applicable California law there has been an invasion of his right of privacy. Defendant contends that since both the California and the United States Constitutions protect freedom of press and speech, the entry of its agents into plaintiff's quarters and the publication of the pictures taken there were privileged.

Since the article by Brandeis and Warren in 4 Harv.L.Rev. 193 (1890), the right of privacy has received more and more attention. Both writers and judges throughout the country have attempted to delineate the boundaries of the action for invasion of privacy. Despite the lack of unanimity in the decisions in the various states and the differences between the writers, the law in California in a large measure has been settled. Since that law applies here, it must be ascertained and applied.

The case of Melvin v. Reid et al., 112 Cal.App. 285, 297 P. 91, usually referred to as the *"Red Kimono"* case, appears to be the cornerstone case in which the right of privacy was defined. The court stated the applicable law as follows (297 P., page 82):

> "The right of privacy may be defined as the right to live one's life in seclusion, without being subjected to unwarranted and undesired publicity."

In this case a motion picture was made of the life of a woman who had been a prostitute and who had been tried for murder and acquitted. The court apparently held that the use of incidents from her life was not actionable because those incidents appeared in public records, but that the use of her name was an invasion of her right of privacy guaranteed by the California Constitution. Among other things the court said the right of privacy is an incident of the person and not of property. It is purely a personal action. It does not exist where the published matter was consented to or where the person is so prominent that by his very prominence he has dedicated his life to the public, thereby waiving his right of privacy. In other words, there can be no privacy in that which is already public. The right of privacy can only be violated by printings, writings, pictures, or publications, not by word of mouth. The court also noted that the right of action accrues when the publication is made for gain or profit, but noted that this is, however, questioned in some cases.

\* \* \*

The defenses interposed will now be considered. Defendant asserts first, and as its major contention, that the intrusion of the plaintiff's quarters and the pictures taken there at the time were privileged under the First Amendment of the United States Constitution, and Article I, Section 9, of the California Constitution.

At the outset defendant is met with the proposition that although freedom of speech and freedom of press are constitutional guaranties, so is the right of privacy. While the courts may be required under some circumstances to balance the rights and privileges when the constitutional guaranties of freedom of speech and press clash with the right of privacy, there would appear to be no basis to give greater weight or priority to any one of these constitutional guaranties.

\* \* \*

Defendant's claim that the plaintiff's house was open to the public is not sustained by the evidence. The plaintiff was administering his so-called treatments to people who visited him. He was not a medical man of any type. He did not advertise. He did not have a phone. He did have a lock on his gate. To obtain entrance it was necessary to ring a bell. He conducted his activities in a building which was his home. The employees of defendant gained entrance by a subterfuge.

If a person's home, or even his business premises, is to be subjected to invasion by subterfuge for the purpose of obtaining facts concerning his private life, then privacy would not exist. It may well be that a professional man violating the law in connection with the practice of his profession should be arrested, prosecuted, and his activities suppressed, but it is inconceivable that the press or even a law enforcement officer can be permitted to obtain entrance by subterfuge for the purpose of photographing or observing those activities.

Defendant's contention that plaintiff's home was open to the public because he had given treatments to some people would lead to the conclusion that all business premises and homes in which illegal activities are carried on become public places because of such illegal activities. This is merely a resort to the proposition that the end justifies the means.

\* \* \*

To maintain the right of privacy and the right to be let alone is rapidly becoming more difficult. Already there are devices which may record the most secret and confidential conversations from substantial distances without entry on the premises and without any kind of equipment on such premises. There can be no peace if neighbors and friends, as well as enemies, vicariously join in the confidential discussions occurring in home, office, and places not open to the public. Merely knowing what your neighbor thinks about you may generate thoughts of mayhem, if not murder.

Those who insist upon absolute freedom of speech and press should remember the warning of Oscar Wilde in De Profundis that what one has done in the secret chamber one has some day to cry aloud from the housetops.

No freedom, including freedom of press or speech, can be permitted completely unbridled. Let it be hoped that it will not be said of us what was said of the Greeks in Rene Sedillot's History of the World:

> "They grew drunk on freedom, on argument and talk. This was the great age of Greek particularism, which produced masterpieces and paved the way for disaster."

While the claim in this case rests upon the theory that there has been an invasion of the right of privacy as protected under the California law, it would appear that the judgment for plaintiff may also be predicated on federal law. Perhaps the publicity required under California law would not be necessary under federal law.

The instant case is not altogether different in principle from the case of York v. Story (9th Cir.), 324 F.2d 450. In that case a woman who went to the police station to make a complaint was photographed in the nude and the pictures passed around among the police officers. The court upheld a cause of action alleged under Section 1983, Title 42, United States Code, stating at page 456:

> "\* \* \* such acts constituted an arbitrary intrusion upon the security of her privacy, as guaranteed to her by the Due Process Clause of the Fourteenth Amendment. \* \* \*

Many writers and judges have urged a broad construction of the Fourth Amendment to protect privacy. However, the right of privacy might be on more solid ground if it were premised on privacy as a part of liberty protected by the Due Process Clause of the Fifth and Fourteenth Amendments.

If a case is alleged and proved under both the laws of California and the federal laws, the judgment may rest upon either or both of such laws. It is concluded that plaintiff has alleged and proved a case under the California law and also under federal law. The publication in Life Magazine on November 1, 1963 of plaintiff's picture taken without his consent in his home on September 20, 1963 was an invasion of his right of privacy under California law for which he is entitled to damages. The acts of defendant also constituted an invasion of plaintiff's right of privacy guaranteed by the Constitution of the United States which would entitle him to relief under Section 1983, Title 42, United States Code.

Plaintiff is entitled to damages for injury to his feelings and peace of mind. The injury is mental and subjective and difficult of ascertainment; however, the trier of fact is accorded a wide and elastic discretion. Plaintiff is awarded general damages in the amount of $1,000.00.

It is also within the discretion of the trier of fact to award exemplary damages. In view of the unusual facts of this case, it is concluded that the award of exemplary damages is not warranted. It cannot be overlooked that defendant's efforts were directed toward the elimination of quackery, an evil which has visited great harm upon a great number of gullible people. Furthermore, if this decision correctly states the law, the publisher will undoubtedly be guided accordingly in the future.

## PROBLEMS

1. Le Mistral, a New York City restaurant, was on a list of restaurants cited by the city's health service administration for health code violations. Television channel 2, a Columbia Broadcasting affiliate, wanted to do a film on restaurants that were guilty of health code violations. It dispatched a camera crew to film the facilities of Le Mistral, unannounced to its owner. The camera crew entered the restaurant with bright cameras shining and cameras "rolling." The owner of Le Mistral ordered the camera crew out of the restaurant and they left after a short delay. Later the owner of Le Mistral sued the Columbia Broadcasting System (CBS) for trespass, demanding compensatory and punitive damages. Decide the case.

2. Sears, Roebuck and Co. was constructing a 110-story building in the city of Chicago. After the construction had progressed to a height of fifty stories, various plaintiffs filed suit to enjoin any further construction of the building. The plaintiffs alleged that the building, if completed, would interfere with television reception in certain areas because the

broadcasting antennas of Chicago television stations were lower than the contemplated structure. Does the building constitute a nuisance? Why?

3. Gallagher and Dodge owned adjacent stores and operated competing businesses. Dodge erected a show case on his property which had the two-fold purpose of displaying his goods and preventing the public from seeing goods which were on display in Gallagher's window. Gallagher claimed that, since one of Dodge's motives was malicious, the show case should be removed. Is Gallagher correct? Why?

4. Hudson has operated a printing press and published a newspaper for twenty-five years. DeFile now purchases a building next to Hudson's printing plant and leases two floors of the building for residential purposes. The building is located in an area in which there are both businesses and residences. The tenants in DeFile's building complain that the printing plant is too noisy from 1:00 to 2:00 a. m., when the newspaper is printed. Do Hudson's activities constitute a nuisance? Why?

5. Wilbur, an attorney, lived in a residential area in Tulsa, Oklahoma. The area was zoned for family dwellings, although the zoning ordinance allowed residents to rent rooms or apartments in dwellings they occupied. The ordinance, however, prohibited residents from advertising that rooms or apartments were available for rent. Adda owned a house across the street from Wilbur and rented rooms chiefly to servicemen and their wives. She displayed a sign in the front of her home which read "Rooms, Meals." Wilbur, without notice to Adda, entered her property and destroyed the sign. When he was subsequently charged with malicious mischief, he argued that he had the right to abate the nuisance. Assuming the sign was a nuisance, is Wilbur correct? Why?

6. Mandell was struck by a defectively installed awning as he walked down Main Street in Hartford. Mandell brought suit against the owner of the building for injuries he sustained, on the grounds that the awning was a nuisance. Mandell did not state the type of nuisance action he was bringing. May he recover? Why?

7. Harry purchased property adjacent to a private nursing home operated by Margaret. Margaret had operated the nursing home approximately fifteen years before Harry moved into the neighborhood. Harry now seeks to have the operation of the nursing home enjoined on the theory that it constitutes a private nuisance. Harry argues that occasional ill-smelling odors and moans and groans coming from the nursing home are mentally upsetting to him and cause him great discomfort. Decide the case.

8. Thaw owns and occupies a residence valued at $300,000 in Brookside Place in West Hartford. It has an elaborate air-conditioning system that cost $46,000. The ordinary, average-sized, single house in West Hartford would use an air-conditioning unit having approximately a 60,000 BTU capacity; the air-conditioning system installed for Thaw's residence has a 300,000 BTU capacity. Nair, a neighbor, claims that the operation of Thaw's air-conditioning unit causes excessive noise which has affected her health. Is the unit a nuisance? Why?

9. Arkow, a New York City resident, recently purchased a new air-conditioning unit for his home. The unit is the type commonly used for

residential purposes and emanates the normal sound made by home air-conditioning units. Gershberg, a neighbor, claims the unit creates a disturbing and unnecessary noise that is detrimental to his health. He files a complaint against Arkow for violating a provision of the New York Penal Law that prohibits the maintenance of a public nuisance. Decide.

10. Friendship Farms Camps, Inc., leased a farm for use as a campground. Youth day camps were initially held on the property, but in later years a number of weekly high school marching band camps were held. The Parsons and the Combs, who lived across the road from Friendship, brought an action against Friendship to abate an alleged nuisance and for damages. They claim that during the summer months loud band music and electronically amplified voices could be heard from 7:00 or 8:00 a. m. until 9:00 or 10:00 p. m. They claimed that the noise interfered with their sleep and use of their property during the evening hours. Decide the case.

Chapter 12

# DUTIES OF LAND OWNERS AND OCCUPANTS

Law favoreth public quiet.

Wingate, *Maxims*

In Chapter 11 we examined the rights of an owner or occupant of real estate. These rights include (1) the right to damages or injunctive relief when someone trespasses or creates a nuisance, (2) the right to privacy, and (3) the right to personal property discovered on the real estate. Owning or occupying real estate also results in certain burdens in the form of duties. The duties may be owed both to persons outside the real estate and to persons entering the real estate. In discussing these duties, we will frequently use examples involving landowners, although the rules apply equally to tenants or other occupants of real estate.

## I. PERSONS OUTSIDE THE REAL ESTATE

### A. INJURIES CAUSED BY CONDITIONS

Greta owned a house on Easy Street that had an old oak tree in the front yard. One day a limb from the tree fell on Henry, who was driving his motorcycle past Greta's house. Must Greta pay for Henry's injuries?

The first question to be determined in such cases is whether the injury was caused by a condition or by an activity on the land. In this case, the injury was caused by a condition, the state of the tree. Under the traditional rule for injuries caused by conditions, the landowner was not liable. The rule was fair in England and frontier America where landowners often owned huge tracts of undeveloped land, and it was not possible for the owner to examine his holdings constantly for potential dangers and to eliminate those dangers.

However, in modern, urbanized America, it is much easier for an owner or occupier to examine and maintain real estate. As a result, courts have determined that the landowner will be held liable for injuries to passersby in two types of cases. First, a landowner will be held liable if the real estate is located in an urban area. Second, even when the real estate is located in a rural area, the owner will be liable if he actually knows that the condition is dangerous or if he has created the condition. Thus even if Greta lived on a large farm, if she knew the limb was rotten or dangerous or if she had planted and cultivated the tree, she would be liable to Henry.

Under either of these modern approaches, owner liability is sometimes extended even to a passerby who enters the land, such as a person who walks onto the land because there is an obstruction on the sidewalk or a person who is misled into entering the property. In Rogers v. Bray,[1] the defendant, worried about vandals, placed a chain across a private road leading to his home. The chain was placed 150 feet in from the street on his private road, but the defendant did not post a sign to indicate that the drive, which appeared to be well used, was in fact a private road. A motorcyclist travelled onto the road, struck the chain and fractured his leg. The court held the defendant liable for not keeping the road reasonably safe.

The modern tendency to hold the owner liable is qualified if the condition threatens an adjoining owner rather than a passerby. Although several courts allow an adjoining owner to recover damages for a noxious (i.e. poisonous or otherwise dangerous) plant or tree, other courts have decided that the only remedy for an adjoining landowner is self-help. Under the self-help approach, if a rotten limb extends from a neighbor's property onto your land, your only remedy is to cut off the limb. The philosophy behind this approach was stated by a Massachusetts court: "The common sense of the common law has recognized that it is wiser to leave the individual to protect himself, if harm results to him from this exercise of another's right to use his property in a reasonable way, than to subject that other to the annoyance, and the public to the burden, of actions at law, which would be likely to be innumerable and, in many instances, purely vexatious."[2]

## B.  INJURIES CAUSED BY ACTIVITIES

Returning to the case of Henry and Greta, let us suppose that Henry was injured, not by a falling limb but by a frisbee thrown by Greta as she was standing on her lot. In accordance with the general principles of tort law discussed in the preceding chapter, Greta will be held liable whenever she intentionally injures a passerby (an intentional tort) or when she fails to exercise reasonable care (negligence).

What should be the result, however, if Henry is injured by Greta's activities on her land which do not fall within intentional tort or negligence theory? For example, Greta decides to fumigate her house with cyanide and, because of an unprecedented wind that no reasonable person would expect, the cyanide blows onto neighboring property and injures Henry. May Henry collect damages from Greta? The answer is to be found within a third area of tort liability, strict liability. Special strict liability rules covering landowners orig-

1.  16 Wash.App. 494, 557 P.2d 28 (1976).    2.  Michalson v. Nutting, 275 Mass. 232, 175 N.E. 490 (1931).

inally developed in England in the 1868 case of Rylands v. Fletcher.[3] In that case, after the defendants constructed a reservoir on their land, water from the reservoir entered an abandoned coal mine and eventually flooded the plaintiff's neighboring mine. Under the law in existence at that time, the plaintiff could not recover on either trespass or nuisance theory, and it was determined that the defendants were not negligent. The court, however, decided that the defendants should still be held liable because they were making abnormal use of their land.

In the United States today such cases could often be resolved by using a trespass or nuisance approach, but most courts have also adopted the special strict liability theory embodied in the *Rylands* decision. Once the theory is accepted, the major legal question becomes, What is an abnormal or non-natural use of the land? Although this is generally a factual question, most courts stress the nature of the community, the character of the real estate, and the dangers in the particular activity.[4] Thus the rule is very close to Justice Sutherland's description of nuisances as "the right thing in the wrong place—like a pig in the parlor instead of the barnyard."[5] For instance, a landowner who allows water to collect in a dangerous place, such as a cellar that is close to neighboring land, will be strictly liable for damage caused by the water, while there will be no strict liability for water collected in household pipes because this is a normal use of the land.

## II.  PERSONS ENTERING THE LAND

Returning to our original example, let us assume that Henry did not receive his injuries as a passerby but, instead, was injured while on Greta's real estate. Is Greta liable for these injuries? At first glance, it might appear fair and logical to apply the same rules to injuries on the land as to injuries outside the land. For example, it might seem proper to decide that when Henry is injured by a dangerous condition such as the falling limb while he is on Greta's land, the result should be the same as if he had been a passerby: if Greta lived in an urban area, if she knew the limb was dangerous, or if she had planted the tree, Henry should receive payment for injuries. Likewise, it might seem logical to hold Greta liable for Henry's injuries resulting from her activities if her actions fall within the defined areas of negligence, intentional tort, or strict liability.

Despite the apparent logic of doing so, courts have not applied the rules governing injuries outside the land to injuries on the real estate because an additional factor must be considered when injuries

3.  L.R. 3 H.L. 330 (1868).

4.  W. Prosser, Law of Torts § 78 at 506, 507 (4th ed. 1971).

5.  Village of Euclid v. Ambler Realty Co., 272 U.S. 365, 47 S.Ct. 114, 71 L. Ed. 303 (1926).

occur on the land: the landowner's use and enjoyment of his own property will be interfered with if he is held accountable for injuries on the land. Because the law traditionally favored free use of one's land, the owner's liability is often limited, depending on the legal status of the person who enters the land. In most cases, the person entering the real estate will fall into one of four categories; that is, there are four possible "hats" that the person might be wearing, each of which alters the owner's duties.

## A. TRESPASSERS

The first hat that the person entering the land might be wearing is that of a trespasser, someone on the land without the permission of the owner. The principle favoring the owner's free use of his land has the greatest appeal in cases of trespass. If the owner is unaware of a trespasser on the land, the general rule is that the owner is not liable for injuries to the trespasser. If the landowner knows that the trespasser is on the property, then at least the landowner must not intentionally injure the trespasser. Most states further require the landowner to exercise reasonable care not to injure known trespassers and to warn them of hidden dangers of which the landowner is aware: "It is true that, unless and until the property owner or the operator of the instrumentality involved, becomes apprised of his presence no duty in regard to the trespasser's safety arises, but when the owner or operator is put on guard as to the presence of the trespasser, the latter immediately acquires the right to proper protection under the circumstances." [6]

Once the principles of liability to a trespasser have been established, the major difficulty is determining whether or not the owner knew the trespasser was on the land. Although this usually is a question of fact, there is one class of cases where the law presumes the owner knows of the trespass, even when the owner is unaware of the individual trespasser's presence. This occurs when the owner knows that trespassers frequently enter his property. If, for example, a homeowner knows that students from a nearby college continually cross his backyard on the way to and from classes, he must exercise reasonable care in his activities and in warning them of known concealed dangers such as a high tension wire.

A special type of trespasser, a person who enters the property to commit a criminal act, has caused legal controversy in recent years. Concerned by the increase in crime, some landowners have developed special security devices to deter criminal trespassers. These devices include shotgun traps, explosive devices, and dangerous animals. In one well-publicized example, owners of a jewelry store in San Fran-

---

**6.** Frederick v. Philadelphia Rapid Transit Co., 337 Pa. 136, 10 A.2d 576 (1940).

cisco, victimized by five break-ins, placed two four-inch-long tarantulas in their window display. Although such devices are often effective deterrents, they also raise a difficult legal issue: May a criminal injured by the security device recover damages from the landowner?

As a general rule, a landowner may use mechanical devices or animals to protect his property only if he could legally have used them if he were there in person. A landowner defending his property in person may not use deadly force to protect only his property because the law values human life more than property rights. Thus a landowner who is not present cannot use deadly force in the form of a mechanical device or an animal to deter petty thieves. See Katko v. Briney, infra. However, several courts have held that the owner may use such devices against a burglar in order to prevent a felony.[7]

## B.  CHILD TRESPASSERS

After graduating from college, William purchased a ten-acre parcel of land in a rural area and excavated a small pond on the land, which he used for swimming and boating. Two years later, a nine-year-old boy, who entered the property without William's permission, drowned after diving from a dock that William had built at one end of the pond. If William were sued for damages by the drowned boy's parents, he might feel confident that he would not be liable under the trespasser rules discussed above. In short, a landowner is not liable for injuries to an unknown trespasser, or even to a known trespasser, unless the injury is caused by a hidden dangerous condition.

However, the question might be raised, Do the usual trespasser rules apply to children? The answer, originally established by the Supreme Court in 1873,[8] was that injuries to child trespassers are governed by a different principle: the attractive nuisance doctrine. The attractive nuisance theory, as the name implies, originally required that the child be attracted to the danger. But this requirement has been dropped by most courts in recent years, and they now require the injured party to prove four elements in order to recover damages under the attractive nuisance theory. Proof of these elements establishes liability only when young children trespassing on land are injured by a structure or other artificial condition.[9] In William's case, the child was young and was injured while using an artificial condition, the dock that William had built at the edge of the man-made pond. Thus, the parents will be allowed to recover damages if they can prove the following four elements.

First, the possessor must know or should know that young children are likely to trespass on the land where the artificial condition

7. W. Prosser, Law of Torts, § 21 (4th ed. 1971).

8. Sioux City & Pacific R. Co. v. Stout, 84 U.S. 657, 21 L.Ed. 745 (1873).

9. Restatement of Torts § 339 (1965). The attractive nuisance doctrine also covers children who are licensees or invitees.

is located. If William's pond were located in a remote area, far from dwellings, it is unlikely that this element could be proven. But if the pond were adjacent to a playground used by young children, the owner should know that young children are likely to trespass.

Second, the landowner must know or should know that the artificial condition exists and must realize or should realize that it involves an unreasonable risk of serious harm or death to young children. Almost any artificial condition can be dangerous in the hands of young children. For example, if William left a beach towel on the dock, a young child might use the towel to "snap" another child and, in so doing, blind him. Although William should know of this danger it is not considered an unreasonable risk. In other words, William is not expected to childproof his property because this would be impractical and virtually impossible. Thus the question in William's case becomes: Is water, like the towel, an ordinary risk or is it an unreasonable risk? Most courts have decided that the risk of drowning in water is not an unreasonable risk because children are taught from a very early age the danger of water. However, if there were other factors involved, William might be liable. For instance, if the dock were located in extremely shallow water and the young child drowned after striking his head on the bottom of the pond, a court would probably determine this to be an unreasonable risk.

Even where the condition obviously involves an unreasonable risk, the landowner will not be liable if he has no reason to know of its existence. In Norton v. City of Easton,[10] the defendant operated a service station and also stored wrecked cars, which he towed for the city to an adjacent lot. A group of boys went to the station to obtain a map, visited the lot, and began looking through the cars. In one wrecked automobile, the boys discovered a box of .22 bullets in the glove compartment. They took the bullets and later put them in a matchbox and lit it. The box exploded and one of the boys, the plaintiff, was blinded. The court decided that the service station owner should not be held liable because he did not know that the bullets were in the glove compartment and had no reason to know of their existence.

Third, it must be proven that the young child, because of his age, did not realize the risk created by the artificial condition. Thus even when the landowner knows that the artificial condition is unreasonably dangerous, he will not be liable if the child who was injured was old enough to appreciate the danger. In Richards v. Marlow,[11] a thirteen-year-old girl slipped while walking on a pipe which had been part of a pier on the defendant's property. The pipe was wet and the girl slipped from the pipe, injuring her mouth. The court denied recovery on the grounds that a thirteen-year-old should realize the risk

---

10. Norton v. City of Easton, 378 A.2d    11. 347 So.2d 281 (La.App.1977).
    417 (1977).

of balancing on the pipe in such conditions. In William's case, the question becomes, Should a nine-year-old realize the risk of diving off the dock? As discussed above, water itself is such an obvious danger that it is not considered an unreasonable risk even to a very young child. However, the risk of diving into shallow water is one which a nine-year-old might not appreciate. This is a question for the jury; but if the injured child has reached a certain age, which usually varies from thirteen to sixteen depending on state law, the judge will not allow a jury verdict for the child.[12]

Fourth, the risk to young children must be great compared to the utility of the artificial condition to the landowner. In William's case, the utility of the pond would possibly outweigh the risk to young children. As one court noted, "ponds are always useful and often necessary, and where they do not exist naturally must be created, in order to store water for stock and domestic purposes, irrigation, etc. Are we to hold that every owner of a pond or reservoir is liable in damage for any child that comes uninvited upon his premises and happens to fall in the water and drown? If so, then upon the same principle must the owner of a fruit tree be held liable for the death or injury of a child who, attracted by the fruit, climbs into the branches, and falls out. But this, we imagine, is an absurdity, for which no one would contend." [13] However, a different conclusion might be reached regarding the dock. The utility of the dock could easily be questioned and the danger more easily removed.

In most states, if the four elements can be proven, landowners such as William will be liable for injuries to young children. In a few states, however, the attractive nuisance doctrine has been rejected. The reasons for the rejection were best stated by the court in Lewis v. Mains: "Sympathy is quickly aroused by the injuries of a child, and that emotion is both natural and proper. In such a mood, courts have sometimes substituted moral or sentimental obligations for legal obligations. In so doing they tend to curtail unreasonably the proper use of property by an owner in order to confer protection upon a person wrongfully thereon. We have never imposed upon a property owner the obligation of due care to protect a trespasser even though the trespasser was a child of tender years. . . . Upon whom then does the duty devolve to protect small children from dangers which they may encounter while trespassing? Surely upon their most natural custodians and protectors, the parents." [14]

See Doren v. Northwestern Baptist Hospital Ass'n, infra.

12. W. Prosser, Law of Torts § 59 at 373, 374 (4th ed. 1971).

13. Peters v. Bowman, 115 Cal. 345, 47 P. 113 (1897).

14. 150 Me. 75, 104 A.2d 432 (1954).

## C. LICENSEES

The third hat that a person entering the real estate might be wearing is that of a licensee. A licensee is defined as a person who enters the land of another without any invitation or else for some purpose not connected with the business conducted on the land. In either case, however, the entry is with the permission or at the toleration of the owner. Thus a licensee differs from a trespasser because he has the owner's permission.

The landowner owes the same duty of care to a licensee as he owes to a known trespasser; that is, in most states the owner must exercise reasonable care not to injure licensees and, furthermore, must warn them of any hidden dangers of which he is aware. In a few states, however, the only duty of the owner is to avoid intentional injury to the licensee: "Generally speaking, the owner of land in Maryland owes no duty with respect to the condition of his land to a trespasser, or even to a licensee, whose presence upon the land is known to him, except to abstain from wilful or wanton misconduct." [15]

To illustrate the duty of reasonable care owed by the landowner, the plaintiff in Reynolds v. Nichols,[16] a guest in his neighbors' home, was stabbed by another guest. The plaintiff sued his neighbors, claiming that the defendants did not exercise reasonable care because they served the other guest alcoholic beverages and failed to restrain him when he attacked the plaintiff. The court held that, although the hosts could be held liable for serving alcoholic beverages to a person they knew had violent propensities, this was not proven here. The court also concluded the defendants had no duty to aid a guest endangered by another guest.

The owner's duty to warn licensees of hidden dangers was at issue in another case, Smith v. Goldman.[17] In *Smith*, the plaintiff was injured when riding his bicycle on a bicycle path located on the defendant's property. He fell from his bike into a pool and was injured by debris which had collected in the pool. The court acknowledged that a landowner has a duty to warn licensees and known trespassers of hidden dangers on the bicycle path. However, the duty does not extend to warning of all hidden debris located near the path which might increase a fallen bicyclist's injuries. A reasonable person riding a bicycle should know that such debris normally exists along bicycle paths. Consequently, the court held for the defendant.

Perhaps the most difficult question facing courts is how to determine the status of the person entering the land; that is, Does the person meet the licensee test? To illustrate the application of the licensee test, we will examine cases involving the three most common

15. Duff v. United States, 171 F.2d 846 (4th Cir. 1949).

16. 276 Or. 597, 556 P.2d 102 (1976).

17. 53 Ill.App.3d 632, 11 Ill.Dec. 444, 368 N.E.2d 1052 (1977).

types of licensees.  First, it is widely recognized that social guests and relatives are licensees.  In Bisnett v. Mowder,[18] a woman was injured while visiting the defendants' home.  After sitting at the edge of the defendants' swimming pool, with her feet dangling in the water, the woman walked across a patio  to pick up her cigarettes.  On the way she slipped and was injured.  The court noted the general rule that a social guest is a licensee and therefore the owner must warn the guest of hidden dangers.  While a licensee should be aware of the danger of slipping on a wet spot near a swimming pool, in this case there were additional factors.  The defendants had recently repainted the patio, thus making the patio more slippery than usual.  In fact, other guests  had slipped on the patio and the owners had given warnings to others to be careful.  Because of these factors, the appellate court concluded that the case should be tried by a jury and remanded it for trial.  This case should be contrasted with Hastings v. DeLeon,[19] where a mother was injured when she slipped on a loose rug which covered a tile floor in her daughter's home.  The court concluded that, although the mother was legally classified as a licensee, the daughter should not be held liable for the injury since the daughter was unaware that the rug was dangerous or unsafe.

A second common type of licensee is the person who visits the property in an attempt to sell something to the owner.  Under our original definition, such a person enters the premises without an express or implied invitation and therefore is a licensee.  In Stacy v. Shapiro,[20] the court decided that a woman hired by a manufacturer to visit housewives, demonstrate the company's products and leave coupons with the housewives, was a licensee: "Clearly the plaintiff had not been invited by anyone.  She went upon the premises in her own interest and that of her employers.  Consequently the housewives upon whom she intended calling did not know that she was coming.  The plaintiff  .  .  .  was only a bare licensee upon the premises."

A final, common type of licensee is the person who visits a business or factory for educational purposes or for a purpose that is not connected with the business on the land.  In Benson v. Baltimore Traction Co.,[21] the graduating class of a local high school was given permission to visit the defendant traction company.  One of the students slipped into an uncovered vat of boiling water, the top of which was level with the floor.  Although at the time of the injury the students were walking through the plant on their own and had not been warned of such dangers, the court decided that the company was not liable because the student was only a licensee.

18.  114 Ariz. 213, 560 P.2d 68 (1977).     20.  212 App.Div. 723, 209 N.Y.S. 305 (1935).

19.  532 S.W.2d 147 (Tex.Civ.App.1976).     21.  77 Md. 535, 26 A. 973 (1893).

## D. INVITEES

The last hat that the person entering the real estate might be wearing is that of an invitee. The invitee is in most cases a business visitor, and a few courts limit invitee status to only those persons whose presence brings potential economic benefit to the landowner. Most courts, however, have adopted a much broader definition that extends invitee status to anyone who has been invited to the premises and who has an implied assurance that the owner has exercised reasonable care to make the premises safe.[22]

The use of this broader definition has resulted in judicial decisions that are widely accepted, although they may appear illogical at first. For instance, social guests are clearly invited to the premises by the landowner, but they are considered to be licensees rather than invitees. The reason given by the courts is that the host makes no implied assurance that reasonable care has been taken to make the premises safe. Instead, the guest is treated as one of the family and, if he is injured by a hidden danger unknown to the owner, cannot recover. However, when members of the public are invited to the premises, even if there is no economic benefit to the owners, they are considered to be invitees because by making the invitation the owners implicitly assure the public that reasonable care has been exercised to make the premises safe. Thus, persons attending free lectures or a college reunion are considered invitees.[23]

The landowner owes a full duty of reasonable care to a visitor who can be classified as an invitee. In other words the policy that favors the owner's free use of the land, which resulted in limiting the owner's duty to trespassers and licensees, bows to the policy of protecting the invitee from injury. Thus, the landowner must exercise reasonable care in conducting activities on the land so as not to injure invitees. In some cases, this requires the landowner to take affirmative action. In one case,[24] a woman who had checked into the Hyatt Hotel in Atlanta committed suicide by jumping from the twenty-first floor. When her husband and daughter sued the hotel, the hotel moved for a summary judgment on the grounds that it owed no legal duty to the woman to prevent the suicide. The court refused to grant summary judgment, noting that the hotel may owe a legal duty in such circumstances and that duty would require the hotel to take affirmative action to prevent suicides. The plaintiffs stressed that the hotel knew other similar suicides had occurred, the woman had been inebriated when she arrived at the hotel, she arrived with no luggage, and the hotel employees observed her wandering around the twenty-first floor in a confused state.

---

22. W. Prosser, Law of Torts § 61 at 386–389 (4th ed. 1971).

23. Id. §§ 60, 61 at 379, 389.

24. Sneider v. Hyatt Corp., 390 F.Supp. 976 (N.D.Ga.1975).

In addition to conducting activities in a reasonable manner, the landowner must exercise reasonable care in warning invitees of hidden dangerous conditions. This duty extends—and this is the major distinction between the duty owed the licensee and the invitee—even to those conditions of which the owner has no actual knowledge, if the court decides that he *should* have known of the danger. The question of whether the owner should have known of hidden dangers is frequently litigated. In Wamser v. City of St. Petersburg,[25] a boy was severely injured when he was attacked by a shark at a beach operated by the city of St. Petersburg, Florida. The court concluded that the city had no duty to warn swimmers of the danger, since this was the first recorded shark attack in the history of the beach and the city had no reason to foresee the danger.

In the common situation where a customer slips and falls on an object in a store, the major legal question is whether the store had reason to know of the danger. In Williams v. Bedford Market, Inc.,[26] a customer claimed that she slipped in a small puddle of water, about two inches wide, on the floor of the store. The court noted that the store would be liable for injuries caused by foreign substances on the floor if (1) the storekeeper or his employees created the dangerous condition or (2) if the owner did not remove the substance within a reasonable time after learning of its existence. These duties do not make the owner an insurer against all injuries to customers. In this case, the court, in concluding that the store was not liable, relied on evidence that the store was mopped and swept every night and that spills were usually cleaned up within five minutes. However the results in such cases are mixed. In Ferrington v. McDaniel,[27] a supermarket was held liable when the plaintiff, who was walking toward a display of Red Seal snuff, which she wanted to buy for her mother, tripped over a box of candy in the aisle.

Even when the owner is aware of the danger, there will be no liability to invitees who know or should know of the danger. In House v. European Health Spa,[28] an invitee at the defendant's health spa slipped on a foreign substance as she entered the shower. During the trial she admitted that on previous visits to the spa the showers were slippery and dirty and that she had slipped before. The court held that she could not recover because of her knowledge of the danger.

In a similar case,[29] when a theater patron slipped on a popcorn box while leaving a theater, the court observed: "Two elements must exist in order to merit recovery—fault on the part of the owner, and ignorance of the danger on the part of the invitee. . . . By enter-

**25.** 339 So.2d 244 (Fla.App.1976).

**26.** 199 Neb. 577, 260 N.W.2d 316 (1977).

**27.** 336 So.2d 796 (La.1976).

**28.** 239 S.E.2d 653 (1977).

**29.** Rogers v. Atlanta Enterprises, 89 Ga.App. 903, 81 S.E.2d 721 (1954).

ing the theatre under the circumstances here, she voluntarily assumed the risk that other patrons might negligently throw such cartons to the floor, and that they often did so, and, knowing that the management would not and did not attempt to clean them up during the progress of the entertainment, she assumed the risk of finding one of them in her path. Her means of knowledge being equal with that of the defendant, it follows that she has failed to show a right of recovery based upon the acts of negligence alleged."

Because of the higher duty of care owed the invitee, many cases hinge on the question whether the plaintiff is considered an invitee or a licensee. This question is complicated by the fact that the status of a person may change; that is, he may switch hats while he is on the premises. The court in Sheridan v. Ravn [30] gave the following example: "A restaurant or a lunch room has a place for the public to come in, has a counter at which they may sit, a place where they may give their order, or pay their bills as the case may be, or any other part of the premises to which the public is invited, either directly or by implication, or because of the position or character of the place, but if a person went behind the counter, for instance, he would cease being an invitee. That is not where he belongs; he would then be a licensee, even though the proprietor said, 'You may come back of the counter and see how I slice the bacon,' or whatever is going on. It would be a matter in which the proprietor wouldn't have any interest, merely for the accommodation of the customer."

In Pagarigan v. Phillips Petroleum Co.,[31] the plaintiff took his car to a service station to have the car radio repaired. When he returned later, he found the defendant station mechanic working in the lubrication room. The mechanic said he would talk about the radio as soon as he finished with the car on which he was working. While the plaintiff was waiting in the lubrication room, a car fell from a hoist and injured him. The defendant argued that the plaintiff could not recover because he was a licensee. The court rejected this argument and ruled for the plaintiff, noting that he retained his invitee status because he entered the lubrication room for a business purpose.

Another legal issue relating to the owner's duty to an invitee has been litigated frequently in recent years. The issue is illustrated by the case of Rosier v. Gainesville Inns Associates.[32] The plaintiffs, who were attending homecoming at the University of Florida, stayed at the Holiday Inn in Gainesville with their children. When they returned to their room at night, they locked their door but did not lock the chain latch. During the night, the wife awoke when an intruder

30. 91 Cal.App.2d 112, 204 P.2d 644 (1949).

31. 16 Wash.App. 34, 552 P.2d 1065 (1976).

32. 347 So.2d 1100 (Fla.App.1977).

entered the room. The husband, in attacking the intruder, was stabbed, and the wife also suffered a minor injury. Before fleeing, the intruder grabbed a key on the floor which he apparently had used to enter the room. When the plaintiffs sued the hotel, the trial court dismissed the complaint and the plaintiffs appealed. The appellate court reversed the trial court decision, noting that a jury could find the hotel liable on the facts. Guests in a hotel are invitees, and there was evidence the hotel knew burglaries had occurred in the past. Consequently, the case was remanded for trial.

In another case,[33] a woman was assaulted in a shopping center parking lot at 9:30 p.m. after leaving work. The court refused to overturn a jury verdict against the mall. The court noted that the defendant mall owner should have known of the danger since the defendant was aware of seventy-seven car thefts in the past year. Once it is determined that the owner should have known of the danger, it is for the jury to decide whether the owner took adequate measures to prevent further criminal activity and to warn customers and employees of the danger.

In contrast to the decisions just mentioned, there are numerous cases in which landowners have not been held liable for injuries resulting from criminal activity. In many of these cases, courts have decided that the act of the criminal rather than the owner's negligence was the proximate cause of the injuries. In Davis v. Allied Supermarkets, Inc.,[34] the plaintiff sued a supermarket after she was injured by a purse snatcher in the supermarket parking lot. She claimed that the business was located in a high crime area and the defendant had failed to provide adequate lighting and security. The court held for the supermarket on the grounds that the damage resulted from the act of the independent third party, the criminal. The court also stressed that it did not want to make the landowner an insurer against losses resulting from criminal activities. Courts may also decide in favor of the owner if the owner had no reason to know of the criminal activity. In Shipes v. Piggly Wiggly St. Andrews, Inc.,[35] a customer who had been assaulted in a supermarket parking lot was denied recovery on the grounds that the store had no reason to expect criminal acts. The store was located in a quiet neighborhood, and the only previous criminal activity in the parking lot was the theft of a tape deck from a car. See McNeal v. Henry, and Earle v. Colonial Theatre Co., infra, which were decided on the same day by the Michigan Court of Appeals.

33. Morgan v. Bucks Associates, 428 F. Supp. 546 (E.D.Pa.1977).

34. 547 P.2d 963 (Okl.1976).

35. 269 S.C. 479, 238 S.E.2d 167 (1977).

## E.  NEW TRENDS

The traditional approach—determining the landowner's liability according to which of the four hats the visitor wears—has offered the landowner a certain measure of immunity from suit, but it has also resulted in a complex body of law full of subtle distinctions.  In the words of Lord Denning in an English case,[36] "A canvasser who comes on your premises without your consent is a trespasser.  Once he has your consent he is a licensee.  Not until you do business with him is he an invitee.  Even when you have done business with him, it seems rather strange that your duty towards him should be different when he comes up to your door from what it is when he goes away.  Does he change his colour in the middle of the conversation?  What is the position when you discuss business with him and it comes to nothing?  No confident answer can be given to these questions.  Such is the morass into which the law has floundered in trying to distinguish between licensees and invitees."

Because of such frustrations, a statute was enacted in England in 1957 that requires a landowner to exercise the same duty of care to both licensees and invitees.  In the United States, courts in three states have followed the English approach.  Courts in six other states, however, seem to be setting the trend for the United States by abolishing the distinction between invitees, licensees and even trespassers.  In one such case, Webb v. City and Borough of Sitka,[37] the plaintiff fell and broke her hip after stubbing her toe on the sidewalk in Sitka, Alaska.  When she sued the city, the trial court, in dismissing the complaint, stated the traditional rule that her status as a licensee or invitee had a bearing on the city's liability.  On appeal, the Alaska Supreme Court decided that the rigid common law classifications were outdated.  The court decided that the better rule is that "a landowner or owner of other property must act as a reasonable person in maintaining his property in a reasonably safe condition in view of all the circumstances, including the likelihood of injury to others, the seriousness of the injury, and the burden on the respective parties of avoiding the risk."  In this case, for example, the court felt that a jury should consider whether the sidewalk was reasonably safe in view of the likelihood of injury to others, the burden of avoiding injury, and the seriousness of potential injury.  The jury should also consider whether the plaintiff's negligence had contributed to the injury.  The case was remanded for a jury trial.  See Rowland v. Christian, infra.

One other new trend should be mentioned—the trend to hold a person liable even though that person is not at fault.  No-fault laws often affect the liability of a landowner.  For example, under workers' compensation statutes, an employer must pay for an employee's

36. Dunster v. Abbott, 2 All Eng.Rep.     37.  561 P.2d 731 (Alaska 1977).
   1572 (1953).

injury incurred on the job even if the employer did not cause the injury.  In recent years, many statutes have been broadened to include many part-time persons hired by a homeowner.  In some states, household employees such as babysitters, handymen, and gardeners are subject to workers' compensation laws.  For example, if a babysitter in one of these states accidently burns himself on the kitchen stove, the homeowner would be liable for medical expenses and disability wages regardless of fault.

Another type of no-fault law is products liability, whereby the seller of a defective product will be liable even if he has exercised all possible care.  This liability has been extended even to cover a customer in a store who is injured by a product before it is sold.  In Embs v. Pepsi-Cola Bottling Co. of Lexington, Kentucky, Inc.,[38] the plaintiff was walking down an aisle in a store when she heard a noise that sounded "like a shotgun."  When she looked down she saw a gash in her leg and green pieces of a Seven-Up bottle on the floor. The plaintiff was immediately taken to the hospital by the store manager, who advised her that several Seven-Up bottles had exploded that week.  The court held all parties in the distributive chain liable even though no Seven-Up was sold to the plaintiff.  "Our expressed public policy will be furthered if we minimize the risk of personal injury and property damage by charging the costs of injuries against the manufacturer who can procure liability insurance and distribute its expense among the public as a cost of doing business; and since the risk of harm from defective products exists for mere bystanders and passersby as well as for the purchaser or user, there is no substantial reason for protecting one class of persons and not the other. The same policy requires us to maximize protection for the injured third party and promote the public interest in discouraging the marketing of products having defects that are a menace to the public by imposing strict liability upon retailers and wholesalers in the distributive chain responsible for marketing the defective product which injures the bystander.  The imposition of strict liability places no unreasonable burden upon sellers because they can adjust the cost of insurance protection among themselves in the course of their continuing business relationship."

38.  528  S.W.2d  703  (Ky.1975).

# CASES

## KATKO v. BRINEY

Supreme Court of Iowa, 1971.
183 N.W.2d 657.

MOORE, Chief Justice.

The primary issue presented here is whether an owner may protect personal property in an unoccupied boarded-up farm house against trespassers and thieves by a spring gun capable of inflicting death or serious injury.

We are not not here concerned with a man's right to protect his home and members of his family. Defendants' home was several miles from the scene of the incident to which we refer infra.

\* \* \*

At defendants' request plaintiff's action was tried to a jury consisting of residents of the community where defendants' property was located. The jury returned a verdict for plaintiff and against defendants for $20,000 actual and $10,000 punitive damages.

\* \* \*

Most of the facts are not disputed. In 1957 defendant Bertha L. Briney inherited her parents' farm land in Mahaska and Monroe Counties. Included was an 80-acre tract in southwest Mahaska County where her grandparents and parents had lived. No one occupied the house thereafter. Her husband, Edward, attempted to care for the land. He kept no farm machinery thereon. The outbuildings became dilapidated.

For about 10 years, 1957 to 1967, there occurred a series of trespassing and housebreaking events with loss of some household items, the breaking of windows and "messing up of the property in general". The latest occurred June 8, 1967, prior to the event on July 16, 1967 herein involved.

Defendants through the years boarded up the windows and doors in an attempt to stop the intrusions. They had posted "no trespass" signs on the land several years before 1967. The nearest one was 35 feet from the house. On June 11, 1967 defendants set "a shotgun trap" in the north bedroom. After Mr. Briney cleaned and oiled his 20-gauge shotgun, the power of which he was well aware, defendants took it to the old house where they secured it to an iron bed with the barrel pointed at the bedroom door. It was rigged with wire from the doorknob to the gun's trigger so it would fire when the door was opened. Briney first pointed the gun so an intruder would be hit in the stomach but at Mrs. Briney's suggestion it was lowered to hit the legs. He admitted he did so "because I was mad and tired of being tormented" but "he did not intend to injure anyone". He gave no explanation of why he used a loaded shell and set it to hit a person already in the house. Tin was nailed over the bedroom window. The spring gun could not be seen from the outside. No warning of its presence was posted.

Plaintiff lived with his wife and worked regularly as a gasoline station attendant in Eddyville, seven miles from the old house. He had observed it for several years while hunting in the area and considered it as being abandoned. He knew it had long been uninhabited. In 1967 the area around the house was covered with high weeds. Prior to July 16, 1967 plaintiff and McDonough had been to the premises and found several old bottles and fruit jars which they took and added to their collection of antiques. On the latter date about 9:30 p.m. they made a second trip to the Briney property. They entered the old house by removing a board from a porch window which was without glass. While McDonough was looking around the kitchen area plaintiff went to another part of the house. As he started to open the north bedroom door the shotgun went off striking him in the right leg above the ankle bone. Much of his leg, including part of the tibia, was blown away. Only by McDonough's assistance was plaintiff able to get out of the house and after crawling some distance was put in his vehicle and rushed to a doctor and then to the hospital. He remained in the hospital 40 days.

Plaintiff's doctor testified he seriously considered amputation but eventually the healing process was successful. Some weeks after his release from the hospital plaintiff returned to work on crutches. He was required to keep the injured leg in a cast for approximately a year and wear a special brace for another year. He continued to suffer pain during this period.

There was undenied medical testimony plaintiff had a permanent deformity, a loss of tissue, and a shortening of the leg.

The record discloses plaintiff to trial time had incurred $710 medical expense, $2056.85 for hospital service, $61.80 for orthopedic service and $750 as loss of earnings. In addition thereto the trial court submitted to the jury the question of damages for pain and suffering and for future disability.

Plaintiff testified he knew he had no right to break and enter the house with intent to steal bottles and fruit jars therefrom. He further testified he had entered a plea of guilty to larceny in the nighttime of property of less than $20 value from a private building. He stated he had been fined $50 and costs and paroled during good behavior from a 60-day jail sentence. Other than minor traffic charges this was plaintiff's first brush with the law. On this civil case appeal it is not our prerogative to review the disposition made of the criminal charge against him.

The main thrust of defendants' defense in the trial court and on this appeal is that "the law permits use of a spring gun in a dwelling or warehouse for the purpose of preventing the unlawful entry of a burglar or thief". They repeated this contention in their exceptions to the trial court's instructions 2, 5 and 6. They took no exception to the trial court's statement of the issues or to other instructions.

In the statement of issues the trial court stated plaintiff and his companion committed a felony when they broke and entered defendants' house. In instruction 2 the court referred to the early case history of the use of spring guns and stated under the law their use was prohibited except to prevent the commission of felonies of violence and where human life is in danger. The instruction included a statement breaking and entering is not a felony of violence.

      *    *    *

The overwhelming weight of authority, both textbook and case law, supports the trial court's statement of the applicable principles of law.

Prosser on Torts, Third Edition, pages 116–118, states:

"*    *    * the law has always placed a higher value upon human safety than upon mere rights in property, it is the accepted rule that there is no privilege to use any force calculated to cause death or serious bodily injury to repel the threat to land or chattels, unless there is also such a threat to the defendant's personal safety as to justify a self-defense. *    *    * spring guns and other man-killing devices are not justifiable against a mere trespasser, or even a petty thief. They are privileged only against those upon whom the landowner, if he were present in person would be free to inflict injury of the same kind."

Restatement of Torts, section 85, page 180, states: "The value of human life and limb, not only to the individual concerned but also to society, so outweighs the interest of a possessor of land in excluding from it those whom he is not willing to admit thereto that a possessor of land has, as is stated in § 79, no privilege to use force intended or likely to cause death or serious harm against another whom the possessor sees about to enter his premises or meddle with his chattel, unless the intrusion threatens death or serious bodily harm to the occupiers or users of the premises. *    *    * A possessor of land cannot do indirectly and by a mechanical device that which, were he present, he could not do immediately and in person. Therefore, he cannot gain a privilege to install, for the purpose of protecting his land from intrusions harmless to the lives and limbs of the occupiers or users of it, a mechanical device whose only purpose is to inflict death or serious harm upon such as may intrude, by giving notice of his intention to inflict, by mechanical means and indirectly, harm which he could not, even after request, inflict directly were he present."

Siedel Cs.Real Est.Law MCB—14

In Volume 2, Harper and James, The Law of Torts, section 27.3, pages 1440, 1441, this is found: "The possessor of land may not arrange his premises intentionally so as to cause death or serious bodily harm to a trespasser. The possessor may of course take some steps to repel a trespass. If he is present he may use force to do so, but only that amount which is reasonably necessary to effect the repulse. Moreover if the trespass threatens harm to property only—even a theft of property—the possessor would not be privileged to use deadly force, he may not arrange his premises so that such force will be inflicted by mechanical means. If he does, he will be liable even to a thief who is injured by such device."

\* \* \*

In addition to civil liability many jurisdictions hold a land owner criminally liable for serious injuries or homicide caused by spring guns or other set devices. See State v. Childers, 133 Ohio 508, 14 N. E.2d 767 (melon thief shot by spring gun); Pierce v. Commonwealth, 135 Va. 635, 115 S.E. 686 (policeman killed by spring gun when he opened unlocked front door of defendant's shoe repair shop); State v. Marfaudille, 48 Wash. 117, 92 P. 939 (murder conviction for death from spring gun set in a trunk); State v. Beckham, 306 Mo. 566, 267 S.W. 817 (boy killed by spring gun attached to window of defendant's chili stand); State v. Green, 118 S.C. 279, 110 S.E. 145, 19 A.L.R. 1431 (intruder shot by spring gun when he broke and entered vacant house. Manslaughter conviction of owner affirmed); State v. Barr, 11 Wash. 481, 39 P. 1080 (murder conviction affirmed for death of an intruder into a boarded up cabin in which owner had set a spring gun).

In Wisconsin, Oregon and England the use of spring guns and similar devices is specifically made unlawful by statute.

\* \* \*

Affirmed.

---

### DOREN v. NORTHWESTERN BAPTIST HOSPITAL ASS'N

Supreme Court of Minnesota, 1953.
240 Minn. 181, 60 N.W.2d 361.

THOMAS GALLAGHER, Justice.

Action by Gerald Doren as father of Joel Doren, a minor, and by Gerald Doren in his own behalf against Northwestern Baptist Hospital Association, a corporation, and Arthur M. Calvin, its receiver, for injuries sustained by Joel Doren on August 23, 1949, when he fell into a pile of live ashes on defendants' premises and for resulting damages sustained by Gerald Doren as the result thereof.

The jury returned a verdict for Gerald Doren as father of Joel Doren in the sum of $15,000 and for Gerald Doren personally in the sum of $5,000. Defendants moved for judgments notwithstanding the verdicts or for a new trial in each case. This is an appeal from the orders denying such motions. The cases were consolidated for trial in the district court and for hearing on appeal here.

The facts are as follows: At the time of the accident Joel Doren was six years of age. Northwestern Baptist Hospital Association, a corporation, hereinafter referred to as defendant, owned and operated the Mounds Park Hospital bordered by Earl street on the west, Frank street on the east, Thorn street on the south, and Burns avenue on the north in the city of St. Paul. The hospital structures consist of one large building, set approximately in the center of the block, to which there is attached to the east thereof another building housing the hospital's heating plant and known as the powerhouse.

\* \* \*

Defendant's employees knew that children were constantly in and about the hospital grounds and in the area in which the ashes were deposited after removal from the furnaces. William Carlson, chief engineer in charge of the powerhouse, testified that during the period of approximately 14 years in which he had been employed at the hospital he had frequently observed children playing on the premises, including the enclosed area in which the ashes were kept; that they often climbed to and sat upon the top of the fence bordering the area; that they played about the hospital grounds on many occasions with the permission of the hospital employees. Joseph McNeice, maintenance mechanic in the powerhouse, testified that he had permitted them to sit on boxes within the area to watch drilling operations taking place there. Other employees testified that they had observed children playing on the premises and at times had not ordered them to leave; that at times they even got in the boiler room to play; and that they could easily get within the fenced area by way of the driveway from Burns avenue or that leading to Thorn street.

It was customary for defendant's employees to remove the ashes and combustible material from the furnaces in the power plant once a week and to pile them within the enclosed area to await their final removal. After dumping them in this area, they would level them to a thickness of five or six inches and pour water upon them to kill any still smoldering. There was testimony that ashes thus handled at times would rekindle and smolder beneath the top surface. They were ordinarily permitted to remain in the yard for several days until their final removal by the haulers. The ashes thus deposited in the area were not otherwise enclosed by protective screen or guard nor segregated from the remaining rubbish and debris. Certain metal drums located there might have been used for their storage but were not.

Just prior to the accident, some 18 or 19 wheelbarrows of ashes had been removed from the power plant and deposited in the area described. They had been leveled out and soaked with water, but apparently those beneath the top surface had rekindled thereafter. In the late afternoon of the day of the accident, Joel Doren and a companion entered the enclosed area through one of the entryways thereto preparatory to climbing on the fence bordering it so that they might watch the older boys playing on the hospital grounds. The accident occurred when Joel, in passing the ash pile on his way toward the fence, tripped and fell into the smoldering ashes. As a result his arms and hands and other parts of his body were severely burned, requiring lengthy hospitalization and resulting in permanent deformities.

The charge to the jury included the following:

" *   *   * in considering the alleged negligence of the defendants it is the law that one who maintains on his premises an artificial condition is liable for resulting injury to young children present thereon, if:

"A. The place where the condition is maintained is one upon which the possessor knows or should know that such children are liable to trespass, and

"B. The condition is one of which the possessor knows or should know which he realizes or should realize as involving an unreasonable risk of death or serious bodily injury to such children, and

"C. The children, because of their youth do not discover the condition or realize the risk involved in their inter-meddling in it or in coming within the area made dangerous by it, and

"D. The utility to the possessor of maintaining the condition is slight as compared to the risk to young children involved therein.

" *   *   * in applying the fore-going rule,   *   *   * whether   *   *   * plaintiff was on the defendants' premises by express or implied invitation, or by mere acquiescence of the defendants, or contrary to the defendants' wishes and as trespasser, *   *   * is immaterial to the plaintiff's right to recover if he has established by a fair preponderance of the evidence each of the foregoing conditions."

*   *   *

This court has discarded the distinction between "attractive nuisance" cases and other negligence cases. It recognizes that, when an artificial condition involving risks to children is maintained where children are known to play, a degree of diligence greater than under ordinary circumstances is required of the property owner. In determining whether the property owner is liable for injuries sustained by a child because of such an instrumentality, it follows Restatement,

Torts, § 339, which sets forth the four conditions to be established as specified by the trial court here.

\*   \*   \*

We feel that the evidence is sufficient here to establish the four conditions which impose liability upon defendant. There can be no dispute that the maintenance of the ash pile with the smoldering ashes beneath its surface constituted an artificial condition involving a risk of serious injury to children playing near it. There can be no dispute that children of the age of Joel would not be likely to discover from the outward appearance of the ash pile the dangers beneath the surface thereof or realize the risk involved in playing near it. There is substantial evidence that defendants, through its employees, knew that children were likely to trespass, and in fact, it is clear that at times they had actually invited the children to remain and play about the premises in and near the enclosed area where the ashes were piled. The utility to defendant of maintaining the condition must be regarded as slight when it is recalled that, if it so desired, it could readily have stored the burning ashes in the metal containers on its premises, thereby eliminating the risk attendant upon the artificial condition maintained.

It is contended that the evidence established as a matter of law that defendant had used more than ordinary care to keep children off its property and, hence, was absolved from negligence. It is true that some precautions were taken to prevent children from gaining access to the premises. Defendant constructed a fence which partially enclosed the area, and at times its employees ordered the children away. However, the evidence also discloses that two open driveways permitted easy access to the dangerous area and that defendant's employees were aware of the fact that children frequently gained entry to this area thereby and at times invited or encouraged the children to play or watch work in progress there. True, defendant did not owe the duty of keeping constant watch over its premises to prevent trespass thereon, but it would seem to be a fact question whether it might not have made the area where the known dangers existed more secure against the children's entry or otherwise more effectively safeguarded the dangerous condition there maintained. Had the jury determined that defendant exercised more than ordinary care to exclude children or to safeguard a dangerous condition, it would follow that the four conditions required had not been established. The jury, however, determined that the four conditions were established, and implicit therein is the determination that defendant had not exercised the degree of care required.

Defendants contend that the trial court erred in failing to instruct the jury that Joel Doren "when he came within the fenced in portion of defendants' property on said date, was a trespasser on the property of the defendant, but inasmuch as Joel Doren was a minor of tender years, the Defendant owed to Joel Doren the duty of exercising ordinary care * * *."

Under the conditions set forth in Restatement, Torts, § 339, upon which liability attaches in cases of this kind, it is immaterial that the child involved was a trespasser.

* * *

Defendants contend that the trial court erred in failing to instruct the jury that it should determine whether Joel Doren was guilty of contributory negligence. If the conditions imposed by Restatement, Torts, § 339, are established, it is obvious that the contributory negligence of a child involved in an accident would rarely constitute the proximate cause thereof. In any event there is nothing in the record here upon which a finding of contributory negligence could be based. Certainly the fact that Joel, only six years of age, in running past the ash pile tripped and fell into it would not make a fact issue on the question.

The rule is well established that a parent is required to exercise that degree of care for a child which a reasonably prudent person would exercise under the same conditions. There is no evidence here which would support a finding that Joel's parents had failed to exercise such care. Mrs. Doren testified that she did not know her children played on the hospital grounds, although she was aware that some children played baseball on one corner thereof, and that she did not know what was within the enclosed area. Gerald Doren specifically denied that he was aware that Joel had ever wandered over to the hospital grounds or was accustomed to playing there.

For recovery of a parent to be barred because of negligence, the evidence must establish that the parent had some knowledge that the child was frequenting dangerous areas and failed to warn with reference thereto or otherwise take adequate precautions to prevent the child from going into such areas. The absence of evidence on this point justified the trial court in directing the jury as it did on this question.

Affirmed.

---

## McNEAL v. HENRY

Court of Appeals of Michigan, 1978.
82 Mich.App. 88, 266 N.W.2d 469.

V. J. BRENNAN, J. The wife of plaintiff Bennie L. McNeal was killed during a fight which occurred inside the Kroger Food Store in Flint, Michigan. Plaintiff filed a wrongful death action in the circuit court of Genesee County. On January 6, 1977, the trial court granted defendant Kroger Company's motion for summary judgment pursuant to GCR 1963, 117.2(1) on grounds that Kroger did not owe the decedent a duty to protect against the kind of sudden and unforesee-able injury occurring here.

\*    \*    \*

Plaintiff alleged that defendant Kroger failed to prevent the death of decedent by failing to react in time to commotion which re-sulted from the fight preceding decedent's death. However, this posi-tion depends upon the fact that defendant actually owed plaintiff a duty relative to this kind of occurrence and harm. We agree with the trial court that the conduct of decedent's assailant was so ex-traordinary that defendant as a matter of law could not be held re-sponsible for providing the kind of protection which would have avoided her death. Consequently, though defendant may have owed a duty of reasonable care to plaintiff as a business invitee, that duty did not extend to the extreme and totally unforeseeable behavior de-cedent's assailant demonstrated by the act of his shooting her.

The trial court was justified in determining as a matter of law that no duty arose on the part of defendant Kroger and consequently that granting summary judgment was appropriate for failure to state a cause of action. As a matter of policy, we do not believe that com-mercial businesses should be required to answer for the type of bi-zarre consequence faced by defendant in this case, even though plain-tiff's complaint clearly and correctly characterized plaintiff herself as a business invitee. Defendant assumed a duty of reasonable care as to her. Defendant did not assume a duty to protect her against the kind of behavior her assailant demonstrated and the consequences of that behavior. We see a real line between the duty to plaintiff and the unforeseeable consequences of her assailant's behavior. We take this opportunity to draw that line.

The grant of summary judgment to defendant by the trial court is sustained.

Affirmed.

---

## EARLE v. COLONIAL THEATRE CO.

Court of Appeals of Michigan, 1978.
82 Mich.App. 54, 266 N.W.2d 466.

BEASLEY, J. On August 23, 1972, while a patron in the now closed Colonial Theatre on the edge of downtown Detroit, plaintiff was shot in the right ear in an unprovoked attack by a stranger. Al-though suffering serious injury and loss of hearing in one ear, plain-tiff recovered and sued defendant for damages, claiming defendant did not exercise reasonable care for his safety. Specifically, plaintiff offered evidence of previous criminal activity in or about the theatre and asserted defendants were thus placed on notice of an unreasona-ble risk of harm to patrons which imposed a duty on defendants to maintain armed security guards for the safety of paying patrons.

The jury returned a verdict of $40,000 for plaintiff. Defendants appeal as of right.

Defendants say that while crime has, unfortunately, become such a way of life as to be generally foreseeable, this does not mean that all businesses have a duty to hire armed guards to protect customers. Defendants say this Court should determine, as a matter of law, that defendants had no duty to maintain armed guards.

In this connection, defendants urge that we consider the economic effect of a holding (albeit by jury verdict) that businesses in high crime areas have a duty to maintain armed guards to secure the safety of patrons and other business invitees. We are not only mindful of this economic effect, but we also are aware that "high crime areas" exist not only in the large cities, but also in the suburbs and many medium-sized cities throughout the state.

Nevertheless, it is also clear that defendants, in conducting their business, undertook certain duties regarding business invitees. Among other things, the court instructed the jury as follows:

> "Now, in considering whether there was an act of negligence, the law provides that when a person is invited on the premises of a business he is a business invitee, and the person doing the inviting has a certain duty to that individual. That duty is, in this state, to use reasonable care for the safety of that person. Now, it is going to be up to you to determine what are the requirements of using reasonable care for the safety of the Plaintiff  *  *  *."

As stated by the court, once such a duty is established, it is for the jury to determine the specific standard of care applicable. In this case, presumably the jury did determine the specific standard of care required of this theatre owner. Under present law, that determination must be affirmed.

V. J. BRENNAN, J. (dissenting). I am forced to dissent from a portion of my brother BEASLEY's majority opinion in this case for the same basic reasons expressed in McNeal v. Henry, 82 Mich.App. 88; 266 N.W.2d 46 (1978). Though I agree that defendants owed plaintiff a duty of reasonable care due to plaintiff's status as a business invitee, I would conceive the legal definition of that duty, which is a matter for the court to decide, in terms which do not extend to the kind of unforeseeable conduct exhibited by plaintiff's assailant. Defendants' duty will not legally extend to this kind of harm. Very simply then, I do not believe that an unprovoked attack by a stranger with a revolver is the kind of harm foreseeably related to defendants' duty to protect their patrons.

Consequently, I would find that, as a matter of law, defendants could not be held responsible for the type of unforeseeable harm consequent to this unprovoked attack. The court was thus in error by denying defendants' motion for directed verdict since that motion properly requested the trial court to decide a legal question, which in my opinion should have been resolved by directing a verdict for defendants. Therefore, I would reverse the court below.

---

## ROWLAND v. CHRISTIAN

Supreme Court of California, 1968.
62 Cal.2d 108, 70 Cal.Rptr. 97, 443 P.2d 561.

PETERS, Justice.

Plaintiff appeals from a summary judgment for defendant Nancy Christian in this personal injury action.

In his complaint plaintiff alleged that about November 1, 1963, Miss Christian told the lessors of her apartment that the knob of the cold water faucet on the bathroom basin was cracked and should be replaced; that on November 30, 1963, plaintiff entered the apartment at the invitation of Miss Christian; that he was injured while using the bathroom fixtures, suffering severed tendons and nerves of his right hand; and that he has incurred medical and hospital expenses. He further alleged that the bathroom fixtures were dangerous, that Miss Christian was aware of the dangerous condition, and that his injuries were proximately caused by the negligence of Miss Christian. Plaintiff sought recovery of his medical and hospital expenses, loss of wages, damage to his clothing, and $100,000 general damages. It does not appear from the complaint whether the crack in the faucet handle was obvious to an ordinary inspection or was concealed.

Miss Christian filed an answer containing a general denial except that she alleged that plaintiff was a social guest and admitted the allegations that she had told the lessors that the faucet was defective and that it should be replaced. Miss Christian also alleged contributory negligence and assumption of the risk. In connection with the defenses, she alleged that plaintiff had failed to use his "eyesight" and knew of the condition of the premises. Apart from these allegations, Miss Christian did not allege whether the crack in the faucet handle was obvious or concealed.

Miss Christian's affidavit in support of the motion for summary judgment alleged facts showing that plaintiff was a social guest in her apartment when, as he was using the bathroom, the porcelain handle of one of the water faucets broke in his hand causing injuries to his hand and that plaintiff had used the bathroom on a prior occasion. In opposition to the motion for summary judgment, plaintiff filed an affidavit stating that immediately prior to the accident he told Miss Christian that he was going to use the bathroom facilities, that she had known for two weeks prior to the accident that the faucet handle that caused injury was cracked, that she warned the manager of the building of the condition, that nothing was done to repair the condition of the handle, that she did not say anything to plaintiff as to the condition of the handle, and that when plaintiff turned off the faucet the handle broke in his hands severing the tendons and medial nerve in his right hand.

\* \* \*

Section 1714 of the Civil Code provides: "Every one is responsible, not only for the result of his willful acts, but also for an injury occasioned to another by his want of ordinary care or skill in the management of his property or person, except so far as the latter has, willfully or by want of ordinary care, brought the injury upon himself. \* \* \*

\* \* \*

One of the areas where this court and other courts have departed from the fundamental concept that a man is liable for injuries caused by his carelessness is with regard to the liability of a possessor of land for injuries to persons who have entered upon that land. It has been suggested that the special rules regarding liability of the possessor of land are due to historical considerations stemming from the high place which land has traditionally held in English and American thought, the dominance and prestige of the landowning class in England during the formative period of the rules governing the possessor's liability, and the heritage of feudalism.

The departure from the fundamental rule of liability for negligence has been accomplished by classifying the plaintiff either as a trespasser, licensee, or invitee and then adopting special rules as to the duty owed by the possessor to each of the classifications. Generally speaking a trespasser is a person who enters or remains upon land of another without a privilege to do so; a licensee is a person like a social guest who is not an invitee and who is privileged to enter or remain upon land by virtue of the possessor's consent, and an invitee is a business visitor who is invited or permitted to enter or remain on the land for a purpose directly or indirectly connected with business dealings between them.

Although the invitor owes the invitee a duty to exercise ordinary care to avoid injuring him the general rule is that a trespasser and licensee or social guest are obliged to take the premises as they find them insofar as any alleged defective condition thereon may exist, and that the possessor of the land owes them only the duty of refraining from wanton or willful injury. The ordinary justification for the general rule severely restricting the occupier's liability to social guests is based on the theory that the guest should not expect special precautions to be made on his account and that if the host does not inspect and maintain his property the guest should not expect this to be done on his account.

An increasing regard for human safety has led to a retreat from this position, and an exception to the general rule limiting liability has been made as to active operations where an obligation to exercise reasonable care for the protection of the licensee has been imposed on the occupier of land. In an apparent attempt to avoid the general rule limiting liability, courts have broadly defined active operations, sometimes giving the term a strained construction in cases involving dangers known to the occupier.

\* \* \*

Another exception to the general rule limiting liability has been recognized for cases where the occupier is aware of the dangerous condition, the condition amounts to a concealed trap, and the guest is unaware of the trap. \* \* \*

The cases dealing with the active negligence and the trap exceptions are indicative of the subtleties and confusion which have resulted from application of the common law principles governing the liability of the possessor of land. Similar confusion and complexity exist as to the definitions of trespasser, licensee, and invitee.

\* \* \*

There is another fundamental objection to the approach to the question of the possessor's liability on the basis of the common law distinctions based upon the status of the injured party as a trespasser, licensee, or invitee. Complexity can be borne and confusion remedied where the underlying principles governing liability are based upon proper considerations. Whatever may have been the historical justifications for the common law distinctions, it is clear that those distinctions are not justified in the light of our modern society and that the complexity and confusion which has arisen is not due to difficulty in applying the original common law rules—they are all too easy to apply in their original formulation—but is due to the attempts to apply just rules in our modern society within the ancient terminology.

Without attempting to labor all of the rules relating to the possessor's liability, it is apparent that the classifications of trespasser, licensee, and invitee, the immunities from liability predicated upon those classifications, and the exceptions to those immunities, often do not reflect the major factors which should determine whether immunity should be conferred upon the possessor of land. Some of those factors, including the closeness of the connection between the injury and the defendant's conduct, the moral blame attached to the defendant's conduct, the policy of preventing future harm, and the prevalence and availability of insurance, bear little, if any, relationship to the classifications of trespasser, licensee and invitee and the existing rules conferring immunity.

\* \* \*

A man's life or limb does not become less worthy of protection by the law nor a loss less worthy of compensation under the law because he has come upon the land of another without permission or with permission but without a business purpose. Reasonable people do not ordinarily vary their conduct depending upon such matters, and to focus upon the status of the injured party as a trespasser, licensee, or invitee in order to determine the question whether the landowner has a duty of care, is contrary to our modern social mores and humanitarian values. The common law rules obscure rather than illuminate the proper considerations which should govern determination of the question of duty.

It bears repetition that the basic policy of this state set forth by the Legislature in section 1714 of the Civil Code is that everyone is responsible for an injury caused to another by his want of ordinary care or skill in the management of his property. The factors which may in particular cases warrant departure from this fundamental principle do not warrant the wholesale immunities resulting from the common law classifications, and we are satisfied that continued adherence to the common law distinctions can only lead to injustice or, if we are to avoid injustice, further fictions with the resulting complexity and confusion. We decline to follow and perpetuate such rigid classifications. The proper test to be applied to the liability of the possessor of land in accordance with section 1714 of the Civil Code is whether in the management of his property he has acted as a reasonable man in view of the probability of injury to others, and, although the plaintiff's status as a trespasser, licensee, or invitee may in the light of the facts giving rise to such status have some bearing on the question of liability, the status is not determinative.

Once the ancient concepts as to the liability of the occupier of land are stripped away, the status of the plaintiff relegated to its proper place in determining such liability, and ordinary principles of negligence applied, the result in the instant case presents no substantial difficulties. As we have seen, when we view the matters presented on the motion for summary judgment as we must, we must assume defendant Miss Christian was aware that the faucet handle was defective and dangerous, that the defect was not obvious, and that plaintiff was about to come in contact with the defective condition, and under the undisputed facts she neither remedied the condition nor warned plaintiff of it. Where the occupier of land is aware of a concealed condition involving in the absence of precautions an unreasonable risk of harm to those coming in contact with it and is aware that a person on the premises is about to come in contact with it, the trier of fact can reasonably conclude that a failure to warn or to repair the condition constitutes negligence. Whether or not a guest has a right to expect that his host will remedy dangerous conditions on his account, he should reasonably be entitled to rely upon a warning of the dangerous condition so that he, like the host, will be in a position to take special precautions when he comes in contact with it.

\*    \*    \*

The judgment is reversed.

## PROBLEMS

1. Eunice and Jane, along with the latter's two-year-old daughter, entered a store to purchase some hosiery. Eunice was accustomed to having a saleswoman by the name of Nell wait on her. Informed that Nell was in an alteration room at the rear of the store, Eunice sought permission to go there. Eunice was granted permission, and, upon entering a partition at the rear of the store leading to the alteration room, she fell down some steps leading to the basement. Eunice was seriously injured and now seeks damages from the store. Is the store liable? Why?

2. Frank was driving his automobile on a public highway when he was involved in a collision with an automobile driven by Merrill. Merrill was negligently exiting a private driveway maintained by Curley's Tavern when the accident occurred. Frank claims the driveway was poorly maintained; trees and poles obstructed Merrill's view, and the surface of the driveway caused Merrill's car to skid. Frank now seeks damages from Curley's Tavern. Is Curley's Tavern liable? Why?

3. Cities Service Company operates a phosphate rock mine in Polk County, Florida. On December 3, 1971, there was a break in a dam in one of Cities Service's settling ponds. As a result, approximately one billion gallons of phosphate slime escaped from the pond into Whidden Creek, which flows into Peace River, thereby killing countless numbers of fish and inflicting other damage. The State of Florida filed a suit against Cities Service for damages, claiming Cities Service is strictly liable for all damages because of its hazardous use of the land. Decide the case, giving reasons for your decision.

4. Depue was in the business of buying cattle, hides, and furs from farmers. Depue visited Flateau's farm for the purpose of buying cattle, but due to his late arrival he decided to inspect the cattle the following morning. Depue's request to stay the night at Flateau's house was denied but he was offered supper, which he accepted. Depue had recently been ill and when he completed dinner, he nearly collapsed. He was assisted into his wagon by Flateau's son who propped Depue up and threw the reins to the horses over Depue's shoulders. Depue was found the next day nearly frozen to death. Depue had to have several fingers amputated and now seeks damages from Flateau. Is he entitled to damages? Why?

5. Wade owned and operated a liquor store in Cordele, Georgia; he also maintained a cigarette vending machine which had been burglarized several times in the past. In an attempt to scare vandals, Wade booby-trapped the vending machine with dynamite. Robert, a minor, attempted to break into the vending machine and was killed by the dynamite charge. Robert's mother sues Wade for wrongful death. Is she entitled to damages? Why?

6. The North Carolina State Highway Commission leased land from Harry for the purpose of excavating and removing land and gravel. Harry and his family lived on a small portion of the land. As a result of the excavation by the Commission, a large pit was created which ultimately filled with water. It reached a depth of 12 feet and was used by neighboring children for swimming. While walking on a sandbar, Harry's thirteen-year-old daughter slipped into deep water and drowned in the pit. Is the State Highway Commission liable for damages? Why?

7.  James, a twenty-one-year-old student, was vacationing at Stratton Mountain in Vermont.  Having skied a total of eight hours prior to this trip, James was looking forward to spending considerable time on the slopes.  While skiing on a novice slope, James fell and hit his head on a rock.  He was paralyzed from the neck down as a result of the fall.  James claims the fall was caused by a bush or branch at the edge of the trail and sues the Stratton Mountain Resort for $1,250,000, claiming the slope was negligent in not maintaining the slopes properly.  Is the resort liable? Why?

8.  Mary was a night student at Atlanta University.  When Mary was leaving class on the night of March 27, 1972, the lights on the front of her classroom building were not on.  Although Mary was familiar with the walkway and walked carefully toward a parking lot, she fell on a brick that protruded from the walk.  Mary was injured by the fall and sued the university for damages.  The university defended the suit by arguing that it did not know of the protruding brick.  Is Mary entitled to damages? Why?

9.  Stafford drove to Food World one rainy afternoon to do her grocery shopping.  As a result of the rain, puddles of water had settled on the grocery store floor.  The floor was a terrazzo floor and became slippery when wet.  The management of the store attempted to keep the floor dry by mopping it at regular intervals and providing a rubber mat on which customers could wipe their feet.  Stafford entered the store, did not wipe her feet, and was injured when she fell in a puddle of water.  Is the store liable for Stafford's injuries?  Why?

10.  Rose went shopping at Colby's, Inc.  After completing her shopping, Rose was leaving the store when she decided to call her sister.  She was directed to a telephone in an unlighted vestibule.  While attempting to read the telephone directory, Rose fell down an unguarded stairway and was seriously injured.  She claims the store failed to warn her of the dangerous conditions and seeks damages.  Is the store liable?  Why?

# Chapter 13

## LEGAL REGULATION OF LAND USE

> Every man holds his property subject to the general right of the community to regulate its use to whatever degree the public welfare may require it.
>
> Theodore Roosevelt, 1910

In pioneer America, the person who acquired fee simple ownership of real estate had almost complete freedom to use the land for any purpose. The owner was free to build a house or factory or store; he could clear the land and farm it; he could erect a gaudy structure and tasteless signs; or he might develop the property into a place of natural beauty.

However, as population increased, the United States became more settled and urbanized. This general trend brought with it a number of restrictions on an individual's freedom to use and develop real estate. Sometimes the restrictions were created through the common law of torts, sometimes through private agreements. In most cases, though, the restrictions came about through government ownership and regulation of real estate. This chapter will cover both the private and the public control of land use. Special types of public control in the form of state and federal land use and environmental laws will be discussed in Chapter 14.

## I. PRIVATE CONTROL OF LAND USE

### A. COMMON LAW TORT REMEDIES

In Chapters 11 and 12, tort remedies that affect the ownership and use of real estate were examined. Four of these torts—nuisance, trespass, strict liability, and negligence—have often been used to limit the use of land.[1] Of these torts, the nuisance theory is the most popular, although a private nuisance action cannot be an unqualified and universal remedy for all abuses of land. For instance, a court will balance the economic harm done to the plaintiff with the economic loss that would result if the defendant is enjoined from using the land for its present purpose. Furthermore, courts can only consider the limited interests that are represented by parties in each private nuisance suit. As the court noted in Boomer v. Atlantic Cement Co.,[2] "it seems manifest that the judicial establishment is neither

---

1. Comment, *Environmental Land-Use Control: Common Law and Statutory Approaches*, 28 U.Miami L.Rev. 135 (1973).

2. 26 N.Y.2d 219, 309 N.Y.S.2d 312, 257 N.E.2d 870 (1970).

equipped in the limited nature of any judgment it can pronounce nor prepared to lay down and implement an effective policy for the elimination of air pollution. This is an area beyond the circumference of one private lawsuit. It is a direct responsibility for government and should not thus be undertaken as an incident to solving a dispute between property owners and a single cement plant—one of many—in the Hudson River Valley."

Despite these problems, the private nuisance action remains more popular than the public nuisance action because public officials often are reluctant to prosecute nuisance cases, and because governmental acquiescence in the nuisance will prevent the government from succeeding in its action. Furthermore, private litigants cannot start a public nuisance action unless they prove that their injury is different in kind from the public injury.[3] For instance in Kuehn v. City of Milwaukee,[4] a professional fisherman on Lake Michigan was denied injunctive relief against city authorities who were dumping garbage into the lake; he could not prove that his injury was unique because the waters of Lake Michigan were used by other members of the public for fishing. In a few states, recent decisions have allowed relief where the private injury is sufficiently different in degree, and this view has been adopted in the Restatement of Torts.[5]

The second tort theory, trespass, is available in cases where the use of one person's land results in a physical invasion of another person's land by visible or even invisible matter. One court held that the intrusion of fluoride particulates from a Reynolds Metals Company plant constituted a trespass: "In this atomic age even the uneducated know the great and awful force contained in the atom and what it can do to a man's property if it is released. In fact, the now famous equation $E = mc^2$ has taught us that mass and energy are equivalents and that our concept of 'things' must be reframed. If these observations on science in relation to the law of trespass should appear theoretical and unreal in the abstract, they become very practical and real to the possessor of land when the unseen force cracks the foundation of his house. The force is just as real if it is chemical in nature and must be awakened by the intervention of another agency before it does harm."[6]

The remaining two tort theories, strict liability and negligence, are available to restrict land use even in cases when the owner did not intend to cause injury. As noted in Chapter 12, strict liability requires proof that the landowner was engaged in ultrahazardous activities or that he was making a non-natural use of the land, whereas a

3. Note, *Private Remedies for Water Pollution*, 70 Colum.L.Rev. 734 (1970).

4. 83 Wis. 583, 53 N.W. 912 (1892).

5. Restatement, Second, Torts § 821C, Comment c at 15 (Tent.Draft No. 17, 1971).

6. Martin v. Reynolds Metals Co., 221 Or. 86, 342 P.2d 790 (1959).

negligence action requires the plaintiff to prove first the standard of care and then that the standard was not met.

The common law theories, taken together, are often ineffective because legal action is frequently slow and expensive—it is difficult to prove the elements of the tort and to obtain an injunction, and courts are reluctant to act before the harm occurs. Yet these actions are important because, in the words of one commentator, they "will continue to be the major tool in individual rights oriented land use disputes." [7]

## B.  VOLUNTARY RESTRICTIONS ON LAND USE

There are three prominent private, voluntary restrictions on land use. Two of these restrictions—the use of easements, and defeasible fees that terminate when a certain event occurs—have been examined in previous chapters. The third type of voluntary restriction utilizes a special type of contract, a covenant running with the land.

Like any other contract, a covenant running with the land involves mutual promises between the parties, but the covenant is unique because it not only binds the parties but also later owners of the land. The covenant is distinguished from an easement in that the easement is an interest in land, while the covenant is merely a contractual promise that passes with the land.[8] The covenant may also be distinguished from the defeasible fee; a defeasible fee will terminate if the promise is not kept, but a breach of covenant results in an action for damages or injunctive relief. For example, in one case a person deeded land to a buyer with the restriction that "this conveyance is upon the condition that no windows shall be placed in the north wall of the house." When the buyer later placed windows in the north wall, the seller commenced an action charging that the buyer must forfeit his estate. The court held for the seller on the grounds that the promise constituted a condition, not a covenant. The court noted that "we cannot help the folly of parties who consent to take estates upon onerous conditions, by converting conditions into covenants.  .  .  .   The grantee was not surprised into the bargain, nor those who hold under him, the condition being inserted in all the deeds  .  .  .   it was a voluntary bargain, and if they did not choose to take the estate they should have rejected it altogether." [9]

1.  **Creation of Covenants.** Covenants must be created by signing a document, often a deed, that complies with the Statute of Frauds. Typically the deed will spell out restrictions on land use or will refer to a recorded plat containing details of the restrictions. In

---

7. Comment, *Environmental Land-Use Control: Common Law and Statutory Approaches*, 28 Miami L.Rev. 135, 152 (1973).

8. C. Smith and R. Boyer, Survey of the Law of Property 348 (2nd ed. 1971).

9. Gray v. Blanchard, 25 Mass. (8 Pick.) 284 (1829).

either event, the written covenant must have three characteristics: (1) the writing must include an intention that the covenant run with the land, for example by use of the words "assigns" or "successor;" (2) the covenant must "touch and concern" the land—that is, the promise must relate to the land in such a way as to affect its value; (3) there must be privity of estate which, although subject to many interpretations, generally means that if a party is to be bound by a covenant, he must hold the same estate as the person who originally made the promise.[10]  If any one of the requirements is not met, then the covenant operates as a binding contract only against the original parties to the contract and does not bind later purchasers of the real estate.  For instance, assume that Orville enters into a written contract to provide transportation to his neighboring landowner, Wilbur. If Wilbur later sells his land to Charles without assigning this right, Charles is not entitled to the transportation because this type of right is personal to Wilbur and does not "touch and concern" the land.[11]

The above requirements have been established by courts at law in damage action suits for breach of covenant.  However, in many cases the plaintiff brings the action in an equity court because he wants the court to issue an injunction to prevent further violations of the covenant.  Courts of equity have traditionally been more liberal in enforcing restrictions on land use and, apart from the writing requirement, require only (1) that the covenant was intended to operate as a restriction on land use and (2) that later purchasers have actual or constructive notice of the restriction.  Thus, the major difference between covenants at law and equitable servitudes is that privity of estate is not required in the courts of equity.[12]

2.  **Interpretation of Covenants.**  The interpretation of covenants has been an especially troublesome problem.  Courts have adopted the following general test: "Restrictive covenants, being in derogation of the common law right to use land for all lawful purposes, are to be narrowly construed and are not to be extended by implication. If their language is of doubtful meaning, it will be construed against rather than in favor of the covenant." [13]  For instance, in Bear v. Bernstein,[14] the courts faced the legal issue of whether a duplex or four-unit apartment house could be built when a restrictive covenant in a deed provided that the land was to be "used only for residential purposes  .  .  .  and that only one residence shall be erected on .  .  .  the lot."  The court noted that a number of courts have interpreted this language to mean there shall not be plurality of occupan-

---

10. C. Smith and R. Boyer, Survey of the Law of Property 345, 348 (2nd ed. 1971).

11. The Wiggins Ferry Co. v. The Ohio and Mississippi Rwy. Co., 94 Ill. 83 (1879).

12. C. Smith and R. Boyer, Survey of the Law of Property 368, 369 (2nd ed. 1971).

13. Rossini v. Freeman, 136 Conn. 321, 71 A.2d 98 (1949).

14. 251 Ala. 230, 36 So.2d 483 (1948).

cy, while many other courts maintain it only prohibits plurality of houses or buildings. The court adopted the second view on the basis of the following standards: "Though it is the duty of the courts to give full force and effect to any restraint placed on the use of property intended by the parties, the rule is that restrictions against its free use and enjoyment are not favored in law and being in derogation of such right, are to be strictly construed against the enforcement thereof. Where the language of the restriction is clear and unambiguous it will, of course, be given its manifest meaning, but its construction will not be extended by implication or include anything not plainly prohibited and all doubts and ambiguities must be resolved against the party seeking enforcement. The fact that eminent courts of our country have entertained diametrically opposing views as to the intent and meaning of such character of restriction but makes it apodictic that such a covenant is to the judicial mind ambiguous and doubtful and emphasizes the necessity of calling into play these well-known rules of construction, resulting in resolving the ambiguity and doubt against the appellee who here seeks to enforce the restraint." See Simons v. Work of God Corp., infra.

Even if a covenant has been stated in clear and unambiguous language, courts consider the following issues in deciding whether to enforce a covenant.

a. *Change in the Neighborhood.* Two types of change in the neighborhood might result in a decision that land use restrictions are no longer enforceable. The first type of change occurs within the restricted area where certain owners act in violation of the restrictions with the apparent acquiescence of other owners. In Watts v. Fritz,[15] a covenant restriction stated that no more than one house could be built on each lot in a subdivision. When Fritz attempted to subdivide his lot so that two houses could be built thereon, Watts claimed that Fritz was acting in violation of the restrictions. The court held for Fritz because there had been other violations within the subdivision: "[T]he evidence showed that there had been several subdividings of lots in the subdivision with the building of more than one dwelling on a lot as originally platted. Plaintiff, himself, acknowledged that one such subdividing and building took place across the street from him after he purchased his property. . . . There is no showing that plaintiff took any action to prevent the subdividing of the lot across the street from him or the building of a dwelling on it other than to talk to the developer and possibly an attorney. No positive preventative action was taken. Minor violations of a restriction will not prohibit the subsequent enforcement of it. However, where there has been acquiescence of prior violations of the very substance of a general plan or particular restriction, the plaintiff will be held to have waived any right he may have had to enforce it."

15. 29 Ill.2d 517, 194 N.E.2d 276 (1963).

The other type of change occurs outside the area restricted by a covenant. If the change in the surrounding area is so great as to make enforcement of the covenant oppressive and inequitable, courts will refuse to enforce the restrictions. In Norris v. Williams,[16] a one-acre parcel of land was restricted to use for residential purposes only. In the thirty years following the creation of the restriction, the parcel was surrounded by businesses, including a bowling alley, restaurant, paint shop, bakery, liquor store, filling station, food store, hardware store, tobacco shop, men's clothing store, pool room, laundry, barber shop and a sewage disposal plant. The court determined that the restriction should no longer be enforced: "Under the circumstances now existing, the covenant made by Grace and his wife in 1917 is no longer effective for the purpose for which it was imposed. It is evident that the purpose of the restriction was to make the locality a suitable one for residences; but, owing to the general growth of the town, and the development of the neighborhood west of the avenue as a business district, this purpose can no longer be accomplished. It is conceded that there is no one who could enforce the restriction. But even if it could be enforced, it would not restore to the locality its residential character. It would, therefore, be oppressive and inequitable to give effect to the covenant. As the changed condition of the locality has resulted from causes other than breach of the covenant, it is clear that to enforce the restriction could have no effect other than to injure and harass the owners without effecting the purpose for which it was intended."

b. *Zoning Ordinances.* In the *Norris* case, the land in question had been zoned for commercial use. This factor alone would not invalidate the restriction, for a covenant may establish a more limited use of the land than allowed by a zoning ordinance. In cases where the zoning ordinance conflicts with the restrictive covenant, however, the zoning ordinance will prevail.

In the case of Lidke v. Martin,[17] the defendants hoped to erect apartment buildings on a lot that was restricted by a covenant to single-family dwellings. The zoning regulations allowed apartment buildings on the property, and the covenant provided that it was not to be "construed as conflicting with any terms or regulations of the present or future Jefferson County zoning ordinance." The court held that the apartments could not be built because this provision merely incorporated into the covenant any sections of the zoning ordinance which provided more restrictive standards than the covenant.

c. *Expiration Time.* Another problem faced by the *Norris* court was that the restriction in question provided that the parcel be used for residential purposes for a period of fifty years. Although the court held that the covenant would not be enforced because of

16. 189 Md. 73, 54 A.2d 331 (1947).     17. 31 Colo.App. 40, 500 P.2d 1184 (1972).

changed conditions, had there been no change in neighborhood conditions, courts would enforce the covenant for the time stated. And if no time is stated, according to the *Norris* court, "it will be implied that some reasonable limitation adapted to the nature of the case was intended, and the restriction will be construed as extending for no longer period of time than the nature of the circumstances and the purposes of the imposition indicate as reasonable." Several states have enacted statutes stipulating that all covenants, conditions, and restrictions are valid for only a limited period of time, for example, thirty years.[18]

d. *Implied Reciprocal Restrictions.* In some cases, the owner of a subdivision will place restrictions on some lots when he sells them but will fail to mention restrictions in the deeds to the other lots. Are the owners of the lots without restrictions legally bound by the covenants? As a general rule, they will be bound if the restrictions are part of a general plan of development and if the purchasers at least had notice of the restrictions. In Allen v. City of Detroit,[19] an owner of eleven lots sold ten of the lots with restrictions limiting their use to residential purposes. The eleventh lot was sold to the City of Detroit without restrictions, and Detroit planned to build a firehouse on the property. However, a court held that the restrictions were binding on Detroit. "The law is well settled that building restrictions of the character shown are in the nature of reciprocal negative easements and may be created upon a division and conveyance in severalty to different grantees of an entire tract. That a portion of the conveyances do not contain the restriction will not defeat the same. Although some of the lots may have written restrictions imposed upon them and others not, if the general plan has been maintained from its inception, if it has been understood, accepted, relied on, and acted upon by all in interest, it is binding and enforceable on all *inter se.* It goes with the land and is equally binding upon all purchasers with notice."

e. *Race Restrictions.* The Fourteenth Amendment prohibits the states from interfering with an individual's rights by engaging in discriminatory conduct, and among the civil rights protected are the rights to acquire, enjoy, own, and dispose of property. This raises the following legal issue: If individuals create discriminatory restrictions, may the states enforce the restrictions? The Supreme Court addressed this issue in Shelley v. Kraemer,[20] where a deed restriction provided that the real estate was not to be "occupied by any person not of the Caucasian race, it being intended hereby to restrict the use of said property . . . against the occupancy as owners or tenants of any portion of said property for resident or other purpose by people of the Negro or Mongolian Race." The Supreme Court held

---

18. Minn.Stat.Ann. § 500.20.

19. 167 Mich. 464, 133 N.W. 317 (1911).

20. 334 U.S. 1, 68 S.Ct. 836, 92 L.Ed. 1161 (1947).

that such restrictions alone do not violate the Fourteenth Amendment as long as no state action is involved. However, the Court concluded that this type of restriction could not be enforced by state courts because the judicial proceedings would constitute state action. "We hold that in granting judicial enforcement of the restrictive agreements in these cases, the States have denied petitioners the equal protection of the laws and that, therefore, the action of the state courts cannot stand. We have noted that freedom from discrimination by the States in the enjoyment of property rights was among the basic objectives sought to be effectuated by the framers of the Fourteenth Amendment. That such discrimination has occurred in these cases is clear. Because of the race or color of these petitioners they have been denied rights of ownership or occupancy enjoyed as a matter of course by other citizens of different race or color. The Fourteenth Amendment declares 'that all persons whether colored or white, shall stand equal before the law of the States, and, in regard to the colored race, for whose protection the amendment was primarily designed, that no discrimination shall be made against them by law because of their color.' "

Beyond enforcing the covenants, state courts may not award damages for breach of the restrictions. In Barrows v. Jackson,[21] the Supreme Court declared that if a state sanctioned the use of restrictive covenants by awarding damages for their breach, the result "would be to encourage the use of restrictive covenants. . . . [which] would constitute state action as surely as it was state action to enforce such covenants in equity."

## II.  PUBLIC CONTROL OF LAND USE

There are two types of governmental control of land use. First, the government itself owns and controls a vast amount of the nation's total acreage. Second, the government regulates privately owned real estate through zoning regulations, discussed below, and through state and federal land use plans and environmental legislation, which are the subject of the next chapter.

### A.  GOVERNMENTAL OWNERSHIP OF REAL ESTATE

The federal government owns over 750 million acres or approximately one-third of the nation's land. Over 179 million acres of this land have been reserved as national parks and forests and over 53 million acres have been set aside for specific uses, for example by the Atomic Energy Commission. The Bureau of Land Management administers more than 465 million acres of federal land not set aside for special uses, the Forest Service administers about one-fourth of federal lands, and the National Park Service and the Bureau of Sport

21. 346 U.S. 249, 73 S.Ct. 1031, 97 L. Ed. 1586 (1953).

Fisheries and Wildlife administer smaller acreages. One-half of public lands are in Alaska, where the United States ownership comprises 96 percent of the state. Most of the remaining federal lands are in eleven western states: in Nevada, the United States owns 87 percent of the state; in Utah, 66 percent; Idaho, 64 percent; Oregon, 53 percent; Wyoming, 48 percent; California, 45 percent; Arizona, 43 percent; Colorado, 36 percent; New Mexico, 34 percent; Montana, 30 percent; and Washington, 30 percent.[22]

Approximately 700 million acres of federal land were part of the original public domain, while the remaining acreage has been acquired from private owners.[23] Federal or state governments use three methods to acquire privately owned land: escheat, condemnation, and dedication.

1. **Escheat.** In feudal law, if a tenant in possession of land died leaving no heirs or if the tenant committed a felony, his land would revert to the lord of the manor or to the crown. In the United States, the escheat doctrine provides that when a person dies leaving no one to inherit his property, the property passes to the state.

2. **Eminent Domain.** The state has the right to condemn, that is, to take, private property for public purposes. This right, called eminent domain, has been described as "an inseparable attribute of sovereignty—an inherent power founded on the primary duty of government to serve the common need and advance the general welfare."[24] According to the Annals of Tacitus, this right goes back at least to Roman times; the term "eminent domain" possibly originated with Grotius, who declared that the state may take or destroy property for the public good, but he noted that "when this is done the state is bound to make good the loss to those who lose their property."[25]

In the United States, the power of the federal government to take private property is recognized in the Fifth Amendment to the Constitution, which provides, "nor shall private property be taken for public use, without just compensation." The Fourteenth Amendment states that "no state shall . . . deprive any person of life, liberty, or property, without due process of law"; this has been interpreted to require states to comply with the Fifth Amendment when they take private property, although in most cases the same result would be reached under state constitutions. For both state and federal condemnation, then, the key questions are these: Is there a public use, and was there just compensation?

---

22. Public Land Law Review Commission, One Third of the Nation's Land 19–30 (1970).

23. Id.

24. Bergen County Sewer Authority v. Borough of Little Ferry, 5 N.J. 548, 76 A.2d 680 (1950).

25. Valentine v. Lamont, 25 N.J.Super. 342, 96 A.2d 417 (1953).

a. *Public Use.* Although the public use requirement is often litigated, as a general rule courts are reluctant to define the term absolutely because, as noted by one court, public use "changes with varying conceptions of the scope and function of government, and other differing circumstances brought about by an increase in population and new modes of communication and transportation." [26] Despite the lack of an absolute definition, the question of whether or not the use is public is a judicial question and a question to be measured by the constitutional standard.[27] In deciding this question, however, courts will not consider whether the public use was necessary or whether other property would be better suited, as these are questions for the governmental authority.

The public use question often arises when the extent of the government's condemnation is in issue. For example, there may be a question whether condemnation proceedings resulted in the government's taking an easement, a fee simple defeasible, or a fee simple absolute. In such cases, a court must determine the nature of the public use, for the general rule is that "in condemnation proceedings an estate of such quality may be taken as is reasonably necessary for the accomplishment of the purpose in aid of which the proceedings are brought." [28]

In many cases the public use issue is raised when the government initially condemns private property and then sells or leases the property to private individuals. This often happens when local governmental agencies engaged in slum clearance projects acquire the slum area by eminent domain and then sell the land to private individuals or companies for redevelopment. In such cases, the public use requirement is generally met because the purpose of the condemnation is to eliminate the slum area. According to one court, "Slum areas, because of the congestion, filth and unsanitary conditions which are their ever-lasting qualities, are the breeding places of crime, immorality and disease. These evils necessarily and inevitably strike at the heart of the happiness and well being of all the people of a community. They cannot run rampant in any part of a community without stretching their tentacles menacingly throughout its entire length and breadth. . . . Any purpose leading toward [slum clearance] . . . is a public purpose." [29]

Condemnation has been upheld as a public use in other cases where a city takes land for parking facilities and then leases the land to a private company,[30] or where the state condemns land adjoining a

26. Barnes v. City of New Haven, 140 Conn. 8, 98 A.2d 523 (1953).

27. Perellis v. Mayor & City Council of Baltimore, 190 Md. 86, 57 A.2d 341 (1948).

28. Valentine v. Lamont, 25 N.J.Super. 342, 96 A.2d 417 (1953).

29. Chapman v. Huntington Housing Auth., 121 W.Va. 319, 3 S.E.2d 502 (1939).

30. Barnes v. City of New Haven, 140 Conn. 8, 98 A.2d 523 (1953).

proposed turnpike for construction of gasoline stations and restaurants which are to be leased to private individuals. One court, discussing restaurants along the turnpike, came to the conclusion: "Undoubtedly many travellers will seek food on their way across the State. It will be a great convenience to them to find it at a place where they can park their vehicles without interfering with traffic and without the necessity of looking for an exit, searching for a restaurant, and then re-entering the turnpike. . . . We think restaurants such as are provided for in the act are part of the turnpike, and that a reasonable amount of land taken for them is land 'needed for the actual construction' of the highway and is devoted to a public use." [31]

b. *Just Compensation.* When the government takes fee simple ownership of real estate, the owner is entitled to the fair market value of the land. The value is determined by considering the most profitable use of the land, even though the land was being used for other purposes at the time of the taking. For instance, in Huie v. Campbell,[32] the city of New York condemned a farm that was used as a dairy farm and a boarding house for summer guests. After the condemnation but before a hearing to determine compensation, bluestone and flagstone were discovered on the property; the owners claimed that the value of these deposits should have been considered in the compensation award. The court agreed, noting that "the owners are entitled to compensation for the value of the premises for any purpose, irrespective of its previous use."

The condemnation of nonprofit facilities, such as churches, museums, hospitals, and libraries, has caused special problems because of the unique nature of these properties. Instead of applying a "fair market value" test, a federal court recently ruled that a "substitute facilities" test should be used, which will determine the value of an equivalent facility.[33]

Additional problems arise when the condemnation of property results in lost profits or, in the reverse situation, when condemnation results in special benefits. Courts will generally disallow evidence of lost profits because such evidence is often too speculative and the business usually can be moved to another location. However, most courts will allow evidence of lost profits if the profits come from the intrinsic nature of the condemned property, such as real estate used as a stone quarry, as a turnpike, or for agricultural purposes. On the other hand, if the owner of the condemned property receives benefits as a result of the condemnation, should the value of the benefit be deducted from the award? Although a number of approaches have

31. Opinion of the Justices, 330 Mass. 713, 113 N.E.2d 452 (1953).

32. 281 App.Div. 275, 121 N.Y.S.2d 86 (1953).

33. United States v. 564.54 Acres of Land, 506 F.2d 796 (3d Cir. 1974).

been developed by the courts, the trend is to deduct all benefits, even those which the owner shares with the general public, from the condemnation award.[34]

If the government condemns only a part of the property, just compensation is measured by the decrease in fair market value caused by the condemnation: "The general rule for arriving at just compensation for property not taken but adversely affected is the so-called 'before and after' rule; and this poses the question: What was the value before the taking, and what is now the market value after the taking? The owner of property, ordinarily, is entitled to receive the difference between these sums." [35]

c. *Taking.* Although "public use" and "just compensation" questions continue to be raised, the most important issue facing modern courts is determining of whether or not there has been a taking. The issue is easily resolved when the government consciously decides to take an individual's property and begins condemnation proceedings. The issue becomes more complicated, however, when the government uses or regulates property in a manner that restricts the owner in his own use and enjoyment without initiating condemnation proceedings. The general rule governing the issue of whether governmental regulation constitutes a taking was stated by Justice Holmes in Pennsylvania Coal Co. v. Mahon:[36] "Government hardly could go on if to some extent values incident to property could not be diminished without paying for every such change in the general law. As long recognized some values . . . must yield to the police power. But obviously the implied limitation must have its limits or the contract and due process clauses are gone. One fact for consideration in determining such limits is the extent of the diminution. When it reaches a certain magnitude, in most if not all cases there must be an exercise of eminent domain and compensation to sustain the act."

For example, in Householder v. Town of Grand Island,[37] a landowner was limited to using two small strips of his property, one merely a foot wide and the other only eight feet wide, because of a municipal ordinance which required a ninety-foot setback from the street. The court decided that the ordinance resulted in a taking: "Such an ordinance is confiscatory and unenforceable. It is an attempt to accomplish by so-called 'set back ordinance' without any compensation what can legally be done, if at all, only by the exercise of the power of eminent domain." On the other hand, in Horizon Adirondack Corp. v. State,[38] a New York court determined that there

---

34. Board of Commissioners of Dona Ana County v. Gardiner, 57 N.M. 478, 260 P.2d 682 (1953).

35. Board of County Commissioners of Santa Fe County v. Slaugher, 49 N. M. 141, 158 P.2d 859 (1945).

36. 260 U.S. 393, 43 S.Ct. 158, 67 L.Ed. 322 (1922).

37. 36 Misc.2d 862, 114 N.Y.S.2d 852 (1951).

38. 88 Misc.2d 619, 388 N.Y.S.2d 235 (1976).

was no taking of 24,000 acres of land owned by a private developer when the land was subjected to strict land use regulation under the Adirondack Park Agency Act. As a result, under the intensity guidelines and use classifications of the act, the developer was allowed to build only 1,608 dwelling units instead of the 6,955 dwellings originally planned.

If the government regulates or uses private land without bringing condemnation proceedings, the private landowner faces special problems in selecting a remedy. When the government's use of the land has interfered with his own use and enjoyment, the owner might claim damages under a tort theory, for example, nuisance. However, tort theories are often unacceptable because the government is immune from tort liability in some cases, or because a court might prefer injunctive relief over damages. As a result, it has become popular for landowners to reverse the normal condemnation procedure— where the government initiates the action—and sue the government using an "inverse" condemnation theory. The leading inverse condemnation case is United States v. Causby,[39] described in Chapter 3. The Causbys could not bring a traditional tort action on a nuisance theory in that case because at the time of the action the United States was immune from tort liability. However, under the Tucker Act, the United States had consented to be sued on the grounds of an unconstitutional taking or breach of contract. The Causbys claimed that the repeated trespasses over their land at altitudes ranging from eighteen to eighty-three feet constituted a taking and an implied contractual duty to pay for the use of the land. The court determined that the United States was liable for damages because it had taken an easement of flight across the claimants' land.

Although inverse condemnation is commonly raised in cases of aircraft interfering with the use of the land, it is also used in a number of other situations, albeit not always successfully. For instance, in one case the plaintiff operated a successful restaurant business that later was almost destroyed when the state installed a median strip in the road in front of the property. Using an inverse condemnation theory, the plaintiff claimed that the state had taken his property because one-half of the traffic could not conveniently reach his property. The court disagreed, noting that there was no taking "when access to property is merely made 'inconvenient' as opposed to being completely blocked.  .  .  .  The plaintiff's restaurant remains directly accessible from the southbound lanes of Orchard Lake Road. Access to or from the northbound lanes is indirect and difficult—but not impossible. Given the authorities, we are forced to conclude that the plaintiff has suffered an inconvenience, not an unconstitutional taking."[40]  See Penn Central Transp. Co. v. City of New York, infra.

---

**39.**  328 U.S. 256, 66 S.Ct. 1062, 90 L.Ed. 1206 (1946).

**40.**  Biff's Grills Inc. v. State Highway Comm., 75 Mich.App. 154, 254 N.W.2d 824 (1977).

3. **Dedication.** Dedication takes place when a private landowner gives the public the ownership of, or the right to use, his real estate. Under the common law, dedication is based upon estoppel and occurs (1) when the landowner shows an intention that his real estate be used for a public purpose and (2) when there is an acceptance in the form of actual public use.[41] In such cases the public has not acquired ownership of the land but merely the right to use it for a particular purpose, which might be for a park, a wharf, a highway, or a school.[42]

The major problem arising from common law dedication is proving the intention of the owner. Smith owns 100 acres of land which he plans to sell; he decides that he will get more money for his property if he creates a park in the center and tells his neighbors that he is dedicating a defined area for public use as a park. If the people in the area actually use the land as a park, there is a common law dedication.[43] On the other hand, if Jones owns a store and paves a strip of his land between the store and the street so that the public will walk by the store windows, there is no dedication because there is no intention to dedicate to the public.[44]

The more common form of dedication is statutory dedication. In many states, statutes provide that a person who records a plat—a map which subdivides a piece of real estate into lots, streets, parks, and common areas—is offering to dedicate the streets, parks, and common areas to the public. After the offer has been made, the city must accept the offer by taking official action or by public use.[45] Statutory dedication may result in public acquisition of title to the real estate, if the statute and the plat so provide.

The creation of a plat raises three common legal problems, the first two of which relate to dedication. First, the language of the plat that dedicates land to the public is often ambiguous. Thus, courts may have to decide (a) whether the owner wanted to dedicate the land to the public or merely to the subdivision lot owners; (b) whether or not the person making the dedication has retained title to the dedicated area; and (c) whether the dedication restricts the land to certain uses. For instance, if a developer creates a subdivision that includes a park, he should specifically state on the plat that the park is not dedicated to the public but is only for the use of the lot owners, if that is his intent. Without such specific language, a court might determine that the public has the right to use the park.

41. W. Burby, Real Property 284 (3rd ed. 1965).

42. Tiffany, Real Property §§ 538, 542 (abr. 3rd ed. 1970).

43. C. Smith and R. Boyer, Survey of the Law of Property 265 (2nd ed. 1971).

44. Nickel v. University City, 239 S.W. 2d 519 (Mo.1951).

45. W. Burby, Real Property 284 (3rd ed. 1965).

A second problem arises when a municipality attempts to force a developer to dedicate land for streets, sewers, parks, and playgrounds. Whether or not a forced dedication will be allowed often depends on the extent of the dedication, although there is a split of authority among the states. For instance, in one case [46] a statute that authorized cities and counties to require subdividers to dedicate land for park or recreational purposes or to pay a fee in lieu of dedication was held to be constitutional. That court noted, "While Illinois has held an ordinance requiring a subdivider to dedicate land for park purposes to be unconstitutional, Montana has reached a contrary conclusion. New York and Wisconsin have affirmed the validity of statutes requiring either dedication or a fee in lieu thereof. In Connecticut the dedication requirement has been upheld but the requirement that a fee be paid in lieu of dedication was struck down on the ground that its use was not confined for the benefit of the subdivision but to the contrary the fees could be utilized to purchase park land for the residents of the entire town. The rationale of the [majority of] cases affirming constitutionality indicate the dedication statutes are valid under the state's police power. They reason that the subdivider realizes a profit from governmental approval of a subdivision since his land is rendered more valuable by the fact of subdivision, and in return for this benefit the city may require him to dedicate a portion of his land for park purposes whenever the influx of new residents will increase the need for park and recreational facilities."

Finally, a developer faces a number of regulatory problems beyond dedication when he creates a subdivision. Largely as a result of unregulated real estate developments in the 1920s, which led to severe losses by individual investors, states have placed stringent restrictions on developers. The Michigan Subdivision and Control Act of 1967 illustrates the degree of control by the state. This act defines a subdivision as the dividing of land for sale, lease, or development whereby five or more parcels of land are created—each of ten acres or less—over a ten-year period. In creating a subdivision, a developer must first prepare a preliminary plat and submit it to a number of governmental agencies for approval. These agencies may include the local municipality, the county road commission, the county drain commission, the department of state highways, the department of conservation, and the health department. Upon approval of the agencies, a final plat is prepared and recorded which includes certificates from a surveyor, the applicant, the county treasurer, the county plat board, the state treasurer and other governmental agencies. If a developer fails to comply with the act, purchasers may void their sales contracts and the developer may be convicted of a misdemeanor.

    4. **Public Trust Doctrine.** Once the government has acquired title to real estate through escheat, eminent domain, or dedication,

---

46. Associated Home Builders of the Greater East Bay, Inc. v. City of Walnut Creek, 4 Cal.3d 633, 94 Cal.Rptr. 630, 484 P.2d 606 (1971).

what is the government's duty with respect to public lands—beyond specific statutory duties?  A theory that has been popular with environmentalists in recent years views the government as the holder of lands in public trust.  The leading case of Illinois Central Railroad v. Illinois [47] involved an 1869 grant of submerged lands by the Illinois legislature to the Illinois Central Railroad.  The lands extended for one mile along the central business district in Chicago and one mile out from the shoreline—thus covering virtually the entire commercial waterfront of Chicago.  After a few years, the legislature brought an action to have the original grant declared invalid.  The U.S. Supreme Court decided for the legislature on the grounds that the title to the navigable waters of Lake Michigan is "different in character from that which the state holds in lands intended for sale.  .  .  .  It is a title held in trust for the people of the state that they may enjoy the navigation of the waters, carry on commerce over them, and have liberty of fishing therein freed from the obstruction or interferences of private parties."  The principle emerging from this opinion has been summarized as follows: "When a state holds a resource which is available for the free use of the general public, a court will look with considerable skepticism upon any governmental conduct which is calculated either to reallocate that resource to more restricted uses or subject public uses to the self-interest of private parties." [48]  While the public trust doctrine has mainly been applied in cases involving submerged lands or parklands, it is possible that the doctrine may be used whenever governmental regulation is questioned.[49]

## B.  GOVERNMENTAL  REGULATION  OF  PRIVATE  REAL ESTATE

Although modern forms of governmental regulation of private real estate and the environment have developed in recent years, the traditional method of regulation in the United States has involved zoning ordinances enacted by municipalities.  Zoning ordinances originally divided towns and cities into three areas: residential, industrial, and commercial.  In recent years, however, zoning ordinances have become much more complex.  A typical ordinance for a mid-size city, for instance, might include the following zones: (1) Agricultural;  (2) Residential, often with a large number of subclassifications for various types of single-family or multiple-family dwellings;  (3) Office;  (4) Public Lands;  (5) Industrial;  and (6) Commercial, often with many subclassifications.

Modern zones are further complicated because they may be either exclusive or cumulative.  If an area is zoned exclusively for

**47.** 146 U.S. 387, 13 S.Ct. 110, 36 L.Ed. 1018 (1892).

**48.** Sax, *The Public Trust Doctrine in Natural Resources Law:  Effective*

*Judicial Intervention*, 68 Mich.L.Rev. 471 (1970).

**49.** Id.

heavy industry, for example, the property could not be utilized for more restrictive uses, such as light industrial, commercial, or residential purposes.  On the other hand, if the ordinance called for cumulative zoning, more restrictive uses would be allowed.  Even if an area is zoned exclusively for one use, however, the ordinance commonly allows certain "accessory" uses.  For instance, if a lot is zoned for single-family dwellings, the owner typically would also be allowed to construct a private garage, swimming pool, garden house, tool shed, private greenhouse, or play house.

In addition to specifying uses, zoning ordinances also include area, height and placement regulations.  These regulations may include minimum lot sizes, minimum usable floor area, minimum usable open space, minimum parking, maximum height, and required setbacks from the front, rear, and sides of the lot.  Zoning regulations are complemented by building codes that specify construction requirements in greater detail.  Thus, in order to obtain a building permit from a municipality, an owner must comply with both the building code and the zoning ordinance.

In zoning cases, legal problems tend to cluster around three basic issues: (1) Is the ordinance valid?  (2) Should an exception be made to the ordinance? and (3) Is the ordinance exclusionary?

1.  **Validity of Zoning Ordinance.**  The "police power" is the power of a state to exercise control in order to protect the health, safety, morals, and welfare of the public.  The United States Constitution delegates specified powers to the federal government, but these powers do not include the police power, which is reserved to the states by the Tenth Amendment.[50]  The definition of the police power is used as the measure to test the validity of zoning ordinances; zoning ordinances are presumed to be valid unless it is shown that they are "arbitrary or unreasonable, or substantially unrelated to the public health, safety, convenience, morals or welfare."[51]

In the well-known case of Village of Euclid, Ohio v. Ambler Realty Co.,[52] Ambler Realty challenged the Euclid zoning ordinance, enacted in 1922, on the grounds that it constituted a deprivation of property without due process of law.  Ambler owned sixty-eight acres of land that allegedly was worth $10,000 an acre for industrial uses but only $2,500 per acre for residential uses, for which it had been zoned.  The Supreme Court upheld the ordinance, noting that "the exclusion of buildings devoted to business, trade, etc., from residential districts, bears a rational relation to the health and safety of the community.  Some of the grounds for this conclusion are promotion of the health and security from injury of children and others by

50. C. Smith and R. Boyer, Survey of the Law of Property 345, 348 (2d ed. 1971).

51. Anderson v. Town of Wilmington, 347 Mass. 302, 197 N.E.2d 682 (1964).

52. 272 U.S. 365, 47 S.Ct. 114, 71 L.Ed. 303 (1926).

separate dwelling houses from territory devoted to trade and industry; suppression and prevention of disorder; facilitating the extinguishment of fires, and the enforcement of street traffic regulations and other general welfare ordinances; aiding the health and safety of the community by excluding from residential areas the confusion and danger of fire, contagion, and disorder which in greater or less degree attach to the location of stores, shops, and factories."

Under the police power, aesthetics may also be considered; for instance, a zoning ordinance which prohibited outdoor advertising signs unrelated to the business conducted on the premises has been upheld.[53]   In the words of the Supreme Court,[54] "Miserable and disreputable housing conditions may do more than spread disease and crime and immorality.   They may also suffocate the spirit by reducing the people who live there to the status of cattle.   They may indeed make living an almost insufferable burden.   They may also be an ugly sore, a blight on the community which robs it of charm, which makes it a place from which men turn.   The misery of housing may despoil a community as an open sewer may ruin a river.   We do not sit to determine whether a particular housing project is or is not desirable.   The concept of the public welfare is broad and inclusive. .   .   .   The values it represents are spiritual as well as physical, aesthetic as well as monetary.   It is within the power of the legislature to determine that the community should be beautiful as well as healthy, spacious as well as clean, well-balanced as well as carefully patrolled."

The proliferation of adult bookstores, theaters and massage parlors has been troublesome to city officials in recent years, especially because officials have generally been unsuccessful in prosecuting pornography cases.   As a result, many cities now use zoning ordinances to limit pornography to certain areas.   Although these ordinances have resulted in a direct confrontation between the rights of cities to restrict land use and the rights of individuals to exercise their First Amendment right to free speech, the Supreme Court upheld such ordinances in 1976.   See Young v. American Mini Theatres, Inc., infra.

Although there has been a trend to allow cities to regulate land as a proper exercise of police power, the limitations of such regulation are illustrated by Fred F. French Investing Co. v. City of New York.[55]   A 1972 amendment to the New York City zoning resolution rezoned two private parks into public parks, and the private park owners received transferable development rights that could be used in developing property elsewhere.   The plaintiff brought an action claiming inverse condemnation.   The court decided that, although

53.   United Advertising Corp. v. Borough of Metuchen, 42 N.J. 1, 198 A.2d 447 (1964).

54.   Berman v. Parker, 348 U.S. 26, 75 S.Ct. 98, 99 L.Ed. 27 (1954).

55.   39 N.Y.2d 587, 385 N.Y.S.2d 5, 350 N.E.2d 381 (1976).

there had been no condemnation because the owners retained ownership of the land, the amendment was an invalid exercise of police power: "While the police power of the state to regulate the use of private property zoning is broad indeed, it is not unlimited." The court noted that the transferable development rights were inadequate compensation because of their uncertain value.

2. **Exceptions to Zoning Ordinances.** Owners of real estate are often allowed to use their land in a manner that conflicts with a zoning ordinance. Such use may be divided into two categories. First, it often happens that the land was already being used for one purpose when a zoning ordinance was adopted which made that use illegal. In order to be fair to the owner and to avoid claims that there was a "taking," most zoning ordinances provide that nonconforming uses may continue after the effective date of the ordinance. Some ordinances contain amortization provisions that allow the nonconforming use to continue for a specified number of years; these provisions have been upheld by most courts. For instance, when a challenge was made to a Los Angeles ordinance requiring that nonconforming uses cease within five years, the court concluded that the ordinance was valid: "The distinction between an ordinance restricting future uses and one requiring the termination of present uses within a reasonable period of time is merely one of degree, and constitutionality depends on the relative importance to be given to the public gain and to the private loss. Zoning as it affects every piece of property is to some extent retroactive in that it applies to property already owned at the time of the effective date of the ordinance. The elimination of existing uses within a reasonable time does not amount to a taking of property nor does it necessarily restrict the use of property so that it cannot be used for any reasonable purpose. Use of a reasonable amortization scheme provides an equitable means of reconciliation of the conflicting interests in satisfaction of due process requirements." [56]

Even if the nonconforming use is permitted to continue, it may not be increased; if there are buildings on the property, they may be repaired but not altered. Whether the nonconforming use has been increased or not is a question of fact for the court. In Franklin Planning & Zoning Comm. v. Simpson Cty. Lumber Co.,[57] the city contended that a landowner who was allowed nonconforming use of his residential property to store building materials could not use the property to store logs. The court held that this was not an increase in the use: "Regardless of our sadness at seeing the elimination of the 'spreading chestnut tree,' and the village smith, it must be admitted that in the interest of progress the law favors the gradual elimination of 'nonconforming' uses of property in our cities. It naturally follows that such nonconforming uses as are tolerated under the law

56. City of Los Angeles v. Gage, 127      57. 394 S.W.2d 593 (Ky.1965).
Cal.App.2d 442, 274 P.2d 34 (1954).

cannot be enlarged. . . . Admitting the saw logs were stacked higher than the brick and not so symmetrically, unless they obstruct the view or impede the natural flow of air we cannot see wherein their storage back of the barn is materially different from the storage of the stacks of brick. Accordingly, we agree with the chancellor that the 'nonconforming use' by Potts of his property has not been enlarged by the storage of saw logs on the property. There is no contention Potts plans a sawmill. It goes without saying that a sawmill in such a residential community would be such an enlargement as appellants oppose."

If the owner abandons his nonconforming use, he must thereafter use the property in accordance with the zoning ordinance. For instance, when the owner of a slaughterhouse that was a nonconforming use removed the smokestack and discontinued his use, the property lost its exemption from the zoning laws.[58]

The second category of exceptions covers those cases when an owner desires to use his land in a manner that conflicts with the ordinance—after the enactment of the zoning ordinance. In most cases, the owner will apply to the zoning board for an authorization (called a variance) to use the land in a manner not allowed by the ordinance. For the variance to be granted, the owner must meet the following tests which have been developed by the courts. First, the owner must prove that his land will not yield a reasonable rate of return if used as zoned. Second, there must be proof that the hardship is unique to the property and does not affect other property in the area. Finally, it must be shown that the variance will not change the essential character of the neighborhood.[59]

If the variance is not granted, perhaps because the plight of the owner is not unique to the area, other remedies might be available. One solution would be to seek amendment of the zoning ordinance— to change the regulations for the entire neighborhood. For instance, rezoning was ordered in a case in which an area zoned for single-family residences was located on a six-lane highway and near gas stations, a Super Burger restaurant, several automobile dealers, and a fish market.[60] However, "spot zoning"—where the city reclassifies a single piece of property for a use inconsistent with the neighborhood —will not be allowed. For example, a zoning ordinance may not be amended to allow the building of a mortuary in a residential area.[61]

Once a decision to rezone has been reached, it is lawful to submit the zoning change to the voters for approval through a referendum. In one case a developer could not build a high-rise apartment on his

58. Beyer v. Mayor of Baltimore, 182 Md. 444, 34 A.2d 765 (1943).

59. C. Smith and R. Boyer, Survey of the Law of Property 428 (2nd ed. 1971).

60. Stokes v. Jacksonville, 276 So.2d 200 (Fla.App.1973).

61. Mueller v. Hoffmeister Undertaking Co., 343 Mo. 430, 121 S.W.2d 775 (1938).

property because a zoning change was not approved at a referendum. The Supreme Court held that the referendum requirement is valid. Although the court noted that if the subject of the referendum was unrelated to the police power it would not be upheld, use of the referendum does not in itself constitute an unconstitutional delegation of power: "Under our constitutional assumptions, all power derives from the people, who can delegate it to representative instruments which they create. In establishing legislative bodies, the people can reserve to themselves power to deal directly with matters which might otherwise be assigned to the legislature." [62]

Many zoning ordinances contain built-in provisions for variation without the need for amendment each time. For example, it is common for ordinances to provide for "special exceptions" which would allow churches, schools, and parks to be established in residential areas. If the ordinance includes such exceptions, the three tests for a variance do not apply and the special use must be permitted. It is also common for zoning ordinances to provide for "floating" zones where, for example, the ordinance provides for a light industrial zone but does not allocate land to this zone until a landowner makes a request.[63]

3. **Exclusionary Zoning.** Exclusionary zoning has become an especially troublesome issue in recent years. Suppose, for example, that Clear Waters is a suburb of a large city. Clear Waters has experienced tremendous expansion in recent years, with an accompanying increase in air and water pollution. Prodded by local environmentalists, the city decides to prevent future growth by passing a zoning ordinance providing that houses cannot be built on lots smaller than one acre and by limiting the issuance of building permits. As might be expected, developers resent the city's action, and local civil rights groups protest that the real intent of the city's action is to prevent low-income, minority families in the nearby city from moving to Clear Waters. Is Clear Waters' action constitutional?

To answer this question, the proper constitutional test must first be determined. The choice of tests is illustrated by the Supreme Court decision in Village of Belle Terre v. Boraas.[64] Belle Terre adopted a zoning ordinance that, in effect, prevented more than two unrelated persons from living together in a single-family dwelling. Six students from the nearby campus at Stony Brook rented a house in Belle Terre; when they were notified that they were violating the zoning ordinance, they brought suit in federal court asking that the

---

62. City of Eastlake v. Forest City Enterprises, Inc., 426 U.S. 668, 96 S.Ct. 2358, 49 L.Ed.2d 132 (1976).

63. C. Smith and R. Boyer, Survey of the Law of Property 428, 429 (2nd ed. 1971).

64. 416 U.S. 1, 94 S.Ct. 1536, 39 L.Ed. 2d 797 (1974).

ordinance be declared unconstitutional because it deprived them of equal protection under the law.  In deciding for the village, the Supreme Court applied the traditional "two-tier" approach to the equal protection issue.  Under this approach, if legislation violates a "fundamental" interest such as the right to free speech or is based on a "suspect classification" such as race, it will be declared unconstitutional unless there is a compelling governmental interest.  If the legislation does not violate a fundamental interest or contain a suspect classification, then the legislation is only required to bear a reasonable relationship to a permissible state objective;  that is, there must be a rational basis for the legislation.[65]

In *Belle Terre*, the Supreme Court adopted the rational basis test in upholding the statute: "It involves no procedural disparity inflicted on some but not on others.  It involves no 'fundamental' right guaranteed by the Constitution, such as voting, the right of association, the right of access to the courts, or any rights of privacy.  We deal with economic and social legislation where legislatures have historically drawn lines which we respect against the charge of violation of the Equal Protection Clause if the law be 'reasonable, not arbitrary' and bears 'a rational relationship to a [permissible] state objective.'  It is said, however, that if two unmarried people can constitute a 'family,' there is no reason why three or four may not.  But every line drawn by a legislature leaves some out that might well have been included.  That exercise of discretion, however, is a legislative, not a judicial, function.  It is said that the Belle Terre ordinance reeks with an animosity to unmarried couples who live together.  There is no evidence to support it; and the provision of the ordinance bringing within the definition of a 'family' two unmarried people belies the charge.  The ordinance places no ban on other forms of association, for a 'family' may, so far as the ordinance is concerned, entertain whomever it likes.  The regimes of boarding houses, fraternity houses, and the like present urban problems.  More people occupy a given space; more cars rather continuously pass by; more cars are parked; noise travels with crowds.  A quiet place where yards are wide, people few, and motor vehicles restricted are legitimate guidelines in a land-use project addressed to family needs.  This goal is a permissible one within Berman v. Parker, supra.  The police power is not confined to elimination of filth, stench, and unhealthy places.  It is ample to lay out zones where family values, youth values, and the

---

**65.** Courts have also developed two approaches which lie between the "compelling interest" and the "rational basis" tests.  Under one approach, adopted by the Court of Appeals in *Belle Terre*, the state must show that the legislation *in fact* advances a permissible state objective.  The second approach utilizes a "sliding scale" analysis whereby the legislation will be scrutinized more closely when it affects interests of greater constitutional significance.  See Note, *Zoning Ordinances Limiting the Number of Unrelated Individuals in a Dwelling Unit*, 88 Harv.L.Rev. 119 (1974); Gibson, *Zoning and the Equal Protection Clause—Village of Belle Terre v. Boraas*, 14 Am.Bus.L.J. 370 (1977).

blessings of quiet seclusion and clean air make the area a sanctuary for people."

Even after the appropriate test has been selected, it is often difficult to determine whether or not the action of a municipality is discriminatory. Specifically, should a court focus on the effect of the action or on the intent of the officials? This was the question faced by the Supreme Court in Village of Arlington Heights v. Metropolitan Housing Development Corp.[66] The Metropolitan Housing Development Corporation (MHDC), a nonprofit developer, contracted to purchase a fifteen-acre parcel of land in Arlington Heights, Illinois for the purpose of building racially integrated housing for low- and moderate-income persons. When the village refused to rezone the parcel from a single-family to a multiple-family classification, MHDC and individual minority plaintiffs filed suit alleging that the village's action constituted a denial of equal protection. Although the Supreme Court remanded the case to a lower court for a determination of whether the Fair Housing Act was violated, the court did consider the equal protection argument involved and noted that the test should be whether there is proof of a racially discriminatory intent or purpose: "Official action will not be held unconstitutional solely because it results in a racially disproportionate impact. . . . Proof of racially discriminatory intent or purpose is required to show a violation of the Equal Protection Clause." In formulating this test, the Court relied heavily on Washington v. Davis,[67] in which the Court had determined that tests for Washington, D.C., police officers were not unconstitutional merely because they had a racially disproportionate impact. To determine whether a discriminatory purpose was a motivating factor, the Court suggested that the following evidence should be considered: (1) the impact of the official action; (2) the historical background of the decision; (3) the sequence of events leading up to the decision; and (4) departure from usual procedures or usual substantive considerations.

Applying this test, the Court decided that the plaintiffs had failed to prove that a discriminatory purpose motivated the village's decision. Although the decision did have a discriminatory impact insofar as minorities comprised forty percent of the income groups eligible for the proposed housing, the Court felt that the events leading up to the decision were not suspicious; and the rezoning request followed normal procedure.

Given the Constitutional background, courts that have considered exclusionary zoning cases have often reached conflicting results.

---

66. 429 U.S. 252, 97 S.Ct. 555, 50 L.Ed. 2d 450 (1977). On remand, the Court of Appeals decided that, even when there is no discriminatory intent, the Fair Housing Act is violated when the acts of a municipality have a "dis-criminatory impact." 558 F.2d 1283 (7th Cir. 1977).

67. 426 U.S. 229, 96 S.Ct. 2040, 48 L.Ed. 2d 597 (1976).

One approach is illustrated by Construction Industry Ass'n, Sonoma City v. City of Petaluma,[68] where the court considered the "Petaluma Plan," a land use plan adopted by Petaluma, a city forty miles north of San Francisco. The plan resulted from the city's concern over a rapid growth rate, which totaled 25 percent in a two-year period. Under the plan, which was limited to the 1972–77 period, the housing development growth rate in the city was not to exceed 500 dwelling units per year, and the development permits were awarded to builders who adapted their plans to other city land use plans. The plan further established a "greenbelt" around the city which served as a boundary for urban expansion.

Dispute arose over the purpose of the Petaluma Plan. According to the city, the plan was designed to ensure that "development in the next five years will take place in a reasonable, orderly, attractive manner, rather than in a completely haphazard and unattractive manner." However, the construction industry claimed that the plan was enacted to limit Petaluma's demographic and market growth rate in housing and the immigration of new residents." Regardless of purpose, the court determined that the effect of widespread adoption of such plans would be a "shortfall in needed housing in the region . . . [of] 25 percent of the units needed . . . a loss of the mobility of current and prospective residents and a deterioration in the quality and choice of housing available to income earners with real incomes of $14,000 per year or less."

When the construction industry and two landowners brought suit, the district court decided that the plan was unconstitutional. The court determined at the outset that the plan involved a fundamental right—the right to travel—and therefore concluded that Petaluma had to show a compelling interest if the plan were to be sustained. The city argued that a compelling interest arose from its inadequate sewage treatment facilities, inadequate water supply and desire to preserve its small town character, but the court rejected the argument that these were compelling interests.

When the case was appealed, the appellate court declined to consider whether the right to travel was violated because the plaintiffs were asserting the right on behalf of third parties and therefore lacked standing, a concept to be considered in the following chapter. The appellate court concluded that the Petaluma Plan was not arbitrary and unreasonable since it did bear a rational relationship to a legitimate state interest: "We conclude therefore that under *Belle Terre* . . . the concept of the public welfare is sufficiently broad to uphold Petaluma's desire to preserve its small town character, its open spaces and low density of population and to grow at an orderly and deliberate pace."

---

**68.** 522 F.2d 897 (9th Cir. 1975).

In addition to its reliance on *Belle Terre*, the California appellate court also cited Golden v. Planning Bd. of Town of Ramapo,[69] in which a New York appellate court upheld a zoning amendment adopted by the town of Ramapo. Under the amendment, development was not permitted until municipal services were available under an eighteen-year capital plan. According to the court, "What we will not countenance, then, under any guise, is community efforts at immunization or exclusion. But, far from being exclusionary, the present amendment merely seeks, by the implementation of sequential development and timed growth, to provide a balanced cohesive community dedicated to the efficient utilization of land. . . . In sum, where it is clear that the existing physical and financial resources of the community are inadequate to furnish the essential service and facilities which a substantial increase in population requires, there is a rational basis for 'phased growth' and hence, the challenged ordinance is not violative of the Federal and State Constitution."

A contrast to the *Petaluma* and *Ramapo* decisions is the leading case of Southern Burlington County N.A.A.C.P. v. Township of Mount Laurel.[70] The township of Mt. Laurel, New Jersey, enacted a zoning ordinance which, by allowing only single-family detached dwellings, excluded low- and moderate-income housing such as apartments, town houses, and mobile homes. Even single-family residences in Mt. Laurel were beyond the means of moderate-income families because the zoning ordinance required large lots and large buildings. The court concluded that "Mount Laurel permits only such middle and upper income housing as it believes will have sufficient taxable value to come close to paying its own governmental way."

The plaintiffs who challenged the ordinance represented poor minority groups, although the court noted that other groups barred by restrictive land use regulations would include young couples, elderly couples, single persons, and large, growing families in the middle-income range. The issue, according to the court, was, "whether a developing municipality like Mount Laurel may validly, by a system of land use regulation, make it physicially and economically impossible to provide low and moderate income housing in the municipality for the various categories of persons who need and want it and thereby, as Mount Laurel has, exclude such people from living within its confines because of the limited extent of their income and resources." The court also noted that the "implications of the issue presented are indeed broad and far-reaching, extending much beyond these particular plaintiffs and the boundaries of this particular municipality."

In deciding this issue under state law—and without considering federal constitutional grounds—the court considered the argument

69. 30 N.Y.2d 359, 334 N.Y.S.2d 138,   70. 67 N.J. 151, 336 A.2d 713 (1975).
285 N.E.2d 291 (1972).

that a municipality may exercise its zoning power to allow uses that are beneficial to the local tax rate; however, the court decided that this reason alone would not suffice. Furthermore, the court decided that ecological or environmental reasons were insufficient grounds to use restrictive zoning because the land in the township was readily amenable to the installation of sewage disposal and water supply facilities.

Consequently, the court reached the following conclusion: "By way of summary, what we have said comes down to this. As a developing municipality, Mount Laurel must, by its land use regulations, make realistically possible the opportunity for an appropriate variety and choice of housing for all categories of people who may desire to live there, of course including those of low and moderate income. It must permit multi-family housing, without bedroom or similar restrictions, as well as small dwellings on very small lots, low cost housing of other types and, in general, high density zoning, without artificial and unjustifiable minimum requirements as to lot size, building size and the like to meet the full panoply of these needs."

# CASES

---

## SIMONS v. WORK OF GOD CORP.

Appellate Court of Illinois, 1962.
36 Ill.App.2d 199, 183 N.E.2d 729.

BURMAN, Justice.

The sole question presented by this appeal is whether the Circuit Court correctly construed a restrictive land covenant appearing in defendant's deed. The decree of the trial court permanently enjoined defendant from using its residence at 854 Castlewood Terrace, Chicago, "for any purpose other than the residence of one single family consisting only of persons related each to the others by blood or marriage and keeping house as one single housekeeping unit."

Defendant is an Illinois not-for-profit eleemosynary corporation whose purpose is "to foster religious and cultural development of men and women; to teach the application of Christian principles to everyday life; to promote Christian morals and benevolence." Pursuant to this corporate purpose defendant purchased several residences in Chicago and furnishes residential and other facilities to members of Opus Dei, a secular institute of the Roman Catholic Church whose members dedicate their lives to God by seeking professional perfection in the modern world. On December 22, 1958, defendant purchased the house and lot at 854 Castlewood Terrace for $36,000.00. Five members of Opus Dei occupy the residence as their home: two are accountants, two are priests, and one a retired physicist.

In 1896 certain negative reciprocal covenants were imposed by deed upon the purchasers of the lots facing Castlewood Terrace. Those covenants appear in defendant's deed and read, in part, as follows:

"3. That not more than one building to be used for a dwelling shall at any time be erected or maintained upon the lot above described.

"4. That no apartment or flat-building or structure built, *used or adapted for the separate housekeeping of more than one family* shall at any time be built *or maintained* upon said lot. (emphasis added.)"

Twelve resident property-owners in the Castlewood subdivision filed a complaint alleging that defendant, with knowledge of the covenants, was occupying the premises for the use and promotion of its religious activities in violation of the restrictions. The issues were submitted to the trial court on stipulation that all issues were to be determined on the pleadings, documents, photographs, depositions, briefs and oral argument.

\* \* \*

Defendant's house can accommodate about ten or twelve permanent residents. It contains seven bedrooms, a living room, and a large ballroom currently in poor condition. Among the numerous rooms in the basement are a kitchen and a dining room. The old dining room on the first floor has been converted into a chapel where daily private masses are held solely for the residents. The five members of Opus Dei currently occupy four of the bedrooms. They are free to move out at any time. The admission of other members of Opus Dei as new residents would require the mutual consent of the existing residents.

Three of the current residents have no regular monetary income. The remaining two, in accordance with vows of poverty, deposit their entire net salaries in a joint bank account from which are paid all of the expenses for clothing, transportation and other necessities for each resident, as well as the operating expenses of defendant's house, including food, utilities, heat and domestic help. The mortgage payments on the residence, the furnishings in the house, and any remodeling or redecorating, are taken care of by defendant corporation. The bank account is in the name of three of the residents and withdrawals require the signatures of two of the residents. Household decisions and questions as to the personal needs of any of the residents are determined by an informal vote of the five residents, a majority governing and no one person having the final voice on any matter. Even the vice president of the defendant corporation was not certain "who runs the house."

It is our view that this group occupancy and cooperative management of the house, without a head of the household, by persons related by neither blood nor marriage, constitutes a use of the property forbidden by clause four of the deed. We are convinced that the framer of the restriction used the word "family" in its ordinary, popular sense, connoting a natural fundamental unit of our society. Generally speaking, this fundamental unit is composed of a father, mother, children, and possibly others related by blood or marriage (servants excepted), who make one home together with a natural head of the family.

In placing a construction upon the clause in question we must also look to the surrounding circumstances, if in them there is any evidence to indicate the construction placed on the words by the parties in the deed. The history of the Castlewood subdivision, as evidenced by the affidavits of each plaintiff and the discussion in Cuneo v. Chicago Title & Trust Co., 337 Ill. 589, 169 N.E. 760 and Kruetgen v. General Outdoor Advertising Co., 288 Ill.App. 619, 6 N.E.2d 469, reveals that each structure on Castlewood Terrace, with the exception now created by defendant, has from its inception been used exclusively as a residence by a natural family and, in some instances, its domestic servants. To us this is a clear manifestation of the intent of the parties to the restriction, an intent which has been uniformly and steadfastly perpetuated throughout the years.

\* \* \*

The reasoning in Seeley v. Phi Sigma Delta House Corp., 245 Mich. 252, 222 N.W. 180, lends support to our view even though its precise holding is not controlling here. The Michigan Supreme Court there held the attempt by a college fraternity to erect a house for its members on property restricted by a covenant limiting its use to "one single private dwelling house" to be in violation of the restriction. Construing the restriction to intend "a building designed as a single dwelling to be used by one family," the court stated, at page 181:

> "A college fraternity may assume some attributes characteristic of a natural family relation, but does so for the comfort of the members and for a convenience of management, and it is obvious that the relation is purely artificial, is a business proposition, and more nearly approximates the character of a club, boarding house, or apartment house, with added recreational privileges, than a family."

It seems to us that substantially the same observations can be made concerning the residents of defendant's house. Though they are bound together by strong religious principles and for a noble purpose, their occupancy is nevertheless a business proposition, designed for convenience of management, and assumes the nature of a boarding house or private club rather than that of a family.

The court was not swayed in Phi Sigma Delta, by the fact that only one kitchen and one dining room would be used by the fraternity. Moreover, the opinion, at page 182, articulates the novelty of cases involving negative reciprocal covenants:

> "Definitions, adopted for legislative purposes in housing codes and zoning ordinances cannot be employed in interpreting or construing a restrictive covenant running with land. The purpose of the restrictive covenant in the case at bar was to maintain the quiet, the privacy, and the family character of a residential district."

In reaching our decision we have not ignored the general rule, urged by defendant, to the effect that whenever a restrictive covenant is involved all doubts and ambiguities should be resolved in favor of natural rights and against restrictions. In our opinion, the language "separate housekeeping" of not "more than one family" is neither unclear nor susceptible equally to more than one interpretation. Calling to mind again the pattern of residential use that has been maintained continuously since the origin of the restrictions, it is clear that none of the parties to the covenants has ever been uncertain as to the meaning, either. The rule favoring a free use of property and demanding that such restrictions be confined to all reasonable limits consistent with the language used does not justify our rendering meaningless the lawful, reasonable and unambiguous restriction before us. "Where the intention is clearly shown by the restriction, and the enforcement of such restriction is necessary for the protection of substantial rights, they will be enforced."

\*    \*    \*

Under the facts and circumstances before us we hold that defendant's use of its property on Castlewood Terrace as a residence for members of Opus Dei is a violation of the restrictive covenants appearing in defendant's deed, and therefore was properly enjoined. Accordingly, the decree of the Circuit Court is affirmed.

Affirmed.

---

### PENNSYLVANIA CENTRAL TRANSP. CO. v. CITY OF NEW YORK

Supreme Court of the United States, 1978.
98 S.Ct. 2646, 57 L.Ed.2d 631.

Mr. Justice BRENNAN delivered the opinion of the Court.

The question presented is whether a city may, as part of a comprehensive program to preserve historic landmarks and historic districts, place restrictions on the development of individual historic landmarks—in addition to those imposed by applicable zoning ordinances—without effecting a "taking" requiring the payment of "just compensation." Specifically, we must decide whether the application of New York City's Landmarks Preservation Law to the parcel of land occupied by Grand Central Terminal has "taken" its owners' property in violation of the Fifth and Fourteenth Amendments.

Over the past 50 years, all 50 States and over 500 municipalities have enacted laws to encourage or require the preservation of buildings and areas with historic or aesthetic importance. These nationwide legislative efforts have been precipitated by two concerns. The first is recognition that, in recent years, large numbers of historic structures, landmarks, and areas have been destroyed without adequate consideration of either the values represented therein or the possibility of preserving the destroyed properties for use in economically productive ways. The second is a widely shared belief that structures with special historic, cultural, or architectural significance enhance the quality of life for all. Not only do these buildings and their workmanship represent the lessons of the past and embody precious features of our heritage, they serve as examples of quality for today. "[H]istoric conservation is but one aspect of the much larger problem, basically an environmental one, of enhancing—or perhaps developing for the first time—the quality of life for people."

New York City, responding to similar concerns and acting pursuant to a New York State enabling act adopted its Landmarks Preservation Law in 1965. The city acted from the conviction that "the standing of [New York City] as a worldwide tourist center and world capital of business, culture, and government" would be threatened if legislation were not enacted to protect historic landmarks and neighborhoods from precipitate decisions to destroy or fundamentally alter their character. The city believed that comprehensive measures to safeguard desirable features of the existing urban fabric would benefit its citizens in a variety of ways: e. g., fostering "civic pride in the beauty and noble accomplishments of the past"; protecting and enhancing "the city's attraction to tourists and visitors"; "support[ing] and stimul[ating] business and industry"; "strengthen[ing] the economy of the city"; and promoting "the use of historic districts, landmarks, interior landmarks, and scenic landmarks for the education, pleasure and welfare of the people of the city."

The New York City law is typical of many urban landmark laws in that its primary method of achieving its goals is not by acquisitions of historic properties, but rather by involving public entities in land use decisions affecting these properties and providing services, standards, controls, and incentives that will encourage preservation by private owners and users. While the law does place special restrictions on landmark properties as a necessary feature to the attainment of its larger objectives, the major theme of the Act is to ensure the owners of any such properties both a "reasonable return" on their investments and maximum latitude to use their parcels for purposes not inconsistent with the preservation goals.

\*   \*   \*

Although the designation of a landmark and landmark site restricts the owner's control over the parcel, designation also enhances the economic position of the landmark owner in one significant respect. Under New York City's zoning laws, owners of real property who have not developed their property to the full extent permitted by the applicable zoning laws are allowed to transfer development rights to contiguous parcels on the same city block. A 1968 ordinance gave the owners of landmark sites additional opportunities to transfer development rights to other parcels. * * *

This case involves the application of New York City's Landmark Preservation Law to Grand Central Terminal (Terminal). The Terminal, which is owned by the Penn Central Transportation Company and its affiliates (Penn Central), is one of New York City's most famous buildings. Opened in 1913, it is regarded not only as providing an ingenious engineering solution to the problems presented by urban railroad stations, but also as a magnificent example of the French Beaux Arts style.

The Terminal is located in midtown Manhattan. Its south facade faces 42nd Street and that street's intersection with Park Avenue. At street level, the Terminal is bounded on the west by Vanderbilt Avenue, on the east by the Commodore Hotel, and on the north by the Pan-American Building. Although a 20-story office tower, to have been located above the Terminal, was part of the original design, the planned tower was never constructed. The Terminal itself is an eight-story structure which Penn Central uses as a railroad station and in which it rents space not needed for railroad purposes to a variety of commercial interests. The Terminal is one of a number of properties owned by appellant Penn Central in this area of midtown Manhattan. The other include the Barclay, Biltmore, Commodore, Roosevelt, and Waldorf-Astoria Hotels, the Pan-American Building and other office buildings along Park Avenue, and the Yale Club. At least eight of these are eligible to be recipients of development rights afforded the Terminal by virtue of landmark designation.

On August 2, 1967, following a public hearing, the Commission designated the Terminal a "landmark" and designated the "city tax block" it occupies a "landmark site." The Board of Estimate confirmed this action on September 21, 1967. Although appellant Penn Central had opposed the designation before the Commission, it did not seek judicial review of the final designation decision.

* * *

Appellants UGP and Penn Central then applied to the Commission for permission to construct an office building atop the Terminal. Two separate plans, both designed by architect Marcel Breuer and both apparently satisfying the terms of the applicable zoning ordinance, were submitted to the Commission for approval. The first, Breuer I, provided for the construction of a 55-story office building, to be cantilevered above the existing facade and to rest on the roof of the Terminal. The second, Breuer II Revised, called for tearing down a portion of the Terminal that included the 42nd Street facade, stripping off some of the remaining features of the Terminal's facade, and constructing a 53-story office building. The Commission denied a certificate of no exterior effect on September 20, 1968. Appellants then applied for a certificate of "appropriateness" as to both proposals. After four days of hearings at which over 80 witnesses testified, the Commission denied this application as to both proposals.

      \*    \*    \*

Before considering appellants' specific contentions, it will be useful to review the factors that have shaped the jurisprudence of the Fifth Amendment injunction "nor shall private property be taken for public use, without just compensation." The question of what constitutes a "taking" for purposes of the Fifth Amendment has proved to be a problem of considerable difficulty. While this Court has recognized that the "Fifth Amendment's guarantee [is] designed to bar Government from forcing some people alone to bear public burdens which, in all fairness and justice, should be borne by the public as a whole," Armstrong v. United States, 364 U.S. 40, 49, 80 S.Ct. 1563, 1569, 4 L.Ed.2d 1554 (1960), this Court, quite simply, has been unable to develop any "set formula" for determining when "justice and fairness" require that economic injuries caused by public action be compensated by the Government, rather than remain disproportionately concentrated on a few persons. Indeed, we have frequently observed that whether a particular restriction will be rendered invalid by the Government's failure to pay for any losses proximately caused by it depends largely "upon the particular circumstances [in that] case."

In engaging in these essentially ad hoc, factual inquiries, the Court's decisions have identified several factors that have particular significance. The economic impact of the regulation on the claimant and, particularly, the extent to which the regulation has interfered with distinct investment backed expectations are of course relevant considerations. So too is the character of the governmental action. A "taking" may more readily be found when the interference with property can be characterized as a physical invasion by Government, see e. g., Causby v. United States, 328 U.S. 256, 66 S.Ct. 1062, 90 L. Ed. 1206 (1946), than when interference arises from some public program adjusting the benefits and burdens of economic life to promote the common good.

"Government could hardly go on if to some extent values incident to property could not be diminished without paying for every such change in the general law," Pennsylvania Coal Co. v. Mahon, 260 U.S. 393, 413, 43 S.Ct. 158, 159, 67 L.Ed. 322 (1922), and this Court has accordingly recognized, in a wide variety of contexts, that Government may execute laws or programs that adversely affect recognized economic values. Exercises of the taxing power are one obvious example. A second are the decisions in which this Court has dismissed "taking" challenges on the ground that, while the challenged Government action caused economic harm, it did not interfere with interests that were sufficiently bound up with the reasonable expectations of the claimant to constitute "property" for Fifth Amendment purposes.

\*   \*   \*

More importantly for the present case, in instances in which a state tribunal reasonably concluded that "the health, safety, morals or general welfare" would be promoted by prohibiting particular contemplated uses of land, this Court has upheld land use regulations that destroyed or adversely affected recognized real property interests.

\*   \*   \*

Stated baldly, appellants' position appears to be that the only means of ensuring that selected owners are not singled out to endure financial hardship for no reason is to hold that any restriction imposed on individual landmarks pursuant to the New York scheme is a "taking" requiring the payment of "just compensation." Agreement with this argument would of course invalidate not just New York City's law, but all comparable landmark legislation in the Nation. We find no merit in it.

It is true, as appellants emphasize, that both historic district legislation and zoning laws regulate all properties within given physical communities whereas landmark laws apply only to selected parcels. But, contrary to appellants' suggestions, landmark laws are not like discriminatory, or "reverse spot," zoning: that is, a land use decision which arbitrarily singles out a particular parcel for different, less favorable treatment than the neighboring ones. In contrast to discriminatory zoning, which is the antithesis of land use control as part of some comprehensive plan, the New York City law embodies a comprehensive plan to preserve structures of historic or aesthetic interest wherever they might be found in the city, and as noted, over 400 landmarks and 31 historic districts have been designated pursuant to this plan.

\*   \*   \*

Rejection of appellants' broad arguments is not however the end of our inquiry, for all we thus far have established is that the New York law is not rendered invalid by its failure to provide "just compensation" whenever a landmark owner is restricted in the exploitation of property interests, such as air rights, to a greater extent than provided for under applicable zoning laws. We now must consider whether the interference with appellants' property is of such a magnitude that "there must be an exercise of eminent domain and compensation to sustain [it]." That inquiry may be narrowed to the question of the severity of the impact of the law on appellants' parcel, and its resolution in turn requires a careful assessment of the impact of the regulation on the Terminal site.

Unlike the governmental acts in *Goldblatt, Miller, Causby, Griggs,* and *Hadacheck,* the New York City law does not interfere in any way with the present uses of the Terminal. Its designation as a landmark not only permits but contemplates that appellants may continue to use the property precisely as it has for the past 65 years: as a railroad terminal containing office space and concessions. So the law does not interfere with what must be regarded as Penn Central's primary expectation concerning the use of the parcel. More importantly, on this record, we must regard the New York City law as permitting Penn Central not only to profit from the Terminal but to obtain a "reasonable return" on its investment.

\* \* \*

Second, to the extent appellants have been denied the right to build above the Terminal, it is not literally accurate to say that they have been denied *all* use of even those pre-existing air rights. Their ability to use these rights has not been abrogated; they are made transferable to at least eight parcels in the vicinity of the Terminal, one or two of which have been found suitable for the construction of new office buildings. Although appellants and others have argued that New York City's transferable development rights program is far from ideal, the New York courts here supportably found that, at least in the case of the Terminal, the rights afforded are valuable. While these rights may well not have constituted "just compensation" if a "taking" had occurred, the rights nevertheless undoubtedly mitigate whatever financial burdens the law has imposed on appellants and, for that reason, are to be taken into account in considering the impact of regulation.

On this record we conclude that the application of New York City's Landmarks Preservation Law has not effected a "taking" of appellants' property. The restrictions imposed are substantially related to the promotion of the general welfare and not only permit reasonable beneficial use of the landmark site but afford appellants opportunities further to enhance not only the Terminal site proper but also other properties.

Affirmed.

---

### YOUNG v. AMERICAN MINI THEATRES, INC.

Supreme Court of the United States, 1976.
427 U.S. 50, 96 S.Ct. 2440, 49 L.Ed.2d 310.

Mr. Justice STEVENS delivered the opinion of the Court.

Zoning ordinances adopted by the city of Detroit differentiate between motion picture theaters which exhibit sexually explicit "adult" movies and those which do not. The principle question presented by this case is whether that statutory classification is unconstitutional because it is based on the content of communication protected by the First Amendment.

Effective November 2, 1972, Detroit adopted the ordinances challenged in this litigation. Instead of concentrating "adult" theaters in limited zones, these ordinances require that such theaters be dispersed. Specifically, an adult theater may not be located within 1,000 feet of any two other "regulated uses" or within 500 feet of a residential area. The term "regulated use" includes 10 different kinds of establishments in addition to adult theaters.

The classification of a theater as "adult" is expressly predicated on the character of the motion pictures which it exhibits. If the theater is used to present "material distinguished or characterized by an emphasis on matter depicting, describing or relating to 'Specified Sexual Activities' or 'Specified Anatomical Areas,'" it is an adult establishment.

The 1972 ordinances were amendments to an "Anti-Skid Row Ordinance" which had been adopted 10 years earlier. At that time the Detroit Common Council made a finding that some uses of property are especially injurious to a neighborhood when they are concentrated in limited areas. The decision to add adult motion picture theaters and adult book stores to the list of businesses which, apart from a special waiver, could not be located within 1,000 feet of two other "regulated uses," was, in part, a response to the significant growth in the number of such establishments. In the opinion of urban planners and real estate experts who supported the ordinances, the location of several such businesses in the same neighborhood tends to attract an undesirable quantity and quality of transients, adversely affects property values, causes an increase in crime, especially prostitution, and encourages residents and businesses to move elsewhere.

Respondents are the operators of two adult motion picture theaters. One, the Nortown, was an established theater which began to exhibit adult films in March 1973. The other, the Pussy Cat, was a corner gas station which was converted into a "mini theater," but denied a certificate of occupancy because of its plan to exhibit adult films. Both theaters were located within 1,000 feet of two other regulated uses and the Pussy Cat was less than 500 feet from a residential area. The respondents brought two separate actions against appropriate city officials, seeking a declaratory judgment that the ordinances were unconstitutional and an injunction against their enforcement. Federal jurisdiction was properly invoked and the two cases were consolidated for decision.

The District Court granted defendants' motion for summary judgment [but the Court of Appeals reversed].

\* \* \*

A remark attributed to Voltaire characterizes our zealous adherence to the principle that the Government may not tell the citizen what he may or may not say. Referring to a suggestion that the violent overthrow of tyranny might be legitimate, he said: "I disapprove of what you say, but I will defend to the death your right to say it." The essence of that comment has been repeated time after time in our decisions invalidating attempts by the Government to impose selective controls upon the dissemination of ideas.

Thus, the use of streets and parks for the free expression of views on national affairs may not be conditioned upon the sovereign's agreement with what a speaker may intend to say. Nor may speech be curtailed because it invites dispute, creates dissatisfaction with conditions the way they are, or even stirs people to anger. The sovereign's agreement or disagreement with the content of what a speaker has to say may not affect the regulation of the time, place, or manner of presenting the speech.

     \*    \*    \*

The question whether speech is, or is not, protected by the First Amendment often depends on the content of the speech. Thus, the line between permissible advocacy and impermissible incitation to crime or violence depends, not merely on the setting in which the speech occurs, but also on exactly what the speaker had to say. Similarly, it is the content of the utterance that determines whether it is a protected epithet or an unprotected "fighting comment." And in time of war "the publication of the sailing of transports or the number and regulation of troops may unquestionably be restrained," see Near v. Minnesota, 283 U.S. 697, 716, 51 S.Ct. 625, 631, 75 L.Ed. 1357, although publication of news stories with a different content would be protected.

     \*    \*    \*

Moreover, even though we recognize that the First Amendment will not tolerate the total suppression of erotic materials that have some arguably artistic value, it is manifest that society's interest in protecting this type of expression is of a wholly different, and lesser, magnitude than the interest in untrammeled political debate that inspired Voltaire's immortal comment. Whether political oratory or philosophical discussion moves us to applaud or to despise what is said, every schoolchild can understand why our duty to defend the right to speak remains the same. But few of us would march our sons and daughters off to war to preserve the citizen's right to see "Specified Sexual Activities" exhibited in the theaters of our choice. Even though the First Amendment protects communication in this area from total suppression, we hold that the State may legitimately use the content of these materials as the basis for placing them in a different classification from other motion pictures.

     \*    \*    \*

Reversed.

## PROBLEMS

1. Inez lived in an East Cleveland home with her son, Dale, his son, Dale, Jr., and another grandson, John. The two boys were first cousins; John, who was ten years old, came to live with his grandmother after his mother's death. An East Cleveland housing ordinance limited the occupancy of a dwelling unit to members of a single family. Inez was informed that John was an "illegal occupant" and that he would have to leave the home. Inez refused to comply with the ordinance and the city filed a criminal charge against her. Is the ordinance constitutional? Why?

2. Mayme owned six lots in Block #2 of an addition to the city of Harrodsburg. All the lots contained a covenant restricting the use of the land to residential purposes. Mayme sold the six lots to various purchasers. Each deed contained the restrictive covenant and a statement that it ran with the land. Thereafter, Kentucky Highway No. 35 was rerouted around the city of Harrodsburg and small portions of the lots were obtained by condemnation proceedings. As a result of the rerouting of the highway, traffic in the area of the lots increased greatly; approximately 500 motor vehicles passed the lots on the highway each hour. The Longs purchased one of the six lots with the intention of operating it as a used car lot. They felt that lot was best suited for business purposes after the rerouting of the highway. All the other lots had been developed for residential purposes and contained residential dwellings. However, a number of commercial enterprises had been built near Block #2. Is the restrictive covenant enforceable against the Longs? Why?

3. The Bakers, husband and wife, own four lots in Lantana Heights in the town of Lantana. The Bakers have filed suit to remove certain covenants, which restrict the use of the property to residential purposes. The lots were bounded on the west by a large tract of land reserved for commercial purposes, and they were located directly across from a tuberculosis hospital. A new shopping center was also being completed across from the property during the year the Bakers purchased the lots. The Bakers argue that because of the commercial nature of the area surrounding their property, in addition to the building of a Baptist church in the subdivision, they cannot sell their property for residential purposes. Should the covenants be removed? Why?

4. In order to erect a power plant, the Union Electric Co. sought to acquire by condemnation land owned by Saale. The land was zoned for agricultural uses, with authorization also for residential purposes. Saale argues that the value of the land should be determined by its potential for industrial use, which would result in a higher valuation. He reasons that since the land will be used for a power plant, an industrial use, it should have the value of industrial property. Is Saale correct? Why?

5. Marie Ida owns land in Mount Ayr, Iowa. Her land is not located in a slum area. The Low-Rent Housing Agency of Mount Ayr, through its power of eminent domain, claims the land of Marie Ida for low-income housing purposes. Marie Ida objects to the condemnation, arguing that the use of her land for low-income housing is not a public use, and that only slum areas can be taken. Is she correct? Why?

6. State University has been given the right to acquire real estate through condemnation proceedings. State decided to acquire ten and one-half acres of Joe's land, which it wants to use to build an eighteen hole golf course. Joe objects, claiming that the university has not proven the necessity of taking his land. Is Joe correct? Why?

7. In 1926, Sam purchased a lot in a new subdivision. Each lot in the subdivision was subject to a restriction, which provided that any house built in the subdivision lot had to cost at least $12,500. Later, as a result of the Great Depression, construction costs decreased and a house that once cost $12,500 could be built for $9,000. Sam brought an action to modify the building restrictions because of the changed conditions resulting from the depression. Will he win? Why?

8. Venerose owned a parcel of land in the village of Larchmont. He entered into a lease with Burger King, which intended to construct and operate a restaurant on the premises in which it would offer its patrons a limited menu, fast service and minimal prices. Burger King applied for a building permit to construct the proposed restaurant. At the time of the application, the zoning ordinance permitted all types of restaurants in that district. However, the Village Board amended the zoning ordinance after the Burger King application to outlaw all fast food restaurants. The Burger King building permit was denied under the amended zoning ordinance, and Burger King has brought suit to obtain a building permit. Will Burger King win? Why?

9. The Castlewood Terrace subdivision was subdivided and platted in 1896. The deeds to the Castlewood Terrace lots contained covenants restricting the use of the lots to single-family residences. Paschen acquired several lots in Castlewood Terrace with full knowledge of a restriction on the types of residences that could be built in the subdivision. Fifty years later, Castlewood Terrace had become surrounded by high-rise multiple-family residences. The value of Paschen's property when used for single-family residences is $110,000, yet the value of the same property is roughly $256,000 if used for high-rise multiple-family residences. Paschen brings suit to have the restrictive covenants removed so that a high-rise multiple-family residence may be built on his property. Pashkow, a neighbor, objects to the removal of the restriction. Who should prevail—Paschen or Pashkow? Why?

10. Garramone leased property which extended over two different zoning areas in the village of Lynbrook, Nassau County, New York. One portion of the property was zoned for commercial use, while the other portion was zoned for residential use. Garramone planned to build a roller skating rink on the leased property. To facilitate off-street parking, Garramone sought a variance on the portion of the property zoned for residential use. The village Board of Appeals granted Garramone a variance on the grounds that a denial would cause him unnecessary hardship. The board noted that, if the skating rink was built on only the commercial portion of the leased property, access to the rear portion would be obstructed and patrons would be required to park in the streets thus causing traffic problems. Adjoining landowners object to the granting of the variance and file suit against the zoning board of appeals. Is the variance legal? Why?

## Chapter 14

## LAND USE REGULATION AND
## ENVIRONMENTAL LAW

Buy land. They ain't makin' any more of it.

Will Rogers

Land use is the single most important element affecting the quality of our environment which remains substantially unaddressed as a matter of national policy. Land is our most valuable resource. There will never be any more of it.

Russell E. Train, Chairman of the Council
on Environmental Quality

Although their solutions may differ, Will Rogers and Russell E. Train have recognized a problem that has recently come to the forefront of our environmental concerns: the limited supply of land in the United States. Recognition of this problem brings with it the demise of Rogers' solution, which views land as a commodity to be bought, developed, and sold, and the emergence of Train's solution—land use planning. This drift toward land use planning represents, in the words of James Rouse, a major developer of shopping centers, ". . . the most radical change in our concept of private property rights we have ever seen in the history of this country."[1]

What is the nature of the solution that will bring this "radical change?" Essentially, land use planning means what it says—planning how to use our land to maximize housing, recreation, and commerce, and to minimize the harmful effects of these activities on the environment. Land use planning has been used for many years in the United States, but only in piecemeal fashion. In the past, for example, a land developer would be primarily concerned with local zoning ordinances and building codes, many of which would differ whenever a development moved beyond the boundaries of one local governmental unit. The land use planning currently envisioned by governmental leaders would place more control of the planning process at the state and, possibly, federal levels; planning would be directed toward larger areas of land, eliminating inconsistent uses of neighboring lands that happen to be in different counties, townships, or cities. The immediate effect on the developer, then, would be the need to clear future developments with regional or state agencies as well as with local governmental units.

In addition to the trend toward state and federal land use planning, a bewildering array of environmental legislation has been enacted at both state and federal levels. This legislation is directed

1. *Stop Signs for Developers Going Up
All Over U. S.*, 76 U. S. News and
World Report 40 (1974).

441

against water pollution, air pollution, and noise pollution and toward the control of pesticides, toxic substances and radiation. In the area of air quality control alone, a developer must consider (1) regulation of indirect sources (buildings and structures) of air pollution under the Clean Air Act; (2) transportation controls relating to management of parking areas, also adopted under the Clean Air Act; (3) Air Quality Maintenance Plans in areas designated by the states as having the potential for excessive air pollution; (4) federal regulations requiring states to implement plans to prevent air pollution emergencies; and (5) federal regulations designed to prevent significant deterioration of existing air quality.[2]

This chapter is intended to provide an overview of land use planning and environmental legislation at both the state and the federal level.

# I.  LAND USE PLANNING

## A.  STATE LAND USE PLANNING

There are four major methods of state land use planning in existence.[3] The first of these involves direct state regulation of land use, a method adopted in Hawaii, Maine, and Vermont. In Hawaii, the State Land Use Commission is authorized to classify land in the state's four counties as "urban," "agricultural" or "conservation." The counties make land use decisions within the "urban" district, while state agencies regulate the other two districts.[4] The Maine land use plan is similar to the Hawaiian scheme with one major exception: the Maine land use commission only has power to regulate the unincorporated areas of the state. The Vermont plan is characterized by a subdelegation of authority to seven regional districts in which commissions administer the land use program. In both Maine and Vermont, land use legislation is designed primarily to regulate corporate developers of housing projects.

A second method of land use planning—involving areas of "critical concern"—is characterized by state regulation of a limited geographical area affected by a land use crisis.[5] Critical area regulation includes the San Francisco Bay Conservation and Development Commission, the Tahoe Regional Planning Agency, the Hackensack Meadowland Development Commission, the Adirondack Park Agency, the Delaware Coastal Zone Act and the California Coastal Zone Act.[6]

2. Mastriana, *Environmental Regulation Checklist for Shopping Center Development*, 9 Nat.Resources Law 81 (1976).

3. This classification system comes from R. Tager, Innovations in State Legislation: Land Use Management 5–7 (1973).

4. The descriptions of direct state regulation systems are paraphrased from Low, *State Land Use Control: Why Pending Federal Legislation Will Help*, 25 Hastings L.J. 1165 (1974).

5. Id. at 1175.

6. Id. at 1175.

The Delaware Coastal Zone Act, for example, was a response to the development of new oil tanker facilities in coastal areas. The legislation prohibits additional oil refineries within a one to six mile zone along the Delaware Bay Coast and the Atlantic Coast and strictly regulates all other new industrial development within the same area.[7]

The land use legislation enacted in Florida might be considered a blend of the first two methods of state land use planning. The Florida Environmental Land and Water Management Act of 1972 is considered "clearly the most promising state action" taken in the last decade.[8] The act may serve as a model for other states because Florida, unlike Hawaii, Maine and Vermont, is a large, populous state with all of the problems found in most other states. Also, Florida modeled its legislation after the American Law Institute's Model Act, which is expected to have a "significant impact on future state legislation." [9]

The Florida land use legislation is directed toward "areas of critical state concern" and "developments of regional impact." An area of "critical state concern" is one that has a significant impact on environmental, historical, natural, or archeological resources of regional or statewide importance. A Florida commission composed of the governor and the cabinet designates the boundaries of the areas of critical concern; all development within those boundaries must comply with state land use guidelines. A "development of regional impact" is a development that is of such character, magnitude, or location as to have a substantial effect on the health, safety, and welfare of citizens of more than one county. These developments would include airports, large subdivisions, shopping centers, power plants, and other major projects. While such developments still must be approved at the local level, the state land use planning agency may challenge the local decision, forcing a review of the decision by a state commission that has the power to deny permission for the development.[10]

The third method of state land use planning is state regulation on the basis of functional criteria. The only example of this method is the Massachusetts Zoning Appeals Law. Under this law, a public agency or nonprofit corporation that has been denied the right to build low-income housing by a local authority may appeal the denial to a state committee that is more likely to consider what is best for the entire region.[11]

The last method of state land use control is use of regional land use planning and control. By 1966, thirty-eight states had adopted regional planning legislation; this legislation is often ineffective,

7. R. Tager, supra note 3, at 5.

8. Low, supra note 4, at 1183.

9. Id. at 1187.

10. Id. at 1181–83.

11. R. Tager, supra note 3, at 6.

however, because it asks for only voluntary participation of local government units, and most regional planning commissions merely serve in an advisory function.[12]   As a result, some states have developed a stronger system of regional land use control.   The Twin Cities Metropolitan Council, for example, was created by the Minnesota legislature to coordinate planning and development in the Minneapolis-St. Paul region, which is composed of seven counties and 320 local governmental units.   The council regulates land use by reviewing and approving development plans of all boards, commissions, and agencies —using a comprehensive development plan prepared as a guide.[13]

In addition to the four major methods of state land use planning, the concept of transferable development rights (TDRs) has recently gained popularity at both state and local levels.   Traditional methods of controlling land use—such as eminent domain or zoning—often are either too expensive or subject to variations in the form of spot zoning, variances, and zone changes.   As a result, a number of governmental units have adopted the approach that the ownership of real estate is a bundle of individual rights, including the right to develop the real estate, and that any of these rights may be sold to someone else.

Several municipalities use the following system based on transferable development rights (TDRs).   (1) A master plan is established that designates which sections of the municipality may be developed; (2) every property owner is given "shares" of development rights as determined by the size or value of his land holdings; and (3) a developer must present the municipality with an appropriate number of TDRs before he may develop real estate.   For instance, the town of St. George, Vermont, has a population of 500 and an area of 2,300 acres.   The town established a master plan that included an area in which future growth would be focused.   For a developer to obtain authority to proceed with a development, he must transfer a specified number of TDRs to the town; to build twenty houses, for example, he might be required to transfer twenty TDRs.   If he lacks the required TDRs, he may purchase the shares from other landowners in the area.   In other cases, transferable development rights are used to preserve ecological resources and landmarks and to encourage the construction of low-income housing.[14]

## B.   FEDERAL LAND USE PLANNING

1.   **Existing Legislation.**   Existing federal land use legislation, which includes at least 112 federal land-oriented programs, may be grouped under two main headings:   natural resources and physical

12.  Low, supra note 4, at 1172.

13.  R. Tager, supra note 3, at 6, 7.

14.  Rose, *The Transfer of Development Rights:   A Preview of an Evolving Concept*, 3 Real Est.L.J. 330 (1975).

development.[15] The following are natural resources agencies and programs: (1) The Council on Environmental Quality is responsible for analyzing land and environmental conditions and trends, reviewing federal programs, and recommending environmental policies. (2) Services of the Department of Agriculture, including the Cooperative State Research Service, Agricultural Stabilization and Conservation Service, Soil Conservation Service, and the Forest Service, administer programs relating to land use. (3) The Bureau of Land Management manages approximately 450 million acres of federal public land. (4) The Environmental Protection Agency is responsible for environmental research, pollution control, solid waste management, and noise abatement. (5) A number of agencies are responsible for water programs. (6) Several agencies are involved in land use in particular areas, such as the Alaska Power Administration and the Bonneville Power Administration. (7) Federal programs dealing with minerals and wildlife are handled by the Bureau of Mines and the Bureau of Sport Fisheries and Wildlife respectively, while the Bureau of Outdoor Recreation administers programs for recreational activity.

The following agencies and programs are related to physical development: (1) The Farmers Home Administration is involved in the development of rural housing. (2) The Department of Housing and Urban Development administers most federal housing programs. The programs relate to all aspects of housing and include the Interstate Land Sales Full Disclosure Act, housing rehabilitation, construction of low- and moderate-income housing, the "701" program for urban development, the "New Community" assistance grants, and the Model Cities program. (3) The Economic Development Administration oversees a number of programs to assist economically distressed areas. (4) The Department of Commerce administers five regional development programs. (5) Several federal agencies sponsor programs to assist the development of sanitation facilities. (6) The Department of Transportation administers most transportation programs and conducts transportation research and planning.

In addition to these programs that directly affect land use, other federal programs, individually or in combination, often affect land use. It is claimed, for example, that urban sprawl has been assisted by federal policies encouraging the purchase of single-family homes. These policies include what has been termed the "familiar litany" of the effect of FHA mortgage insurance for homeowners, the interstate highway system, and the allowance of a tax deduction for home mortgage interest.[16]

15. National Land Use Policy Legislation: An Analysis of Legislative Proposals and State Laws, Senate Comm. on Interior and Insular Affairs; 93rd Congress, 1st Session, at 99. The descriptions of existing federal programs are paraphrased from this analysis. See also pp. 23–39 for a chronological summary of major enactments, statements, and actions related to land use policy.

16. Holland, *National Growth Policy: Notes on the Federal Role*, 1973, Urban Law Annual 59 (1973).

2. **Proposed Legislation.** The existence of so many separate programs affecting land use is one reason for the potential development of additional federal land use legislation. This legislation, it is claimed, would prevent clashes between agencies viewing development from different perspectives; it would also attempt to coordinate what is now, in the word of an Interior Department official, the "shotgunning [of] $40–$50–$60 billion to 80,000 jurisdictions (through revenue sharing) without any plan or theory." [17] For these and other reasons, environmentalists herald federal land use proposals as comparable in importance to the National Environmental Policy Act of 1969, the Clean Air Act Amendment of 1970, and the Federal Water Pollution Control Act Amendments of 1972. [18]

Federal land use proposals to date have represented three different strategies. [19] The first of these strategies would utilize a "stick" approach whereby federal legislation would require comprehensive state level planning. If a state failed to implement planning within a reasonable time, it would be punished by the loss of federal funds in other areas. The second approach, adopted by opponents of federal control of land use, would be to provide federal funds for state planning with no strings attached. The third strategy, the "carrot" approach, represents a compromise and has been the most promising proposal to date. In 1972, a bill using this approach passed the Senate but died in the House of Representatives. Again in 1973, a similar bill (S.268) was passed by the Senate but was not considered by the House. Yet when federal land use legislation is enacted, it will probably be similar to S.268; thus, this proposal deserves to be examined in greater detail.

The stated purpose of S.268 was "To establish a national land use policy, to authorize the Secretary of the Interior to make grants to assist the states to develop and implement State land use programs, to coordinate Federal programs and policies which have a land use impact, to coordinate planning and management of adjacent non-Federal lands, and to establish an Office of Land Use Policy Administration in the Department of the Interior, and for other purposes." [20] These objectives would be achieved under a program administered by a new bureaucracy in the Department of the Interior—the Office of Land Use Policy Administration. One of the major functions of this office would be to administer the "carrot"—a grant-in-aid program to assist the states in developing a state land use program which would control developments in areas of critical environmental concern as

17. The Ann Arbor News, April 23, 1975, at 30.

18. Healy, *National Land Use Proposal: Land Use Legislation of Landmark Environmental Significance*, 3 Environmental Affairs 355 (1974).

19. Haskell, *Land Use and the Environment: Public Policy Issues*, 5 Environment Reporter 1 (1974).

20. S. 268, 93rd Cong., 1st Sess. (1973).

well as other large-scale developments with more than a local environmental impact.

The "carrot" approach has three main characteristics.[21] First, the role of the federal government is to guide the states in making their own land use decisions. Second, the proposal encourages states to work with local government in areas involving more than local concern. Third, public participation is required in the planning process. Because the thrust of the proposal would be to allow states to make land use decisions, the state land use programs discussed above will achieve special importance.

## C. LEGAL CHALLENGES TO LAND USE PLANNING

There are a variety of legal challenges that might be raised with regard to state and federal land use plans. While these challenges in general are likely to include the traditional legal challenges to zoning ordinances, probably the foremost legal problem confronting the statutes will be the question of whether or not a land use plan constitutes an unlawful taking of private property without just compensation. That very problem underlies the following hypothetical situation posed by Rep. Paul J. Fannin of Arizona during a Senate floor debate of S.268 in 1973. "A man purchases, in good faith, three hundred acres of land containing a lake which he intends to develop for resort purposes. He reflects on its development potential. The land use bill becomes law; and because it is found that the lake in question is of vital importance to a species of endangered waterfowl, it is found to be an 'area of critical environmental concern.' The state, therefore, outlaws any development of the property containing the lake as being incompatible with its designation. As a consequence, the land loses three-quarters of its market value. Under these circumstances, does the designation constitute a taking or impairment of property rights which is compensable under the law of each and every state?"[22]

This issue was faced in In re Spring Valley Development,[23] a case of considerable interest because it involves a challenge to the Maine state land use system that utilizes direct control of land use by the state. Spring Valley Development was the name of a 92-acre subdivision, planned by Lakesites, Inc., on one side of a pond in Raymond, Maine. Development of the property by Lakesites was brought to a halt by an order of the Maine Environmental Improvement Commission after a hearing authorized by the Maine land use act. Lakesites' appeal of the commission's decision to the Supreme Judicial Court of Maine was based in part on a "taking" issue; the claim was made that requiring a subdivider to comply with the criteria of the legislation denied him the "ability to sell or offer for sale his land."[24] The

21. Healy, supra note 18, at 358.

22. 52 Cong.Digest 289 (1973).

23. 300 A.2d 736 (Me.1973).

24. Brief for Appellant at 13.

court summarily rejected this assertion, noting that nothing in the record indicated that the legislation constituted an unreasonable burden on the property that would amount to a taking. The court also cited an earlier Maine decision, which held that only a restriction that deprived property of all commercial value constituted a taking, and concluded that ". . . the record demonstrates only that the appellant's land cannot be sold for residential purposes while subdivided to the extent and in the manner Lakesites originally planned."

In addition to the "taking" issue, Lakesites raised other constitutional issues that are likely to be used in attacks on land use statutes elsewhere. First, is the state land use plan a constitutional exercise of a state's police power? The Maine court, after stating a presumption that all acts of the legislature are constitutional, concluded that the limitation of property use embodied in the Maine land use scheme was within the state's police power to preserve the quality of air, soil, and water. In reaching this conclusion, the court quoted a 1907 opinion that "if the owners of large tracts can waste them at will without State restriction, the State and its people may be helplessly impoverished and one great purpose of government defeated."

Second, is the land use legislation unconstitutionally vague, making compliance impossible? Language in the Maine legislation that was particularly troublesome required the state commission to approve developments which had "no adverse effect on natural environment." Utilizing the test that the standard "must be sufficiently distinct so that the public may know what conduct is barred," the court decided that the language quoted, coupled with more specific provisions throughout the act, was sufficiently clear.[25]

Third, does the land use plan deny a developer equal protection of the law? Lakesites claimed that its equal protection rights were violated because persons who plan to subdivide more than twenty acres, such as Lakesites, must receive commission approval, but subdividers of less than twenty acres had no such requirements. Lakesites noted, for example, that a twenty-one-acre subdivision containing five residences must receive approval, yet a nineteen-acre subdivision containing nineteen residences needs no approval. The court rejected this argument by concluding that the act involved no irrational or arbitrary discrimination against large subdividers: "It is elementary that the Legislature may in its judgment create classifications so long as they are not arbitrary and are based upon actual differences in classes which differences bear a substantial rational relation to the public purpose sought to be accomplished by the statute."

Fourth, does the land use legislation, in failing to require a comprehensive plan, constitute spot zoning? In Maine, the statutes au-

25. See Note, *Environmental Law*, 22 Kansas L.R. 127 (1973) for a critical analysis of this conclusion.

thorizing municipalities to enact zoning ordinances require that the ordinances be based upon a master plan. Lakesites argued that "effect upon local environment is cumulative" [26] so that a prior developer who is given commission approval without reference to a comprehensive plan takes more than his share of the environmental capacity. The result, Lakesites argued, is spot zoning, which gives a privileged status to some developers.[27] The court rejected this argument on the grounds that the basic purpose of the land use statute and the zoning legislation differs. While both seek to restrict the use of land, the land use act was "not directed toward promoting an orderly community growth relating one area of a community to all other areas. It is not concerned with where a development takes place in general but only that the development takes place in a manner consistent with the needs of the public for a healthy environment."

## II. ENVIRONMENTAL LAW

### A. STATE ENVIRONMENTAL PROTECTION LEGISLATION

Individual states have enacted a wide variety of legislation over the years in an attempt to control contamination of the environment. This legislation includes the four types of state land use planning strategies discussed above. State legislation directly related to control of environment quality may be divided into two categories: (1) traditional legislation, which delegates control to state administrative agencies; and (2) modern legislation, which gives individual citizens the opportunity to participate in environmental law enforcement. To illustrate these two approaches, we will discuss the legislation enacted in Illinois, representing the most comprehensive form of the traditional approach, and Michigan laws, representing the modern approach.

1. **Illinois Legislation.** The Illinois Environmental Protection Act represents an attempt to control all types of environmental pollution by regulating the sources of pollution. Under the act, three bodies are created. The Environmental Protection Agency investigates cases for possible violation of environmental law and prosecutes cases before the second body, the Pollution Control Board. The Pollution Control Board, in addition to adjudicating these cases, establishes rules and regulations designed to achieve environmental standards. The Illinois Institute for Environmental Quality conducts long-range planning and research into control of contaminants.

In order to enforce the rules and regulations, a complaint is first filed with the Pollution Control Board, and the violator is given written notice to appear before the board on a future date. The violator may also file a written answer to the complaint. After the hearing,

**26.** Brief for Appellant at 20.  **27.** See Note, supra note 25, at 132.

the board will issue a final order on the basis of all evidence presented at the hearing as well as other factors, such as the social and economic value of the polluter to the community. The board has the power to order a stop to violations of the rules and regulations and to fine violators $10,000 for each violation and an additional $1,000 a day for every day the violation continues. Decisions of the board may be appealed directly to an appellate court.

In addition to the above provisions, the Illinois statute gives the Environmental Protection Agency the power to seal any facility without a board hearing if an emergency should arise. The board may require anyone intending to construct facilities that might emit pollutants to obtain a permit, after submitting plans to the agency. And the Illinois act allows the board to issue variances whenever a regulation imposes an "arbitrary or unreasonable hardship" on a violator.[28]

2. **Michigan Legislation.** Michigan, like other states, has statutes that empower various agencies to control environmental quality. However, Michigan was a leader in also allowing direct citizen action under the Environmental Protection Act of 1970. This Act is summarized in Ray v. Mason County Drain Comm., infra. The Michigan approach has been followed in Minnesota, Massachusetts, Connecticut, South Dakota, Florida, and Indiana.

## B. FEDERAL ENVIRONMENTAL PROTECTION LEGISLATION

1. **National Environmental Policy Act.** The year 1970 was critically important in the history of federal environmental protection. In that year the National Environmental Policy Act was signed into law. In this act, Congress described the national environmental policy: "The Congress, recognizing the profound impact of man's activity on the interrelations of all components of the natural environment, particularly the profound influences of population growth, high-density urbanization, industrial expansion, resource exploitation, and new and expanding technological advances and recognizing further the critical importance of restoring and maintaining environmental quality to the overall welfare and development of man, declares that it is the continuing policy of the Federal Government, in cooperation with State and local governments and other concerned public and private organizations, to use all practicable means and measures, including financial and technical assistance, in a manner calculated to foster and promote the general welfare, to create and maintain conditions under which man and nature can exist in productive harmony, and fulfill the social, economic, and other requirements of present and future generations of Americans. . . . The Congress recognizes that each person should enjoy a healthful environment and that each per-

---

28. See Comment, *The Illinois Environmental Protection Act—A Comprehensive Program for Pollution Control*, 66 Nw.U.L.Rev. 345 (1971).

son has a responsibility to contribute to the preservation and enhancement of the environment."

Congress directed that regulations and public laws of the United States be interpreted according to this policy. Further, federal agencies were given the duty of including an environmental impact statement "in every recommendation or report on proposals for legislation and other major Federal actions significantly affecting the quality of the human environment." The statement must cover "(i) the environmental impact of the proposed action, (ii) any adverse environmental effects which cannot be avoided should the proposal be implemented, (iii) alternatives to the proposed action, (iv) the relationship between local short-term uses of man's environment and the maintenance and enhancement of long-term productivity, and (v) any irreversible and irretrievable commitments of resources which would be involved in the proposed action should it be implemented." Most litigation to date has focused upon the issues of whether a statement is necessary and—if a statement has been prepared—whether it is adequate. See Daly v. Volpe, infra.

The Environmental Policy Act also created the three-member Council on Environmental Quality. Among the duties of the council are the following: (1) to assist the President in preparing an annual Environmental Quality Report; (2) to gather and analyze information concerning conditions and trends in environmental quality; (3) to review federal programs to determine whether they are contributing toward the achievement of the act's environmental policy; (4) to develop and recommend national policies to improve environmental quality; (5) to document and define changes in the natural environment; and (6) to report to the President at least once a year on the condition of the environment.

2. **Environmental Protection Agency.** The year 1970 also brought the establishment of the Environmental Protection Agency (EPA) for the purpose of coordinating the government's environmentally related activities. According to the President, the functions of the EPA include establishing and enforcing environmental protection standards consistent with national environmental goals; conducting research on the adverse effects of pollution and on methods and equipment for controlling it; gathering information to strengthen environmental protection programs and recommend policy changes; assisting others, through grants, technical assistance, and other means, in arresting pollution of the environment; and assisting the Council on Environmental Quality in developing and recommending to the President new policies for the protection of the environment.

The impact of the Environmental Protection Agency's efforts have been described as follows: "Cars rolling off Detroit's assembly lines now have antipollution devices as standard equipment. The dense black smokestack emissions that used to symbolize industrial

prosperity are rare, and illegal, sights.  Plants that once blithely ran
discharge water out a pipe and into a river must apply for permits
that are almost impossible to get unless the plants install expensive
water treatment equipment.  All told, the EPA has made a sizable
dent in man-made environmental filth." [29]  On the other hand, the
agency has been criticized for the additional costs imposed on business and on utility consumers for these environmental controls.  In
1975, $7.7 billion was spent on capital expenditures to control air and
waste pollution, and the Council on Environmental Quality has pre-
dicted that existing legislation will require an outlay of $258 billion
from 1975 through 1984.

The work of the Environmental Protection Agency has become
especially important in recent years with the enactment of a number
of federal statutes relating to the environment.  Environmental legislation covering air and water pollution is especially important in land
use planning.  "Control of both air and water pollution depends on
land control to a great degree.  Evidence of this is presented by
present clean air regulations which control the placement of shopping
centers and other public attractions if the consequential increase in
traffic would cause a violation of the air quality standards.  The effects of land use on water quality are equally obvious.  Erosion, fertilizer and animal excretion runoff, sewage disposal, and destruction
of the acquifer are examples of how improper land use is tied into
water pollution." [30]

a. *Air.*  Congress originally enacted the Clean Air Act in 1963,
although the act has been amended on several occasions.  Title I of
the act presents the Congressional finding that "the growth in the
amount and complexity of air pollution, brought about by urbanization, industrial development, and the increasing use of motor vehicles,
has resulted in mounting dangers to the public health and welfare, including injury to agricultural crops and livestock, damage to and the
deterioration of property, and hazards to air and ground transportation."  Title I requires the administrator of the EPA to (1) prepare a
list of air pollutants that have an adverse effect on public health and
welfare;  (2) issue air quality criteria and control techniques for air
pollutants on the list;  and (3) publish regulations prescribing national primary and secondary ambient air standards for the listed pollutants.  (Primary standards are designed for the protection of public
health and secondary standards are those required to protect the public welfare from the adverse effects of an air pollutant.)  After pro-
mulgation of the standards, states are required to adopt plans for implementation which must then be approved by the EPA administrator.  The plan for the primary standards must be adopted, at the lat-

29. *The Tricks of the Trade-Off*, Business Week 72 (April 4, 1977).

30. *Environmental Land Use Control:
Common Law and Statutory Approaches*, 28 U. of Miami L.R. 135
(1973).

est, within three years of approval of the primary standards, and secondary standards must be attained within a reasonable time. The Clean Air Act gives the administrator power to enforce the plans either by issuing cease and desist orders or by a civil enforcement action in federal district court. The act also provides for a fine of up to $50,000 and imprisonment for up to two years in certain cases of knowing violation. Under Title II of the Clean Air Act, which covers emission standards for moving sources, the administrator of the EPA is directed to prescribe standards for air pollutants from motor vehicles.

b. *Water.* The most important legislation relating to water pollution is the Federal Water Pollution Control Act, originally enacted in 1948 and later amended on several occasions. The goals of the 1972 amendments are that "the discharge of pollutants into navigable waters be eliminated by 1985" and that a level of water quality be achieved by July 1, 1983 that will both provide for the protection and propagation of fish and wildlife, and provide for water recreation. The 1972 amendments also state that industries must use the "best practicable" water pollution control technology by July 1, 1977, and the "best available" technology by July 1, 1983, although provisions for extending the deadlines were enacted in 1977. In order to achieve the legislative goals, the discharge of pollutants from certain sources without a permit is prohibited. The permits, which limit the "quantities, rates and concentration of chemical, physical, biological, and other constituents which are discharged," are issued by the EPA or by states that have EPA-approved permit programs. Penalties for violating the law range from a $2,500 to $50,000 maximum fine per day and up to two years in prison.

## C.  JUDICIAL REVIEW OF ADMINISTRATIVE DECISIONS

As state and federal environmental legislation illustrates, administrative agencies have been given a leading role in protecting the environment. The work of administrative agencies in other areas has been strongly criticized in recent years because agencies often lack personnel and funding or have close ties to the industry being regulated. One critic, for example, has observed: "As the oldest independent federal regulatory agency, the Interstate Commerce Commission has set longevity records in its systematic failure to protect or further the public interest in surface transportation. Long ago, the ICC found itself surrounded by a special interest constituency that viewed the agency as an opportunity for protection from competition and for insulation from consumer demands." [31]

Because of potential abuses, it is important that agency decisions be subject to review by the courts. In conducting their review,

31.  R. Fellmuth, The Interstate Commerce Commission: The Public Interest and the I.C.C. vii–viii (1970).

courts will not only determine whether the agency followed the procedures mandated by the relevant statute but will also review the actual decision of the agency. Under Section 10 of the Administrative Procedure Act, a reviewing court may set aside an agency action that is found to be any one of the following: "(A) arbitrary, capricious, an abuse of discretion, or otherwise not in accordance with law; (B) contrary to constitutional right, power, privilege, or immunity; (C) in excess of statutory jurisdiction, authority, or limitations, or short of statutory right; (D) without observance of procedure required by law; (E) unsupported by substantial evidence in a case subject to sections 556 and 557 of this title or otherwise reviewed on the record of an agency hearing provided by statute; or (F) unwarranted by the facts to the extent that the facts are subject to trial de novo by the reviewing court." In deciding whether an administrative decision is arbitrary, capricious, or an abuse of discretion, a court "must consider whether the decision was based on a consideration of the relevant factors and whether there has been an error of judgment. * * * Although this inquiry into the facts is to be searching and careful, the ultimate standard of review is a narrow one. The court is not empowered to substitute its judgment for that of the agency." [32]

In many cases, a court will refuse to review an agency case because any one of the four following criteria has not been met.

1. **Standing.** In order to challenge an administrative decision, a plaintiff must first prove that he has standing to bring the action, that is, that he has been hurt by the agency's action. In Ass'n of Data Processing Service Organizations, Inc. v. Camp,[33] the petitioners, who sold data processing services to businesses, challenged a ruling of the Comptroller of the Currency to the effect that national banks may make data processing services available to bank customers and other businesses. In holding that the petitioners had standing, Justice Douglas applied the following tests: "Generalizations about standing to sue are largely worthless as such. One generalization is, however, necessary and that is that the question of standing in the federal courts is to be considered in the framework of Article III which restricts judicial power to 'cases' and 'controversies.' . . . The first question is whether the plaintiff alleges that the challenged action has caused him injury in fact, economic or otherwise. . . . The question of standing . . . concerns, apart from the 'case' or 'controversy' test, the question whether the interest sought to be protected by the complainant is arguably within the zone of interests to be protected or regulated by the statute or constitutional guarantee in question."

In Sierra Club v. Morton, infra, the Supreme Court decided that the Sierra Club did not have standing to maintain the action. The

**32.** Citizens to Preserve Overton Park, Inc. v. Volpe, 401 U.S. 402, 91 S.Ct. 814, 28 L.Ed.2d 136 (1971).

**33.** 397 U.S. 150, 90 S.Ct. 827, 25 L.Ed. 2d 184 (1970).

court noted that, while the interest of the person bringing the action may reflect aesthetic, conservationist, and recreational values, the party seeking review must still allege that he individually has suffered an injury.

2. **Ripeness.** Judges are reluctant to render advisory opinions on matters that are not actually in controversy because it is felt that that adjudicatory process should be reserved for actual rather than hypothetical problems. It is often stated that this policy stems from Article III of the U.S. Constitution, which limits judicial power to "cases" and "controversies." [34] A leading administrative law decision relating to ripeness is Abbott Laboratories v. Gardner,[35] in which the Supreme Court decided that a regulation of the Commissioner of Food and Drugs could be judicially reviewed even before it was enforced. According to the Court, "Without undertaking to survey the intricacies of the ripeness doctrine it is fair to say that its basic rationale is to prevent the courts, through avoidance of premature adjudication, from entangling themselves in abstract disagreements over administrative policies, and also to protect the agencies from judicial interference until an administrative decision has been formalized and its effects felt in a concrete way by challenging parties. The problem is best seen in a two-fold aspect, requiring us to evaluate both the fitness of the issue for judicial decision and the hardship to the parties of withholding court consideration."

3. **Exhaustion of Remedies.** As a general rule, the courts will not review an administrative decision until the party has tried—and completely exhausted—all of the administrative remedies. However, exhaustion of remedies will not be required if the requirement would result in irreparable injury, if the administrative agency does not have jurisdiction over the matter, or if it is improbable that the party will obtain adequate relief through administrative remedies.[36] For instance, in McKart v. United States,[37] McKart was prosecuted in a criminal action for refusing to submit to induction. In defense, he challenged his classification by the selective service board—even though he did not first attempt an administrative appeal of the board's decision. The Supreme Court initially noted that the exhaustion of remedies doctrine is designed to avoid disrupting the administrative process, for "it is generally more efficient for the administrative process to go forward without interruption." However, the court held that this interest must "clearly outweigh the severe burden imposed upon the registrant if he is denied judicial review." In this case the burden of going to jail without judicial review, coupled with the fact that the issue was one of interpreting a statute rather than

**34.** K. Davis, Administrative Law and Government 81 (1975).

**35.** 387 U.S. 136, 87 S.Ct. 1507, 18 L.Ed. 2d 681 (1967).

**36.** K. Davis, Administrative Law and Government 46, 84 (1975).

**37.** 395 U.S. 185, 89 S.Ct. 1657, 23 L.Ed. 2d 194 (1969).

abuse of discretion by the selective service board, outweighed the interests underlying the exhaustion rule.

4. **Reviewability.** The last threshold question a court must face is whether the issue is subject to review by the courts. The Administrative Procedure Act, section 701, states that issues are not reviewable when "(a) statutes preclude judicial review; or (b) agency action is committed to agency discretion by law." One of the major reasons why judges decide that a matter is "committed to agency discretion" is that the administrative decision involves expertise beyond the ability or capacity of the court.[38] For instance, in Kletschka v. Driver,[39] the court decided against review of a decision by the Veterans Administration to transfer Dr. Kletschka from Syracuse to Houston, a transfer that allegedly deprived Dr. Kletschka of a research grant. "It would not be feasible for the courts to review decisions by the V.A. awarding or refusing to award research grants. Each such decision . . . requires considerable expertise in the scientific, medical, and technical aspects of each application. A reviewing court would have to master considerable technical data before it could even attempt to determine whether one application, Dr. Kletschka's for example, was so superior to the others that its rejection by the V.A. was an abuse of discretion. Furthermore, even if these technical aspects were mastered it would be difficult for the court to review the judgments of relative personal competence which necessarily play a role in the agency determination." The court also noted that the case involved "strained personal relationships" between Dr. Kletschka and other staff members and that if the administrative decision were reviewed, it would open the door to a "vast quantity of litigation." See Environmental Defense Fund v. Hardin, infra.

# CASES

---

### RAY v. MASON COUNTY DRAIN COMM.

Supreme Court of Michigan, 1975.
393 Mich. 294, 224 N.W.2d 883.

WILLIAMS, J. This is a significant case of first impression relating to Michigan's world-famous Environmental Protection Act (EPA). The question involved is the kind of findings of fact required of the trial judge by GCR 1963, 517 and § 3(1) of the EPA in deciding an action brought under the EPA.

---

38. K. Davis, Administrative Law and Government 57 (1975).     39. 411 F.2d 436 (2nd Cir. 1969).

In the instant case the trial judge failed to make specific findings of facts. Rather than attempt a review *de novo*, we remand for full and specific findings of fact  *  . * .

*  *  *

Michigan's EPA was the first legislation of its kind and has attracted worldwide attention. The act also has served as a model for other states in formulating environmental legislation. The enactment of the EPA signals a dramatic change from the practice where the important task of environmental law enforcement was left to administrative agencies without the opportunity for participation by individuals or groups of citizens. Not every public agency proved to be diligent and dedicated defenders of the environment. The EPA has provided a sizable share of the initiative for environmental law enforcement for that segment of society most directly affected—the public.

The act provides private individuals and other legal entities with standing to maintain actions in the circuit courts for declaratory and other equitable relief against anyone "for the protection of the air, water and other natural resources and the public trust therein from pollution, impairment or destruction".

The act also empowers the circuit courts to grant "equitable relief or  *  *  * impose conditions on the defendant that are required to protect the air, water and natural resources  *  *  *".

But the EPA does more than give standing to the public and grant equitable powers to the circuit courts, it also imposes a duty on individuals and organizations both in the public and private sectors to prevent or minimize degradation of the environment which is caused or is likely to be caused by their activities. The EPA prohibits pollution, destruction, or impairment of the environment unless it can be shown that "there is no feasible and prudent alternative" and that defendant's conduct "is consistent with the promotion of public health, safety and welfare in light of the state's paramount concern for the protection of its natural resources  *  *  *".

The Legislature in establishing environmental rights set the parameters for the standard of environmental quality but did not attempt to set forth an elaborate scheme of detailed provisions designed to cover every conceivable type of environmental pollution or impairment. Rather the Legislature spoke as precisely as the subject matter permits and in its wisdom left to the courts the important task of giving substance to the standard by developing a common law of environmental quality. The act allows the courts to fashion standards in the context of actual problems as they arise in individual cases and to take into consideration changes in technology which the Legislature at the time of the act's passage could not hope to foresee.

*  *  *

## DALY v. VOLPE

United States Dist. Court of Washington, 1972.
350 F.Supp. 252.

BEEKS, Chief Judge.

Plaintiffs, individual residents and property owners in or near the proposed corridor of I–90, a federally funded interstate highway through the State of Washington, seek to enjoin its construction. They base their claim on essentially two grounds: First, that selection of the location of this corridor was arbitrary and capricious, and second, that defendants violated the provisions of certain federal statutes.

The facts of this case are not essentially in dispute. The state proposes to construct a section of I–90 in the vicinity of North Bend, Washington. The first corridor location hearing was held on April 8, 1957. The issues lay dormant until July 30, 1969, when the location design engineer sent letters to interested parties, requesting comment on corridor A–3, a segment of the proposed highway that would parallel the location of the existing highway, U.S. 10, and also pass through the town of North Bend. A second location hearing was held on December 3, 1969. Meetings with interested groups were held through the summer of 1970. Late in August 1970, the state made public an "Environmental Report of the Upper Snoqualmie Valley," which did not discuss alternative routes, but did provide a summary of information which bore on choosing a route most favorable to the environment. This "Environmental Report" was distributed at the third corridor location hearing of September 1, 1970. Following this last hearing, the state and federal defendants for the first time advocated construction through corridor E–3, which would completely bypass North Bend to the south.

The "Environmental Report" and an "Advance Planning Study" were transmitted to the Federal Highway Administration (FHWA) division engineer on September 25, 1970. The state's request for approval of corridor E–3 was submitted November 4, 1970, and its draft environmental impact study was sent to FHWA on November 25, 1970. Corridor E–3 was approved November 30. A second draft environmental statement of January 13, 1971, and a "Final Environmental Statement" of February 8, 1971, were subsequently sent to FHWA. Neither of these environmental reports considered the ecological effects of the highway on Kimball Creek Marsh, a non-publicly owned refuge for waterfowl close to which the proposed highway will pass.

\*   \*   \*

Plaintiffs next contend that defendants failed to follow the required procedures with respect to drafting and filing an environmental impact statement. NEPA, which became law on January 1, 1970, requires that "all agencies of the Federal Government shall—

\* \* \*

(C) include in every recommendation or report on proposals for legislation and other major Federal actions significantly affecting the quality of the human environment, a detailed statement by the responsible official on—

(i) the environmental impact of the proposed action,

(ii) any adverse environmental effects which cannot be avoided should the proposal be implemented,

(iii) alternatives to the proposed action,

(iv) the relationship between local short-term uses of man's environment and the maintenance and enhancement of long-term productivity, and

(v) any irreversible and irretrievable commitments of resources which would be involved in the proposed action should it be implemented.

Prior to making any detailed statement, the responsible Federal official shall consult with and obtain the comments of any Federal agency which has jurisdiction by law or special expertise with respect to any environmental impact involved. Copies of such statement and the comments and views of the appropriate Federal, State, and local agencies, which are authorized to develop and enforce environmental standards, shall be made available to the President, the Council on Environmental Quality and to the public as provided by section 552 of Title 5, and shall accompany the proposal through the existing agency review processes; \* \* \*

Such "detailed statement" should "be prepared at the earliest practicable point in time" so that the statement can provide "significant inputs to the decisionmaking process."

\* \* \*

a. *The "Environmental Report" and "Advance Planning Study"*

Neither the "Environmental Report" nor the "Advance Planning Study" complies with NEPA, although the state should be commended for the polished and professional quality of both reports. The court's objection is not that they were poorly done, but that they fail to ask and answer all of the pertinent questions. The two reports, singly and in combination, fail to adequately analyze the five subjects identified by NEPA. The discussion of the environmental impact of the proposed location is not acceptable; it inadequately discusses the effects of corridor E–3 on the surrounding environment, particularly on Kimball Creek Marsh. Adverse environmental effects should be listed and discussed in a single section of the statement, and not scattered throughout the report. The court believes that the alternatives to the proposed corridor are adequately discussed in the "Advance

Planning Study," which may be incorporated by reference in the new environmental impact study. Neither report sufficiently discusses the relationship between local short-term uses of man's environment and long-term productivity. Finally, there is virtually no discussion of irreversible and irretrievable commitments of resources involved in locating the highway in corridor E–3.

### b. The First Draft Environmental Impact Statement

The state's first draft environmental impact statement was drafted in the form required by statute, but was ambiguous and self-contradictory. Paragraph one, concerning the environmental impact of the highway, failed to discuss Kimball Creek Marsh, and was too general and ambiguous. In redrafting an impact statement, state defendants may use information from the "Environmental Report", as pertinent, but must specifically discuss the effects of corridor E–3 on the area which that report concerned.

The second paragraph was inadequate. All adverse environmental effects should be listed, and harmful effects which cannot be avoided must be discussed to indicate what measures can be taken to minimize the harm. The state's draft environmental impact statement was far too general and not sufficiently detailed. This paragraph may include relevant information found in the "Advance Planning Study," e. g., on page 3.

Alternative routes were sufficiently discussed in the state's "Advance Planning Study," which may, as previously mentioned, be incorporated by reference into paragraph three of the new environmental impact statement.

Paragraph four of the draft impact statement is too general and not sufficiently detailed. The subjects discussed are relevant to the requirements of NEPA, but are conclusory rather than analytical. Relevant portions of the "Advance Planning Study" (e. g., pp. 3 and 25–33) and of the "Environmental Report" (e. g., pp. 14–19) may be reproduced in paragraph four of the new statement.

The fifth paragraph of the draft impact statement is totally unsatisfactory. It should list, among other things, (1) the cost of land, construction materials, labor, and other economically measurable costs which cannot be retrieved once a highway is constructed; and (2) the resources which may be irretrievably lost, and the nature of each such loss, to which a dollar value cannot be readily assigned— for example, the loss of forested recreational land.

Aside from these deficiencies, the state's first draft environmental impact statement was inadequately considered by FHWA. Indeed, the decision approving route E–3 came the first business day following receipt of the statement. The statute contemplates more deliberation than the time required to use a rubber stamp.

\* \* \*

It is the judgment of the court that defendants have failed to conform to the procedural requirements of 42 U.S.C.A. § 4332(2)(C).

\* \* \*

---

## SIERRA CLUB v. MORTON

Supreme Court of the United States, 1972.
405 U.S. 727, 92 S.Ct. 1361, 31 L.Ed.2d 636.

Mr. Justice STEWART delivered the opinion of the Court.

The Mineral King Valley is an area of great natural beauty nestled in the Sierra Nevada Mountains in Tulare County, California, adjacent to Sequoia National Park. It has been part of the Sequoia National Forest since 1926, and is designated as a national game refuge by special Act of Congress. Though once the site of extensive mining activity, Mineral King is now used almost exclusively for recreational purposes. Its relative inaccessibility and lack of development have limited the number of visitors each year, and at the same time have preserved the valley's quality as a quasi-wilderness area largely uncluttered by the products of civilization.

The United States Forest Service, which is entrusted with the maintenance and administration of national forests, began in the late 1940's to give consideration to Mineral King as a potential site for recreational development. Prodded by a rapidly increasing demand for skiing facilities, the Forest Service published a prospectus in 1965, inviting bids from private developers for the construction and operation of a ski resort that would also serve as a summer recreation area. The proposal of Walt Disney Enterprises, Inc., was chosen from those of six bidders, and Disney received a three-year permit to conduct surveys and explorations in the valley in connection with its preparation of a complete master plan for the resort.

The final Disney plan, approved by the Forest Service in January 1969, outlines a $35 million complex of motels, restaurants, swimming pools, parking lots, and other structures designed to accommodate 14,000 visitors daily. This complex is to be constructed on 80 acres of the valley floor under a 30-year use permit from the Forest Service. Other facilities, including ski lifts, ski trails, a cog-assisted railway, and utility installations, are to be constructed on the mountain slopes and in other parts of the valley under a revocable special-use permit. To provide access to the resort, the State of California proposes to construct a highway 20 miles in length. A section of this road would traverse Sequoia National Park, as would a proposed high-voltage power line needed to provide electricity for the resort. Both the highway and the power line require the approval of the Department of the Interior, which is entrusted with the preservation and maintenance of the national parks.

Representatives of the Sierra Club, who favor maintaining Mineral King largely in its present state, followed the progress of recreational planning for the valley with close attention and increasing dismay.  They unsuccessfully sought a public hearing on the proposed development in 1965, and in subsequent correspondence with officials of the Forest Service and the Department of the Interior, they expressed the Club's objections to Disney's plan as a whole and to particular features included in it.  In June 1969 the Club filed the present suit in the United States District Court for the Northern District of California, seeking a declaratory judgment that various aspects of the proposed development contravene federal laws and regulations governing the preservation of national parks, forests, and game refuges, and also seeking preliminary and permanent injunctions restraining the federal officials involved from granting their approval or issuing permits in connection with the Mineral King project.  The petitioner Sierra Club sued as a membership corporation with "a special interest in the conservation and the sound maintenance of the national parks, game refuges and forests of the country," and invoked the judicial-review provisions of the Administrative Procedure Act, 5 U.S.C.A. § 701 et seq.

\* \* \*

The first question presented is whether the Sierra Club has alleged facts that entitle it to obtain judicial review of the challenged action.  Whether a party has a sufficient stake in an otherwise justiciable controversy to obtain judicial resolution of that controversy is what has traditionally been referred to as the question of standing to sue.  Where the party does not rely on any specific statute authorizing invocation of the judicial process, the question of standing depends upon whether the party has alleged such a "personal stake in the outcome of the controversy," as to ensure that "the dispute sought to be adjudicated will be presented in an adversary context and in a form historically viewed as capable of judicial resolution."  Where, however, Congress has authorized public officials to perform certain functions according to law, and has provided by statute for judicial review of those actions under certain circumstances, the inquiry as to standing must begin with a determination of whether the statute in question authorizes review at the behest of the plaintiff.

The Sierra Club relies upon § 10 of the Administrative Procedure Act (APA), 5 U.S.C.A. § 702, which provides:

> "A person suffering legal wrong because of agency action, or adversely affected or aggrieved by agency action within the meaning of a relevant statute, is entitled to judicial review thereof."

Early decisions under this statute interpreted the language as adopting the various formulations of "legal interest" and "legal wrong" then prevailing as constitutional requirements of standing.  But, in

Association of Data Processing Service Organizations, Inc. v. Camp, 397 U.S. 150, 90 S.Ct. 827, 25 L.Ed.2d 184, and Barlow v. Collins, 397 U.S. 159, 90 S.Ct. 832, 25 L.Ed.2d 192, decided the same day, we held more broadly that persons had standing to obtain judicial review of federal agency action under § 10 of the APA where they had alleged that the challenged action had caused them "injury in fact," and where the alleged injury was to an interest "arguably within the zone of interests to be protected or regulated" by the statutes that the agencies were claimed to have violated.

In *Data Processing*, the injury claimed by the petitioners consisted of harm to their competitive position in the computer-servicing market through a ruling by the Comptroller of the Currency that national banks might perform data-processing services for their customers. In *Barlow*, the petitioners were tenant farmers who claimed that certain regulations of the Secretary of Agriculture adversely affected their economic position vis-à-vis their landlords. These palpable economic injuries have long been recognized as sufficient to lay the basis for standing, with or without a specific statutory provision for judicial review. Thus, neither *Data Processing* nor *Barlow* addressed itself to the question, which has arisen with increasing frequency in federal courts in recent years, as to what must be alleged by persons who claim injury of a noneconomic nature to interests that are widely shared. That question is presented in this case.

The injury alleged by the Sierra Club will be incurred entirely by reason of the change in the uses to which Mineral King will be put, and the attendant change in the aesthetics and ecology of the area. Thus, in referring to the road to be built through Sequoia National Park, the complaint alleged that the development "would destroy or otherwise adversely affect the scenery, natural and historic objects and wildlife of the park and would impair the enjoyment of the park for future generations." We do not question that this type of harm may amount to an "injury in fact" sufficient to lay the basis for standing under § 10 of the APA. Aesthetic and environmental well-being, like economic well-being, are important ingredients of the quality of life in our society, and the fact that particular environmental interests are shared by the many rather than the few does not make them less deserving of legal protection through the judicial process. But the "injury in fact" test requires more than an injury to a cognizable interest. It requires that the party seeking review be himself among the injured.

The impact of the proposed changes in the environment of Mineral King will not fall indiscriminately upon every citizen. The alleged injury will be felt directly only by those who use Mineral King and Sequoia National Park, and for whom the aesthetic and recreational values of the area will be lessened by the highway and ski resort. The Sierra Club failed to allege that it or its members would be affected in any of their activities or pastimes by the Disney development. Nowhere in the pleadings or affidavits did the Club state that its members use Mineral King for any purpose, much less that they use it in any way that would be significantly affected by the proposed actions of the respondents.

\*    \*    \*

As we conclude that the Court of Appeals was correct in its holding that the Sierra Club lacked standing to maintain this action, we do not reach any other questions presented in the petition, and we intimate no view on the merits of the complaint. The judgment is

Affirmed.

---

### ENVIRONMENTAL DEFENSE FUND, INC. v. HARDIN

United States Court of Appeals Dist. of Columbia, 1970.
428 F.2d 1093.

BAZELON, Chief Judge:

This case requires the court to consider under what circumstances there may be a judicial remedy for the failure of an administrative agency to act promptly, and what form that remedy may take.

The shipment of pesticides in interstate commerce is regulated by the Federal Insecticide, Fungicide, and Rodenticide Act (FIFRA), which is administered by the Secretary of the Department of Agriculture. The Act requires pesticides and other "economic poisons" to carry labels bearing certain information, including any warnings necessary to prevent injury to people. A pesticide which fails to comply with the labelling requirement, or which cannot be rendered safe by any labelling, is "misbranded," and the Secretary must refuse or cancel its registration as an economic poison approved for shipment in interstate commerce.

The statute establishes an elaborate procedure by which a registration may be cancelled, that begins when the Secretary issues a notice of cancellation to a registrant. Since the statutory procedures can easily occupy more than a year, the statute also gives the Secretary the power to suspend a registration immediately if he finds such action "necessary to prevent an imminent hazard to the public." Such an interim suspension triggers an expedited version of the procedure that can lead to cancellation.

Petitioners here are five organizations engaged in activities relating to environmental protection. On the basis of extensive evidence of the harmful effects of the pesticide DDT on human, plant, and animal life, they filed a petition with the Secretary of the Department of Agriculture requesting (1) the issuance of notices of cancellation for all economic poisons containing DDT, and (2) the suspension of registration for all such products pending the conclusion of cancellation proceedings. The Secretary issued notices of cancellation with respect to four uses of DDT, solicited comments concerning the remaining uses, and took no action on the request for interim suspension. Petitioners filed this appeal, seeking to compel the Secretary to comply with their request.

\* \* \*

## I. STANDING

\* \* \*

The injury alleged by petitioners is the biological harm to man and to other living things resulting from the Secretary's failure to take action which would restrict the use of DDT in the environment. Numerous scientific studies and several reports to government agencies have concluded that DDT has a wide spectrum of harmful effects on nontarget plant and animal species; it increases the incidence in animals of cancer and reproductive defects; and its residues persist in the environment and in the human body long enough to be found far in time and space from the original application.

Consumers of regulated products and services have standing to protect the public interest in the proper administration of a regulatory system enacted for their benefit. The interest asserted in such a challenge to administrative action need not be economic. Like other consumers, those who "consume"—however unwillingly—the pesticide residues permitted by the Secretary to accumulate in the environment are persons "aggrieved by agency action within the meaning of a relevant statute." Furthermore, the consumers' interest in environmental protection may properly be represented by a membership association with an organizational interest in the problem.

On the basis of petitioners' uncontroverted allegations, it appears that they are organizations with a demonstrated interest in protecting the environment from pesticide pollution. Therefore they have the necessary stake in the outcome of a challenge to the Secretary's inaction to contest the issues with the adverseness required by Article III of the Constitution.

## II. REVIEWABILITY

Related to the question of standing is respondents' argument that the decision to suspend the registration of a pesticide as an "imminent hazard" is committed by statute to unreviewable administrative discretion. Even if petitioners have standing to seek review of some administrative decisions under the FIFRA, respondents contend that they cannot seek review of a decision on emergency suspension. Preclusion of judicial review is not lightly to be inferred, however; it requires a showing of clear evidence of legislative intent. That evidence cannot be found in the mere fact that a statute is drafted in permissive rather than mandatory terms. Although the FIFRA provides that the Secretary "may" suspend the registration of an economic poison that creates an imminent hazard to the public, we conclude that his decision is not thereby placed beyond judicial scrutiny.

## III.  RIPENESS

The main thrust of respondents' argument is that the Secretary has issued no final order reviewable in this court.  Petitioners asked the Secretary to take certain actions; he complied in part, and indicated that he was considering further compliance.  Since he has neither granted nor denied much of the relief requested, respondents contend that his response to petitioners' request has not yet ripened into a reviewable order.

An order expressly denying the request for suspension or for cancellation would clearly be ripe for review.  The doctrines of ripeness and finality are designed to prevent premature judicial intervention in the administrative process, before the administrative action has been fully considered, and before the legal dispute has been brought into focus.  No subsequent action can sharpen the controversy arising from a decision by the Secretary that the evidence submitted by petitioners does not compel suspension or cancellation of the registration of DDT.  In light of the urgent character of petitioners' claim, and the allegation that delay itself inflicts irreparable injury, the controversy is as ripe for judicial consideration as it can ever be.

\* \* \*

At some point administrative delay amounts to a refusal to act, with sufficient finality and ripeness to permit judicial review.  The present record does not permit us to determine whether that point has been reached here.  On remand, the Secretary should either decide on the record whether to issue the remaining requested cancellation notices, or explain the reasons for deferring the decision still further.  In light of that record, and in view of his disposition of the request for interim relief, the court will be in a better position to evaluate the impact of any further delay and decide whether judicial relief is appropriate.

Remanded for further proceedings in accordance with this opinion.

---

## PROBLEMS

1.  Waldo serves on the city council of Plains.  The council is considering a land use program that utilizes transfer development rights similar to those used in St. George, Vermont (described in the text).  He asks whether you think the St. George program is a good one.  What problems, if any, do you foresee in the St. George program?  Why?

2.  Environmental legislation enacted in recent years often contains provisions that allow private citizens to sue polluters.  Examples of such legislation include the Michigan Environmental Protection Act and the

Federal Water Pollution Act. What is the purpose of these provisions? Without these provisions, what problems would a private citizen face in seeking court action to stop pollution? Why?

3. The U.S. government signed a contract to purchase helium from a corporation but later decided to cancel the contract. If you worked for the corporation, how could you use the environmental laws discussed in this chapter to delay or avoid completely the cancellation of the contract? Why?

4. Leroy lives near a factory owned and operated by Smog, Unlimited. As a result of factory operations, the air in Leroy's neighborhood and the water in a local river have become polluted. Assuming there are no environmental protection statutes relating to the company's activities, what legal theories could Leroy raise if he sued the company to stop the pollution? What problems would he encounter with each theory? Why?

5. On June 15, 1971, the U.S. Secretary of the Interior announced that a sale of oil and gas leases in eastern Louisiana would take place in December, 1971. A sixty-seven-page environmental impact statement was filed that discussed in great detail the environmental impact of the oil drilling operations that would result from the sale. An environmental group claims that the statement is inadequate because it does not discuss the environmental effect of alternative courses of action outside the authority of the Secretary of the Interior—such as the possible elimination of oil import quotas. Is the environmental group correct? Why?

6. Students Challenging Regulatory Agency Procedures (SCRAP), a student environmental group, sued the Interstate Commerce Commission, challenging an ICC price increase in the cost of shipping goods that boosted the cost of shipping recyclable materials. SCRAP contended that the price increase had the effect of discouraging the use of recyclable goods and that it should not become effective until an environmental impact statement is filed. What defenses should the ICC raise? Are these good defenses? Why?

7. The Scenic Hudson Preservation Conference, an association of nonprofit organizations, and the towns of Putnam Valley and Yorktown, New York, sued the Federal Power Commission (FPC) and the Consolidated Edison Company of New York, asking the court to set aside FPC orders authorizing Consolidated Edison to build Storm King, a hydroelectric project on the Hudson River. The Storm King project was to be located in an area of extreme beauty and major historical significance. The Federal Power Act provides that court review of FPC orders may be obtained by any party aggrieved by the orders. Do the plaintiffs have standing? Why?

8. A company distributed a fungicide product, Panogen, which was registered under a federal statute as an "economic poison." After an accident involving Panogen, the Department of Agriculture suspended the registration on the grounds that Panogen was dangerous to the public. The company immediately requested an administrative hearing but, before the hearing, filed suit asking a court to set aside the suspension. How should the court decide the case? Why?

9. The Atomic Energy Commission established a procedure for considering environmental protection in its decision-making process. Under

the procedure, hearing boards that reviewed staff recommendations were not required to consider environmental issues unless they were raised by the parties involved in the hearing.  Furthermore, hearing boards were prohibited from conducting independent evaluations of environmental factors if other agencies had certified that their own standards were satisfied.  Does this procedure violate the National Environmental Policy Act? Why?

10.  Andrews owned a marsh in Maine that was considered important in the conservation and development of aquatic and marine life, game birds, and other waterfowl.  Andrews wanted to deposit fill dirt in the marsh because, unless filled, it had no commercial value.  His application to the State Wetlands Control Board for a permit to fill the marsh was denied, and now Andrews brings suit to force the board to issue the permit.  Should the permit be issued?  Why?

## Part Four

# LANDLORD AND TENANT

### Chapter 15

### LANDLORD AND TENANT

A house she hath, 'tis made of such good fashion,
The tenant ne'er shall pay for reparation,
Nor will the landlord ever raise her rent
Or turn her out of doors for non-payment:
From chimney tax this cell is free
To such a house who would not tenant be?

17th Century English Tombstone

## I. INTRODUCTION

An "estate" is the interest which one has in real or personal property. Interests in real property are usually divided into two categories: (1) freehold estates, which are characterized by their indefinite duration since no one knows when the estate will end; and (2) leasehold estates, which usually last for a definite period of time. A freehold estate is considered to be an interest in real property, and the owner of the estate has both title and the right to take possession of the land. A leasehold estate is personal property and the owner, the tenant, has the right to take possession of the property for a stated period, although he does not have title. When the lease ends, the right to possession reverts back to the landlord; the landlord's interest during the period of the lease is called a "reversionary interest."

The two common freehold estates are the fee simple, which represents absolute ownership of the property, and the life estate. The four types of leasehold estates are the estate for years, the periodic tenancy, the tenancy at will, and the tenancy by sufferance. We will first review these leasehold estates and then examine the contract used to create a leasehold estate—the lease. Then we will review the remedies available to the landlord or tenant when there has been a breach of duty established by the lease or by law. Finally, we will discuss the landlord's tort liability to the tenant or to visitors on the premises.

## II. TYPES OF ESTATES

### A. ESTATE FOR YEARS

The most common type of leasehold estate is the estate for years, an estate that has a definite beginning and a definite end. The length of time between the beginning and end may be one day or it may be 10,000 years. But in some states, if the lease is to last beyond a certain period (for example, more than one hundred years in Massachusetts), it is considered to be a fee simple estate. Where such statutes have been enacted, 99-year leases are common. If a state does not limit the length of the lease, the parties may select any period of time. In one case, for example, the court decided that an estate for years was created when one person leased property to another in the year 1800 for a term of 2,000 years at an annual rent of $10.07.[1]

Unless the lease provides for termination under specified conditions, the estate for years will terminate at the end of the period. The rights of the tenant cease automatically at midnight on the last day of the term, and in the absence of a special statutory requirement, the landlord is not required to send the tenant a notice to leave since the lease itself serves as the notice. If the tenant dies before the end of the term, his interest passes as personal property under his will or the laws of intestate succession.

## B. PERIODIC TENANCY

A periodic tenancy, sometimes called an estate from year to year, lasts for a period of time that is automatically renewed until the landlord or tenant gives notice that it will end. The periodic tenancy can be created by the express agreement of the landlord and tenant, or its creation may be implied. For example, if the landlord and tenant sign a lease which states everything except the term of the lease, it is implied that they intended a periodic tenancy. An implied periodic tenancy is also created when the tenant takes possession of the property under a defective lease. In Laughran v. Smith,[2] the tenants took possession of the rental property on May 1 under a five-year lease which was void because the landlord never signed it. The court decided that by "the entry, occupation, and payment of rent they became tenants from year to year, with the right to terminate the lease on the 30th day of April of any year on giving due notice."

The most common method of creating a periodic tenancy occurs when a tenant remains on the premises at the conclusion of an estate for years. By remaining in possession (or "holding over") the tenant is considered to have made an offer to rent the premises under a periodic tenancy. The landlord has two options: (1) he may reject the offer and treat the tenant as a trespasser, in which case the landlord is entitled to rent for the holdover period; or (2) he may accept the offer, in which case the rent and the length of the renewable periods are determined by the original lease. However, if the original

1. Monbar, Inc. v. Monaghan, 18 Del.     2. 75 N.Y. 205 (1878).
   Ch. 395, 162 A. 50 (1932).

lease was for a term of more than a year, the periodic tenancy is considered to be from year to year.

The rule making the tenant liable for another term is sometimes harsh. For instance, if a tenant remains in his apartment for three days after the end of a one-year lease, he would be liable for another full year's rent. Yet the objective of the rule is to protect tenants as a class. As one court noted: "The rule imposes a penalty upon the individual tenant wrongfully holding over, but ultimately operates for the benefit of tenants as a class by its tendency to secure the agreed surrender of terms to incoming tenants who have severally yielded possession of other premises in anticipation of promptly entering into the possession of the new. . . . [A]s the value of any piece of property is largely dependent upon its actual or potential continuing yield in periodic rent, the social and economic importance of the landlord being able certainly to deliver, and the prospective tenant so to obtain possession on the stipulated day, is obvious." [3]

In some situations the holdover tenant remains on the property involuntarily because of circumstances beyond his control; when this happens the tenant will not be liable for a new term. In Regan v. Fosdick,[4] the tenant was unable to leave an apartment until nineteen days after the term ended because the tenant's child had scarlet fever and was quarantined on the premises under a board of health order. When the landlord later brought suit on the theory that the tenancy had been renewed, the court decided in favor of the tenant because the tenant was forced to remain on the premises by circumstances beyond his control.

Regardless of the method used to create a periodic tenancy, the usual method of termination is by a notice to quit, given by either the landlord or the tenant. At common law, a six-month notice was required to terminate a year-to-year tenancy, while the notice for tenancies with shorter periods was determined by the length of the period. For instance, a one-month notice was required to terminate a month-to-month tenancy. Today the time period for giving notice in most states is determined by statute. To compute the time period, days are counted beginning with the day after the notice was served and ending with the last day of the rental period.

Although the notice does not have to use legal terminology, it must be clear and unambiguous. For example, in one case [5] a tenant leased property under a year-to-year lease ending May 1 each year. The tenant wrote to his landlord, "I want to tell you that I will have to give up the apartment when the lease expires, June 1, 1921, as I shall break up housekeeping. I expect to return East early in May to

3. A. H. Fetting Mfg. Jewelry Co. v. Waltz, 160 Md. 50, 152 A. 434 (1930).

4. 19 Misc. 489, 43 N.Y.S. 1102 (1897).

5. Torrey v. Adams, 254 Mass. 22, 149 N.E. 618 (1925).

see about things and trust this will be satisfactory to you." The tenant moved from the apartment in May but was held liable for rent for the rest of the year because the notice "must be so certain that it cannot reasonably be misunderstood, and if a particular day is named therein for the termination of the tenancy that day must be the one corresponding to the conclusion of the tenancy, or the notice will be treated as a nullity. The notice would have been sufficient if in any form of words it had provided for the termination of the lease on May 1, 1921."

## C. TENANCY AT WILL

A tenancy at will is characterized by its indefinite duration; it may be terminated at any time after either the landlord or the tenant gives proper notice. In most states the tenant has a statutory right to remain on the premises for a specified period (for example, thirty days) after notice is given.

A tenancy at will may be created expressly by contract between the parties or it may be implied. For example, a landlord owns an apartment building that he wants to sell. If potential buyers would prefer to purchase the building free of long-term leases, the landlord might lease each apartment under a tenancy at will which expressly provides that "the lease shall last until the landlord sells the property." Even if this clause was omitted from the lease, a tenancy at will might be implied if the landlord and tenant made no agreement specifying the term of the lease.

## D. TENANCY AT SUFFERANCE

A tenancy at sufferance results when a person in possession of real estate refuses to leave after his rights to occupy the property have ceased. This is technically not an estate, because the tenant has no right or permission to remain on the real estate; however, neither is the occupancy a trespass because the tenant's original entry onto the property was rightful.

For example, Lanny leased an apartment to Bennett for one year; the lease was to end September 1, 1979. If Bennett does not leave the apartment by September 1, he becomes a tenant at sufferance and becomes liable for damages under one of four theories: (1) The landlord could elect to treat Bennett's holding over as a periodic tenancy, with rent to continue as provided in the lease. (2) In some states, statutes allow the landlord to collect double or triple the previous monthly rent when a tenant refuses to leave. (3) The landlord may decide to evict the tenant and collect damages based on the reasonable rental value of the property. (4) Lanny could demand an increased rent and, if the tenant continues to remain in possessior without protest after receiving the demand, he has impliedly agreed to pay at the increased rate.[6]

## E. LICENSE

In many business transactions, it is important to determine whether a leasehold estate or a license has been created. A lease gives the tenant an estate in the form of an exclusive right to possession of the property; a license, which is permission to enter the premises for a specified purpose, gives the licensee no right, title or interest in the property.

In Timmons v. Cropper,[7] for example, Cropper, the proprietor, signed a "Location Agreement" under which he agreed to lease to Timmons space in his building for pinball machines. The agreement was to be automatically renewed on a year-to-year basis unless a 60-day notice was given by either party. The lease provided that "proprietor leases unto Timmons appropriate space for the operation of automatic amusement equipment" and also provided that, if Cropper breached the contract, Timmons had the right to an injunction forbidding Cropper from installing anyone else's pinball machines on the premises. Cropper later breached the agreement and Timmons brought suit to restrain Cropper from installing another party's pinball machines. The court refused to issue an injunction because Timmons was only a licensee and such relief was not available to a licensee: "The agreement here does not delineate any identifiable space to which it is to apply. Neither does it pretend to grant to plaintiff exclusive possession even of appropriate space. . . . The present agreement establishes the licensor-licensee relationship."

## F. COOPERATIVES

The cooperative is a unique leasehold in which the tenants own the landlord. Usually the landlord is a corporation, and the capital from the sale of stock in the corporation is used as a down payment in purchasing an apartment building. Apartments in the building are then leased to the shareholders, who pay enough rent to cover the corporation's mortgage, operating costs, taxes, and other expenses. As in the case of other leaseholds, each tenant's interest in the cooperative, represented by the lease and stock certificate, is regarded as personal property. For example, restaurateur Toots Shor purchased stock in a New York cooperative and received a proprietary lease, but he was later evicted for nonpayment of monthly charges. In a subsequent dispute among Shor's creditors over his interest in the cooperative, a creditor with a lien on his real estate claimed that the lien had priority. The court disagreed on the grounds that, under the law of

---

6. David Properties, Inc. v. Selk, 151 So.2d 334 (Fla.App.1963).

7. 40 Del.Ch. 29, 172 A.2d 757 (Del. 1961).

New York and other states, an interest in a cooperative is personal property.[8]

While many principles of landlord and tenant law govern the cooperative arrangement, there are four special legal issues that relate specifically to the cooperative. First, under a normal leasehold, the rights and duties of the parties are spelled out in the lease. In the cooperative, many of the rights and duties are also included in the lease (called a proprietary lease); but since the cooperative is usually incorporated, the shareholder-tenant should also examine closely the articles of incorporation and by-laws. The by-laws, for example, will cover matters such as the right to sell the certificates, the sales price, and the grounds for terminating the shareholder's rights.

Second, the person investing in a cooperative should remember that, as the name implies, the housing arrangement is a group enterprise with a philosophy of "all for one and one for all." For example, if certain tenants neglect or refuse to pay their monthly charges, the other members must make up the difference in order to avoid a mortgage foreclosure or a sale to pay delinquent taxes.

Third, interests in a cooperative are often difficult to transfer after an increase in the corporation's equity in the property. To illustrate, we might assume that ten investors each purchase $2,000 worth of stock in a cooperative corporation, which uses the money as a down payment to purchase a ten-unit apartment building for $200,000. The corporation borrows the remaining $180,000 and gives the lender a mortgage. As the years pass, the value of the building increases to $250,000 while the mortgage is reduced to $100,000. The corporation's equity is now worth $150,000, or $15,000 per shareholder. If one of the shareholders decides to sell his interest, in most states he must find a purchaser who is able to pay cash because his individual interest is personal property that cannot be used to secure a mortgage. To avoid this result, the shareholder-tenants might decide to refinance the mortgage and thus reduce the equity to make the interests more salable.

The last important legal issue in a cooperative arrangement is whether laws regulating the sale of securities apply to the sale of shares in a cooperative. This question was considered by the Supreme Court in United Housing Foundation, Inc. v. Forman,[9] where fifty-seven residents of Co-op City, the largest cooperative in the United States, sued the corporations that built, promoted, and operated the cooperative, claiming violations of the antifraud provisions of the Securities Act of 1933 and the Securities Exchange Act of 1934. To lease an apartment in Co-op City, prospective tenants had to purchase eighteen shares of stock at $25 per share for each room in the

8. State Tax Comm. v. Shor, 43 N.Y.2d 151, 400 N.Y.S.2d 805, 371 N.E.2d 523 (1977).

9. 421 U.S. 837, 95 S.Ct. 2051, 44 L.Ed. 2d 621 (1975).

apartment. The shares could not be sold to a nontenant, and on leaving Co-op City, a tenant could not sell his shares for more than $25 per share plus a fraction of the mortgage principal he paid during the tenancy. The Supreme Court decided that there was no sale of securities because of the nonprofit nature of the arrangement. "What distinguishes a security transaction—what is absent here—is an investment where one parts with his money in the hope of receiving profits from the efforts of others, and not where he purchases a commodity for personal consumption or living quarters for personal use." In its decision the Supreme Court left open the question of whether securities laws would apply had the shareholders been allowed to sell their shares for a profit.

## III.  LANDLORD'S CHOICE OF TENANT

### A.  INITIAL SELECTION OF TENANT

The Civil Rights Act of 1866 provides that a landlord may not discriminate on the basis of race in selecting tenants. Furthermore, under the Civil Rights Act of 1968, a landlord may not discrminate on the basis of race, color, religion, national origin, sex, or marital status in leasing a dwelling. However this act does not apply in certain situations, such as when an owner rents a single-family house or when the owner lives in the apartment building and there are no more than four apartments in the building. State and local fair housing legislation often adds additional categories of prohibited discrimination. For example, in several states it is illegal for a landlord to refuse to rent to families with children or to a person with a physical handicap or to a recipient of public welfare benefits. There are also special state statutes that apply to the rental of public housing, which prohibit discrimination against persons who have illegitimate children or a criminal record.[10]

Despite the federal and state legislation, landlords still have considerable leeway in selecting tenants. For instance, in Kramarsky v. Stahl Management,[11] a landlord refused to rent an apartment to a black divorcee, who was general counsel to the New York Commission on Human Rights, because he felt she might cause trouble as a tenant. When the prospective tenant brought suit, the landlord proved that he was not discriminating on the basis of race or marital status: 60 percent of his apartments were rented to unmarried persons and 30 percent to blacks. The court decided that discrimination on the basis of intelligence is legal. According to the court, a landlord "may decide not to rent to singers because they are too noisy, or not to rent to baldheaded men because he had been told they give wild parties. He can bar his premises to the lowest strata of society, should he choose, or to the highest, if that be his personal desire."

10. Conn.Gen.Stat.Ann. § 8–45, 45a (1971).          11. 92 Misc.2d 1030, 401 N.Y.S.2d 943 (1977).

## B. RETALIATORY EVICTION

After the landlord has selected a tenant and leased an apartment, does the landlord have complete freedom to refuse to renew the lease so long as he does not violate fair housing legislation? The traditional answer was yes. In Aluli v. Trusdell,[12] for example, the landlord brought suit to evict a tenant who was leasing an apartment under a month-to-month periodic tenancy. The tenant claimed that the reason for the eviction was his activities as an organizer and member of a tenant's union. Although the tenant alleged that the eviction would deprive him of his First Amendment rights to freedom of speech and association, the court decided in favor of the landlord: "If it is true that he is seeking possession of the rented premises for the sole reason that he disagrees or dislikes the tenant's communicative or associative activities, is not the landlord also protected by the First Amendment in expressing these disagreements or dislikes? * * * [T]he landlord-tenant relationship is a contractual one in our jurisdiction. If we accept the tenant's contention, it would mean that we would be substantially altering this relationship and impairing the traditional right of a landlord to recover possession of the demised premises under the terms of a lease."

In many states the traditional rule has been modified by statutes that prohibit a landlord from raising rent, decreasing services, or terminating a lease in retaliation because (1) the tenant attempted to enforce rights under the lease or state law, (2) the tenant reported health or building code violations to a government authority, or (3) the tenant joined a tenants' union. Even where there is no statute, in some states the courts have developed the retaliatory eviction defense, as illustrated by Toms Point Apartments v. Goudzward, infra.

## IV.    REQUIRED LEASE PROVISIONS

The lease is a unique legal hybrid: it not only is a contract between the landlord and tenant but also is an instrument which conveys a property interest—a leasehold estate—to the tenant. The reasons for this dual nature are historical. In early English law, the lease was regarded merely as a contract. But in the fifteenth and sixteenth century when England was dependent on an agrarian economy and it became important to stabilize the lease of agricultural land, the lease came to be regarded solely as a conveyance of the landlord's entire interest for the term of the lease. Later, however, with the coming of the industrial revolution, residential and commercial leases in heavily populated urban areas became predominant, and these leases are more similar to contracts than to conveyances. The net result

12. 54 Hawaii 417, 508 P.2d 1217 (1973). However the holding in *Aluli* was limited in Windward Partners v. Delos Santos, 577 P.2d 326 (1978).

is that courts today use both property and contract law concepts in fashioning the rights and duties of the landlord and tenant.[13]

Every lease should be written in order to facilitate proof of its terms in the event of a later dispute. In most states, however, leases are legally required to be in writing only when the term is for more than one year. The required writing must include four essential provisions: names and signatures of the parties, a description of the property, the term of the lease, and the amount of rent. If the lease is not written or if any of the essential terms is missing, it usually will be invalid. But if the tenant takes possession of the property under an invalid lease, a tenancy at will is created; and if the tenant takes possession and pays rent, there is a periodic tenancy. If the tenant takes possession, pays rent, and makes improvements on the property, the lease will be enforced under the doctrine of substantial performance. In one case, a court held that there was substantial performance when the tenant took possession, paid rent, planted rose bushes, installed expensive carpet, and painted the house.[14]

## A. NAMES AND SIGNATURES

The lease must name both the landlord and the tenant. The spouse of the landlord should also be named in order to avoid problems arising under dower and curtesy laws. Like the contract for the sale of real estate, the lease must be signed by the party to be charged, although in some states a lessee who has not signed will be bound by the lease if he has taken possession of the property.

## B. DESCRIPTION OF PROPERTY

Because the lease is a conveyance of property as well as a contract, the lease must describe the property with the same certainty required in a deed or a mortgage. Furthermore, the landlord should specifically reserve any rights which are not to pass to the tenant. For example, the lease conveys to the tenant the exclusive right to possess the real estate, and not even the landlord can enter the premises without the tenant's permission. Consequently, if the landlord wants to enter the property to show an apartment to prospective tenants, the right should be specifically reserved in the lease.

In addition to the described property, the tenant receives a number of incidental rights necessary for the use and enjoyment of the premises unless the lease states otherwise. For instance, when a tenant leases an apartment in a building, he is entitled to use the building's halls and stairways to reach his apartment, even though the right is not specified in the lease. If the whole building is leased, the tenant has the right to use the outside walls and roof for advertising

13. Restatement, Second, Property, Landlord and Tenant, Introduction, 4, 5 (1977).

14. Wallace v. Scoggin, 18 Or. 502, 21 P. 558 (1889).

purposes. In a recent Connecticut case the landlord leased a building to a tenant for a five-year term and then leased the roof to another party for advertising. The court decided that the lease gave the tenant the right to the roof, even though it was not specifically mentioned in the lease, and that rents which the landlord received for leasing the roof should go to the tenant.[15]

In some cases a tenant who leases a building has the implied right to use the landlord's adjoining land and buildings. In McDaniel v. Willer,[16] the landlord operated a general store and used a building on a nearby lot to store fertilizer. When he leased the store, the tenant was given the right to use the storage building even though that right was not mentioned in the lease.

## C. THE LEASE TERM

The date the lease begins and duration of the tenancy should be clearly stated in the lease. If they are not, and if a court cannot ascertain the intended term, the lease will be considered a tenancy at will or a periodic tenancy.

## D. RENT

The lease must state the consideration (rent) that the landlord is receiving in exchange for possession of the property. If no rent is stated in the lease, the leasehold will either be considered a gift from the landlord or the tenant will be liable for the reasonable value of his possession of the property. The lease should also state the time and place for the rent payment. If no time is stated, then payment is due on the last day of the period. For instance, if rent is paid monthly, the rent would be due on the last day of the month. If no place is stated, payment is due at the rented premises.

Any method may be used to calculate rent as long as a specific amount may be determined by the use of the formula. Each of the following methods are permissible: (1) a specific dollar amount; (2) a graduated rental calling for predetermined periodic increases in the rent; (3) a cost-of-living index method by which the rent is adjusted on the basis of the index; (4) a percentage method by which the rent is based on the volume of the tenant's business on the leased property; and (5) an appraisal method which calculates rent as a percentage of the appraised value of the rental property.[17]

It is common practice for the landlord to require a tenant to make an additional advance payment, called a security deposit, to

15. Monarch Accounting Supplies, Inc. v. Prezioso, 170 Conn. 659, 368 A.2d 6 (1976).

16. 216 S.W.2d 144 (Mo.App.1948).

17. Restatement, Second, Property, Landlord and Tenant § 12.1, Comment a (1977).

cover the tenant's liability for unpaid rent, unpaid utility bills, or damage to the premises. In approximately half the states, security deposits are regulated by statute. Although the statutes are not identical, there are several common features. First, the statutes define the security deposit (for instance, as any amount which must be paid in advance apart from the actual rent) and limit the amount of the deposit, often to one month's rent. Second, the statutes limit the use of the security deposit. In some states the deposit cannot be used to reimburse the landlord for ordinary wear and tear that may reasonably be expected in the normal course of apartment living. Third, the legislation limits the landlord in his interim use of the deposit; the landlord may have to post bond to cover the deposit or place the deposit in a special bank account and pay interest to the tenant. Finally, the statutes prescribe the procedure for collecting a security deposit. In some states, a landlord must mail a claim for damages to the tenant within a specified period or else waive his right to damages. Also in many states the landlord has the burden of bringing suit to justify his retention of the security deposit.

## E. LEASE FORMALITIES

A lease containing the four required provisions will be valid between the landlord and tenant. However, in many states two additional requirements must be met if the lease is to be recorded: (1) the lease must be witnessed, and (2) the signatures must be acknowledged by the landlord and tenant before a notary public. Almost all states have established provisions for recording leases. As one example, in Wisconsin all leases may be recorded, but only leases for more than one year must be recorded to be valid against later purchasers.[18]

## V.  SUGGESTED LEASE PROVISIONS

Although not required by law, there are a number of provisions that should be included in the lease to avoid expensive, time-consuming litigation in the future. The issues most likely to cause a dispute may be grouped into three categories that will be discussed below: the condition of the premises, the tenant's use of the property, and the transfer of lease rights.

In most cases the rules we discuss can be changed by an appropriate lease provision. However, the ability to alter legal rights and duties by contract is sometimes restricted by the doctrine of unconscionability. An unconscionable contract or provision is one that is unfair to one of the parties, who is in a weak bargaining position. A contract between a party in a strong position, who can dictate the contract terms on a "take it or leave it" basis, and a weaker party, who is in need of the subject matter of the contract, is termed a contract of adhesion. For example, in Weidman v. Tomaselli,[19] a clause

18. Wis.Stat.Ann. §§ 706.05, 706.01, 706.-
    08.

19. 81 Misc.2d 328, 365 N.Y.S.2d 681 (1975).

in an apartment lease provided that if the tenant breached the lease agreement, he would pay additional rent of $100 to cover attorney's fees and court costs incurred by the landlord. When the tenant later breached the agreement and the landlord brought suit for the $100, the court listed the requirements necessary to prove a contract of adhesion: "A contract of adhesion is a contract in relation to a necessity of life, drafted by or for the benefit of a party for that party's excessive benefit, which party uses its economic or other advantage to offer the contract in its entirety solely for acceptance or rejection by the offeree. Thus, the elements of a contract of adhesion are (1) a necessity of life; (2) a contract for the excessive benefit of the offeror; (3) an economic or other advantage of the offeror; and (4) the offer of the proposed contract on a take-it-or-leave-it basis." The court decided that this lease was an adhesion contract with an unconscionable clause and refused to enforce the clause. According to the court: "Given the overwhelming need for housing, the respondents must do exactly as the petitioner demands, or shelter will be denied. Had the petitioner demanded that the respondents fall to their knees and grovel before him, the respondents perforce would have swallowed their pride and done so, or be condemned to remain outside, never to come in from the cold. Here, the petitioner demanded that the respondents grovel not physically, but legally. The petitioner's unbargainable price is that the respondents agree to clause after clause of terms to the excessive benefit of the petitioner."

## A. CONDITION OF PREMISES

On September 1, 1979, Pete leased a building to Rose for one year; the lease stated that Rose was to take possession on that date. After Rose took possession of the property, she discovered that she could not use the building because the plumbing needed repair. Who has the duty to repair the plumbing, Pete or Rose? The answer to this question often depends on whether the plumbing was defective when the lease was made on September 1 or became defective after Rose took possession.

1. **Conditions Existing When Lease Made.** The traditional rule applied to the sale of property generally and to leases in particular is *caveat emptor* or "let the buyer beware." In lease cases, the rule was based on the assumption that the tenant could inspect the premises and discover any problems, such as defective plumbing, before signing the lease. If the tenant refused to make the inspection or decided to rent the property despite the defect, the tenant could not later force the landlord to correct the defect, unless the lease specifically imposed that duty on the landlord.

A major exception to the traditional rule has developed in recent years as a result of state statutes and cases involving for the most part the lease of residential property. The exception provides that even when a lease does not impose the duty on the landlord, he must provide premises which are suitable for residential use.[20] For example, in Lemle v. Breeden,[21] Lemle rented a home in Honolulu from Breeden. Shortly after moving into the apartment, Lemle realized that there were rats in the home. Before vacating the premises, Lemle and his family spent three nights camped in the living room where they were unable to sleep because they were apprehensive of the rats. They could hear them scurrying across the roof, and the rats could enter the house through various openings. The court held that Lemle was entitled to recover an advance payment of rent and his security deposit because the landlord had breached an implied warranty of habitability: "The application of an implied warranty of habitability in leases gives recognition to the changes in leasing transactions today. It affirms the fact that a lease is, in essence, a sale as well as a transfer of an estate in land and is, more importantly, a contractual relationship. From that contractual relationship an implied warranty of habitability and fitness for the purposes intended is a just and necessary implication. It is a doctrine which has its counterparts in the law of sales and torts and one which when candidly countenanced is impelled by the nature of the transaction and contemporary housing realities. Legal fictions and artificial exceptions to wooden rules of property law aside, we hold that in the lease of a dwelling house, such as in this case, there is an implied warranty of habitability and fitness for the use intended."

     2. **Conditions Arising After Tenant Takes Possession; The Duty to Repair.** At common law, the tenant assumed any risks that arose after he took possession of the premises on the theory that these risks should fall on the party in possession of the property. Thus if a tornado destroyed the building that Rose leased from Pete, she would still be liable for rent for the remainder of the lease term, the tenancy being considered primarily a lease of the land rather than the building.[22]

     The common law rule placing the risk of loss on the tenant no longer applies in many states which have adopted statutes providing that the tenant's duty to pay rent ceases if the premises are destroyed by a natural force.[23] More importantly, the landlord bears the risk of changed conditions if he has a duty to keep the premises in repair, a duty that has increasingly been imposed on the landlord. We will now examine the nature of that duty.

     At common law, the landlord, who had no right to enter the leased premises, had no duty to make repairs on the property. The

---

**20.** Restatement, Second, Property, Landlord and Tenant § 5.1 (1977).

**21.** 51 Hawaii 426, 462 P.2d 470 (1969).

**22.** However, if Rose rented only one apartment in a large apartment complex, she would not be liable for rent after the destruction of the apartment building because in this case she would not be renting the real estate.

**23.** Restatement, Second, Property, Landlord and Tenant § 5.4 (1977).

tenant also had no duty to make major repairs, although he was required to make "tenantable repairs" to prevent waste. These were described in the ancient case of Suydam v. Jackson:[24] "At common law the lessor was, without express covenant to that effect, under no obligation to repair, and if the demised premises became, during the term, wholly untenantable by destruction thereof by fire, flood, tempest or otherwise, the lessee still remained liable for the rent unless exempted from such liability by some express covenant in his lease. But the lessee was under an implied covenant, from his relation to his landlord, to make what are called 'tenantable repairs.' . . . The lessee was not bound to make substantial, lasting or general repairs, but only such ordinary repairs as were necessary to prevent waste and decay of the premises. If a window in a dwelling should blow in, the tenant could not permit it to remain out and the storms to beat in and greatly injure the premises without liability for permissive waste; and if a shingle or board on the roof should blow off or become out of repair, the tenant could not permit the water, in time of rain, to flood the premises, and thus injure them, without a similar liability. He being present, a slight effort and expense on his part could save a great loss; and hence the law justly casts the burden upon him."

The common law rule has been altered in recent years by statutes or case law involving residential leases. Under the modern approach, the landlord is responsible for keeping the property in the condition required by housing codes. Many states go further and require the landlord to repair defects that make the apartment uncomfortable, even when there has been no building code violation. The underlying theory is that a landlord gives an implied warranty of habitability; that is, he promises that the apartment will be fit for residential use. This implied warranty is the logical consequence of modern living patterns.[25] See Green v. Sumski, infra.

There are limitations to the landlord's implied duty to keep the premises repaired. For instance, the landlord has no duty to repair when a tenant, a third party, or a natural force has caused the condition. The landlord also has no duty to make minor repairs that do not make the apartment unlivable or do not constitute a substantial violation of the housing code.[26] Furthermore, the tenant must notify the landlord of the changed conditions and give the landlord a reasonable time to make corrections.[27]

3. **Lease Provisions.** The above rules governing conditions in existence when the lease was made and conditions arising after the tenant takes possession will apply only in the absence of a lease pro-

**24.** 54 N.Y. 450 (1873).

**25.** Javins v. First Nat. Realty Corp., 428 F.2d 1071 (D.C.Cir. 1970).

**26.** Restatement, Second, Property, Landlord and Tenant § 5.5 (1977).

**27.** Garner v. La Marr, 88 Ga.App. 364, 76 S.E.2d 721 (1953).

vision. In other words the landlord and tenant may rewrite these rules and establish their own list of rights and duties. However, a lease provision which is unconscionable or violates public policy will not be enforced. Thus, if a tenant lives in a city where there are very few residential apartments available and a landlord offers a lease to the tenant containing a waiver of the implied warranty of habitability on a "take it or leave it" basis, it is unlikely that the waiver would be enforced by a court.[28]

Lease provisions altering the duties imposed by law should be drafted with great care. For example, we might assume that a tenant makes a general promise in the lease to make all necessary repairs or to leave the premises in the condition they were in when he took possession. If the property was destroyed by a trespasser or by a natural cause such as a hurricane, most courts would hold the tenant responsible for rebuilding or repairing the property.[29]

## B.  TENANT'S USE OF PROPERTY

1. **No Lease Provision.** In the absence of a lease provision restricting use, the tenant may use the property for any legal purpose consistent with the nature of the property or the intentions of the parties. In Edwards v. Roe,[30] a landlord tried to evict an unmarried female tenant on the grounds that she was using the premises to engage in sexual intercourse with a male friend. The court held that the tenant was not acting illegally because, since it was not a commercial activity, she was not engaged in prostitution and because New York law does not proscribe normal sexual intercourse between unmarried consenting adults. The court also held that the tenant could not be evicted under a statute allowing eviction when the premises is used for immoral purposes: "If the test be personal to me, I hold that, without a showing—and there is none—that she has harmed anyone, respondent has done nothing immoral. And if the test be the response of the 'ordinary' or 'average' man or woman, assuming that it makes sense to posit the existence of such a person, I hold that, given the ethical standards of the day, respondent has done nothing immoral."

In order to make the best use of the property, the tenant may make physical changes but may not make structural alterations, even when the alterations increase the value of the real estate. For example, if a tenant has leased a building for use as a coffee shop, he could install a counter and stoves but could not tear down or build partitions on the property. However, the rule against alterations has been

---

**28.** Restatement, Second, Property, Landlord and Tenant § 5.6 (1977).

**29.** Bradley v. Holliman, 134 Ark. 588, 202 S.W. 469 (1918).

**30.** 68 Misc.2d 278, 327 N.Y.S.2d 307 (1971).

criticized in recent years, and it is likely that in the future more courts will allow alterations which are necessary for the tenant to make reasonable use of the property.[31]

A tenant who has made physical changes in the property must restore the property to its original condition, when possible. However the tenant is not responsible for changes due to normal wear and tear which result from reasonable use of the property. Consequently, the tenant would not be responsible for refinishing wooden floors that had become scuffed through the tenant's normal use, but he would have to repair damage caused by his using skateboards on the floors.[32]

2. **Lease Provisions.** The parties to a lease can and usually should insert a clause in the lease specifying the use to be made of the property. In Lyon v. Bethlehem Engineering Corp.,[33] the lease limited the use of the building to "the following purposes, and those only: Restaurant, stores, store-rooms and offices  .  .  .  and sales-rooms." The tenant allowed Roxy Theatres Corporation to attach an electric sign, forty feet tall and sixty feet long, on the roof of the building. The court, in holding that this use violated the lease, observed that a tenant, "in the absence of restrictions contained in a lease, may use a leased building in any lawful way not materially different from that to which it is adapted, and for which it was constructed. The right to exclusive occupation granted by a lease entitles a tenant to use the premises in the same manner that the owner might have used them.  .  .  . The landlord may, however, by express provisions in a lease, limit and restrict the use of a building to specific purposes. He has a legal right to control the uses to which his building may be put and may do so by appropriate provisions in a lease."

In lease provisions restricting use, often the key word is "only." If the lease provision states that the property is to be used for a billiards hall but omits the word "only," the tenant is free to make other uses of the property. If the landlord decides to restrict the use of the property "for a billiard hall only," the tenant may use the property only for billiards and related purposes. For instance, the tenant could not use the premises as a pancake shop but could sell and rent cue sticks because this would be related to the permitted use. As discussed below, if the lease provision limits the tenant to only one use and the use becomes illegal, the lease is invalid.

Frequently a lease clause will provide that the tenant may not use the premises in a manner that competes with the landlord's business. Alternatively the lease might provide that the landlord will not compete with the tenant in using or leasing property. For example, if a tenant rented space in a shopping mall for a natural food store

31. Restatement, Second, Property, Landlord and Tenant § 12.2 (1977).

32. Id.

33. 253 N.Y. 111, 170 N.E. 512 (1930).

under a long term lease, the tenant might insist on such a clause to prevent the landlord from renting space to competing natural food stores. Are promises by the landlord or tenant not to compete with the other's business legal? There are two views. In many states the promises are valid, although they must be limited in scope to protection of the other party's interests.[34] In other states the promises are unenforceable, often because of state antitrust statutes.[35]

3. **Interference With Use.** Once the tenant's use has been established by law or by the lease, the tenant has the right to carry out his use of the property without interference. Interference with use usually comes from the landlord, from outsiders, or from the government.

a. *Interference by Landlord.* Interference by the landlord may be passive or active. Passive interference occurs when, as discussed above, the landlord fails to meet his duty to keep the property in good condition, thus making it unusable. Active interference is when the landlord or someone under his control interferes with the tenant's use of the property. For example, in an apartment complex with a swimming pool, the landlord might interfere with the tenant's use of his apartment by throwing wild poolside parties late at night or by failing to prevent other tenants from throwing poolside parties, since the landlord retains control of common areas such as the pool.

The landlord is liable regardless of whether the interference is passive or active and whether it is caused by the landlord directly or by persons under his control. The reason usually given by the courts is that the landlord gives the tenant an implied covenant of quiet enjoyment; this promise is breached when there is landlord-related interference with the tenant's quiet enjoyment of the property. As discussed below, a tenant who is actually forced to leave the premises as a result of the landlord's breach—a constructive eviction—is no longer liable for rent.

b. *Interference by Outsiders.* Two types of outsiders might interfere with the tenant's use of his property. The first type is an outsider with a legal interest superior to that of the tenant. To illustrate, let us assume that a landlord, in purchasing a house, mortgaged the property to First Bank. After the mortgage was recorded, the landlord leased the house to a tenant for a term of three years. In this case First Bank's prior, recorded interest is superior to the tenant's leasehold interest; if First Bank foreclosed on the mortgage, it could evict the tenant.[36] A tenant who signs a lease and then learns of the superior interest before taking possession may hold the land-

---

34. Goldberg v. Tri-States Theatre Corp., 126 F.2d 26 (8th Cir. 1942).

35. See Mich.Comp.Laws Ann. § 445.761 (1967).

36. But if the landlord gave the mortgage to the bank after the lease was signed and recorded, the bank's interests would be inferior to those of the tenant and it could not evict the tenant on foreclosure.

lord liable on the theory that he has breached a covenant of title. However, after the tenant has taken possession, the landlord is liable only if the tenant's use (that is, quiet enjoyment) has been interfered with by the third party. In our case this would occur if First Bank foreclosed its mortgage and evicted the tenant.[37]

The other type of outsider is one with no legal interest in the property or with an interest inferior to that of the tenant. If this type of outsider interferes with the tenant's use, the tenant, as "owner" for the term of the lease, must take action directly against the outsider and cannot hold the landlord liable. Many courts hold that this rule applies even when the tenant initially attempts to take possession of the property. For instance, if the tenant was to take possession under a one-year lease beginning September 1, and the previous tenant wrongfully refused to leave the apartment, these courts would require the tenant to commence proceedings to remove the wrongdoer.[38] However, other courts have adopted the "English rule," which places the duty to remove holdover tenants on the landlord.[39]

c. *Interference by Government.* A tenant is not liable when a lease restricts him to a particular purpose if that purpose becomes illegal as the result of government action. Thus a tenant would not be liable when a lease provides that property is to be used "as a retail liquor store only" if the state or federal government later enacts legislation such as the Volstead Act making it illegal to sell liquor.

A tougher question arises when government action causes the tenant's business to become unprofitable, even though the tenant can continue his use. Under the contract law doctrine of frustration of purpose, if an unforeseeable event defeats the purpose of the contract even though performance is still physically and legally possible, the parties will be excused from performance. This rule originated in the "Coronation Cases." Several persons rented rooms in order to watch a procession scheduled in connection with the coronation of Edward VII. When the king became ill, the procession was cancelled and the renters claimed they were no longer liable on their contracts. In the resulting litigation, the court held that performance of the contract was excused because the reason for making the contracts had been destroyed. In the United States, although there is some authority to the contrary, courts have been reluctant to apply the frustration of purpose doctrine to leases.

37. Restatement, Second, Property, Landlord and Tenant §§ 4.2, 4.3 (1977).

38. Teitelbaum v. Direct Realty Co., 172 Misc. 48, 13 N.Y.S.2d 886 (1939).

39. Dieffenbach v. McIntyre, 208 Okl. 163, 254 P.2d 346 (1952).

## C.  TRANSFER OF LEASEHOLD INTERESTS

1.  **Assignee's Rights and Duties.**  Either the landlord or the tenant may assign his entire interest in the leasehold to a third party, the assignee.  The effect of an assignment is that the assignee steps into the shoes of the party who has made the assignment and takes over the rights and duties of the assignor.  For example, in Ernst v. Conditt,[40] Ernst leased a tract of land to Rogers, who used the property to operate a Go-Cart track.  Rogers later assigned the lease to Conditt, stating in their agreement that "I hereby sublet the premises to A. K. Conditt."  Conditt took possession of the property but refused to pay rent to Ernst.  When Ernst brought suit, the court decided that Conditt, as an assignee, took over both the rights and duties of Rogers.  The court would have reached the same conclusion if the landlord, Ernst, had sold his reversionary interest to a third party who then sued Conditt; the third party would take over the rights of Ernst (for example, the right to collect rent), but the assignee would be liable for the duties imposed by the lease agreement or by law (for example, a duty in the lease to keep the Go-Cart track repaired).

In stepping into the assignor's shoes, the assignee acquires no greater rights than the assignor possessed, and he takes the rights subject to any defense that could be raised by the other party to the contract.  To illustrate, in Martinique Realty Corp. v. Hull,[41] the landlord owned a 55-unit apartment building in Passaic, New Jersey.  One of the tenants leased an apartment for a five-year term and prepaid over $8,400 of the agreed rent.  The landlord later sold the property to a third party, who was unaware that the tenant had prepaid the rent.  When the new owner sued the tenant for failing to make monthly rental payments, the court held that the tenant was not liable: "This is but an illustration of the general rule that the assignee of a contract right takes subject to all defenses valid against his assignor.  .   .   .   It is long settled that the purchaser of a lessor's interest in property has a duty to make inquiry as to the extent of the rights of any person in open, notorious and exclusive possession of the premises; if this duty is not discharged, then notice is imputed to the purchaser of all facts which a reasonably prudent inquiry would have revealed."

2.  **Assignor's Rights and Duties.**  A landlord or tenant who assigns his interest to a third party gives his leasehold rights to the third party but remains obligated to perform the lease duties if the third party defaults.  Thus in the *Ernst* case above, if the landlord could not collect the rent from the assignee, Conditt, he could collect from the original tenant, Rogers.

There are two exceptions to the rule that the assignor remains liable on the lease obligations.  First, the assignor is not liable if the

**40.**  54 Tenn.App. 328, 390 S.W.2d 703    **41.**  64 N.J.Super. 599, 166 A.2d 803
    (1965).                                        (1960).

other party to the lease agrees to release the assignor from liability and to accept the assignee in his place. This is called a novation. Second, once an assignment has been made, the assignor remains liable only for promises made in the lease but is not liable for obligations imposed by law. For instance, in many cases a landlord does not expressly promise to keep the property in good repair but the obligation to do so is imposed by law. If the landlord sells his interest to a third party, it is the general rule that the landlord's duty to keep the property repaired ceases, unless he had already breached his obligation at the time of sale.[42]

3. **Sublease.** An assignment should be distinguished from a sublease. With an assignment, the tenant transfers the entire interest to a third party. With a sublease, the tenant transfers only a part of the leasehold estate. For example, the tenant might transfer only a part of the remaining lease term (one year of the remaining two years) or only a part of the property (two rooms out of five).[43] In subleasing the property, the tenant has carved a new leasehold estate out of his own leasehold. The rights and duties of the subtenant are governed by the agreement between the tenant and subtenant; the subtenant does not step into the shoes of the tenant under the original lease because he is not taking the leasehold estate created by that lease. The original tenant, however, remains liable to the landlord under the original lease.

To illustrate the practical ramifications of the distinction between an assignment and a sublease, let us return to the *Ernst* case. Ernst, the landlord, sued the third party, Conditt, for unpaid rent. When the original tenant transferred his interest to Conditt, he used the language "I hereby sublet" to Conditt. In the lawsuit Conditt's defense was that, as a subtenant rather than an assignee, he did not take over the duties of the original tenant under the lease and therefore was not liable to the landlord for rent. The court held that, regardless of what the parties called the transfer, this was in reality an assignment and that Conditt was liable. In reaching this decision the court cited earlier authority to the effect that if "the instrument purports to transfer the lessee's estate for the entire remainder of his term it is an assignment, regardless of its form or of the parties' intention. Conversely, if the instrument purports to transfer the lessee's estate for less than the entire term—even for a day less—it is a sublease, regardless of its form or of the parties' intention."

The distinction between an assignment and a sublease is also important if the tenant holds the property under a tenancy at will. A tenancy at will exists only as long as the landlord and tenant want it

42. Restatement, Second, Property, Landlord and Tenant § 16.3 (1977).

43. But some courts consider an assignment of a portion of the premises a partial assignment rather than a sublease.

to continue; and most courts hold that by transferring his interest, whether by assignment or sublease, the tenant has shown that he no longer wants the estate to continue, thus terminating the lease. However, a few courts have decided that a tenant at will can sublease the property without termination because "no conclusion that the tenant has expressed his will to terminate the tenancy can be drawn from the fact that he sublets a portion of the property. On the contrary, such conduct clearly evidences his intent to maintain the tenancy and enjoy its benefits." [44]

4. **Lease Clause.** It is common practice for a landlord to insert a clause in the lease prohibiting assignments or subleases. While such clauses are generally valid, courts try whenever possible to interpret them narrowly because the law favors the ability to transfer property freely. For example, if the lease stated only that the tenant could not sublease an apartment, the clause would not prevent the tenant from assigning the lease, because an assignment is different from a sublease. Furthermore, if the lease provides that the tenant may not assign or sublease his interest without the consent of the landlord, several courts, although still a minority, hold that the landlord cannot withhold his consent unless he has a "fair, solid and substantial cause or reason." [45] In one case, a landlord testified that he refused to allow a sublease to a widow because, as he stated in a deposition, "I will not rent to a single lady or widow on account of I had a bad experience right now. I had Mrs. Hope Beck in my apartment, never a complaint, never trouble. Mrs. Beck got married and I had nothing else than trouble with her husband. This is the only reason. And I tell you again the only reason why I wouldn't take no single lady in the apartment." The court held that this reason was "illogical, arbitrary and unreasonable." [46]

# VI. REMEDIES

## A. TENANT'S REMEDIES

A tenant has several remedies available when there has been interference with his leasehold rights. The remedies vary considerably depending on the nature of the interference, yet most of them fall into three broad categories. The first two categories, termination of the lease and damages, represent the traditional remedies available to the tenant. The third category, rent-related remedies, has been developed recently in a minority of states, although it is likely that most states will eventually adopt these methods.

---

44. Public Service Co. v. Voudoumas, 84 N.H. 387, 151 A. 81 (1930).

45. Mitchell's, Inc. v. Nelms, 454 S.W. 2d 809 (Tex.Civ.App.1970). See also Restatement, Second, Property, Land-lord and Tenant § 15.2 (1977), which adopts the minority view.

46. Stern v. Taft, 49 Ohio App.2d 405, 361 N.E.2d 279, 3 O.O.3d 463 (1976).

1. **Termination of Lease.** In virtually every case of interference with leasehold rights, the tenant may terminate the lease by vacating the premises; after termination, the tenant is no longer obligated to pay rent. In some cases, the tenant may terminate the lease even if the landlord is not at fault—for example, when a natural force destroys the property or a governmental act makes the tenant's use of the property illegal.

But in most cases the termination will result because the landlord has breached duties arising under the lease or by law. Perhaps the most common example is the situation in which the landlord's breach interferes with the tenant's use and enjoyment of the property to such an extent that the tenant is forced to leave the property and terminate the lease. The courts describe the landlord's breach as a constructive eviction of the tenant and, as in the case of an actual eviction, the evicted tenant is relieved of his obligation to pay rent.

As an illustration of constructive eviction, in Washington Chocolate Co. v. Kent,[47] Washington Chocolate Company leased half a basement in a warehouse from Kent and used the property to store cocoa beans in burlap sacks. Kent retained control of the rest of the building. Government authorities later discovered that the beans stored in the basement were infested with rats. The company immediately notified Kent, who attempted to eliminate the rats but was unsuccessful. As a result, the government seized and destroyed 6,832 pounds of beans, and the company abandoned the premises. When the company sued Kent for the value of the beans and related expenses, such as expenses charged by the government, Kent countersued for rental payments allegedly due. The court held that because Kent retained control of the building and the rats constituted a nuisance, he had breached the implied covenant of quiet enjoyment and was liable to the company for damages. Furthermore, because the company had been constructively evicted from the premises by the presence of rats, it was not liable for rent arising after it abandoned the property.

2. **Damages.** The second traditional remedy is damages. The damage remedy is available when the landlord has breached a duty imposed by the lease or by law. The damage remedy can be used in conjunction with termination, as illustrated by the *Washington Chocolate Co.* case above. Alternatively the tenant may decide to sue for damages while continuing the lease. For instance, in Garcia v. Freeland Realty, Inc.[48] the tenant, Garcia, discovered that his children were eating paint and plaster that was flaking off the walls in his apartment. When the landlord refused to plaster and paint the walls, Garcia did the job himself and sued the landlord for the cost of his supplies and labor. The court awarded damages after noting that "lead poisoning is limited mainly to the children of the poor in New

47. 28 Wash.2d 448, 183 P.2d 514 (1947). 48. 63 Misc.2d 937, 314 N.Y.S.2d 215 (1970).

York City; and that the eating of such plaster and paint flakes by children leads to lead poisoning with the consequences of mental retardation and death." In some cases like *Garcia,* courts have decided that equitable relief, such as specific performance, is a suitable alternative to damages.

3. **Rent-Related Remedies.** The traditional remedies of lease termination and damages are often unsuitable, especially in cases involving a residential lease. Termination requires the tenant to move his family and belongings out of his home and to search for a new residence, which is a difficult task in areas where the occupancy rates are high. And to collect damages, the tenant has the burden of commencing what might be a time-consuming and expensive legal proceeding.

The obvious solution is to allow the tenant to use the only real leverage he has against the landlord—his rental payments—to correct a defect in the apartment or to force the landlord to meet his duties. However, in most states rent-related remedies are not allowed for the reason, now largely historical, that a lease is primarily a transfer of an interest in real estate and the promise to pay for that real estate (rent) is independent of other promises which might be given in the lease. However, a number of states have rejected the "independent covenants" approach and have decided that, at least for residential leases, the promise to pay rent is dependent on the landlord's meeting his lease obligations. Three types of remedies have been developed in states following the modern "dependent covenants" approach: rent withholding, rent application, and rent abatement.[49]

a. *Rent Withholding.* Under several state statutes and a few court decisions, the tenant may withhold rent until the landlord fulfills his obligations. State laws are not uniform on the procedure to be followed by the tenant. In some states the tenant may retain the rent, while in others he must deposit his rent in court or in an escrow account.

b. *Rent Application.* Under several state statutes, the tenant may use the rent to remedy the landlord's breach of duty. For example, the California statute provides that a tenant may, after notice to the landlord of a defect in the premises, repair the defect and apply up to one month's rent toward the repair.[50] The same result has been reached under a few city ordinances that require landlords to set aside a security deposit that could be used to keep the premises repaired.

c. *Rent Abatement.* Several state statutes allow a tenant to reduce his rent in certain situations. The Massachusetts legislation, for instance, provides that if an apartment violates housing laws, the ten-

**49.** Restatement, Second, Property, Landlord and Tenant §§ 11.1–11.3 (1977).

**50.** Cal.Civ.Code § 1942.

ant only has to pay fair value for his use of the property rather than the agreed rent.

A more drastic form of rent abatement has been reached in states using traditional remedies, under the theory of partial actual eviction. This theory provides that if the landlord evicts the tenant from a part of the premises, the tenant owes no rent, even if the tenant uses the rest of the property. Thus if the tenant rents a house and lot and the landlord later refuses to allow the tenant to use the basement, the tenant can continue to use the house without paying rent.

## B.  LANDLORD'S REMEDIES

1. **General Remedies.** In addition to the landlord's rights against a holdover tenant, discussed above with periodic tenancies, the landlord may, upon the tenant's default, use the traditional remedies of damages and termination. In enforcing these remedies a landlord is often tempted to use self-help; that is, the landlord might try to evict the tenant personally or to seize and sell the tenant's property (which is called the right of distress). However, the landlord's ability to use self-help is very limited. In most states, the landlord who enters the property to evict a tenant will be held criminally liable under statutes prohibiting "forcible entry". The landlord who evicts a tenant might also be liable for damages if he commits an intentional tort, such as assault and battery. What constitutes force under the forcible entry statutes varies from state to state, although it is clear that force has been used when a person, threatening and cursing the occupant, "kicked down the door, entered the house, and fell over something, by which his leg was unfortunately broken, instead of his neck." [51]

Distress is often allowed under state statutes that authorize the landlord to seize and sell the tenant's property for unpaid rent. But such statutes have been declared unconstitutional in recent years if they allow seizure of the tenant's property without notice and without an opportunity for a hearing.[52]

Although the landlord is limited in using self-help, most states allow him to bring an action to oust the tenant under a statute entitled (depending on the state) "Summary Proceedings" or "Forcible Entry and Detainer." Shortly after the landlord files a complaint pursuant to these statutes, the matter will be heard by the court; if the landlord prevails, the court will issue a writ ordering a local official to remove the tenant on a specified date, usually a few days after the hearing.

2. **Abandonment.** A tenant's abandonment of the premises before the end of the lease term gives the landlord a choice of three

---

51. State v. Jacobs, 94 N.C. 950 (1886). See Prosser, Law of Torts § 23 (4th ed. 1971).

52. Ragin v. Schwartz, 393 F.Supp. 152 (W.D.Pa.1975).

options.  We might assume, for example, that Terri has leased an apartment from Pam for one year.  After two months, Terri leaves the apartment and mails the keys to Pam.  Terri's actions constitute an offer to surrender the premises to Pam and terminate the lease.  Pam's first option is to accept the offer, thus relieving Terri from further liability for rent.

Pam's second option would be to do nothing, in which case Terri remains liable for the rent.  However in recent years several courts, although still a minority, have decided that the lease is more of a contract than a sale of real estate and that the contract rule of mitigation of damages should apply.  Under this rule the nonbreaching party to the contract, the landlord, must attempt to reduce damages by re-letting the premises to a new tenant.  The reasons for adopting the mitigation rule were reviewed by a Nebraska court: "The traditional view is that a lease creates an interest or estate in land and, therefore, the lessor need not concern himself with a lessee's abandonment of his own property.  A modern lease of a business building ordinarily involves multiple and mutual running covenants between lessor and lessee.  It is difficult to find logical reasons sufficient to justify placing such leases in a category separate and distinct from other fields of the law which have forbidden a recovery for damages which the plaintiff by reasonable efforts could have avoided.  The perpetuation of the distinction between such a lease and a contract in the application of the principle of mitigation of damages, is no longer supportable.  We, therefore, hold that a landlord may not unreasonably refuse to accept a qualified and suitable substitute tenant for the purpose of mitigating the damages recoverable from a tenant who has abandoned the leased premises prior to the expiration of the term." [53]

Pam's third approach as a nonbreaching landlord is to retake possession of the premises and to attempt to mitigate damages voluntarily, even though most states do not require mitigation.  This can be a risky practice for the landlord, because if the landlord fails to notify the tenant that she is taking possession and attempting to re-let the premises on the tenant's behalf, a court will probably treat the landlord's actions as an acceptance of the tenant's offer to surrender the property.  "The landlord, upon an abandonment by the tenant, may retake possession of the premises on behalf of the tenant, re-let the premises for the tenant's account, and hold the tenant for the difference.  If the landlord simply takes possession of the premises and re-lets them at a lower rent, such act is inconsistent with the absolute dominion of the tenant, and constitutes an acceptance of the implied offer to surrender, and terminates the lease.  But if he notifies the tenant that the retaking is on behalf of the tenant, and that he in-

53. Bernstein v. Seglin, 184 Neb. 673,
171 N.W.2d 247 (1969).

tends to sublet to another on behalf of the tenant to mitigate damages, the re-letting does not operate as an acceptance of the abandonment, and no surrender by operation of law results. . . . Normally, the notice must be given before the re-letting to allow the tenant to object or to make other arrangements if he so desires." [54]

## VII. LANDLORD'S TORT LIABILITY

As a general rule, when someone is wrongfully injured as the result of activities or defective conditions on leased property, the tenant is liable as possessor of the property and the landlord is generally not liable. If there was a dangerous condition in existence when the property was leased, the landlord escapes liability under the principle of caveat emptor; if the condition arose during the lease, the tenant, who is in exclusive possession and control of the property, must correct it. However, in recent years courts have developed exceptions to these general principles, discussed below. If the exceptions apply, the landlord becomes liable to the tenant or to a third party injured on the premises. See Borders v. Roseberry, infra.

### A. HIDDEN DANGERS KNOWN TO LANDLORD

If a landlord knows or should know of hidden dangers on the premises, he is under a duty to disclose these dangers to the tenant. In Rhoades v. Seidel,[55] August Seidel rented a house to Rhoades. After taking possession, Rhoades contracted typhoid fever which, he alleged, was caused by a noxious gas coming from an open sewer in the cellar. When Rhoades brought suit, the court held that Seidel was not liable. According to the court, both parties knew of the existence of the open sewer when the lease was made; and at that time Seidel did not know and had no reason to know that a noxious gas would emanate from the sewer.

### B. INJURY OUTSIDE THE PREMISES

A landlord is liable to persons injured outside the premises as the result of a defect which existed when the lease was made. In one case [56] a landlord leased a two-story brick building to a tenant who agreed to keep the building repaired. When the lease was made, the building was old and in a dangerous condition, with cracked walls and sagging windows. Shortly thereafter, the building collapsed, damaging a car parked in front of the building. The tenant was held liable for his negligence in maintaining the building, but "the landlord also is liable where the injury resulted from the permanent condition of

**54.** Dorcich v. Time Oil Co., 103 Cal. App.2d 677, 230 P.2d 10 (1951).

**55.** 139 Mich. 608, 102 N.W. 1025 (1905).

**56.** Barrett v. Stoneburg, 238 Iowa 1068, 29 N.W.2d 420 (1947).

the building (not the use thereof by the tenant) and such condition existed at the time of the lease."

## C. PREMISES LEASED FOR PUBLIC ADMISSION

A landlord will be liable if he leases property that is to be used for the admission of the public and if a dangerous condition existed when the lease was made. To illustrate this rule, in Webel v. Yale Univ.,[57] a woman visited a beauty shop to have her hair waved. While in the shop she went to the ladies room, the floor of which was seven inches higher than the floor of the shop. The raised floor caused the woman to fall and she sued the landlord, Yale University, for her injuries. The court decided that if the woman could prove the alleged facts, she could recover from Yale on the grounds that the landlord leased "premises on which he knows or should know that there are conditions likely to cause injury to persons entering upon them, that the purpose for which the premises are leased involves the fact that people will be invited upon the premises as patrons of the tenant, and that the landowner knows or should know that the tenant cannot reasonably be expected to remedy or guard against injury from the defect."

## D. LANDLORD RESERVES CONTROL

A landlord often retains control over parts of the premises such as hallways and stairways that are for the common use of all tenants. The landlord is liable for injuries that result when the common area is not properly maintained. In one case [58] an eighty-three-year-old tenant opened her oven and a mouse jumped out. Frightened of the mouse, she fell and fractured her hip. She claimed that the landlord was liable for her injuries on the ground that he negligently maintained the areas under his control by permitting those areas to become infested with mice. In affirming a decision in favor of the tenant, the court stated the rule that "where a portion of the premises is reserved for common use and is under the landlord's control, a duty is imposed upon him to use ordinary care to keep such portion in a safe condition. The fact that the actual injury occurred on the demised premises should make no difference if the cause of the injury was the landlord's negligent maintenance of a common area."

## E. LANDLORD'S REPAIR OF PREMISES

A landlord is liable for injuries which result when he has a duty to repair the premises but fails to do so. For example, a landlord with a statutory duty to repair an apartment will be liable if the ceiling falls and injures a tenant.[59]

**57.** 125 Conn. 515, 7 A.2d 215 (1939).

**58.** Mangan v. F. C. Pilgrim Co., 32 Ill.App.3d 563, 336 N.E.2d 374 (1975).

**59.** Altz v. Lieberson, 233 N.Y. 16, 134 N.E. 703 (1922).

A landlord will also be liable when he voluntarily makes repairs in a negligent manner, even when he had no duty to keep the premises repaired. Thus a landlord who voluntarily repaired a second floor porch banister was held liable when the banister gave way, causing the tenant's young daughter to fall eighteen feet onto a hard surface.[60]

## F.  LIABILITY FOR TENANT'S ACTIVITIES

In certain circumstances, a landlord will be liable for the acts of his tenants. In Uccello v. Laudenslayer,[61] the court held that a landlord could be held liable to a third party who was injured by a vicious dog which the tenant kept on the premises. However, the court limited such liability to cases in which the landlord has actual knowledge of the dog's vicious nature and when he has the right to terminate the tenancy.

## G.  LANDLORD'S LIABILITY FOR CRIMINAL ACTS

In Samson v. Saginaw Professional Bldg., Inc.,[62] the landlord leased the fourth floor of a professional building to a mental health clinic. One morning a secretary who worked for an attorney with offices on the fifth floor entered the elevator on her way to a local coffee shop. A patient receiving treatment at the clinic was the only other person in the elevator, and as the elevator started down, he pushed the emergency stop button, robbed the secretary, and began stabbing her with a knife. He then restarted the elevator and ran away when it reached the ground floor, although he was later apprehended. Should the landlord be held liable for the criminal act of the mental patient?

In resolving cases such as this, two questions have been especially troublesome. First, does the landlord have a duty to the tenant to use reasonable care in preventing criminal conduct? In answering this question, courts generally examine closely those situations in which a landlord may be held liable for defective conditions; in most cases, they have decided that a duty exists. The reasons usually cited are that the landlord has a duty to keep the property (for example, door locks and security systems) repaired or that the landlord has control of common areas. In Samson, the court concluded that "the landlord has retained his responsibility for the common areas of the building which are not leased to his tenants. The common areas such as the halls, lobby, stairs, elevators, etc., are leased to no individual tenant and remain the responsibility of the landlord. It is his responsibility to insure that these areas are kept in good repair and reasonably safe for

---

**60.** Henderson v. Dolas, 217 S.W.2d 554 (Mo.1949).

**61.** 44 Cal.App.3d 504, 118 Cal.Rptr. 741 (1975). See also Restatement, Second, Property, Landlord and Tenant § 18.4 (1977).

**62.** 393 Mich. 393, 224 N.W.2d 843 (1975).

the use of his tenants and invitees. The existence of this relationship between the defendant and its tenants and invitees placed a duty upon the landlord to protect them from unreasonable risk of physical harm."

But even if we assume that a landlord has a duty to a tenant and has breached the duty (for example, by not installing an adequate security system), a second major question must be answered: Was the injury caused by the landlord's negligence or, instead, by the intervening act of an independent third party, the criminal? The law requires that if a person is to be held liable for his wrongful act, the act must not only be the cause in fact of the injury but also the proximate (or legal) cause of the injury. Proximate cause is one which, in a natural sequence of events unbroken by an intervening event, results in an injury. Without limiting liability to proximate causes, the chain of liability would be endless—the "fatal trespass done by Eve was cause of all our woe." [63] As a general rule, when a person's negligent act provides the opportunity for another person to commit a criminal act, the criminal act is an intervening event which relieves the negligent party from liability.

However, an important exception has developed in cases where the negligent party should have foreseen the likelihood that the crime would be committed; relying on this exception, many courts have decided that landlords should be held liable. In *Samson*, the court held that the "fact that such an event might occur in the future was foreseeable to this defendant. It had even been brought to its attention by other tenants in the building. The magnitude of the risk, that of a criminally insane person running amok within an office building filled with tenants and invitees, was substantial to say the least." In other cases, courts have held that the criminal act was foreseeable because the leased property was located in a high crime area or because of prior criminal activity on the property. See Johnston v. Harris, infra.

## H. EXCULPATORY CLAUSES

A landlord faced with increasing liability for injuries on the leased premises will be tempted to include an exculpatory clause in the lease. In Crowell v. Housing Authority of City of Dallas,[64] a tenant was killed by carbon monoxide from a defective gas heater in his apartment. When his son sued the landlord, the Dallas Housing Authority, it raised in defense an exculpatory clause in the lease which provided: ". . . nor shall the Landlord nor any of his representatives or employees be liable for any damage to person or property of the Tenant, his family, or his visitors, which might result from the condition of these or other premises of the Landlord, from theft or

---

63. W. Prosser, Law of Torts 236 (4th ed. 1971).

64. 495 S.W.2d 887 (Tex.1973).

from any cause whatsoever." The court stated as a general rule that agreements "exempting a party from future liability for negligence are generally recognized as valid and effective except where, because of the relationship of the parties, the exculpatory provision is contrary to public policy or the public interest. If the contract is between private persons who bargain from positions of substantially equal strength, the agreement is ordinarily enforced by the courts. The exculpatory agreement will be declared void, however, where one party is at such disadvantage in bargaining power that he is practically compelled to submit to the stipulation." In applying the rule in this case, the court decided that the exculpatory clause was contrary to public policy and void because the landlord dictated the terms of the lease and the tenant had no choice but to accept the terms because decent housing was not otherwise available.

# CASES

---

## TOMS POINT APARTMENTS v. GOUDZWARD

District Court, Nassau County, Third District, 1972.
72 Misc.2d 629, 339 N.Y.S.2d 281.

RALPH DIAMOND, Judge.

This is a holdover proceeding in which the landlord-petitioner seeks possession of the demised premises. The tenant's defense is retaliatory eviction.

The basic facts are not in dispute. The parties entered into a lease on August 17, 1966, for a two-year period commencing September 1, 1966. The lease was renewed twice, each time for a two-year period. The last renewal expired August 31, 1972.

In October, 1971, the tenant invited a group of fellow-tenants to meet in her apartment to consider the possibility of forming a tenant's organization to deal with the landlord with respect to several grievances.

In April, 1972, and again in June, 1972, the tenant was advised that her lease would not be further renewed. Despite notice tenant failed to vacate the premises. On the 5th day of October, 1972, this proceeding was begun.

At the trial, the tenant raised the affirmative defense of "retaliatory eviction". She claimed that the landlord's refusal to renew her lease was solely in retaliation for her actions with her fellow tenants in opposing the landlord. The landlord contends that the tenant has failed to sustain the burden of proof required and, further, that the defense of retaliatory eviction does not apply in this case.

Tenant seeks to dismiss the action and have the Court order the landlord to renew the lease on terms equal to those offered other tenants.

The Court has before it the question whether a landlord has the right to pick his tenants and refuse to renew the tenancy of a person he finds undesirable for any reason, or whether that right is affected by the defense of retaliatory eviction.

The defense of retaliatory eviction in New York State is a comparatively new one. Retaliatory eviction has been defined in many ways. In Markese v. Cooper, 70 Misc.2d 478, 333 N.Y.S.2d 63, the Court stated that retaliatory eviction is the nomenclature that has developed to define the action of a landlord who evicts his tenant because of the tenant's reporting of a housing code violation. The Court in that case went on to say that it might have been called anything, "vengeful eviction" or, simply, "getting even". The Court in Hosey v. Club Van Cortlandt, D.C., 299 F.Supp. 501, described retaliatory eviction as an act by a landlord evicting a tenant when the overriding reason was to retaliate against the tenant for exercising his constitutional right.

The defense of retaliatory eviction in a holdover proceeding was not available at common law, nor do we in New York have any statutes specifically prohibiting retaliatory eviction. A few states have recently enacted such statutes. Illinois has declared it to be against public policy for a landlord to "terminate or refuse to renew a lease or tenancy of property used as a residence on the ground that the tenant has complained to any government authority of a bona fide violation of any applicable building code, health ordinance, or similar regulation." Rhode Island and Michigan allow a tenant-defendant, in an action based upon termination of a lease, to interpose the defense that the alleged termination was intended as a penalty for the tenant reporting a violation of any health or safety code, or any ordinance. Maryland has provided that retaliatory action will be stayed for a period of six months after a tenant has reported a major defect in the premises. California's new Civil Code Section 1942.5 states that a landlord, whose dominant purpose is retaliation against a lessee for complaining to a government agency or for exercising other rights, "may not recover possession of a dwelling in any action or proceeding, cause the lessee to quit involuntarily, increase the rent, or decrease any services, within 60 days". New Jersey provides for criminal punishment of any landlord who takes reprisals against a tenant for reporting violations of any health or building code.

\*    \*    \*

In reviewing the New York, Federal, and out of state cases discussed above, the Court finds that the basis for accepting the defense of retaliatory eviction is as follows:

A tenant has the constitutional right such as to discuss the conditions of the building he is living in with his co-tenants; to encourage them to use legal means to remedy improper conditions; hold meetings; form tenants' associations; and inform public officials of their complaints. These rights would for all practical purposes be meaningless if the threat of eviction would coerce the most justifiable complaints into a submissive silence.

Failure to recognize the defense of retaliatory eviction might result in the continuation of undesirable housing conditions contrary to the strong public policy of creating and/or maintaining proper housing in New York State. Our Court should not by the granting of an eviction of a complaining tenant encourage the landlord to evade his responsibility to abide by the law.

The Court is in accord with the reasoning behind the acceptance of the defense of retaliatory eviction in an action by a landlord to recover possession. Once having accepted that concept, the Court is faced with the problem as to what elements are necessary to create a valid retaliatory eviction defense. In reviewing the cases we find no definite guidelines to follow.

It seems to this Court that *all* of the following should be present for the tenant to prevail:

1. The tenant must have exercised a constitutional right in the action he undertook.

2. The grievance complained of by the tenant must be bona fide, reasonable, serious in nature, and have a foundation in fact. However, the grievance need not have been adjudicated by the agency reviewing the complaint.

3. The tenant did not create the condition upon which the complaint is based.

4. The grievance complained of must be present at the time the landlord commences his proceeding.

5. The overriding reason the landlord is seeking the eviction is to retaliate against the tenant for exercising of his constitutional rights.

Applying the facts in the present case to the above criteria, the Court finds that at the time the landlord commenced this action and, at the present time, none of the original grievances existed. The tenant testified that the tenants' association never came into being; that the tenants had collected the interest due them; that the problem with the superintendent had been resolved. Moreover, the tenant failed to show any current complaint against the landlord.

In Edwards v. Habib, 130 U.S.App.D.C. 126, 397 F.2d 687, 702, the Court cautioned that even if a tenant can prove a retaliatory defense, he would not be entitled to remain in possession in perpetuity. "If this illegal purpose is dissipated, the landlord can, in the absence of legislation or a binding contract, evict his tenants or raise their rents for economic or other legitimate reasons, or even for no reason at all."

The Court finds that the tenant has failed to prove the elements necessary to sustain the alleged retaliatory eviction defense. Accordingly, the decision of the Court is as follows:

Final Judgment in favor of the landlord against the tenant. Execution of the warrant stayed to February 28, 1973.

--------

### GREEN v. SUPERIOR CT. OF CITY & CTY. OF SAN FRANCISCO

Supreme Court of California, 1974.
10 Cal.3d 616, 111 Cal.Rptr. 704, 517 P.2d 1168.

\*    \*    \*

1. *The facts of the instant case.*

We begin with a brief review of the facts of the instant case, which reveal a somewhat typical unlawful detainer action. On September 27, 1972, the landlord Jack Sumski commenced an unlawful detainer action in the San Francisco Small Claims Court seeking possession of the leased premises and $300 in back rent. The tenant admitted non-payment of rent but defended the action on the ground that the landlord had failed to maintain the leased premises in a habitable condition. The small claims court awarded possession of the premises to the landlord and entered a money judgment for $225 against the tenant.

The tenant then appealed the decision to the San Francisco Superior Court, where a de novo trial was held pursuant to section 117j of the Code of Civil Procedure. In support of his claim of uninhabitability, the tenant submitted a copy of an October 1972 inspection report of the San Francisco Department of Public Works disclosing some 80 housing code violations in the building in question, as well as an order of the department scheduling a condemnation hearing for January 19, 1973. In addition, in testimony at trial, petitioner and his roommate detailed a long list of serious defects in the leased premises which had not been repaired by the landlord after notice and which they claimed rendered the premises uninhabitable. Some of the more serious defects described by the tenants included (1) the collapse and non-repair of the bathroom ceiling, (2) the continued presence of rats, mice, and cockroaches on the premises, (3) the lack of any heat in four of the apartment's rooms, (4) plumbing blockages, (5) exposed and faulty wiring, and (6) an illegally installed and dangerous stove. The landlord apparently did not attempt to contest the presence of serious defects in the leased premises, but instead claimed that such defects afforded the tenant no defense in an unlawful detainer action.

The superior court judge ultimately agreed with the landlord's contention, holding that the "repair and deduct" provisions of Civil Code section 1941 et seq. constituted the tenant's exclusive remedy under these circumstances. Accordingly, the superior court entered judgment for the landlord, awarding him $225 and possession of the premises.

\* \* \*

2. *The transformation of the landlord-tenant relationship and developments in analogous areas of law compel the recognition of a common law implied warranty of habitability in residential leases in California.*

At common law, the real estate lease developed in the field of real property law, not contract law. Under property law concepts, a lease was considered a conveyance or sale of the premises for a term of years, subject to the ancient doctrine of caveat emptor. Thus, under traditional common law rules, the landlord owed no duty to place leased premises in a habitable condition and no obligation to repair the premises. These original common law precepts perhaps suited the agrarianism of the early Middle Ages which was their matrix; at such time, the primary value of a lease lay in the land itself and whatever simple living structures may have been included in the leasehold were of secondary importance and were readily repairable by the typical "jack-of-all-trades" lessee farmer. Furthermore, because the law of property crystallized before the development of mutually dependent covenants in contract law, a lessee's covenant to pay rent was considered at common law as independent of the lessor's covenants. Thus even when a lessor expressly covenanted to make repairs, the lessor's breach did not justify the lessee's withholding of the rent.

In recent years, however, a growing number of courts have begun to re-examine these "settled" common law rules in light of contemporary conditions, and, after thorough analysis, all of these courts have discarded the traditional doctrine as incompatible with contemporary social conditions and modern legal values. This emerging line of decisions, along with a veritable flood of academic commentaries, demonstrates the obsolescence of the traditional common law rule absolving a landlord of any duty to maintain leased premises in a habitable condition during the term of the lease.

The recent decisions recognize initially that the geographic and economic conditions that characterized the agrarian lessor-lessee transaction have been entirely transformed in the modern urban landlord-tenant relationship. We have suggested that in the Middle Ages, and, indeed, until the urbanization of the industrial revolution, the land itself was by far the most important element of a lease transaction; this predominance explained the law's treatment of such leases as conveyances of interests in land. In today's urban residential leases, however, land as such plays no comparable role. The typical city dweller, who frequently leases an apartment several stories above the actual plot of land on which an apartment building rests, cannot realistically be viewed as acquiring an interest in land; rather, he has contracted for a place to live. As the Court of Appeal for the District of Columbia observed in Javins v. First National Realty Corp. (1970) 138 U.S.App.D.C. 369, 428 F.2d 1071, 1074: "When American city dwellers, both rich and poor, seek 'shelter' today, they seek a well known package of goods and services—a package which includes not merely walls and ceilings, but also adequate heat, light and ventilation, serviceable plumbing facilities, secure windows and doors, proper sanitation, and proper maintenance."

In the past, California courts have increasingly recognized the largely contractual nature of contemporary lease agreements and have frequently analyzed such leases' terms pursuant to contractual principles. Similarly, leading legal scholars in the field have long stressed the propriety of a more contractually oriented analysis of lease agreements. Our holding in this case reflects our belief that the application of contract principles, including the mutual dependency of covenants, is particularly appropriate in dealing with residential leases of urban dwelling units.

Modern urbanization has not only undermined the validity of utilizing general property concepts in analyzing landlord-tenant relations, but it has also significantly altered the factual setting directly relevant to the more specific duty of maintaining leased premises. As noted above, at the inception of the common law rule, any structure on the leased premises was likely to be of the most simple nature, easily inspected by the lessee to determine if it fit his needs, and easily repairable by the typically versatile tenant farmer. Contemporary urban housing and the contemporary urban tenant stand in marked contrast to this agrarian model.

       \*    \*    \*

The crucial issue in this case thus becomes whether a landlord's breach of a warranty of habitability directly relates to the issue of possession. Holding that such breach was irrelevant to the question of possession, early California cases refused to permit a defense that the landlord had breached a covenant to repair premises. These decisions, however, rested primarily upon the ancient property doctrine of "independent covenants," under which a tenant's obligation to pay rent was viewed as a continuing obligation which was not excused by the landlord's failure to fulfill any covenant of repair he may have assumed. As indicated earlier in this opinion, the entire foundation of the "independent covenants" doctrine rested on the central role played by land in the lease transaction of the Middle Ages; the doctrine simply reflected the fact that in those early times covenants regarding the maintenance of buildings were generally "incidental" to the furnishing of land, and did not go to the root of the consideration for the lease. In that setting, a landlord's breach of such an "incidental" covenant to repair was reasonably considered insufficient to justify the tenant's refusal to pay rent, the tenant's main obligation under the lease.

The transformation which the residential lease has undergone since the Middle Ages, however, has completely eroded the underpinnings of the "independent covenant" rule. Today the habitability of the dwelling unit has become the very essence of the residential lease; the landlord can as materially frustrate the purpose of such a lease by permitting the premises to become uninhabitable as by withdrawing the use of a portion of the premises. Thus, in keeping with the contemporary trend to analyze urban residential leases under modern contractual principles, we now conclude that the tenant's duty to pay rent is "mutually dependent" upon the landlord's fulfillment of his implied warranty of habitability. Such was essentially the holding of the Court of Appeal in Hinson v. Delis as well as a number of the out-of-state cases which have recently adopted the implied warranty of habitability rule. (See p. 1178 ante.) As the Supreme Judicial Court of Massachusetts stated most recently: "The old common law treatment of the lease as a property conveyance and the independent covenants rule which stems from this treatment have outlived their usefulness."

Once we recognize that the tenant's obligation to pay rent and the landlord's warranty of habitability are mutually dependent, it becomes clear that the landlord's breach of such warranty may be directly relevant to the issue of possession. If the tenant can prove such a breach by the landlord, he may demonstrate that his nonpayment of rent was justified and that no rent is in fact "due and owing" to the landlord. Under such circumstances, of course, the landlord would not be entitled to possession of the premises.

\* \* \*

We have concluded that a warranty of habitability is implied by law in residential leases in this state and that the breach of such a warranty may be raised as a defense in an unlawful detainer action. Under the implied warranty which we recognize, a residential landlord covenants that premises he leases for living quarters will be maintained in a habitable state for the duration of the lease. This implied warranty of habitability does not require that a landlord ensure that leased premises are in perfect, aesthetically pleasing condition, but it does mean that "bare living requirements" must be maintained. In most cases substantial compliance with those applicable building and housing code standards which materially affect health and safety will suffice to meet the landlord's obligations under the common law implied warranty of habitability we now recognize. As the *Hinson* court observed: "[m]inor housing code violations standing alone which do not affect habitability must be considered *de minimis* and will not entitle the tenant to reduction in rent.   \*   \*   \* "

In the instant case, the tenant defended the unlawful detainer action on the grounds that the premises were not in a habitable condition; in support of this claim, as noted above, he presented a city housing inspection report detailing some 80 violations of local housing and building codes, including major defects in the building's plumbing and electrical facilities. At trial the tenant also testified that he had repeatedly informed the landlord of plumbing blockages, a collapsed bathroom ceiling, lack of heat in four rooms, exposed and faulty wiring and an illegally installed and dangerous stove, but that the landlord had failed to make any repairs within a reasonable period of time. Although this evidence of substantial defects in the premises was not controverted at trial, the court granted judgment for the landlord, on the theory that, whatever the condition of the premises, the tenant's exclusive remedy was provided by section 1941 et seq. of the Civil Code. As discussed above, that conclusion was erroneous and thus we must remand this case to the trial court so that it may determine whether the landlord has breached the implied warranty of habitability as defined in this opinion.

If the trial court does find a breach of implied warranty, the court must then determine the extent of the damages flowing from this breach. Recent decisions have suggested that in these circumstances the "tenant's damages shall be measured by the difference between the fair rental value of the premises if they had been as warranted and the fair rental value of the premises as they were during occupancy by the tenant in the unsafe or unsanitary condition."

       \*   \*   \*

In summary, we have concluded that the traditional common law rule which imposed no warranty of habitability in residential leases is a product of an earlier, land-oriented era, which bears no reasonable relation to the social or legal realities of the landlord-tenant relationship of today. The United States Supreme Court has observed that "the body of private property law   \*   \*   \*, more than almost any other branch, of law, has been shaped by distinctions whose validity is largely historical," and on previous occasions in recent years our own court has responded to the changes wrought by modern conditions by discarding outworn common law property doctrines. (See Rowland v. Christian (1968) 69 Cal.2d 108, 70 Cal.Rptr. 97, 443 P.2d 561.) In taking a similar step today, we do not exercise a novel prerogative, but merely follow the well-established duty of common law courts to reflect contemporary social values and ethics. As Justice Cardozo wrote in his celebrated essay "The Growth of the Law" chapter V, pages 136–137: "A rule which in its origin was the creation of the courts themselves, and was supposed in the making to express the *mores* of the day, may be abrogated by courts when the *mores* have so changed that perpetration of the rule would do violence to the social conscience. * * * This is not usurpation. It is not even innovation. It is the reservation for ourselves of the same power of creation that built up the common law through its exercise by the judges of the past."

    * * *

---

## BORDERS v. ROSEBERRY

Supreme Court of Kansas, 1975.
216 Kan. 486, 532 P.2d 1366.

PRAGER, Justice:

This case involves the liability of a landlord for personal injuries suffered by the social guest of the tenant as the result of a slip and fall on the leased premises. The facts in this case are undisputed and are as follows: The defendant-appellee, Agnes Roseberry, is the owner of a single-family, one-story residence located at 827 Brown Avenue, Osawatomie, Kansas. Several months prior to January 9, 1971, the defendant leased the property on a month to month basis to a tenant, Rienecker. Just prior to the time the tenant took occupancy of the house the defendant landlord had work performed on the house. The remodeling of the house included a new roof. In repairing the house the repairmen removed the roof guttering from the front of the house but failed to reinstall it. The landlord knew the guttering had been removed by the workmen, intended to have it reinstalled, and knew that it had not been reinstalled. The roof line on the house was such that without the guttering the rain drained off the entire north side of the house onto the front porch steps. In freezing weather water from the roof would accumulate and freeze on the steps. The landlord as well as the tenant knew that the guttering had not been reinstalled and knew that without the guttering, water from the roof would drain onto the front porch steps and in freezing weather would accumulate and freeze. The tenant had complained to the landlord about the absence of guttering and the resulting icy steps.

On January 9, 1971, there was ice and snow on the street and ice on the front steps. During the afternoon the tenant worked on the front steps, removing the ice accumulation with a hammer. The plaintiff-appellant, Gary D. Borders, arrived on the premises at approximately 4:00 p. m. in response to an invitation of the tenant for dinner. It is agreed that plaintiff's status was that of a social guest of the tenant. There was ice on the street and snow on the front steps when plaintiff arrived. At 9:00 p. m. as plaintiff Borders was leaving the house he slipped and fell on an accumulation of ice on the steps and received personal injuries. There is no contention that the plaintiff Borders was negligent in a way which contributed to cause his injuries. After a pretrial conference the case was tried to the court without a jury. Following submission of the case the trial court entered judgment for the defendant, making findings of fact which are essentially those set forth above. The trial court based its judgment upon a conclusion of law which stated that a landlord of a single-family house is under no obligation or duty to a social guest, a licensee of his tenant, to repair or remedy a known condition whereby water dripped onto the front steps of a house fronting north, froze and caused plaintiff to slip and fall. The plaintiff has appealed to this court.

The sole point raised on this appeal by the plaintiff, Gary D. Borders, is that the trial court committed reversible error in concluding as a matter of law that a landlord of a single-family house is under no obligation or duty to a social guest of his tenant to repair or remedy a known condition whereby water dripped from the roof onto the front steps of a house fronting north, froze and caused the social guest to slip and fall.

At the outset it should be emphasized that we do not have involved here an action brought by a social guest to recover damages for personal injuries from his host, a possessor of real property. The issue raised involves the liability of a lessor who has leased his property to a tenant for a period of time. Furthermore, it should be pointed out that the plaintiff, a social guest of the tenant, has based his claim of liability against the landlord upon the existence of a defective condition which existed on the leased property *at the time the tenant took possession.*

Traditionally the law in this country has placed upon the lessee as the person in possession of the land the burden of maintaining the premises in a reasonably safe condition to protect persons who come upon the land. It is the tenant as possessor who, at least initially, has the burden of maintaining the premises in good repair. The relationship of landlord and tenant is not in itself sufficient to make the landlord liable for the tortious acts of the tenant. When land is leased to a tenant, the law of property regards the lease as equivalent to a sale of the premises for the term. The lessee acquires an estate in the land, and becomes for the time being the owner and occupier, subject to all of the responsibilities of one in possession, both to those who enter onto the land and to those outside of its boundaries. Professor William L. Prosser in his Law of Torts, 4th Ed. § 63, points out that in the absence of agreement to the contrary, the lessor surrenders both possession and control of the land to the lessee, retaining only a reversionary interest; and he has no right even to enter without the permission of the lessee. There is therefore, as a general rule, no liability upon the landlord, either to the tenant or to others entering the land, for defective conditions existing at the time of the lease.

The general rule of non-liability has been modified, however, by a number of exceptions which have been created as a matter of social policy.  *  *  *

*  *  * It is clear that the exceptions pertaining to undisclosed dangerous conditions known to the lessor (exception 1), conditions dangerous to persons outside of the premises (exception 2), premises leased for admission of the public (exception 3), and parts of land retained in the lessor's control (exception 4) have no application in this case. Nor do we believe that exception 5, which comes into play when the lessor has contracted to repair, has been established by the court's findings of fact. It does not appear that the plaintiff takes the position that the lessor contracted to keep the premises in repair; nor has any consideration for such an agreement been shown. As to exception 6, although it is obvious that the repairs to the roof were not completed by installation of the guttering and although the landlord expressed his intention to replace the guttering, we do not believe that the factual circumstances bring the plaintiff within the application of exception 6 where the lessor has been negligent in making repairs. As pointed out above, that exception comes into play only when the lessee lacks knowledge that the purported repairs have not been made or have been negligently made. Here it is undisputed that the tenant had full knowledge of the icy condition on the steps created by the absence of guttering. It seems to us that the landlord could reasonably assume that the tenant would inform his guest about the icy condition on the front steps. We have concluded that the factual circumstances do not establish liability on the landlord on the basis of negligent repairs made by him.

In his brief counsel for the plaintiff vigorously argues that the law should be changed to make the landlord liable for injuries resulting from a defective condition on the leased premises where the landlord has knowledge of that condition. He has not cited any authority in support of his position, nor does he state with particularity how the existing law pertaining to a landlord's liability should be modified. We do not believe that the facts and circumstances of this case justify a departure from the established rules of law discussed above.

The judgment of the district court is affirmed.

———

### JOHNSTON v. HARRIS

Supreme Court of Michigan, 1972.
387 Mich. 569, 198 N.W.2d 409.

T. M. KAVANAGH, Chief Justice.

Plaintiff was an elderly tenant in decedent's 4-unit apartment building located in the Detroit inner city. Returning home at about 7:30 p. m. on October 7, 1965, plaintiff approached the front door. As he reached for the doorknob, the door was jerked open and he was assaulted, struck and robbed by an unknown youth who was lurking in the poorly lighted, unlocked vestibule.

Plaintiff commenced action in Wayne circuit court against defendants' decedent, asserting that the assault, robbery and consequent injuries were proximately caused by the failure of decedent to provide adequate lighting and door locks.

Plaintiff offered proof of the dim lighting of the porch and vestibule and the continuously unlocked outer door of the vestibule. He showed, through the testimony of a public lighting expert, the relationship between poor lighting and the high incidence of night crime. He further showed this to be a high crime area.

At the conclusion of plaintiff's proofs the trial court, sitting without a jury, granted defendants' "motion for a directed verdict of no cause of action," stating it was not persuaded "that there was any degree of fault on the part of the landlord which could be declared to be the contributing or direct proximate cause for the injury that befell the plaintiff   *   *   *."

The Court of Appeals concluded from a review of the record that as to duty and breach, plaintiff had established a *prima facie* case. However, it found no adequate proof of a proximate cause and therefore affirmed the trial court. Plaintiff was granted leave to appeal to this Court.

The controlling issue is: where plaintiff has presented a *prima facie* case to a judge without a jury that a landlord had a duty to provide adequate porch and vestibule lighting and a lock on the front door of his apartment building, was the landlord's breach of that duty a proximate cause of plaintiff's mugging by a criminal who was lurking in the poorly lighted and unlocked vestibule of the apartment building?

\*   \*   \*

We are of the opinion that Restatement, Second, Torts, § 442B, p. 469, cited by the Court of Appeals, is not applicable to the instant case. Rather, in point are §§ 302B, 448 and 449, supra.

Section 302B provides:

> "An act or an omission may be negligent if the actor realizes or should realize that it involves an unreasonable risk of harm to another through the conduct of the other or a third person which is intended to cause harm, even though such conduct is criminal."

Section 448 provides:

> "The act of a third person in committing an intentional tort or crime is a superseding cause of harm to another resulting therefrom, although the actor's negligent conduct created a situation which afforded an opportunity to the third person to commit such a tort or crime, *unless the actor at the time of his neg-*

*ligent conduct realized or should have realized the likelihood that such a situation might be created, and that a third person might avail himself of the opportunity to commit such a tort or crime."* (Emphasis supplied.)

Section 449 provides:

"If the likelihood that a third person may act in a particular manner is the hazard or one of the hazards which makes the actor negligent, such an act whether innocent, negligent, intentionally tortious, or criminal does not prevent the actor from being liable for harm caused thereby."

\* \* \*

Contrary to the statement of the trial court, we hold that actionable negligence may lie in these circumstances.

\* \* \*

Reversed and remanded for new trial.

BRENNAN, Justice (dissenting).

I disagree. I believe the majority extends the rule of tort law too far.

Public safety is the business of government.

Today's decision concedes the failure of government to make the streets and homes of certain areas reasonably safe and in effect transfers the governmental function of public protection to the unfortunate owners of real property in such places.

Already overburdened by taxes largely laid to pay for public safety, these owners will now be required to maintain additional lighting, guards, enclosures, alarms, locks and take every other precaution to avoid reasonably foreseeable conditions which attract criminals to carry out their nefarious deeds.

At a time when concerned citizens and public officials are seeking ways to involve the broader community in resolving the plight of so-called "high crime areas", our Court would place an additional burden upon the land and the resources of such areas.

The intrusion of private industry into the business of public safety has been one of the most unfortunate phenomena of the 1960's and the 1970's. Already, there are subdivisions which operate their own patrol cars; private police and private guards are multiplying; vigilante forces of private citizens roam the streets with walkie-talkies; store owners and apartment managers arm themselves and set traps for burglars; and now this Court would give further impetus to such developments by imposing civil liability on the unfortunate victims of crime in "high crime areas."

No member of this Court lives in such an area. None are voting to increase his own insurance premium, or that of his neighbors. What we do in the name of liberality is regressive. It is a mistake.

## PROBLEMS

1. Shakespeare leased property to Sinclair Refining Company for a term of five years at a rental of $50 per month. Thirty-three days before the end of the term, Sinclair notified Shakespeare that it would be vacating the premises, but Sinclair did not actually move until four months after the end of the term. Sinclair claims that it is liable only for four months rent, since the original lease called for a monthly rental. Shakespeare claims that Sinclair is liable for an additional five year's rent as a holdover tenant. Who is correct? Why?

2. Dewar rented a sleeping room, one of twenty-four such rooms, at the local Elks Lodge for $35 per month. After several months the Lodge gave Dewar notice to vacate the room within the next few days. When Dewar refused to vacate, the lodge removed his belongings and locked him out. Dewar sued the Elks for damages, claiming that the lodge did not give the notice required for month-to-month tenancies. Assuming this claim is true, how can the lodge best defend this case? Why?

3. Larry owns a house which he leased to Tom for one year. Six months after Tom took possession, the bathroom floor began to sink as the result of termite infestation, and Tom could no longer use the bathroom. Tom claims that Larry, as landlord, has the duty to repair the termite damage. Larry claims that tenants like Tom must continue to pay rent even if the whole house crumbles as the result of termite damage. Who is correct? Why?

4. Bonnie leased a restaurant to Clyde for a twenty-five-year term. In the lease, Clyde promised not to assign or sublease the property without Bonnie's consent. Shortly after taking possession of the property, Clyde borrowed $20,000 from Last Bank and gave the bank a mortgage on his leasehold interest. Does the mortgage violate the lease? Why?

5. In 1939, Lena leased a building to Mary which was to be used "solely as a filling station and not for restaurant or lunch counter purposes" for a five-year period at a rental of $100 per month. After three years, Mary offered to restore possession of the property to Lena. Mary claimed that World War II government regulations that froze the sale of automobiles and rationed the sale of gasoline made it impossible for her to use the leased property as a filling station. Lena refused to terminate the lease and claimed that Mary must pay rent for the full five-year term. Is Lena correct? Why?

6. Clarence owned a large apartment complex. Approximately 20 percent of his apartments were leased to blacks. Clarence required all prospective tenants to prove that their weekly income, after taxes and debts had been subtracted, was at least 90 percent of the monthly rent. A group of black welfare recipients were refused apartments because they did not meet this test. They sued Clarence, claiming that the test violated the 1866 Civil Rights Act and the 1968 Fair Housing Act, both of which prohibit racial discrimination. Is Clarence liable? Why?

7. On August 25, 1978, Chauncey, a university student, leased an apartment near the university from Snidely on a month-to-month basis. The state statute provided that a landlord must give a one-month notice to quit in order to terminate a month-to-month tenancy. Snidely served

Chauncey with a notice to quit on February 25, 1979, ordering him to leave the apartment on March 25, 1979. Is this a valid notice? Why?

8. In January, Pilgrim Properties hired Sam as custodian and furnished him with an apartment in the building where he worked. Two months later, Sam was fired for failing to perform his janitorial duties, but he refused to give up the apartment. Pilgrim brought suit to recover possession. What type of property interest does Sam have? Will Pilgrim win? Why?

9. · Dickey leased a vacant piece of real estate to Minit-Man Corp. (MM) for ten years. The lease provided that the property was to be used for "the business of washing and cleaning automobiles . . . and for no other purpose." MM was to pay rent equal to 12½ percent of its annual gross sales with a minimum payment of $1,800 per year. MM installed a car wash on the property but discontinued the business after five years. Although MM continued to pay the minimum rental, Dickey brought suit to evict MM on the grounds that MM had defaulted by discontinuing the business. Is Dickey correct? Why?

10. Matina owned a two-story building. The first story was leased to a shoe store, and the second floor was leased to Scheidel for a club. Scheidel hired Stumpka, a professional window washer, to wash the outside of the second floor windows. After washing the windows at least once a month for over two years, Stumpka was seriously injured in a fall from the second story window. The fall resulted when decayed wood in the window frame failed to hold his safety belt. Are Matina and Scheidel liable for Stumpka's injuries? Why?

# Appendix A

## CHECK LIST FOR USE IN REAL ESTATE TRANSACTIONS *

### 1. Parties

List the names of the parties whose interests are to be affected. Consider the need of mentioning trade names. Obtain the business and home address and phone number of the necessary parties. Be informed as to the marital status and the competency of the parties. Where a party is a corporate entity obtain exact name, the location of the principal office—whether it has the power to do what the agreement calls for. If a foreign corporation, determine whether it is qualified to do business here, if that qualification should be necessary. Obtain names of the agents or officers of the corporation and be satisfied with the proof of their authority.

If a party is executor, administrator, guardian, trustee, or trustee in bankruptcy, receiver, assignee for benefit of creditors one should obtain information as to date of appointment, whether he has power to act. If he has been appointed by will or other instrument, examine such instrument to determine extent of his powers. Consider whether it is necessary to obtain a court order authorizing or approving the sale.

If a party is an heir or devisee, ascertain whether estate or inheritance taxes have been paid, whether debts have been paid, legacies paid, whether the heirship has been sufficiently proved.

If a party is an unincorporated association or business trust, obtain copy of the articles or trust agreement to determine authority and power. Ascertain whether real property is acquired, or can be acquired in the association name or the members. Examine the powers of managers or trustees to convey real estate, and if you believe that the beneficiaries have sufficient control over the trustees, that the result is a partnership, make sure that they are also parties. If the party is a business trust, ascertain whether less than all the trustees are empowered to act.

If a party is a partnership, see whether it is a general, limited, trading or non-trading firm. Obtain the names and addresses of all partners, and the names of the persons in whom legal title is vested. Obtain copy of the partnership agreement to see whether there are any limitations on the authority of a partner to act for copartners. If the conveyance by a partnership is more than carrying on in the usual way the business of the partnership, all partners should join.

---

* This check list and the forms in Appendix B (with the exception of the mechanic's lien and will forms), are from E. Belsheim, Modern Legal Forms. These forms, and the legal dictionary in Appendix C, have been reprinted with the permission of West Publishing Company.

If a party acts by agent or Attorney-in-fact, be sure that the power of attorney is sufficient and see that it is recorded prior to the execution and recording of the instrument of transfer.

### 2.  Description and Identification of Property

A street number alone is unsatisfactory and may be inaccurate. Obtain, if possible the legal description.

Surveys are most useful, and if there is none, arrange for it and determine who is to pay for it.  Select the most competent surveyors. Sometimes, photographs of the property are useful too.

Be sure that subdivision plans have been approved by planning board in the town or city where the land is located.  Or, have the board certify that approval is not necessary where there is an existing way and such is the fact.

Check the matter of streets, roads and alleys.  See whether, if ways have not been accepted by the municipality in question, the costs have been or will be charged to contractor, and, if the property is in a subdivision whether the ways have not been paved.  Make sure that there is on file a competent bond or other good security guaranteeing the completion.  Check the matter of betterment taxes, if any, and what the liability is on the buyer if the buyer is represented by you.

Explore the matter of easements or the like.

Explore the matter of party walls, if the circumstances suggest such thing.  Make sure as to whether an adjoining lot owner may, under any party wall agreement, change, extend the length, height, depth and thickness.

### 3.  Parties in Possession

Obtain names and addresses, and full information as to tenants; examine leases held by tenants or sub-tenants.  Is there an option exercisable in any tenant?  Are the leases properly executed where the property is purchased (and you represent the buyer) subject to the leases?  May the leases be assigned?  Are they required to be recorded, and, if so, have they been recorded?  Have the tenants kept the rentals up to date?  Are the rents to be prorated?  See whether any tenants are violating the terms of a lease and whether any zoning ordinances are being violated or, whether they are using the property improperly so as to affect the insurance coverage.  Notify tenants of change in ownership when the transfer is complete.

### 4.  Condition of the Property

Possibly the contract should provide for license for the purchaser, or his agents, architects, engineers, to enter for the purpose of testing, measuring, and the like.

Have the buildings inspected to determine their age and adaptability. Are they safe for tenants and invitees? Is the steel to be tested for corrosion?

Have an examination made of elevators, furnaces, boilers, electrical wiring, gas, water and sewer lines. Have test made for floor loads if this is essential.

Make sure that the local building codes and zoning ordinances are complied with, and whether additions, alterations and the like, may be made.

Ascertain whether there are any existing orders requiring fire escapes or changes in sanitary facilities.

Procure estimates of cost of demolition, repair, alteration, if any such are contemplated.

Have the buildings appraised for insurance purposes.

Check as to whether the vendor is to keep the property in its present state of repair up to the time of closing, and whether he has the right to make new leases, without consent of the purchaser, before closing.

### 5. Delivery of Possession

Check as to what occupancies and tenancies the delivery is subject.

If the property is or may be vacant prior to the closing consider what effect the vacancy may have on insurance.

Determine whether provision for a watchman or caretaker should be employed while the property is vacant, and at whose expense.

If the purchaser is to take possession prior to closing, determine whether the taking of possession may constitute an acceptance by the purchaser. And determine who is to pay taxes, insurance and cost of repairs, whether purchaser may commence alterations or improvements, which of the parties has the risk of loss. And determine who is entitled to the rentals. What are the rights and obligations in the event the matter is not closed?

### 6. Personal Property

If personal property is to be included in a sale obtain a complete description of it and check the following items especially: air conditioning equipment, awnings, bookcases, cabinets, carpets, lighting fixtures, curtains and curtain rods, draperies, electric fans, other electrical equipment, fire-place grates and andirons, fuel, furniture, ironing boards, kitchen cabinets, lamps, linoleum, radiant heaters, refrigerators and the like, rugs, screen doors, shelves, sprinkling equipment, stationary tubs, storm doors and windows, stoves and heaters, supplies, tools and equipment, trade fixtures, venetian blinds, ventilators, wash tubs, window shades, window screens.

Make certain whether any property is held under conditional sale or subject to chattel mortgage (see Uniform Commercial Code Article 9); whether there are any attachments, factors' liens against the property.

If the Bulk Sales law must be complied with, see to the inventory, cost of items, the sworn list of creditors, etc.

### 7. The Purchase Price

Determine the amount of deposit and who is to hold it. Make provision, if desirable, for an adjustment of the price if the price is dependent upon the quantity of land involved. Provide for the medium, time and place of payment, and period of grace, if any.

See to whom payment is to be made—if more than one vendor, determine how a check is to be made payable. Determine whether a check may be made payable to an agent or attorney.

If closing is delayed or postponed, see whether interest is to be paid on the purchase price.

If the purchase price is to be paid in installments, provide for the amounts and due date of each installment, and whether the unpaid installments are to be evidenced by a note or notes and secured by mortgage. Calculate how interest is to be computed and provide for it—whether on a monthly, quarterly, semi-annual or annual basis. Provide as to the method of application of installments—whether they are to be applied, for example, first on the interest, and then on principal, or whether the payments are to be applied separately on the interest and principal.

Provide for the right, if it is to be, for the purchaser to prepay or anticipate the payments, and whether any premium is to be paid by the purchaser in such event.

Also, provide, if it be desirable, for an acceleration of the entire principal immediately upon default of payment, at the vendor's option. Also, provide that any waiver of default by the vendor in payment of any installment shall not extend to any subsequent default.

### 8. Apportionment

Determine which items are to be apportioned such as: taxes and assessments, fuel and supplies, insurance premiums, maintenance charges, rentals, survey expenses, utility charges, title expense for curing defects, water and sewer charges, and any other items, if so desired.

### 9. Purchaser's Assumption of Existing Mortgage

Obtain copy of mortgage and note to ascertain any unusual provisions, such as assigning rents, and other matters. Ascertain whether there are any defaults, whether further advances have been made and added to the debts, such as taxes, insurance and the like. Check the balance and the interest and obtain from the mortgagee a state-

ment as to the daily accumulation of interest up to time of closing.
Check as to whether the mortgage may be paid prior to maturity.

### 10. Deed to be Delivered

If warranty deed, specify it, otherwise a "good and sufficient
deed" is understood, in most places, to mean a quitclaim deed.

If a fiduciary's deed, make any references desirable as to form.

Check whether the deed is to contain any special exceptions,
reservations or restrictions.

Provide for the date title is to be good.

Request old deed for title reference and description or obtain adequate references for title examination.

### 11. Examination of Title by Purchaser

If any defects appear which may be cured by affidavits, i. e., identity of persons, deaths, heirship, and the like, request vendor to obtain
them.

Consider the relationship of encumbrances to each other, and
whether discharges are properly on record, if any are claimed to be
discharged.

Obtain certificate of municipal liens, assessments and the like.

Check for any state liens, inheritance taxes, or receipts or waiv-
ers; also for federal liens.

Check all building, zoning and other restrictions.

Check the insurance coverages—fire, extended coverage, plate
glass window, rentals, and all other pertinent insurance protection.
Provide as to abatement of the purchase price in the event of loss or
damage to the extent not protected by insurance. Provide for options,
in the agreement, as to rescission and restitution of payments made
by the buyer, in the event of loss and damage, to repair and rebuild
on the part of the vendor, or require the purchaser to repair and rebuild upon an abatement of the purchase price to the extent the loss
or damage is not compensated for by insurance.

### 12. Miscellaneous

It may be desirable to state whether specific performance is to
be prohibited, whether payments are to be forfeited, or whether there
should be liquidated damages, other remedies of the respective parties.

Usually, there is a provision for the payment of a broker's commission of a stated percentage, by the vendor, if a broker has been
employed, or a rate established by a Real Estate Board for members.
This provision may be varied according to circumstances—in the event,
for example, that properties are exchanged instead of sold and purchased for à price in dollars and cents.

A provision against assignability may be included if desired.

Escrow conditions may be inserted.

# Appendix B

# FORMS

---

## LISTING AGREEMENT

To: [*Name and address of broker*]

In consideration of your agreement to list in your office and of your services in undertaking to find a purchaser for the following described real estate in _____ Township of _____ County, State of _____: [*here describe*], I hereby grant to you the exclusive right to sell or to contract to sell said real estate within a period of _____ days from the date hereof, for the price of $_____, said amount to be paid in the following manner: $_____ in cash, $_____ by the purchaser taking the property subject to a mortgage in that amount, and the balance by the purchaser executing and delivering to me a purchase money mortgage for the amount thereof with interest at _____ per cent [*or otherwise specify terms*].

I hereby agree to furnish complete abstract or title insurance policy of title to said real estate and to execute a deed of general warranty in due form of law, conveying a marketable title to the same, in which my wife or husband shall join, to such person as you shall have sold or agreed to sell the same, and for your services, I hereby agree to pay you the regular _____% commission on the purchase thereof, the receipt of which is hereby acknowledged, upon any sale or contract for sale of said real estate made while this agreement remains in force, whether such sale be made by yourselves or by myself or whether at the price and upon the terms stated above, or at a different price or upon other terms accepted by me.

It is further agreed that upon any sale or contract for the sale of said real estate made by me after the termination of this agreement to any person with whom you have had negotiations for sale of the same and of which I shall have been advised, I will pay you the full rate of commission, as above indicated.

You are hereby authorized to place one neat "For Sale" sign on said real estate and to remove all other signs therefrom.

Dated _____, 19__.

_____
Owner

_____
Address

Accepted:

_____
Broker

By _____
Salesman

518

## REAL ESTATE SALES CONTRACT

1. **Real Property.** The undersigned _____ residing at _____, hereinafter called the Purchaser, hereby offers and agrees to purchase from _____, residing at _____, hereinafter called the Seller, the premises locally known as _____, situated in _____, County of _____ and State of _____, and more particularly described as _____.

Together with and including all buildings and other improvements thereon and all rights of seller in and to any and all streets, roads, highways, alleys, driveways, easements, and rights of way appurtenant thereto.

2. **Personal Property.** All heating, plumbing and lighting fixtures, all flowers, shrubs, trees, linoleum, window shades, venetian blinds, curtain rods, storm windows and storm doors, screens and awnings, whatever and if any, belonging to and now in or on said premises, are included in this sale and shall become the property of the purchaser at closing.

3. **Purchase Price.** The Purchaser shall pay to the Seller for the above described real and personal property the sum of $_____ payable as follows:

On signing this instrument as a deposit . . . . . . . . . . . . . . $_____

On the delivery of the deed as hereinafter provided, in
    cash or certified check, the sum of . . . . . . . . . . . . . . . $_____

By assuming and agreeing to pay according to its terms,
    the principal balance of a mortgage in the amount
    of . . . . . . . . . . . . . . . . . . . . . . . . . . . . . . . . . . . . . . . . . . $_____
    which mortgage is not a first lien on said premises,
    bearing interest at the rate of _____ per cent per
    annum and payable _____

By giving Seller a purchase money bond and mortgage
    in the amount of . . . . . . . . . . . . . . . . . . . . . . . . . . . . . $_____
    which bond and mortgage shall be in statutory form
    and a _____ lien on said premises, and which shall
    run for a term of _____ years, bearing interest at
    the rate of _____ per cent per annum and payable
    as follows: _____.

4. **Title Policy.** The Seller shall deliver to the Purchaser within 30 days a commitment for a policy of title insurance to be issued by the _____ Guaranty Company and to be delivered to the Purchaser at the closing, for an amount not less than the purchase price hereunder, guaranteeing title in the condition required herein.

5. **Defects in Title.** If objection to the title is made, based upon a written opinion of the Purchaser's attorney that the title is not in

the condition required hereunder, the Seller shall have 30 days from the date he is notified in writing of the particular defects claimed either (a) to remedy the title, or (b) to refund the deposit, in full termination of this agreement, if he is unable to remedy the title or obtain title insurance. If the Seller remedies the title within the time specified, the Purchaser agrees to complete the sale within 10 days of written notification thereof. If the Seller fails to remedy the title or to give the Purchaser the above written notification within such 10 days, the deposit shall be refunded forthwith in full termination of this agreement.

6. **Mortgage Commitment.** The Purchaser agrees, on acceptance by the Seller, to apply forthwith and in good faith for a _____ year _____ mortgage commitment in the amount of $_____ at _____ per cent. If such mortgage commitment is not obtained by _____, 19__, either party may cancel this contract by giving written notice of such cancellation to the other party, in which event the money paid on account hereof shall be returned to Purchaser and this contract shall become null and void and neither party hereto shall have any claim against the other.

7. **Adjustments at Closing.** Rentals, mortgage interest, taxes computed on a fiscal year basis including all items in the current county tax bill excepting returned school taxes, insurance premiums (fire and extended coverage), water and sewer charges, and all other matters not herein otherwise provided for shall be prorated and adjusted as of date of delivery of deed. The Seller shall assign to purchaser all right, title, and interest in and to any and all reserves held in escrow by the mortgagee for payment of taxes, interest, and other items and the Purchaser shall repay to the Seller the amount of such reserves. The Purchaser will accept title subject to, and will pay all assessments and installments of assessments for local improvements that are not payable as of date of delivery of deed.

8. **Rights of Tenants.** The Seller shall deliver and the Purchaser shall accept possession of such property at the date of closing subject to the rights of tenants, a list of which is hereto attached. All the leases to tenants named therein shall be assigned to the Purchaser and the security rental deposits, if any, shall be transferred to the Purchaser. The Seller shall in addition represent that there are no prepaid rentals other than those disclosed in such leases.

9. **Date of Closing.** If this offer is accepted by the Seller and if title can be conveyed in the condition required hereunder, the Purchaser agrees to complete the sale within 30 days after delivery of the commitment for the policy of title insurance. At least three-days notice of the date of closing shall be given to the Seller by the Purchaser. In the event of default by the Purchaser, the Seller may declare a forfeiture hereunder and retain the deposit as liquidated damages.

10.  **Place of Closing.**  The closing of the sale shall take place at the office of the _____ Guaranty Company.

11.  **Notices.**  All notices, deliveries, or tenders given or made in connection herewith shall be deemed completed and legally sufficient if in writing and if mailed or delivered to the respective party for whom the same is intended at his address herein set forth.

12.  **Term of Offer.**  If acceptance by the Seller is not made in writing on or before _____, 19__, this offer shall be deemed withdrawn, and the deposit shall be returned to the Purchaser.

13.  **Representations.**  This instrument, on acceptance by the Seller, shall constitute the entire agreement between the parties hereto relating to said sale and purchase and supersedes all prior or other agreements and representations in connection with said sale and purchase.

14.  **Binding Effect.**  The covenants herein shall bind the heirs, personal representative, administrators, executors, assigns, and successors of the respective parties.

Dated _____, 19__.

_____                              _____
Witness                                                                    Purchaser

### Receipt

Received from the Purchaser the deposit money above mentioned which will be returned forthwith if the foregoing offer is not accepted within the time above set forth.

                                                                    _____
                                                                    Broker
                                                                    _____
                                                                    Address

### Acceptance

The foregoing offer is hereby accepted and the Seller agrees to sell the property described upon the terms stated.  Receipt of the deposit money is acknowledged.

The Seller agrees to pay the broker for services rendered and for value received a commission of _____% of the sale price, which shall be due only if the sale is consummated and shall be payable at the closing of title.

By the execution of this instrument, the Seller acknowledges the receipt of a copy of this agreement.

Dated _____, 19__.

_____                              _____
Witness                                                                    Seller

## MORTGAGE NOTE

US $_____                                        _____, Florida
                                                                *City*

                                                             _____, 19__

FOR VALUE RECEIVED, the undersigned promise to pay _____, or order, the principal sum of _____ Dollars, with interest on the unpaid principal balance from the date of this Note, until paid, at the rate of _____ percent per annum.  The principal and interest shall be payable at _____, or such other place as the holder hereof may designate in writing, in consecutive monthly installments of _____ Dollars (US $_____), on the _____ day of each month beginning _____, 19__, until the entire indebtedness evidenced hereby is fully paid, except that any remaining indebtedness, if not sooner paid, shall be due and payable on the _____ day of _____.

If any monthly installment under this Note is not paid when due and remains unpaid after a date specified by a notice sent by certified mail to the undersigned at the address stated below, which date shall be not less than thirty days from the date such notice is mailed, the entire principal amount outstanding hereunder and accrued interest thereon shall at once become due and payable at the option of the holder hereof.  Failure to exercise such option shall not constitute a waiver of the right to exercise such option if the undersigned is in default hereunder.  In the event of any default in the payment of this Note and if suit is brought hereon, the holder hereof shall be entitled to collect in such proceeding all reasonable costs and expenses of suit, including, but not limited to, reasonable attorney's fees.

The undersigned shall pay to the holder hereof a late charge of _____ percent of any monthly installment not received by the holder hereof within _____ days after the installment is due.

The undersigned shall have the right to prepay the principal amount outstanding in whole or in part, provided that the holder hereof may require that any partial prepayments shall be made on the date monthly installments are due and shall be in the amount of that part of one or more installments which would be applicable to principal.  Any partial prepayment shall be applied against the principal amount outstanding and shall not extend or postpone the due date of any subsequent monthly installments or change the amount of such installments, unless the holder hereof shall otherwise agree in writing. If, within five years from the date of this Note, the undersigned makes any prepayments in any twelve month period beginning with the date of this Note or anniversary dates thereof ("loan year") with money lent to the undersigned by a lender other than the holder hereof, the undersigned shall pay the holder hereof (a) during each of the first three loan years _____ percent of the amount by which the sum of prepayments made in any such loan year exceeds 20 percent of the original principal amount of this Note and (b) during the fourth and fifth loan years _____ percent of the amount by which the sum of prepayments made in any such loan year exceeds 20 percent of the original principal amount of this Note.

Presentment, notice of dishonor, and protest are hereby waived by all makers, sureties, guarantors and endorsers hereof. This Note shall be the joint and several obligation of all makers, sureties, guarantors and endorsers, and shall be binding upon them and their heirs, personal representatives, successors and assigns.

The indebtedness evidenced by this Note is secured by a Mortgage, dated of even date herewith, and reference is made thereto for rights as to acceleration of the indebtedness evidenced by this Note.

_____[Seal]

_____ _____[Seal]

_____ _____[Seal]

Property Address

## MORTGAGE

### (New York Statutory Form)

This mortgage, made the _____ day of _____, nineteen hundred and _____, between _____, [insert residence], the mortgagor, and _____ [insert residence], the mortgagee.

Witnesseth, that to secure the payment of an indebtedness in the sum of _____ dollars, lawful money of the United States, to be paid on the _____ day of _____, nineteen hundred and _____, with interest thereon to be computed from _____ at the rate of _____ per centum per annum, and to be paid _____, according to a certain bond or obligation bearing even date herewith, the mortgagor hereby mortgages to the mortgagee [description].

And the mortgagor covenants with the mortgagee as follows:

1. That the mortgagor will pay the indebtedness as hereinbefore provided.

2. That the mortgagor will keep the buildings on the premises insured against loss by fire for the benefit of the mortgagee; that he will assign and deliver the policies to the mortgagee; and that he will reimburse the mortgagee for any premiums paid for insurance made by the mortgagee on the mortgagor's default in so insuring the buildings or in so assigning and delivering the policies.

3. That no building on the premises shall be removed or demolished without the consent of the mortgagee.

4. That the whole of said principal sum and interest shall become due at the option of the mortgagee: after default in the payment of any installment of principal or of interest for _____ days; or after default in the payment of any tax, water rate or assessment for _____ days after notice and demand; or after default after no-

tice and demand either in assigning and delivering the policies insuring the buildings against loss by fire or in reimbursing the mortgagee for premiums paid on such insurance, as hereinbefore provided; or after default upon request in furnishing a statement of the amount due on the mortgage and whether any offsets or defenses exist against the mortgage debt, as hereinafter provided.

5.   That the holder of this mortgage, in any action to foreclose it, shall be entitled to the appointment of a receiver.

6.   That the mortgagor will pay all taxes, assessments or water rates, and in default thereof, the mortgagee may pay the same.

7.   That the mortgagor within _____ days upon request in person or within _____ days upon request by mail will furnish a written statement duly acknowledged of the amount due on this mortgage and whether any offsets or defenses exist against the mortgage debt.

8.   That notice and demand or request may be in writing and may be served in person or by mail.

9.   That the mortgagor warrants the title to the premises.

In Witness Whereof, this mortgage has been duly executed by the mortgagor.

In presence of:

_____

_____

## WARRANTY DEED

[*Parties*] This indenture, made this _____ day of _____, 19__, between _____, of _____, party of the first part, and _____, of _____, party of the second part:

[*Consideration*] Witnesseth, that the party of the first part, in consideration of the sum of _____ Dollars, to him in hand paid by the party of the second part, the receipt whereof is hereby acknowledged,

[*Operative Words*] does hereby grant, bargain, sell, and convey unto the party of the second part [*his heirs and assigns, forever*] all that tract or parcel of land lying and being in _____ and described as follows, to wit: [*Description*].

[*Habendum*] To have and to hold the same, together with all the hereditaments and appurtenances thereunto belonging or in any wise appertaining, to the party of the second part, his heirs and assigns, forever.

[*Covenants*] And the party of the first part, for himself, his heirs, executors and administrators, does hereby covenant with the party of the second part, his heirs and assigns, that he, the party of the first part, is well seised in fee of the lands and premises aforesaid; that he has good right to sell and convey the same in manner and form aforesaid; that the same are free from all incumbrances; and that he and his heirs, executors and administrators will warrant and defend the same to the party of the second part, his heirs and assigns, against the lawful claims and demands of all persons.

[*Testimonium*] In witness whereof, the party of the first part has hereunto set his hand and seal the day and year first above written.

In presence of                                        _____ [*Seal*]

_____

_____

[*Acknowledgment*]

## SPECIAL WARRANTY DEED

This indenture [*as in Warranty Deed down to and including habendum*].

And the party of the first part, for himself and his heirs, executors and administrators, does hereby covenant with the party of the second part, his heirs and assigns, that he, the party of the first part, has not made, done, executed or suffered any act or thing whereby the above described premises or any part thereof now are or at any time hereafter shall or may be imperiled, charged or incumbered in any manner whatsoever; and the title to the above granted premises against all persons lawfully claiming the same from, through or under him the party of the first part will forever warrant and defend.

In witness whereof, *etc.*

## QUITCLAIM DEED

This indenture [*as in Warranty Deed, down to and including consideration*] does by these presents remise, release and quitclaim unto the party of the second part [*his heirs and assigns, forever*] all that [*description*].

To have and to hold the above quitclaimed premises, together with all and singular the hereditaments and appurtenances thereunto belonging or in any wise appertaining, to the party of the second part, his heirs and assigns, forever.

In witness whereof, *etc.*

## CLOSING STATEMENT

Property Sold _____ Closing Date _____
Seller _____ Purchaser _____
Address _____ Address _____

### CREDITS TO SELLER

Purchase Price . . . . . . . . . . . . . . . . . . . . . .$_____
Pro-rated Insurance . . . . . . . . . . . . . . . . .$_____
_____ . . . . . . . . . . . . . . . . . . . . . .$_____
    Total due Seller (Gross) . . . . . . . . . .$_____   $_____

### CREDITS TO PURCHASER

Earnest Money .....................$_____
To satisfy First Mortgage .............$_____
To satisfy Barrett Law ...............$_____
To satisfy Taxes_____ .............$_____
Pro-rated Rents .....................$_____
To record Affidavits, etc. ..............$_____
_____ .....................$_____
_____ .....................$_____
_____ .....................$_____

    Total Credits to Purchaser .......$_____   $_____
    Net Total due Seller from Purchaser ............$_____

### ADDITIONAL EXPENSES PAID BY SELLER

Realtor's Commission (less earnest
    money deposit with Realtor) ......$_____
Revenue Stamps .....................$_____
Abstract Bill .......................$_____
_____ .....................$_____

    Total Additional Expenses ........$_____   $_____
    Net to Seller ..............................$_____
Plus excess of Earnest Money over
    Commission ...........................$_____
    Total net to Seller .........................$_____

### TOTAL DUE SELLER FROM PURCHASER
### PAID AS FOLLOWS:

Check _____ ..................$_____
Check _____ ..................$_____
Check _____ ..................$_____
    Total .........................$_____

### ADDITIONAL EXPENSES PAID BY PURCHASER

To record Deed .....................$_____
Additional Insurance ................$_____
_____ .....................$_____
    Total Additional Expenses ........$_____

        Above Statement Checked and Approved:
        _____ Seller
        _____ Purchaser
        _____ Realtor

Closed at _____
Closing Attorney _____
Realtor _____

## STATEMENT OF INSURANCE

| Policy No. Company | Kind | Amount | Date Issue | Expiration | Term Premium | Unearned Premium |
|---|---|---|---|---|---|---|
|  |  |  |  |  |  |  |
|  |  |  |  |  |  |  |
|  |  |  |  |  |  |  |
|  |  |  |  |  |  |  |
|  |  |  |  |  |  |  |

## TENANTS

| Name | Rent | Payable | Paid to | Unearned Rent |
|---|---|---|---|---|
|  |  |  |  |  |
|  |  |  |  |  |
|  |  |  |  |  |
|  |  |  |  |  |
|  |  |  |  |  |

Total Rent Due $_____

## MECHANIC'S LIEN

### (Michigan Statutory Form)

State of Michigan  
County of _____ } ss.

A B, of _____, being duly sworn, says, that he furnished certain labor (or materials or engineering or surveying services) or leased equipment in and for building (or altering, improving, repairing, erecting or ornamenting, as the case may be) a certain _____ situated on the land hereinafter described, in pursuance of a certain contract of which C D, is the owner (or part owner or lessee, contractor, subcontractor or other person, as the case may be). The performance of such labor (or the furnishing of such materials, or engineering or surveying services) or the use of leased equipment was begun on the _____ day of _____ 19__, and the last of such labor was performed (or such materials furnished, or engineering or surveying services) or the use of leased equipment on the _____ day of _____ 19__; and there is justly and truly due deponent therefor from the said C D, over and above all legal setoffs, the sum of _____ dollars, for which amount deponent claims a lien on said land (or building or swimming pool) of which _____ is the owner (or part owner, or lessee) which premises are described as follows:

_____

_____

_____    _____

A.  _____              B. _____

Owner's name _____

Residence No. _____ (Street or avenue)

City, township or village _____

Subscribed and sworn to before me this _____ day of _____ 19__.

## WILL OF HENRY FORD

I, HENRY FORD, of "Fairlane", Dearborn, Michigan, do hereby revoke all instruments of a testamentary nature heretofore made by me, and do hereby make, publish, and declare this to be my Last Will and Testament, in manner and form following:

### I.

I direct my executors hereinafter named to pay all my just debts and funeral expenses, as well as the cost and expenses of the administration of my estate, as soon after my death as shall be practicable.

### II.

I have heretofore provided generously for my wife, CLARA J. FORD, and am satisfied that she is now in a position of complete financial independence. I wish my wife to have, however, and I hereby bequeath to her, all of my personal effects in and about our home "Fairlane", at Dearborn, Michigan, including all household furniture, automobiles, and everything used in connection with our home; and, further, any other article or articles of a personal nature which she may wish to retain because of the sentimental value. I believe that our home, known as "Fairlane", located at Dearborn, Michigan, is held as an estate by the entireties by myself and my wife, CLARA J. FORD, but if by chance title to any portion of the property included in such home estate is found to be in me alone, then I hereby give and devise to my wife, CLARA J. FORD, all of the real estate included in such home estate and not so held by the entireties.

### III.

There has been heretofore organized, under the laws of the State of Michigan, during my lifetime, a corporation known as THE FORD FOUNDATION, the purposes of such corporation being set forth fully in its Articles of Incorporation. To this FOUNDATION I give and bequeath all of my shares of stock in the Ford Motor Company, which are non-voting shares known as Class "A" stock, save such as it may be necessary to sell to pay the obligations of my estate, the FOUNDATION to have full and unqualified title, without limitation, to such shares, with all the incidents thereto, including the right to expend either the principal or the income therefrom for the purposes of said corporation.

## IV.

All of my real estate other than such real estate as may be a part of our home "Fairlane", I give and devise to THE FORD FOUNDATION, save such as it may be necessary to sell to pay the obligations of my estate, without qualification or limitation, to be used for the purposes for which the FOUNDATION is organized.

## V.

I wish to divide all of my voting stock, known as Class "B" stock, in the Ford Motor Company, into five equal parts to be disposed of in the following manner: I bequeath one of such five parts to my son, EDSEL B. FORD, without qualification or limitation. The other four parts I bequeath for the benefit of my four grandchildren, HENRY FORD II, BENSON FORD, JOSEPHINE CLAY FORD, and WILLIAM CLAY FORD, the present children of my son, EDSEL B. FORD, to be held in the manner provided in paragraph VI hereof.

## VI.

Heretofore, on the 4th day of November, 1935, ELEANOR CLAY FORD entered into four declarations of trust whereby she declared that she held certain property in trust for each of my said four grandchildren. I bequeath one of said five parts of my voting stock, known as Class "B" stock, in the Ford Motor Company, to the person who shall at the time of my decease be Trustee under each of said four trusts; or, if there be no Trustee under some of said trusts, or some of them be terminated, then to my executor under this Will, as Trustee, to be handled, managed, and disposed of in the same manner and with the same powers as are provided by said respective declarations of trust, except that in case any of said trusts are terminated at the time of my decease by reason of any of my grandchildren becoming twenty-five years old, I bequeath the interest of such grandchild herein provided for directly to him or to her.

## VII.

I give, devise, and bequeath all the rest and remainder of my estate to my son, EDSEL B. FORD, and his heirs.

## VIII.

I hereby designate and appoint my son, EDSEL B. FORD, to be Executor of this my Last Will and Testament, and direct that no bond or other security shall be required from him for the faithful performance of his duty as such Executor or as Trustee under this Will.

## IX.

I hereby give to my said Executor full power to sell, lease without limit as to period or terms, and mortgage, pledge, invest, re-invest, exchange, manage, control, and, in any way, use, and deal with, any and all property of my estate, without application to any court or authority for leave or confirmation, unless the same shall be expressly required by law and shall be unwaivable even by this provision of my Will, and to that end, said Executor may sell such property for cash or upon credit, upon such terms as to him may seem sufficient; continue present investments; invest and re-invest any such property or securities in such a manner as he shall deem adequate and safe, free from any limitations imposed by law; borrow on the credit of, exchange, pledge, or mortgage any of such property; deposit any securities with Voting Trustees or for other purposes; exercise any and all rights which have accrued or may accrue appurtenant to any securities; and use the principal and income of my estate not herein specifically devised or bequeathed as he may deem advisable; and compromise any and all claims in favor of my estate or against it. Further, I hereby give identical power to the Trustee or Trustees under the trusts provided in Paragraph VI hereof as to the property placed in trust under that paragraph.

## X.

I realize that my estate may be subject to heavy death duties and taxes both by the Federal and State Governments and other Governments which may have tax jurisdiction over my properties. I desire and hereby direct that my Executor shall as far as possible arrange that my specific bequests made herein to my wife, CLARA J. FORD, and my specific bequest of my voting shares in the Ford Motor Company, known as Class "B" stock, shall be given to the legatees intact and without diminution. If for the purpose of paying obligations of my estate it shall be necessary to sell any part of it, it is my desire and will that my Executor shall have free discretion to sell, or borrow on the security of, or dispose of as in his judgment he may deem proper, all other property for the purpose of meeting such obligations.

IN WITNESS WHEREOF, I have hereunto set my hand and seal this 3rd day of February A.D. 1936.

Henry Ford (SEAL)

The foregoing instrument was signed, sealed, published, and declared by HENRY FORD, the above named Testator, as and for his Last Will and Testament, in our presence, and we at his request, in his presence, and in the presence of each other, have hereunto subscribed our names as subscribing witnesses thereto this 3rd day of February A.D. 1936; and we, the said subscribing witnesses, further say that we are well acquainted with said HENRY FORD and are satisfied from our own knowledge that he is of sound and disposing mind and memory.

Frank Campsall who resides at Dearborn, Michigan

H. R. Waddell who resides at Dearborn, Michigan

I, CLARA J. FORD, wife of HENRY FORD, Testator in the foregoing Will, do hereby acknowledge that full provision has been made for me by said testator during his lifetime, and I have agreed with him, in consideration of the provisions made therein, and hereby consent and agree to accept the provisions made in the foregoing Will in lieu of dower in his estate and in lieu of any and all other rights to which I might by law be otherwise entitled.

Clara J. Ford (SEAL)

Signed, sealed, and delivered by
CLARA J. FORD in the presence of:

Frank Campsall
H. R. Waddell

STATE OF MICHIGAN ⎫
COUNTY OF WAYNE ⎬ SS.
⎭

On this 6th day of February A.D. 1936, before me, a Notary Public in and for said County, personally appeared CLARA J. FORD, known to me to be the person named in and who executed the foregoing instrument and who acknowledged the same to be her free act and deed.

Edward L. Davis<br>Notary Public, Wayne County, Michigan

NOTARY PUBLIC, WAYNE COUNTY, MICH.
My Commission Expires March 11, 1936

## CODICIL

I, HENRY FORD, of "Fairlane", Dearborn, Michigan, hereby declare this to be a first codicil to my Last Will and Testament, bearing date the third day of February, A.D. 1936.

Whereas, since the date and execution of my said Will, my son, Edsel B. Ford, the Executor therein named, has departed this life: Now, I do hereby revoke the appointment of Edsel B. Ford as Executor as aforesaid and do appoint Clara J. Ford to be the Executor thereof in his place and stead. And I do hereby also direct and declare that my said Will shall be read and construed so as to have the same effect and operation in every respect as if the name of the new Executor had been originally inserted therein. And I do hereby ratify and confirm my said Will in every other respect.

IN WITNESS WHEREOF, I have hereunto set my hand and seal this 1st day of June, A.D. 1943.

Henry Ford (SEAL)

The foregoing instrument was signed, sealed, published, and declared by HENRY FORD as and for a codicil to his Last Will and Testament, in our presence, and we at his request, in his presence, and in the presence of each other, have hereunto subscribed our names as subscribing witnesses thereto this 1st day of June, A.D. 1943; and we, the said subscribing witnesses, further say that we are well acquainted with said HENRY FORD and are satisfied from our own knowledge that he is of sound and disposing mind and memory.

Frank Campsall who resides at Dearborn, Michigan

Chas. E. Sorensen who resides at Detroit, Michigan

# APPENDIX C
# DICTIONARY OF LEGAL TERMS

(Abridged and Adapted from Black's Law Dictionary.)

---

# A

**AB INITIO.** Latin. From the beginning. E. g., void ab initio. An agreement is said to be "void ab initio" if it has at no time had any legal validity.

**ABROGATE.** To annul; to repeal. A statute may abrogate a rule of the common law.

**ABSTRACT OF TITLE.** A condensed history of the title to land, consisting of a synopsis or summary of the material or operative portion of all the conveyances, of whatever kind or nature, which in any manner affect said land, or any estate or interest therein, together with a statement of all liens, charges, or liabilities to which the same may be subject, and of which it is in any way material for purchasers to be apprised.

**ACCEPTANCE. In contracts and sales.** The act of a person to whom a thing is offered or tendered by another, whereby he receives the thing with the intention of retaining it, such intention being evidenced by a sufficient act.

**In negotiable instruments.** Acceptance of a bill of exchange. The act by which the person on whom a bill of exchange is drawn (called the "drawee") assents to the request of the drawer to pay it, or, in other words, engages, or makes himself liable to pay it when due. 2 Bl.Comm. 469. Under the negotiable Instruments Law, "the acceptance must be in writing and signed by the drawee."

**ACCESSION.** An addition to one's property by increase of the original property or by production from such property. Instances are: The growth of a tree on A.'s land, although the tree overhangs the land of B.; the birth of a calf to the cow of A.; the innocent conversion of B.'s material by A. into a thing of different kind, so that its former identity no longer exists, as where A. innocently converts the wheat of B. into bread.

**ACCIDENT.** An unusual event, not expected by the person affected by it.

**In equity.** "An occurrence in relation to a contract which was not anticipated by the parties when the same was entered into, and which gives an undue advantage to one of them over the other in a court of law. Jeremy, Eq. 358. This definition is objected to, because, as accidents may arise in relation to other things besides contracts, it is inaccurate in confining accidents to contracts; besides, it does not exclude cases of unanticipated occurrence resulting from the negligence or misconduct of the party seeking relief. In general, courts of equity will relieve a party who cannot obtain justice at law in consequence of an accident which will justify the interposition of a court of equity. The jurisdiction which equity exerts in case of accident is mainly of two sorts: Over bonds with penalties to prevent a forfeiture where the failure is the result of accident, as sickness, or where the bond has been lost, but, if the penalty be liquidated damages, there can be no relief; and, second, where a negotiable or other instrument has been lost, in which case no action lay at law, but where equity will allow the one entitled to recover upon giving proper indemnity. In some states it has been held that a court of law can render judgment for the amount, but requires the defendant to give a bond of indemnity. Relief against a penal bond can now be obtained in almost all common-law courts." Bouvier, Law Dict.

**ACCOMMODATION PAPER.** An accommodation bill or note is one to which the accommodating party, be he acceptor, drawer, or indorser, has put his name, without consideration, for the purpose of benefiting or accommodating some other party who desires to raise money on it and is to provide for the bill or note when due.

**ACCORD AND SATISFACTION.** An agreement between two persons, one of whom has a right of action against the other, that the latter should do or give, and the former accept, something in satisfaction of the right of action different from, and usually less than, what might be legally enforced. When the agreement is executed, and satisfaction has been made, it is called "accord and satisfaction." Accord and satisfaction is the substitution of another agreement between the parties in satisfaction of the former one, and execution of the latter agreement. Such is the definition of this sort of defense usually given. But a broader application of the doctrine has been made in later times, where one promise or agreement is set up in satisfaction of a prior one, unless it has been expressly accepted as such; as, where a new promissory note has been given in lieu of a former one, to have the effect of a satisfaction of the former, it must have been accepted on an express agreement to that effect.

**ACCOUNT.** A detailed statement of the mutual demands in the nature of debt and credit between parties, arising out of contracts or some fiduciary relation.

**Account closed.** An account to which no further additions can be made on either side, but which remains still open for adjustment and set-off, which distinguishes it from account stated.

**Account current.** An open or running or unsettled account between two parties.

**Account rendered.** An account made out by the creditor, and presented to the debtor for his examination and acceptance. When accepted, it becomes an account stated.

**Account stated.** The settlement of an account between the parties, with a balance struck in favor of one of them; an account rendered by the creditor, and by the debtor assented to as correct, either expressly or by implication of law from the failure to object.

**ACKNOWLEDGMENT.** In conveyancing. The act by which a party who has executed an instrument of conveyance as grantor goes before a competent officer, or court, and declares or acknowledges the same as his genuine and voluntary act and deed. The certificate of the officer on such instrument that it has been so acknowledged.

The term is also used of the act of a person who avows or admits the truth of certain facts which, if established, will entail a civil liability upon him. Thus, the debtor's acknowledgment of the creditor's demand or right of action will revive the enforceability of a debt barred by the statute of limitations.

**ACTION.** A lawsuit. A right of action; i. e., a right to bring suit.

**ACT OF GOD.** Any misadventure or casualty is said to be caused by the "act of God," when it happens by the direct, immediate, and exclusive operation of the forces of nature, uncontrolled and uninfluenced by the power of man, and without human intervention, and is of such a character that it could not have been prevented or escaped from by any amount of foresight or prudence, or by any reasonable degree of care or diligence, or by the aid of any appliances which the situation of the party might reasonably require him to use. Any accident produced by any physical cause which is irresistible, such as lightning, tempests, perils of the seas, inundations, earthquakes; and also the sudden death or illness of persons.

**ADJUDICATION.** The giving or pronouncing of a judgment in a case; also the judgment given. The term is principally used in bankruptcy proceedings; the adjudication being the order which declares the debtor to be a bankrupt.

**ADMINISTRATION.** The management and settlement of the estate of an intestate decedent.

**ADMINISTRATOR.** In the most usual sense, is a person to whom letters of administration—that is, an authority to administer the estate of a deceased person—have been granted by the proper court. He resembles an executor, but is appointed by the court, without any nomination by the deceased. An administrator of the estate is appointed, if the deceased has made no will, or has named no executor in his will.

**ADMIRALTY.** That system of law governing civil and criminal maritime cases.

**ADVERSE POSSESSION.** The actual, open, and notorious possession and enjoyment of real property, or of any estate lying in grant, continued for a certain length of time, held adversely and in denial and opposition to the title of another claimant, or under circumstances which indicate an assertion or color of right or title on the part of the person maintaining it, as against another person who is out of possession.

**AFFIANT.** The person who makes and subscribes an affidavit. The word is used, in this sense, interchangeably with "deponent." But the latter term should be reserved as the designation of one who makes a deposition.

**AFFIDAVIT.** A written or printed declaration or statement of facts, made voluntarily, and confirmed by the oath or affirmation of the party making it, taken before an officer having authority to administer such oath.

**A FORTIORI.** Latin. By a stronger reason.

**AGENCY.** A relation, created either by express or implied contracts or by law, whereby one party (called the principal) delegates the transaction of some lawful business or the power to do certain acts for him or in relation to his rights or property, with more or less discretionary power, to another person (called the agent, attorney in fact, or proxy) who undertakes to manage the affair and render him an account thereof.

**AGENT.** One who represents and acts for another under the relation of agency.

**ALIAS.** Latin. At other times.

**In practice.** An alias writ is one issued in a case wherein another writ the same in substance has been issued before. For instance, there may be an alias attachment, an alias summons, etc.

The word commonly precedes the assumed names under which a party to an action, usually a defendant in a criminal action, is known as the names are stated in the pleadings. For instance, "John Jones, alias John Smith," would indicate "John Jones, at other times known as John Smith."

**ALIBI.** Latin. Elsewhere. In criminal cases, the defendant frequently pleads that he was elsewhere at the time of the perpetration of the alleged crime. In such a case, he is said to plead an alibi.

Apparently through the ignorance of some of those persons reporting court news to the daily papers, the word has been often very incorrectly and inexcusably used to signify a justification or an excuse.

**ALIENATION.** The transfer of property from one person to another.

**ALLEGATION.** The assertion, declaration, or statement of a party to an action, made in a pleading, setting out what he expects to prove.

**ALLEGE.** To state, recite, assert, or charge; to make an allegation.

**ANIMO CONTRAHENDI.** Latin. With the intention of contracting.

**ANIMUS TESTANDI.** Latin. An intention to make a last will and testament.

**ANNUL.** To cancel; make void; destroy. To annul a judgment or judicial proceeding is to deprive it of all force and operation, either ab initio or prospectively as to future transaction.

**ANSWER. In pleading.** Any pleading setting up matters of facts by way of defense. In chancery pleading, the term denotes a defense in writing, made by a defendant to the allegations contained in a bill or information filed by the plaintiff against him. In pleading, under the Codes of Civil Procedure, the answer is the formal written statement made by a defendant setting forth the ground of his defense; corresponding to what, in actions under the common-law practice, is called the "plea."

**ANTENUPTIAL CONTRACT.** A contract made prior to marriage, usually between the prospective wife and the prospective husband, under which the wife gains certain advantages or suffers certain detriments. In some instances, the prospective wife, in consideration of the settling of a certain amount of real estate or of personalty upon her, gives up her right of dower in the property of the husband.

**APPEAL. In civil practice.** The complaint to a superior court of an injustice done or error committed by an inferior one, whose judgment or decision the court above is called upon to correct or reverse. The removal of a cause from a court of inferior to one of superior jurisdiction, for the purpose of obtaining a review and retrial.

**APPEARANCE.** A technical coming into court as a party to an action, as plaintiff or as defendant. The party may actually appear in court, or he may, by his attorney, enter his appearance by filing written pleadings in the case, or by filing a formal written entry of appearance. The term first came into use at a time when the only appearance known was the actual physical appearance of a party in court.

**APPELLANT.** A party who takes an appeal from one court to another.

**APPELLEE.** The party in a cause against whom an appeal is taken; that is, the party who has an interest adverse to setting aside or reversing the judgment.

**APPRAISE. In practice.** To fix or set a price or value upon; to fix and state the true value of a thing, and, usually, in writing.

**APPURTENANCES.** Things that belong to another thing regarded as the principal thing. Things appurtenant pass as incident to the principal thing. Sometimes an easement consisting of a right of way over one piece of land will pass with another piece of land as being appurtenant to it.

**ARBITRATION. In practice.** The investigation and determination of a matter or matters of difference between contending parties, by one or more unofficial persons, chosen by the parties, and called "arbitrators," or "referees."

**ARREST OF JUDGMENT. In practice.** The act of staying a judgment, or refusing to render judgment in an action at law, after verdict, for some matter intrinsic appearing on the face of the record, which would render the judgment, if given, erroneous or reversible.

**ASSUMPSIT.** Latin. He undertook; he promised. A promise or engagement by which one person assumes or undertakes to do some act or pay something to another. It may be either oral or in writing, but is not under seal. It is express, if the promisor puts his engagement in distinct and definite language; it is implied, where the law infers a promise (though no formal one has passed) from the conduct of the party or the circumstances of the case.

**In practice.** A form of action which lies for the recovery of damages for the non-performance of a parol or simple contract, or a contract that is neither of record nor under seal.

The ordinary division of this action is into (1) common or indebitatus assumpsit, brought for the most part on an implied promise; and (2) special assumpsit, founded on an express promise.

The action of assumpsit differs from trespass and trover, which are founded on a tort, not upon a contract; from covenant and debt, which are appropriate where the ground of recovery is a sealed instrument, or special obligation to pay a fixed sum; and from replevin, which seeks the recovery of specific property, if attainable, rather than of damages.

**ASSURANCE. In conveyancing.** A deed or instrument of conveyance. The legal evidences of the transfer of property are in England called the "common assurances" of the kingdom, whereby every man's estate is assured to him, and all controversies, doubts, and difficulties are either prevented or removed.

**ATTACHMENT.** The act or process of taking, apprehending, or seizing a person's property, by virtue of a writ, and bringing the same into the custody of the law, used either for the purpose of bringing a person before the court, of acquiring jurisdiction over the property seized, to compel an appearance, to furnish security for debt or costs, or to arrest a fund in the hands of a third person who may become liable to pay it over. Also the writ or other process for the accomplishment of the purposes above enumerated, this being the more common use of the word.'

**ATTESTATION.** The act of witnessing an instrument in writing, at the request of the party making the same, and subscribing it as a witness. Execution and attestation are clearly distinct formalities; the former being the act of the party, and the latter of the witnesses only.

**Attestation clause.** The clause commonly placed at the conclusion of an instrument, in which clause the witnesses certify that the instrument has been executed before them.

**ATTESTING WITNESS.** One who signs his name to an instrument as a witness thereto at the request of the parties, for the purposes of proof and identification.

**ATTORNEY.** In the most general sense, this term denotes an agent or substitute, or one who is appointed and authorized to act in the place or stead of another.

It is "an ancient English word, and signifieth one that is set in the turne, stead, or place of another; and of these some be private * * * and some be publike, as attorneys at law." Co. Litt. 51b.

One who is appointed by another to do something in his absence, and who has authority to act in the place and turn of him by whom he is delegated.

When used with reference to the proceedings of courts, the term always means "attorney at law."

**AUCTION.** A sale of property, conducted in public or after a notice to the general public, to the highest bidder.

**AUCTIONEER.** One who conducts an auction.

**AUTHORITIES.** Legislative enactments, judicial opinions, legal textbooks, and articles in law periodicals are recognized as authorities on the law. The weight given each of these classes of authorities is far from being equal to that given each of the others. Legislative enactments, if valid under the Constitution, represent the final word on what the present law is. Judicial opinions, until overruled, constitute another primary authority. Textbooks and legal articles, though important, are only secondary authorities, guiding into and interpreting the primary authorities, the statutes and decisions.

**AWARD,** v. To grant, concede, adjudge to. Thus, a jury awards damages; the court awards an injunction.

**AWARD,** n. The decision or determination rendered by arbitrators or commissioners, or other private or extrajudicial deciders, upon a controversy submitted to them; also the writing or document embodying such decision.

# B

**BAGGAGE.** Such articles of necessity or convenience as are carried by passengers for their general use. It includes clothing, books of the student, tools of the workman, etc.

**BAIL,** v. To procure the release of a person from legal custody, by undertaking that he shall appear at the time and place designated and submit himself to the jurisdiction and judgment of the court.

**BAIL,** n. **In practice.** The sureties who procure the release of a person under arrest, by becoming responsible for his appearance at the time and place designated. Those persons who become sureties for the appearance of the defendant in court.

**BAILEE.** In the law of contracts, one to whom goods are bailed; the party to whom personal property is delivered under a contract of bailment.

**BAILMENT.** A delivery of goods or personal property, by one person to another in trust for the execution of a special object upon or in relation to such goods, beneficial either to the bailor or bailee or both, and upon a contract, express or implied, to perform the trust and carry out such object, and thereupon either to redeliver the goods to the bailor or otherwise dispose of the same in conformity with the purpose of the trust.

**BAILOR.** The party who bails or delivers goods to another, in the contract of bailment.

**BANKRUPT.** A person who has committed an act of bankruptcy; one who has done some act or suffered some act to be done in consequence of which, under the laws of his country, he is liable to be proceeded against by his creditors for the seizure and distribution among them of his entire property.

**BARTER.** A contract by which parties exchange goods or commodities for other goods. It differs from sale, in this: That in the latter transaction goods or property are always exchanged for money.

**BATTERY.** Any unlawful beating, or other wrongful physical violence or constraint, inflicted on a human being without consent.

**BENEFICIARY.** A person having the enjoyment of property of which a trustee, executor, etc., has the legal possession. The person to whom a policy of insurance is payable.

**BEQUEATH.** To give personal property by will to another.

**BEQUEST.** A gift by will of personal property; a legacy.

**BID.** An offer by an intending purchaser to pay a designated price for property which is about to be sold at auction.

**BILL.** A formal declaration, complaint, or statement of particular things in writing. As a legal term, this word has many meanings and applications, the more important of which are enumerated below.

**BILL IN EQUITY.** The first written pleading in a proceeding in equity. The complaint in a suit in equity.

**BILL OF LADING. In common law.** The written evidence of a contract for the carriage and delivery of goods sent by sea for a certain freight. The term is often applied to a similar receipt and undertaking given by a carrier of goods by land. A bill of lading is an instrument in writing, signed by a carrier or his agent, describing the freight so as to identify it, stating the name of the consignor, the terms of the contract for carriage, and agreeing or directing that the freight be delivered to the order or assigns of a specified person at a specified place.

**BILL OF PARTICULARS. In practice.** A written statement or specification of the particulars of the demand for which an action at law is brought, or of a defendant's set-off against such demand (including dates, sums, and items in detail), furnished by one of the parties to the other, either voluntarily or in compliance with a judge's order for that purpose.

**BILL OF SALE. In contracts.** A written agreement under seal, by which one person assigns or transfers his right to or interest in goods and personal chattels to another. An instrument by which, in particular, the property in ships and vessels is conveyed.

**BONA FIDE.** Latin. In good faith.

# C

**CAPITAL. Partnership.** "The capital of a partnership is the aggregate of the sums contributed by its members to establish or continue the partnership business." Gilmore on Partnership, p. 132.

**Corporations.** In reference to a corporation, it is the aggregate of the sum subscribed and paid in, or secured to be paid in, by the shareholders, with the addition of all gains or profits realized in the use and investment of those sums, or, if loss have been incurred, then it is the residue after deducting such losses.

**CAPITAL STOCK.** The common stock or fund of a corporation. The sum of money raised by the subscriptions of the stockholders, and divided into shares. It is said to be the sum upon which calls may be made upon the stockholders, and dividends are to be paid.

**CARRIER.** One who carries passengers or the goods of another. See **Common Carrier; Private Carrier.**

**CAUSE OF ACTION.** Matter for which an action may be brought. The ground on which an action may be sustained. The right to bring a suit.

**CAVEAT EMPTOR.** Latin. Let the buyer take care. This maxim summarizes the rule that the purchaser of an article must examine, judge, and test it for himself, being bound to discover any obvious defects or imperfections.

**CERTIFICATE OF DEPOSIT. In the practice of bankers.** This is a writing acknowledging that the person named has deposited in the bank a specified sum of money, and that the same is held subject to be drawn out on his own check or order, or that of some other person named in the instrument as payee.

**CERTIFICATE OF STOCK.** A certificate of a corporation of joint-stock company that the person named is the owner of a designated number of shares of its stock; given when the subscription is fully paid and the "scrip certificate" taken up.

**CERTIORARI.** A discretionary writ of review or inquiry. It is an appellate proceeding for reexamination and review of actions of an inferior court or tribunal or as auxiliary process to enable an appellate court to obtain further information in a pending cause. It is available for review of official, judicial or quasi-judicial actions.

**CESTUI QUE TRUST.** Anglo-French. He who has a right to a beneficial interest in and out of an estate the legal title to which is vested in another. The person who possesses the equitable right to property and receives the rents, issues, and profits thereof, the legal estate of which is vested in a trustee. It has been proposed to substitute for this uncouth term the English word "beneficiary," and the latter has come to be quite frequently used.

**CHAMPERTY.** A bargain made by a stranger with one of the parties to a suit, by which such third person undertakes to carry on the litigation at his own cost and risk, in consideration of receiving, if he wins the suit, a part of the land or other subject sought to be recovered by the action.

**CHANCELLOR.** In American law, this is the name given in some states to the judge (or the presiding judge) of a court of chancery. In England, besides being the designation of the chief judge of the Court of Chancery, the term is used as the title of several judicial officers attached to bishops or other high dignitaries and to the universities.

**CHANCERY.** Equity; equitable jurisdiction; a court of equity; the system of jurisprudence administered in courts of equity.

**CHARTER.** An instrument emanating from the sovereign power, in the nature of a grant, authorizing the formation of a corporation. Under modern statutes, a charter is usually granted by the state secretary of state, who acts under general statutory authority conferred by the state legislature.

**CHARTER PARTY.** A contract by which an entire ship, or some principal part thereof, is let to a merchant for the conveyance of goods on a determined voyage to one or more places.

**CHATTEL.** An article of personal property; any species of property not amounting to a freehold or fee in land.

**CHATTEL MORTGAGE.** An instrument of sale of personalty conveying the title of the property to the mortgagee with terms of defeasance; and, if the terms of redemption are not complied with, then, at common law, the title becomes absolute in the mortgagee.

**CHECK.** A draft or order upon a bank or banking house, purporting to be drawn upon a deposit of funds, for the payment at all events of a certain sum of money to a certain person therein named, or to him or his order, or to bearer, and payable instantly on demand.

**CHOSE IN ACTION.** A right to personal things of which the owner has not the possession, but merely a right of action for their possession. 2 Bl.Comm. 389, 397; 1 Chit.Pr. 99.

A right to receive or recover a debt, demand, or damages on a cause of action ex contractu, or for a tort connected with contract, but which cannot be made available without recourse to an action.

**CHOSE IN POSSESSION.** A thing in possession, as distinguished from a thing in action.

**CIVIL.** In contradistinction to "criminal," it indicates the private rights and remedies of men, as members of the community, in contrast to those which are public and relate to the government; thus, we speak of civil process and criminal process, civil jurisdiction and criminal jurisdiction.

**CIVIL LAW.** The "Roman law" and the "civil law" are convertible phrases, meaning the same system of jurisprudence; it is now frequently denominated the "Roman civil law."

**CLIENT.** A person who employs or retains an attorney, or counsellor, to appear for him in courts, advise, assist, and defend him in legal proceedings, and to act for him in any legal business.

**CLOSE.** A portion of land, as a field, inclosed, as by a hedge, fence, or other visible inclosure.

**CODE.** A collection or compendium of laws. A complete system of positive law, scientifically arranged, or promulgated by legislative authority.

**COGNOVIT.** Latin. He knew. The written authority of a debtor and his direction for entry of judgment against him. Defendant has confessed judgment and justice of the claim against him.

**COLLATERAL.** By the side; at the side; attached upon the side. Not lineal, but upon a parallel or diverging line. Additional or auxilliary; supplementary; co-operating.

**COLLATERAL SECURITY.** A security given in addition to the direct security, and subordinate to it, intended to guarantee its validity or convertibility or insure its performance; so that, if the direct security fails, the creditor may fall back upon the collateral security. Collateral security, in bank phraseology, means some security additional to the personal obligation of the borrower.

**COLOR.** An appearance or semblance, as distinguished from a reality. Hence, color of title.

**COMITY OF NATIONS AND STATES.** The most appropriate phrase to express the true foundation and extent of the obligation of the laws of one nation within the territories of another. It is derived altogether from the voluntary consent of the latter; and it is inadmissible when it is contrary to its known policy, or prejudicial to its interest. In the silence of any positive rule affirming or denying or restraining the operation of foreign laws, courts of justice presume the tacit adoption of them by their own government, unless repugnant to its policy, or prejudicial to its interests. It is not the comity of the courts, but the comity of the nation, which is administered and ascertained in the same way and guided by the same reasoning, by which all other principles of the municipal law are ascertained and guided.

**COMMERCIAL LAW.** A phrase used to designate the whole body of substantive jurisprudence applicable to the rights, intercourse, and relation of persons engaged in commerce, trade, or mercantile pursuits. It is not a very scientific or accurate term. As foreign commerce is carried on by means of shipping, the term has come to be used occasionally as synonymous with "maritime law;" but, in strictness, the phrase "commercial law" is wider, and includes many transactions or legal questions which have nothing to do with shipping or its incidents.

**COMMERCIAL PAPER.** The term "commercial paper" means bills of exchange, promissory notes, bank checks, and other negotiable instruments for the payment of money, which, by their form and on their face, purport to be such instruments as are, by the law-merchant, recognized as falling under the designation of "commercial paper."

**COMMISSION.** A warrant or authority or letters patent, issuing from the government, or one of its departments, or a court, empowering a person or persons named to do certain acts, or to exercise jurisdiction, or to perform the duties and exercise the authority of an office (as in the case of an officer in the army or navy).

Also, in private affairs, it signifies the authority or instructions under which one person transacts business or negotiates for another.

In a derivative sense, a body of persons to whom a commission is directed. A board or committee officially appointed and empowered to perform certain acts or exercise certain jurisdiction of a public nature or relation; as a "commission of assize."

**In commercial law.** The recompense or reward of an agent, factor, broker, or bailee, when the same is calculated as a percentage on the amount of his transactions or on the profit to the principal. But in this sense the word often occurs in the plural.

**COMMISSION MERCHANT.** A factor.

**COMMITTEE.** A term applied, in some states, to the guardian of an insane person.

**COMMODATUM.** Latin. A loan of goods for use without pay, the goods to be returned in kind.

**COMMON CARRIER. Of goods.** "One who holds himself out to transport for hire the goods of such as choose to employ him." Goddard on Bailments and Carriers, § 191.

**Of passengers.** "Such as hold themselves out for hire to carry all persons indifferently who apply for passage." Id. § 317.

**COMMON COUNTS.** Certain general counts or forms inserted in a declaration in an action to recover a money debt not founded on the circumstances of the individual case, but intended to guard against a possible variance, and to enable the plaintiff to take advantage of any ground of liability which the proof may disclose within the general scope of the action. In the action of assumpsit, these counts are as follows: For goods sold and delivered, or bargained and sold; for work done; for money lent; for money paid; for money received to the use of the plaintiff; for interest, or for money due on an account stated.

**COMMON LAW.** As distinguished from the Roman law, the modern civil law, the canon law, and other systems, the common law is that body of law and juristic theory which was originated, developed, and formulated and is administered in England, and has obtained among most of the states and peoples of Anglo-Saxon stock.

As distinguished from law created by the enactment of legislatures, the common law comprises the body of those principles and rules of action, relating to the government and security of persons and property, which derive their authority solely from usages and customs of immemorial antiquity, or from the judgments and decrees of the courts recognizing, affirming, and enforcing such usages and customs, and in this sense, particularly the ancient unwritten law of England.

As distinguished from equity law, it is a body of rules and principles, written or unwritten, which are of fixed and immutable authority, and which must be applied to controversies rigorously and in their entirety, and cannot be modified to suit the peculiarities of a specific case, or colored by any judicial discretion, and which rests confessedly upon custom or statute, as distinguished from any claim to ethical superiority.

**COMPLAINANT.** The plaintiff in code pleading or in equity.

**COMPLAINT. In civil practice.** In those states having a Code of Civil Procedure, the complaint is the first or initiatory pleading on the part of the plaintiff in a civil action. It corresponds to the declaration in the common law practice.

**In criminal law.** A charge, preferred before a magistrate having jurisdiction, that a person named (or a certain person whose name is unknown) has committed a certain offense, with an offer to prove the fact, to the end that a prosecution may be instituted. It is a technical term, descriptive of proceedings before a magistrate.

**COMPOSITION.** An agreement, made upon a sufficient consideration between an insolvent or embarrassed debtor and his creditors, whereby the latter, for the sake of immediate payment, agree to accept a dividend less than the whole amount of their claims, to be distributed pro rata, in discharge and satisfaction of the whole.

**COMPOS MENTIS.** Latin. Sound of mind.

**COMPOUNDING A FELONY.** The offense committed by a person who, having been directly injured by a felony, agrees with the criminal that he will not prosecute him, on condition of the latter's making reparation, or on receipt of a reward or bribe not to prosecute.

The offense of taking a reward for forbearing to prosecute a felony; as where a party robbed takes his goods again, or other amends, upon an agreement not to prosecute.

**COMPROMISE.** An arrangement arrived at, either in court or out of court, for settling a dispute upon what appears to the parties to be equitable terms, having regard to the uncertainty they are in regarding the facts or the law and the facts together.

**CONDITIONAL SALE.** A sale under the terms of which the passage of title is made to depend upon the performance of a condition. Usually the condition precedent to the passage of title is payment of the purchase price by the purchaser.

**CONFESSION OF JUDGMENT.** The act of a debtor in permitting judgment to be entered against him by his creditor, for a stipulated sum, by a written statement to that effect or by warrant of attorney, without the institution of legal proceedings of any kind.

**CONFLICT OF LAWS.** An opposition, conflict, or antagonism between different laws of the same state or sovereignty upon the same subject-matter.

A similar inconsistency between the municipal laws of different states or countries, arising in the case of persons who have acquired rights or a status, or made contracts, or incurred obligations, within the territory of two or more states.

That branch of jurisprudence, arising from the diversity of the laws of different nations in their application to rights and remedies, which reconciles the inconsistency, or decides which law or system is to govern in the particular case, or settles the degree of force to be accorded to the law of a foreign country (the acts or rights in question having arisen under it), either where it varies from the domestic law, or where the domestic law is silent or not exclusively applicable to the case in point. In this sense it is more properly called "private international law."

**CONNIVANCE.** The secret or indirect consent or permission of one person to the commission of an unlawful or criminal act.

**CONSANGUINITY.** Kinship; blood relationship; the connection or relation of persons descended from the same stock or common ancestor.

**CONSERVATOR.** A guardian of an insane person's estate.

**CONSIDERATION.** The inducement to a contract. The cause, motive, price, or impelling influence which induces a contracting party to enter into a contract.

Any benefit conferred, or agreed to be conferred, upon the promisor, by any other person, to which the promisor is not lawfully entitled, or any prejudice suffered, or agreed to be suffered, by such person, other than such as he is at the time of consent lawfully bound to suffer, as an inducement to the promisor, is a good consideration for a promise.

**CONSIGNEE.** In mercantile law. One to whom a consignment is made. The person to whom goods are shipped for sale.

**CONSIGNMENT.** The act or process of consigning goods; the transportation of goods consigned; an article or collection of goods sent to a factor to be sold; goods or property sent, by the aid of a common carrier, from one person in one place to another person in another place.

**CONSIGNOR.** One who sends or makes a consignment. A shipper of goods.

**CONSPIRACY.** In criminal law. A combination or confederacy between two or more persons formed for the purpose of committing, by their joint efforts, some lawful or criminal act, or some act which is innocent in itself, but becomes unlawful when done by the concerted action of the conspirators, or for the purpose of using criminal or unlawful means to the commission of an act not in itself unlawful.

**CONSTRUCTIVE.** That which is established by the mind of the law in its act of construing facts, conduct, circumstances, or instruments; that which has not the character assigned to it in its own essential nature, but acquires such character in consequence of the way in which it is regarded by a rule or policy of law; hence, inferred, implied, made out by legal interpretation.

**Constructive assent.** An assent or consent imputed to a party from a construction or interpretation of his conduct; as distinguished from one which he actually expresses.

**CONTRA.** Latin. Opposite, contrary. Where a decision is said to be contra, it is on the opposite side of the question.

**CONTRACT.** "In its broadest sense, an agreement whereby one or more of the parties acquire a right, in rem or in personam, in relation to some person, thing, act, or forbearance." Clark on Contracts (3d Ed.) p. 1.

**CONTRIBUTION.** The sharing of a loss or payment among several. The act of any one or several of a number of codebtors, cosureties, etc., in reimbursing one of their number, who has paid the whole debt or suffered the whole liability, each to the extent of his proportionate share. In equity, a bill is brought by a surety that has paid the whole debt, for contribution by his cosureties. Such an action is also had at law.

**CONVERSION.** An unauthorized assumption and exercise of the right of ownership over goods or personal chattels belonging to another, to the alteration of their condition or the exclusion of the owner's rights.

**Constructive conversion.** An implied or virtual conversion, which takes place where a person does such acts in reference to the goods of another as amount in law to the appropriation of the property to himself.

**CONVICT.** Under the criminal law, to find guilty of an offense as charged in the indictment or information.

**CORPORATION.** An artificial person or legal entity, created by or under the authority of the laws of a state or nation, composed in same rare instances of a single person and his successors, being the incumbents of a particular office, but ordinarily consisting of an association of numerous individuals, who subsist as a body politic under a special denomination, which is regarded in law as having a personality and existence distinct from that of its several members, and which is, by the same authority, vested with the capacity of continuous succession, irrespective of changes in its membership, either in perpetuity or for a limited term of years, and of acting as a unit or single individual in matters relating to the common purpose of the association, within the scope of the powers and authorities conferred upon such bodies by law.

**CORPOREAL PROPERTY.** Such as affects the senses, and may be seen and handled by the body, as opposed to incorporeal property which cannot be seen or handled, and exists only in contemplation. Thus, a house is corporeal, but the annual rent payable for its occupation is incorporeal. Corporeal property is, if movable, capable of manual transfer; if immovable, possession of it may be delivered up. But incorporeal property cannot be so transferred, but some other means must be adopted for its transfer, of which the most usual is an instrument in writing.

**CORPUS.** Latin. Body.

**CORPUS DELICTI.** Latin. The body of the wrong; the essential fact of the crime. The general rule is that no one can be convicted of a crime unless the actual doing of the crime has been proved. Laymen are accustomed to regard the requirements of this general rule as being much more rigid than they really are, and some convictions are on record in which the proof of the corpus delicti, while not entirely absent, was comparatively slight.

**COSTS.** A pecuniary allowance, made to the successful party (and recoverable from the losing party), for his court costs in prosecuting or defending a suit or a distinct proceeding within a suit. Costs do not include attorney's fees, excepting where the parties have stipulated for them, or where a statute provides for their being included in costs.

**COUNSEL.** The one or more attorneys or counselors appearing for a party in a cause. Both theoretically and actually, attorneys are officers of the court, and, by virtue of their office, are expected to give advice to the court, through their briefs and arguments, as to the law involved in the case in hand. Thus they are, in a very real sense, counsel.

**COUNT, n. In pleading.** The different parts of a declaration, each of which, if it stood alone, would constitute a ground for action, are the counts of the declaration. Used also to signify the several parts of an indictment, each charging a distinct offense.

**COUNTERCLAIM.** A claim presented by a defendant in opposition to or deduction from the claim of the plaintiff. A species of set-off or recoupment introduced by the codes of civil procedure in several of the states, of a broad and liberal character.

**COURT. In practice.** An organ of the government, belonging to the judicial department, whose function is the application of the laws to controversies brought before it and the public administration of justice.

**COURT ABOVE—COURT BELOW.** In appellate practice, the "court above" is the one to which a cause is removed for review, whether by appeal, writ of error, or certiorari; while the "court below" is the one from which the case is being removed.

**COVENANT.** An agreement, convention, or promise of two or more parties, by deed in writing, signed, sealed, and delivered, by which either of the parties pledges himself to the other that something is either done or shall be done, or stipulates for the truth of certain facts. A promise contained in such an agreement.

**COVERT.** Covered, protected, sheltered. A pound covert is one that is closed or covered over, as distinguished from pound overt, which is open overhead. A feme covert is so called, as being under the wing, protection or cover of her husband.

**COVERTURE.** The condition or state of a married woman.

**CRIME.** A crime is an act committed or omitted, in violation of a public law, either forbidding or commanding it; a breach or violation of some public right or duty due to a whole community, considered as a community in its social aggregate capacity, as distinguished from a civil injury.

# D

**DAMAGE.** Loss, injury, or deterioration, caused by the negligence, design, or accident of one person to another, in respect of the latter's person or property.

**DAMAGES.** 1. The plural of damage.
2. Compensation claimed or awarded in a judicial proceeding for damage or for the invasion of a legal right. Bauer on Damages, p. 1.

**DEBT.** A sum of money due to certain and express agreement; as by bond for a determinate sum, a bill or note, a special bargain, or a rent reserved on a lease, where the amount is fixed and specific, and does not depend upon any subsequent valuation to settle it.

**DECEIT.** A fraudulent and cheating misrepresentation, artifice, or device, used by one or more persons to deceive and trick another, who is ignorant of the true facts, to the prejudice and damage of the party imposed upon.

**DECLARATION.** The complaint in a civil proceeding at common law. It is the first pleading filed by the plaintiff upon beginning his action.

**DECREE. In practice.** The judgment of a court of equity or admiralty, answering to the judgment of a court of common law.

**DEED.** A sealed instrument, containing a contract or covenant, delivered by the party to be bound thereby, and accepted by the party to whom the contract or covenant runs.

**DE FACTO.** Latin. In fact; in deed; actually.

**DEFENDANT.** The party sued in an action. The person against whom the declaration or complaint is filed, and who is so named in such declaration or complaint.

**DE JURE.** Latin. Of right; legitimate; lawful; by right and just title.

**DEL CREDERE.** An agreement by which a factor, when he sells goods on credit, for an additional commission (called a "del credere commission"), undertakes that the purchase price will be paid the seller. The del credere factor is usually held to have undertaken a primary and absolute liability, but some cases hold that he is a mere surety.

**DELICTUM.** Latin. A tort.

**DELIVERY.** The physical or constructive transfer of an instrument or of goods from the hands of one person to those of another.

**DEMISE.** 1. A conveyance of an estate to another for life, for years, or at will; a lease.

2. Death or decease.

**DEMURRER. In pleading.** The formal mode of disputing the sufficiency in law of the pleading of the other side. In effect it is an allegation that, even if the facts as stated in the pleading to which objection is taken be true, yet their legal consequences are not such as to put the demurring party to the necessity of answering them or proceeding further with the cause.

An objection made by one party to his opponent's pleading, alleging that he ought not to answer it, for some defect in law in the pleading. It admits the facts, and refers the law arising thereon to the court.

It imports that the objecting party will not proceed, but will wait the judgment of the court whether he is bound so to do.

**In equity.** An allegation of a defendant, which, admitting the matters of fact alleged by the bill to be true, shows that as they are therein set forth they are insufficient for the plaintiff to proceed upon or to oblige the defendant to answer, or that, for some reason apparent on the face of the bill, or on account of the omission of some matter which ought to be contained therein, or for want of some circumstances which ought to be attendant thereon, the defendant ought not to be compelled to answer to the whole bill, or to some certain part thereof.

**DE NOVO.** Latin. Anew.

**DEPONENT.** One who makes oath to a written statement.

**DEPOSIT. In banking law.** The act of placing or lodging money in the custody of a bank or banker, for safety or convenience, to be withdrawn at the will of the depositor or under rules and regulations agreed on; also the money so deposited.

**DEPOSITION.** The testimony of a witness taken upon interrogatories, not in court, but intended to be used in court.

**DEPOSITUM.** Latin. A bailment having for its purpose that the bailee keep the goods for the bailor without reward.

**DESCENT.** Hereditary succession.

**DESCRIPTIO PERSONÆ.** Latin. Description of the person.

**DETUR DIGNIORI.** Latin. Let it be given to him who is more worthy.

**DEVASTAVIT.** Latin. He laid waste. The allegation, "He laid waste," in a suit brought against executor, administrator, guardian, or trustee, gave rise to the naming of the wrong "devastavit." In such a case, the defendant is alleged to have mismanaged and wasted assets of the estate intrusted to him and thereby caused a loss.

**DEVISE.** A testamentary disposition of land or realty; a gift of real property by the last will and testament of the donor.

**DICTUM.** Latin. The word is generally used as an abbreviated form of obiter dictum, "a remark by the way;" that is, an observation or remark made by a judge in pronouncing an opinion upon a cause, concerning some rule, principle, or application of law, or the solution of a question suggested by the case at bar, but not necessarily involved in the case or essential to its determination; any statement of the law enunciated by the court merely by way of illustration, argument, analogy, or suggestion.

**DISCOUNT.** In a general sense, an allowance or deduction made from a gross sum on any account whatever. In a more limited and technical sense, the taking of interest in advance. By the language of the commercial world and the settled practice of banks, a discount by a bank means a drawback or deduction made upon its advances or loans of money, upon negotiable paper or other evidences of debt payable at a future day, which are transferred to the bank.

**DISHONOR. In mercantile law and usage.** To refuse or decline to accept a bill of exchange, or to refuse or neglect to pay a bill or note at maturity.

**DIVIDEND.** A fund to be divided. The share allotted to each of several persons entitled to share in a division of profits or property. Thus, dividend may denote a fund set apart by a corporation out of its profits, to be apportioned among the shareholders, or the proportional amount falling to each. In bankruptcy proceedings, a dividend is a proportional payment to the creditors out of the insolvent estate.

**DOMICILE.** That place in which a man has voluntarily fixed the habitation of himself and family, not for a mere special or temporary purpose, but with the present intention of making a permanent home, until some unexpected event shall occur to induce him to adopt some other permanent home.

**DORMANT PARTNER.** See **Partners.**

**DOWER.** The provision which the law makes for a widow out of lands or tenements of her husband, for her support and the nurture of her children. Co. Litt. 30a. Dower is an estate for life of the widow in a certain portion of the estate of her husband, to which she has not relinquished her right during the marriage.

**DRAWEE.** A person to whom a bill of exchange is addressed, and who is requested to pay the amount of money therein named.

**DRAWER.** The person drawing a bill of exchange and addressing it to the drawee.

**DUEBILL.** A brief written acknowledgment of a debt. It is not made payable to order, like a promissory note.

**DURESS.** Unlawful constraint exercised upon a person, whereby he is forced to do some act against his will.

# E

**EARNEST.** The payment of a part of the price of goods sold, or the delivery of part of such goods, for the purpose of binding the contract.

**EASEMENT.** A right in the owner of one parcel of land, by reason of such ownership, to use the land of another for a special purpose not inconsistent with a general property in the owner. 2 Washb. Real Prop. 25.

A private easement is a privilege, service, or convenience which one neighbor has of another, by prescription, grant, or necessary implication, and without profit; as a way over his land, a gateway, watercourse, and the like. Kitch. 105.

**EJECTMENT.** An action of which the purpose is to determine whether the title to certain land is in the plaintiff or is in the defendant.

**ELECTION.** The act of choosing or selecting one or more from a greater number of persons, things, courses, rights, or remedies.

**EMANCIPATION.** The act by which an infant is set at liberty from the control of parent or guardian and made his own master.

**EMBEZZLEMENT.** The fraudulent appropriation to his own use or benefit of property or money intrusted to him by another, by a clerk, agent, trustee, public officer, or other person acting in a fiduciary character.

**EMBLEMENTS.** The vegetable chattels called "emblements" are the corn and other growth of the earth which are produced annually, not spontaneously, but by labor and industry, and thence are called "fructus industriales."

**EMINENT DOMAIN.** Eminent domain is the right of the people or government to take private property for public use.

**ENTIRETY.** The whole, in contradistinction to a moiety or part only. When land is conveyed to husband and wife, they do not take by moieties, but both are seised of the entirety. Parceners, on the other hand, have not an entirety of interest, but each is properly entitled to the whole of a distinct moiety.

The word is also used to designate that which the law considers as one whole, and not capable of being divided into parts. Thus, a judgment, it is held, is an entirety, and, if void as to one of the two defendants, cannot be valid as to the other. So, if a contract is an entirety, no part of the consideration is due until the whole has been performed.

**EO NOMINE.** Latin. By that name.

**EQUITABLE.** Just, fair, and right. Existing in equity; available or sustainable only in equity, or only upon the rules and principles of equity.

**EQUITABLE ASSIGNMENT.** An assignment which, though invalid at law, will be recognized and enforced in equity; e. g., an assignment of a chose in action, or of future acquisitions of the assignor.

**EQUITY.** In one of its technical meanings, equity is a body of jurisprudence, or field of jurisdiction, differing in its origin, theory, and methods from the common law.

In a still more restricted sense, it is a system of jurisprudence, or branch of remedial justice, administered by certain tribunals, distinct from the common-law courts, and empowered to decree "equity" in the complex of well-settled and well-understood rules, principles, and precedents.

Equity also signifies an equitable right; i. e., a right enforceable in a court of equity. Hence a bill of complaint which did not show that the plaintiff had a right entitling him to relief was said to be demurrable for want of equity; and certain rights now recognized in all the courts are still known as "equities," from having been originally recognized only in the court of chancery.

**EQUITY OF REDEMPTION.** The right of the mortgagor of an estate to redeem the same after it has been forfeited, at law, by a breach of the condition of the mortgage, upon paying the amount of debt, interest and costs.

**ERROR.** A mistaken judgment or incorrect belief as to the existence or effect of matters of fact, or a false or mistaken conception or application of the law.

Such a mistaken or false conception or application of the law to the facts of a cause as will furnish ground for a review of the proceedings upon a writ of error; a mistake of law, or false or irregular application of it, such as vitiates the proceedings and warrants the reversal of the judgment.

"Error" is also used as an elliptical expression for "writ of error"; as, in saying that error lies; that a judgment may be reversed on error.

**Assignment of errors.** In practice. The statement of the plaintiff's case on a writ of error, setting forth the errors complained of; corresponding with the declaration in an ordinary action. A specification of the errors upon which the appellant will rely, with such fullness as to give aid to the court in the examination of the transcript.

**Harmless error.** In appellate practice. An error committed in the progress of the trial below, but which was not prejudicial to the rights of the party assigning it, and for which, therefore, the court will not reverse the judgment; as, where the error was neutralized or corrected by subsequent proceedings in the case, or where, notwithstanding the error, the particular issue was found in that party's favor, or where, even if the error had not been committed, he could not have been legally entitled to prevail.

**Reversible error.** In appellate practice. Such an error as warrants the appellate court in reversing the judgment before it.

**ESCROW.** The state or condition of a deed which is conditionally held by a third person, or the possession and retention of a deed by a third person pending a condition; as when an instrument is said to be delivered "in escrow."

**ESTATE.** The interest which any one has in lands, or in any other subject of property.

In another sense, the term denotes the property (real or personal) in which one has a right or interest; the subject-matter of ownership; the corpus of property.

In a wider sense, the term "estate" denotes a man's whole financial status or condition—the aggregate of his interests and concerns, so far as regards his situation with reference to wealth or its objects, including debts and obligations, as well as possessions and rights.

**ESTOPPEL.** A bar or impediment raised by the law, which precludes a man from alleging or from denying a certain fact or state of facts, in consequence of his previous allegation or denial or conduct or admission, or in consequence of a final adjudication of the matter in a court of law.

**EVICTION.** Dispossession by process of law; the act of depriving a person of the possession of lands which he has held, in pursuance of the judgment of a court.

**EVIDENCE.** Any species of proof, or probative matter, legally presented at the trial of an issue, by the act of the parties and through the medium of witnesses, records, documents, concrete objects, etc., for the purpose of inducing belief in the minds of the court or jury as to their contention.

**EXCEPTION.** In practice. A formal objection to the action of the court, during the trial of a cause, in refusing a request or overruling an objection; implying that the party excepting does not acquiesce in the decision of the court, but will seek to procure its reversal, and that he means to save the benefit of his request or objection in some future proceeding.

**EXCHANGE.** In conveyancing. A mutual grant of equal interests (in lands or tenements), the one in consideration of the other.

**In commercial law.** A negotiation by which one person transfers to another funds which he has in a certain place, either at a price agreed upon or which is fixed by commercial usage.

**In law of personal property.** Exchange of goods is a commutation, transmutation, or transfer of goods for other goods, as distinguished from "sale," which is a transfer of goods for money.

**EX CONTRACTU.** Latin. From or out of a contract. In both the civil and common law, rights and causes of action are divided into two classes—those arising ex contractu (from a contract); and those arising ex delicto (from a delict or tort).

**EX DELICTO.** Latin. From a delict, tort, fault, crime, or malfeasance. In both the civil and the common law, obligations and causes of action are divided into two great classes—those arising ex contractu (out of a contract); and those ex delicto.

**EX DOLO MALO NON ORITUR ACTIO.** Latin. Out of fraud no action arises; fraud never gives a right of action. No court will lend its aid to a man who founds his cause of action upon an immoral or illegal act.

**EXECUTED.** Completed; carried into full effect; already done or performed; taking effect immediately; now in existence or in possession; conveying an immediate right or possession. The opposite of executory.

**EXECUTION. In contracts.** (1) The signing of a contract not under seal, or the signing, sealing, and delivering of a contract under seal. (2) The doing or accomplishing of the things stipulated in a contract to be done.

**In criminal law.** The legal putting to death of a convict, in conformity with the terms of his sentence.

**In civil practice.** The writ in which the court authorizes and orders the sheriff or similar officer to put into effect the court's final decree or judgment.

"Final execution is one which authorizes the money due on a judgment to be made out of the property of the defendant." Bouvier's Law Dictionary.

**EXECUTOR.** A person appointed by a testator to carry out the directions and requests in his will, and to dispose of the property according to his testamentary provisions after his decease.

**EXECUTORY.** That which is yet to be executed or performed; that which remains to be carried into operation or effect; incomplete; depending upon a future performance or event. The opposite of executed.

**EXEMPLARY.** Punitive, punitory, for punishment.

**EXEMPLARY DAMAGES.** Damages on an increased scale, awarded to the plaintiff over and above what will barely compensate him for his property loss, where the wrong done to him was aggravated by circumstances of violence, oppression, malice, fraud, or wanton and wicked conduct on the part of the defendant, and are intended to punish the defendant for his evil behavior.

**EXEMPTION.** A privilege allowed by law to a judgment debtor, by which he may hold property to a certain amount, or certain classes of property, free from all liability to levy and sale on execution or attachment.

**EX GRATIA.** Latin. Out of grace; as a matter of favor or indulgence; gratuitous.

**EX MERO MOTU.** Latin. Of his own mere motion; of his own accord.

**EXONERATION.** Latin, exonere; disburden; take the load off of. The lifting of a burden from a person or property.

**In administration of estates.** The taking of the burden of a mortgage debt, in certain instances, from mortgaged real estate, and the placing of the burden upon personalty.

**In suretyship.** The right of exoneration is an equitable right of a surety to have the burden of the debt lifted from his shoulders and placed upon those of the principal debtor. When a surety is sued by the creditor, he has sometimes filed a bill in equity, asking that the creditor be enjoined from prosecuting the action at law against the surety before suing the principal, and offering a bond to indemnify the creditor against loss.

**EX PARTE.** Latin. On one side only; by or for one party; done for, in behalf of, or on the application of, one party only.

**EXPRESS.** Made known distinctly and explicitly, and not left to inference or implication. Declared in terms; set forth in words. Manifested by direct and appropriate language, as distinguished from that which is inferred from conduct. The word is usually contrasted with "implied."

**EX TURPI CONTRACTU NON ORITUR ACTIO.** Latin. Out of an immoral or illegal contract an action does not arise. A contract founded upon an illegal or immoral consideration cannot be enforced by action. 2 Kent, Comm. 466.

# F

**FACTOR.** A commercial agent, employed by a principal to sell merchandise consigned to him for that purpose, for and in behalf of the principal, but usually in his own name, being intrusted with the possession and control of the goods, and being remunerated by a commission.

**FEE SIMPLE. In English law.** A freehold estate of inheritance, absolute and unqualified. It stands at the head of estates as the highest in dignity and the most ample in extent; since every other kind of estate is derivable thereout, and mergeable therein.

**FEE TAIL.** An estate of inheritance, descending only to a certain class or classes of heirs; e. g., an estate is conveyed or devised "to A. and the heirs of his body," or "to A. and the heirs male of his body," or "to A., and the heirs female of his body." Such estates have been common in England, but never very common in the United States. State statutes have dealt variously with estates tail, some statutes converting them into estates in fee simple. The entire plan of the estate tail is contrary to the spirit of American progress, contemplating, as the plan does, the continuance of the tenure in one class of persons, regardless of the changes in ownership often required by the progress of the community as a whole.

**FELONY. In American law.** The term has no very definite or precise meaning, except in some cases where it is defined by statute. For the most part, the state laws, in describing any particular offense, declare whether or not it shall be considered a felony. Apart from this, the word seems merely to imply a crime of a graver or more atrocious nature than those designated as "misdemeanors."

**FEME.** L. Fr. A woman.

**Feme covert.** A married woman.

**Feme sole.** A single woman.

**FICTION.** An assumption or supposition of law that something which is or may be false is true, or that a state of facts exists which has never really taken place.

**FIDUCIARY.** As an adjective it means of the nature of a trust; having the characteristics of a trust; Analogous to a trust; relating to or founded upon a trust or confidence.

**FINAL PROCESS.** A writ of execution. Such process is final, as contrasted with earlier process in the action. Process prior to judgment is known as mesne process.

**FINAL SETTLEMENT.** The rendering of a final account by an executor or an administrator, at the closing of the business of the estate, approved by the probate court, and followed by the discharge of the executor or administrator.

**FIRE INSURANCE.** A contract under the terms of which the insurer agrees to indemnify the insured against loss caused by fire during a period specified in the contract.

**FIXTURES.** (Authorities differ so much in their definitions of this term that it is deemed best to include several definitions, presenting varying conceptions.)

"A fixture is a thing which, though originally a chattel, is, by reason of its annexation to land, regarded as a part of the land, partaking of its character and belonging to its owner. Whether a chattel annexed to land is, in a particular case, to be so regarded as a part thereof, is determined usually by the mode of its attachment to the land, and the character of the chattel, as indicating the presumed intention of the annexor." Tiffany on Real Property, c. 9 (IV).

"Personal chattels affixed to real estate, which may be severed and removed by the party who has affixed them, or by his personal representative, against the will of the owner of the freehold. There is much dispute among the authorities as to what is a proper definition." Bouvier's Law Dict.

**F. O. B.** Free on board. "If a quotation is f. o. b., the seller undertakes for the price named to deliver the goods on board car or ship at a designated place, free of charges to the buyer." Whitaker's Foreign Exchange, p. 335.

**FORCIBLE DETAINER.** The offense of violently keeping possession of lands and tenements, with menaces, force, and arms, and without the authority of law.

**FORCIBLE ENTRY.** An offense against the public peace, or private wrong, committed by violently taking possession of lands and tenements with menaces, force, and arms, against the will of those entitled to the possession, and without the authority of law.

**FORECLOSURE.** A proceeding by which the rights of the mortgagee of real property are enforced. This procedure varies greatly in different states. The property is commonly put up at public auction and sold to the highest bidder. The mortgagee gets out of the proceeds the amount of his debt, with costs. The remaining portion of the proceeds, if any, goes to the debtor, the mortgagor. If the property sells at a price less than the amount of the debt and costs, judgment is given against the mortgagor for the deficiency.

Foreclosure is now generally by court proceeding in the case of real estate mortgages, though formerly all mortgages were subject to "strict foreclosure"; i. e., foreclosure without judicial process.

**FORFEITURE. In bonds.** A bond is given as the absolute and sealed promise of the obligor to pay a certain sum of money, with a defeasance clause following the obligation. This clause states that, upon the happening of a certain event, such as the conveying of certain land or the faithful performance of the duties of a certain office during a specified term, the bond is to become null and void. If the condition subsequent stated in such defeasance clause does not occur, the obligor has forfeited his bond.

**In insurance.** In a fire insurance policy, it is often stated that the policy shall be forfeited upon the occurrence of a certain event, such as nonpayment of the premium, storage of gasoline on the premises, vacancy of the premises, etc. A life insurance policy usually provides that it shall be forfeited for nonpayment of premiums. In the event of the happening of such a condition subsequent in an insurance policy, the insurer may declare a forfeiture or may waive the forfeiture and permit the insurance to continue.

**FORGERY. In criminal law.** The falsely making or materially altering, with intent to defraud, any writing which, if genuine, might apparently be of legal efficacy or the foundation of a legal liability.

**FORMS OF ACTION.** Classes or kinds of action under the common law. "This term comprehends the various classes of personal action at common law, viz. trespass, case, trover, detinue, replevin, covenant, debt, assumpsit, scire facias, and revivor, as well as the nearly obsolete actions of account and annuity, and the modern action of mandamus. They are now abolished in England by Judicature Acts of 1873, and 1875, and in many of the states of the United States, where a uniform course of proceeding under codes of procedure has taken their place. But the principles regulating the distinctions between the common-law actions are still found applicable even where the technical forms are abolished." Bouvier's Law Dict.

**FRANCHISE.** A special privilege conferred by government upon an individual or corporation, and which does not belong to the citizens of the country generally, of common right.

**FRAUD.** Fraud consists of some deceitful practice or willful devise, resorted to with intent to deprive another of his right, or in some manner to do him an injury. As distinguished from negligence, it is always positive, intentional.

**FREEHOLD.** An estate in land or other real property, of uncertain duration; that is, either of inheritance or which may possibly last for the life of the tenant at the least (as distinguished from a leasehold), and held by a free tenure.

**FRUCTUS INDUSTRIALES.** Latin. Industrial fruits or fruits of industry. Those fruits of a thing, as of land, which are produced by the labor and industry of the occupant, as crops of grain; as distinguished from such as are produced solely by the powers of nature.

**FRUCTUS NATURALES.** Latin. Those products which are produced by the powers of nature alone; as wool, metals, milk, the young of animals.

**FUNGIBLE THINGS.** Movable goods, which may be estimated and replaced according to weight, measure, and number, things belonging to a class, which do not have to be dealt with in specie.

**FUTURE ESTATE.** An estate to begin in possession at or after the termination of the present estate; e. g., A. holds a life estate in a tract of land, and B. has a reversion therein, B.'s possession to begin on the termination of A.'s estate. B.'s reversion is one kind of future estate. The remainder is another common species of future estate.

# G

**GARNISH,** v. To issue process of garnishment against a person.

**GARNISHEE,** n. One garnished.

**GARNISHMENT. In the process of attachment.** A warning to a person in whose hands the effects of another are attached not to pay the money or deliver the property of the defendant in his hands to him, but to appear and answer the plaintiff's suit.

**GENERAL AND SPECIAL ISSUE.** The former is a plea which traverses and denies, briefly and in general and summary terms, the whole declaration, indictment, or complaint, without tendering new or special matter.

**GENERAL VERDICT.** A verdict whereby the jury find either for the plaintiff or for the defendant in general terms; the ordinary form of verdict.

**GRATIS DICTUM.** Latin. A voluntary assertion; a statement which a party is not legally bound to make, or in which he is not held to precise accuracy.

**GRAVAMEN.** Latin. The burden or gist of a charge.

**GUARANTY,** n. A promise to answer for the payment of some debt, or the performance of some duty, in case of the failure of another person, who, in the first instance, is liable to such payment or performance.

**GUARDIAN.** A guardian is a person lawfully invested with the power, and charged with the duty, of taking care of the person and managing the property and rights of another person, who, for some peculiarity of status, or defect or age, understanding, or self-control, is considered incapable of administering his own affairs.

# H

**HEARSAY.** A term applied to that species of testimony given by a witness who relates, not what he knows personally, but what others have told him, or what he has heard said by others.

**HEIR. At common law.** A person who succeeds, by the rules of law, to an estate in lands, tenements, or hereditaments, upon the death of his ancestor, by descent and right of relationship.

**HEREDITAMENTS.** Things capable of being inherited, be it corporeal or incorporeal, real, personal, or mixed, and including not only lands and everything thereon, but also heirlooms, and certain furniture which, by custom, may descend to the heir together with the land.

# I

**IMPLIED.** This word is used in law as contrasted with "express"; i. e., where the intention in regard to the subject-matter is not manifested by explicit and direct words, but is gathered by implication or necessary deduction from the circumstances, the general language, or the conduct of the parties.

**INCHOATE.** Imperfect; unfinished; begun, but not completed; as a contract not executed by all the parties.

**INCORPOREAL.** Without body; not of material nature; the opposite of "corporeal."

**INDEMNITY.** An indemnity is a collateral contract or assurance, by which one person engages to secure another against an anticipated loss or to prevent him from being damnified by the legal consequences of an act or forbearance on the part of one of the parties or of some third person.

**INDENTURE.** A deed to which two or more persons are parties, and in which these enter into reciprocal and corresponding grants or obligations towards each other; whereas a deed poll is properly one in which only the party making it executes it, or binds himself by it as a deed, though the grantors or grantees therein may be several in number.

**INDICIA.** Latin. Signs; indications.

**INDICTMENT.** The formal written accusation of a crime, as presented by a grand jury. The indictment holds a place, in criminal pleading, analogous to the place held, in a civil case, by the declaration or complaint. The plaintiff, in a criminal case, is the state, and the proof introduced by the state must, in order to convict, sustain one or more of the counts named in the indictment, just as, in a civil case, the proof introduced by the plaintiff must sustain one or more counts in the declaration or complaint. In a criminal case, the state must sustain its case by proof beyond a reasonable doubt; in a civil case, the plaintiff need prove his case only by a preponderance of the evidence.

**INDORSEE.** The person to whom a bill of exchange, promissory note, bill of lading, etc., is assigned by indorsement, giving him a right to sue thereon.

**INDORSEMENT.** The act of a payee, drawee, accommodation indorser, or holder of a negotiable instrument in writing his name upon the back of same, with or without further words, whereby the property in same is transferred to another.

**INDORSER.** He who makes an indorsement.

**INFANT.** A person within age, not of age, or not of full age; a person under the age of twenty-one years; a minor.

**INFORMATION.** In the criminal law, an accusation made the basis of a prosecution for a crime, but not itself the result of a finding by a grand jury.

**IN HÆC FŒDERA NON VENIMUS.** Latin. We did not enter into these bonds; we did not make this contract.

**IN INVITUM.** Latin. Against an unwilling party.

**INIQUUM EST INGENUIS HOMINIBUS NON ESSE LIBERAM RERUM SUARUM ALIENATIONEM.** Latin. Literally, it is unjust to freeborn men that the alienation of their own property should not be free. A better and freer translation would be: It is unjust that freeborn men should be unable freely to alienate their own property. This maxim states a reason underlying the rule against restraints upon alienation.

**INJUNCTION.** A prohibitive writ issued by a court of equity, at the suit of a party complainant, directed to a party defendant in the action, or to a party made a defendant for that purpose, forbidding the latter to do some act, or to permit his servants or agents to do some act, which he is threatening or attempting to commit, or restraining him in the continuance thereof, such act being unjust and inequitable, injurious to the plaintiff, and not such as can be adequately redressed by an action at law.

**INJURY.** Any wrong or damage done to another, either in his person, rights, reputation, or property.

**IN LIMINE.** Latin. On or at the threshold; at the very beginning; preliminarily.

**INNKEEPER.** The proprietor or keeper of a hotel or inn.

**IN PARI DELICTO.** Latin. In equal fault; equally culpable or criminal.

**In pari deiicto, potior est conditio possidentis [defendentis].** In a case of equal or mutual fault (between two parties), the condition of the party in possession [or defending] is the better one. This maxim is often applied to cases in which a plaintiff seeks to procure, under an illegal contract, money or other property in the possession of the defendant, or to get a judgment or decree of any kind, under such a contract.

**IN PERSONAM.** Latin. Against the person. Actions or rights in personam are contrasted with actions or rights in rem, which are directed at specific property or at a specific right or status. A. sues B., in an action at law, for $100. This is one instance of an action in personam. All suits in equity were originally in personam, the bill and the decree being addressed directly to the person of the defendant and seeking to control his conduct.

**IN RE.** Latin. In the matter; e. g., "In re Jones" means "in the matter of Jones."

**IN REM.** Latin. Against a thing; against the status; directed at specific property, or at a specific right or status. An action in admiralty against a certain vessel is in rem. A suit for the foreclosure of a mortgage is, in a sense, in rem. A divorce suit, while in a certain sense in personam, is actually directed against the status of marriage and is, in part, a suit in rem.

**INSOLVENCY.** The condition of a person who is insolvent; inability to pay one's debts; lack of means to pay one's debts. Such a relative condition of a man's assets and liabilities that the former, if all made immediately available, would not be sufficient to discharge the latter. Or the condition of a person who is unable to pay his debts as they fall due, or in the usual course of trade and business.

**INSOLVENT.** Latin, insolvens; not paying.

**In bankruptcy.** In the federal Bankruptcy Act the following rule is stated: "A person shall be deemed insolvent within the provisions of this act whenever the aggregate of his property, exclusive of any property which he may have conveyed, transferred, concealed or removed, or permitted to be concealed or removed, with intent to defraud, hinder or delay his creditors, shall not, at a fair valuation, be sufficient in amount to pay his debts." Section 1, cl. 15.

**In sales.** The Uniform Sales Act gives the following rule: "A person is insolvent within the meaning of this act who either has ceased to pay his debts in the ordinary course of business or cannot pay his debts as they fall due, whether he has committed an act of bankruptcy or not, and whether he is insolvent within the meaning of the federal bankruptcy law or not." Section 76.

**IN SPECIE.** Latin. In kind. Specific; specifically.

**IN STATU QUO.** Latin. In the condition or state (in which it was).

**INSURABLE INTEREST.** Such a real and substantial interest in specific property as will sustain a contract to indemnify the person interested against its loss. If the assured had no real interest, the contract would be a mere wager policy.

**INSURANCE.** A contract whereby, for a stipulated consideration, one party undertakes to compensate the other for loss on a specified subject by specified perils. The party agreeing to make the compensation is usually called the "insurer" or "underwriter"; the other, the "insured" or "assured"; the written contract, a "policy"; the events insured against, "risks" or "perils"; and the subject, right, or interest to be protected, the "insurable interest." Insurance is a contract whereby one undertakes to indemnify another against loss, damage, or liability arising from an unknown or contingent event.

**INSURED.** **In fire and other property insurance.** The person whose property interest is insured.

**In life insurance.** The person whose life is insured.

**INSURER.** The underwriter or insurance company with whom a contract of insurance is made.

**INTERPLEADER.** When two or more persons claim the same thing (or fund) of a third, and he, laying no claim to it himself, is ignorant which of them has a right to it, and fears he may be prejudiced by their proceeding against him to recover it, he may file a bill in equity against them, the object of which is to make them litigate their title between themselves, instead of litigating it with him, and such a bill is called a "bill of interpleader."

**INTER ALIA.** Among other things. A term anciently used in pleading, especially in reciting statutes, where the whole statute was set forth at length. Inter alia enactatum fuit. Among other things it was enacted.

**INTER SE, or INTER SESE.** Latin. Between or among themselves.

**INTERSTATE COMMERCE COMMISSION.** A commission appointed by the President of the United States by authority of the Interstate Commerce Act of 1887. It is a corporate body, so that it may sue or be sued in the courts, and, by court action, its decisions, when valid, are enforced. Its work involves the rates and practices of interstate carriers.

**INTERVENER.** An intervener is a person who voluntarily interposes in an action or other proceeding with the leave of the court.

**INTESTATE.** Without making a will.

# J

**JOINT.** United; combined; undivided; done by or against two or more unitedly; shared by or between two or more.

A "joint" bond, note, or other obligation is one in which the obligors or makers (being two or more in number) bind themselves jointly, but not severally, and which must therefore be prosecuted in a joint action against them all. A "joint and several" bond or note is one in which the obligors or makers bind themselves both jointly and individually to the obligee or payee, and which may be enforced either by a joint action against them all or by separate actions against any one or more at the election of the creditor.

**JOINTLY.** Acting together or in concert or cooperation; holding in common or interdependently, not separately. Persons are "jointly bound" in a bond or note when both or all must be sued in one action for its enforcement.

**Jointly and severally.** Persons who bind themselves "jointly and severally" in a bond or note may all be sued together for its enforcement, or the creditor may select any one or more as the object of his suit.

**JOINT–STOCK COMPANY.** A partnership with a capital divided into transferable shares.

**JOINT TENANCY.** "Exists when a single estate in land is owned by two or more persons claiming under one instrument; its most important characteristic being that, unless the statute otherwise provides, the interest of each joint tenant, upon his death, inures to the benefit of the surviving joint tenant or tenants, to the exclusion of his own heirs, devisees, or personal representatives." Tiffany on Real Property, p. 368.

**JUDGMENT.** The official and authentic decision of a court of justice upon the respective rights and claims of the parties to an action or suit therein litigated and submitted to its determination.

**JUDGMENT DEBTS.** Debts, whether on simple contract or by specialty, for the recovery of which judgment has been entered up, either upon a cognovit or upon a warrant of attorney or as the result of a successful action.

**JUDGMENT IN PERSONAM.** A judgment against a particular person, as distinguished from a judgment against a thing or a right or status. The former class of judgments are conclusive only upon parties and privies; the latter upon all the world.

**JUDGMENT IN REM.** A judgment in rem is an adjudication, pronounced upon the status of some particular subject-matter, by a tribunal having competent authority for that purpose. It differs from a judgment in personam, in this: That the latter judgment is in form, as well as substance, between the parties claiming the right; and that it is so inter partes appears by the record itself.

**JUDGMENT NOTE.** A promissory note, embodying an authorization to any attorney, or to a designated attorney, or to the holder, or the clerk of the court, to enter an appearance for the maker and confess a judgment against him for a sum therein named, upon default of payment of the note.

**JUDGMENT N. O. V.** Judgment non obstante veredicto in its broadest sense is a judgment rendered in favor of one party notwithstanding the finding of a verdict in favor of the other party. Originally, at common law, judgment non obstante veredicto was a judgment entered for plaintiff "notwithstanding the verdict" for defendant. The generally prevailing rule now is that either plaintiff or defendant may have a judgment non obstante veredicto.

**JUDICIAL.** Belonging to the office of a judge; as judicial authority.

**JURAT.** The clause written at the foot of an affidavit, stating when, where, and before whom such affidavit was sworn.

**JURISDICTION.** The power and authority constitutionally conferred upon (or constitutionally recognized as existing in) a court or judge to pronounce the sentence of the law, or to award the remedies provided by law, upon a state of facts, proved or admitted, referred to the tribunal for decision, and authorized by law to be the subject of investigation or action by that tribunal, and in favor of or against persons (or a res) who present themselves, or who are brought, before the court in some manner sanctioned by law as proper and sufficient.

**JURY.** (From the Latin jurare, to swear.) A body of persons selected and summoned by law and sworn to try the facts of a case and to find according to the law and the evidence. In general, the province of the jury is to find the facts in a case, while the judge passes upon pure questions of law. As a matter of fact, however, the jury must often pass upon mixed questions of law and fact in determining the case, and in all such cases the instructions of the judge as to the law become very important.

# K

**KIN.** Relationship; relationship by blood or marriage. The term is sometimes restricted to relationship by blood.

**KNOWLEDGE.** Information. "Knowledge" is a broader term than "notice," including, not only facts of which one is put on notice, but also facts of which one gets knowledge by means other than notice.

# L

**LACHES.** Negligence, consisting in the omission of something which a party might do, and might reasonably be expected to do, towards the vindication or enforcement of his rights. The word is generally the synonym of "remissness," "dilatoriness," "unreasonable or unexcused delay"; the opposite of "vigilance"; and means a want of activity and diligence in making a claim or moving for the enforcement of a right (particularly in equity) which will afford ground for presuming against it, or for refusing relief, where that is discretionary with the court.

**LANDLORD.** He of whom lands or tenements are holden. He who, being the owner of an estate in land, has leased the same for a term of years, on a rent reserved, to another person, called the "tenant."

**LAPSE,** n. **In the law of wills.** The failure of a testamentary gift in consequence of the death of the devisee or legatee during the life of the testator.

**LARCENY.** **In criminal law.** The wrongful and fraudulent taking and carrying away by one person of the mere personal goods of another from any place, with a felonious intent to convert them to his (the taker's) use, and make them his property, without the consent of the owner.

**LAW MERCHANT.** The system of rules, customs, and usages generally recognized and adopted by merchants and traders, and which either in its simplicity or as modified by common law or statutes, constitutes the law for the regulation of their transactions and the solution of their controversies.

**LEASE.** A conveyance of lands or tenements to a person for life, for a term of years, or at will, in consideration of a return of rent or some other recompense. The person who so conveys such lands or tenements is termed the "lessor," and the person to whom they are conveyed, the "lessee"; and when the lessor so conveys lands or tenements to a lessee, he is said to lease, demise, or let them.

**LEASEHOLD.** An estate in realty held under a lease; an estate for a fixed term of years.

**LEGACY.** A bequest or gift of personal property by last will and testament.

**LEGAL TENDER.** That kind of coin, money, or circulating medium which the law compels a creditor to accept in payment of his debt, when tendered by the debtor in the right amount.

**LESSEE.** He to whom a lease is made.

**LESSOR.** He who grants a lease.

**LET, v.** In conveyancing. To demise or lease. "To let and set" is an old expression.

**LETTERS OF ADMINISTRATION.** The formal instrument of authority and appointment given an administrator by the proper court, empowering him to enter upon the discharge of his duties as administrator.

**LETTERS TESTAMENTARY.** The formal instrument of authority and appointment given to an executor by the proper court, empowering him to enter upon the discharge of his office as executor.

**LEVY, v.** To raise; execute; exact; collect; gather; take up; seize. Thus, to levy (raise or collect) a tax; to levy (raise or set up) a nuisance; to levy (acknowledge) a fine; to levy (inaugurate) war; to levy an execution—i. e., to levy or collect a sum of money on an execution.

**LIEN.** A qualified right of property which a creditor has in or over specific property of his debtor, as security for the debt or charge or for performance of some act.

**LIFE ESTATE.** An estate whose duration is limited to the life of the party holding it, or of some other person; a freehold estate, not of inheritance.

**LIFE TENANT.** One who holds an estate in lands for the period of his own life or that of another certain person.

**LIMITATION. In conveyances.** A defining or limiting, either by express words or by implication of law, of the time during which the estate granted is to be enjoyed; e. g., "to A. and his heirs forever,"

limits an estate in fee simple to A.; "to B. for life, remainder to C. and his heirs," limits a life estate to B., with a remainder in fee simple to C.

**In statutes of limitation.** Under statutes of limitation, a certain limit of time is set, after the running of which, subsequent to the accruing of a cause of action, no action can be brought successfully, if the statute is pleaded.

**LIMITED PARTNERSHIP.** A partnership consisting of one or more general partners, jointly and severally responsible as ordinary partners, and by whom the business is conducted, and one or more special partners, contributing in cash payments a specific sum as capital to the common stock, and who are not liable for the debts of the partnership beyond the fund so contributed.

**LIQUIDATED.** Ascertained; determined; fixed; settled; made clear or manifest. Cleared away; paid; discharged.

**LIQUIDATED ACCOUNT.** An account whereof the amount is certain and fixed, either by the act and agreement of the parties or by operation of law; a sum which cannot be changed by the proof; it is so much or nothing; but the term does not necessarily refer to a writing.

**LIQUIDATED AND UNLIQUIDATED DAMAGES.** The former term is applicable when the amount of the damages has been ascertained by the judgment in the action, or when a specific sum of money has been expressly stipulated by the parties to a bond or other contract as the amount of damages to be recovered by either party for a breach of the agreement by the other.

**LIS PENDENS.** Latin. A suit pending; that legal process, in a suit regarding land, which amounts to legal notice to all the world that there is a dispute as to the title. In equity the filing of the bill and serving a subpoena creates a lis pendens, except when statutes require some record.

**LOCATIO.** Latin. A hiring of goods for a reward.

**LOCUS PŒNITENTIÆ.** Latin. A place for repentance; an opportunity for changing one's mind; a chance to withdraw from a contemplated bargain or contract before it results in a definite contractual liability. Also used of a chance afforded to a person, by the circumstances, of relinquishing the intention which he has formed to commit a crime, before the perpetration thereof.

**LODGING HOUSE.** A private house at which lodging is given for a consideration, as contrasted with a public house or inn or hotel.

**L. S.** An abbreviation for "locus sigilli," the place of the seal; i. e., the place where a seal is to be affixed, or a scroll which stands instead of a seal.

# M

**MAINTENANCE.** An unauthorized and officious interference in a suit in which the offender has no interest, to assist one of the parties to it, against the other, with money or advice to prosecute or defend the action.

**MALFEASANCE.** The wrongful or unjust doing of some act which the doer has no right to perform, or which he has stipulated by contract not to do. It differs from "misfeasance" and "nonfeasance" (which titles see).

**MALUM IN SE.** Latin. A wrong in itself; an act or case involving illegality from the very nature of the transaction, upon principles of natural, moral, and public law. An act is said to be malum in se when it is inherently and essentially evil—that is, immoral in its nature and injurious in its consequences—without any regard to the fact of its being noticed or punished by the law of the state. Such are most or all of the offenses cognizable at common law (without the denouncement of a statute); as murder, larceny, etc.

**MALUM PROHIBITUM.** Latin. A wrong prohibited; a thing which is wrong because prohibited; an act which is not inherently immoral, but becomes so because its commission is expressly forbidden by positive law; an act involving an illegality resulting from positive law. Contrasted with malum in se.

**MANDAMUS.** Latin, we command. A legal writ compelling the defendant to do an official duty.

**MANDATE.** A bailment of property in regard to which the bailee engages to do some act without reward. Story, Bailm. § 137.

**MATERIALMAN.** One who furnishes materials to be used in the construction or repair of ships or houses.

**MATURITY. In mercantile law.** The time when a bill of exchange or promissory note becomes due.

**MECHANIC'S LIEN.** A species of lien created by statute in most of the states, which exists in favor of persons who have performed work or furnished material in and for the erection of a building. Their lien attaches to the land as well as the building, and is intended to secure for them a priority of payment.

**MERGER.** The fusion or absorption of one thing or right into another; generally spoken of a case where one of the subjects is of less dignity or importance than the other. Here the less important ceases to have an independent existence.

**MESNE.** Intermediate.

**Mesne process.** Process issued between the beginning of a suit and final process.

**Mesne profits.** Profits from the use of land during wrongful occupancy, recovered, in ejectment or trespass, by the owner from the defendant in the action.

**MINOR.** An infant or person who is under the age of legal competence. A term derived from the civil law, which described a person under a certain age as less than so many years. Minor viginti quinque annis, one less than twenty-five years of age.

**MISDEMEANOR. In criminal law.** A general name for criminal offenses of every sort, punishable by indictment or special proceedings, which do not in law amount to the grade of felony.

**MISFEASANCE.** A misdeed or trespass. The doing what a party ought to do improperly. The improper performance of some act which a man may lawfully do.

Misfeasance, strictly, is not doing a lawful act in a proper manner, omitting to do it as it should be done, while malfeasance is the doing an act wholly wrongful, and nonfeasance is an omission to perform a duty, or a total neglect of duty. But "misfeasance" is often carelessly used in the sense of "malfeasance."

**MISREPRESENTATION.** An intentional false statement respecting a matter of fact, made by one of the parties to a contract, which is material to the contract and influential in producing it.

**MORTGAGE.** An estate created by a conveyance absolute in form, but intended to secure the performance of some act, such as the payment of money, and the like, by the grantor or some other person, and to become void if the act is performed agreeably to the terms prescribed at the time of making such conveyance.

A conditional conveyance of land, designed as a security for the payment of money, the fulfillment of some contract, or the performance of some act, and to be void upon such payment, fulfillment, or performance.

A debt by specialty, secured by a pledge of lands, of which the legal ownership is vested in the creditor, but of which, in equity, the debtor and those claiming under him remain the actual owners, until debarred by judicial sentence or their own laches.

The foregoing definitions are applicable to the common-law conception of a mortgage. But in many states, in modern times, it is regarded as a mere lien, and not as creating a title or estate. It is a pledge or security of particular property for the payment of a debt, or the performance of some other obligation, whatever form the transaction may take, but is not regarded as a conveyance in effect, though it may be cast in the form of a conveyance.

**MUTUUM.** Latin. In the law of bailments. A loan for consumption; a loan of chattels, upon an agreement that the borrower may consume them, returning to the lender an equivalent in kind and quantity.

# N

**NEGLIGENCE.** The omission to do something which a reasonable man, guided by those considerations which ordinarily regulate the conduct of human affairs, would do, or doing something which a prudent and reasonable man would not do. It must be determined in all cases by reference to the situation and knowledge of the parties and all the attendant circumstances.

Negligence, in its civil relation, is such an inadvertent imperfection, by a responsible human agent, in the discharge of a legal duty, as immediately produces, in an ordinary and natural sequence, a damage to another.

**NEGLIGENCE VEL NON.** (A phrase of mixed English and Latin.) Negligence or not.

**NEGOTIABLE.** An instrument embodying an obligation for the payment of money is called "negotiable" when the legal title to the instrument itself and to the whole amount of money expressed upon its face, with the right to sue therefor in his own name, may be transferred from one person to another without a formal assignment, but by mere indorsement and delivery by the holder or by delivery only.

**NEMO PLUS JURIS AD ALIUM TRANSFERRE POTEST QUAM IPSE HABERET.** Latin. No one can transfer to another more of right than he himself has. This maxim, like most maxims, must not be taken as true without any limitations. It is well known that the bona fide purchaser of real or personal property, or the holder in due course of a negotiable instrument, does in many cases take a greater right than his transferor has had.

**NIL DEBET.** Latin. He owes nothing. A plea that the defendant owes nothing.

**NISI PRIUS.** Latin. Literally, unless before. The expression has now so far departed from its original Latin signification as to mean substantially "at the trial." The words were originally words of some importance in the writ directing the sheriff to summon jurors. "A practice obtained very early, * * * in the trial of trifling causes, to continue the cause in the superior court from term to term, provided the justices in eyre did not sooner (nisi prius justiciari) come into the county where the cause of action arose, in which case they had jurisdiction when they so came." Bouvier's Law Dict.

**NOMINAL AND SUBSTANTIAL DAMAGES.** Nominal damages are a trifling sum awarded to a plaintiff in an action, where there is no substantial loss or injury to be compensated, but still the law recognizes a technical invasion of his rights or a breach of the defendant's duty, or in cases where, although there has been a real injury, the plaintiff's evidence entirely fails to show its amount.

**NOMINAL PARTNER.** A person who appears to be a partner in a firm, or is so represented to persons dealing with the firm, or who allows his name to appear in the style of the firm or to be used in its business, in the character of a partner, but who has no actual interest in the firm or business.

**NON ASSUMPSIT.** Latin. The general issue in the action of assumpsit, being a plea by which the defendant avers that "he did not undertake" or promise as alleged.

**NON COMPOS MENTIS.** Latin. Not sound of mind; insane.

**NON EST FACTUM.** Latin. It was not made.

**NONFEASANCE.** The neglect or failure of a person to do some act which he ought to do.

**NON SEQUITUR.** Latin. It does not follow. An inference which does not follow from the premise.

**NONSUIT.** Not following up the cause; failure on the part of a plaintiff to continue the prosecution of his suit. An abandonment or renunciation of his suit, by a plaintiff, either by omitting to take the next necessary steps, or voluntarily relinquishing the action, or pursuant to an order of the court. An order or judgment, granted upon the trial of a cause, that the plaintiff has abandoned, or shall abandon, the further prosecution of his suit.

**NOTARY PUBLIC.** A public officer whose function is to attest and certify, by his hand and official seal, certain classes of documents, in order to give them credit and authenticity in foreign jurisdictions; to take acknowledgments of deeds and other conveyances, and certify the same; and to perform certain official acts, chiefly in commercial matters.

**NUDUM PACTUM.** Latin. A naked pact; a bare agreement; a promise or undertaking made without any consideration for it.

**NUISANCE.** That class of wrongs that arise from the unreasonable, unwarrantable, or unlawful use by a person of his own property, either real or personal, or from his own improper, indecent, or unlawful personal conduct, working an obstruction of or injury to the right of another or of the public, and producing such material annoyance, inconvenience, discomfort, or hurt that the law will presume a consequent damage.

# O

**OATH.** An external pledge or asseveration, made in verification of statements made or to be made, coupled with an appeal to a sacred or venerated object, in evidence of the serious and reverent state of mind of the party, or with an invocation to a supreme being to witness the words of the party and to visit him with punishment if they be false.

**OBITER DICTUM.** Latin. A remark made, or opinion expressed, by a judge, in his decision upon a cause, "by the way"; that is, incidentally or collaterally, and not directly upon the question before him, or upon a point not necessarily involved in the determination of the cause, or introduced by way of illustration, or analogy or argument.

**OMNIS RATIHABITIO RETROTRAHITUR ET MANDATO PRIORI ÆQUIPARATUR.** Latin. Every ratification relates back and is equivalent to a prior authority. Broom, Max. 757, 871.

**ORDINANCE.** The term is used to designate the enactments of the legislative body of a municipal corporation.

**OSTENSIBLE AGENCY.** An implied or presumptive agency, which exists where one, either intentionally or from want of ordinary care, induces another to believe that a third person is his agent, though he never in fact employed him.

**OSTENSIBLE PARTNER.** A partner whose name is made known and appears to the world as a partner, and who is in reality such.

**OUTLAWED.** When applied to a promissory note, means debarred by the statute of limitations.

**OYER. In modern practice.** A copy of a bond or specialty sued upon, given to the opposite party, in lieu of the old practice of reading it.

# P

**PAR. In commercial law.** Equal; equality. An equality subsisting between the nominal or face value of a bill of exchange, share of stock, etc., and its actual selling value. When the values are thus equal, the instrument or share is said to be "at par"; if it can be sold for more than its nominal worth, it is "above par"; if for less, it is "below par."

**PARI PASSU.** Latin. By an equal progress; ratably; without preference.

**PARTICEPS.** Latin. A participant; a sharer; anciently, a part owner, or parcener.

**PARTICEPS CRIMINIS.** Latin. A participant in a crime; an accomplice. One who shares or co-operates in a criminal offense, tort, or fraud.

**PARTITION.** The dividing of lands held by joint tenants, coparceners, or tenants in common, into distinct portions, so that they may hold them in severalty. And, in a less technical sense, any division of real or personal property between co-owners or co-proprietors.

**PARTNERSHIP.** A voluntary contract between two or more competent persons to place their money, effects, labor, and skill, or some or all of them, in lawful commerce or business, with the understanding that there shall be a proportional sharing of the profits and losses between them.

**PART PERFORMANCE.** The doing some portion, yet not the whole, of what either party to a contract has agreed to do.

**PATENT, n.** A grant of some privilege, property, or authority, made by the government or sovereign of a country to one or more individuals.

**In English law.** A grant by the sovereign to a subject or subjects, under the great seal, conferring some authority, title, franchise, or property; termed "letters patent" from being delivered open, and not closed up from inspection.

**In American law.** The instrument by which a state or government grants public lands to an individual.

A grant made by the government to an inventor, conveying and securing to him the exclusive right to make and sell his invention for a term of years.

**PAWN, n.** A bailment of goods to a creditor, as security for some debt or engagement; a pledge. Story, Bailm. art. 7.

**PAYEE.** The person in whose favor a negotiable instrument is made or drawn; the person to whom a negotiable instrument is made payable.

**PAYER, or PAYOR.** One who pays, or who is to make a payment; particularly the person who makes or is to make payment of a negotiable instrument.

**PERFORM.** To perform an obligation or contract is to execute, fulfill, or accomplish it according to its terms. This may consist either in action on the part of the person bound by the contract or in omission to act, according to the nature of the subject-matter; but the term is usually applied to any action in discharge of a contract other than payment.

**PERFORMANCE.** The fulfillment or accomplishment of a promise, contract, or other obligation according to its terms.

**Part performance.** The doing some portion, yet not the whole, of what either party to a contract has agreed to do.

**Specific performance.** Performance of a contract in the specific form in which it was made, or according to the precise terms agreed upon. This is frequently compelled by a bill in equity filed for the purpose. 2 Story, Eq. Pl. § 712 et seq. The doctrine of specific performance is that, where damages would be an inadequate compensation for the breach of an agreement, the contractor will be compelled to perform specifically what he has agreed to do. Sweet.

**PERJURY. In criminal law.** The willful assertion as to a matter of fact, opinion, belief, or knowledge, made by a witness in a judicial proceeding as part of his evidence, either upon oath or in any form allowed by law to be substituted for an oath, whether such evidence is given in open court, or in an affidavit, or otherwise, such assertion being known to such witness to be false, and being intended by him to mislead the court, jury or person holding the proceeding.

**PERPETUITY.** "A future limitation, whether executory or by way of remainder, and of real or personal property, which is not to vest till after the expiration of, or which will not necessariy vest within, the period prescribed by law for the creation of future estates, and which is not destructible by the person for the time being entitled to the property subject to the future limitation, except with the concurrence of the person interested in the contingent event." Lewis, Perp. c. 12.

**PER SE.** Latin. By himself or itself; in itself; taken alone; inherently; in isolation; unconnected with other matters.

**PERSONALTY.** Personal property; movable property; chattels.

**PERSONAL PROPERTY.** See **Personalty.**

**PIGNUS.** Latin. A pledge. A collateral pledge.

**PLAINTIFF.** A person who brings an action; the party who complains or sues in a personal action and is so named on the record.

**PLAINTIFF IN ERROR.** The party who sues out a writ of error to review a judgment or other proceeding at law.

**PLEA. In common-law practice.** A pleading; any one in the series of pleadings. More particularly, the first pleading on the part of the defendant. In the strictest sense, the answer which the defendant in an action at law makes to the plaintiff's declaration, and in which he sets up matter of fact as defense, thus distinguished from a demurrer, which interposes objections on grounds of law.

**In equity.** A special answer showing or relying upon one or more things as a cause why the suit should be either dismissed or delayed or barred.

**PLEAD.** To make, deliver, or file any pleading; to conduct the pleadings in a cause. To interpose any pleading in a suit which contains allegations of fact; in this sense the word is the antithesis of "demur." More particularly, to deliver in a formal manner the defendant's answer to the plaintiff's declaration, or to the indictment, as the case may be.

**PLEADING.** The peculiar science or system of rules and principles, established in the common law, according to which the pleadings or responsive allegations of litigating parties are framed, with a view to preserve technical propriety and to produce a proper issue.

The process performed by the parties to a suit or action, in alternately presenting written statements of their contention, each responsive to that which precedes, and each serving to narrow the field of controversy, until there evolves a single point, affirmed on one side and denied on the other, called the "issue," upon which they then go to trial.

The act or step of interposing any one of the pleadings in a cause, but particularly one on the part of the defendant; and, in the strictest sense, one which sets up allegations of fact in defense to the action.

**PLEDGE,** n. A bailment of goods to a creditor, as security for some debt or engagement; a pawn. Story, Bailm. art. 7.

**PLEDGEE.** The party to whom goods are pledged, or delivered in pledge.

**PLEDGOR.** The party delivering goods in pledge; the party pledging.

**POLICE POWER.** The power vested in a state to establish laws and ordinances for the regulation and enforcement of public order and tranquillity. The power vested in the legislature to make, ordain, and establish all manner of wholesome and reasonable laws, statutes, and ordinances, either with penalties or without, not repugnant to the constitution, as they shall judge to be for the good and welfare of the commonwealth, and of the subjects of the same. The police power of the state is an authority conferred by the American constitutional system upon the individual states, through which they are enabled to establish a special department of police; adopt such regulations as tend to prevent the commission of fraud, violence, or other offenses against the state; aid in the arrest of criminals; and secure generally the comfort, health, and prosperity of the state, by preserving the public order, preventing a conflict of rights in the common intercourse of the citizens, and insuring to each an uninterrupted enjoyment of all the privileges conferred upon him by the laws of his country. It is true that the legislation which secures to all protection in their rights, and the equal use and enjoyment of their property, embraces an almost infinite variety of subjects. Whatever affects the peace, good order, morals, and health of the community comes within its scope; and every one must use and enjoy his property subject to the restrictions which such legislation imposes. What is termed the "police power" of the state, which, from the language often used respecting it, one would suppose to be be an undefined and irresponsible element in government, can only interfere with the conduct of individuals in their intercourse with each other, and in the use of their property, so far as may be required to secure these objects.

**POLICY OF INSURANCE.** A mercantile instrument in writing, by which one party, in consideration of a premium, engages to indemnify another against a contingent loss, by making him a payment in compensation, whenever the event shall happen by which the loss is to accrue.

**POST–DATE.** To date an instrument as of a time later than that at which it is really made.

**POWER OF APPOINTMENT.** A power or authority conferred by one person by deed or will upon another (called the "donee") to appoint, that is, to select and nominate, the person or persons who are to receive and enjoy an estate or an income therefrom or from a fund, after the testator's death, or the donee's death, or after the termination of an existing right or interest.

**POWER OF ATTORNEY.** An instrument authorizing a person to act as the agent or attorney of the person granting it.

**PREFERENCE.** The payment of money or the transfer of property to one creditor in preference to other creditors. Where the debtor is solvent, he may legally make such a preference. Under the federal Bankruptcy Act, a debtor is said to have made a preference if, being insolvent, he has made a transfer of any of his property and the effect of the enforcement of such transfer will be to enable any one of his creditors to obtain a greater percentage of his debt than any other of such creditors of the same class.

**PREMIUM.** The sum paid or agreed to be paid by an assured to the underwriter as the consideration for the insurance; being a certain rate per cent. on the amount insured.

**PRESCRIPTION.** The acquisition of incorporeal hereditaments by user or enjoyment for a very long time; i. e. "from time immemorial," or for a certain time set by a statute of limitations. For instance, A. continues to cross the land of B. by a certain path each day for twenty years, the period within which an action must be brought or other means taken to cause a discontinuance of A.'s user, under the laws of the state in which B.'s land lies. A. then has the right "by prescription" to continue to cross the land of B. His easement is complete.

**PRESENTMENT.** The production of a bill of exchange to the drawee for his acceptance, or to the drawer or acceptor for payment; or of a promissory note to the party liable, for payment of the same.

**PRESUMPTION.** An inference affirmative or disaffirmative of the truth or falsehood of any proposition or fact drawn by a process of probable reasoning in the absence of actual certainty of its truth or falsehood, or until such certainty can be ascertained.

**PRIMA FACIE.** Latin. At first sight; on the first apearance; on the face of it; so far as can be judged from the first disclosure; presumably.

A litigating party is said to have a prima facie case when the evidence in his favor is sufficiently strong for his opponent to be called on to answer it.

**PRINCIPAL.** In the law of agency. The employer or constitutor of an agent; the person who gives authority to an agent or attorney to do some act for him.

**PRIVATE CARRIER.** One who carries passengers or the goods of another without holding himself out to the general public as serving all persons that apply. The private carrier is contrasted with the common or public carrier.

**PROBATE.** The act or process of proving a will. The proof before an ordinary, surrogate, register, or other. duly authorized person that a document produced before him for official recognition and registration, and alleged to be the last will and testament of a certain deceased person, is such in reality.

**PROCEDURE.** The method and mechanism, so to speak, by which proceedings in a court are conducted.

**PROCESS. In practice.** This word is generally defined to be the means of compelling the defendant in an action to appear in court.

**PROCURATION.** Agency; proxy; the act of constituting another one's attorney in fact; action under a power of attorney or other constitution of agency. Indorsing a bill or note "by procuration" (or per proc.) is doing it as proxy for another or by his authority.

**PROMISSORY NOTE.** A promise or engagement, in writing, to pay a specified sum at a time therein limited, or on demand, or at sight, to a person therein named, or to his order, or bearer.

**PROMOTERS.** In the law relating to corporations, those persons are called the "promoters" of a company who first associate themselves together for the purpose of organizing the company, issuing its prospectus, procuring subscriptions to the stock, securing a charter, etc.

**PROSECUTE.** To follow up; to carry on an action or other judicial proceeding; to proceed against a person criminally.

**PRO TANTO.** Latin. For so much; as far as it goes.

**PROTEST.** A notarial act, being a formal statement in writing made by a notary under his seal of office, at the request of the holder of a bill or note, in which such bill or note is described, and it is declared that the same was on a certain day presented for payment (or acceptance, as the case may be), and that such payment or acceptance was refused, and stating the reasons, if any, given for such refusal, whereupon the notary protests against all parties to such instrument, and declares that they will be held responsible for all loss or damage arising from its dishonor.

**PROXY.** A person who is substituted or deputed by another to represent him and act for him, particularly in some meeting or public body. Also the instrument containing the appointment of such person.

# Q

**QUA.** Latin. As; in the character or capacity of. E. g., "the trustee qua trustee."

**QUANTUM MERUIT.** Latin. As much as he deserved.

**In pleading.** The common count in an action of assumpsit for work and labor, founded on an implied assumpsit or promise on the part of the defendant to pay the plaintiff as much as he reasonably deserved to have for his labor.

**QUASI.** Latin. As if; as it were; analogous to. This term is used in legal phraseology to indicate that one subject resembles another, with which it is compared, in certain characteristics, but that there are also intrinsic differences between them.

**QUASI CONTRACT.** In the civil law. A contractual relation arising out of transactions between the parties which give them mutual rights and obligations, but do not involve a specific and express convention or agreement between them.

**QUIA EMPTORES.** Latin. The English statute (18 Edw. I) prohibiting subinfeudation.

**QUIET,** v. To pacify; to render secure or unassailable by the removal of disquieting causes or disputes. This is the meaning of the word in the phrase "action to quiet title," which is a proceeding to establish the plaintiff's title to land by bringing into court an adverse claimant and there compelling him either to establish his claim or be forever after estopped from asserting it.

**QUITCLAIM DEED.** A deed of conveyance operating by way of release; that is, intended to pass any title, interest, or claim which the grantor may have in the premises, but not professing that such title is valid, nor containing any warranty or covenants for title.

**QUO WARRANTO.** Latin. By what warrant? A name commonly applied, in the United States, to an "information in the nature of a quo warranto," an action compelling the defendant to show by what warrant he exercises certain powers or privileges. The proceeding is used to test the right of a person to public office, or the right of a private or public corporation to exercise certain franchises.

# R

**RATIFICATION.** The confirmation of a previous act done either by the party himself or by another; confirmation of a voidable act.

**REAL ESTATE.** See **Real Property.**

**REALTY.** See **Real Property.**

**REAL PROPERTY.** A general term for lands, tenements, and hereditaments; property which, on the death of the owner intestate, passes to his heir. Real property is either corporeal or incorporeal.

**RECEIPT.** A receipt is the written acknowledgment of the receipt of money, or a thing of value, without containing any affirmative obligation upon either party to it; a mere admission of a fact in writing.

Also the act or transaction of accepting or taking anything delivered.

**RECEIVER.** A receiver is an indifferent person between the parties appointed by the court to collect and receive the rents, issues, and profits of land, or the produce of personal estate, or other things which it does not seem reasonable to the court that either party should do; or where a party is incompetent to do so, as in the case of an infant. The remedy of the appointment of a receiver is one of the very oldest in the court of chancery, and is founded on the inadequacy of the remedy to be obtained in the court of ordinary jurisdiction.

**RECOGNIZANCE.** An obligation of record, entered into before some court of record, or magistrate duly authorized, with condition to do some particular act; as to appear at the assizes, or criminal court, to keep the peace, to pay a debt, or the like. It resembles a bond, but differs from it in being an acknowledgment of a former debt upon record.

**RECOUPMENT.** Recoupment is a right of the defendant to have a deduction from the amount of the plaintiff's damages, for the reason that the plaintiff has not complied with the cross-obligations or independent covenants arising under the same contract.

"Recoupment" differs from "set-off" in this respect: that any claim or demand the defendant may have against the plaintiff may be used as a set-off, while it is not a subject for recoupment unless it grows out of the very same transaction which furnishes the plaintiff's cause of action.

**RECOVERY.** The collection of a debt through an action at law.

**Right of recovery.** A plaintiff is said to have a right of recovery when he has a right of action under the facts of a given case.

**REDEMPTION.** (From the Latin, redemptio; a buying back.) A buying back of property from the original purchaser by the original seller. A mortgage purports to convey title to the mortgagee, subject to a right of redemption in the mortgagor; i. e., the mortgagor has an "equity of redemption" in the property. The mortgagor has a right and a power to defeat the efficacy of his mortgage as a complete conveyance of the title, by paying the amount of the debt secured by the mortgage, thus meeting the condition subsequent stated in the "defeasance clause" of the mortgage.

**REIMBURSEMENT.** The equitable and legal right of reimbursement of a surety is the surety's right to be reimbursed by his principal in the amount of the principal's debt paid by the surety.

**RELATOR.** The person upon whose complaint, or at whose instance, an information or writ of quo warranto is filed, and who is quasi the plaintiff in the proceeding.

**RELEASE.** The relinquishment, concession, or giving up of a right, claim, or privilege, by the person in whom it exists or to whom it accrues, to the person against whom it might have been demanded or enforced.

**REMAINDER.** An estate limited to take effect and be enjoyed after another estate is determined. As, if a man seised in fee-simple grants lands to A. for twenty years, and, after the determination of the said term, then to B. and his heirs forever, here A. is tenant for years, remainder to B. in fee.

**REMAND.** Where a decision of a trial court is reversed in an appellate court, it is frequently sent back or "remanded" to the trial court for a new trial. In some cases, as where the plaintiff has been given judgment on a state of facts that could not, in any view, justify such judgment, the appellate court may reverse the judgment without remanding.

**REMEDIAL.** Of or pertaining to the legal remedy, or to the form or procedural details of such remedy.

**REMEDY.** The means by which the violation of a right is prevented, redressed, or compensated. Though a remedy may be by the act of the party injured, by operation of law, or by agreement between the injurer and the injured, we are chiefly concerned with one kind of remedy, the judicial remedy, which is by action or suit.

**REMITTITUR DAMNA.** Latin. Usually shortened to **Remittitur.** An entry made on record, in cases where a jury has given greater damages than a plaintiff has declared for, remitting the excess.

**RENT.** The compensation, either in money, provisions, chattels, or labor, received by the owner of the soil from the occupant thereof.

**REPLEVIN.** A personal action ex delicto brought to recover possession of goods unlawfully taken (generally, but not only, applicable to the taking of goods distrained for rent), the validity of which taking it is the mode of contesting, if the party from whom the goods were taken wishes to have them back in specie, whereas, if he prefer to have damages instead, the validity may be contested by action of trespass or unlawful distress.

**REPLEVIN BOND.** A bond executed to indemnify the officer who executed a writ of replevin and to indemnify the defendant or person from whose custody the property was taken for such damages as he may sustain.

**RESCISSION.** Rescission, or the act of rescinding, is where a contract is canceled, annulled, or abrogated by the parties, or one of them.

**RESIDENCE.** Living or dwelling in a certain place permanently or for a considerable length of time. The place where a man makes his home, or where he dwells permanently or for an extended period of time.

**RESIDUARY.** Pertaining to the residue; constituting the residue; giving or bequeathing the residue; receiving or entitled to the residue.

**RESIDUARY DEVISEE.** The person named in a will, who is to take all the real property remaining over and above the other devises.

**RESIDUARY ESTATE.** The remaining part of a testator's estate and effects, after payment of debts and legacies; or that portion of his estate which has not been particularly devised or bequeathed.

**RESIDUARY LEGATEE.** The person to whom a testator bequeaths the residue of his personal estate, after the payment of such other legacies as are specifically mentioned in the will.

**RESPONDEAT SUPERIOR.** Latin. Let the master answer. This maxim means that a master is liable in certain cases for the wrongful acts of his servant, and a principal for those of his agent.

**RESPONDENT.** The party who makes an answer to a bill or other proceeding in chancery.

The party who appeals against the judgment of an inferior court is termed the "appellant"; and he who contends against the appeal, the "respondent."

**REVERSE.** An appellate court uses the term "reversed" to indicate that it annuls or avoids the judgment, or vacates the decree, of the trial court.

**REVOCATION.** The recall of some power, authority, or thing granted, or a destroying or making void of some deed that had existence until the act of revocation made it void. It may be either general, of all acts and things done before; or special, to revoke a particular thing.

**RIGHT OF ACTION.** The right to bring suit; a legal right to maintain an action, growing out of a given transaction or state of facts and based thereon.

**RIGHT OF ENTRY.** A right of entry is the right of taking or resuming possession of land by entering on it in a peaceable manner.

**RIGHT TO REDEEM.** The term "right of redemption" or "right to redeem," is familiarly used to describe the estate of the debtor when under mortgage, to be sold at auction, in contradistinction to an absolute estate, to be set off by appraisement. It would be more consonant to the legal character of this interest to call it the "debtor's estate subject to mortgage."

# S

**SATISFACTION.** The act of satisfying a party by paying what is due to him (as on a mortgage, lien, or contract), or what is awarded to him, by the judgment of a court or otherwise. Thus, a judgment is satisfied by the payment of the amount due to the party who has recovered such judgment, or by his levying the amount.

**SCIENTER.** Latin. Knowingly.

**SCINTILLA.** Latin. A spark; a remaining particle; the least particle.

**SCIRE FACIAS.** Latin. You may cause to know. In practice, a judicial writ, founded upon some record, and requiring the person against whom it is brought to show cause why the party bringing it should not have advantage of such record, or (in the case of a scire facias to repeal letters patent) why the record should not be annulled and vacated.

The most common application of this writ is as a process to revive a judgment, after the lapse of a certain time, or on a change of parties, or otherwise to have execution of the judgment, in which cases it is merely a continuation of the original action.

**SCROLL or SCRAWL.** A mark intended to supply the place of a seal, made with a pen or other instrument of writing.

**SEAL.** An impression upon wax, wafer, or some other tenacious substance capable of being impressed.

**SEISIN.** Possession with an intent on the part of him who holds it to claim a freehold interest.

**SET-OFF.** A counterclaim or cross-demand; a claim or demand which the defendant in an action sets off against the claim of the plaintiff, as being his due, whereby he may extinguish the plaintiff's demand, either in whole or in part, according to the amount of the set-off.

**SET UP.** To bring forward or allege, as something relied upon or deemed sufficient; to propose or interpose, by way of defense, explanation, or justification; as, to set up the statute of limitations—i. e., offer and rely upon it as a defense to a claim.

**SEVERANCE.** The cutting of the crops, such as corn, grass, etc., or the separating of anything from the realty. Brown.

**SHELLEY'S CASE, RULE IN.** "That rule is that, where a life estate is given to A. with a future interest to A.'s heirs (the use of the particular word 'heirs' being necessary), the whole gift is construed as one 'to A. and his heirs,' at once giving an estate to A. in fee." Albert M. Kales, in 5 Am.Law & Proced. 105.

**SILENT PARTNER.** Popular name for dormant partners or special partners.

**SIMPLE CONTRACT.** A contract based upon consideration and not upon form.

**SPECIAL INDORSEMENT.** An indorsement in full, which specifically names the indorsee.

**SPECIAL PARTNER.** A member of a limited partnership, who furnishes certain funds to the common stock, and whose liability extends no further than the fund furnished.

**SPECIAL PROPERTY.** Property of a qualified, temporary, or limited nature; as distinguished from absolute, general, or unconditional property. Such is the property of a bailee in the article bailed, of a sheriff in goods temporarily in his hands under a levy, of the finder of lost goods while looking for the owner, of a person in wild animals which he has caught.

**SPECIALTY.** A writing sealed and delivered, containing some agreement.

**SPECIAL VERDICT.** A special finding of the facts of a case by a jury, leaving to the court the application of the law to the facts thus found.

**SPOLIATION. In torts.** Destruction of a thing by the act of a stranger, as the erasure or alteration of a writing by the act of a stranger, is called "spoliation." This has not the effect to destroy its character or legal effect.

**SS.** An abbreviation used in that part of a record, pleading, or affidavit, called the "statement of the venue." Commonly translated or read "to wit," and supposed to be a contraction of "scilicet."

**STATUS.** The status of a person is his legal position or condition.

**STATUTE,** n. An act of the legislature.

**STATUTE OF FRAUDS.** A celebrated English statute, passed in 1677, and which has been adopted, in a more or less modified form, in nearly all of the United States. Its chief characteristic is the provision that no action shall be brought on certain contracts unless there be a note or memorandum thereof in writing, signed by the party to be charged or by his authorized agent.

**STATUTE OF LIMITATION.** A statute prescribing limitations to the right of action on certain described causes of action; that is, declaring that no suit shall be maintained on such causes of action unless brought within a specified period after the right accrued.

**STATUTORY UNDERTAKING.** A penal bond, given, as required by statute, in connection with certain legal proceedings. "Common examples of statutory undertaking are: The bond given by a plaintiff in an injunction suit, as security to the defendant for damages caused by the issuance of an interlocutory injunction, such damages, within the amount of the penalty, to be collected by the defendant if the injunction is found to have been wrongfully issued; and the bond given for a very similar purpose in attachment or replevin." Bauer on Damages, p. 98, note.

**STOCK. In corporation law.** The capital or principal fund of a corporation or joint-stock company, formed by the contributions of subscribers or the sale of shares, and considered as the aggregate of a certain number of shares severally owned by the members or stockholders of the corporation; also the proportional part of the capital which is owned by an individual stockholder; also the incorporeal property which is represented by the holding of a certificate of stock, and in a wider and more remote sense, the right of a shareholder to participate in the general management of the company and to share proportionally in its net profits or earnings or in the distribution of assets on dissolution.

**STOPPAGE IN TRANSITU.** The act by which the unpaid vendor of goods stops their progress and resumes possession of them, while they are in course of transit from him to the purchaser, and not yet actually delivered to the latter.

**STRICTISSIMI JURIS.** Latin. Of the strictest right or law.

**SUBAGENT.** An under-agent; a substituted agent; an agent appointed by one who is himself an agent.

**SUBINFEUDATION.** Under the feudal system, an inferior lord sometimes carved out of an estate which he held of a superior lord, a part which he granted to an inferior tenant, whose lord he in turn became. This under-feudalizing, so to speak, used in order to evade restraints on alienation, was known as subinfeudation, and was prohibited by the Statute of Quia Emptores (St. 18 Edw. I).

**SUBPŒNA.** Latin. Sub, under, and pœna, punishment or penalty. In the Latin writs early used in England, one was commanded to appear "sub pœna," and these words have given the name to writs of those types in which they appeared.

**Of a witness.** A process commanding a witness to appear in court at a certain time to testify in a given cause.

**In chancery practice.** A process commanding a party or parties to a suit in equity to appear and answer matters alleged against them in the bill.

**SUBROGATION.** The substitution of one thing for another, or of one person into the place of another with respect to rights, claims, or securities.

Subrogation denotes the putting a third person who has paid a debt in the place of the creditor to whom he has paid it, so that he may exercise against the debtor all the rights which the creditor, if unpaid, might have done.

**SUBSCRIBE. In the law of contracts.** To write under; to write the name under; to write the name at the bottom or end of a writing.

**SUBSTANTIVE LAW.** The part of the law which the courts are established to administer, as opposed to the rules according to which the substantive law itself is administered. That part of the law which creates, defines, and regulates rights, as opposed to adjective or remedial law, which prescribes the method of enforcing rights or obtaining redress for their invasion.

**SUI GENERIS.** Latin. Of its own kind or class.

**SUI JURIS.** Latin. Of his own right; having legal capacity to manage his own affairs.

**SUIT.** "Suit" is a generic term, of comprehensive signification, and applies to any proceeding in a court of justice in which the plaintiff pursues, in such court, the remedy which the law affords him for the redress of an injury or the recovery of a right.

**SUMMARY,** adj. Immediate; peremptory; off-hand; without a jury; provisional; statutory.

**SUMMON. In practice.** To serve a summons; to cite a defendant to appear in court to answer a suit which has been begun against him; to notify the defendant that an action has been instituted against him, and that he is required to answer to it at a time and place named.

**SUMMONS. In practice.** A writ, directed to the sheriff or other proper officer, requiring him to notify the person named that an action has been commenced against him in the court whence the writ issues, and that he is required to appear, on a day named, and answer the complaint in such action.

**SURETY.** A surety is one who at the request of another, and for the purpose of securing to him a benefit, becomes responsible for the performance by the latter of some act in favor of a third person, or hypothecates property as security therefor.

# T

**TENANCY IN COMMON.** A tenancy under which each cotenant has a distinct and several estate in the property. Under such a tenancy, the survivor from among the cotenants does not take the entire property as in the case of a joint tenancy.

**TENANT.** In the broadest sense, one who holds or possesses lands or tenements by any kind of right or title, whether in fee, for life, for years, at will, or otherwise. Cowell.

In a more restricted sense, one who holds lands of another; one who has the temporary use and occupation of real property owned by another person (called the "landlord"), the duration and terms of his tenancy being usually fixed by an instrument called a "lease."

**TENDER.** An offer of money; the act by which one produces and offers to a person holding a claim or demand against him the amount of money which he considers and admits to be due, in satisfaction of such claim or demand, without any stipulation or condition.

Also, there may be a tender of performance of a duty other than the payment of money.

**TENOR.** In pleading the "tenor" of a document is sometimes said to be shown when an exact copy is set out in the pleading. Also, the word is often used to denote the true meaning or purport of an instrument.

**TENURE. In the law of public officers.** The period during which an officer holds office.

**In the law of real property.** The legal mode in which one owns an estate in lands.

**TERM. Of court.** The word "term" when used with reference to a court, signifies the space of time during which the court holds a session. A "session" signifies the time during the term when the court sits for the transaction of business, and the session commences when the court convenes for the term, and continues until final adjournment, either before or at the expiration of the term. The "term" of the court is the time prescribed by law during which it may be in "session." The "session" of the court is the time of its actual sitting.

**TESTATOR.** One who makes or has made a testament or will; one who dies leaving a will.

**TITLE.** The means whereby the owner of lands or of personalty has the just possession of his property. See Co. Litt. 345; 2 Bl.Comm. 195.

**TORT.** Wrong; injury; the opposite of right. So called, according to Lord Coke, because it is "wrested," or crooked, being contrary to that which is right and straight. Co. Litt. 158b.

In modern practice, "tort" is constantly used as an English word to denote a wrong or wrongful act, for which an action will lie, as distinguished from a "contract." 3 Bl.Comm. 117.

A tort is a legal wrong committed upon the person or property independent of contract. It may be either (1) a direct invasion of some legal right of the individual; (2) the infraction of some public duty by which special damage accrues to the individual; (3) the violation of some private obligation by which like damage accrues to the individual. In the former case, no special damage is necessary to entitle the party to recover. In the two latter cases, such damage is necessary. Code Ga.1882, § 2951.

**TORT–FEASOR.** One who commits or is guilty of a tort.

**TORTIOUS.** Wrongful; of the nature of a tort. Formerly certain modes of conveyance (e. g., feoffments, fines, etc.) had the effect of passing not merely the estate of the person making the conveyance, but the whole fee simple, to the injury of the person really entitled to the fee; and they were hence called "tortious conveyances." Litt. par. 611; Co. Litt. 271b, note 1; 330b, note 1. But this operation has been taken away. Sweet.

**TRANSITORY ACTION.** An action that is personal—i. e., brought against the person of the defendant —and possible to be brought in any county in which service of process upon the defendant is obtained.

**TRESPASS.** Any misfeasance or act of one man whereby another is injuriously treated or damnified. 3 Bl.Comm. 208.

An injury or misfeasance to the person, property, or rights of another person, done with force and violence, either actual or implied by law.

In the strictest sense, an entry on another's ground, without a lawful authority, and doing some damage, however inconsiderable, to his real property. 3 Bl. Comm. 209.

**In practice.** A form of action, at the common law, which lies for redress in the shape of money damages for any unlawful injury done to the plaintiff, in respect either to his person, property, or rights, by the immediate force and violence of the defendant.

**Trespass de bonis asportatis.** (Trespass for goods carried away.) In practice. The technical name of that species of trespass for injuries to personal property which lies where the injury consists in carrying away the goods or property.

**Trespass on the case.** The form of action, at common law, adapted to the recovery of damages for some injury resulting to a party from the wrongful act of another, unaccompanied by direct or immediate force, or which is the indirect or secondary consequence of such act. Commonly called "case," or "action on the case."

**Trespass quare clausum fregit.** (Trespass wherefore he broke the close, or trespass for breaking the close.) The common-law action for damages for an unlawful entry or trespass upon the plaintiff's land.

**TROVER.** In common-law practice, the action of trover (or trover and conversion) is a species of action on the case, and originally lay for the recovery of damages against a person who had "found" another's goods and wrongfully converted them to his own use. Subsequently the allegation of the loss of the goods by the plaintiff and the finding of them by the defendant was merely fictitious, and the action became the remedy for any wrongful interference with or detention of the goods of another.

**TRUST.** An equitable or beneficial right or title to land or other property, held for the beneficiary by another person, in whom resides the legal title or ownership, recognized and enforced by courts of chancery.

**TRUST DEED.** An instrument in use in many states, taking the place and serving the uses of a common-law mortgage, by which the legal title to real property is placed in one or more trustees, to secure the repayment of a sum of money or the performance of other conditions.

**TRUSTEE.** The person appointed, or required by law, to execute a trust; one in whom an estate, interest, or power is vested, under an express or implied agreement to administer or exercise it for the benefit or to the use of another.

**TRUSTEE PROCESS.** The name given in the New England states, to the process of garnishment or foreign attachment.

# U

**ULTRA VIRES.** Latin. Beyond the powers. A term used to express the action of a corporation which is beyond the powers conferred upon it by its charter, or the statutes under which it was instituted. 13 Am.Law Rev. 632.

**UNDERTAKING.** A promise, engagement, or stipulation. Each of the promises made by the parties to a contract, considered independently and not as mutual, may, in this sense, be denominated an "undertaking."

**UNDERWRITER.** The person who insures another in a fire or life policy; the insurer.

A person who joins with others in entering into a marine policy of insurance as insurer.

**UNIFORM STATUTES.** In general, statutes of substantially uniform substance, passed by various states, with the purpose of making the law of the subject uniform throughout the country. Such statutes have been drafted by the Commission on Uniform State Laws of the American Bar Association, and recommended for passage by the Legislatures of the various states. The most important of such statutes are the Negotiable Instruments Act, the Sales Act, and the Partnership Act, which have all been enacted in many of the states.

**UNILATERAL.** One-sided; ex parte; having relation to only one of two or more persons or things.

**USURY.** Unlawful interest; a premium or compensation paid or stipulated to be paid for the use of money borrowed or returned, beyond the rate of interest established by law. Webster.

# V

**VALID.** Of binding force. A deed, will, or other instrument, which has received all the formalities required by law, is said to be valid.

**VALIDITY.** This term is used to signify legal sufficiency, in contradistinction to mere regularity.

**VENDEE.** A purchaser or buyer; one to whom anything is sold. Generally used of the transferee of real property, one who acquires chattels by sale being called a "buyer."

**VENDITIONI EXPONAS.** Latin. You may expose to sale. This is the name of a writ of execution, requiring a sale to be made, directed to a sheriff when he has levied upon goods under a fieri facias, but returned that they remained unsold for want of buyers; and in some jurisdictions it is issued to cause a sale to be made of lands, seized under a former writ, after they have been condemned or passed upon by an inquisition. Frequently abbreviated to "vend. ex."

**VENDOR.** The person who transfers property by sale, particularly real estate, "seller" being more commonly used for one who sells personalty.

**VENIRE.** Latin. To come; to appear in court. This word is sometimes used as the name of the writ for summoning a jury, more commonly called a "venire facias."

**VENIRE FACIAS DE NOVO.** Latin. A fresh or new venire, which the court grants when there has been some impropriety or irregularity in returning the jury, or where the verdict is so imperfect or ambiguous that no judgment can be given upon it, or where a judgment is reversed on error, and a new trial awarded.

**VERDICT.** The formal and unanimous decision or finding of a jury, impaneled and sworn for the trial of a cause, upon the matters or questions duly submitted to them upon the trial.

**VESTED.** Accrued; fixed; settled; absolute; having the character or giving the rights of absolute ownership; not contingent; not subject to be defeated by a condition precedent.

**VINDICTIVE DAMAGES.** Exemplary damages are damages on an increased scale, awarded to the plaintiff over and above what will barely compensate him for his property loss, where the wrong done to him was aggravated by circumstances of violence, oppression, malice, fraud, or wanton and wicked conduct on the part of the defendant, and are intended to solace the plaintiff for mental anguish, laceration of his feelings, shame, degradation, or other aggravations of the original wrong, or else to punish the defendant for his evil behavior or to make an example of him, for which reason they are also called "punitive" or "punitory" damages or "vindictive" damages, and (vulgarly) "smart money."

**VOID.** Null; ineffectual, nugatory; having no legal force or binding effect; unable, in law, to support the purpose for which it was intended.

**VOIDABLE.** That may be avoided, or declared void; not absolutely void, or void in itself. Most of the acts of infants are "voidable" only, and not absolutely void.

**VOLUNTARY.** Free; without compulsion or solicitation.

Without consideration; without valuable consideration; gratuitous.

**VOLUNTEER. In conveyancing,** one who holds a title under a voluntary conveyance; i. e., one made without consideration, good or valuable, to support it.

A person who gives his services without any express or implied promise of remuneration in return is called a "volunteer," and is entitled to no remuneration for his services, nor to any compensation for injuries sustained by him in performing what he has undertaken. Sweet. Also one who officiously pays the debt of another.

# W

**WAGER.** A wager is a contract by which two or more parties agree that a certain sum of money or other thing shall be paid or delivered to one of them on the happening of an uncertain event or upon the ascertainment of a fact which is in dispute between them.

**WAIVER.** The renunciation, repudiation, abandonment, or surrender of some claim, right, privilege, or of the opportunity to take advantage of some defect, irregularity, or wrong.

**WARD.** An infant or insane person placed by authority of law under the care of a guardian.

**WARRANT, v. In contracts.** To engage or promise that a certain fact or state of facts, in relation to the subject-matter, is, or shall be, as it is represented to be.

**WARRANT, n.** A writ or precept from a competent authority in pursuance of law, directing the doing of an act, and addressed to an officer or person competent to do the act, and affording him protection from damage, if he does it.

**WARRANTY. In real property law.** A real covenant by the grantor of lands, for himself and his heirs, to warrant and defend the title and possession of the estate granted, to the grantee and his heirs, whereby either upon voucher, or judgment in the writ of warrantia chartæ, and the eviction of the grantee by paramount title, the grantor was bound to recompense him with other lands of equal value.

**In sales of personal property.** A warranty is a statement or representation made by the seller of goods, contemporaneously with and as a part of the contract of sale, though collateral to the express object of it, having reference to the character, quality, or title of the goods, and by which he promises or undertakes to insure that certain facts are or shall be as he then represents them.

A warranty is an engagement by which a seller assures to a buyer the existence of some fact affecting the transaction, whether past, present, or future.

**In contracts.** An undertaking or stipulation, in writing, or verbally, that a certain fact in relation to the subject of a contract is or shall be as it is stated or promised to be.

A warranty differs from a representation in that a warranty must always be given contemporaneously with, and as part of, the contract; whereas, a representation precedes and induces to the contract. And, while that is their difference in nature, their difference in consequence or effect is this: that, upon breach of warranty (or false warranty), the contract remains binding, and damages only are recoverable for the breach; whereas, upon a false representation, the defrauded party may elect to avoid the contract, and recover the entire price paid. Brown.

**WILL.** A will is the legal expression of a man's wishes as to the disposition of his property after his death.

An instrument in writing, executed in form of law, by which a person makes a disposition of his property, to take effect after his death.

**WRIT OF ENTRY.** A real action to recover the possession of land where the tenant (or owner) has been disseised or otherwise wrongfully dispossessed.

**WRIT OF ERROR.** A writ issued from a court of appellate jurisdiction, directed to the judge or judges of a court of record, requiring them to remit to the appellate court the record of an action before them, in which a final judgment has been entered, in order that examination may be made of certain errors alleged to have been committed, and that the judgment may be reversed, corrected, or affirmed, as the case may require.

A writ of error is defined to be a commission by which the judges of one court are authorized to examine a record upon which a judgment was given in another court, and, on such examination, to affirm or reverse the same, according to law.

# Y

**YEAR BOOKS.** Books made up of reports of English cases from Edward II, 1292, to Henry VIII, early in the sixteenth century. They constitute an important source of information on the early English common law.

# INDEX

References are to Pages

†